RESTRUCTURING ASIAN ECONOMICS FOR THE NEW MILLENNIUM

RESEARCH IN ASIAN ECONOMIC STUDIES

Series Editor: M. Dutta

RESEARCH IN ASIAN ECONOMIC STUDIES VOLUME 9-B

RESTRUCTURING ASIAN ECONOMICS FOR THE NEW MILLENNIUM

EDITED BY

J. R. BEHRMAN

University of Pennsylvania, Philadelphia, PA, USA

M. DUTTA

Rutgers University, New Brunswick, NJ, USA

S. L. HUSTED

University of Pittsburgh, Pittsburgh, PA, USA

P. SUMALEE

Chulalongkorn University, Bangkok, Thailand

C. SUTHIPHAND

Chulalongkorn University, Bangkok, Thailand

P. WIBOONCHUTIKULA

Chulalongkorn University, Bangkok, Thailand

Emerald

United Kingdom – North America – Japan – India – Malaysia – China

Emerald Group Publishing Limited
Howard House, Wagon Lane, Bingley BD16 1WA, UK

First edition 2001.

British Library Cataloguing in Publication Data
A catalogue record for this book is available from the British Library

ISBN: 978-0-762-30710-4

Printed and bound in Great Britain by
CPI Antony Rowe, Chippenham and Eastbourne

CONTENTS

SECTION FIVE

SECTION SIX

LIST OF CONTRIBUTORS

Nittayagasetwat Aekkachai	Chulalongkorn University, Bangkok, Thailand
Momtaz Uddin Ahmed	Dhaka University, Dhaka, Bangladesh
Juanjai Ajanant	Chulalongkorn University, Bangkok, Thailand
Robert H. Aten	EPSO/USAID, Jakarta, Indonesia
Tubtimtong Bangorn	Chulalongkorn University, Bangkok, Thailand
Romeo M. Bautista	International Food Policy Research Institute, Washington, DC, USA
Teerana Bhongmakapat	Chulalongkorn University, Bangkok, Thailand
Chaivichayachat Bundit	Chulalongkorn University, Bangkok, Thailand
Do Loc Diep	National Center for Social Sciences and Humanities, Hanoi, Vietnam
Moataz El-Said	International Food Policy Research Institute, Washington, DC, USA
James P. Gander	University of Utah, Salt Lake City, UT, USA
Wattana S. Janjaroen	Chulalongkorn University, Bangkok. Thailand
Hiroki Kawai	Kieo University, Tokyo, Japan
Saleem M. Khan	Bloomsburg University, Bloomsburg, PA, USA

Hiro Lee	Nagoya University, Nagoya, Japan
Yang-Taek Lim	Hanyang University, Seoul, Korea
Jung-Chao Liu	State University of New York at Binghamton, NY, USA
Dominique van der Mensbrugghe	The World Bank, Washington, DC, USA
Linda Fung Yee Ng	The Chinese University of Hong Kong, Hong Kong, China
Wiboonchutikula Paitoon	Chulalongkorn University, Bangkok, Thailand
Somchai Ratanakomut	Chulalongkorn University, Bangkok, Thailand
Lakshmi Raut	Chulalongkorn University, Bangkok, Thailand
Amit S. Ray	Jawaharlal Nehru University, New Delhi, India
Stephen Reynolds	University of Utah, Salt Lake City, UT, USA
Sherman Robinson	International Food Policy Research Institute, Washington, DC, USA
David Roland-Hoist	Mills College, London, U.K.
Siripen Supakankunti	Chulalongkorn University, Bangkok. Thailand
Sunti Tirapat	Chulalongkorn University, Bangkok, Thailand
Chyau Tuan	The Chinese University of Hong Kong, Hong Kong, China

Shujiro Urata	Waseda University, Tokyo, Japan
Piyasiri Wickramasekara	International Labour Office, Geneva, Switzerland
Changsheng Xu	Huazhong University of Science & Technology, Wuhan China
Li-Lai Xu	LaTrobe University, Victoria, Australia

FOREWORD

The forty chapters in six sections in RESTRUCTURING ASIAN ECONOMIES FOR THE NEW MILLENNIUM present the revised versions of presentations made at the international conference on "*A Macroeconomic Core of An Open Economy for Progressive Industrialization and Development of Asian Economies in the New Millennium*", jointly organized by the Faculty of Economics, Chulalongkorn University and the American Committee on *Asian Economic Studies (ACAES*), on December16–18, 1998 in Bangkok. Conferees included a large number well-known economists, experts in economic policy-making and researchers in allied fields, who presented papers, served on panel discussions and participated in discussions and deliberations regarding the Asian financial crisis and strategies for industrialization and development in the future. Invited speakers, panelists, and discussants came from the United States, Germany, Australia, Japan, Korea, People's Republic of China, Hong Kong, Taiwan, Indonesia, the Philippines, Singapore, Vietnam, India, Bangladesh joined their peers from Thailand at this three-day event. This book is the final output of the scholarly exercises at the conference which was a superb success.

The Asian economic crisis and future development is a hot subject among academics and policy-makers worldwide. Several countries in Asia came to face severe economic recession in the wake of their financial and foreign exchange crisis which began in 1997. The recession was deep and the challenges for managers of respective economies for an optimum specification of monetary and fiscal policy guideliens became all too great. Many came to wonder whether the so-called "*Asian Miracle*" all of a sudden became a part of history. If so, how will Asia recover from the crisis and experience high growth and continuing development as in the past quarter of the century? Can such a crisis be forewarned? Which development paths should Asia seek so that the crisis will not be repeated in the future? In other words, the challenge is to formulate rational economic policies for Asia'a newly industrialized/industrializing economies so that their industrialization and development can sustainably progress as Asia enters the Twenty-First Century.

The book addresses the above issues by covering many topics including financial meltdown and industrial development, money and financial markets, exchange rates, capital flows, economic reforms, human capital development, impact of the financial crisis on growth and poverty incidence, as well as other development problems in Asia-Pacific countries. This conference featured a keynote speech by M. R. Chatu Momgol SONAKUL, Governor of the Bank of Thailand on "Optimal monetary and exchange policy under global financial crisis" (see chapter one section). A roundtable discussion on "*Asian Economies in the New Millennium*", chaired by KIM Duk-choong of Seoul (now Minister for Education, Government of Korea) was joined by Juergen SCHROEDER of University of Mannheim, Mannheim, Hiromitsu ISHI of Hitotsubashi University, Tokyo, HUANG Fan-zhang of State Planning Commission of PRC, Beijing, Peter J. LLOYD of University of Melbourne, Victoria,

M. G. QUIBRIA of Asian Development Bank, Manila, Jang-Hee YOO and Chul –Woo MOON of EWHA University, Seoul, Tzong-shiana YU of Chinese Institute of Economics and Business, Taipei, Anwar Nasution of University of Indonesia, Jakarta (now Deputy Governor of Bank Indonesia), and Pasuk PHONGPAICHIT ofChulalongkorn University, Bangkok plus a dinner lecture for Thailand's Ministry of Finance on policies and measures to cope with the Thai financial crisis were special features of the conference program. The subject of this book is definitely very timely and should be of great interest to scholars, policy-makers, and the general public who follow the economic development in Asia. RESTRUCTURING ASIAN ECONOMIES FOR THE NEW MILLENNIUM should contribute to a broader perspective and at the same time, a deeper understanding of the subject.

Thienchay Kiranandana, Ph.D.
Professor of Economics, and
President of Chulalongkorn University
Bangkok, Thailand

PREFACE

RESTRUCTURING ASIAN ECONOMIES FOR THE NEW MILLENNIUM

Since the 1970s researchers in economics have been engaged in studying Asia's newly industrialized/industrializing economies and literature in economics is very rich reporting their findings. As Asian economies in the Northeast and Southeast Asia recorded spectacularly high rates of growth of their respective gross domestic products with high rates of savings and investments as percentages of their respective gross domestic products with reasonably moderate rates of inflation, many hailed it as "The Asian Miracle". In the late 1990s, came the now-famous Asian financial crisis and challenged several of Asia's success stories, and many scholars came to be overwhelmed. Few wrote a treatise forecasting the crisis. There were hardly any warning from national and/or international think tanks. Again a miracle? Happily, financial crisis in most affected Asian economies has been contained.

There is a need for sustained, in-depth research of economic happenings in Asian economies and that is a challenge to all students of economics, be they in Asia or in any other continent. Let there be no search for what one may call the final truth. Let us search for the truth as it affects the economies of Asia we study. The traditional agriculture-dominated Asian economies have accepted the challenge of industrialization, and that too at an accelerated rate. Their economic agenda is to be an able and competitive actor in the world market as they adopt an economic program of industrialization and internationalization. They want to import physical capital form the relatively capital-abundant mature industrialized economies and pay for them by way of exporting a share of their newly manufactured industrial products to the world market, and thus earning export-revenue in convertible currencies. This is an import-export led growth model, not an export-led one, as some have called it. The economic gains are shared by partners at both ends, indeed a win-win situation. In the new millennium Asian economies, indeed economies of all continents, will face newer challenges and we must pursue our studies to find our best answers to them.

In two parts, A and B, RESTRUCTURING ASIAN ECONOMIES FOR THE NEW MILLENNIUM presents 40 research papers in six sections with a foreword by Thienchay Kiranandana, President of Chulalongkorn University, Bangkok, Thailand, himself a distinguished economist.

Section one includes six chapters. Chapter 1 presents a learned discourse by Governor M. R. Chatu Mongol Sonakul of Bank of Thailand on optimal monetary and exchange policy under global financial crisis. M. Dutta follows in chapter 2 with a discussion on a macroeconomic core of open economies in Asia for progressive industrialization in the new millennium. In chapter 3, Jürgen Schröder makes a presentation on The Euro, Dollar and International Monetary System inviting his readers to examine the eventful economic impacts of the emerging new global money market and to be ready for the impacts that there will be. Peter J. Lloyd in chapter 4 presents a forceful discussion of the architecture of the multilateral organizations, the IMF, OECD, G-7, World Bank, BIS, WTO and poses the question if there are too many of them. In chapter 5, Mardi Dungey and Vance L. Martin specify a model and present their statistical findings regarding the contagion in the East Asian Currency Crisis, and in chapter 6, Steven Husted writes on the long-run equilibrium exchange rate behavior with focus on Asian/Yen exchange rates before the crash.

Section two consists of nine chapters. In chapter 7, Jere R. Benhrman presents a discussion of "Schooling in Asia" analyzing micro evidence on determinants and effects and policy implications, relative to selected countries in South and Southeast Asia. Chapter 8 adds a discourse by Peter G. Warr on growth, crisis and poverty in Southeast Asia. In chapter 9, Hiromitsu Ishi writes on macroeconomic fundamentals of postwar economic growth of Japan with an analysis of the story of a great success and recent economic frustrations in Asian economies. In chapter 10, Jang-Hee Yoo and Chul Woo Moon discuss the causes and challenges of the Korean financial crisis during 1997–1998. Fan-zhang Huang in chapter 11 dwells on the current economic situation and trends in China with an analysis of employment related issues in the process of industrialization. Tzhong-shian Yu follows in chapter 12 writing on the evolution of commercial banking and financial markets in Taiwan and pointing to the challenges of the financial crisis for all Asian economies. In chapter 13, Anwar Nasution writes on Indonesia and argues that a long and bumpy road to Indonesia's economic recovery lies ahead. Chapter 14 is a thematic presentation on the challenges for the Asian economies in the new millennium by Pasuk Phongpaichit. M. G. Quibria in Chapter 15 writes on challenges to human resource development in Asia.

Section three presents six studies. Chapter 16 offers an econometric study of Thailand's experiences relative to equilibrium real exchange rate, real exchange rate misalignment and the current account by Shuji Kasajima and Sukanda Lewis. In chapter 17, Chartchai Parasuk and Wimonrat Sukcharoen analyze appropriateness of flexible exchange rate regime in economic adjustments for Asian economies. Rungsun Hataiseree follows in chapter 18 examining monetary conditions and monetary policy in small open economies with empirical results of Thailand under floating rate regime. Chayodom Sabhasri and Gene Janevathanavitya in chapter 19 report a study on the optimum currency index in the context of selected Asian countries. Sung Yeung Kwack presents in chapter 20 an empirical evaluation of the Asian financial crisis relative to the balance sheets of banking and corporate sectors. In chapter 21, Masumi Kishi offers a study of the Thai financial crisis and the role of public financial institutions.

Section four includes 8 chapters. Chapter 22 presents a study on microeconomic foundations of macroeconomic crisis with risk analysis of Asian non-Financial firms with comparisons to Latin America by Stephen Reynolds, Somchai Ratanakomut and James P. Gander. In chapter 23, Sunti Tirapat and Nittayagasetwat Aekkachai predict a firm's financial distress using micro and macro variables for Thailand. Teerana Bhongmakapat, in chapter 24, offers an analysis of the management of the Thai crisis with focus on asset bubbles, globalization and macroeconomic policy. Chapter 25 presents a study of China's macroeconomic stabilization policies in the process of high growth, system transition and opening to the outside world by Changsheng Xu. Do Loc Diep follows in chapter 26 with a discourse on foreign exchange policy in the context of monetary-financial crisis in Asia and economic renewal of Vietnam. Chapter 27 presents a study by Chyau Tuan and Linda Fund Yee Ng on the post-industrialization economic growth of Hong Kong from the perspectives of a mega-city. Jung-Chao Liu and Li-Lai Xu in chapter 28 analyze China's foreign exchange rate policy in the context of the Asian financial crisis. In chapter 29, Saleem M. Khan offers an analytic study on the concept of a new regionalism in South Asia.

Section five consists of 5 chapters on studies on foreign investment. In chapter 30, Yang-Taek Lim presents a much comprehensive analysis of the role of foreign direct investment for Korea's economic recovery and future directions in foreign investment promotion policy. Amit S. Ray offers in chapter 31 a study based on the evidence from the Indian chemical industry and has posed the question if foreign firms are technologically more active and progressive as they invest in less developed countries. Shujiro Urata and Hiroki Kawai in chapter 32 offers an empirical study on locational determinants of

Japanese foreign direct investment. In chapter 33, Momtaz Uddin Ahmed analyzes trends, patterns and policies of foreign direct investment and technology flows in Asia and the Pacific region in the 1990s. Wiboonchutikula Paitoon, Tubitimtong Bangorn, Lakshmi Raut and Chaivichayachat Bundit follow in chapter 34 with an exhaustive and comprehensive study of Thailand's capital flows.

In conclusion, section six has 6 chapters. In chapter 35, Hiro Lee, David Roland-Hoist and Dominique van der Mensbrugghe present a study on general equilibrium assessments of trade liberalization in APEC countries. Juanjai Ajanant, in chapter 36, projects an economic perspective of trade and industrialization of Thailand in 2020. In chapter 37, Romeo M. Bautista, Sherman Robinson and Moataz El-Said make use of SAM and CGE analytic frameworks and present alternative industrial development paths for Indonesia. Robert H. Aten follows in chapter 38 with an extended study of the Indonesian economy in the context of imperfect competition and progression of techonolgical advancement. In chapter 39, Wottana S. Janjaroen and Siripen Supakankunti study health services systems and the consequences from the general agreement of trade in services (GATS). In the concluding chapter 40, Piyasiri Wickramasekara presents a comprehensive study of the implications for employment, labor markets and poverty as the economic crisis confronts the economies. in the Asia-Pacific region.

M. DUTTA, EDITOR

SECTION FOUR

22. MICROECONOMIC FOUNDATIONS OF MACROECONOMIC CRISIS: RISK ANALYSIS OF ASIAN NON FINANCIAL FIRMS WITH COMPARISONS TO LATIN AMERICA

Stephen Reynolds, Somchai Ratanakomut and James Gander

INTRODUCTION

Progressive industrialization and development in Asian countries must arise out of the current stagnation and decline in the aftermath of the 1997 financial-economic crisis among Southeast and East Asian countries, especially Thailand, Korea, and Indonesia and, to a lesser degree, in other countries as well. The crisis was sudden and unanticipated in its onset. Unanticipated, too, was the persistence of stagnation and decline in Japan. Why was this the case? Were there early-warning signals of impending crisis? We examine the riskiness of the capital structures of major industrial and service firms to find answers to these questions. A comparison is made with firms in Latin American countries to provide perspective on the integration with mature, global financial markets. Countries such as Brazil and Venezuela are in crisis too; there may be similarities.

Restructuring Asian Economics for the New Millennium, Volume 9B, pages 413–426.

ISBN: 0-7623-0710-2

An important distinctiveness of our paper is its focus on micro financial data as opposed to macro data. To date, macro explanations of the crisis have dominated. Answers have been sought in terms of foreign exchange markets, monetary institutions, foreign trade, and aggregate foreign direct investment flows. For example, the analysis by the International Monetary Fund (IMF, 1998) relies on macroeconomic variables, as does that by several other analysts, e.g. Baer, Miles and Moran (1998: 98–102), Garnaut (1998: 1–11) and Montiel and Reinhart (1998). The micro theoretic analysis of Krugman (1998) is a partial exception but it focuses on financial firms and looks at no micro data. The national case studies in the McLeod and Garnaut (1998) volume also give minimal attention to micro data outside of the financial sector.

We focus on non-financial firms, using their individual balance sheet and income statement items to define their capital structures and to measure financial or economic risk (Damodaran, 1997). Each approach (the macro and the micro) has its own advantages and disadvantages. They are complementary. The macro is complete but it over aggregates. The micro is fundamental but, due to sampling problems, it is seldom complete. In other words, it is usually not possible to include in a sample all of the firms in a given industry. Yet, in our data set, most of the large firms are represented. In what follows, we discuss the data and method of analysis, then the empirical results and some conclusions.

DATA AND METHOD

The data (Compustat Services, 1997) on short-term debt, long-term debt, shareholder equity, and profit (net income) covering the years 1986 to 1996 were obtained by Standard and Poors as public data. There are many case-wise missing values, particularly for 1996. Also, the number of firms for which there are data varies from 35 firms to 307 firms. To use as much data as possible, we pooled the time-series and cross-sectional data for each country, when analyzing our various ratios. For example, a given financial ratio can have many firms for a given year or a few firms for several years, or some combination of each. We examined the ratios for 1995 only and found that the frequency patterns are generally the same. So, pooling across years for individual countries seemed an acceptable method to describe riskiness and capital structures. The data are in the currency of the country and in nominal values. Since we are examining ratios, deflators and currency exchange rates would cancel out. We accept that there are unknown errors in the data. If they are systematic, we would expect them to understate the riskiness of the firms' capital structures in order to improve the firms' credit terms, but we recognize that any required personal guarantees by major shareholders work to the contrary.

The focus is on the financial risk analysis of industrial, agriculture, mining, public utility and service firms over the period 1986–1996, across several countries and developing regions. This period of time is used to determine the financial behavior of firms just prior to the crisis of 1997. The key question is: "Was there any warning of impending macroeconomic crisis that could have been detected from the micro data?"

Our measure of risk, the risk index (RISKID), is the ratio of short-term borrowing to net income (or profit after taxes). We take as a normalized value a ratio equal to one. Values of RISKID greater than one are absolutely risky, independent of the currency in which they are denominated. (This paper does not directly address the issues that arise out of the currency in which debt is denominated.) The presumption is that a year's net profit could, in principle, pay off the short-term debt if it cannot be renewed. Other measures of the ability to pay are cash and other liquid assets. However, net profit represents an addition to total assets and, as such, can show up in any number of items in the asset account including cash. So, net profit captures the ability-to-pay principle. The log of RISKID is regressed on the profit rate of return on sales, a dummy variable for time (0 for 1986–1990 and 1 for 1991–1996), several dummy variables for industrial and services SIC groupings (see the appendix for SIC definitions) and dummy variables for several countries of the regions.

The theory motivating the regression is based on the principle of substitution between short-term debt (STD) and long-term debt (LTD) and the probability of renewal of STD. It can be argued that if the probability of renewal were certain ($p = 1$), short term and long term interest rates were equal and transaction costs were zero, then STD and LTD would be perfect substitutes and the firm would be indifferent about the composition of its total debt. The level of total debt would be the outcome of selecting the optimum level of output and the corresponding inputs of labor, capital (financed by the total debt), and other inputs. When p is less than one and the short-term interest rate (r_s) is less than the long-term interest rate (r_l), the early 1990s experience, STD is preferred over LTD. As p increases to 1, STD is substituted for LTD. As r_s falls relative to r_l, STD is substituted for LTD.

Since we do not have data on p, r_s, and r_l, we take as a proxy for all three variables the dummy variable for time: DVTIME = 0 for 1986–1990 when p is assumed to be low and DVTIME = 1 for 1991–1996 when p is assumed to be high. The exact specification of our regression is derived indirectly from a two-stage profit maximization model, where in the first stage a conditional profit function is derived based on the composition of the total debt and in the second stage the level of profit is determined by the composition of the total debt. The STD and LTD are endogenously determined along with the size of the firm (sales) and the level of profit. To operationalize the model, profit is used as a normalizing variable to arrive at the RISKID as the dependent variable and the profit rate on sales (PROFSALE), DVTIME, and the industry dummy variables as the independent variables. As DVTIME increases, implicitly p increases, so the RISKID is expected to increases: the short-term debt-to-profit ratio rises.

Separate regressions for each of seven Southeast and East Asia countries were previously reported (Reynolds, Ratanakomut & Gander, 1998) but are included in this paper for ease of comparison. In those previous regressions, we used RISKID on firm size (in sales), net profit, and dummy variables for time and SIC groupings. In the present paper, we are pooling data from the same seven countries to obtain a Southeast and East Asian regional analysis and from seven countries to obtain a Latin American regional analysis. In addition, three other Asian countries, Japan, Taiwan and India, whose economies differ significantly in their levels of industrial maturity, their openness to the global economy and their degree of financial liberalization, are included.

Pooling country data made it necessary to factor out currency differences from our variables. For some unknown reason, Compustat files on currency conversion could not be electronically copied or read. Furthermore, the countries differ in the variability of their currency exchange rates and in their exchange regimes. So, conversion (at what rate?) into a numeraire currency may increase the difficulty of interpreting the econometric results. Therefore, rather than use sales and profit independently as in our previous study of individual countries, here we use, instead, the ratio of profit to sales as a determinant of riskiness, RISKID.

The division of the time period into 1986–1990 and 1991–1996 is made to reflect changes in policy regimes. Some form of increased financial liberalization occurred in each of the seven pooled, Southeast and East Asian countries around the period 1990–1992 (Kitamura & Tanaka, 1997). At approximately the same time, the bubble burst in Japan's economy, the United States expansionary monetary policy put downward pressure on world interest rates, and India initiated a policy shift toward greater openness of its economy (Jayasuriya, 1998). It is hypothesized that liberalization led to increasing the riskiness of the firms' capital structures in the post-liberalization period compared to the pre liberalization period.

At the descriptive level of analysis, we report frequency distributions for each country and for each region on the variable RISKID. Also reported are the frequency distributions for two indexes of capital structure: the ratio of short-term debt to long-term debt (STDTOLTD) and the ratio of long-term debt to equity (DEBEQU). These distributions are useful for comparisons among countries and across regions.

EMPIRICAL RESULTS

The corresponding descriptive data on the mean, standard deviation, and the percent of observations with a ratio equal to or less than one are given in Table 1. The data in the table includes all the values except that the RISKID is limited to only positive values.

The RISKID distributions are decidedly L-shaped (skewed to the right) for all regions and all countries with the exceptions of Venezuela, Peru, Argentina, Chile, and Korea. The sample sizes vary and the range of values for RISKID

Table 1. Frequencies for Financial Ratios.

Country or Region	RISKID			STDTOLTD			DEBEQU			
	M	SD	%≤1	M	SD	%≤1	M	SD	%≤1	N-Range
Brazil	15.0	116.8	36	75.2	851.2	56	0.4	1.1	92	225–318
Venezuela	5.0	5.6	0	0.9	1.1	65	0.8	1.1	76	12–17
Peru	5.9	8.3	38	25.2	73.7	58	0.2	0.3	94	12–18
Chile	1.4	1.8	64	1.7	3.8	73	0.4	0.4	96	76–78
Colombia	3.1	6.1	56	3.4	5.4	40	0.2	0.2	100	48–55
Argentina	16.0	74.3	26	2.1	4.7	61	0.2	0.2	100	57–68
Mexico	5.6	17.7	40	14.4	147.8	63	0.5	1.4	89	230–305
LatAm (all, above)	9.0	72.4	41	34.1	529.1	60	0.4	1.1	92	660–859
Taiwan	7.8	25.2	35	22.2	87.2	50	0.2	0.2	100	64–76
India	1.7	4.7	56	0.2	1.0	96	1.2	0.9	48	121–505
Japan	52.2	450.4	8	22.6	396.6	40	2.7	197.1	81	9687–10855
SE & E Asia (all, below)	8.9	67.5	38	25.5	465.0	51	0.3	0.9	93	4755–6163
Thailand	9.7	35.3	24	41.0	653.6	34	0.4	1.4	89	751–1045
Korea	29.5	62.7	2	1.1	1.2	58	1.2	0.9	61	83–88
Malaysia	7.8	33.9	37	30.3	625.4	48	0.2	0.7	95	1232–1834
Indonesia	5.3	11.4	24	30.2	208.2	44	0.4	0.5	89	234–253
Singapore	2.1	3.9	44	20.2	343.6	66	0.3	0.9	94	994–1368
Hong Kong	7.6	93.0	48	16.5	138.0	54	0.3	0.8	95	1277–1513
Philippines	3.0	4.7	40	1.5	3.2	63	0.4	0.4	90	49–62

Notes: Observations are included only when profits are positive. Extreme values are included.

varies, but the L-shape persists. This shape seems to be a nearly universal phenomenon. The proportionality hypothesis suggests that as profit increases, the short-term debt increases proportionally (Cohen & Klepper, 1992; Kallunki, Martikainen & Perttunen, 1996; Turner, 1997). This hypothesis has to be rejected. Generally, there are many firms with low RISKID ratios and only a few with high RISKID ratios.

Table 1 shows the RISKID results more dramatically. Japanese firms stand out as having on the average a very high RISKID ratio with a large standard deviation and only 8% of the firms having a ratio equal to or less than one, i.e. in a range considered financially safe or not risky. Korean firms also have high RISKID ratios with only 2% considered safe. For comparison, Brazilian and Argentinean firms are also, generally, in a very risky position, although 36% and 26%, respectively, are considered safe. Regionally, Latin America and Southeast and East Asia have relatively high riskiness and are not substantially different. Countries with relatively safe firms are Chile, India, and Singapore. Other Asian countries with relatively more risky firms are Thailand, Malaysia, Indonesia and Hong Kong (where average riskiness is high, but 48% of firms are safe).

The short-term to long-term debt ratios, STDTOLTD, have similar L-shaped frequency distributions for regions and countries with the exception of Venezuela and Peru. Table 1 shows the mean ratios are very high, double digits, for most countries and regions. There are only seven exceptions among the 19 values. The ratios exceed a value of twenty-five for Brazil, Peru, Thailand, Malaysia and Indonesia. However, in only five countries (Colombia, Japan, Thailand, Malaysia and Indonesia) do less than 50% of firms have ratios less than or equal to one, indicating that the high mean ratios are often due to extreme values. Korea has one of the lowest mean ratios (but note a long-term debt-to-equity ratio, three to six times that of other Southeast and East Asian countries). Thailand and Brazil have the highest mean ratios.

The long-term debt equity ratios, DEBEQU, for the firms of the seven Southeast and East Asian countries (except the Philippines) exhibit L-shaped frequency distributions. So, too, do the ratios for the firms of Japan, Taiwan, and India. In contrast, the firm data does not exhibit consistent L-shaped frequency distributions for Latin American countries. Table 1 shows relatively high mean debt/equity ratios in Korea, India, Japan (extraordinarily high but more strongly impacted by extreme values) and possibly Venezuela. The rest of the countries have relatively low ratios, on the average, and in each of those countries 89% or more of the observations are less than or equal to one.

Taken together, the frequency distributions for the three measures of risk and capital structure do not show large or systematic differences between the two regions, respectively, seven Latin American and seven Southeast and East Asian countries. Marginally, the firms of the Latin American region appear more vulnerable to risk as expressed in the ratios' means but with lower percentages of exposed firms. By the measures used here of the risk vulnerability of firms in each country, there is greater variation among the countries within each of the respective groupings than collectively between them. Furthermore, the frequency distributions for firms in Taiwan do not seem to differentiate it from the seven Southeast and East Asian countries.

These micro results are somewhat different than the usual macro results. The micro data does signal the countries that had more risky firms in the decade before the crisis: Japan, Korea, Thailand, Malaysia and Indonesia for Asia. For Latin American countries, those that were vulnerable to risk as signaled by the micro data, are Venezuela, Brazil, Peru, and Argentina.

The regression results for the RISKID for Latin America, Southeast and East Asia, Japan, Taiwan, and India are given in Table 2. Our earlier results (Reynolds, Ratanakomut & Gander, 1998) for individual Southeast and East Asian countries are reproduced here for comparison purposes as Table 3. Due to the currency conversion problems when pooling across countries, the two tables use a slightly different, but equivalent, set of independent variables. Table 2 shows that the (log of) RISKID is inversely and significantly related to the profit rate on sales for both regional groupings of countries and, also, for Japan and Taiwan. The higher is the rate of profit, the lower the riskiness of the firms. The levels of significance are very high (low alpha-levels for a two-tailed test) for Latin American countries, Taiwan, and Japan. The dummy variable on time is significant and positive in sign for the firms of the Southeast and East Asia countries, Japan, and India. This indicates the increased riskiness of industrial and service firms in the post-liberalization period, on the eve of crisis; a result that has certainly been borne out by recent financial events. Importantly, the dummy variable on time is not significant for the firms in Taiwan, where financial liberalization followed a more measured pace (Kuo and Liu, 1998) nor for those of Latin America where liberalization followed the crisis of the early 1980s.

About one-third of the industry dummy variables are statistically significant. Blank spaces in the table indicate insignificant coefficients and the results are not reported. Thus, there is considerable variation in the level of riskiness across industry groupings. This suggests that the structure and degree of competition among industries will influence the degree of riskiness. For example, public utilities are relatively less risky, in their respective economies, among the seven countries in Southeast and East Asia compared to the status of similar firms in Latin America and in Japan. The same pattern also exists for

Table 2. Risk Analysis for Countries and Regions
LOG (RISKID) Regressions, Pooled Data, 1986–1996.

VARIABLE	LATAM	SE & E ASIA	JAPAN	TAIWAN	INDIA
Constant	0.33 (1.683)	–1.81 (–1.702)	1.89 (36.986)	1.46 (3.942)	–4.16 (–4.091)
PROFSALE	–5.57 (–10.262)	–0.01 (–2.381)	–1.17 (–19.307)	–11.70 (–6.625)	–6.35 (–1.487)
DVTIME	0.03 (.213)	0.23 (3.724)	0.17 (4.869)	–0.32 (–1.022)	2.22 (2.330)
DVAGR		–0.37 (–2.116)	1.49 (5.876)		
DVMIN	0.87 (3.264)	–0.91 (–3.434)			
DVBLDG	1.59 (3.472)	0.36 (2.375)	0.95 (13.196)		
DVLMF			0.18 (2.564)		3.28 (2.609)
DVMMF	0.44 (2.461)	–0.36 (–3.074)	0.27 (4.865)		
DVHMF	0.84 (4.247)		0.20 (3.710)	1.32 (3.836)	
DVWH			1.57 (17.228)		
DVBU			0.56 (5.612)	22.37 (6.919)	
DVRE	1.07 (2.083)				
DVHT		–0.42 (–2.777)	–0.35 (–2.045)		
DVHH					
DVPU	0.52 (2.307)	–0.80 (–5.716)	0.17 (2.005)		
DVNC					
DVBRA					
DVARG					
DVCHL					
DVCOL					
DVVEN	1.00 (2.060)				

Table 2. Continued.

VARIABLE	LATAM	SE & E ASIA	JAPAN	TAIWAN	INDIA
DVPER					
DVTHA		1.17			
		(13.050)			
DVKOR		2.90			
		(12.668)			
DVMYS		0.44			
		(5.255)			
DVSGP					
DVPHL		0.68			
		(2.390)			
DVIDN		0.92			
		(6.319)			
R^2	0.21	0.08	0.09	0.57	0.24
F	8.47	20.79	74.86	9.45	3.49
	(p = 0.000)	(p = 0.000)	(p = 0.000)	(p = 0.000)	(p = 0.001)
N	660	4755	9687	66	121

Notes: Mexico and Hong Kong are the reference groups for the country dummy variables. Statistically insignificant coefficients for the dummy variables are suppressed. Reference group for industry dummy variables is an assortment of industries not fitting our classifications.

medium manufacturing firms in Latin America, Japan, and Southeast and East Asia. The building industry is consistently relatively risky in their national contexts but relatively, to other national firms, more risky in Latin America and Japan compared to countries in Southeast and East Asia. For Southeast Asia, particularly for Thailand, this is a little surprising in light of the overbuilding of residential and commercial properties in and around Bangkok.

The dummy variables for the various countries in each region are also reported in Table 2. For Latin American countries, only Venezuela shows a significant risk differential relative to Mexico. Of course Mexico, whose firms do not look particularly risky in comparison to several of the Asian countries, experienced its own crisis in 1995 under substantially different macroeconomic conditions than in the recent Asian crisis (Hale, 1998). On the other hand, there are significant risk differentials among the seven countries of Southeast and East Asia, relative to Hong Kong, for each country except Singapore. Within that group Korea stands out as having the highest level of riskiness among its firms, then Thailand, and then Indonesia. This pattern is not surprising given what we now know about the financial crisis of 1997.

Table 3 shows the results of our earlier look at data on the firms of the seven Southeast and East Asian countries, individually (Reynolds, Ratanakomut & Gander, 1998). The econometric analysis reported there yields consistent and statistically significant results: a more risky short-term capital structure (as the dependent variable) is associated with larger firm size, lower firm profitability and financial liberalization. Among the countries in question, the analysis identifies firms in Korea, Thailand and Indonesia, in contrast to the other countries, as developing more risky capital structures, i.e. being more vulnerable to risk – in the decade before the crisis.

CONCLUSIONS

The microeconomic analysis demonstrates that in the decade prior to the crisis of 1997 – independent of issues regarding the currency of denomination of their debt – non-financial business firms of many Southeast and East Asian countries had taken on excessive short-term debt. This made them vulnerable to any disruption of their ability to rollover that debt on attractive terms. In the post liberalization period, firms' financial structures became more risky, i.e. more vulnerable to such disruption. This was commonly and individually the case across all of the seven countries of the Southeast and East Asian group, in India and in Japan – but not in Taiwan nor in the Latin American group of countries (although there are signs of high riskiness in a few countries there, too).

On the eve of the crisis, among the firms of several of the Asian countries, riskiness was high in an absolute sense (inability to pay short-term debt out of current profits) and in a relative sense, in comparisons with contemporaneous Latin America and with the capital structures of the 1980s. The unrecognized, high and increasing riskiness of the industrial and service firms constitutes an element of the microeconomic foundations of the crisis. Things were not "all right" in the productive sector. The capital structures of firms implied a crisis "waiting to happen" in several of the subsequently most impacted countries. Their vulnerability to market disruption, if not the timing of crisis, could have been foreseen since the microeconomic analysis identifies, in advance of macroeconomic signals, the highly – and increasingly – risky capital structures of industrial and service firms, especially, in Korea, Thailand, Indonesia and Japan prior to the crisis. In assessing macroeconomic policy regimes, this analysis indicates the importance of attention to the short-run profitability and borrowing behavior of industrial and service firms, the foundations of macroeconomic performance in progressive industrialization and development.

Table 3. LOG (RISKID) Regressions, Pooled Data, Seven Southeast and East Asian Developing Countries 1986–1996.

VAR	KOR	MYS	IDN	THA	SGP	HKG	PHL
Constant	2.86	0.21	1.06	1.30	0.23	–0.64	0.60
	(9.969)	(0.820)	(2.537)	(7.066)	(0.935)	(–3.936)	(1.681)
SALES	–3.0E-08	2.5E-07	3.9E-10	7.0E-08	8.2E-07	3.7E-08	4.7E-08
	(–0.585)	(3.073)	(3.562)	(4.469)	(4.515)	(2.928)	(2.087)
TOTINC	–2.2E-06	–4.6E-06	–5.4E-09	–6.1E-07	–7.0E-06	–3.4E-07	–8.1E-07
	(–5.284)	(–6.704)	(–3.245)	(–5.391)	(–7.523)	(–5.971)	(–3.083)
DVTIME	1.08	–0.18	0.28	0.39	0.38	0.41	1.38
	(4.297)	(–1.372)	(0.967)	(3.431)	(2.625)	(3.731)	(3.213)
DVAGR		–0.20	0.07	–0.30	–0.88		
		(–0.648)	(0.146)	(–0.792)	(–1.221)		
DVMIN		0.82		–2.41	–5.04		–0.88
		(1.362)		(–6.324)	(–3.432)		(–1.929)
DVBLDG	–0.12	0.30		–0.10	0.71	0.72	
	(–0.251)	(0.960)		(–0.204)	(2.182)	(2.609)	
DVLMF	0.34	0.10	–0.50	–0.60	–1.00	0.62	–0.33
	(0.507)	(.348)	(–1.265)	(–2.841)	(–3.399)	(2.844)	(–0.388)
DVMMF	–0.82	–0.17	-.98	–0.74	–0.81	0.84	
	(–2.745)	–0.635	(–2.474)	(–3.598)	(–2.671)	(2.776)	
DVHMF	–0.36	0.80	–1.02	0.07	–0.51	0.89	–3.55
	(–1.199)	(2.668)	(–1.984)	(0.322)	(–1.916)	(3.831)	(–3.655)
DVWH		0.53	–0.11	–0.53	–0.90	0.08	
		(0.968)	(–0.189)	(–1.712)	(–2.268)	(0.314)	
DVBU		0.87	0.54	–6.5E-04	–0.17	0.44	–1.25
		(3.053)	(1.219)	(–0.002)	(–0.596)	(2.429)	(–1.687)
DVRE		1.15	–2.45	–0.53	–1.03	1.09	
		(1.810)	(–2.792)	(–1.559)	(–1.835)	(2.978)	
DVHT		0.11	–1.15	–1.25	–0.33	–0.15	
		(0.291)	(–1.828)	(–4.084)	(–1.037)	(–0.600)	
DVHH		1.48		–1.84			
		(2.252)		(–4.141)			
DVPU	–0.76	0.74	–0.95	–0.67	–0.83	–0.31	0.83
	(–1.948)	(1.749)	(–1.425)	(–2.022)	(–2.497)	(–1.406)	(–0.883)
DVNC	–1.02	0.74	–0.31	–0.25	–0.54	0.67	
	(–1.122)	(0.982)	(–0.208)	(–0.454)	(–0.571)	(1.645)	
R^2	0.58	0.08	0.22	0.11	0.14	0.09	0.40
F	10.09	6.59	4.75	7.35	9.80	8.98	3.76
N	83	1232	234	971	899	1277	55

Notes: For a two-tailed test, t > absolute 1.96, is significant at 5% level or less. Coefficients for 18 of 21 economic variables are significant, as are 26 of 67 industry coefficients.
Source: (Reynolds, Ratanakomut and Gander, 1998, 1999).

The analysis also suggests a differential industrial policy, since the level of riskiness varies across industrial sectors.

REFERENCES

Baer, W., Miles, W. R., & Moran, A. B. (1998). *The End of the Asian Myth: Why Were the Experts Fooled?* CIBER Working Paper, Urbana-Champaign: University of Illinois, College of Commerce and Business Administration, Office of Research. (12 May): 98–102.

Center for International Economics (CIE), Faculty of Economics (1998). *The Study of Trade and Investment Policies in Developing Countries (Thailand).* Bangkok: Chulalongkorn University.

Cohen, W. M., & Klepper, S. (1992). The Anatomy of Industry R&D Intensity Distributions. *American Economic Review, LXXXII*(4), 773–799.

Compustat Services (1997). Industrial/Commercial File. *Global Vantage*. Englewood, Colorado: Standard & Poor's, Inc.

Damodaran, A. (1997). *Corporate Finance: Theory and Practice*. New York: John Wiley & Sons.

Garnaut, R. (1998). The Financial Crisis: A Watershed in Economic Thought About East Asia. *Asian-Pacific Economic Literature, XII*(1), 1–11.

Hale, D. D. (1998). Will Mexico's Recovery from Crisis Be a Model for East Asia? In: R. H. McLeod & R. Garnaut (Eds), *East Asia in Crisis: From Being a Miracle to Needing One?* New York: Routledge.

International Monetary Fund (IMF) (1998). World Economic Outlook. Washington, D.C.: International Monetary Fund.

Jayasuriya, S. (1998). India. In: R. H. McLeod & R. Garnaut (Eds), *East Asia in Crisis: From being a miracle to needing one?* New York: Routledge.

Kallunki, J.-P., Martikainen, T., & Perttunen, J. (1996). The Proportionality of Financial Ratios: Implications for Ratio Classifications. *Applied Financial Economics, VI*(6), 535–541.

Kitamura, K., & Tanaka, T. (Eds) (1997). *Examining Asia's Tigers: Nine Economies Challenging Common Structural Problems*. Tokyo: Institute of Developing Economies.

Krugman, P. (1998). What Happened to Asia?
http://web.mit.edu/krugman/www/DISINTER.htm

Kuo, S. W. Y., & Liu, C. Y. (1998). Taiwan. In: R. H. McLeod & R. Garnaut (Eds), *East Asia in Crisis: From Being a Miracle to Needing One?* New York: Routledge.

McLeod, R. H., & Garnaut, R. (Eds) (1998). *East Asia in Crisis: From being a miracle to needing one?* New York: Routledge.

Montiel, P. J., & Reinhart, C. M. (1998) (forthcoming). The Dynamics of Capital Movements to Emerging Economies During the 1990s. In: S. Griffith-Jones & M. Montes (Eds), *Short-Term Capital Movements and Balance of Payments Crises*. Oxford: Oxford University Press.

Reynolds, S. E., Ratanakomut, S., & Gander, J. P. (1998). The Private Sector in Financial Crisis: The Short-term and Long-Term Capital Structure of Firms in Southeast and East Asia. Seventh Southeast Asia Business Research Conference, May 30–31, University of Michigan, Ann Arbor. Forthcoming in *Journal of Asian Business, XV*(1), (March 1999).

Tirapat, S., & Nittayagasetwat, A. (1998). A Prediction of Firms' Financial Distress Using Macro and Micro Variables: A Case of Thailand. A paper presented at The 22nd American Committee on Asian Economic Studies (ACAES) International Conference on Asian

Economics, December 16–18, Bangkok, Thailand, sponsored jointly by Chulalongkorn University and ACAES in cooperation with the Asian Development Bank.

Turner, J. L. (1997). The Impact of Materiality Decisions on Financial Ratios. *Journal of Accounting, Auditing and Finance*, *NS12* (Spring), 125–147.

APPENDIX

Industry and Country Definitions of Dummy Variables

Note: The Standard Industrial Codes (SIC) have been omitted to save space. They are available from the authors upon request. To minimize the number of dummy variables and to reduce the number of empty cells, some aggregation was used. Where possible, the aggregates reflect either a common technology or raw materials or outputs. Admittedly some arbitrariness exists.

DVAGR = Agriculture and Forestry Products.

DVMIN = Mining, Oil and Gas, and Minerals.

DVBLDG = Building Construction, Highways, Bridges, and Related Trades.

DVLMF = Light Manufacturing Products: Food, Dairy, Beverages, Tobacco, Textiles, Apparel, Lumber, Furniture, Paper, and Printing.

DVMMF = Medium Manufacturing Products: Chemicals, Rubber, Leather, Stone, Glass, and Clay.

DVHMF = Heavy Manufacturing Products: Primary Metals, Fabricated Metals, Machinery, Electrical, Transportation Equipment, and Petroleum Refining.

DVWH = Wholesale Goods: Durable and Nondurable.

DVBU = Business and Commercial Services: Credit, Real Estate, Advertising, Consulting, and Engineering.

DVRE = Retail Stores: Apparel, Furniture, Other Household Goods, and Miscellaneous Retail.

DVHT = Hotels and Lodging, Amusement and Recreation Services, and Personal Services.

DVHH = Health Services, Legal and Social Services, and Educational Services (schools).

DVPU = Public Utilities: Railroad, Motor Freight, Water Transportation, Air, Pipeline, and Communication.

DVNC = Nonclassified Establishments.

DVBRA = Brazil

DVARG = Argentina

DVCHL = Chile

DVCOL = Colombia

DVEN = Venezuela
DVPER = Peru
DVTHA = Thailand
DVKOR = Korea
DVMYS = Malaysia
DVSGP = Singapore
DVPHL = Philippines
DVIND = Indonesia

23. A PREDICTION OF FIRMS' FINANCIAL DISTRESS USING MACRO AND MICRO VARIABLES: A CASE OF THAILAND

Sunti Tirapat and Nittayagasetwat Aekkachai[1]

1. INTRODUCTION

In 1997, the Asian financial crisis began. From Thailand, the crisis rapidly spread throughout the region. The swiftness and the confounding effect of the "tom yam" crisis have raised several interesting economic issues. What are the roots of problems? Why is the crisis "contagious"? What triggered the speculative attack? These issues have already been investigated by prominent economic scholars. Numerous causes of the crisis have been proposed ranging from the role of financial panic by Rechel and Sachs (1998) to a nexus of moral hazard problems by Corsetti, Pensenti and Roubini (1998). The speculative attack literature is reviewed by Flood and Marion (1998). The contagious nature of the crises has been investigated by Eichengreen, Rose and Wyplosz (1996) and recently by Glick and Rose (1998).

The crisis, however, has provided an opportunity to investigate another area of interest, the prediction of bankruptcy. The impact of the crisis has resulted in massive numbers of bankrupt Thai firms in 1996.[2] A study of the prediction of financially-distressed firms is certainly useful and of interest for both academicians and practitioners. Prior studies on predicting bankruptcy focus primarily on the financial variables such as financial ratios, cash flows, or

Restructuring Asian Economics for the New Millennium, Volume 9B, pages 427–446.
2001 by Elsevier Science B.V.
ISBN: 0-7623-0710-2

accounting opinions.[3] Many studies have been conducted for developed countries because data is readily available. In emerging markets, this line of research is scarce since in growing economies, bankrupt firms are actually nonexistent.[4] The crisis provides us a unique opportunity to investigate the prediction model of developing countries (or emerging markets) under financial crisis.

The prediction of financially-distressed firms in emerging markets, in our view, should be different from the traditional bankruptcy prediction models in that the economic conditions should play an important role. Firms that are more sensitive to economic shocks should be more prone to financial distress than firms that are less sensitive. This study attempts to incorporate the macroeconomic factors into the prediction of financially distressed firms.

The paper is organized as follows: Section 2 reviews prior research; the sample and methodology are discussed in Section 3; results of the model are reported in Section 4; and the discussion of the findings and conclusions are in Section 5.

2. PRIOR RESEARCH

2.1 Prediction of Bankruptcy

Bankruptcy prediction models were pioneered by Beaver (1966), Altman (1968), and Altman, Haldeman and Narayanan (1977). These studies, based on discriminant analysis, document that financial variables are related to bankruptcy. Since then, prediction of corporate failure has been a topic of much interest, and more recent works have extended this line of research in three areas: statistical techniques, definitions of bankruptcy, and a greater variety of explanatory variables. For the first area, Olson (1980) utilized the logit and probit analysis to estimate the probability of bankruptcy. The adjustments of estimation bias resulting from oversampling – such as weights based on prior probabilities in the estimation process and optimal cut-off point – are discussed in Zmijewski (1984). The problems of pooling data due to a small number of samples are addressed in Zavgren (1983) and Mensah (1984).

The second area of extension has dealt with the definitions of bankruptcy. For example, a model that distinguishes between financially distressed firms that survive and financially-distressed firms that ultimately go bankrupt has been investigated. Gilbert, Menon and Schwartz (1990) find different explanatory financial variables for these two groups of firms. In addition, a sample firm may be classified into more than two categories (bankrupt or nonbankrupt), and the classification probabilities can be estimated by the multinomial logit technique. For example, Poston, Harmon and Gramlich (1994) assigned firms into one of three groups according to each firm's financial condition: turnarounds, business failures, and survivors. They find that financial ratios are not so useful in distinguishing between financially distressed firms that are able to turnaround and those that are unable to avoid failure. Johnsen and Melicher (1994), on the other hand, suggest that by using multinomial logit models, the classification errors can be significantly reduced.

The third area covers other variables that are related to firm failure in addition to the financial variables. For example, Hopwood, McKeown and Mutchler (1989) and Flagg, Giroux and Wiggins (1991) find that a qualified opinion is significant in distinguishing financially-distressed firms. Some studies include macroeconomic variables to control for changes in the business environment. Rose and Giroux (1982) examine 28 business cycle indicators and find that economic conditions affect the failure process. Finally, industry differences are controlled by matching bankrupt and nonbankrupt firms by industry classification, or by standardizing firm-specific financial ratios with industry norms, as tested by Barnes (1987) and Platt and Platt (1990), for example.

2.2 *Prediction of Currency and Banking Crises*

Another strand of related research concerns the prediction of currency and banking crises; see for example Demirguc-Kunt and Detragiache (1997), Eichengreen and Rose (1998). These studies are motivated by the recent spate of crises[5] in Europe (Finland, Sweden), Latin America (Mexico, Argentina) and Asia (Thailand, Indonesia). Kaminsky and Reinhart (1996), analyzing a sample of 20 crises, report the importance of macroeconomic factors in a crisis. They document that output, the stock market and the real exchange rate usually peak about a year before the onset of banking crises. Real interest rates and bank deposits rise in the period leading up to the crisis. Demirguc-Kunt and Detragiache (1997) apply a multivariate logit model to the determinants of banking in a sample of developed as well as developing countries between 1980 and 1994. They find that in general, low growth and high inflation are associated with the probability of a banking crisis. Eichengreen and Rose (1998) restrict their sample to cover only banking crises in emerging markets from 1975 through 1992. They apply a multivariate probit model to nine economic variables: four of their variables are "international" in nature, three are "domestic" and two are "external" in nature. Their results suggest that banking crises in emerging countries tend to occur in response to a conjuncture of unfavorable developments in international markets and domestic imbalances. Specifically, rising industrial-country interest rates precipitate banking crises: a one percent increase in interest rates is associated with an increase in the probability of banking crises of around three percent.

Kaminsky, Lizondo and Reinhart (1997) examine the empirical evidence on 25 currency crises and compare the merits of alternative approaches in providing early indications of the crises. They document that the best track record includes exports, deviations of the real exchange rate from the trend, the ratio of broad money supply to gross international reserves, output and equity prices. Kaminsky and Reinhart (1996) also investigate 76 currency crises and 26 banking crises and find that banking and currency crises are closely related in the aftermath of financial liberalization, with banking crises generally preceding currency crashes.

SECTION 3. DATA AND METHODOLOGY

Sample and Data

The sample includes firms listed in the Stock Exchange of Thailand (SET) that experienced financial distress in 1996. We define financially-distressed firms as firms that either (i) were closed down by governmental authorities (all the closed firms were banks and finance companies) or (ii) were required by the Bank of Thailand or SET to submit restructuring plans (these companies were designated as C or SP[6] by the exchange). There were 459 firms listed in the SET in 1996, of which 55 were financially distressed by our definition. We exclude firms that were first listed in the SET in 1995 or later and exclude firms with incomplete data. The resulting sample consists of 396 nonfinancially-distressed firms and 55 financially-distressed firms. The characteristics of firms in the sample are reported in Table 1.

Table 1. Description of Firms in the Sample (Units: Thousand Baht).

Description	Full Sample	Distressed	Non-distressed
Firm size	19,736,583.97	21,690,440.67	19,377,074.33
Average EBIT	499,938.28	–84,358.06	608,901.65
Equity	3,357,872.92	2,683,971.35	3,481,870.81
Total debt	16,453,198.47	19,006,469.32	15,980,877.58

Method

Although some prior research, e.g. Rose, Andrews and Giroux (1982), has included macroeconomic variables in the prediction model, our study is different in an important aspect. The purpose of incorporating macroeconomic variables is not to control for changes in the business environment but rather to capture the sensitivity to change in macroeconomic factors. This perspective, in our view, is more consistent with the Thai situation.

The sensitivity of firms to economic conditions is expected to play a major role in differentiating the financially-distressed companies from the non-distressed ones. For example, an enterprise which has a high systematic risk corresponding to macroeconomic conditions, e.g. growth of industrial production, inflation, changes in interest rates, and changes in money supply (M2), may be exposed to the possibility of financial distress.

The study by Thomson (1992) uses Maddala's (1986) two-step logit regression approach as a link between official bank failure and bank insolvency. Therefore, logistic discriminant analysis used in this study will apply ideas from both articles in which the expected return on a firm's stock calculated from the macro-factor model is designed as a link to the micro-crisis model. In other words, the firm's expected return calculated from the multi-factor (or macroeconomic factors) model represents the macro effects incorporated into the micro-crisis prediction model. In general, the micro-crisis model and the related macro factors imply the following specifications:

$$Prob\ (Y_i = 1) = \frac{1}{1 + e^{-Z_i}} \tag{1}$$

$$\text{where} \quad Z_i = a + bE(r_i) + \sum_j c_j X_{ji} + e_i$$

$$E(r_i) = \alpha_i + \sum_k \beta_{ki} E(F_k).$$

As Y_i is assigned to be 1 if firm i is financially distressed and to be 0 if firm i is financially healthy, the probability with which firm i is classified as a financially-distressed firm is given by $Prob(Y_i = 1)$.

The probability, $Prob\ (Y_i = 1)$, depends on the logistic function of a linear relationship of a set of variables including $E(r_i)$ and X_{ji}. In addition, Z_i is a linear function in which a, b, and c are coefficients of variables, and e_i is an error term.

The expected return of the firm i, $E(r_i)$, can be calculated from a multi-factor model in which the expected macroeconomic factors, F_k, are used to develop the model. The details of this ex ante equation will be discussed later with the macroeconomic specifications of the multi-factor model.

Financial Variables

The exogenous variables, X_{ji}, are financial characteristics of the firm i. Shivaswamy, Hoban and Matsumoto (1993) study 13 research papers and summarize the frequency of financial ratios used in those papers. The most frequently used ratios are: current ratio, leverage ratio, and profitability ratio. Altman and Altman et al. (1968, 1977, 1979, 1981, 1983, 1984, 1985, 1994) develop numerous models predicting bankruptcy and financial distress. In particular, Altman (1984) surveys studies on business failure models in various countries and reviews the utilization of variable profiles employed in those studies. The most frequently used financial ratios are: working capital to total assets, retained earnings to total assets, earnings before interest and taxes to total assets, market value of equity to total liabilities, and sales to total assets.

However, the literature in this area of finance and accounting shows that the researchers usually base their models on the capital, assets, management, earnings, and liquidity of a firm, which are the so-called CAMEL categories. Following Salchenberger, Cinar and Lash (1992), the financial ratios are categorized only from each element of the CAMEL framework. The set of variables, X_j, following the CAMEL categories is selected as follows:

- *Capital:* X_1 = book value of stockholders' equity/total assets (*SETA*)
- *Assets:* X_2 = retained earnings/total assets (*RETA*)
- *Management:* X_3 = operating income/net sales (*OINS*)
- *Earnings:* X_4 = net income/total assets (*NITA*)
- *Liquidity:* X_5 = net working capital/total assets (*WCTA*)

In addition, the market value of equity to total assets ratio reflects the actual market value (market value = market price x number of outstanding shares) and the firm's size as perceived by the market. Therefore, the sixth financial characteristic in addition to the CAMEL framework can be specified as:

- *Market:* X_6 = market capitalization/total assets (*MCTA*)

These six variables will be used as the financial characteristics of the firms in the sample and these characteristics are exogenous to the model.

Multi-Factor Model

The expected return of the firm *i*, $E(r_i)$, will be calculated from a multi-factor model in which the expected macroeconomic factors, F_k, are used to develop the model. Demirguc-Kunt and Detragiache (1997), mentioned above, use 10 variables as macroeconomic factors in their logit model. However, only four variables (real quarterly GDP growth, real short-term interest rate, inflation, and M2 money supply to international reserves) are significant variables which can explain the probability of banking crises. These four macroeconomic factors have also been widely used econometrically. For the sample of Thai economic conditions, monthly growth of the production manufacturing index will give more observations than will the use of quarterly real GDP growth. To avoid multicollinearity, therefore, the macro-factors, F_k, are selected as follows:

- F_1 = growth of the production manufacturing index (PMI)
- F_2 = inflation or changes in the consumer price index (CPI)
- F_3 = changes in interest rates (INT)
- F_4 = changes in M2 money supply (MS2)

The expected changes in the above economic conditions will be used to calculate the expected returns of firm *i* according to the following equation:

$$E(r_i = \alpha_i + \beta_{1i}E(F_1) + \beta_{2i}E(F_2) + \beta_{3i}E(F_3) + \beta_{4i}E(F_4)$$

where β_i is the intercept and β_{1i}, β_{2i}, β_{3i}, and β_{4i}, are coefficients of variables representing the systematic risks or the sensitivity of firm *i* to the changes in industrial production, consumer price index, interest rates, and M2 money supply, respectively. It should be noted that for the specification in Equation (1), the expected return is a complete reflection of the sensitivity of the firm to macroeconomic conditions as well as the expected macroeconomic conditions. Alternatively, the effect of the sensitivity of the firm to macroeconomic factors on the probability of the firm's financial distress can be specified as follows:

$$Prob\ (Y_i = 1) = \frac{1}{1 + e^{-Z_i}} \qquad (2)$$

$$\text{where} \quad Z_i = a + \sum_k b_k\beta_{ki} + \sum_j c_jX_{ji} + e_i$$

The above model tests the effect of the sensitivity of firms to four macroeconomic conditions: growth of industrial production, inflation, changes in interest rates, and changes in M2 money supply. The model combines the exogenous factors of the firm's financial characteristics on the probability of the firm's financial distress.

The systematic risks, β_{ki}, of firm i are obtained from the time-series regression of the monthly returns of the firm i at time t_i, r_{it} on the monthly macroeconomic factors at time t_i F_{jt}. The equation is such that:

$$r_{it} = \alpha_i + \beta_{1i}F_{1t} + \beta_{2i}F_{2t} + \beta_{3i}F_{3t} + \beta_{4i}F_{4t} + e_{it}$$

where e_{it} is the error term of the firm i at time t.

4. RESULTS

The descriptive statistics of variables are reported in Table 2 while the results of the macro-related micro-crisis prediction model (Equation 1) are presented in Table 3. The results indicate that the expected return variable corresponding to the expected changes in macroeconomic factors is significantly different from zero. The sign is as expected, showing that a firm with a higher expected rate of return has a lower probability of financial distress than another firm having a lower expected rate of return. In other words, if stock market participants foresee the good quality of a firm with a low probability of financial distress, they will expect that the stock price of the firm would appreciate. The strong significance of this variable (at the 5% significance level) also indicates the importance of macroeconomic conditions and those conditions can strongly influence the probability of the firm's financial distress.

The results of the alternative specification (Equation 2) are also reported in Table 3. The results indicate that the only significant macro factor is the sensitivity of the firms to inflation or changes in the consumer price index. In other words, only the systematic risk of a firm exposed to inflation affects the probability of the firm's financial distress. The sign suggests that the more a firm faces inflation risk, the higher the firm's vulnerability to the risk of financial distress.

For both the ex ante return and ex post beta models, the financial characteristics such as market capital to total assets (MCTA), stockholders' equity to total assets (SETA), retained earnings to total assets (RETA), net income to total assets (NITA), and working capital to total assets (WCTA) are significant at the 1% significant level. The relationship is such that the greater the MCTA, SETA, and WCTA ratios and the lower the NITA ratio, the lower the probability of financial distress. The possible anomaly in this case is from the positive relationship (positive sign) between NITA and the probability of financial distress. However, this unusual result is noted in other research

Table 2. Descriptive Statistics of Variables for the Full Sample (396 Firms), the Non-distressed Sample (341 Firms), and the Distressed Sample (55 Firms).

Model Variable	Full Sample Max	Full Sample Min	Full Sample Mean[a]	Non-distressed Max	Non-distressed Min	Non-distressed Mean[b]	Distressed Max	Distressed Min	Distressed Mean[b]	Mean Difference[c]
Macroeconomic Factor										
E(r)	3.5138	−11.5892	−0.2962	3.5138	−2.5304	−0.2214	0.9808	−11.5892	−0.7602	0.5389
			(0.7625)			(2.3034)**			(4.1558)***	(6.43)***
PMI	5.6707	−1.4410	0.0374	1.6086	−1.4410	0.0243	5.6707	−0.8706	0.1185	−0.0942
			(0.4828)			(−0.8186)			(−1.3443)	(4.45)***
CPI	26.3030	−17.5141	1.1273	17.8946	−17.5141	0.6371	26.3030	−6.9741	4.1660	−3.5288
			(5.1035)			(−3.8041)***			(−4.8949)***	(2.03)***
INT	0.4366	−1.6489	−0.0664	0.4366	−0.5001	−0.0586	0.1775	−1.6489	−0.1143	0.0557
			(0.1446)			(1.6537)			(2.6697)***	(4.19)***
MS2	26.6999	−18.5894	1.5073	11.7656	−18.5894	1.3140	26.6999	−5.3813	2.7060	−1.3921
			(3.4242)			(−2.0503)**			(−2.8224)***	(2.49)***
Financial Characteristic										
SETA	1.0030	−2.1488	0.4201	1.0030	−2.1488	0.4601	0.7051	−1.1681	0.1718	0.2883
			(0.2428)			(7.2561)***			(7.4099)***	(1.06)
RETA	1.3293	−3.0053	0.1007	1.3293	−3.0053	0.1328	0.4259	−2.9265	−0.0980	0.2308
			(0.2990)			(3.1289)***			(4.6004)***	(3.06)***
OINS	7.1950	−17.1278	0.0893	7.1950	−17.1278	0.1193	0.4200	−3.4021	−0.0965	0.2158
			(1.1016)			(1.8335)*			(1.2886)	(2.76)***
NITA	0.5458	−2.0747	0.0111	0.5458	−2.0747	0.0242	0.1492	−1.8470	−0.0696	0.0937
			(0.1855)			(2.2041)**			(3.2132)***	(2.97)***
WCTA	5.3238	−44.2817	−0.4050	5.3238	−44.2817	−0.2145	0.3336	−7.5143	−1.5864	1.3719
			(2.4283)			(4.6441)***			(3.8645)***	(1.67)**
MCTA	8.7957	0.0049	0.6563	8.7957	0.0049	0.7062	1.2109	0.0300	0.3469	0.3593
			(0.8728)			(5.6603)***			(2.8584)***	(10.18)***

Notes:
The macro-economicmacroeconomic variables are from monthly data during 1987–1995.
a: Standard deviation is in parenthesis.
B: *T-value*, for H_0: variances are equal, is in parenthesis.
c: *F-value*, for H_0: means are not significantly different from zero, is in parenthesis.
***, ** and * denote statistical significancet at the 0.01, 0.05 and 0.10 levels, respectively.

Table 3. The Macro-Related Micro-Crisis Prediction Models: Estimated Parameters and Wald Chi-Square Statistics in Parentheses.

Model Variable	Model I	Model II
	$Prob\ (Y_i=1)=\frac{1}{1+e_i^{-Z}}$	$Prob\ (Y_i=1)=\frac{1}{1+e_i^{-Z}}$
	where $Z_i=a+bE(r_i)+\sum_j c_jX_{ji}+e_i$	where $Z_i=a+\sum_k b_k\beta_{ki}+\sum_j c_jX_{ji}+e_i$
	$E(r_i)=\alpha_i+\sum_k \beta_{ki}E(F_k)$	
Constant	–0.3848	(1.4004)
	–0.6154	(3.1258)*
Macroeconomic Factor		
E(r)	–0.4708	
	(4.6232)**	
PMI		–0.2412
		(0.3743)
CPI		–0.0948)
		(7.0439)***
INT		–16.8401
		(1.4794)
MS2		–0.0168
		(0.0863)
Financial Characteristic		
SETA	–2.7514	–2.5258
	(8.7628)***	(7.1956)***
RETA	–2.5490	–3.0003
	(7.2959)***	(9.6941)***
OINS	–0.1012	–0.0824
	(0.1910)	(0.2308)
NITA	–5.0874	–5.3884
	(7.0904)***	(7.7590)***
WCTA	–0.3619	–0.3335
(12.8779)***	(11.18.1677)***	
MCTA	–2.1294	–1.9035
(8.5778)***	(7.1550)***	
–2 Log L	234.872	229.033
Model Chi-Square	84.258***	90.097***

Notes:
***, **, and * denote statistical significance at the 0.01, 0.05 and 0.10 levels, respectively.

studies, and it is widely argued that the result is due to "window dressing" adjustments of a firm's net income.

Tables 4–9 show the predictive ability of the macro-related micro-crisis prediction models at various cut-off points. Since type I errors are more costly than type II errors, the study attempts to determine a cut-off point which correctly discriminates the distressed firms at the approximate number of non-distressed firms or, in other words, which type I errors are approximately close to type II errors. On average, the cut-off point at 0.10 seems to be optimal, indicating that a firm which has the probability of financial distress of 10% or over will be classified as a distressed firm, and a firm which has the probability under 10% will be classified as a non-distressed firm. The prediction results for the ex ante (expected return) model (Equation 1) are shown in Tables 4–6. At the cut-off point of 0.1, the total prediction accuracy equals to 76.01% for the full-sample test, 78.67% for the in-sample test, and 74.85% for the out-sample test as shown in Tables 4–6. The prediction results for the ex post (beta) model (Equation 2) are shown in Tables 7–9. At the cut-off point of 0.1, the total prediction accuracy equals to 70.45% for the full-sample test, 80.08% for the in-sample test, and 74.38% for the out-sample test as shown in Tables 7–9. The out-sample predictive ability of approximately 74% for both models makes for a promising result from this study.

5. CONCLUSIONS

This study employs the 1997 economic crisis in Thailand as a case study. Using econometric approaches, the macro-related micro-crisis prediction model is developed and the warning indicators are issued from the hypothesis tested in the macroeconomic crisis and the corporate bankruptcy models. This study uses the logit regression as a tool to develop the model which attempts to portray corporate bankruptcy caused by economic collapse as systematic risk. The firm-specific risk, e.g. the firm's capital, assets, management, earnings, and liquidity (CAMEL), is also included in the corporate bankruptcy model.

The macro-related micro-crisis prediction model developed in this study has two specifications. The first specification uses firms' expected returns calculated from the expected changes in macroeconomic variables and firms' sensitivities to those macro variables as proxies of macro-related factors, while the second specification uses firms' sensitivities to macro variables as proxies for macro factors. The contribution of the macro-related micro-crisis prediction model is to bridge a firm's sensitivity to macroeconomic conditions and its financial characteristics in order to predict the firm's financial distress.

Table 4. The Full-sample Test[a] for Model I.

$$Prob\ (Y_i = 1) = \frac{1}{1 + e^{-Z_i}}$$

$$\text{where} \quad Z_i = a + bE(r_i) + \sum_j c_j X_{ji} + e_i$$

$$E(r_i) = \alpha_i + \sum_k \beta_{ki} E(F_k)$$

Cutoff Point	Distressed Prediction				Non-distressed Prediction				Total Prediction			
	Accuracy[b]		Error[c]		Accuracy[d]		Error[e]		Accuracy		Error	
	Amount	%	Amount	%	Amount	%	Amount	%	Amount	%	Amount	%
0.00	55	100.00	0	0.00	0	0.00	341	100.00	55	13.89	341	86.11
0.10	18	32.73	37	67.27	283	82.99	58	17.01	301	76.01	95	23.99
0.20	4	7.27	51	92.73	335	98.24	6	1.76	339	85.61	57	14.39
0.30	2	3.64	53	96.36	339	99.41	2	0.59	341	86.11	55	13.89
0.40	1	1.82	54	98.18	340	99.71	1	0.29	341	86.11	55	13.89
0.50	1	1.82	54	98.18	340	99.71	1	0.29	341	86.11	55	13.89
0.60	0	0.00	55	100.00	341	100.00	0	0.00	341	86.11	55	13.89
0.70	0	0.00	55	100.00	341	100.00	0	0.00	341	86.11	55	13.89
0.80	0	0.00	55	100.00	341	100.00	0	0.00	341	86.11	55	13.89
0.90	0	0.00	55	100.00	341	100.00	0	0.00	341	86.11	55	13.89
1.00		0.00		0.00		0.00		0.00	0	0.00	0	0.00

Notes:
a: The sample is divided into two subsamples: 60% of the full sample as the in-sample (learning sample) and 40% of the full sample as the out-sample (holdout sample).
b: Distressed prediction accuracy is coded as (1,1) or a distressed firm (1) is correctly classified.
c: Type I error is coded as (1,0) or a distressed firm (1) is misclassified as a non-distressed firm (0).
d: Non-distressed prediction accuracy is coded as (0,0) or a non-distressed firm (0) is correctly classified.
e: Type II error is coded as (0,1) or a non-distressed firm (0) is misclassified as a distressed firm (1).

Table 5. The In-sample Test[a] for Model I.

$$Prob\ (Y_i = 1) = \frac{1}{1 + e^{-Z_i}}$$

$$\text{where} \quad Z_i = a + bE(r_i) + \sum_j c_j X_{ji} + e_i$$

$$E(r_i) = \alpha_i + \sum_k \beta_{ki} E(F_k)$$

Cutoff Point	Distressed Prediction				Non-distressed Prediction				Total Prediction			
	Accuracy[b]		Error[c]		Accuracy[d]		Error[e]		Accuracy		Error	
	Amount	%	Amount	%	Amount	%	Amount	%	Amount	%	Amount	%
0.00	34	100.00	0	0.00	0	0.00	191	100.00	34	15.11	191	84.89
0.10	27	79.41	7	20.59	150	78.53	41	21.47	177	78.67	48	21.33
0.20	20	58.82	14	41.18	167	87.43	24	12.57	187	83.11	38	16.89
0.30	19	55.88	15	44.12	178	93.19	13	6.81	197	87.56	28	12.44
0.40	17	50.00	17	50.00	187	97.91	4	2.09	204	90.67	21	9.33
0.50	17	50.00	17	50.00	188	98.43	3	1.57	205	91.11	20	8.89
0.60	12	35.29	22	64.71	190	99.48	1	0.52	202	89.78	23	10.22
0.70	8	23.53	26	76.47	190	99.48	1	0.52	198	88.00	27	12.00
0.80	4	11.76	30	88.24	190	99.48	1	0.52	194	86.22	31	13.78
0.90	3	8.82	31	91.18	191	100.00	0	0.00	194	86.22	31	13.78
1.00	0	0.00	34	100.00	191	100.00	0	0.00	191	84.89	34	15.11

Notes:

a: The sample is divided into two subsamples: 60% of the full sample as the in-sample (learning sample) and 40% of the full sample as the out-sample (holdout sample).

b: Distressed prediction accuracy is coded as (1,1) or a distressed firm (1) is correctly classified.

c: Type I error is coded as (1,0) or a distressed firm (1) is misclassified as a non-distressed firm (0).

d: Non-distressed prediction accuracy is coded as (0,0) or a non-distressed firm (0) is correctly classified.

e: Type II error is coded as (0,1) or a non-distressed firm (0) is misclassified as a distressed firm (1).

Table 6. The Out-sample Test[a] for Model I.

$$Prob\ (Y_i = 1) = \frac{1}{1 + e^{-Z_i}}$$

$$\text{where}\quad Z_i = a + bE(r_i) + \sum_j c_j X_{ji} + e_i$$

$$E(r_i) = \alpha_i + \sum_k \beta_{ki} E(F_k)$$

Cutoff Point	Distressed Prediction				Non-distressed Prediction				Total Prediction			
	Accuracy[b]		Error[c]		Accuracy[d]		Error[e]		Accuracy		Error	
	Amount	%	Amount	%	Amount	%	Amount	%	Amount	%	Amount	%
0.00	21	100.00	0	0.00	0	0.00	150	100.00	21	12.28	150	87.72
0.10	16	76.19	5	23.81	112	74.67	38	25.33	128	74.85	43	25.15
0.20	10	47.62	11	52.38	138	92.00	12	8.00	148	86.55	23	13.45
0.30	7	33.33	14	66.67	141	94.00	9	6.00	148	86.55	23	13.45
0.40	4	19.05	17	80.95	144	96.00	6	4.00	148	86.55	23	13.45
0.50	4	19.05	17	80.95	147	98.00	3	2.00	151	88.30	20	11.70
0.60	4	19.05	17	80.95	147	98.00	3	2.00	151	88.30	20	11.70
0.70	1	4.76	20	95.24	148	98.67	2	1.33	149	87.13	22	12.87
0.80	1	4.76	20	95.24	148	98.67	2	1.33	149	87.13	22	12.87
0.90	1	4.76	20	95.24	148	98.67	2	1.33	149	87.13	22	12.87
1.00	0	0.00	21	100.00	150	100.00	0	0.00	150	87.72	21	12.28

Notes:
a: The sample is divided into two subsamples: 60% of the full sample as the in-sample (learning sample) and 40% of the full sample as the out-sample (holdout sample).
b: Distressed prediction accuracy is coded as (1,1) or a distressed firm (1) is correctly classified.
c: Type I error is coded as (1,0) or a distressed firm (1) is misclassified as a non-distressed firm (0).
d: Non-distressed prediction accuracy is coded as (0,0) or a non-distressed firm (0) is correctly classified.
e: Type II error is coded as (0,1) or a non-distressed firm (0) is misclassified as a distressed firm (1).

Table 7. The Full-sample Test[a] for Model II.

$$Prob\,(Y_i = 1) = \frac{1}{1 + e^{-Z_i}}$$

$$\text{where} \quad Z_i = a + \sum_k b_k \beta_{ki} + \sum_j c_j X_{ji} + e_i$$

Cutoff Point	Distressed Prediction				Non-distressed Prediction				Total Prediction			
	Accuracy[b]		Error[c]		Accuracy[d]		Error[e]		Accuracy		Error	
	Amount	%	Amount	%	Amount	%	Amount	%	Amount	%	Amount	%
0.00	55	100.00	0	0.00	0	0.00	341	100.00	55	13.89	341	86.11
0.10	46	83.64	9	16.36	233	68.33	108	31.67	279	70.45	117	29.55
0.20	41	74.55	14	25.45	289	84.75	52	15.25	330	83.33	66	16.67
0.30	30	54.55	25	45.45	313	91.79	28	8.21	343	86.62	53	13.38
0.40	22	40.00	33	60.00	326	95.60	15	4.40	348	87.88	48	12.12
0.50	17	30.91	38	69.09	335	98.24	6	1.76	352	88.89	44	11.11
0.60	12	21.82	43	78.18	338	99.12	3	0.88	350	88.38	46	11.62
0.70	9	16.36	46	83.64	339	99.41	2	0.59	348	87.88	48	12.12
0.80	4	7.27	51	92.73	340	99.71	1	0.29	344	86.87	52	13.13
0.90	1	1.82	54	98.18	341	100.00	0	0.00	342	86.36	54	13.64
1.00	0	0.00	55	100.00	341	100.00	0	0.00	341	86.11	55	13.89

Notes:

a: The sample is divided into two subsamples: 60% of the full sample as the in-sample (learning sample) and 40% of the full sample as the out-sample (holdout sample).

b: Distressed prediction accuracy is coded as (1,1) or a distressed firm (1) is correctly classified.

c: Type I error is coded as (1,0) or a distressed firm (1) is misclassified as a non-distressed firm (0).

d: Non-distressed prediction accuracy is coded as (0,0) or a non-distressed firm (0) is correctly classified.

e: Type II error is coded as (0,1) or a non-distressed firm (0) is misclassified as a distressed firm (1).

Table 8. The In-sample Test[a] for Model II.

$$Prob\ (Y_i = 1) = \frac{1}{1 + e^{-Z_i}}$$

$$\text{where} \quad Z_i = a + \sum_k b_k \beta_{ki} + \sum_j c_j X_{ji} + e_i$$

Cutoff Point	Distressed Prediction				Non-distressed Prediction				Total Prediction			
	Accuracy[b]		Error[c]		Accuracy[d]		Error[e]		Accuracy		Error	
	Amount	%	Amount	%	Amount	%	Amount	%	Amount	%	Amount	%
0.00	28	100.00		0.00	0	0.00	208	100.00	28	11.86	208	88.14
0.10	24	85.71	4	14.29	165	79.33	43	20.67	189	80.08	47	19.92
0.20	21	75.00	7	25.00	183	87.98	25	12.02	204	86.44	32	13.56
0.30	18	64.29	10	35.71	199	95.67	9	4.33	217	91.95	19	8.05
0.40	14	50.00	14	50.00	203	97.60	5	2.40	217	91.95	19	8.05
0.50	9	32.14	19	67.86	204	98.08	4	1.92	213	90.25	23	9.75
0.60	8	28.57	20	71.43	205	98.56	3	1.44	213	90.25	23	9.75
0.70	7	25.00	21	75.00	205	98.56	3	1.44	212	89.83	24	10.17
0.80	3	10.71	25	89.29	207	99.52	1	0.48	210	88.98	26	11.02
0.90	1	3.57	27	96.43	208	100.00	0	0.00	209	88.56	27	11.44
1.00	0	0.00	28	100.00	208	100.00	0	0.00	208	88.14	28	11.86

Notes:

a: The sample is divided into two subsamples: 60% of the full sample as the in-sample (learning sample) and 40% of the full sample as the out-sample (holdout sample).

b: Distressed prediction accuracy is coded as (1,1) or a distressed firm (1) is correctly classified.

c: Type I error is coded as (1,0) or a distressed firm (1) is misclassified as a non-distressed firm (0).

d: Non-distressed prediction accuracy is coded as (0,0) or a non-distressed firm (0) is correctly classified.

e: Type II error is coded as (0,1) or a non-distressed firm (0) is misclassified as a distressed firm (1).

Table 9. The Out-sample Test[a] for Model II.

$$Prob\ (Y_i = 1) = \frac{1}{1 + e^{-Z_i}}$$

$$\text{where } Z_i = a + \sum_k b_k \beta_{ki} + \sum_j c_j X_{ji} + e_i$$

Cutoff Point	Distressed Prediction				Non-distressed Prediction				Total Prediction			
	Accuracy[b]		Error[c]		Accuracy[d]		Error[e]		Accuracy		Error	
	Amount	%	Amount	%	Amount	%	Amount	%	Amount	%	Amount	%
0.00	27	100.00	0	0.00	0	0.00	133	100.00	27	16.88	133	83.13
0.10	18	66.67	9	33.33	101	75.94	32	24.06	119	74.38	41	25.63
0.20	15	55.56	12	44.44	113	84.96	20	15.04	128	80.00	32	20.00
0.30	11	40.74	16	59.26	122	91.73	11	8.27	133	83.13	27	16.88
0.40	9	33.33	18	66.67	127	95.49	6	4.51	136	85.00	24	15.00
0.50	6	22.22	21	77.78	129	96.99	4	3.01	135	84.38	25	15.63
0.60	3	11.11	24	88.89	131	98.50	2	1.50	134	83.75	26	16.25
0.70	3	11.11	24	88.89	132	99.25	1	0.75	135	84.38	25	15.63
0.80	2	7.41	25	92.59	132	99.25	1	0.75	134	83.75	26	16.25
0.90	1	3.70	26	96.30	133	100.00	0	0.00	134	83.75	26	16.25
1.00	0	0.00	27	100.00	133	100.00	0	0.00	133	83.13	27	16.88

Notes:

a: The sample is divided into two subsamples: 60% of the full sample as the in-sample (learning sample) and 40% of the full sample as the out-sample (holdout sample).

b: Distressed prediction accuracy is coded as (1,1) or a distressed firm (1) is correctly classified.

c: Type I error is coded as (1,0) or a distressed firm (1) is misclassified as a non-distressed firm (0).

d: Non-distressed prediction accuracy is coded as (0,0) or a non-distressed firm (0) is correctly classified.

e: Type II error is coded as (0,1) or a non-distressed firm (0) is misclassified as a distressed firm (1).

The results are promising and confirm that macroeconomic conditions are important factors to determine a firm's possibility of financial crises. The expected-return variable shows strong significance in the ex ante specification (Equation 1) and the sensitivity-to-inflation variable is also significant at the 0.01 level in the ex post specification (Equation 2). Since 1996–1997, the Thai economy was in a steep decline causing negative returns for equity investors. The empirical findings show that, in an economic crisis, the higher or less negative a firm's return, the lower the probability of the firm's financial distress. Inflation is the most crucial variable in which the higher a firm's sensitivity to inflation, the more likely the firm's exposure to financial distress.

For testing the predictive ability of the model, the study uses the cut-off point at 0.10 to separate financially-distressed firms from non-distressed firms. The rationale is to limit type I errors to approximately the same number of type II errors, because type I errors are quite costly, relative to type II errors. For both specifications, the predictive ability or accuracy ranges between 70–80% of the sample. An out-sample test of predictive ability confirms that the model has an accuracy of about 74% of the holdout sample.

The 1997 Thai financial crisis is a remarkable case study for academic research. The contribution of this research is to develop the prediction model and warning signals of upcoming crises at both the corporate level and the economy as a whole, so that policymakers can seek protective measure in order to immunize the economy and protect against contagious, potentially lethal financial diseases.

NOTES

1. Financial support for this research was provided by The Listed Company Association, Thailand.

2. During 1992–1995, the growth of average net incomes of firms listed in the Stock Exchange of Thailand was around 22%, while in the 1996 it declined to –31.30%.

3. Studies that use only financial ratios include early works such as Beaver (1966), Altman (1968), and Altman, Haldeman and Narayanan (1977). Much of the recent work is discussed in Zavgren (1983). Studies that incorporate accountant opinions include Hopwood et al. (1989) and Flagg et al. (1991).

4. For example, in Thailand less than 10 companies listed in the Stock Exchange of Thailand were financially distressed during 1987–1994.

5. Caprio and Klingebiel (1996) document 49 banking crises in the 1970s and 1980s, and 33 crises occurred over the first six years of the present decade.

6. The SET posts a supervision sign of "C" (the filing for compliance) or "SP*" (the suspension or the temporary prohibition of trading until the causes of delisting are eliminated) against a listed company, and the firm must submit the SET documents supporting the company's financial position.

REFERENCES

Altman, E., Haldeman, R., & Narayana, P. (1977). ZETA Analysis: A new model to identify risk of corporations. *Journal of Banking and Finance*, June, 29–54.

Altman, E. I. (1983). Multidimensional Graphics and Bankruptcy Prediction: A Comment. *Journal of Accounting Research, 21*(1), (Spring), 297–299.

Altman, E. I. (1968). Financial Ratios, Discriminant Analysis and the Prediction of Corporate Bankruptcy. *Journal of Finance, 23*(4), (September), 589–609.

Altman, E. I. (1994). Corporate distress diagnosis: Comparisons using linear discriminant analysis and neural network (the Italian experience). *Journal of Banking and Finance, 18*, 505–529.

Barnes, P. (1987). The Analysis and Use of Financial Ratios: A Review Article. *Journal of Business, Finance and Accounting, 14*(4), 449–461.

Beaver, W. H. (1966). Financial Ratios as Predictors of Failure, Empirical Research in Accounting: Selected Studies. *Journal of Accounting Research, 4* (Supplement).

Caprio, G., & Klingebiel, D. (1996). *Dealing with Bank Insolveneies: Cross Country Experience.* The World Bank: Washington, D.C.

Corsetti, G., Pesenti, P., & Roubini, N. (1998). What Caused the Asian Currency and Financial Crisis? Unpublished manuscript.

Demirguc-Kunt, A., & Detragiache, E. (1997). The Determinants of Banking Crises: Evidence from Developing and Developed Countries. International Monetary Fund Working Paper.

Eichengreen, B., Rose, A. K., & Wyplosz, C. (1996). Contagious Currency Crises. NBER Working Paper No. 5681.

Eichengreen, B., & Rose, A. K. (1998). Staying Afloat when the Wind Shifts: External Factors and Emerging-Market Banking Crises. NBER Working Paper No.6370.

Flagg, J. C., Giroux, G. A., & Wiggins, C. E. Jr. (1991). Predicting Corporate Bankruptcy Using Failing Firms. *Review of Financial Economics. 1*(1), 67–78.

Flood, R., & Marion, N. (1998). Perspectives on the Recent Currency Crisis Literature. NBER Working Paper No. 6380.

Gilbert, L. R., Krishnagopal, M., & Schwartz, K. B. (1990). Predicting Bankruptcy for Firms in Financial Distress. *Journal of Business Finance & Accounting, 17*(1), (Spring), 161–171.

Glick, R., & Rose, A. K. (1998). Contagion and Trade: Why Are Currency Crises Regional? NBER Working Paper No. 6806.

Hopwood, W., McKeown, J. C., & Mutchler, J. F. (1989). A Test of the Incremental Explanatory Power of Opinions Qualified for Consistency and Uncertainty. *the Accounting Review, 66*(1), 28–48.

Johnsen, T., & Melicher, R. W. (1994). Predicting Corporate Bankruptcy and Financial Distress: Information Value Added by Multinomial Ligit Models. *Journal of Economics & Business, 46*(4), 269–286.

Kaminsky, G., & Reinhart, C. M. (1996). The Twin Crises: The Causes of Banking and Balance-of-Payment Problems. Federal Reserve Board and International Monetary Fund. Unpublished manuscript.

Kaminsky, G., Lizondo, S., & Reinhart, C. M. (1997). Leading Indicators of Currency Crises. International Monetary Fund Working Paper.

Maddala, G. S. (1986). Econometric Issues in the Empirical Analysis of Thrift Institutions' Insolvency and Failure. Invited Research Working Paper 56. Federal Home Loan Bank Board, October.

Ohlson, J. A. (1980). Financial Ratios and the Probabilistic Prediction of Bankruptcy. *Journal of Accounting Research, 18*(1), (Spring), 109–130.

Platt, H. E., & Platt, M. B. (1991). A note of The Use of Industry-Relative Ratios in Bankruptcy Prediction. *Journal of Banking and Finance, 15*, 1183–1194.

Poston, K. M., Harmon, W. K., & Gramlich, J. D. (1994). A Test of Financial Ratios as Predictors of Turnaround versus Failure among Finanially Distressed Firms. *Journal of Applied Business Research. 10*(1), 41–56.

Radelet, S., & Sachs, J. (1998). The Onest of the East Asian Financial Crisis. NBER Working Paper No. 6680.

Rose, R. S., Andrews, W. T., & Giroux, G. A. (1982). Predicting Business Failure: A Macroeconomic Perspective. *Journal of Accounting, Auditing and Finance*, Fall, 20–31.

Salchenberger, L. M., Cinar, E. M., Lash, N. A. (1992). Neural Networks: A New Tool for Predicting Thrift Failures. *Decision Sciences, 23*, 899–916.

Shivaswamy, M., Hoban, J. P., & Matsumoto, K. (1993). A Behavioral Analysis of Financial Ratios. *The Mid-Atlantic Journal of Business, 29*(2), (March), 7–24.

Thomson, J. B. (1992). Modeling the Bank Regulator's Closure Option: A Two-step Logit Regression Approach. *Journal of Financial Services Research.*

Zavgren, C. (1983). The Prediction of Corporate Failure: the State of the Art. *Journal of Accounting Literature, 2*, 1–35.

Zmijewski, M. E. (1984). Methodological Issues Related to the Estimation of Financial Distress Prediction Models. *Journal of Accounting Research, 22* (Supplement), 59–85.

24. MANAGING THE THAI CRISIS: ASSET BUBBLES, GLOBALIZATION AND MACROECONOMIC POLICY[1]

Teerana Bhongmakapat[2]

I. INTRODUCTION

Before the world economy enters the new millenium, it has witnessed surprising currency and financial crises. East Asian countries have been severely hit by crises, initiating from Thailand in 1996, despite lessons learned a few decades earlier on new development experiences that developing countries or late comers might catch up with developed countries with remarkable growth and industrialization. A chapter in history has just become outdated and inconsistent with the so-called "convergence hypothesis."

Why are these economies, with strong macroeconomic fundamentals, all a sudden plagued with the most severe crises in recent history? Why do successes easily and suddenly become failures? Were there any successes or miracles after all? The onset or the causes of Asian crises have recently been widely debated, and a number of studies have conjectured various explanations to the new experience of booms and busts. Certain countries seriously hit by the crises have to be under the policy packages sponsored by the IMF and other institutions, such as the World Bank, Asian Development Bank and several countries.

Restructuring Asian Economics for the New Millennium, Volume 9B, pages 447–476.

ISBN: 0-7623-0710-2

Thailand is the first and among the hardest hit economies. It has to be under the IMF program with financial supports amounting to 17.1 billion U.S.$. Indonesia and South Korea are equally hard hit by the crises, although they receive larger financial bailouts from the IMF-led institutions. Malaysia refuses the IMF assistance and its economic turmoil is also apparent. Crises in these countries are argued to essentially be rooted in flawed domestic fundamentals, particularly weak financial institutions, government over guarantees, over-valuation of assets, bad investment, lack of transparency, and cronyism.

Of course, once a crisis develops, it is typical to see fingers pointing at many different factors. Although there are many factors behind the crisis in Thailand and their contagion effect evident throughout East Asia, at least three major observations should receive further attention. One, while the crisis relates to fundamentals, it was not foreseen as chaotic bubbles, but rather a slowdown in economic growth. In the case of Thailand, Teerana Bhongmakapat (1990) accepted that there were several forces that would hinder Thailand's economic successes and its average growth rate tended to decline from 8.6% during 1990–1995 to 5.9% during the second half of the 1990s. Competitiveness Subcommittee (1995) also warned that it was critical to stay away from bubbles but did not anticipate it as a likely chaotic outcome within a few years to come. The Thai crisis is involved very much with serious lack of confidence in policy management, policy makers and politics (see also Teerana Bhongmakapat, 1997a, c); Corsetti, Pesenti & Roubini, 1998; Warr, 1998).[4] Such lack of confidence relates to pessimism and market reaction that can instantaneously produce discrete changes in country risk; while investors started to worry about emerging markets, including Thailand which was anticipated in 1996 to face the problems of sustained export slowdown, oversupplies in property markets, and rigid exchange rates. This implies that the crisis is quite unpredictable and characterized by self-fulfilling expectations. Two, external factors of the crises are of concern. In most studies and policy discussions, currency and financial crises have been essentially treated as consequences of weak domestic fundamentals. The domestic dimension is the main reason why the IMF program aims at correcting domestic fundamentals, not external roots of the problems, whereas several multilateral meetings have just recently signified the hot issue of global crisis and initiatives toward global financial reform. Financial liberalization was however highly accepted as one of the factors leading to the financial turmoil, largely because it occurred very rapidly without enough preparation and accompanying institutional changes (See Goldstein & Turner, 1996; Dwor-Frecaut, Mallikamas & Pootrakool, 1998). Together with a weak financial system at home, globalization of finance should be given more attention, since it may aggravate or even precede the crises.

Financial flu that spreads from Thailand to other countries in the region, and to Russia and Eastern Europe, is evidence of the new era of globalized markets. In addition, whereas the Asian crisis starts from Thailand, there are certain external factors that put pressure on exchange rates and supply of foreign credits, such as spillover effects due to rising global interest rates and probably contagious effects from the Mexican financial collapse. It is crucial to see whether or not the role of global finance, such as world interest rates and the Tequila effect, explains the Thai crisis. If it is true, policy discussions may have to redirect toward correcting global finance.

Three, it involves short-term capital movements and the panic in asset markets. Japan is a case in point. Asset bubbles and collateral damages are viewed to be a major element of the financial meltdown in Thailand and some other countries in East Asia. Thailand's asset bubble was financed by capital inflows that moved very easily through the Bangkok International Banking Facility (BIBF) which is a "half-way" approach to financial liberalization.[5] In Thailand, it is generally believed that asset bubbles lead to output collapses and financial crashes, not capital flows that rather affect asset prices and business activities. Speculation on asset prices during the first half of the 1990s led to overvaluation of wealth and collateral for bank credits. It may be the case that speculative bubbles accumulated the likelihood of financial collapse, but it is unclear whether movements in asset prices are either the cause or the consequence of the crisis. Miller and Luangaram (1998) argue that the asset bubble busted before the crisis and may not be the convincing explanation. Moreover, the sudden stops of capital inflows can destabilize domestic capital markets tremendously, and the resulting asset collapse would put the economy into deep recessions. Therefore, asset prices and private capital flows played an important role in the crisis process, and both could reinforce one another. The association between asset prices and capital movements matters greatly and requires further elaboration in understanding the Thai crisis and its "ways out."

The purpose of this chapter is to examine external causes of the crises and relevant policy implications. The emphasis is on the role of asset prices in globalized financial markets. Asset price deflation may encourage capital outflows, but, on the contrary, capital outflows are likely to dampen asset values. This chapter, therefore, studies causal relationships between asset prices, such as exchange rates and equity prices, and short-term private capital movements. An examination is made as to whether capital flows or asset values are exogenous. Different directions of causal relationships would imply different policy strategies in dealing with the crisis.

In addition, signifying the modern role of globalization in financial markets, the Mexican crisis and its contagion effects on Thailand's asset prices are explored. This is different from a number of previous studies that mostly examine contagion effects within regions. (See, for example, Masson, 1998; Alba, Bhattararacharya, Claessens, Ghosh & Hernandez, 1998; Glick & Rose, 1998). The findings may lay support for global corrections if the Mexican crisis is transmitted to the Thai economy through the channels of international asset markets. In terms of policy, the argument that domestic weaknesses are responsible for the Thai financial meltdown dominates the policy recommendations made by the IMF and Thai authorities, especially during the first year of the program. The existence of volatile capital flows and contagion across from Mexico to emerging markets in East Asia, if any, will suggest that domestic macro policies are not sufficient, though necessary, and additional global reforms may have to be seriously considered to suit the new era of globalization.

This chapter is organized into four sections. Section II conceptualizes theoretical understanding on capital movements and asset values that are possibly contributing to the capital-market crises. Section III examines statistical co-movements between asset prices and capital flows, as well as contagion effects. Section IV discusses macroeconomic policy lessons and alternatives in coping with the Thai crisis. Macroeconomic policies here are traditionally defined as those for stabilization. Finally, we conclude in Section V.

II. ASSET BUBBLES, CAPITAL MOVEMENTS AND THE CRISIS: A THEORETICAL PERSPECTIVE

Recently, there has been growing literature on the role of the credit market and the banking sector that may aggravate the adverse impact of fundamental shocks. A number of studies postulate procyclical behavior for bank credits, asset prices and business activities. Falling asset prices will affect firms' net worth and their capacity to borrow. Firms with financial distress have to liquidate their assets, causing asset prices to collapse. This will further jeopardize asset values and lead to a continuum of large shocks and recessions. At the other end, credit limitation or reduced supply of credits, both foreign and domestic, will lower prices of assets which will cause further damages on debt capacity and banks' ability to lend.

In the dynamic model constructed by Kiyotaki and Moore (1997), durable assets serve both as factors of production and collaterals for loans, and the expansion of credit-constrained firms has to be subject to their ability to acquire collateral in forms of land or other durable assets. Credit-constrained firms holding and using land as collateral will find themselves suffering from even a small, temporary negative shock that cause prices of assets to deteriorate. For example, a small productivity shock in one sector will have spillover effects on the (common) land market. Lower land prices will have an indirect effect on firms' net worth in other sectors, generating much larger fluctuations in output and asset values than the initial shock.

The closed-economy model of Kiyotaki and Moore has been modified nicely by Edison, Luangaram and Miller (1998) to explore responses to the ending of land price bubble and the fall of exchange rates. The extension may fit the current crisis in Asia, especially in Thailand which has apparently witnessed a dramatic reduction in land prices and exchange rates[6]. They argue that financial collapses where prudent firms are brought down by imprudent firms are likely if asset values fall. The scramble for liquidity will result in "knock-on" effects as firms liquidate their land to satisfy collateral requirements, whereas the further fall in asset price will intensify the financial crisis. The bust in the bubble can, therefore, easily force firms with liquidity constraints into insolvency.

Following the Tequila crisis, Calvo presented a series of studies theorizing the problems of capital flows and globalized capital markets. (See, for example, Calvo, 1998a, b; Calvo & Mendoza, 1998.) Calvo (1998b) conjectures that a slowdown, especially a sudden stop, in capital flows would generate a crisis in capital markets. The sudden-stop crisis is possible even with current account deficits being financed by direct foreign investment, but equity and long-term bond financing might shield the economy from it. Much literature on capital-market crises relates to the functioning of the banking system and the transmission mechanism through which the financial institutions might amplify initial shocks. (See Sachs, Tornell & Velasco, 1996; Eichengreen & Rose, 1998; Goldstein & Turner, 1996; Goldfajn & Valdes, 1997; Fama, 1985.)

Globalization of finance is a salient feature of modern crises, and market imperfection is central to the problem. As stated by Wyploz (1998): "the combination of financial deregulation, contagion and erratic market behavior suggests that financial markets are not the epitome of perfection that they are often made to be." Asymmetric information and incomplete markets exist in both domestic and world capital markets, of course. Sachs, Tornell and Velasco (1996) argued that, as in the Mexican Peso Crisis, international banks had a tendency to lend excessively to certain developing countries that were considered to emerge.

The rapid buildup of international lending could easily lead to crises if the perceived credit risk was sufficiently lower than its actual level, and international lending was cut back or unable to roll over. Goldstein and Turner (1996) and Wyploz (1998) are among others who considered financial liberalization as a very good predictor of currency and financial crises, as it has been in Latin America in the 1980s, in Europe in the early 1990s and recently in Asia. It is very important to know that once there is the withdrawal or sudden stop of capital flows, liquidity crisis would ensue, and it could lead the affected economy into insolvency and severe crisis that probably take several years to get back on track.

Capital inflows generate both returns from improved efficiency as well as costs from greater financial risk. The point is that the bust of capital flows following the boom period is a very good indicator of currency and banking crises. The sharp decline in net capital inflows can produce even larger results. From a modeling perspective, to come up with large discrete results, like bubbles, it usually requires very large movements in initial shocks or fundamentals; otherwise an expectations-based model or a model with multiple equilibria is to be constructed.[7] However, with a unique way of modeling, the problem of initial shocks in capital flows has been analyzed nicely by Chan-Lau and Chen (1998) who developed a model of private debt financing. Assuming that the financial system is subject to inefficiency due to costly loan monitoring, they considered a credit crunch or a reduction in the amount of loans intermediated by the inefficient financial system. One of their findings is that changes in asset values would greatly affect economic vulnerability and the severity of the financial crash.

It is realistic to take the decline in capital inflows, including the foreign supply of credit, as an exogenous shock due to the fact that, in the Asia crisis, the large and sudden reversal in private capital inflows stood in sharp contrast to favorable macro fundamentals. Furthermore, the financial system in Thailand and other Asian countries is relatively inefficient due to its stage of financial development and the slow adjustment to the new world of financial globalization that rapidly require improvements in banking standard, transparency, supervisory/regulatory framework, and competitiveness.

Let us first look at a simplified version of the model of Chan-Lau and Chen, then a standard IS-LM-BP model with greater financial risk and costs of external financing will be depicted.

Figure 1 is an interpretation of the Chan-Lau-Chen (C-C) model where DF is the demand schedule for financial intermediation and SF is the maximum supply of credit by foreign depositors being dependent on the perceived fundamental strength of the economy. On the demand side of the credit market, the optimal amount of the financial intermediary is subject to expected profits. With loan monitoring, the optimal amount that yields the local maximum

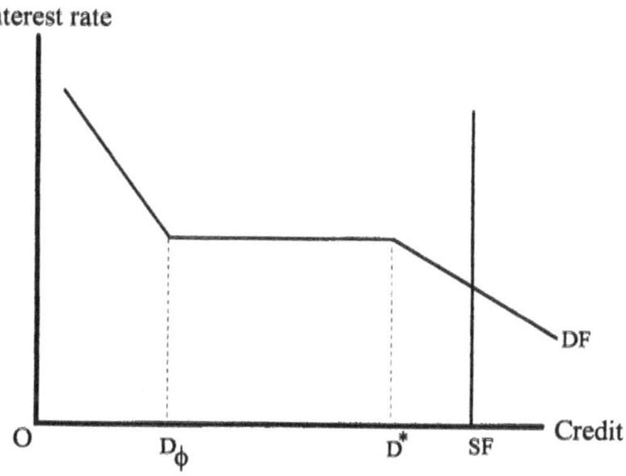

Fig. 1. An Interpretation of Chan-Lau and Chen (1998).

expected profit is Dϕ. However, the amount of equilibrium intermediation, where demand for credit equals supply of foreign credit, can increase, unmonitored, after the switching point D*. Suppose D* is the amount of intermediation that yields the same expected profit as at Dϕ, and the supply of foreign credit is between Dϕ and D*, then only Dϕ will be demanded.

The problem arises when the "safety buffer," SF-D*, shrinks and forces capital flows to move out. When SF falls below D*, even marginally, the amount of credit demanded is only Dϕ, but the size of capital outflow jumps substantially by D*– Dϕ. Therefore, a moderate reduction in foreign credit supply can drastically increase capital outflows, and certain fundamentals that affect supply of foreign credit and the local optimal of credit demand, Dϕ, are vital to the analyses.

In the C-C model, falling asset values, increasing (risk-free) foreign interest rates and other negative fundamental shifts can trigger the crisis. For example, as simplified in Fig. 1, an increase in interest rates in the capital-rich countries will discourage investment in the less attractive emerging markets, leading to a reduction in SF. The shock will force the safety buffer, SF-D*, to decline, and increase the likelihood of the crisis.

However, technically, the C-C model requires a discontinuous demand curve for credit when the expected profit from intermediary is at its local maximum. The model is good in explaining the credit market once firms become insolvent, not in the process of liquidity crunch. When the firms are at the brink of bankruptcy and the economy is in for a long recession, the demand for loans will be low. The downward pressure on demand for loans, however, may not be the right answer to the declined interest rates usually observed when the recession is at the bottom. In the case of Thailand, declining interest rates are not really the result of lower output growth, but rather the expected appreciation of the domestic currency, and the lower risk or panic in the banking system.

During the period of liquidity crunch and bank run, the rise in interest rates indicates the tight credit market as the leftward shift in the credit supply curve exceeds the downward movement in the demand for loans. This is the case, though insolvent firms may demand less credits at their stage of bankruptcy.

Consider the standard macro analysis to gain an understanding on the likelihood of a crisis when the supply of foreign capital is contracted due to less attractive returns and higher risk premium. In this setup, we ignore the costs of improving the quality of loans (for example loan monitoring costs), and we don't have a discontinuous demand curve for loans. However, during the tough time of liquidity

crisis, interest rates tend to rise, and firms apparently make a complaint on high interest costs and lack of liquidity.

In Figure 2, the credit market has typical demand and supply schedules. External factors, such as world interest rates and country risk, are considered to discourage capital inflows. Risk can be affected by various fundamentals, including world interest rate and exogenous shock in capital flows, together with self-fulfilling expectations. An excessive increase in the risk premium relates to massive movements of capital flows, and, hence, the crisis becomes

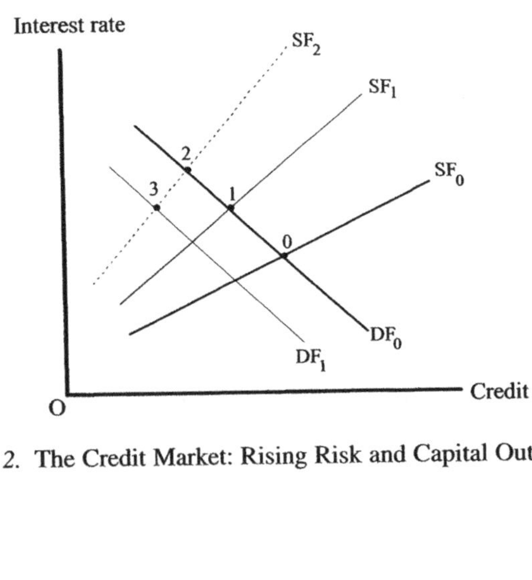

Fig. 2. The Credit Market: Rising Risk and Capital Outflows.

highly probable. It may harshly lead to high interest rates (liquidity crisis), depreciation (currency crisis), and output collapse (deep recession).

Suppose DF and SF are, respectively, the demand for loans and supply of credit. The initial equilibrium in the credit market is at point 0. Perceived country risk is assumed to rise due to pessimism toward fundamental changes, globally or domestically.[8] The SF curve shifts from SF_0 to SF_1 since the rates of returns on domestic assets are relatively lower than foreign assets. At this stage, it is likely that portfolio investments will react promptly, while other major financial flows, such as debts and direct investment, may delay for some time. The shift in the supply of foreign funds dries up liquidity for domestic uses, and damages balance sheets of banks and business firms by putting pressures on domestic interest rates, exchange rates and production costs. The potentially troubled firms and bad debts will weaken the banking system and sharply raise financial risks for the whole economy. Again, the credit supply cure moves further to the left, for instance, from SF_1 to SF_2, perhaps mainly due to outflows of institutional portfolio investment, and difficulties in receiving additional funds or rolling over debts. The liquidity or credit crunch that hurts firms' cash flows and retards growth will lead to a reduction in demand for credits, thereby shifting DF_0 to DF_1. The severity of recession will determine the magnitude of interest rate reduction. Thus, when the economy is building the new base toward recovery, interest rates or other asset prices should fall. Moreover, with some signs of recovery, risk is perceived to be lower, and the SF curve will gradually move down.

It is worth elaborating somewhat with the familiar IS-LM-BP model, as shown in Fig. 3. The initial shock of greater financial risk adversely affects the supply of foreign capital flows, and causes the BP curve to move upward. When the exchange rate is held fixed, the loss in international reserves is evident, and in the end, domestic money supply will decline. As in the case of Thailand, the eroding balance of payments is one of the major reasons why the baht would have to float and excessively depreciate. If exchange rates are allowed to float, the ensuing depreciation will have at least three consequences that signify the currency and financial crisis, assuming that exchange rate depreciation with high volatility has a negligible impact on net exports in the short run.

First, it raises the debt burden as debt contracts are largely dominated in dollars or foreign exchanges. The banks being that dependent would all a sudden become insolvent, while corporations that take bank loans would also find themselves enable to pay foreign debts, particularly those with short-term maturity. The problem of bad debt will jeopardize the functioning of the banking system and reduce the velocity of money, leading to the anti-clockwise rotation of the LM curve. Second, its supply-side effect through higher import

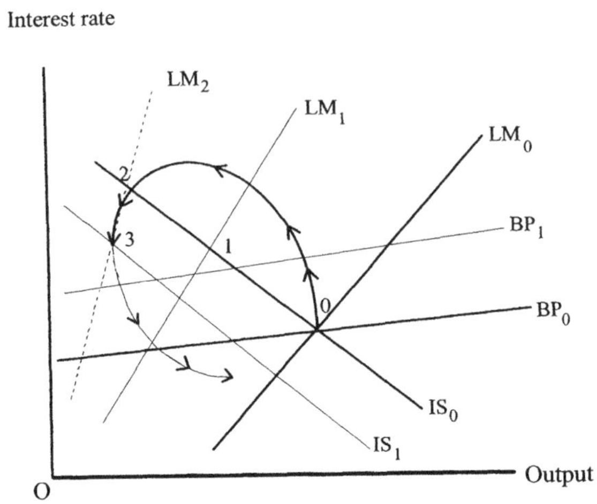

Fig. 3. The IS-LM-BP Model: Rising Risk and Capital Outflows.

prices generates inflation. A resulting decline in supply of real balances will contract liquidity and shift the LM curve to the left. Suppose, from the two reasons cited, greater risk shifts the LM curve from LM_0 to LM_1. Third, asset prices are likely to fall due to asset liquidation and changes in exchange rates, as well as stock prices. The collapse in asset or wealth will raise default risks and adversely affect private spending, causing the IS curve to shift leftward from IS_0 to IS_1. Hence, capital inflows are discouraged and move the LM curve to the left, say, from LM_1 to LM_2. The equilibrium will then move along the path shown by the dark arrow during the bust period, and the recovery path is the dashed arrow.

III. ASSET PRICES, PRIVATE CAPITAL FLOWS AND CONTAGION: ECONOMETRIC ANALYSES

Theoretically, fluctuations in asset prices can be either causes or consequences of changes in private capital flows. In light of sharp movements in asset prices, self-fulfilling prophecy and contagion under capital-market imperfections are crucial, while fundamental changes alone cannot explain the ups and downs in the bubble manner. Here, using Thailand's data, we basically investigate the movements of asset prices, private capital flows, and their simple cointegrations.

Asset Price Movements

In Thailand, information on prices of assets, particularly land and other physical assets, is poor and, to a large extent unavailable. Still, we are able to lay out some information on asset deflation/inflation in the stock market, real estate sector, and foreign exchange market. Stock price index is a barometer for market sentiments and perceived value for firms listed in the Stock Exchange of Thailand. The real estate sector makes up for a large part of national wealth, which implies that changing property values can significantly erode or inflate national wealth. Although the official data on land and property prices are not available, we will make use of the Jones Lang Wootton and Government Housing Bank data on office, retail spaces and housing in Bangkok. (See Renaud, Zhang & Koeberle, 1998). Exchange rates as relative prices of foreign financial assets are briefly covered.

After falling during the Gulf war and the coup d'etat done by National Peacekeeping Force, the Thai stock market became bullish again, particularly in 1993. The average stock price index began to fall sharply and steadily from 1354 in the third quarter of 1995 to 246 in the third quarter of 1998. (See Table 1.) The slowdown in the stock market, especially for property

Table 1. Average Stock Prices.

	1993	1994	1995	1996	1997	1998
SET Index						
Annual	1019.3	1391.7	1293.2	1168.3	597.6	353.6
Q1	932.2	1409.2	1256.8	1344.1	754.5	471.9
Q2	862.0	1297.2	1301.9	1295.7	602.9	361.0
Q3	947.5	1431.8	1353.7	1111.7	591.5	246.2
Q4	1334.1	1425.5	1258.3	924.5	442.9	329.6*
SET Index for Property Development						
Annual	1274.2	1475.9	1016.2	792.6	270.1	69.2*
Q1	1126.9	1840.1	1017.2	977.6	417.7	108.3
Q2	1014.1	1436.1	998.9	876.4	262.7	84.0
Q3	1182.0	1358.9	1098.4	761.5	253.8	33.6
Q4	1771.5	1271.5	947.8	557.1	147.2	42.0*

* As of November 25, 1998.

Sources: Stock Exchange of Thailand and TISCO Securities Research.

development, was in fact evident during 1994 and 1995, before witnessing the stock market crisis of 1996–1998.

In early 1995, the Mexican Peso crisis and the Baring case shook the stock market, and the baht was attacked with the fear of problems similar to the Mexican peso. The speculative attack was short-lived, and it failed to see any sizeable devaluation, but rather an appreciation of the baht. This was mainly because speculators wrongly anticipated baht devaluation, even though the dollars were declining. Pessimism on exports slowdown and high inflation was simply false. However, shortly after the general election in November 1995, the Banharn Administration faced serious credibility problems, while the dollars began to rise and a failing domestic bank led to lack of confidence concerning the supervising and monitoring system in the financial sector. With political difficulties under Banharn and Chavalit governments, the stock market continued to plunge further and the baht was severely under attack, even though a regional market crash had not yet been realized. The abolishment of the basket peg regime, once praised by international communities, led to the serious problem of the currency crisis and unhedged external debts.[9] Defaults and rumors on debt moratoria were intensified, and banks were in a panic. In fact, just before the time of switching exchange rate regime, Somprasong, a major land developer, and Finance One, a major finance company, were expected to go bankrupt. Such greater risk, being aggravated later by regional crises in the region, has continued to put the stock market deeper in crisis since mid-1997.

For the property market, share prices of real estate companies can be taken as a leading indicator of property market, and the property developers experienced a slight slowdown in 1994 and 1995, the period that stock prices for most listed companies had not yet declined. One of the main reasons why the property share prices slowed down somewhat was an anticipation of oversupply. The oversupply can be explained by (a) the continued corporate optimism on Thai economy, (b) high liquidity and heavy loans for the property sector, especially through fincos that extended their large lending to this sector, and (c) lag in project development and/or completion behind relatively volatile demand. According to Jones Lang Wootton, new office space supply reached its peak in 1993–1995, while the supply of retail space was strongest in 1994 and slightly declined in 1995 and 1996. (See Renaud, Zhang & Koeberle, 1998). Housing completion in Bangkok, as reported by Government Housing Bank, was the greatest during 1994–1997. As a result, vacancy rates or oversupply in office, retail spaces and residential property were massive in 1997 and 1998.

In the early 1990s, with enormous capital inflows, foreign reserves were used as a shock absorber, and exchange rates were stabilized to reduce the exchange risk for exporters and the real sector. The high convertibility of the baht indicated that exchange rates might have to be flexible, or otherwise domestic interest rates had to respond to capital flows. It was essentially not possible to manage a macroeconomy by targeting both the exchange and interest rates together, despite a robust economy which was growing very well. Financial liberalization policy committed during 1994 and 1995 lifted the need to reform stabilization policy accordingly. The baht was first attacked in early 1995, but it was by no means vulnerable. However, with pessimism and weaknesses in domestic fundamentals together with rising dollars, the baht was severely attacked by professional speculators in December 1996 and February and May 1997. The basket peg regime finally could not hold on and had to give in to a floating regime on July 2, 1997. Since that time, the baht has been excessively volatile, collapsing from 25.9 baht per dollar in 1997Q2 to 56.70 baht per dollar in December 1997, before reaching the level of 36 baht per dollar in November 1998 . (See also Fig. 4.) In 1998, the contagious currency crisis that spread to Indonesia and other economies in the region had also blocked the tendency for the baht to appreciate and quickly approach its long-run equilibrium.

Figure 4 shows an exchange rate position index (EPI), or an indicator of exchange rate vulnerability, that incorporates exchange rate movements

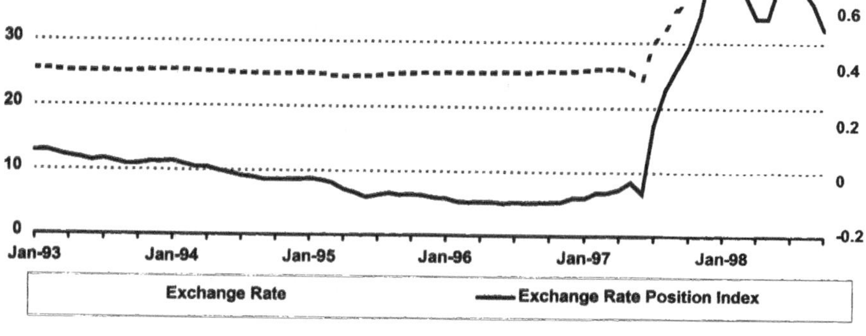

Fig. 4. Exchange Rate and Exchange Rate Position Index.

together with changes in international reserves. When international reserves deplete, EPI indicates currency depreciation or greater vulnerability of the baht, although the currency is held unchanged. Here, this composite index is arbitrarily defined as exchange rate minus 0.3 times percentage changes in international reserves, i.e.

$$[e(t)/e() - 1] - 0.3\ [FR(t)/FR(0) - 1],$$

where e(t) and FR(t) are, respectively, exchange rates and foreign reserves at time t. The period of January 1995 is chosen as the base (t=0). This index is used in our statistical analysis in conjunction with exchange rates. In Figure 4, from 1995 to mid-1997, the baht was stronger than its market rates but started to depreciate quickly in the second quarter of 1997. However, with the complete data set on foreign exchange swap transactions used by the Bank of Thailand in defending the baht attacks, the EPI would move more dramatically due to losses in net international reserves in 1997.

Private Capital Flows

After the second oil shock and the beginning of the low dollar period in the mid-1980s, Thailand and other East Asian economies became the leading destinations for private capital flows. During the last ten years, Thailand and neighboring countries were evidently different from Latin America because of the dominant role of direct investment. However, strong domestic investment and low country risks encouraged massive private capital inflows that, in turn, brought about optimism toward investment and growth.

The financial crisis and private capital flows are related, particularly short-term debts and portfolio investment. In the period prior to the crisis, portfolio investment dropped substantially in 1996. (See Table 2.) This may be due to worries concerning an overheating economy, legal actions against stock market manipulation, and intensified competition in other stock markets, such as China. Portfolio investment dropped in 1996 and later went up in 1997, partly in response to heavy baht depreciation.

On the other end, bank lending rose sizably during 1994 and 1995. BIBF regulation played a big part. It provided low costs of borrowing with tax advantages, so multinational corporations channeled their external funds in the form of loans through the BIBFs, and they were not counted as foreign direct investment. The increasing role of BIBFs, obviously, reduced the maturity of external debts, leading to the problem of maturity mismatches. With a reduction in 1996, bank lending finally collapsed in 1997.

The high ratio of short-term capital flows was the main factor behind the crisis. Total private capital flows began to fall in 1996 due to the reduction in

Table 2. Net Private Capital Flows to Thailand.

	(Billion baht)						
	1992	1993	1994	1995	1996	1997	1998*
Private Capital Flows	237.2	260.9	301.9	517.6	460.6	–274.6	–277.0
Direct Investment	50.2	36.4	22.7	29.1	36.8	105.1	127.7
Portfolio Investment	14.1	122.6	27.5	81.7	88.2	138.7	34.6
– Equity Securities	11.5	67.9	–10.3	52.8	28.4	122.0	27.9
– Debt Securities	2.6	54.8	37.8	29.0	59.8	16.7	6.7
Bank Lending	49.1	91.0	349.9	279.7	126.8	–224.9	–283.4
– BIBFs	—	193.2	253.4	202.4	115.9	–77.6	–210.7
Others	123.8	10.9	–98.2	127.2	208.7	–293.5	–156.0
Official Flows	3.5	5.0	4.0	27.5	33.0	60.4	30.7
International Reserves	21.2	25.4	30.3	37.0	38.7	27.0	26.8
(As % of GDP)							
Private Capital Flows	8.4	8.2	8.3	12.4	10.0	–5.7	—
Direct Investment	1.8	1.1	0.6	0.7	0.8	2.2	—
Portfolio Investment	0.5	3.9	0.8	2.0	1.9	2.9	—
– Equity Securities	0.4	2.1	–0.3	1.3	0.6	2.5	—
– Debt Securities	0.1	1.7	1.0	0.7	1.3	0.3	—
Bank Lending	1.7	2.9	9.6	6.7	2.8	–4.7	—
– BIBFs	—	6.1	7.0	4.8	2.5	–1.6	—
Others	4.4	0.3	–2.7	3.0	4.5	–6.1	—
Official Flow	0.1	0.2	0.1	0.7	0.7	1.3	—

* January-June.

Source: Bank of Thailand

Contagion from Mexico

bank lending and portfolio investment. Bank lending distinctly collapsed further in 1997 since it probably took some time to withdraw or roll over. Private capital inflows reduced from 460.6 billion baht in 1996 to net outflows of 274.6 and 277.0 billion baht in 1997 and the first half of 1998, respectively. Decreased bank lending was clearly to be blamed.

Although the root of the Thai crisis involved, to a large extent, domestic elements of financial crises typically found in recent history, more often than not, it has not been considered as an integral part of possible global crises in the modern era of financial globalization. Was the Thai crisis self-inflicted and had nothing to do with the previous crisis in Mexico? It is evident that the Thai crisis has contagious effects to other countries in the region through trade and financial linkages, but it is important to pose a question as to whether or not there exists a possible relationship between the recent East Asian crisis and the earlier Tequilla crisis. If it were true, we could have underestimated contagion from Mexico, or any other part of the world, to financial markets around the globe, and therefore, international measures might have to be seriously called for.

Here, we examine contagion from Mexico to the Thai stock market. Contagion is also measured in a strong sense as a shift in structural transmission across equity markets. (See Forbes & Rigobon (1998).) Co-movements between stock markets may reflect only standard channels of international shocks and a weak definition of contagion. In the strong sense, co-movements alone simply establish linkages rather than "contagion," which is defined as a measure for the excess variation in the co-movements not explained by standard relationships.

International propagation of shocks in the case of contagious Mexican crisis is specified below:

$$SET = \alpha + \beta\ (1 + D)\ SEMX + \gamma i^* + \varepsilon, \qquad (1)$$

$$SET = \alpha + \beta SEMX + \lambda DSEMX + \gamma i^* + \varepsilon, \qquad (2)$$

where SET and SEMX are stock price indices in the Thai and Mexican stock markets, respectively, i^* is international interest rate and D is a dummy variable for the period of the Mexican crisis, being equal to 1 during 1994–1995, and 0 otherwise. DSEMX is D times SEMX. International interest rate is considered as a variable that leads to the common (or "monsoonal") effects to both Mexican and Thai markets, and the sign of γ is expected to be negative. The U.S. three-month interbank rate is i^*. For the residual, it may be interpreted as Thailand's country risk, which is assumed to be independently distributed or i.i.d. Here, the contagion is captured by changes in β from the pre-crisis to the crisis period, i.e. λ in equation (2).

The estimation result is shown below. Normally, stock prices in Mexico and Thailand move in the opposite direction, implying that financial rates of return in these two countries are substitutes, i.e. competing in terms of attracting foreign funds. But this relationship switches in a meaningful manner, as λ is positive and significant. We have found contagion, in a strong definition, from the Mexican stock market to the Thai stock market: during the crisis, falling Mexican stock did hurt the Thai market. For the spillover effect, γ, is negative as expected, and higher U.S. interest rates hurt the stock market in an emerging economy like Thailand. The findings not only illustrate the role of external factors of the Thai crisis, but also demonstrate a strong likelihood that contagion might very well go worldwide, rather than within geographical proximity.[10]

$$SET = 1924.1 - 0.2406\ SEMX + 0.1709\ DSEMX - 101.57i^*$$
$$(5.9639)\quad(-2.6265)\qquad(4.0954)\qquad(-2.0157)$$
$$R^2 = 0.8138,\ F = 68.7349,\ D.W. = 0.8224,\ N = 63\ (1993.08\text{–}1998.10).$$

Equity Prices and Private Capital Flows

In discovering whether private capital flows determined asset prices, or vice versa, we apply pairwise Granger causality tests on variables related to both factors. Private capital flows include portfolio equities, portfolio debts, bank lending (BIBFs included), and BIBFs. These private capital flows are rather short-term foreign direct investment. Portfolio equities tend to react quickly to changes in market sentiments, whereas portfolio debts and bank lending may have longer maturity and require some time to withdraw or not to renew the debts. Observations on capital flows are in terms of U.S. dollars.

Equity prices and exchange rates are used as asset prices in the analysis. Stock market values, or market capitalization, are in U.S. dollars. For unavailable property prices which are not available, stock price index for listed real estate companies are used as a proxy. We apply the Granger causality test technique on the monthly data from January 1993 to October 1998. In cases where no relationships are found between variables, we report alternative results where data are transformed into a three-month moving average (equations with asterisks, *). This transformation may help avoid irregular fluctuations.

Table 3 shows the estimation results of causality tests between equity prices and various types of private capital flows. The Thai stock market tended to be Granger-affected by portfolio equities but not the other way around. Portfolio equities determined real estate stock prices, and clearly were exogenous in the sense of Granger. On the contrary, portfolio debts and bank lending were Granger-caused by the equity market. For BIBFs, equity prices of property sectors were exogenous, whereas BIBFs, essentially short-term loans, Granger-caused the SET index and market capitalization. The relationship between BIBFs and the SET index was two-fold. The conclusion we may draw here is that short-term private capital flows, particularly portfolio equities, are likely to affect equity prices, while variations in longer-term private capital flows, such as portfolio debts and bank lending (BIBFs excluded) are likely to follow those of equity prices.

Table 4 tests the relationships between private capital flows and exchange rates as well as the EPI index. For portfolio equities, portfolio debts and BIBFs, private capital flows Granger-caused exchange rates and the EPI index. But,

Table 3. Equity Prices and Net Private Capital Flows: Causality Tests.

Null Hypothesis	F statistic	Probability
Equity Prices and Portfolio Equities		
(1)* $P_e \nrightarrow PIE$	1.7755	0.1623
$PIE \nrightarrow P_e$	2.2020	0.0979
(2)* $V_e \nrightarrow PIE$	2.5555	0.0644
$PIE \nrightarrow V_e$	3.6519	0.0178
(3)* $P_{ep} \nrightarrow PIE$	1.8569	0.1474
$PIE \nrightarrow P_{ep}$	3.5115	0.0209
Equity Prices and Portfolio Debts		
(1) $P_e \nrightarrow PID$	5.4258	0.0023
$PID \nrightarrow P_e$	0.7628	0.5195
(2) $V_e \nrightarrow PID$	1.8629	0.1463
$PID \nrightarrow V_e$	1.1039	0.3549
(3) $P_{ep} \nrightarrow PID$	4.4121	0.0073
$PID \nrightarrow P_{ep}$	1.2320	0.3064
Equity Prices and Net Bank Lending		
(1) $P_e \nrightarrow NBL$	6.4784	0.0007
$NBL \nrightarrow P_e$	0.4013	0.7526
(2) $V_e \nrightarrow NBL$	3.3527	0.0249
$NBL \nrightarrow V_e$	1.3118	0.2793
(3) $P_{ep} \nrightarrow NBL$	5.5700	0.0020
$NBL \nrightarrow P_{ep}$	0.1104	0.9537
Equity Prices and Net Bank Lending (BIBF)		
(1)* $P_e \nrightarrow BIBF$	2.9733	0.0393
$BIBF \nrightarrow P_e$	3.1346	0.0325
(2)* $V_e \nrightarrow BIBF$	0.8373	0.4791
$BIBF \nrightarrow V_e$	3.1816	0.0308
(3) $P_{ep} \nrightarrow BIBF$	3.9978	0.0118
$BIBF \nrightarrow P_{ep}$	0.5458	0.6529

only the behavior of bank lending yielded mixed results. Exchange rates and bank lending Granger-caused each other, whereas fluctuations in EPI led to variations in bank lending.

Table 4. Exchange Rates and Net Private Capital Flows: Causality Tests.

Null Hypothesis	F statistic	Probability
Exchange Rates and Portfolio Equities		
(1) *ER $\nrightarrow$ PIE	0.3040	0.8224
PIE $\nrightarrow$ ER	3.0409	0.0363
(2)*EPI $\nrightarrow$ PIE	0.4995	0.6842
PIE $\nrightarrow$ EPI	3.2150	0.0296
Exchange Rates and Portfolio Debts		
(1)* ER $\nrightarrow$ PID	1.1892	0.3222
PID $\nrightarrow$ ER	2.4743	0.0709
(2)* EPI $\nrightarrow$ PID	1.1889	0.3223
PID $\nrightarrow$ EPI	2.5787	0.0627
Exchange Rates and Net Bank Lending		
(1) ER $\nrightarrow$ NBL	3.7310	0.0160
NBL $\nrightarrow$ ER	2.8719	0.0440
(2) EPI $\nrightarrow$ NBL	3.5440	0.0199
NBL $\nrightarrow$ EPI	1.6680	0.1839
Exchange Rates and Net Bank Lending (BIBF)		
(1) ER $\nrightarrow$ BIBF	1.5702	0.2063
BIBF $\nrightarrow$ ER	4.5511	0.0062
(2) EPI $\nrightarrow$ BIBF	0.6712	0.5732
BIBF $\nrightarrow$ EPI	3.5861	0.0190

Other than the interactions between private capital flows and asset prices, it is one step beyond to see whether or not private capital flows responded to other fundamental variables, particularly domestic and global interest rates as commonly adhered to. Table 5 provides the empirical results of causality tests between various types of private capital flows and monetary conditions, both domestic and international. Monetary conditions are defined as indicators incorporating interest rates and changes in exchange rates, that is,

$[i(t)/i(0) - 1] - 0.3\,[e(t)/e(0) - 1]$, for domestic monetary condition (MCI), an

$[i^*(t)/i^*(0) - 1] + 0.3\,[e^*(t)/e^*(0) - 1]$, for foreign monetary condition (MCI*).

The i(t), i*(t), e(t), and e*(t) are domestic interest rates, foreign interest rates, exchange rates of baht/U.S. dollars, and Japanese yen/U.S. dollars at time t,

Table 5. Monetary Conditions and Private Capital Flows: Causality Tests.

Null Hypothesis	F statistic	Probability
Portfolio Equities		
(1) MCI $\nrightarrow$ PIE	1.4363	0.2415
PIE $\nrightarrow$ MCI	1.6692	0.1836
(2) MCI* $\nrightarrow$ PIE	0.4882	0.6918
PIE $\nrightarrow$ MCI*	0.4615	0.7102
Portfolio Debts		
(1) MCI $\nrightarrow$ PID	4.4289	0.0072
PID $\nrightarrow$ MCI	1.4437	0.2394
(2) MCI* $\nrightarrow$ PID	2.9158	0.0418
PID $\nrightarrow$ MCI*	0.7997	0.4991
Net Bank Lending		
(1) MCI $\nrightarrow$ NBL	6.6673	0.0006
NBL $\nrightarrow$ MCI	2.9050	0.0423
(2) MCI* $\nrightarrow$ NBL	0.7871	0.5060
NBL $\nrightarrow$ MCI*	0.3526	0.7874
Net Bank Lending (BIBF)		
(1) MCI $\nrightarrow$ BIBF	3.0088	0.0374
BIBF $\nrightarrow$ MCI	2.0121	0.1222
(2) MCI* $\nrightarrow$ BIBF	1.4566	0.2358
BIBF $\nrightarrow$ MCI*	0.5274	0.6653

respectively. The period of January, 1995 is selected as base, $t=0$. Domestic interest rates are three-month interbank rates, while foreign interest rates are defined as three-month interbank rates in the U.S. money market. The results reveal that both domestic and foreign monetary conditions Granger-caused portfolio debts, whereas domestic, rather than foreign monetary conditions, Granger-caused bank lending, including BIBFs. The implication is that, relative to monetary conditions in the U.S., domestic monetary conditions have a significant role regarding changes in the debt markets.

Based upon our findings and series of data, it can be said that the fast-moving portfolio investment caused fluctuations in the Thai stock market, particularly real estate, resulting in sudden stops in foreign loans. These stops led to the currency crash and financial crisis. Moreover, domestic interest rate policy, as well as global monetary conditions, could be the critical factors that affected capital flows. The implication is that changing monetary conditions, in turn, would tremendously help ease the crisis and its contagion. In any case, leaving out the global element of the crisis is surely a big mistake.

IV. MACROECONOMIC POLICIES

In coping with the Thai crisis, the initial macroeconomic framework, including the IMF-sponsored program, aimed, principally, at restoring confidence in exchange rates and fixing flawed domestic fundamentals. Devaluation was perceived as necessary to reduce the current account deficit, but excessive baht depreciation Thailand experienced shortly after the float led to strong arguments in favor of high interest rates. With heavy external debt and large current account deficits, contractionary demand management was seen as necessary, whereas weak financial institutions and bail-out over guarantees justified the IMF-supported package to close down insolvent financial firms and liquidate assets.

The framework, however, is heavily criticized, and certain lessons can be drawn. The program aims at correcting domestic fundamentals but with little emphasis on global markets and self-fulfilling prophecy. In the following section, we discuss stabilization policies for alleviating the Thai crisis which involves volatile exchange rates, heavy foreign debts, the deep domestic recession and social costs of the crisis.

Domestic money, though having a small and limited role in solving the crisis, is much affected by global factors; monetary policy as a domestic measure is central to macro policy discussions in the crisis-hit economies, such as Thailand and its neighbors. Tight monetary policy was recommended to help restore confidence and stabilize exchange rates for fear of excessive baht depreciation. (See Fischer, 1998; Dornbusch, 1998a; Goldfajn & Baig, 1998.) Fischer (1998) stated clearly: "All *[IMF-supported]* programs *[in Thailand, Korea and Indonesia]* have called for a substantial rise in interest rates to attempt to halt the downward spiral of currency depreciation. And all [these] programs have called for forceful, up-front action to put the financial system on a sounder footing as soon as possible." Whether or not tight monetary policy is the right dose remains debatable. (See Sachs, 1997; Radelet & Sachs, 1998; Stiglitz, 1998c.)

Before the collapse of the baht, speculative attacks signaled for the need to manage either exchange rates or interest rates. Flexible exchange rates were implied if the authorities were reluctant to pursue an exceptionally high interest rate policy for a pretty long period of time. Unhedged foreign borrowing discouraged the authority from giving up in the fight to defend the currency, but swap transactions to maintain international reserves greatly made information asymmetric between speculators and firms. The former received the information from money traders, while the latter simply followed official figures and words. The actual information on swap transactions in foreign reserves suggested that the baht should be more flexible rather than pushing interest rates higher.[11] In fact, before the crisis, interest rates were almost twice as high as in Malaysia.

The attempts to have "sound" monetary policy to restore confidence, or at least the reluctance to adopt counter-cyclical monetary policy, led to excessively high interest rates that produced harmful effects on the health of corporate and financial sectors. The one-month repurchase rate jumped from 13.00% in January 1997 to around 20–24% during the second half of 1997 and early 1998. Real interest rates also rose considerably for several months during the crisis. The growth of broad money, M2A, dropped on an annual basis from 18.1% in 1995 to 12.7 and 2.1% in 1996 and 1997, respectively.

It is very natural and proper for interest rates to rise in response to higher risk premiums. But adopting tight monetary policy at the onset of the crisis with huge debt and money panic could fail to stabilize exchange rates and manage the crisis for a number of reasons.

First, although both current account and balance of payments are negative, macroeconomic management demands a trade-off between internal and external balances. The initial framework that worked on fiscal and monetary contractions put an emphasis on achieving external balance by accepting the costs of output collapse. This is probably due to the beliefs that tight monetary policy effectively combats the problems of capital flights and overheating economy. But, at the other end, tight money raises default risks and retards output amid the crisis, even though it normally relates to currency appreciation. Capacity utilization reduced sharply from 79.4 in December 1995 to 58.5 and 50.7 in December 1997 and September 1998. Certainly, monetary contraction cut back private investment and consumer spending, not largely through interest costs of new projects, but through economy-wide pessimism and defaults of financial institutions which upset confidence in the baht. Domestic interest rates would rise due to higher risk premiums related to the monetary contraction. More importantly, high interest rates discouraged stock markets or asset prices that related to private capital flows (see Table 4).

Second, excessive currency depreciation and liquidity crunches occurred simultaneously, suggesting that the crisis might not be the result of the over expansion in the money supply. The sudden collapse of the baht had much to do with self-fulfilling prophecy and pessimism on the government's capabilities in stopping the panic in domestic and international asset markets. Immediately after the general election in November 1997, the new administration and economic team led by the Prime Minister Chuan Leekpai helped restore confidence remarkably, as supported by the average value of the baht declining from 40.70 baht per dollar in the fourth quarter of 1997 to 43.70 baht per dollar in the first half of 1998 amid the severe regional crisis in Indonesia and South Korea. Sachs (1997) convincingly postulated the self-fulfilling prophecy in the money market which caused the liquidity crisis and deep recession. Financial institutions failed to function properly while non-viable finance companies were closed down and sent a shock wave to the remaining financial sector. Although money supply contracted and inflation rates were high, a seasonally-adjusted index of income velocity of broad money (M2A) further declined from 100 in the base period (December 1996) to 99 and 92 in December 1997 and September 1998, respectively. Reduced velocity and greater bank panic generated excess demand for real balances, thereby not supporting tight monetary policy. As experienced in Thailand, since mid-1998, easing monetary conditions together with new initiatives to stop the bank panic have reinforced interest rates to decline dramatically, and such policy actions have caused the baht to appreciate pretty quickly.

Third, the weak financial system requires a serious reform to improve banking standards, and correct any moral hazard problems associated with the financial system. To right the wrong practices, a smooth process of adjustment is as essential as other processes of structural adjustment and trade liberalization. But to quickly reform the financial sector, tight money would make the process difficult and perhaps impose greater default risks on the entire banking sector which has remained unattractive to foreign investors who have great concerns over unpredictable risks and possible global financial meltdown.

As a result, it is imperative not to make monetary policy rigid so that macroeconomic adjustment can respond well to foreign capital shocks and financial reforms. However, this does not mean that monetary policy should be pursued at the expense of exchange rate depreciation. Based on our findings, exchange rates are Granger-caused by private capital flows, but not the other way around (see Table 4). Exchange rates should be allowed to find a new equilibrium in the aftermath of the currency collapse. With self-fulfilling expectations, attempts at affecting exchange rates through altering the money supply may incur considerable costs, but it matters very briefly. In any case, the "optimal" level of exchange rates is essentially unknown.

To have liquidity with a minimal impact on exchange rates, the "helicopter policy" is inferior to measures specifically aimed at debt restructuring and recapitalization. Successful developments in these two areas greatly resolve the problems of insolvent banks and enormous bad debts. Asset prices would not overly decline when financial intermediation can function and massive asset liquidation remains intact as the diffusion of bankruptcy is contained.

The Thai crisis is rooted in the private sector, making it difficult for the government to resolve the problem. The government basically lacks policy instruments to effectively handle bad debts, including the externals, not to mention the political implications of government bail-outs. As a result, official authorities are reluctant to launch new initiatives but are much more comfortable with social expenditure programs. This is why fiscal policy has many limitations in fixing the financial crisis. The IMF-supported program requires the explicit inclusion of financial burden into the government budget. By the same token, fiscal budget is difficult to ease out collateral damages or to stabilize asset prices that have been reduced substantially.

Initially, fiscal policy targeting was to downsize the budget so as to cut down current account deficits. In 1997, the government, in consultation with the IMF staff, intended for a budget surplus by 1% of GDP. This is acceptable, given that current account surplus is critical for the ability to pay back enormous foreign debts.[12] However, tight money and output recession suggested that fiscal adjustment had to be made to stabilize output growth. Revised fiscal targets allowed (central government) budget deficits to rise to 1.4 and 2.7% of GDP for fiscal years 1997 and 1998, respectively. For fiscal year 1999, the budget deficit target is changed from 1.0 to 3.0% of GDP.

Nevertheless, easing indicative targets on government budget deficits should not be counted as expansionary fiscal policy, but rather a target change due to insufficient revenue collection. Theoretically, based on substantial current account surpluses by some 13.5 and 11% of GDP in 1998 and 1999, greater budget deficits should be made to stimulate the economy. In practice, conservative fiscal targets are consistent with the need to maintain fiscal discipline and assure manageable public debts. Fiscal policy, to a large extent, has been constrained by political consequences and public debt management implications to respond anti-cyclically to movements of capital flows, asset prices and output growth.

As we have discussed so far, macroeconomic policies may play a stabilizing role in the Thai crisis. But limitations do remain, especially in their reaction to the capital-market crisis rooted in the private sector and global conditions. This is tantamount to saying that a resolution to a crisis and its contagion cannot overlook international measures. If the Thai crisis were really domestic, correcting domestic fundamentals would be the first-best solution for us, even when living in the world of self-fulfilling expectations. But complications arrive when it is not. With global causes and implications, externalities exist, and it calls for global corrections. Domestic macro policies may no longer be effective without global measures. In terms of policy management, global measures provide additional instruments for a crisis-hit country to achieve a demanding set of targets comprised of domestic interest rates, exchange rates, capital flows, and the output gap.

What international measures should be undertaken to cease such a crisis? In terms of policies that can manage capital flows and exchange rates, the Chilean measure is popular and preferred in the sense that it helps correct the unpleasant pattern of the flows that rely heavily on short-term capital. It also works through changing incentive structures, making it more desirable to quantitative controls and regulations that Thailand imposed during 1997. In any case, both approaches aimed at changing incentives and regulations can be very costly since they symbolize interventions that can greatly confuse the market and hurt capital inflows necessary for an economic recovery. Worse, the measures are likely to be ineffective, as Thai capital market is a very small player in the global market.

The implication is that decisions toward global financial reform and macro policy coordination should be supported for small economies to gain maximum benefits from financial globalization. Time and energy are required in architecting a global financial reform that well balances risks and returns of capital flows or truly generates benefits for all countries concerned.

In the meantime, collusive actions to quickly stabilize hard currencies can yield astonishing results. Macro policy coordination on interest rates or exchange rates by the U.S., the EU and Japan would greatly prevent the global crisis and currency crashes in various economies around the globe. As suggested by McKinnon (1998), interest rate policies correctly responding to exchange rate misalignments in a cooperative manner would be needed to overcome the East Asian currency crisis. Recent actions promptly made by the Fed to cut down interest rates not only cool down the conceivable likelihood of global deflation and credit crunch, but also substantially raise the ability to pay U.S.-dominated foreign debts, thereby reducing Thailand's country risk. Baht appreciation has also kept prices of equities and real assets from further collapses. The Fed policy is a good example: international and domestic objectives are not always contradictory. During the period of dissenting proposal for global reform, international macro policy coordination is thus a practical solution that can readily save the global economy without independently threatening potential benefits provided by the world capital market.

V. CONCLUDING REMARKS

The domestic causes of the Thai crisis have often been emphasized by a number of observers. Such views have serious implications for macroeconomic management in Thailand and other crisis-hit countries in East Asia. The IMF-supported program has followed along this line of thinking. However, if global factors, contagious effects and self-fulfilling prophecy are introduced into the Thai crisis, it will be difficult and essentially require international measures to put an end to the crisis.

This study, with econometric techniques, tests the hypotheses concerning (1) contagion from the Mexican crisis and (2) Granger-causalities between equity prices and exchange rates, on the one hand, and certain types of financial flows, on the other. The study shows that, although debt flows generally cause variations in asset prices, portfolio equity flows are exogenous in the sense of Granger. It is of importance to note that the Mexican crisis had a contagious effect on the Thai equity market. This leads to a vital question: whether domestic measures are sufficient in tackling this contagious crisis, given that it is much affected by external factors.

Regarding domestic measures, contractionary monetary policy is not good enough for the crisis which requires substantial financial reform and measures to halt the self-fulfilling panic in the globalized capital market. As the crisis is rooted in the private sector, it is difficult and politically unpopular to solve various problems, bad debts and insolvency included. Fiscal expansion also faces some limitation due to declining tax revenues and a need to maintain fiscal disciplines together with well-managed public debts. It is difficult for domestic macroeconomic policies to be actively counter-cyclical, although certain capabilities for crisis management do exist

Global measures need to be found. Through them, global financial reforms should be agreed upon. Due to externalities in the global capital market, certain policy measures that can correct them are desired. One problem is it is difficult to come up with consensus blueprints that benefit a large number of global members in any near future. In the meantime, collective actions to coordinate macroeconomic policies undertaken by hard-currency countries can readily manage an onset of the contagious or self-fulfilling crisis that may spread worldwide. Recently, cooperative policy action made by the Fed to reduce interest rates has virtually stabilized asset prices from their falls and raised the ability of Thai firms and financial institutions to repay their debts. In essence, it has quickly helped prevent the world economy from further damages caused by the potential global crisis. In the difficult process of halting the contagious crisis, international macro coordination is a must and is very much attached to global conditions.

NOTES

1. Paper presented to the American Committee on Asian Economic Studies (ACAES)-Chulalongkorn University International Conference, Bangkok, Thailand, 16–18 December 1998.

2. Associate Professor of Economics, Chulalongkorn University. The author is grateful to Dr. Suchittra Chamnivickorn for comments, and Dr. Man Juttijudata for most statistical work.

3. For seminal studies and influential views, see Fischer (1998), Krugman (1998c), Sachs (1997), Radelet and Sachs (1998), Stiglitz (1998a and c), Corsetti, Pesenti and Roubini (1998) and Edison, Luangaram and Miller (1998).

4. Dornbusch (1998b) viewed the Thai economy with strong fundamentals but related the initial problem of the Thai crisis partly to the relationship between politicians and the weak banking system.

5. The BIBF scheme aims at reducing transaction costs of capital movements and, therefore, facilitates the speed of capital flows. Ammar Siamwalla (1997) asserted that the BIBF contributed to the property boom and excess supply in the real estate sector. (See also Corsetti, Pesenti & Roubini, 1998).

6. According to Fischer (1998) and Krugman (1998c), the role of domestic financial institutions and property prices is an essential element in understanding the crisis in Asia. Both views focus on the domestic dimension of the problems, however.

7. See Goldfjan and Valdes (1997) and Masson (1998) for models with expectations and multiple equilibria, respectively.

8. In the Asian and Tequila crises, we observe the co-movements of stock prices and exchange rates of economies in the same regions. However, contagion may not be significant only through regional links, but also market sentiments worldwide. When a local market is collapsing, global investors may have to maintain their rates of returns and risks by withdrawing their funds from some other markets. Valdes (1996) argued that lack in liquidity in a crisis-hit country would lead financial intermediaries to liquidate their assets invested in other countries, and, thus, might trigger a crisis elsewhere.

9. Before the baht was floated, the market expected the fair value of the baht at 30–32 baht per dollar. But after the float on July 2, 1998, the baht immediately collapsed and recorded a low at 56.50 baht per dollar on January 12, 1998. Actually, pessimism kept increasing when the baht depreciated and even anticipated 50–70 baht per dollar.

10. For studies that found contagious crisis within East Asia, see Glick and Rose (1998) on trade links, and Alba, Bhattaracharya, Claessens, Ghosh and Hernandez (1998) on asset price co-movements.

11. This is the matter of trade-off. Fisher (1998) as well as Corsetti, Pesenti and Roubini (1998) argued that the Thai monetary policy was not sufficiently tight.

12. At the time of switching the exchange rate regime, external debts were seen as critical and required macro policy responses. Assuming that real interest rates and

growth were 7 and 4%, respectively, the current account surplus amounted to roughly 1.7% of GDP, and a 1% budget surplus was called for. (See Teerana Bhongmakapat, 1997b, c).

REFERENCES

Alba, P., Bhattacharya, A., Claessens, S., Ghosh, S., & Hernandez, L. (1998). Volatility and Contagion in a Financially Integrated World: Lessons from East Asia's Experience. Paper presented at the PAFTAD 24th conference on Asia-Pacific Financial Liberalization and Reform, held by School of Development Economics, NIDA, May 20–22.

Bhongmakapat, T. (1990). Prospects and Strategies of the Thai Economy in the Next Decade. Symposium on Directions for Policy Reforms for the Thai Economy in the Next Decade, Faculty of Economics, Chulalongkorn University, Bangkok, January 23–24, in Thai.

Bhongmakapat, T. (1997a). Thailand and Macroeconomic Policy: Toward the Floating Exchange Rate System. Paper prepared for Lecture on Exchange Rates and Interest Rate Policy in the Recent Crisis held by Economics Research Center, Faculty of Economics, Chulalongkorn University, July 3, in Thai.

Bhongmakapat, T. (1997b). It's Time to Resolve the External Debt Crisis. *Krungthep Thurakij*, July 26, in Thai.

Bhongmakapat, T. (1997c). 1997: Stop Leading to Crisis. *Krungthep Thurakij*, August 20, in Thai.

Calvo, G. A. (1998a). *Balance of Payments Crises in Emerging Markets: Large Capital Inflows and Sovereign Governments.* Mimeo., University of Maryland, March.

Calvo, G. A. (1998b). *Capital Flows and Capital-Market Crises: The Simple Economics of Sudden Stops.* Mimeo., University of Maryland, July.

Calvo, G. A., & Mendoza, E. G. (1998). *Rational Herd Behavior and the Globalization of Securities Markets.* Mimeo., University of Maryland and Duke University, March.

Chan-Lau, J., & Z. Chen (1998). Financial Crisis and Credit Crunch as a Result of Inefficient Financial Institution – with Reference to the Asian Financial Crisis. Working Paper No. 98/127, International Monetary Fund.

Competitiveness Subcommittee (1995). White Paper for Strengthening Thailand's International Competitiveness, Bangkok: Office of the Prime Minister, in Thai.

Corsetti, G., Pesenti, P., & Roubini, N. (1998). *What Caused the Asian Currency and Financial Crisis?* Mimeo., New York University, September.

Dornbusch, R. (1998a). *After Asia: New Directions for the International Financial System.* Mimeo., MIT, July.

Dornbusch, R. (1998b). *Asian Crisis Themes.* Mimeo., MIT.

Dwor-Frecaut, D., Mallikamas, V., & Pootrakool, K. (1998). Thailand's Balance of Payments and Financial Crisis: Export Competitiveness, Investment Efficiency, and Financial Fragility. In: J. Witte & S. Koeberle (Eds), *Competitiveness and Sustainable Economic Recovery in Thailand.* Bangkok: National Economic and Social Development Board and World Bank Thailand Office.

Edison, H. J., Luangaram, P., & Miller, M. (1998). Asset Bubbles, Domino Effects and "Lifeboats": Elements of the East Asia Crisis. International Finance Discussion Paper No.606, Board of Governors of the Federal Reserve System, March.

Eichengreen, B., & Rose, A. K. (1998). Staying Afloat When the Wind Shifts: External Factors and Emerging Banking Crises. NBER Working Paper No.6370, January.

Fama, E. F. (1985). What's Different About Banks. *Journal of Monetary Economics, 15*, 29–39.

Fischer, S. (1998). The Asian Crisis: A View from the IMF. Addressed at the Midwinter Conference of the Bankers' Association for Foreign Trade, Washington, D. C., January 22.

Forbes, K., & Rigobon, R. (1998). *Contagion or Vulnerability.* Mimeo., MIT, September.

Glick, R., & Rose, A. K. (1998). *Contagion and Trade: Why Are Currency Crises Regional?* Mimeo, University of California at Berkeley, August.

Goldfajn, I., & Baig, T. (1998). *Monetary Policy in the Aftermath of Currency Crises: The Case of Asia.* Mimeo., International Monetary Fund, October.

Goldfajn, I., & Valdes, R. O. (1997). Capital Flows and the Twin Crises: the Role of Liquidity. Working Paper No. 97/87, International Monetary Fund.

Goldstein, M., & Turner, P. (1996). Banking Crisis in Emerging Economies: Origins and Policy Options. BIS Economic Papers No. 46, Bank for International Settlements.

Kane, E. J. (1998). Capital Movements, Asset Values, and Banking Policy in Globalized Markets. NBER Working Paper No.6633, July.

Kaminsky, G., & Reinhart, C. (1996). The Twin Crises: the Causes of Banking and Balance-of-Paymets Problems. International Finance Discussion Paper No. 544, Board of Governors of the Federal Reserve System, August.

Kiyotaki, N., & Moore, J. (1997). Credit Cycles. *Journal of Political Economy, 105*(2), 211–248.

Kochhar, K., Loungani, P., & Stone, M. R. (1998). The East Asian Crises: Macroeconomic Developments and Policy Lessons. Working Paper No. 98/128, International Monetary Fund, August.

Krugman, P. (1998a). *Currency Crises.* Mimeo., MIT.

Krugman, P. (1998b). Saving Asia: It's time to get radical. *Fortune*, September 7.

Krugman, P. (1998c). *What Happened to Asia.* Mimeo., MIT.

Li, L., & Hu, Z. F. (1998). Responses of the Stock Market to Macroeconomic Announcements Across Economic States. Working Paper No. 98/79, International Monetary Fund, May.

McKinnon, R. I. (1998). Exchange Rate Coordination for Surmounting the East Asian Currency Crisis. Keynote Speech delivered at the Sixth Convention of the East Asian Economic Association, Kitakyushu, September 4–5.

Masson, P. (1998). Contagion: Monsoonal Effects, Spillovers, and Jumps Between Multiple Equilibria. Working Paper No. 98/142, International Monetary Fund, September.

Miller, M., & Zhang, L. (1998). *Handling Liquidity Crises: Is More Money More Hazard?* University of Warwick and CEPR, London, May.

Miller, M., & Luangaram, P. (1998). *Financial Crisis in East Asia: Bank Runs, Asset Bubbles and Antidotes.* National Institute Economic Review, CLARE Group.

Panitchpakdi, S. (1998). Thailand's Exchange Rate Crisis: How It Relates to the Asian and Global Economy. Keynote Speech at the Third Biennial Pacific Rim Allied Economic Organization Conference, Bangkok, January 16.

Radelet, S., & Sachs, J. (1998). *The East Asian Financial Crisis: Diagnosis, Remedies, Prospects.* Mimeo., Harvard Institute for International Development.

Sachs, J. (1997). The Wrong Medicine for Asia. *New York Times*, November 3.

Sachs, J., Tornell, A., & Velasco, A. (1996). Financial Crises in Emerging Markets: The Lesson from 1995. Brookings Paper on Economic Activity, August.

Siamwalla, A. (1997). Why Are We in This Mess? *Bangkok Post*, November 12.

Stiglitz, J. (1998a). Bad Private-Sector Decisions. *Wall Street Journal*, February 4.

Stiglitz, J. (1998b). Boats, Planes and Capital Flows. *Financial Times*, March 25.

Stiglitz, J. (1998c). The Role of International Financial Institutions in the Current Global Economy. Address to the Chicago Council on Foreign Relations, Chicago, February 27.

Valdes, R. (1996). *Emerging Market Contagion: Evidence and Theory.* Mimeo., MIT.

Warr, P. G. (1998). Thailand: What Went Wrong? In: J. Witte & S. Koeberle (Eds), *Competitiveness and Sustainable Economic Recovery in Thailand.* Bangkok: National Economic and Social Development Board and World Bank Thailand Office.

Wyploz, C. (1998). *Globalized Financial Markets and Financial Crises.* Graduate Institute of International Studies, Geneva and CEPR, London, April.

25. CHINA'S MACROECONOMIC STABILIZATION POLICIES IN THE PROCESS OF HIGH GROWTH, SYSTEM TRANSITION AND OPENING TO THE OUTSIDE WORLD[1]

Changsheng Xu[2]

1. INTRODUCTION

China's reform and opening to the outside world began at the end of 1978 when the famous Third Plenary Session of the 11th Central Committee of Chinese Communist Party was held. Now at its 20th anniversary, we are reviewing the experiences and lessons of the past two decades and looking forward to the future of the new millennium. Since the erupting of the Asian financial crisis, China's economic policies and experiences have attracted much attention of the world. Among them, the macroeconomic stabilization policies are perhaps the most interesting. It is generally thought that control on the inflow of short-term foreign capital and inconvertibility of capital account of payment balance have made China escape from this crisis. In my view, these accounted for part of the matter, but not all. Many other discreet macroeconomic stabilization policies

Restructuring Asian Economics for the New Millennium, Volume 9B, pages 477–490.

ISBN: 0-7623-0710-2

which China adopted are even more important. Perhaps they can offer some useful reference to other developing countries.

When we discuss China's macroeconomic stabilization policies, there are three related questions: (1) Are they successful in the past two decades? If the answer is affirmative, what are they? (2) Are there any unsolved problems or difficulties? If there are, what are they? (3) What are the trends of change in the next one or two decades? This paper tries to answer these questions step by step.

2. TARGETS OF CHINA'S MACROECONOMIC STABILIZATION POLICIES

There have been three processes simultaneously going on in China in the past 20 years: (1) the industrialization of the country or changing from a low income developing country to a NIC; (2) the marketization or the system transition from a planned economy to the Socialist Market Economy; (3) the change from a closed economy to an opening one in the process of globalization. These three processes will last for a long-time. By contrast to the other tansitional economies such as Russia and some East European countries, the first process – industrialization – was basically completed long ago. On the other hand, compared with other developing countries within the market system such as Mexico, Brazil, Malaysia, Indonesia and Thailand, the second process – marketization or system transition – does not exist. So China's macroeconomic policies have to face more complicacies than any other developing or transitional countries. They have three main targets: (1) to keep a high rate of economic growth in the process of industrialization; (2) to avoid serious inflation or unemployment and to keep social stability in the process of high growth and system transition; (3) to keep international payments basically in balance and to guard against the outside shock in the process of opening to the outside world while joining the global economic system. Obviously, this is a very difficult job. In the official language of the Chinese government, "we should deal well with the relation among reform, development and stability". According to the explanation of the Chinese government, "Development is the aim, reform is the motive force and stability is the precondition". So the slogan it puts forward is "Deepening the reform, widening the openness, speeding up development and keeping stability". In actual practice, these principles have basically been carried out by the Chinese government, although it went astray in certain occasions.

3. CHINA'S MACROECONOMIC STABILIZATION POLICIES AND THEIR EXPERIENCES IN THE PAST TWO DECADES

Firstly, I would like to point out that China's macroeconomic stabilization policies are generally successful in the past two decades. We could make this judgment from the following four aspects:

(1) They have promoted the lasting high economic growth. As Table 1 shows, the average annual growth rate of real GDP from 1979 to 1997 is 9.8% in

Table 1. The Growth Rate of Real GDP of China and the Main Countries and Regions of the World (%) (1979–1997).

Average Annual Growth Rate	1979–1988	1989–1997	1979–1997
World	3.4	3.2	3.3
Developed Countries	2.7	2.2	2.5
U.S.	2.7	2.3	2.5
Japan	3.8	2.4	3.1
Canada	3.2	1.7	2.5
E.U.	2.3	2.0	2.2
Germany	1.8	2.6	2.2
U.K.	2.5	1.6	2.1
France	2.2	1.8	2.0
Italy	2.7	1.4	2.1
Developing countries	4.3	5.7	5.0
Asia	6.8	7.8	7.3
China	**10.1**	**9.5**	**9.8**
Taiwan	8.1	6.5	7.3
HongKong	8.2	4.8	6.6
Korea	8.1	7.3	7.7
Singapore	7.3	8.5	7.9
Thailand	6.7	7.8	7.2
Indonesia	4.9	7.8	6.3
Malaysia	5.8	8.7	7.2
India	4.7	5.8	5.2
Latin America	2.7	3.1	2.9
Brazil	3.2	2.2	2.7
Mexico	3.0	3.1	3.1
Africa	2.3	2.6	2.4
Russia		–6.9*	

* Average Annual growth Rate of 1991–1997.

Sources: State Statistics Bureau of China (SSBC), Statistical Bulletin of 1998. World Development Report, World Bank, 1997.

China, while in the same period, this rate for the whole world is 3.3%, for the developed countries 2.5%, the developing countries 5.0%, and Asian countries 7.3%.

(2) They have ensured the progress of the reform. Twenty years ago, China's production and price of products and services were controlled by the central government according to plan. Now, more than 95% of them are decided by the market. The framework of the market system has been initially established. In the process of the system transition, the living standard and welfare of nearly all people have improved to some extent. The society has remained stable in the main. This situation is very different from Russia and the other transitional countries.

(3) They have protected China's economy from outside shock and the spread of the Asian financial crisis in the process of opening. The openness of China's economy has made great progress. The total value of imports and exports has increased from U.S.$ 20.64 billion in 1978 to 325.1 billion in 1997, with the average annual growth rate of 15.6% (see Table 2). It is 36% of China's GDP in 1997. China has become the 10th largest trading country (region) up from the 27th in 1978. In the total value of world trade, the share of China's import has risen to 2.5% in 1997 from 0.9% in 1978,

Table 2. Total Value of Imports and Exports in China.
(Unit: Billion U.S. Dollar)

Year	Total	Exports	Imports	Balance
1978	20.64	9.75	10.89	–1.14
1980	38.14	18.12	20.02	–1.90
1985	69.60	27.35	42.25	–14.90
1986	73.85	30.94	42.91	–11.97
1987	82.65	39.44	43.22	–3.77
1988	102.79	47.52	55.27	–7.75
1989	111.68	52.44	59.14	–5.50
1990	115.44	62.09	53.35	8.74
1991	135.63	71.84	63.79	8.05
1992	165.53	84.94	80.59	4.35
1993	195.70	91.74	103.96	–12.22
1994	236.62	121.01	115.61	5.40
1995	280.85	148.77	132.08	16.69
1996	289.90	151.06	138.84	12.22
1997	325.10	182.70	142.40	40.30

Sources: SSBC, China Statistical Yearbook, CSPH, 1997, p. 588.

Table 3. Total Value of Foreign Capital Inflow to China.

(Unit: Billion U.S. Dollar)

Year	Total Value	Foreign Loans	FDI	Other Invesments
1979–83	14.438	11.755	1.802	0.881
1984	2.705	1.286	1.258	0.161
1985	4.647	2.688	1.661	0.298
1986	7.258	5.014	1.874	0.370
1987	8.452	5.805	2.314	0.333
1988	10.226	6.487	3.194	0.545
1989	10.059	6.286	3.392	0.381
1990	10.289	6.534	3.487	0.268
1991	11.554	6.888	4.366	0.300
1992	19.202	7.911	11.007	0.284
1993	38.960	11.189	27.515	0.256
1994	43.213	9.267	33.767	0.179
1995	48.133	10.327	37.521	0.285
1996	54.804	12.669	41.726	0.409
1997	64.00		45.30	

Sources: SSBC, China Statistical Yearbook, CSPH, 1997, p. 605.

and the share of China's export has risen to 3.3% in 1997 from 0.8% in 1978. The total inflow of foreign capital is U.S.$348.3 billion in 1978–1997, about 63% of which is FDI (see Table 3). China has become the second largest country just behind the U.S. and the No. 1 in developing countries in absorbing foreign capital. Its reserve of foreign exchange is U.S.$139.9 billion in 1997 (see Table 4), or No. 2 in the world. These figures of foreign trade, capital inflow and reserve show the great achievement of opening in the past 20 years in China.

Table 4. Foreign Exchange Reserves.

(Unit: Billion U.S. Dollar)

Year	1979	1981	1983	1985	1987	1989	1990	1991	1992	1993	1994	1995	1996	1997
FER	0.840	2.708	8.901	2.644	2.923	5.550	11.093	21.712	19.443	21.199	51.620	73.520	105.029	139.90

Sources: SSBC, China Statistical Yearbook, CSPH, 1997, p. 624.

Table 5. Growth Rate and Inflation Rate of China (1978–1998).

Year	1978	1979	1980	1981	1982	1983	1984	1985	1986	1987	1988
Growth Rate of Real GDP(%)	11.7	7.6	7.9	4.5	8.5	10.2	14.5	12.9	8.5	11.1	11.3
Inflation Rate (CPI, %)	7.0	2.0	6.0	2.4	1.9	1.5	2.8	8.8	6.0	7.3	18.5
Year	1989	1990	1991	1992	1993	1994	1995	1996	1997	1998	
Growth Rate of Real GDP (%)	4.3	3.9	7.0	12.8	13.4	11.8	10.2	9.7	8.8	7.8	
Inflation Rate (CPI, %)	17.8	2.1	2.9	5.4	13.3	21.7	14.8	6.1	0.8	–2.6	

Sources: SSBC, Statistical Yearbook of China and Statistical Bulletin, related years, China Statistical Publishing House (CSPH).

(4) Finally, along with the above processes of economic growth, reform and opening, the institutions and tools of the macroeconomic management themselves have also changed very much. The direct control under the former planned economy has reduced sharply, while the indirect control through the market has considerably increased. The relative importance of these two ways of control has altered. The order of the three most powerful macroeconomic management agencies of Chinese government are now the People's Bank of China (the central bank), then the Ministry of Public Finance, then the State Committee of Planning and Development; while in 1980s they were the State Committee of Planning, then the Ministry of Public Finance, then the People's Bank of China.

What are the successful experiences of China's macroeconomic stabilization policies in the past two decades? In my view, the following four points are worthy of mentioning:

3.1. Seeking High Economic Growth Without Disturbing Macroeconomic Stability

The path of high economic growth in China in the past two decades was not smooth nor steady. There were three and half economic cycles since 1978 (see Table 5 and Fig. 1). From 1978 to 1997, the main task of China's macroeconomic policy was to fight inflation while keeping high speed of

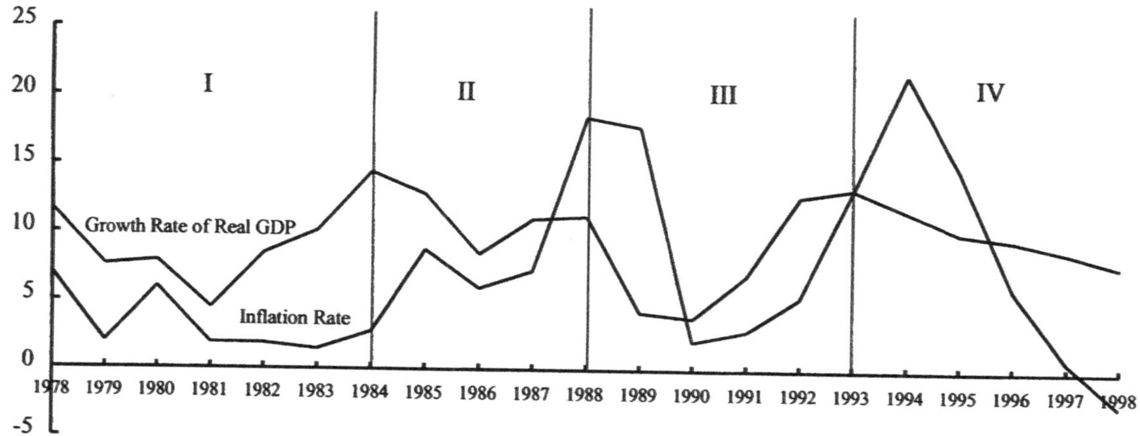

Fig. 1. Business Cycles of China (1978–1997).
Sources: SSBC, Statistical Yearbook of China and Statistical Bulletin, related years, China Statistical Publishing House (CSPH).

economic growth. In Fig. 1, the growth rate of GDP and the inflation rate are highly co-related (the time lag is about 1 year). In the peaks of these cycles, 1983–1984, 1987–1988, 1992–1994, when the annual growth rates of GDP were over 10%, the inflation rates were 8.8% in 1985, 18.5% in 1988, 21.7% in 1994. The accelerated expansion of the economy was always interrupted by the high inflation. When the society could not bear the serious inflation (annual rate of over 10%), the central government had to adopt tightening policies and slow down the step of economic growth. But the tightening policies made the economy glide down sharply, for example, the growth rate of GDP went down to 4.5% in 1981 from 11.7% in 1978, 8.5% in 1986 from 14.5% in 1984, 3.9% in 1990 from 11.3% in 1988, and about 7.8% in 1998 from 13.4% in 1993.

It was fortunate that the Chinese government checked the inflation effectively in time when the economy became too hot. Especially in 1993–1994 when the inflation rate went beyond 20% and the price of real estate and securities went too high, symptoms of economic bubble became very conspicuous. The central government adopted the "moderate tightening" fiscal and monetary policy in time in June 1993, and gradually realized the "soft landing" in 1997, ending with the growth rate of real GDP at 8.8%, and the inflation rate at only 0.8%. Without this effective tightening policy in the preceding, it would be very difficult for China to escape from the Asian financial crisis and keep Renminbi (RMB) from the pressure of depreciation up to the present.

It should be pointed out that China's macroeconomic policies have undergone some adjustments since 1994. The central government tried to avoid the excessively sharp fluctuations of the former three cycles, and made the economy grow more stably and sustainably. It adopted a development strategy called "progress with stability", namely, to seek the highest possible growth rate under low inflation. We could see this point from the first "Code of China People's Bank" (the central bank) approved in March 1995. It says: "The function of monetary policy is to stabilize the value of money, and to promote economic growth through it." This should be the correct summary of the development experiences of both China and other countries.

3.2. Deepening Reform Under Conditions of Macro-Stability

The way of China's reform and transition to market economy from the planned economy is characterized with "gradualism", which is different from the "big bang" or "shock therapy" in Russia and some East European countries. Gradualism includes some customary methods with Chinese characteristics, such as introducing the competition mechanism before the reform of property rights; reforming the price system before reforming the enterprises; deregulating the pricing of products and services step by step, practicing "the dual track system" in the transitional period; developing the non-state-owned enterprises (non-SOEs) and the township and village enterprises (TVEs) before reforming the SOEs, so as to create the competitive market condition for the reform of SOEs; and decentralizing decision-making power from the central government to the local government and SOEs. According to my understanding, the key point of all these measures is to take sufficient consideration of the social bearability to the economic reform. Reform actually means large-scale redistribution of benefits of different groups of people. Inevitably it will incur great disruptions in economic life and will take a long time. The Chinese government is perfectly aware of this, it has been doing its best to guarantee that the absolute living level of most inhabitants should improve with each reform measure, although their relative income may vary. If some people became worse-off after the reform, they would be subsidized. For example, when the price of some farm products was raised to benefit the peasants, the government would give city and town residents some price subsidy in turn. So there never appeared absolute decrease of income as a result of reform in China. Actually the welfare of nearly all the people has improved to some degree, and abject poverty has substantially decreased since the reform. This means the Chinese government has carried out sound social policy in the process of reform. Perhaps this is the essence of what is called Socialist Market Economy.

3.3. Widening Opening to the Outside World Under the Conditions of Stability

As mentioned above, China's degree of openness to the outside world has increased greatly in the past 20 years. It has become an important power in the global economic system. This is because the Chinese government has been upholding open policy as a basic development strategy. But China is a developing country. It is in a disadvantageous position in competition in the international market where monopoly forces hold sway. So the open policy has both its benefit and cost or risk. And China is the largest developing country, its domestic market is huge, so it is impossible for China to rely entirely on the outside market as some small countries do. Thus it is crucial for China to implement the open policy under conditions of stability.

China's stabilization policies in the process of opening consist of four elements: (1) Relying on domestic savings as the main source, while absorbing foreign capital with all kinds of favorable policies, and actively encouraging

FDI while controlling the inflow of short-term foreign private capital. Since 1992, China's foreign capital inflow and FDI have increased sharply (see Table 4). But the relative share of China's foreign debt is not large; it was less than 14% of GDP in 1997, and 85% of which was long-term debt. (2) Relying on domestic market in the main, while actively gaining access to the international market. In 1980's, China's foreign trade had a deficit every year. But in 1990's, with the increase of the export capacity and the relative decrease of the import as a result of the macroeconomic tightening policy after 1993, most years witnessed a surplus in foreign trade (except 1993), which amounted to U.S.$40.3 billion in 1997. (3) Owing to surplus of both capital account and current account in recent years, the foreign exchange reserves of China has gone up rapidly (see Table 5) to about U.S.$140 billion in 1997. The central bank kept these reserves through reducing the domestic money supply. It has become a massive force protecting China against the shock of the Asian financial crisis. (4) Although China has realized the convertibility of RMB in current account and adopted the system of managed floating exchange rate since 1994, the capital account is still inconvertible. This policy successfully protected China from the shock of the international floating capital (the "hot money") during the recent financial crisis.

These active yet steady policies for opening are the result of deliberate and sensible choice by Chinese government and perhaps also worthy of emulation by other developing economies.

3.4. Using Necessary Administrative Measures to Safeguard Stability

In using the policy tools, the Chinese government sometimes employed necessary administrative measures beside macroeconomic levers because the new market system has not been established or consolidated. For example, the three chief weapons of monetary policy – the open market operation, the discount rate and the reserve rate system – are still not in force. In this case, direct control of lending and the interest rate are necessary to ensure economic stability. Actually, China's reform of the macroeconomic management system had not been carried out until 1994. That means, if the microeconomic foundation was not firmly established, the slackening of macroeconomic management would induce economic chaos or even crisis. This is just the lesson of Russia and other transitional countries with the "big bang" or "shock therapy".

In a word, the above four experiences of China show that macroeconomic stability is the necessary precondition for development or reform or opening.

For the sake of stability, both direct and indirect, economic and administrative measures could be used when needed.

4. NEW CHALLENGES AND TRENDS OF CHINA'S MACROECONOMIC STABILIZATION POLICIES

As mentioned above, the main task of China's macroeconomic policies has been fighting inflation concurrent with high growth and system transition. But since the second half of 1997, both internal and external economic situations have changed dramatically. Domestically, China's economy has turned from seller's market to buyer's market, and is confronted with general over-production and glut. It is reported that, among the 601 kinds of staple commodities, 74.2% is in surplus, while those in balance between supply and demand is only 25.8%. The general price level has declined continuously for more than 12 months. Deflation has taken the place of inflation. This situation is partly the outcome of the achievement of the past 20 years of reform and development, that is to say, productivity has increased substantially. Of course it is also related to the macroeconomic tightening policies since 1993 to some extent. Meanwhile, the Asian financial crisis has worsened China's external conditions. The growth rate of foreign trade and foreign capital inflows have declined obviously this year. More seriously, because of the lag of the system reform of the SOEs and the state-owned banks (SOBs) as well as the worsening of both domestic and foreign macroeconomic situation, the loss of the SOEs and the bad assets of the SOBs become increasingly severe, financial risk is rising higher and higher, and unemployment becomes a serious economic and social problem. So China's macroeconomic policy has to turn to fight recession and deflation and to guard against the external shock and the internal financial risk at the same time.

Since the beginning of 1998, China's macroeconomic policy has turned to stimulate domestic demand with active or expansionary fiscal and monetary policies. Its key goal is to keep the growth rate of real GDP at 8% without devaluation of Renminbi (RMB). The central government has increased investment of 100 billion yuan of RMB to infrastructure construction and 270 billion yuan to replenish the equity capital of the four largest SOBs. The commercial banks have also augmented 100 billion yuan of loan to the infrastructure construction. The central bank has reduced the interest rate for six times since 1997, three times in 1998, and lowered the reserve-deposit ratio from 13% to 8%. The commercial banks have opened and expanded the consumer durables credit and the resident mortgages. These policies are very necessary for the economic recovery in the short-run and will come into effect gradually.

Now there are three crucial tasks to which we must pay attention. Firstly, the degree of stimulating aggregate demand should be moderate, or inflation would appear again one or two years later with over-expansion, and the mistake of the former three cycles would be repeated. So, the principle of seeking high growth under stability should be firmly held. According to the experience of the economic growth in the past 20 years and the present situation, China's annual growth rate of real GDP should be about 8% in the next one or two decades. Thus the real growth rate of 8% and the inflation rate below 5% should be the appropriate goals of macroeconomic control in the recent future.

Secondly, the short-run policies of stimulating demand should be combined with the long-run structural adjustment on the supply side. The latter includes the industrial structure among the primary, secondary and tertiary industries, and between the basic industries and the processing industries; the organizational structure between SOEs and non-SOEs; and the regional economic structure among the eastern, middle and western regions. For the balanced and sustainable development, the investment should be inclined to agriculture, basic industries (transportation, communication, and information industries), high technology industries, non-SOEs and the middle and western regions.

Thirdly, with the economic expansion, China's demand for imports will increase, while the surplus of the foreign trade earnings would decrease or deficit would occur. So keeping the basic balance of the international payments is very important. We should develop new export market and introduce foreign capital (specially FDI) continuously with all kinds of favorable policies, including letting Renminbi (RMB) devaluate or float if really necessary.

We have a long way to go in reforming the institution of China's macroeconomic management which is the foundation for implementation of macroeconomic policies. Both our capital market and money market are imperfect, and the SOBs are not commercial banks in the real sense of the term. The interest rate is not shaped by the market, and there exist huge bad assets and increasing financial risk. So the central bank of China has three tasks to accomplish: (1) Carrying out a stable monetary policy for the sustainable high growth under low inflation; (2) Promoting the commercialization of the SOBs, the maketization of interest rate and the establishment of full-fledged financial market; (3) Tightening up the supervision of the rising financial industry and guarding against financial risk.

In the realm of fiscal system, with increasing unemployment and the establishment of the social security system, the government expenditure of social welfare and transfer payments will increase rapidly. But government revenue is not large enough to bear the burden. The government revenue in China has declined from 35% in 1978 to only 11% of GDP in 1996, much lower than the average level of both developed and developing countries. This is because of the decrease of profit and tax from SOEs. Thus, the fiscal deficit would go up sharply. So the fiscal power of the government should be raised. That means an effective taxation system (specially income tax system) should be established as fast as possible, and the tax rate should be raised appropriately.

As to the policies towards the international economy, with entering WTO in the future, the domestic market of China would become even more open to the world, foreign trade would be more free, the capital market of China would be more exposed to the outside world, and the RMB would ultimately become an international money. There will appear new challenge to China's macroeconomic situation. We should draw a lesson from the recent Asian financial crisis, insist on a stable monetary policy and a sound fiscal policy within the country, while constantly paying attention to and manage the balance of payments strictly, and adopt a flexible exchange rate system to deal with any disequilibrium condition if it should occur.

NOTES

1. At the International Conference on "A Macroeconomic Core of an Open Economy for Progressive Industrialization and Development in Asia in the New Millennium" Sponsored by ACAES and Chulalongkorn University Bangkok, Thailand, December 16–18, 1998.
2. Tel: 0086-27-87543752 Fax: 0086-27-87548040 E-mail: chshxu@mail.hust.cn

REFERENCES

Angarg, H. (1998). Macroeconomic Policy: From Moderate Austerity to Enlarging Domestic Demand. *Reform (China), 5* (September).

General Adjustment (1998). A Common Subject and A Necessary Choice – An Analysis of China's Macroeconomy. *Economic Research Journal, 9* (September).

Guoguang, L. et al. (1998). Conversation by Writing in commemoration of the 20th Anniversary of Reform and Opening Up. *Economic Research Journal (China), 11* (November).

Jing-Lian, W. (1998). An Appraisal of Economics Situation and A Proposal of Economic Policy. *Economics Information (China), 9* (September).

Macroeconomic Research Group, China Center for Economic Research, Beijing University (1998). Macro-situation, Financial Risk and External Shock – An analysis of Current China's Macroeconomy. *Economic Research Journal, 3* (March).

Peng, L. (the former Primmer) (1998). Work Report of Government (March 5, 1998). *People Daily (China)*, (March 21).

Research Group of Economic Institute of CASS (1998). General Adjustment: A Common Subject and A Necessary Choice – An Analysis of China's Macroeconomy. *Economy Research Journal (China), 9* (September).

Seeking for the Effective Policy Combination under Multi-economic Goal (1998). An Analysis of China's Macroeconomic Situation and Our Proposal. *Economic Research Journal, 4* (April).

Shi-Yong, G. (1998). The Economic System Reform and the Economic Development of Contemporary China. *Economic Daily (China)*, (November 26).

Stiglitz, J. E. (1998). Going towards the New Paragon of Development: Strategy, Policy and Press. Conference of Trade and Development of U.N., Geneva, (November).

Tao, Y. (1998). On Macroeconomy in Transitional Period form controlling Inflation to Enlarging Domestic Demand. *Reform (China), 6* (November 26).

The Government in the Changing World (19978). World Development Report 1997, New York.

The Reform Strategy of the Second Step of China (1998). *Economic Daily (China)*, (November).

The World Bank (1993). The East Asian Miracle: Economic Growth and Public Policy. Oxford University Press, Oxford.

Xiang-Nong, D. ((1998). The Historic Responsibility of the China People's Bank. *People Daily (China)*, (November).

Yingqiu, L. (1998). High Growth Low Inflation: Goal and Result of Macro control – The Theoretical Reflections of Experience of China's Sustained High Economic Growth in Recent Five Years, Economic Research Journal, *1* (January).

26. MONETARY-FINANCIAL CRISIS IN ASIA AND ECONOMIC RENEWAL IN VIETNAM: CASE STUDY ON FOREIGN EXCHANGE POLICY

Do Loc Diep[1]

INTRODUCTION

Studies on causes and effects of monetary and financial crisis in the region show that exchange rate is one of important reasons that is both direct cause and the consequence of this crisis and a linchpin to get out of the crisis. This has been obviously seen at the expectation by international community to the recovery capacity of Japanese yen or on the possibility of not devaluating the Chinese Juan. Recently, with the Japanese yen getting stronger, indexes of a wide range of regional and global stock markets have risen.

Most of nations stricken by monetary and financial crisis have their mistakes in the foreign exchange policy. One of major errors of these countries is identified as failing to ensure flexibility of exchange rate in the market mechanism.

One valuable lesson Vietnam may learn from the regional monetary and financial crisis is on foreign exchange policy. The Vietnamese authorities have also taken initial interception solutions in advance to reduce pressures on exchange rate and prevent the economy from possible unnecessary shocks. But

Restructuring Asian Economics for the New Millennium, Volume 9B, pages 491–511.

ISBN: 0-7623-0710-2

the next step as a challenge facing Vietnam is to have an active policy on exchange rate so as to provide the sustainable growth of our economy. This is a problem to be resolved in selecting targets of macro-economic policy. To this end, Vietnam should have a consistent vision both from macro and micro-economic aspects. Just for this reason, in this paper we would like to set forth some ideas with the title "Monetary financial crisis in Asia and economic renewal in Vietnam, case study on foreign exchange policy towards Vietnam currency".

I. EXCHANGE RATE AND EVOLUTION OF FOREIGN EXCHANGE POLICY IN THE PAST YEARS

In transiting into market economy and expanding international economic relations for economic development, the system of fixed and multi-rate of exchange in the previous period of centralized planning economy in Vietnam has failed to respond to economic rules of the market economy and thus is no longer a tool of efficient control of the economy.

In addition, it is an impediment to dynamic force required to develop the economy in general and external economic relations in particular including foreign trade, aggravating thus instability, sluggishness and recession of the economy. Since the 6th Party's Congress, as transiting into market economy with the macro-economic adjustment by the State the system of unreasonable and negative exchange rate of the previous period has been gradually improved on the basis of respecting requirements of market mechanism to be in line with actual situation in the process of economic conversion.

During this process, Vietnam government's policy is to orchestrate the renovation of foreign economic fundamental, where foreign exchange policy is one of most important orientation. This foreign exchange policy is designed to develop a system of floating-oriented exchange rates under control instead of the previous system of fixed and multi-rate of exchange.

1. 1988–1991 Period

In October 1988, Chairman of Council of Ministers (presently the Prime Minister) issued Directive No 271-CT stipulating that the rate of exchange of Vietnam Dong against convertible foreign currencies established by State Bank of Vietnam in consult with the National Monetary-Financial Committee shall be in line with the market rate of exchange and only permitted to fluctuate in the range from 10% to 20% as compared to the market exchange rate. Then, in March 1989, Vietnam Government revoked the system of Government's

Table 1. Official Exchange Rate and Market Exchange Rate During 1988–1996 Period.

Year	Official exchange rate VND/US$	Market exchange rate VND/US$	Comparison percentage
1988	900	5,000	18
1989	3,900	4,100	95
1990	6,300	6,500	96
1991	9,767	11,975	82

Source: Fjorde and Vylder, International Economics – Theories and Practices, 1991.

subsidies through the rate of exchange for foreign trade activities, at the same time non-commercial rate of exchange is adjusted to be in line with official exchange rate with a fluctuation range of 20%. After enforcing new regulations on exchange rate, the rate of exchange VND/U.S.$ increased remarkably and constantly, nominal exchange rate approaches closely to market exchange rate (see Table 1).

Fluctuation of exchange rate during 1988–1991 period was very close to the inflation variations, making the actual exchange rate almost unchanged. This has a positive impact on the recovery of balance inside and outside the economy, on increasing the competitiveness of domestic goods, promoting export growth and increase in supply of foreign currency. Therefore, deficit in balance of trade and the balance of payments has gradually declined year after year. Favorable variations of exchange rate coupled with a range of monetary-financial solutions such as monetary restrictions, expenses reduction, credit restrictions, increase of interest rate and other economic policies have cut the inflation short and gradually brought the economy out off recession and into growth phase.

In late 1991, the price shock of gold and U.S. dollar along with the collapse of a wide range of credit funds have led to a sharp increase of market exchange rate (see Table 2) and then a danger of inflation recurrence loomed over the economy.Being scared of inflation recurrence, the State Bank has applied a lot of restricting solutions such as sales of State-treasury bonds, change in exchange reserve (sales of U.S. dollars to buy Vietnam dongs) to devaluate U.S. dollar, granting loans to alleviate consequence of the collapse of credit funds system.

As a result, market exchange rate has been gradually declined and became stable in 1992. Results of such adjustment on exchange rate among others

Table 2. Situation of Change in Inflation, Exchange Rate, Balance of Trade, Balance of Payments and Exchange Reserve in 1989–1992.

Indexes	1989	1990	1991	1992
Inflation rate (%)	34.7	67.4	67.5	17.5
Rate of exchange VND/U.S.$ (value as of the end of the year)	4,300	6,800	11,975	10,840
Balance of trade (U.S.$ million)	–350	–41	–64	12
Balance of payment (U.S.$ million)	–220	–141	–50	218
Exchange reserve (U.S.$ million)	111	94	91	165

Source: Macro-economic management in the Economic Renovation process – International Conference on Trade, Hanoi, 20–21 April 1994.

macro-economic indicators as inflation, trade balance, payment balance . . . have been appraised by most economists as one of the successes of the macro-economic policy beside other achievements of macro-economic nature in the issues in terms of inflation, balance of trade, balance of payments and so on.

According to them, inflation has been pushed backwards, the purchasing power of domestic currency has been gradually stabilized, the balance of payments now runs a surplus (in 1992 the payment balance surplus is about U.S.$0.2 billion). So the then stable exchange rate was reasonable (about VND 10,500 = U.S.$1). Moreover, some people even praise these successes of foreign exchange policy and are of the opinion that the value of Vietnam dong should be increased to be in line with the surplus situation of the balance of payments and to meet the demands for investment expansion to speed up the economic growth.

2. *1992–1997 Period (Before the Crisis)*

But the successes in restoring the stability of exchange rate in late 1991 & in early 1992 and the achievements of Renovation for preventing inflation have obliterated the obsessions on inflation's consequences and impending danger of its recurrence, and it remains to be a factor to encourage policy's makers selecting a set of policies on exchange rate for purpose of preventing inflation and maintaining the stabilization of nominal exchange rate.

Real fluctuation of nominal exchange rate in the period from 1992 until the regional monetary financial crisis has proved this identification.

Table 3. Correlation Between Nominal Exchange Rate and Actual Exchange Rate and Rate Equal to Nominal Purchasing Power Parity.

Indexes	1992	1993	1994	1995	1996
Nominal exchange rate	10,720	10,832	11,050	10,965	11,044
Nominal exchange rate (taking 1992 rate as origin)	1.00	1.010	1.030	1.023	1.030
CPI (U.S.)	1.02	1.02	1.02	1.02	1.02
CPI (U.S.) (taking 1992 index as origin)	1.00	1.02	1.04	1.06	1.08
CPI (Vietnam)	1.175	1.052	1.144	1.02	1.127
CPI (Vietnam) (taking 1992 index as origin)	1.00	1.052	1.203	1.356	1.147
Actual exchange rate	10,720	10,570	9,547	8,575	8,415
Actual exchange rate (taking 1992 rate as origin)	1.00	0.98	0.89	0.80	0.78
Exchange rate of purchasing power parity	10,720	11,256	12,757	14,472	15,115

Source: Economic Studies, Institute of Domestic Economic Studies, September, 1997, p. 24.

Table 3 shows that the exchange rate from 1992 until the regional monetary financial crisis has been stable in general while actual exchange rate has declined by 25%.

The stability of nominal exchange rate in these years has temporarily contributed positively to prices and inflation stabilization and attracting foreign investment, promoting economic growth with relatively high speed. (nearly 9% per ann.)

Nominal exchange rate maintained nearly stable in inflation conditions of inflation, although being controlled, it still continues more seriously as compared to inflation of U.S. and major commercial partners of Vietnam and therefore it makes domestic currency to be over-valued and creates potential factors threatening unsustainable economic growth, accrued factors causing instability and economic crisis.

Theoretically, to keep purchasing power parity of a country's currency and competitiveness of goods/services of that country as compared to foreign goods and services, that country has to ensure the stability of the actual exchange rate, but not the nominal exchange rate. This can be obtained by changing nominal exchange rate in such a way that reflects changes in the correlation between domestic and related-countries inflation. (exchange rate is equal to purchasing power).

Table 4. Balance of Trade, 1992–1997.

Indexes	Units	1992	1993	1994	1995	1996	1997
Export	U.S.$ million	2,552	2,952	4,054	5,449	7,255	9,268
Export	U.S.$ million	2,540	3,924	5,826	8,155	11,144	11,743
Import Surplus	U.S.$ million	12	–972	–1,772	–2,702	–3,889	–1,900

Source: Ministry of Planning and Investment General Statistical Office, 1998.

In fact, the adjustment of nominal exchange rate in direction to reduce actual exchange rate as shown in above Table 3, has resulted in a decline of international competitiveness of Vietnam goods/service, making thus the trade balance and payment balance shift from surplus in the late previous stage into deficit (see Table 4), starting the process of accumulation of unbalance outside the economy and gradually move to lose the balance inside the economy. Because the exchange rate have impact not only on matters of external economic relations but also on domestic economy through monetary market. Positive effects caused by stable nominal exchange rate in attracting foreign investment has gradually transferred into encouraging foreign currency loans to overcapitalize in ineffective projects due to undervalued foreign currency increasing import of fund-intensive technologies/equipment, a resources considered as scarce in Vietnam against the strategy on reaching macro-economic targets on the basis of exploiting efficiently locally available resources – a comparative advantage in favour to Vietnam (labor-intensive technological equipment).

Negative impacts of rate in this time on export have been aggravated because Chinese government has taken the initiative to devalue the Chinese Juan sharply in 1994 (34%), generating thus a competitive advantage for Chinese goods/services in domestic and international market. Sharp decline of exchange rate between Vietnam dong and Chinese Juan made Chinese goods/services cheap, encouraged the improvement of Chinese goods quality to import across the border trading, nullified tariff barrier and administrative solutions aiming to prevent this situation. In 1992, Vietnam has officially imported U.S.$85 million of Chinese goods, but actual import value must be threefold – fourfold if taking into account of smuggled goods. The figure of the year 1994 was surely much higher due to Chinese Juan was devalued by 34%.

Theoretically, when balance of trade and balance of payments are persistently in deficit, the government of a country have to carry out policy on monetary restriction, conversion into inflation decline and restrict growth process. The facts of Vietnam have shown that after 1995, the inflation has declined down to one digit and sometimes deflation state has occurred in these years.

The above-mentioned effort to stabilize the exchange rate has continued to deplete the exchange reserve of Vietnam which is inherently very small. This has increased the pressure of Vietnam dong devaluation in a passive way. It's difficult to forecast adverse impact from the devaluation of VND, especially in near future when Vietnam opens up its monetary-financial market.

In brief: Exchange rate analysis in 1988–1997 period shows: Vietnam dong value in foreign exchange market in past times was stable and tended to increase unreasonably. This is not a promising result, but it covers a lot of matters required to be solved. Domestic currency has been over-valued causing damages to competitiveness of Vietnamese goods and services in international commerce. It has not only adverse impacts in terms of restricted export, encouraged import (including smuggled import) but also produces a significant pressure on domestic production, particularly industries, agriculture production for export and substituted products for imports.

This situation does not only make external balance but also internal balances going into adverse direction. Pressure on VN dong devaluation is increased but its seriousness is difficult to be identified because this pressure is not clearly expressed in the conditions where our monetary financial conditions of Vietnam are still in the process of conversion under strict control of the government and remains as locked system. Achievements from renewal and rather high economic growth rate are partly concealing the problems of instability generated by the growth process.

3. Reasons Explaining the Behavior of Exchange Rate in the Past Time

There are a lot of reasons leading to the evaluation and then the stability of VND exchange rate on the market in the past time. Of which, these reasons are noteworthy to be mentioned:

Firstly, the dollar-inflow to Vietnam has been rapidly increased because of the Vietnam's foreign trade and investment boom. Vietnam's export volume has been growed at rate of over 20% per annum. Total export turnover in 1997 has been increased up to more than U.S.$9 billion, a fourfold increase as compared to 1990. Short-term capital flow such as money transfer, remittance from overseas expatriates, incomes from labor service, tourism, donation, charity, aids from governments and NGO and direct foreign investment long – term borrowings from international credit institutions and international finance community increase more and more. Increase of exchange supply results in a fall in VND/U.S.$ exchange rate on the market and Vietnam dong's appreciation.

Secondly, demands for foreign exchange utilization are restricted. At first, we lose sources of loans to make up import surplus (about one billion of rubles per annum) and trade agreements of preferential terms from former SEV countries, after that because Vietnam imports are always restricted.

Since September 1992, Vietnam Government has taken actions prohibiting import of 17 commodities, increasing tariffs and controlling quota for imports. Restriction of import capacity particularly by administrative and non – economic solutions will produce a decline in demand for foreign currency. This situations tends to advocate the devluation of exchange of VND/U.S.$ and VN dong's appreciation (paradox of policy on customs barrier and quota).

Thirdly, Vietnam competent authorities and State Bank want to maintain – exchange rate between VND vs. U.S.$ at a low stable level to attract foreign investment and reduce pressure of inflation that tends to lead to a recurrence of inflation. Shocks caused by inflation in the initial period of conversion and the danger impending for an inflation recurrence in 1991 have produced a psychology for prevention and getting rid of any possible pressure from inflation. The problem is that exchange rate is tightly associated with inflation. Because of pressure, the Government has used a rather large amount of foreign currency to stabilize exchange rate with a view to avoiding a decline in nominal value of VN dong i.e. a stabilization of nominal rate of exchange and increase of VN dong value in a non-substantial manner. The gap between official exchange rate and market exchange rate fluctuation reaches maximal permitted band, this is not completely a realistic band of exchange market because this market in Vietnam remains closed and strictly controlled by non-market solutions.

According to "Economic Times" issued in January 26, 1994, in six exchanges trading sessions at official stock – exchange centers, the amount of foreign exchange sold out only provides less than 50% of required exchange amount, the State Bank had tried to sell out most of exchange deficit between supply and demand but exchange rate at close hours at transaction equal to the centers increase by a mere 10–20% as compared to the previous week.

This fact shows that the State Bank's operations in recent time for exchange rate stabilization is not yet reasonable. It has deformed the correlation of balance in exchange market, that resulted in significant gaps between exchange supply and demand as well as an increase of deficit in trade balance and payments balance (Table 4). Using exchange rate to suppress inflation and to conceal actual depreciation of domestic currency only bring about the reduction of competitiveness of Vietnam goods in both domestic and overseas market, i.e. more difficulties for exports in contrast with favorable conditions for unstoppable imports, and it's not for this reason that the Vietnam dong can appreciate.

4. Consequences of the Said Situation

Vietnam currency continues to be highly evaluated on exchange market that resulting in adverse consequences for the economy:

(a) Comparative advantage of the economy in international trade activities will not be exploited in an optional manner in both aspects:

Firstly, due to under-valued exchange rate between VND vs. U.S.$, if VN dong is increased in value, some potential comparative advantage of the country will disappear. Vietnam is a country newly coming to the first stage of economic growth based on market mechanism and external economic relations' expansion. Export staples mainly consist of agricultural products, raw materials (oil) and a little of industrial consumer's goods, so Vietnam is clearly not under direct pressure of exchange rate fluctuation. However, the increase of export value based on these traditional commodities, the advantage of which is increasingly depreciated, so their price on the world's market is not stable and recently, tends to decline. This situation have an adverse impact on comparative advantage of Vietnam.

Secondly, the exploitation of comparative advantage requires the encouragement went on exporting commodities that production process is able to attract and on using the best of the rather abundant resources in the economy.

In general, this can be fulfilled only when relative prices of these resources reflect their scarcity or availability. The unreasonably high over-valued domestic currency in the past has made the foreign exchange value (fund resource) cheaper is the reason for increasing waste and ineffective utilization of precious foreign currencies. Undervalued foreign exchange will stimulate the importation of goods import in favor not only for production but also to consumption purposes.

It is more serious that instead of encouraging import of technologies, which require more funds and scarce and precious resources while abundant & available resources (workforce) remain unemployed.

(b) Actual exchange rate declines that results in increase of import, causing pressure on domestic production and conflict with the strategy of sustainable economic growth based on export and gradually substituting import. To overcome this problem, the Government has to strengthen the customs barrier and import quota. This is an impediment to free development of international trade and often faces the protest from other countries, moreover it conflicts with just the strategy of door opening and Vietnam integrating into the world community.

After 1995, as Vietnam has joined ASEAN and has taken part in AFTA, these customs barriers become more and more restricted.

Moreover, as administrative and non – economic solutions, they are not suitable to market mechanism and facing protests of importers, increasing the smuggling import and illegal ventures through border trading, continue to increase the Vietnam dong value and in conflict against just the targets designed by these solutions. So in fact, this policy gains a little efficiency. In addition, increase of customs duties and import quota will also result in and increase of domestic goods price, which causes more difficulties to domestic producers. Benefits gained by the State – budget from increasing customs duties are not enough to make up advantages that Vietnam have not due to export recession and losses incurred by consumers. Moreover, this policy also causes a lot of social vices in the redistribution of other profits form quota.

(c) The longer a nominal exchange rate is maintained constant, the more the pressure is increased and it is expected that a devaluation of Vietnam currency would take place, and the extent of necessary adjustment in the future is larger and more difficult. And if it requires to be implemented in a passive way without any reserved resource, it is difficult for Vietnam to prevent its economy from heavy shocks and a higher price must be paid which can lead to trouble and crisis. This is a fertile ground for the speculation growth and exclusion of validity of monetary policy.

Actual status and consequences generated by the policy on exchange rate over the past period have been aggravated when the monetary financial crisis in the region happened and posed Vietnam before difficult-to-treat and emergency problems in the settlement of exchange rate.

II. IMPACT OF THE CRISIS IN ASIA AND THE PROBLEM OF EXCHANGE RATE FOR VIETNAM DONG

5. Impact of the Crisis on Problem of Exchange Rate in Vietnam

The direct impact of the monetary financial crisis in the region that we identify firstly is its impact on the exchange rate issue. The crisis has made currencies

Table 5. Rate of Decline of Currencies in the Region from July, 1997 to October, 1997 (as Compared to U.S. Dollar).

Index	Rupiah	Ringgit	SDG	Baht	Peso
1st July, 1997	2,433	2.5245	1.43	24.7	26.37
31st October, 1997	3,580	3.580	1.585	40.6	35.42
Rate of decline (%)	32.0	28.9	9.7	39.2	25.6

Source: Bulletins of Vietnam News Agency in corresponding months in 1997.

of a wide range of countries in the region suffering a remarkable decline as compared to U.S.$ and VN dong.

This situation has further over-value the VND – a currency which is already overstated in value. As compared to pre-crisis period taken as a whole, VND has been pushed up to a higher value than its actual value by 60%–70%.

Given that regional countries are Vietnam's key trade partners, that have almost similar structure of exports, Vietnam export is found in a very disadvantaged situation. Vietnam goods and services will lose their competitiveness in both domestic, regional and global market, their export is restricted and import is encouraged. These impacts will become more and more serious if the government fails to have prompt decisions for exchange rate adjustment. However, as the fluctuation in exchange rate never have instant impacts but often after a certain time, so in the initial stage of crisis, Vietnam export & import will be continued to be maintained at present for the reasons as follows:

(1) Contracts signed before the crisis have not expired.
(2) Countries in the region and in the world still have to tackle directly with the crisis.

Stepping into the year 1998, although Vietnam has taken temporary and emergency actions for the problem of exchange rate but the situation becomes more and more adverse. Export turnover in 1998 is expected to be in a sharp decline in terms of growth rate (total turnover of 1998 is estimated to be about U.S.$9,300 million as compared to U.S.$9,268 million realized in 1997, an increase of 0.4% as compared to 22% in 1997.

Because Vietnam is still in a transition to market economy, new trade relations have been opened partially and monetary financial market is not full fledged and remains close, therefore Vietnam is not likely to be immersed into crisis waves. It may be considered as an accidental luck, but it is not quite for

Table 6. Price of U.S. Dollar in Late 1997 at Private Exchange Bureau.

Rate of exchange	7/1997	8/1997	9/1997	10/1997	11/1997	12/1997
VND/U.S.$ Hanoi	11,710	11,760	12,860	12,510	12,850	13,800
VND/U.S.$ HCM City	11,730	11,740	11,880	12,530	12,820	13,780

Source: Vietnam Economic Times 97–98, Domestic market in 1997 and forecase for 1998, p. 33.

this reason that Vietnam can be seen as having reasonable policies for crisis prevention and it can be conducted that more care should be taken to control on door opening. But by psychological impact coupled with the actual status of high valuation of domestic currency in the previous time trouble of investors and of the public about the Vietnam dong devaluation has been increased. This trouble has resulted in a sharp increase of demand on dollars in Vietnam right after the crisis happening and the price pressure from dollar has been increased remarkably in the market..

It is forecast that the possibility of VND depreciation will be higher, which result in an increase of hazard in terms of investment from foreign exchange capital and decrease of attractiveness of Vietnam market. Investment will be in a decline, particularly from foreign capital. This has been shown clearly in investment in late 1997 and early 1998. The situation in investment is more serious as the investing countries involved in crisis will withdraw their invested capital to overcome the crisis. Hence, registered investment in 1997 has sharply declined, equaling to only 64% as compared to 1996 Projects licensed or projects commenced to be implemented or are underway of capital works have slow down their progress, even some projects had to be shutdown due to lack of capital. The problem is the investment recession will lead to a decline of export and increase its pressure on exchange rate issue.

6. Impact of Emergency Solution to the Rate of Exchange taken by Vietnam after the Explosion of the Crisis

There are different viewpoints assessing the crisis causes, but when pondering on the important and direct reason leading to the crisis, anyone can blame that concerned governments have failed to adjust the exchange rate in a flexible manner.

Development history of the exchange rate system since the 1970s has shown that the policy of Government fixing exchange rate by its control mechanism is no longer an effective macro-management tool and many countries have adopted a more flexible exchange rate system (a floating exchange rate system with somewhat control). This system requires that the exchange rate be fixed on the basis of the demand for and supply of foreign exchange on the market an on the international economic relations between countries. The intervention by the government on the exchange rate is limited to a certain band, thereby bringing about stability in the market at a given time for the purpose of concrete macro economic targets at each period. This does not mean that the exchange rate will be fixed in ignorance of the supply and demand for foreign currency and the determinants to exchange rate.

In exchange rate policies of various countries, the misleading element which resulted in the regional crisis is that the fixed exchange rate was maintained for a long time, regardless of many changes taking place inside the country and all over the globe. To be more specific, these countries has overstated the positive benefit of the stable exchange rate in the past, such as investment encouragement, promoting rapid economic growth. They have ignored the shortcomings of such exchange rate in the context of myriad changes taking place inside and outside the country. When economic relations, especially in trade and international investment sector, undergo changes, the exchange rate should be adjusted to accommodate with such changes. The United States and Japan are two economic powers playing a key role in controlling economic growth of underdeveloped and developing countries in Asia. The changes in U.S.–Japan relations which are mirrored in the exchange rate have direct effect on trade and investment of the two countries. The economic conditions of U.S. and Japan and the economic relations between the two powers have changed so much in the past few years, and such changes are reflected by the ups and downs in exchange rate between the U.S.$ and the Japanese Yen. Given the potential and the standing of the U.S. in the world market an in the international economic relations, the U.S. is capable of adjusting its exchange rate to create the most favorable advantages for attaining the set macro-economic targets. If the fixed exchange rate has been very beneficial in increasing export by Southeast Asian countries in 1994–1995, when the U.S.$ depreciated in value, the appreciation of the U.S.$ against the Japanese Yen and the German Mark in recent years have had counter-effects. In combination with increasing inflation in the rapid growth period, the pegging of nominal exchange rate to a stable level while the U.S.$ appreciates has widened the gap with the real exchange rate, this in its turn has lowered the competitiveness of goods and services of these countries.

With demand sagging, and with the competition from neighboring countries as China and Vietnam intensifying, the unreal appreciation of Southeast Asian currencies has made export in these countries drop sharply while import is picking up, and as a result of these, current account deficit and foreign debts increase at an accelerating rate. These factors lead to an increasing pressure on devaluation of currencies in these countries. Nevertheless, these countries continue to retain the fixed exchange rate which has brought about good opportunity for speculators. And it is the currency speculator that has added the last drop on the already full water glass, triggering the explosion of the crisis.

In the transition and economic development process taking place in the last few years, Vietnam has adopted an exchange rate system similar to those of other countries in the region. At the end of 1992 and at the beginning of 1993, the VND exchange rate was allowed to approach the market rate which reflected better its true purchasing power, the move succeeded in creating goods conditions for the economy. Since then until the explosion of the crisis, the Vietnamese Government pursued a stable nominal exchange rate without any major change. It could be said that the floating exchange rate under management applied in Vietnam in the past actually remained to be a fixed one, and the rate has revealed a number of constraints, hindering the sustainable development of the economy.

Given the causes and lessons learnt from the regional financial crisis, the VND may not be devalued downright like those of neighboring countries and the VND may not fall into the cyclone of the crisis since the Vietnam's monetary and financial markets remain absolutely closed. Nevertheless, the Vietnamese Government and the State Bank of Vietnam have taken a number of preventive actions to avoid any unnecessary shock to the economy. Therefore, on 13 October, 1997, the State Bank of Vietnam decided to widen the transaction band between the official exchange rate and the transaction exchange rate (at the inter-bank market) to 10%, an increase of 5% in comparison with the increase in February 1997. The move has helped the market exchange rate to be adjusted in a way that devalues the VND. As soon as the decision by the State Bank of Vietnam was issued, the market exchange rate increased from 11,000 VND/1 U.S.$ to 11,819 VND/1 U.S.$ in 13 October 1997 and then to 12,520 VND /1 U.S.$ in 23 October 1997 (an increase of nearly 14%). This move seems to serve as the acid-test to gauge the reactions by the market and by the economy for the purpose of further policies on exchange rate. Thereafter, the exchange rate got close to the one specified by the State Bank, and slightly decreased (12,290 VND/1 U.S.$ on 28 October 1997). The rate rose to 14,000 VND/1 U.S.$ by the end of the year (13 December 1997) as result of the seasonal and cyclical change of exchange rate which often take place at the end of the year and then decreased to 13,330 VND/1 U.S.$ at the end of December, 1997. The price index on the market witnessed no major change and the it can be accordingly concluded that the adjustment by the State Bank of Vietnam did not impose any adverse impacts on the monetary market and any pressure on inflation. The movement of the market exchange rate confirms that the adjustment by the State Bank of Vietnam is well-oriented and very suitable to meet the imperative requirements of the foreign exchange market and of the exchange rate.

On 16 Feb. 1998, the State Bank of Vietnam decided to fix the official exchange rate from 11,175 VND/1 U.S.$ to 11,800VND/1 U.S.$, a 5.6% increase. The adjustment has brought about similar effects like those of the previous one, and the market has proven that the exchange rate will continue to move on an upturn trend without indicating a sign of inflation, but the market, in contrast, has even shown sign of deflation. Meanwhile, factors leading to the slow-down of the economy continue to emerge.

On 7 August, 1998, the State Bank of Vietnam decided to narrow the foreign currency transaction band to 7% and increased the official exchange rate to 12,998 VND/1 U.S.$. After the move, the market rate at some moments increased to 15,000 VND/1 U.S.$ but then come back and fluctuated around the control level (around 14,000 VND/1 U.S.$) and has shown slight decrease in the past recent few weeks.

In parallel with measures taken to adjust exchange rates, on 14 January 1998, the Prime Minister has issued the Decision No. 37-TTg stipulating a number of changes to the foreign currency management, and on 17 August 1998, the Government released the Decree No. 63/CP for the purpose of spurring economic growth, ameliorating the payment balance, gradually making the VND a convertible one, and improving the foreign currency management system in Vietnam.

After three adjustments, the VND has been devalued by 19% and by 20% in market rate. This rate is close to the power purchasing parity exchange rate as of 1995. Also, the rate helps stabilize the real exchange rate and increase the competitiveness of the Vietnamese goods and services, but remains around 10% lower than what it should be as of the end of 1997 (which should be around 15,540 VND/1 U.S.$ given the inflation rate of 3.6% in 1997), while the fallout of the regional financial and monetary crisis on the exchange rate has not been taken into account.

The adjustment of the exchange rate announced by the State Bank of Vietnam has a two-side effect to export. On the one hand, it stimulates export, accelerates the payment for goods and services, and increases profit of export companies. On the other hand, not all export companies or export goods production enterprises are benefiting from the adjustment. Enterprises producing goods for exports which mainly rely on imported materials and foreign currency capital have to use the windfall earned from the exchange rate adjustment to compensate for the increasing costs in foreign currency borrowings and in imported materials. The difficulty facing these enterprises will be harder when the exchange rate continues to be adjusted on an increasing trend and when the material stock piled up in the previous stage starts to run out.

Another positive effect of the exchange rate adjustment is the drop in import and improvement of the trade balance. In 1997, the trade deficit was reduced to a level equivalent to 64% of that in 1996 (U.S.$ 2,500 million against U.S.$ 3,900 million in 1996); and as of October 1998, the deficit has been reduced by 7% in comparison with the same period last year.

However, the devaluation of the VND has made the foreign debt burden heavier. As of October 1998, with the foreign debt totaling U.S.$ 22 billion, the devaluation has increased the burden by VND 600 billion. Added with VND 250 billion in interest and depreciation, the debt has increased by VND 850 billion. The effect has stymied enterprises having foreign debts and, in some cases, has pushed them further into the red.

The decrease in import combined with the speculation of foreign currency will reduce the purchasing power in relation with the growth rate. After excluding inflation factor, the increase of the aggregate retail goods in 1997 is only equal to two thirds of that in 1996. However, the plump in consumption is not only absolutely attributed to the exchange rate adjustment but also to the fall in agriculture product price which has decreased the income of farmers, and then the purchasing power of 80% of the country's population.

In general, it can be agreed with the statement by Mr. Le Duc Thuy[1] saying that this adjustment of the official exchange rate will bring about great results at the macro level. The exchange rate has been adjusted on the basis of prudent consideration of domestic and foreign factors and can capture the foreseeable future. Mr. Le Duc Thuy added that the recent adjustments of the exchange rate have helped to overcome the overvaluation of the VND, thereby eliminating the likelihood of a sudden devaluation of the VND. The combination of the exchange rate adjustment with the issuance of decrees, regulations on foreign exchange management and with other economic policies as interest rate, stamping imported goods . . . have proven to be very effective in scaling down the adverse effects of the adjustment. The fever and thirst for dollar and the uneasy concerns of the public which lead to dollar speculation will gradually abate.

The likely increase in debt burden of money bleeding enterprises as a result of the exchange rate adjustment seems to be inevitable. Such effect is likely to be more severe if the over-evaluation of the VND is maintained for long. The wider the adjustment gap is, the more costly we have to pay, meanwhile the adjustment, as a rule of development, is sooner or later be adjusted. However, if the action is taken when necessary and when the adjustment level has not been too large, it would be far less damaging than when the currency is devalued in an passive manner. The severity of the monetary and financial turbulence can be taken as a good example for this.

In general, the recent adjustments of exchange rate by State Bank of Vietnam are well oriented and logical. Anyway, these are only the urgent actions taken to solve imperative issues related to the exchange rate for the purpose of establishing a solid foundation for a long-term and stable policy on exchange rate.

7. The Challenges to Exchange Rate Management in Vietnam

After three adjustments, the VND has been devalued by 26% (the transaction band is also taken into account). Since the inflation from 1997 to mid-1998 is now running at 8.5% while the annual inflation rate of U.S.$ is 2.5% and the U.S.$ has, in the past two years, appreciated by 20% in relation with other hard currencies, the devaluation of 26% of the VND has therefore been devalued by 6% only. When the power purchasing parity is taken into account, the VND has even appreciated by 14% (it is estimated that to reflect accurately the power purchasing parity, the rate should be 14,814 VND/1 U.S.$). On the other hand, given the free fall in value of regional currencies, the VND has appreciated much at a much higher level. This can be used to explain why the benefit in export gained from the recent adjustment of the exchange rate is negligible but its effects which result in the indebtedness and loss of enterprises are serious. Nevertheless, it needs to be reiterated that the loss and debt of these enterprises are partially attributed to the inappropriate foreign exchange policy applied in the past. The foreign exchange policy of over-evaluating the domestic currency which fails to measure the price of foreign currency capital has created a misleading disillusion on cheap foreign currency capital source and has encouraged investor to borrow foreign currency capital for investment purposes. Since the cost of foreign currency capital is not fully accounted into the product costs, it has created an unreal profit for enterprises and then increased the inertia in improving the competitiveness of these enterprises. Worse than that, as analyzed above, it does not encourage investor to use the borrowing in an effective manner but encourages them to use capital intensive technology but not labor intensive technology which can help to use up the cheap labor force available in Vietnam.

Auxiliary measures supporting the exchange rate policies as: interest rate, foreign currency management and control, more stringent procedures on imports . . . have contributed to stabilizing the foreign currency market and the monetary market without causing any major disturbance to the market. The new interest rate structure initially put commercial banks in a more active position in deciding mobilizing interest rates, minimizing exchange rate risks, absorbing more domestic and foreign currency savings and deposits, stabilizing market exchange rate, assuring depositors, reducing the withdrawal of deposit to buy foreign currency for speculation purposes. Thanks to the stabilization of exchange rate on the inter-bank market and to the concentration of management on foreign currency to key agencies, the increase of money supply in beginning months of 1998 to buy foreign currency for imperative needs in import and for build-up of foreign reserve has not resulted in major disturbances on the market. The strengthening of anti-smuggling actions has helped to prevent the outflow of foreign currency, and to cool the artificial demand for foreign currency which often leads to exchange rate fevers in the past few years. As such, it can be said that the closing of the market rate to the official one and the stabilization of the rate are mainly attributable to administrative policies but not to the real improvement in the foreign currency management activities. Since in Vietnam, 90% of the foreign exchange is under strict control, leaving a mere 10% to the influence of the free market, the market force, or in other words the supply and demand, is therefore has not been fully manifested. This means that the present stability on the foreign currency market is chiefly temporary and the market is highly vulnerable to bad effects which can occur at any time if the control on the market is loosened and related issues are not dealt with properly in due time.

These analyses reveal that Vietnam is now facing with big challenges in opting long-term solution of exchange rate issue. The recent adjustments are only temporary to solve burning issues related to the rate of exchange. The actual competitiveness of the economy has not been ensured by a comprehensive and long-term strategy. It is definite that when neighboring economies start to bounce back, with the exchange rate maintained at the present level, Vietnam will face harder difficulties in export since the country is a far less competitive in terms of structure, quality and price of goods and services. In import, the obstacle is even more severe since Vietnam has to officially abide by the stipulations of AFTA. Tariffs and administrative barriers for imported goods will be phased out while the goods produced by countries in the region and all over the world are much cheaper. The domestic market will accordingly be strongly affected. This means that the maintenance of the present exchange rate fails to be a solution which can basically cure the long-existing exchange rate headache, and worse, it threatens to push Vietnam back to the disadvantageous position as it used to be previously. Uneven accumulative factors will increase. And things will be more severe when the stock exchange – an effort to open up the monetary and capital market – is put into operation.

However, if the exchange rate is adjusted in a way that further devalues the VND, many enterprises will be driven to an impasse by the rise in debts and production costs. Furthermore, the fall in foreign investment as a result of the crisis and of the poor market conditions in Vietnam has been aggravated by the exchange rate adjustments. The economy is therefore facing a slowdown in growth rate and then possibly a recession.

The option by Vietnam is not easy. On the one hand, the benefit gained from the exchange rate adjustment is modest since the exported goods and services of Vietnam are not much influenced by the changes in exchange rate, while the world market price of these goods is now on a downturn. In addition, the pressure on devaluation of VND is not fully revealed since VND remains to be an inconvertible currency and the foreign currency market, the monetary and capital market are not mature and totally closed as a result of administrative procedures imposed by the State. On the other hand, the effect of the exchange on debts, FDI, and on purchasing power of local currency are visible and explicit, and thus having strong impact on investors, on the general public. Before the crisis, Vietnam suffered from a trade deficit in many consecutive years, the payment account deficit and foreign debts kept rising to an alarming level considered to be dangerous for the economy. The weakness of production enterprise, especially of state-owned enterprises and the instability of investment structure has imposed harder pressure on the option of an exchange rate which is more suitable to the present situation.

Therefore, many have argued to maintain a stable nominal exchange rate. According to them, the past exchange rates were good in terms of promoting economic growth, creating job, reducing unemployment rate, increasing the purchasing power of the domestic currency, curbing inflation and improving the living standard. They argue that the recent adjustments are mainly taken under the psychological effect of the crisis but not on the basis of thorough and prudent calculation of concerned authorities, the benefits gained are therefore negligible while the damage is serious. As such, it is recommended by them that the VND should not be further devalued but maintained as what it is now.

I think that such arguments are not based on the nature of the problem. It can not be denied that the benefits in terms of export promotion remain limited. However, not only because the exported goods of Vietnam is less sensitive to exchange rate change and because the competitiveness of the goods and services are low, but the adjustment level conducted are insufficient to accurately reflect the purchasing power of the VND. The VND remains to be overstated in value and the competitiveness of Vietnam's goods and services is much lower than that of other countries, especially those of neighboring countries and China. Though export goods which are mainly low quality agricultural products, rude oil, unprocessed materials produced by low productivity factories, farms, have contributed much in the initial stage of economic development, it is now high time that the goods were improved in both terms of quality and structure to maintain high growth rate. As for this, the experience of crisis-stricken countries is a valuable lesson for Vietnam to learn from. The adjustment of the exchange rate has been the right remedy to the illness and no illness can be cured without bitter medicines. If the adjustment is delayed until the adjustment gap is much wider, and especially when the adjustment become a must and is conducted in a passive position, the consequence is absolutely much more devastating. In the long-run, the adjustment of exchange rate will encourage the efficient and proper utilisation of foreign currency capital. These issues have been warned by domestic and foreign currency a long time ago, but the conception on the seriousness of the issue and remedial action by relevant agencies are slow.

8. Long-Term and Strategic Orientations on the Exchange Rate in Vietnam

The foreign exchange policy serves as a tool to support the long-term development strategy. The foreign exchange policy therefore cannot be aimed at short-term objectives that often emerge in a given period. It should be constructed to facilitate the achievement of more strategic objectives.

Given the present context in Vietnam, promoting investment, creating jobs, increasing export, curbing inflation for the purpose of economic growth are among the top priority objectives. Nevertheless, the achievement of these objectives is closely related to foreign exchange policy. The adoption of a foreign exchange policy may have either positive or adverse effect on these objectives, which then affect the ultimate goal of sustainable development.

This implies that the long-term foreign exchange policy largely depends on the development strategy of the economy. And the development strategy, in its turn, depends much on the option of a development model.

Experience in many countries and what is happening in Vietnam prove that: in the context of internationalisation and globalisation of the monetary and financial market, when elaborating the sustainable growth and development strategy, no one can ignore the great benefit brought about by trade and by international labor, specialisation (through import, export and international investment). The success or failure of countries in the industrialisation process have confirmed the usefulness of the development model which stresses on export. The achievements gained by the Vietnam economy in the past few years are strongly linked with the adoption of such a model. The continuation of open-door policy and integration into the international community and in the region, and the sustainable development goal require Vietnam to pursue an foreign exchange policy which encourages export since export is regarded as the driving force for the growth process.

The determination of a competitive exchange rate of VND is necessary, rational and inevitable. Such rate will help to promote export, to prevent cheap imported goods from flooding the domestic market, and to ensure that foreign debts are used effectively and properly.

In my opinion, the answer to the exchange rate question in Vietnam should contain two components: on the one hand, the exchange rate should be gradually adjusted to be in line with the purchasing power of VND, on the other hand necessary conditions should be prepared to devalue the VND in an appropriate way to generate advantage for export. Regarding this issue, the active solution to exchange rate issue taken by China can be considered a good lesson. It should be noted that the lesson makes sense only when it is applied appropriately in real conditions in Vietnam and in suitable cases.

The low inflation rate, the inconvertibility of VND, the close of and the strict control over foreign currency market and monetary and financial market are the goods conditions enabling Vietnam to adjust its exchange rate while mitigating the loss and damages to the economy.

However this orientation can be implemented only in the conditions of combination with other related policies. Particularly policies in terms of interest rate, exchange control, investment and restructuring of economic system in general and export in particular.

NOTES

1. This paper is prepared for the presentation at the conference on "A macro-economic Core of Open Economy for Progressive Industrialization and Development in Asia in a New Millennium", The 22nd ACAES International Conference on Asia Economies, December 16–18, 1998, Co-sponsored by the American Committee on Asian Economic Studies (ACAES) and Chulalongkorn University, in Bangkok, Thailand.

2. In the intervew by Mr. Le Duc Thuy, Deputy Governor of the state Bank of Vietnam, with journalists on 3 September 1998.

27. THE POST-INDUSTRIALIZED ECONOMIC GROWTH OF HONG KONG: PERSPECTIVES FROM A MEGA-CITY FORMATION

Chyau Tuan and Linda Fung Yee Ng

I. INTRODUCTION

In the World Bank international conference "Rethinking the Asian Miracle" conducted in December, 1997, Stiglitz (1997) included the issue of "a mega-city formation" as an engine of East Asian economic growth among the other five issues to be investigated by the World Bank. Such an agenda in the World Bank policy studies seems to confirm the significance and the need for further understanding of the economics of the urban areas and the unique role of cities that may play in the context of economic growth.

In fact, during the 1990s, Krugman's studies (1991, 1993), in combining spatial economics and economic geography, have attracted attention toward the study of the spatial (city/region/land) problems and economies of agglomeration, which further reiterated the importance of economics of urban area and its implications on economic growth. In a recent study, Quigley (1998) reviewed the four periods of intense study of cities and further investigated the relations between urban diversity, size, and economic growth.

Along the line, the aims of this paper are first, to study the post-industrialization growth of Hong Kong since the 1990s in terms of its restructuring to a service-based economy; second, to postulate the formation of

Restructuring Asian Economics for the New Millennium, Volume 9B, pages 513–532.
2001 by Elsevier Science B.V.
ISBN: 0-7623-0710-2

a mega-city (core-periphery system) from the perspectives of manufacturing relocation to Guangdong; third, to provide some supporting evidence for such a mega-city formation; and fourth, to study the agglomerative implications on economic growth with special reference to the mega-city economy in general, and the Hong Kong core in particular. Policy aspects to facilitate such a post-industrialization growth are discussed.

II. HONG KONG'S POST-INDUSTRIALIZATION DEVELOPMENT IN THE 1990s

1. The Restructuring Hong Kong Macroeconomy Since the 1980s

Due to the push of high land and labor prices in Hong Kong and the pull of cheap resources in mainland China, especially in the Pearl River Delta (PRD) region[1] in Guangdong and the Special Economic Zones (SEZs), Hong Kong's outward investment to Guangdong mainly in the form of outward processing of manufacturing has continued since the early 1980s upon the economic opening of mainland China. The decline of Hong Kong's manufacturing was marked by its restructuring beginning from 1987 in its input-output content and employment (Tuan & Ng, 1995d) and in industrial concentration (Ng, 1995). The manufacturing contribution to Hong Kong's GDP was observed to decline from 23.7% in 1980 to 22.0% in 1987, 17.6% in 1990, and eventually to only 7.2% in 1996. As a result, the Hong Kong macroeconomy has restructured to a service-oriented economy with the service sector as a whole generated almost 90% of the economy's GDP and being ranked top in the World.[2]

The restructuring of the manufacturing sector since the 1980s indicated that Hong Kong has undergone a process of de-industrialization when Hong Kong is taken as a self-entity but has evolved into a service-oriented metropolitan on one hand through diffusion of outward direct foreign investment (DFI) (Tuan & Ng, 1995b); and yet, Hong Kong is reshaping its course toward the formation of a mega-city economy when the nearby PRD in Guangdong is taken into account (Tuan, Ng & Wong, 1998).

Since the 1980s, the service sector also has restructured in industry structure and competitive patterns (Ng, 1995). Hong Kong has, in fact beginning from 1987, gradually transformed into a post-industrialized economy being dominated by (1) evolved trade related industries such as import/export, transportation, storage, and communications; (2) tourism related industries such as hotel, restaurants, and retailing; and (3) fast growing "new" services sub-sectors to include financial/business services and real estates.

Hence, the cross-border manufacturing-led expansion of re-exports and transsshipments has not only strengthened local trading industries but also nurtured the diversification and development of the service sector in the 1990s. In addition, the government's view on recognizing local comparative advantages and liberalization policy since the late 1980s have encouraged the formation of a regional financial center which further enhances the rapid rise and vigorous development of these service industries (Tuan & Ng, 1998a). Further, Hong Kong has developed through the liberalization of its financial market into the world's fourth largest international financial center, in terms of the number of financial institutions and the amount of syndicate loans, and served the Asian region in various aspects of financing. Even confronted by extensive outward investment to the PRD, Hong Kong, however, was able to maintain its sustained growth in the 1990s through the long-term growth of re-export trade and induced trade derivatives (Tuan & Ng, 1998b). Hong Kong has quickly entered into an era of post-industrialization development and growth since the early 1990s.

2. *Contributions of the Service Sector to the Macroeconomy*

From 1987 to 1996, the contributions of the service sector to GDP were found to increase rapidly. When classified by two major service sub-sectors; namely, (1) traditional services including the trade-related industries and tourism related industries and (2) the newly-developed services including financing, real estates, and business services, Table 1 presents the profile of the service sector and the statistics illustrating the shares of GDP of each sub-sectors. From Table 1, the percentage share in GDP of the traditional service industry was 31.7% in 1987 and increased slightly to 34.3% in 1996. The financial/ business services and real estates sub-sectors recorded an increase from 13.8% in the share of GDP to 20% during the same period.

Table 1 also provides the significance in terms of the contributions in the value-added of the major service industries. Import/export trade is still the most important industry among the traditional services to provide 14.3% of GDP in 1987 and 17.3% in 1996. The other two subgroups of the traditional services associated with local consumption and service exports (such as tourism) including retail sales/wholesale and restaurants/hotel showed decreasing contributions from 8.4% in 1987 to 6.8% in 1996. Furthermore, it was also observed that the two major industry subgroups (financing and real estates) in the newly-developed service sub-sector showed increasing contributions to GDP from 6.5% and 7.3%, respectively, in 1987 to 9.5% and 10.5%, respectively, in 1996.

Table 1. Value-Added Contributions to GDP of Service Sub-Sectors in Hong Kong.

	Traditional Services			'New' Services (%)	
	(1)	(2)	(3)	(4)	(5)
1987	14.3	8.4	8.6	6.5	7.3
1996	17.3	6.8	10.2	9.5	10.5

Notes:
(1) Denotes import/export trade.
(2) Denotes two sub-sectors to include retails/wholesales and restaurants/hotels.
(3) Denotes transportations, storage, and communications.
(4) Denotes financing.
(5) Denotes real estates.
Source: Compiled from Hong Kong Monthly Digest of Statistics, HKSAR, 1998.

3. The Problem of the Linked Exchange Rate Regime: Lessons from the Recent Asian Financial Crisis

In the third quarter of 1984, the Hong Kong Government adopted a linked exchange rate policy to stabilize the foreign exchange rate fluctuations arising from the perceived uncertainty at that time due to the return of sovereignty of Hong Kong to China in 1997. Since then, the Hong Kong dollar has been managed by the Hong Kong Monetary Authority[3] and pegged to the U.S. currency at 1:7.8. The long period of negative interest rate since the late 1980s and the resultant rapid increase in asset prices have never changed the Government's attitude on the pegged rate regime. Even after the Asian financial crisis, the Hong Kong Government has consistently reiterated its intention in the defense and support of the linked exchange rate regime.

The recent Asian Financial Crisis has adversely affected almost all Asian countries and Hong Kong seems to be of no exception. While it is believed that as Hong Kong has evolved into a trade and finance-dominated economy, the extensive depreciation of exchange rates in other Asian countries and the resulting relative appreciation of the Hong Kong dollar due to its linked exchange rate have affected adversely not only the trade sector but especially its service exports.[4] Tuan and Ng (1998c) studied the effects of exchange rate changes on service exports performance and found that service exports proxied by the number of visitor arrivals to Hong Kong was found negatively affected by the exchange rate appreciation of the Hong Kong dollar. The number of tourists would further affect positively the performance of local retail sales. In fact, Hong Kong has experienced an economic downturn since the fourth quarter of 1997[5] due to the financial crisis.

4. Economic Vulnerability under the Linked Exchange Rate

The first wave of the Asian financial crisis and its association with global capital movements affecting the economy in October, 1997 were investigated and presented by Tuan (1997). Recently, it was further observed that the Asian financial crisis has created directly and indirectly the following effects on the local economy that:

(i) the number of passenger visits was observed to drop by 21% during the first half of 1998 as compared to the same period in last year. Service exports reflected by tourists spending decreased by –9.2% in the first quarter and –36.5% in the first six months of 1998;
(ii) a drastic drop in local average property prices by at least 50% since October, 1997;
(iii) the stock market price measured by the Hang Seng Index plunged from the high of over 16,000 points in August, 1997 to 6544 points in August, 1998 representing a drop of over 60% in one year. The recent record of the index in first half of December, 1998 recorded to fluctuate from around 9,950 to 10,900;
(iv) real GDP in the first quarter of 1998 was –2.8% representing the first negative record in fifteen years. The second quarter and third quarter of real GDP growth were even lower at –5.2% and –7.1%, respectively, a record low since the establishment of the Hong Kong GDP accounts. It was estimated that Hong Kong would further suffer continuous negative growth in 1998 and 1999 with estimated ranges of –4.5% to –5.5% and –1.7% to –2.5%, respectively;
(v) local consumption contracted by 2.5% and 5% in the first and second quarter of 1998, respectively; and local retail sales decreased by –14.3% in the first half of 1998 and by –19.6% in the third quarter of 1998 when compared with the same period of 1997;
(vi) the inflation rate measured by the composite price index in July, 1998 was 3.2% representing the lowest in twelve years and continued to drop to 0.1% in October, 1998;

(vii) a continuous rising inter-bank rate (at 2-digit) until November, 1998 and a record high unemployment rate of 5.3% in the third quarter of 1998.

Indeed, given a small open economy under restructuring, Hong Kong needs to adjust itself to the newly developed global competitive environment generated by the financial crisis. The resultant strong Hong Kong currency and its persistent over-valuation will most likely reduce the output produced by the service sector with the absence of a significant manufacturing sector, especially the tradable services which has become a major sector in generating income for the economy. Consequently, this would have further extended Hong Kong's period of recession.

In fact, the current Asian financial turmoil might have provided an opportunity for Hong Kong to reconsider its direction of sustainable economic growth in the coming 21st century. Given the fact that the growth of portfolio investment and short-term international capital flows will be slowed down in the global markets and in particular in the Asian emerging economies, the perspectives of Hong Kong as a "financial center" in the region will become less clear than the years before that of the turmoil.[6]

Even some actions have been considered recently or would be taken to strengthen and regulate the Hong Kong financial market, the less favorable business environment for the international financial industry seems to indicate that the growth of the Hong Kong financial market will soon reach its limit. The expectations to have the "regional financial center" to act as the locomotive in leading the economy's stable growth seems to be less realistic. It is generally expected by the business sector in Hong Kong that the business operating environment will continue to deteriorate after the crisis and in the coming years of 1999 and 2000.

III. THE FORMATION OF A MEGA-CITY ECONOMY (A CORE-PERIPHERY SYSTEM)

Manufacturing cross-border operations performed by Hong Kong firms in the nearby Guangdong area, that is, in PRD in particular, have ever since enhanced the economic integration and development between the two areas. Although the two areas remain institutionally and politically separated due to the "One-country Two-system" arrangement, from the aspects of economic development and growth, Hong Kong and the nearby cities of Guangdong, including Shenzhen, Zuihai, and the other PRD cities, are evolving toward a mega-city economy with Hong Kong as its core.

1. The Process of DFI Diffusion to Guangdong

The economic opening of China since 1979 has attracted heavy flow of direct foreign investment (DFI) to the Mainland especially from Hong Kong. Explanations have been provided to describe the flow of DFI from Hong Kong especially to the nearby Guangdong including the traditional theories of DFI such as the life-cycle hypothesis, and investment climate.[7]

(1) The economic opening China has provided ample investment opportunities to Hong Kong manufacturers since the late 1979. The push factors resulting from market imperfections and high resource costs of land and labor in Hong Kong and the pull factors of immobile cheap land and labor resources in the mainland have enhanced the outward processing activities of Hong Kong manufacturing firms. During the 1980s, it was first observed that Hong Kong manufacturers relocated mainly the middle-stream labor-intensive operations to the PRD area in order to expand its production frontier (Tuan & Ng, 1994). Further relocation of the whole manufacturing establishment and even of service firms have been observed since the mid-1990s (Tuan, Ng & Wong, 1998).

(2) The life-cycle theory seemingly explained the relocation of Hong Kong manufacturing firms in that the manufacturing product has reached a declining stage so that movement to Guangdong might represent an extension of the life-cycle of the products (Tuan, 1989) and the career of local entrepreneurs (Tuan, Ye & Wong, 1986). Being mainly consisting of small and medium firms, the strategy of entering new markets with existing technology/products and the entrepreneurship of Hong Kong manufacturing firms can only be realized and the careers of the small entrepreneurs being prolonged in the nearby Guangdong, given especially their existing limited facilities and the small size of their capital.

(3) Governmental policies in the economic opening of China and the establishments of special economic zones (SEZs) and preferential treatments or tax policies by the mainland government and the "passive" industrial policies of the Hong Kong government (Tuan & Ng, 1995b) have reinforced the pull and push factors for the relocation of Hong Kong manufacturing to Guangdong. The lack of public participations in business research/development in a small enterprise-dominated economy, such as Hong Kong can only result in stagnation of manufacturing product upgrading and technology advancement (Tuan & Ng, 1995a). To maintain its share of labor intensive products in the global market, relocation of manufacturing to Guangdong is the only remaining choice.

2. *The Hong Kong-PRD as a Mega-City Economy*

According to the existing observations on the DFI diffusion process and its pattern of geographical distribution, the two decades of outward DFI from Hong Kong to Guangdong has made the nearby PRD area an integrated economic "sub-urban" of Hong Kong (Tuan & Ng, 1995b). Theories derived from urban and regional economics predict that the distance factor might have played an important role in affecting the investment diffusion process from the center to its peripheries. Distance as a frictional factor would inversely affect the amount of DFI flows. In other words, areas further away will receive less DFI due to increasing transportation costs and time spent on transactions, etc. Tuan and Ng (1995b) studied the diffusion of DFI from Hong Kong to Guangdong with a simple gravity model and found that DFI flows related inversely with distance while market potential and labor supply in mainland were the other significant factors.

From a 1998-data base of a population of 37,724 foreign enterprises operating in Guangdong,[8] 82% of the enterprises were manufacturing firms with 90% of them owned by Hong Kong businessmen. Most of the joint ventures (Hong Kong owned or others) is of small and medium size with an average investment of U.S.$4.16 million and employment size of 160 persons per firms. When considering the distance factor in affecting DFI, the location or geographical distribution of these firms revealed a clear pattern of diminishing intensity in the degree of DFI diffusion from Hong Kong to Shenzhen, the other PRD cities, and then to other periphery areas (Fig. 1), a result found to be consistent with the findings of the gravity model. It was observed that 50% of the joint ventures were located in the nearby special economic zones (SEZs) and the proximate city Dongwang and 68.7% in the PRD region as a whole.

3. *Hong Kong's Manufacturing Outward Investment to the PRD: Implications on the Formation of the Mega-City Economy*

In order to verify the pattern of location distribution and the diffusion pattern of DFI to the PRD at the time of start-up and the outside PRD areas of the East-West wing areas and the mountain areas in Guangdong, a sample survey was performed in 1997 to investigate a random sample of 2,500 firms in Hong Kong (Tuan, Ng & Wong, 1998). Of the 361 returned questionnaires, 175 of the respondents belonged to manufacturing firms. Some major related findings of the survey with regard to the geographical distribution of Hong Kong manufacturing in China revealed the fact that the relocation of manufacturing

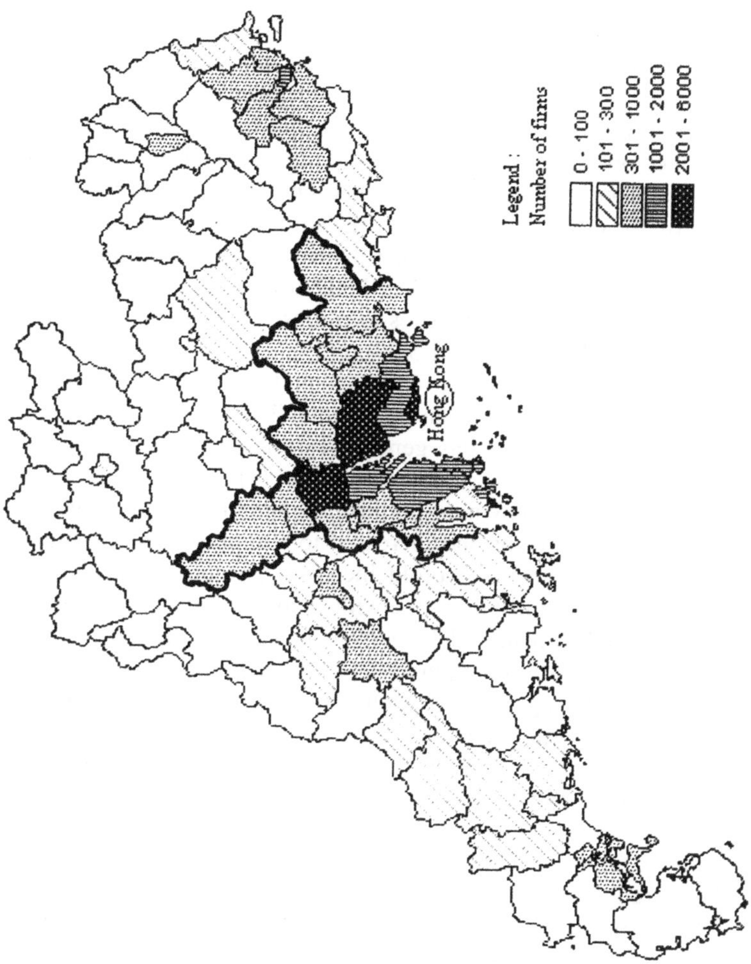

Source: The Study

Fig. 1. A Conceptual Sketch of the HK-PRD Core-Periphery System and its Networked Clusters.

firms mainly at the Guangdong area and its first concentration at the PRD region have facilitated the formation of a mega-city economy from a spatial view point.

Statistical results from the survey showed that (1) most of the firms started up with one plant. However, the number of locations for firm establishment increased from 54 to 76 representing an increase of 40.7%; (2) 89% of the firms were found to first establish their plants in the PRD with 45.2% in the SEZs (Shenzhen & Zuihai) and 43.8% in the other PRD towns. 4.8% of the firms were located at other Guangdong area. Only 6.2% were found first established their plants in other provinces of China; and (3) in considering the existing multi-sites resulted from further relocation, the choice of the firm location revealed a pattern of diffusion from the SEZs to other PRD cities, and subsequently (especially after 1987) to other provinces rather than outside the PRD in Guangdong. The SEZs and other PRD towns covered 29.3% and 45.5%, respectively, of the total plants sites locations; while Shanghai, Beijing and other provinces in China occupied 5.2%, 0.5%, and 16.2%, respectively. Hence, the boundary of the "mega-city" seems to end at the PRD region if the diffusion process of DFI can serve as an effective indicator.

Further, the relocation of firms has generated economies in production in terms of expansion of production scale and contents. (1) Firm scale measured by the average number of employment per firm for the PRD firms at the time of establishment was 174 persons and increased to 800 persons at the time of the survey, representing almost a fivefold increase. The employment of the Hong Kong staff remained almost the same with an average of 13.4 persons per firm at the time of establishment and 13 persons in 1997. (2) Firms were first found to conduct their cross-border operations by relocating mainly the middle stream of the manufacturing process including manufacturing processing/assembly, production inspection, and packaging/package design to Guangdong (Tuan & Ng, 1994). In terms of production content, the 1997 survey further found that the PRD firms had extended the production operations toward both the upper- and lower-stream of the production process. When comparing with the time of start-up, the most rapid expansion were found in the upper-stream operations of research/development and prototype manufacturing (increased by 213% and 77%, respectively) and the lower-stream operations of shipping/exporting and after-sales services (increased by 36% and 73%, respectively).

In terms of management functions, the survey findings suggested that the subsidiaries of the Hong Kong firms at the PRD eventually became more actively engaged in various functions of management and decision making relative to the start-up stage. The survey results showed that the PRD subsidiaries were more participative in management decisions such as on personnel and local market sales but least on financing, international sales, and receiving orders.

There are some further important facts needed to be considered with regard to the flow of DFI from Hong Kong to Guangdong and hence the economic integration and geographical alliances in forming a mega-city economy where significant agglomerative economies might be associated.

(1) The continuation and extension of the economic opening of China to the whole country in the 1990s have provided especially the coastal areas with preferential policies and various kinds of promotion activities in attracting DFI. However, Guangdong remains to be the region attracting the majority of the DFI from Hong Kong even though Shanghai and Chiangsu, in fact, can provide better technological and industrial facilities, while Beijing possesses superior political advantages by being accessible to policy makers in the Central Government. The same DFI allocation pattern from Taiwan firms which investment amount has ranked second among all investing countries/regions is also being observed that more intensive DFI flows moved to Guangdong rather than to its nearby Fujan or Shanghai region.

(2) The diffusion of DFI to Guangdong has not significantly upgraded its production technology. The major production techniques adopted by the Hong Kong manufacturers in Guangdong remained to be quite labor-intensive with insignificant growth in industry TFP (Ng & Tuan, 1997).

Government statistics show that in 1995, the three sub-areas of PRD, that is, Shenzhen, Zuihai, and other PRD cities were found to constitute by area and population 23.57% and 38.32%, respectively, of that of Guangdong. However, in terms of income generation, the three sub-areas together generated 90.34% of the GDP of Guangdong (or measured about 60.3% that of Hong Kong's GDP).

IV. THE MEGA-CITY ECONOMY AND FACILITATION OF POST-INDUSTRIALIZATION ECONOMIC GROWTH

1. The Mega-City Area: Agglomerative Implications

Using the theory of pattern of land use (Alonso, 1968) in explaining the process of the recent economic development of Hong Kong with its nearby Guangdong (PRD) area suggested that high land and rental prices at the core have served as push factors for manufacturing to relocate to distant or periphery areas to search for lower land costs. Business/financial services which could afford the higher land/rental prices would remain at the center. The relocation of the manufacturing operations and the outward processing activities of Hong Kong manufacturing in the nearby Guangdong is seemingly described by such a land use pattern.

Further to Richardson's suggestions (1995) regarding the economies and diseconomies of urban agglomeration, Quigley (1998) provides and interprets the agglomerative implications of size and diversity of cities by four major factors as (1) scale economies in production and consumption, (2) shared inputs in production and consumption, (3) transaction costs in production and consumption, and (4) statistical economies in production and consumption. Applying Quigley's model to the Hong Kong-PRD case, it is suggested that diversity and size of economic activities provided by the core (Hong Kong) with its "sub-urban" or periphery (PRD region) will achieve agglomeration economies through the five factors of scale economies, shared inputs, transaction costs, statistical economies, and knowledge spillovers.

Table 2 summaries the agglomerative implications of diversity and size and also gives the source or provider of the economies due to agglomeration in the Hong Kong-PRD context. The size and the heterogeneity of cities will bring forth economies in both production and consumption. The advantages of a larger size and heterogeneous city, though having its limits, will include higher urban output, productivity, and national income. In the context of the Hong Kong-PRD economy, such advantages will attract more inward DFI to its economic core as well as the "sub-urban". Evidence from the firm relocation of Hong Kong manufacturers showed that significant expansion in production scale and output in the PRD plants and rapid growth in labor productivity for the whole manufacturing were obtained through the cross-border activities at the PRD region (Tuan & Ng, 1995d). Continuous growth of DFI and in labor-intensive manufacturing in particular, in the PRD during the last two decades seemingly provided further evidence to the mega-city postulation.

2. *Implications on Economic Growth: Perspectives on Economic Prospects After the Financial Crisis*

Models explaining the formation of cities recently have emphasized on the significance of diversity in enhancing economic efficiency and national growth through the heterogeneous features of modern cities.[9] Following the underlying logic of these models, the Hong Kong-PRD mega-city economy being postulated in this paper suggests that economic efficiency and growth should be achieved through diversity and enlargement of production scale at both micro and macro levels. The Hong Kong case is, in fact, found parallel to what Chinitz (1961) described when he compared the city development of New York

Table 2. Hong Kong-PRD Mega-City: Agglomerative Implications.

Factor	Example	Provider
1. Scale Economies		
* in production	larger plant size	PRD
	Guangdong and China market	PRD
* in consumption	mega-city public goods (parks, sports stadiums)	HK-PRD
2. Shared Inputs		
* in production	legal, accounting, marketing, financing, transportation, communications services	HK
* in consumption	cultural and living facilities (theater, restaurants, parks)	HK
3. Transaction Costs		
* in production	labor resource matching	HK-PRD
	capital market matching (credit/loans, production)	HK
	small and medium firms network	HK-PRD
	global/regional trade network	HK
	China trade network	HK-PRD
* in consumption	shopping district for World commodities	HK
4. Statistical Economies		
* in production	complete three tier industries stabilities from a heterogeneous economy (prices, employment) stable economic environment	HK-PRD
* in consumption	substitute goods	HK-PRD
5. Knowledge Spillovers	business/management knowhow, financing, marketing, international business	HK
	China economics and trade	HK-PRD

Source: The Study.

and Pittsburgh in that an urban environment with many firms and heterogeneous production is more conducive to economic growth. Such an argument was based upon "the superior competitive conditions fostered in an environment with smaller firms, more entrepreneurial activity, and a more adaptable investment and banking infrastructure" (Quigley, 1998). In understanding the economies of cities, Quigley (1998) further suggests the "using of variation between cities as the vehicle for analyzing and evaluating the nature and causes of economic growth".

3. Sectoral Economic Prospects after the Crisis: Survey Findings

With the postulated Hong Kong-PRD mega-city economy in mind, in order to assess whether such a conceptual framework would contribute to economic stability and growth, especially given the detrimental impacts exerted by the recent Asian financial crisis, the expectation of the local business sector on the their business prospects after the crisis was investigated. A survey was conducted in July, 1998 to randomly sample the chief executives of 3,500 medium/large-size business firms from the population provided by the Hong Kong Business Directory, 1997.[10]

A total of 267 questionnaires were returned representing a response rate of 7.62%, out of which 59 respondents belonged to manufacturing and 218 respondents belonged to the service sector accounting for respectively 18.35% and 81.65% of the total responding firms. The respondent firms were found to have an average of 213.4 persons in employment size and 23.26 years in the length of establishment. Further, 90.5% of the respondents were locally registered. A profile of the sampled firms was summarized in Table 3.

Table 4 illustrates the views of the sampled firms on economic prospects by industry groups measured by the degree of pessimistic views of firms in the next twelve months. The respondent firms, especially service firms, felt extreme pessimism toward their activities and economic prospects in the coming year. Research results showed that the most pessimistic views were

Table 3. Profiles of the Sampled Manufacturing and Services Firms.

	Total (n = 267)	Manufacturing (n = 59)	Services (n = 218)
Average employment size (persons)	213.4	230.0	208.8
Length of establishment (years)	23.2	19.1	24.2
Hong Kong registrated firms (%)	90.5	91.5	90.2
Firms with production/operations in Mainland (%)	55.4	86.4	47.2
Proportion of output produced in Mainland (%)	33.2	69.1	22.9
Firms with clients/sales in Mainland (%)	58.8	66.1	57.1
Mainland related operations/sales to total sales/operations (%)	18.4	22.7	17.3
Hong Kong related operations/sales to total operations/sales (%)	52.4	42.8	56.4

Source: The Study.

Table 4. Expectations on Economic Prospects by Industry Sectors in 1999: Survey Findings.

Industry Sector[a]	Total (n = 267)		Manufacturing (n = 59)		Services (n = 218)	
	%	Ranking	%	Ranking	%	Ranking
Retail Sales	83.0	1	75.9	1	84.9	1
Hotel/Boarding	77.1	2	69.0	4	79.3	2
Tourism	73.3	3	58.6	8	77.4	3
Domestic Exports	72.9	4	75.4	2	72.2	4
Real Estate	66.8	5	62.1	6	68.1	6
Restaurants	66.5	6	57.9	9	68.9	5
Import/Export (Re-exports)	63.6	7	69.6	3	62.0	8
Import/Export (Transhipment)	62.5	8	67.9	5	61.1	9
Transportation	62.2	9	62.1	6	62.3	7
Financial Services	53.5	10	46.6	10	55.4	10
Retained Imports	51.3	11	41.8	12	53.8	11
Other Trade (Off-shore/Triangle)	43.7	12	46.4	11	42.9	12
PRD Manufacturing Exports	35.9	13	35.1	13	36.1	13

Note: [a] Measures the pessimistic views of the sector in percentages.
Source: The Study.

found in retail sales (83.0%), tourists directly related industry groups of hotel/boarding (77.1%) and tourism (73.3%) and indirectly related industry groups of transportation (62.2%) and restaurants (66.5%).[11] Other than domestic exports (72.9%) being ranked the fourth pessimistic industry among all groups, the trade related industry groups were found lower on the list. The three least affected industry groups were retained imports, off-shore/triangle trade, and manufacturing exports from the PRD region.

While the local manufacturing sector basically held similar views toward the degree of pessimistic prospects for various industry groups, statistics from Table 4 show that the local manufacturing sector considered itself being more pessimistic (in domestic exported with rank = 4 and import/exports for re-exports and for transshipment with rank = 3 and = 5, respectively) than that of the service sector (other than retail sales with ranking = 1).

Such survey results seemingly revealed the fact that given some external disturbances, a larger size "city" with more diversity as in the case of the Hong Kong metropolitan by taking into account of the nearby PRD region would be expected to provide more stable growth in production and trade.

4. The HK-PRD Mega-City Economy: A Venue of Future Growth

As Hong Kong has evolved into a dominated-service economy being more vulnerable to external disturbances, its continuous/stable growth would have to rely on the expansion of economic activities to Shenzhen, Zuihai, Dongwang, and the nearby PRD cities to form a mega-city economy in the form of a core-periphery system with Hong Kong as the core and the PRD region as the periphery. The perceived very modest impacts of the Asian financial crisis on the economic prospects of off-shore/PRD trade (43.7%) and PRD manufacturing exports (35.9%) (Table 4) seemingly demonstrated such an importance.

The diffusion of Hong Kong's economic activities into its nearby Guangdong will not only enhance Hong Kong's competitiveness in the World market but will also promote economic growth and stabilize the service-based economy which is highly vulnerable to external shocks. The above survey result tends to support the previous suggestion that any future and stable growth in Hong Kong by exploiting the comparative advantages of the region would have to consider a core-periphery system or mega-city economy as an ultimate solution.

The sampled chief executive officers of the business firms were further requested to reveal their anticipations on the formation of a mega-city economy, that is, Hong Kong with the PRD cities, in ten years according to five different likelihood of occurrences (that is, to choose from the event from "it is not possible" to "it must occur"). Table 5 illustrates the survey results that a majority of the respondents (70.8%) considered the event to be either "possible" (38.2%), "highly possible" (26.2%) or "it must occur" (6.4%). The responses of both the manufacturing and service sectors in this regard were

Table 5. Expectations on the Likelihood of Mega-City Formation: Survey Findings.

	Total (n = 267)	Manufacturing (n = 59)	Services (n = 218)
It is not possible	6.4	7.0	6.2
Slightly possible	22.8	17.5	24.3
Possible	38.2	35.1	39.0
Highly possible	26.2	28.1	25.7
It must occur	6.4	12.3	4.8

Source: The Study.

similar and with manufacturing firms responding more positively (75.5%) than that of services (69.5%).

V. DISCUSSION

By developing into a service-based economy where little manufacturing has remained, Hong Kong seemingly has paid high costs during the recent financial turmoil. The burden of preserving the existing pegged rate cannot be underestimated. A lesson being learnt immediately from the crisis, perhaps, seems to be that a small economy like Hong Kong is not able to handle without shocks the speedy and free movements of global short-term capital flows. The rapid growth of the real estates industries and hence the resultant high asset rental and prices until 1997 were partly the consequence of the inflow of regional capital since the 1980s. Stable economic growth to rely mainly on the growth of the financial sector aiming at serving the region may not be too realistic in the longer run.

Given the fact that the Hong Kong Special Administrative Region (SAR) has determined to defend and maintain the current pegged exchange rate as a target, continuous downward adjustments in the asset prices/rentals, wages, and other prices are the sole ways to restore Hong Kong's comparative advantages in the global market.[12,13] Further, with a less favorable environment for sustainable growth to be faced by the financial service sub-sectors, the remaining hope has to rely on the growth of the traditional service sector. Nevertheless, the uphold of the current pegged rate is going to adversely affect the tourism related industries such as retail, restaurants, and hotel/boarding (Tuan and Ng, 1998c).

Consequently, the only way to boost the growth of the remaining service sub-sectors (that is trade-related sectors such as import/export, transportation, storage, and communications) in generating higher income, employment, and further in facilitating stable growth for the Hong Kong economy is to draw efforts in building up high value-added manufacturing. Such efforts should include strengthening the development of manufacturing research and development (R&D) activities in Hong Kong and enhancing the competitiveness of manufacturing operation base in the PRD region (Tuan and Ng, 1995b). Hong Kong has no technological infrastructure with respect to commercialized (mid-stream) R&D which is required for any innovation-led, technology intensive and high value-added manufacturing. While Hong Kong has relocated her fabrication and assembly operations to PRD, government's efforts to facilitate the manufacturing sector to enrich its pre-lot size production R&D activities in Hong Kong will foster the contributions in value-added of the sector. In this connection, the extension of the scope of any future growth policy should not be limited only to the HKSAR itself as it is now under the current context.

The intensive outward processing activities have expanded the scale of production of the Hong Kong manufacturers since 1987 by using the same technology of production (Tuan and Ng, 1995b; Ng and Tuan, 1997), which further enhanced its export trade and trade derivatives activities (Tuan and Ng, 1998b), and hence, attained growth by the outward shifting of the production possibility frontier of the Hong Kong economy. Aftermath, in considering further economic growth, the mega-city development is likely to be the only effective and realistic strategy to enable another 'big push' of the production possibility frontier. As a longer-run measure, any consideration of the future stability, growth, and global competitiveness of the Hong Kong economy in the next millennium should incorporate measures in facilitating the economic integration of HKSAR with its neighboring cities in the PRD region in the context of a mega-city economy so as to fostering manufacturing and its derived trade activities.

The HKSAR, being the core of the mega-city, will continue to demonstrate its strength in operating as a regional financial center, in trade related services, and in a few remaining high value-added local manufacturing with comparative advantages, and further benefit from the trading and financing of the merchandise produced in the peripheral PRD/Guangdong region. Infrastructural linkages and inter/intra-regional cooperations between the HKSAR and the Guangdong governments in enhancing the continuous development and further diversification of agglomeration economies for the Hong Kong-PRD region are urgently called for. More liberalization trade policies on the part of the China government especially applicable to Hong Kong is much crucial in creating a more favorable trading environment for Hong Kong and the rest of the World. Development and training of human capital for the support of the mega-city area development are also important. The future of the economic stability and growth of Hong Kong would have to rely on the continuous stability and growth of China in general, and the economic diversity, size, and production scale provided by the mega-city economy in particular.

NOTES

1. See Figure 1 for the geographic location of the Pearl River Delta region in Guangdong being bounded by bold line.

2. According to the World Development Report, 1997, in 1993, out of the 15 high-income countries/economies which reported statistics on the share of their service

sector to GDP in a group of 26 high-income economies and 15 small open economies, Hong Kong reported the highest share of 83%.

3. Since 1984, the Hong Kong dollar has been linked to the U.S. dollar at 7.8:1 and is allowed to deviate from a narrow margin set by the Hong Kong Monetary Authority who will ensure the pegged rate by managing its fluctuation to move within the set margin of 7.75 to 7.8.

4. In the case of Hong Kong, the service exports to GDP ratio reported to be 24.2% in 1996 was found to exceed that of commodity exports by 7% in the same year. Therefore, the effects of exchange rate changes in service trade, in particular in its service exports, is of special significance.

5. The recent Government released statistics on the first three quarters of GDP growth in 1998 were –2.5%, –5%, and –7.1%, respectively.

6. After the revealing of the failure of the Long Term Capital Management (LTCM) on September 20, 1998, the Federal Reserve has participated in the rescue action. Less favorable news about the performance of global hedge funds have continued. It is expected that more regulations will be imposed on these funds and other institutional investors in the financial markets. The IMF may also extend its coordination function from trade and current accounts to the international capital market. Financial loans made by commercial banks to finance investors' leverage investments will become more conservative. These changes seem to result in contraction of the volume of turnover and limit the future growth of any regional financial markets.

7. See Tuan and Ng (1995b) for discussions of the theoretical considerations of direct foreign investment.

8. The database was the first of its kind as released by the Guangdong Authority for academic research purpose in 1998.

9. See Quigley (1998) for more detailed discussion.

10. The survey study of opinion of business leaders in Hong Kong was financed by the Department of Economic Analysis, Mainland Affairs Commission, Central Government of Taiwan. The survey findings reported in this paper represented some partial results of the survey submitted to the Department of which acknowledgment should be given.

11. The remaining percentages represented optimistic or unchanged views.

12. It is also the HKSAR Government's target to assure the Hong Kong residents with "affordable" housing prices as presented in the first (October, 1997) and the second (October, 1998) government Chief Executive's reports.

13. Hong Kong has experienced the first period of deflation since the fourth quarter of 1998 and is expected to continue in 1999.

REFERENCES

Alonso, W. (1968). *Location and Land Use*. Cambridge: Harvard University Press.

Chinitz, B. J. (1961). Contrasts in Agglomeration: New York and Pittsburgh. *American Economic Review, 51*, 279–289.

Krugman, P. (1991). Increasing Returns and Economic Geography. *Journal of Political Economy, 99*(3), 483–499.

Krugman, P. (1993). First Nature, Second Nature, and Metropolitan Location. *Journal of Regional Science, 33*(2), 129–144.

Ng, L. F. Y. (1995). Changing Industrial Structure and Competitive Patterns of Manufacturing and Non-manufacturing in a Small Open Economy: An Entropy Measurement. *Managerial and Decisions Economics*, *16*, 547–563.

Ng, L. F. Y., & Tuan, C. (1997). Evolving Outward Investment, Industrial Concentration, and Technology Change: Implications for Post-1997 Hong Kong. *Journal of Asian Economics*, *8*(2), 315–332.

Quigley, J. M. (1998). Urban Diversity and Economic Growth. *Journal of Economic Perspectives*, *12*(2), 127–138.

Richardson, H. W. (1995). Economies and Diseconomies of Agglomeration. In: H. Giersch (Ed.), *Urban Agglomeration and Economic Growth*. Berlin: Springer-Veriag.

Stiglitz, J. E. (1997). Rethinking the East Asian Miracle. Paper presented at the World Bank Conference, Tokyo, December, 1997.

Tuan, C. (1989). The 1989 Hong Kong Manufacturing Strategies Survey. *Economic Reporter*, *50*, 18–19.

Tuan, C. (1997). The October 1997 Financial Turmoil in Hong Kong: Its Causes and Impacts. *Hong Konga-Macau Studies*, *7*(11), 1–8 (in Chinese).

Tuan, C., & Ng, L. F. Y. (1994). Economic Liberalization in China and Structural Adjustment of Hong Kong Manufacturing. *Seoul Journal of Economics*, *7*(2), 124–144.

Tuan, C., & Ng, L. F. Y. (1995a). Evolution of Hong Kong's Electronics Industry under Passive Industrial Policy. *Managerial and Decision Economics*, *16*, 509–523.

Tuan, C., & Ng, L. F. Y. (1995b). Hong Kong's Outward Investment and Regional Economic Integration with Guangdong: Process and Implications. *Journal of Asian Economics*, *6*(3), 385–405.

Tuan, C., & Ng, L. F. Y. (1995c). Manufacturing Evolution under Passive Industrial Policy and Cross-border Operations in China: The Case of Hong Kong. *Journal of Asian Economics*, *6*(1), 71–88.

Tuan, C., & Ng, L. F. Y. (1995d). The Turning Point of the Hong Kong Manufacturing Sector: Impact of Outward Investment to the Pearl River Delta. *Journal of International Trade and Economic Development*, *4*(2), 153–170.

Tuan, C., & Ng, L. F. Y. (1998a). Regionalization of Financial Market and Manufacturing Evolution in Hong Kong: Contribution and Significance. *Journal of Asian Economics*, *9*(1), 119–137.

Tuan, C., & Ng, L. F. Y. (1998b). Export Trade, Trade Derivatives, and Economic Growth of Hong Kong: A New Scenario. *The Journal of International Trade and Economic Development*, *7*(1), 111–137.

Tuan, C., & Ng, L. F. Y. (1998c). The Asian Financial Turmoil and its Impacts upon the Hong Kong Economy: With Special Reference to Service Exports. International Conference on Asian Crisis: A Global Perspective. Deakin University, Australia, October, 1998.

Tuan, C., Ng, L. F. Y., & Wong, C. S. (1998). Mega City Formation and Regional Development. *China Industrial Economy*, *7*, 52–58 (in Chinese).

Tuan, C., Wong, D. S. N., & Ye, C. S. (1986). Chinese Entrepreneurship under Capitalism and Socialism: Hong Kong and Guangzhou Cases. Monograph, No.68, Hong Kong: Center of Asian Studies, University of Hong Kong.

28. THE ASIAN FINANCIAL CRISIS AND CHINA'S EXCHANGE RATE POLICY

Jung-Chao Liu and Li-Lai Xu

INTRODUCTION

South-East and East Asian economies have recently been the envy of many other developing countries. For some time, they seemed to have mastered the mysteries of economic growth, development, and even governance. Today, however, most of those same economies are in recession with massive unemployment, widespread bankruptcy, extensive poverty, and balance of payment deficits. The change was sudden, marked by the devaluation of the baht in Thailand on July 2, 1997, followed by successive currency devaluations in neighboring countries of South-East and East Asia. When the Asian financial crisis spread to South Korea and Japan, many foresaw eventual spillover effects in Hong Kong and China. Despite repeated promises by the Chinese government that its own currency, the RMB or yuan, will not be devalued, the world financial community remains uncertain about the future actuality.

The objective of this article is to provide facts and other background information about China's exchange rate policy for understanding the rationale not to devalue the RMB. In Section I, China's exchange rate system will be briefly described. In Section II, we examine the issue of over-versus- under-valuation of the RMB. In Section III, we review the relationship between the exchange rate and export performance during the 1994–1997 period. Section IV outlines the factors affecting China's recent dramatic increase in the official

Restructuring Asian Economics for the New Millennium, Volume 9B, pages 533–544.
2001 by Elsevier Science B.V.
ISBN: 0-7623-0710-2

foreign exchange reserve. In Section V, we consider various pressures on the depreciation of the RMB. Finally, we present some brief conclusions in Section VI.

I. CHINA'S EXCHANGE RATE SYSTEM

Prior to January 1, 1994, China practiced the dual-exchange-rate system. One exchange rate was official, the other was called a swap rate as determined by the foreign exchange swap market in Shanghai. To illustrate how the dual-exchange rate system works, if a firm earns 100 U.S. dollars (U.S.$), the entire proceeds must be sold to a bank at the official rate, which in 1993 was 5.8 RMB per U.S.$. In other words, the firm would receive: 100 U.S.$100 × 5.8, or 580 RMB. The firm was then awarded a foreign exchange quota (say, 80% of the total proceeds) which it would sell at the rate of 1 U.S.$ = 2.7 RMB, a rate determined according to the day-to-day fluctuation of supply and demand of U.S.$s at the Shanghai Foreign Exchange Swap Centre. Since the total quota retained by the firm is U.S.$100 × 0.8 = U.S.$80, if the firm sold the quota, it could receive U.S.$80 × 2.7 = RMB216. In other words, foreign companies and any Chinese business or individual could sell U.S.$ at the Swap Centre in 1993 at the swap rate of U.S.$100 = RMB580 + RMB216 = RMB796. If the price of a quota rose from RMB2.7 to 2.9 per U.S. dollar, then the swap rate would go to RMB796 to RMB816. To calculate the non-official swap rate per dollar, we must follow the formula:

$$\text{Swap rate} = \text{official rate} + (\text{U.S.\$}1 \times 0.8 \times 2.7) = \text{RMB}7.96.$$

The system was converted to a single exchange rate system on January 1, 1994. This new system is proclaimed to be based on a floating exchange rate system with government supervision. Under the new system, the People's Bank of China declares the exchange rate of U.S. dollar versus RMB each morning according to the rate established on the previous trading date through inter-bank transactions. At the same time, the bank takes the world market into consideration before declaring exchange rates of RMB versus other major currencies. On April 4, 1994, the unified national inter-bank foreign exchange market was formally established. Each market participant, including individual firms, buys and sells foreign currencies through the banks. Initially, the currencies traded were limited to U.S. dollars and Hong Kong dollars, but later, on March 1, 1995, they were expanded to include the Japanese yen.

When the two exchange rates were combined into one in 1994, the two rates should have been collated together, because the official rate was 1: 5.8 and the quota price was 2.7. Multiplying 2.7 by 0.80 gives 2.16, and the combined rate should have been 7.96. Instead, the new exchange rate was declared to be 1:8.5, by simply adding 5.8 and 2.7. Furthermore, another 6% is added in anticipation of the inflation trend. The end result is that the RMB was devalued to 1:8.7, or 33.3% in one action. After 1994, the exchange rate of RMB versus U.S. dollar hovered within the range of 1:8.3 to 1:8.5. Under the managed floating exchange rate system, the RMB showed quite a stable but slightly rising trend for a considerable time after 1994.

II. IS THE RMB OVER-VALUED?

It is well known that the relative prices of non-traded goods to traded goods are lower in developing than in developed countries. Thus, the actual market exchange rate must be corrected to reflect the purchasing power of each country. Various calculations of the purchasing power parity (PPP) exchange rate have shown a significant under-valuation of the RMB. The discrepancy between the market rate and the PPP rate is understandable because most of China's non-tradable goods and services are cheaper than the implied prices as calculated from the market exchange rate. To judge whether the RMB is over- or under- valued, we cannot entirely rely on the PPP-determined long-run exchange rate. Instead, we must take into account the short-run variation in prices of tradable goods. Let us see how Chinese economists have viewed this issue.

Yang (1998) observes that China's price increases in recent years have been concentrated in non-tradable goods. The prices of tradable goods, patently a crucial factor affecting trade, did not rise very much. For example, in 1992, following a 70% increase in investment activity, prices of production materials increased by 50%. And again, in 1993, production materials increased in price by 40%, causing a large increment in steel importation. International trade showed a deficit of 12.0 billion U.S. dollars, which induced a 33.3% depreciation of the RMB by year-end, when the dual-exchange-rate system was converted to the single-rate system. For the three-year period after 1994, materials prices remained basically stable, but prices of consumer goods increased 48% without affecting export and exchange rates very much. In 1997, the domestic consumer prices increased less then 3% and the materials' prices declined, which caused the RMB to appreciate. On the whole, the RMB tended to register a slight upward adjustment, signifying that it was, if anything, under-valued.

Yi and Fan (1997) have calculated the tradable PPP between the U.S. dollar and the RMB, which registers 1:7.0 at the end of 1993, 1:7.3 in 1994, and 1:7.5 in 1995. By extrapolating the trend of increase at 0.2 yuan per year, the exchange rate in 1997 should be 1:7.9. The actual rate, however, was 1:8.3, or 0.4 yuan higher. Therefore, their conclusion is, as with Yang's findings above, that the RMB was not over-valued. If anything, by 1997, it was under-valued. In other respects, the open door and reform policy of China have the effect of shrinking the technology gap between China and the developed countries. As a result, the production efficiency of her tradable goods has improved. The price index of tradable goods has, in fact, been declining. This could be another reason why the relatively high domestic inflation did not pose a threat to the RMB of actual depreciation (instead, it has been rising).

III. APPRECIATION OF THE EXCHANGE RATE AND INCREASE IN EXPORTS

There is a consensus among Chinese economists that the devaluation of the RMB in 1994 resulted in a significant increase in exports (Kwan, 1997). However, the continued increase in exports during the 1994–1997 period cannot be taken for granted, because the exchange rate actually appreciated 4.5% during that same period. To be more precise, exports doubled from 91.74 billion to 182.73 billion U.S. dollars during the period, despite a steady trend of currency appreciation.

There are several factors that can explain this seemingly contradictory phenomenon of exports rising with appreciating exchange rates. First, the domestic procurement prices of export goods by the government had declined significantly during the 1994–1997 period. This was due, in part, to an over-production of such goods in the face of pressures to reduce the selling prices. A decline in prices stimulated exports, despite a slight increase in the value of the RMB. The second factor, again stemming from the domestic economic situation, is the inter-dependency of financial debt among state-owned enterprises (e.g. the debt of enterprise A to B is unpaid because of C's debt to A, which is called a triangular debt). In order to circumvent possible delinquency, firms resorted to exports for ensuring reliable payments. The third factor has to do with the foreign trade system reform. After 1992, in accordance with the new reform provision, foreign trade firms were relieved of fulfilling government-dictated export plans. Thus, foreign trade firms turned to town-and-village enterprises, which generally supplied low-cost commodities for export. Statistics showed that these town-and-village enterprises were indeed the main source of export goods, constituting an 80% increase in exports. The fourth factor is an external one. The appreciation of the RMB versus the U.S. dollar was offset by the depreciation of the U.S. dollar versus the Japanese yen and the German mark. Consequently, the RMB did not appreciate vis-à-vis

Japan and Europe, and therefore exports to Japan and Europe were not adversely affected. The fifth factor can be attributed to structural changes in export products from China. The increase of China's exports resulted mostly from an increase in processed products. Her share in foreign trade increased from 45% in 1991 to about 55% in 1996. The processed products are those which use imported foreign materials. The appreciation of the RMB made imported raw materials cheaper. Exports became attractive, in effect, because of a resulting decline in costs.

What is at stake is whether the same phenomena will recur or persist as a result of a relative appreciation of the RMB with respect to currencies of South-East and East Asian countries. To the extent that China competes in the same market with these countries with lower currency values, her export performance will be affected by new variables and uncertainties.

IV. OFFICIAL INTERNATIONAL CURRENCY RESERVES

In the 1980s, China's official international currency reserve consisted of two components: (1) was the national account settlement and (2) the account of the Bank of China. The national account settlement is the cumulative surplus or deficit of the balance of payments. A surplus is registered as a reserve that is the equivalent of lending abroad, whereas a deficit is tantamount to borrowing from abroad. The lending and borrowing represent the credit and liability of a nation, generally speaking. In contrast, the Bank of China account is merely the foreign currency component of its balance sheet. The reason the Bank of China's account is relevant is that for a long time it was delegated by the People's Bank, (the central bank of China), to be the sole institution to administer and manage foreign exchange and currency businesses on its behalf. However, the foreign exchange reserve kept in the Bank of China during the 1980s was never greater than 10 billion U.S. dollars.

This peculiar arrangement between the Bank of China and the People's Bank of China was terminated in 1992. The Bank of China's foreign currency account ceased to be counted as a part of China's official foreign exchange reserve. As the table below illustrates, the official reserve of China declined in 1992 and 1993, reflecting the change in accounting method mentioned above.

Beginning in 1994, China's system of managing foreign currency has undergone an important reform. Thereafter, foreign currencies were not allowed to be kept in individual firms. A bank settlement system was initiated. The foreign currencies accumulated and circulated in firms to that point were absorbed by various banks and became a part of the national foreign exchange

Table 1. China's Balance of Payments.

(Unit: 100 million U.S. dollars)

Year	Export	Import	Balance of Trade	Balance of Current Account	Foreign Direct Investment	Balance of Foreign Debt	Balance of Capital Account	Foreign Currency Reserve	Errors & Omissions
1991	718.4	637.9	80.5	132.72	43.7	605.1	2.2	217.1	6
1992	849.4	805.9	43.5	64.02	110.1	693.2	–2.5	194.4	–82.72
199	917.4	1,039.6	–122.2	–119.01	275.2	835.7	234.72	212	–98.04
1994	1,210.4	1,156.9	53.5	76.57	337.7	928.1	326.44	516.2	–97.74
1995	1,488.4	1,321	167	16.18	380.8	1,065.9	386.74	736	–178.1
1996	1,510.7	1,388.30	122.4	72.4	417.3	1,162.6	399.67	1,050.9	–155.59
1997	1,827.3	1,423.2	404.1	198.7	452.8	1,319*	301*	1,399	–117

Note: Figures with * in the table are estimated from the data of October 1997.
Source: *Quarterly Statistics*, The People's Bank of China, 1996–1997.

reserve. As a result (also shown by the table below), the foreign currency reserve increased dramatically, from 21.2 billion U.S. dollars at the beginning of 1994 to 51.6 billion U.S. dollars by the end of 1994, for an increase of 143% in just one year. In the subsequent two years of 1995 and 1996, the foreign currency reserve of China continued to increase to 73.6 and 105.1 billion U.S. dollars, respectively. Such figures represent the second largest foreign reserve holding country in the world, after Japan. In 1997, this trend of regular increases continued. Moreover, the annual rate of increase of 1997 over 1996 was 34.8 billion U.S. dollars, or a staggering 33.2%.

Looking back, one might attribute the sudden rise of the official reserve in 1994 as the result of a change in accounting method and not necessarily of a rise in international competitiveness. However, the spectacular increase of official reserves after 1994 must be explained differently. In the wake of 1994, both the current account and the non-official capital account had surpluses simultaneously, which was the main reason behind the continuing large increase in the official foreign exchange reserve. The capital account surplus (non-official) was predominantly due to direct foreign investment that was attracted to China because of low labor costs, extensive market potential, and favorable tax policies. As to the current account surplus, Wu (1998) points out various policies of export promotion and import restriction as contributing to such an export surplus. From the table, we can see a conspicuous change which took place in 1993–1994, when the trade balance shifted from a deficit of 12.2

billion U.S. dollars to a surplus of 5.4 U.S. billion dollars.[1] Likewise, the capital account (non-official) changed from a 0.25 billion U.S. dollar deficit in 1992 to a 23.5 billion U.S. dollar surplus in 1993 and again increased to a 32.6 billion U.S. dollar surplus in 1994.

It cannot be denied that the enormous increase in the official foreign exchange reserves made it possible to keep the exchange rate of the RMB stable, but China also had to pay a significant cost in lost opportunity.[2] Since the central bank had to use the RMB to buy foreign currencies, the effectiveness of the government's fiscal and monetary policies was inevitably undermined by the accumulation of foreign exchange reserves. Equally significant is the argument that holding an excessive amount of foreign exchange reserves is tantamount to keeping wealth in the form of foreign assets. These resources might otherwise be invested in China for improving the domestic standard of living.

V. PRESSURES TO DEVALUATE THE RMB

1. A Decline in the Growth of Exports

From January to May of 1998, the growth rate of exports was slowing down. Moreover, in May, exports showed an actual decline for the first time in recent years. It is important to note that exports represent a significant portion of China's GDP. In 1997, for example, it constituted 20.3% of the GDP. The people who advocates devaluing the RMB argue that it is necessary for enhancing the competitiveness of export goods in the world market. To achieve the government's set goal of 8% economic growth, they argue that China must rely on exports.

However, if we scrutinize carefully the factors that contributed to the decline of export growth, it is not difficult to find that blame should not be directed against the currency depreciation of the Southeast and East Asian countries. Being mostly exporters from their processing industry, Southeast and East Asian countries had to import expensive raw materials to produce their export goods. As a result, the cost of imported materials accounts for 60% of the total value of their exports. This being the case, any gain accruable from depreciation is largely offset by the higher cost associated with more expensive raw materials to be imported. Furthermore, the financial crisis increases the cost of getting loans, in some cases prohibitively so, for engaging in regular production activities. Concern about the timely delivery tends to discourage buying from Southeast Asian firms. The net result of these factors is that China's exports to the U.S. and Europe did not decrease, but increased.

As to the depreciation of the Japanese yen, China was not adversely affected because commodities exported by China and Japan are different enough to be independently competitive in the international markets. As a matter of fact, the depreciation of the Japanese yen benefitted China because it lowered the cost of equipment China had to import from Japan. This, in time, lowered the production costs of China's export goods. In addition, Japan is China's biggest creditor. Hence the depreciation of the Japanese yen had the effect of reducing the burden of China's yen-denominated debt as to both principal and interest.

The decline of China's export growth was mainly in those countries that suffered a financial crisis. For example, the main cause for the decline in export growth in May 1998 was the sudden decline of exports to Japan (although the Japanese yen depreciated in June). The real cause was not the depreciated yen, but the bursting of equity and real estate bubbles in Japan, resulting in her worst post-war recession, with a shrinkage in GDP and domestic demand. Under these circumstances, even if the RMB were devalued, the likelihood of export expansion to Japan would be nil. In fact, a more effective way to stimulate exports is through the granting of a tax credit on export products. And indeed, China reduced the tax credit rate to 9% from 17%; but she has recently raised it back to 17% for selective commodities, such as textiles. Since raw materials and semi-finished products occupy about 50% of China's exports, if all the export goods were allowed to receive a 17% tax credit out of total taxes charged, the effect would be to reduce the effective tax rate to 8.5%, which is equivalent to a 17% depreciation of the RMB.

2. *The Hidden Danger of Foreign Debt*

As mentioned above, the spectacular increase in China's foreign exchange reserve in recent years has been due partly to a huge capital inflow consisting mostly of direct foreign investment. Other things being equal, the RMB should be expected to appreciate as a result of this inflow of capital. The situation would be reversed if repayments of foreign debt (including interest) surpassed the inflow of capital.

It is important to emphasize that most of the foreign capital entering China since the early 1990s has consisted of direct long-term investments.[3] Because of large direct foreign investments, the private capital account has shown a surplus. For the three years, 1994–1996, in particular, the capital account surpluses were 33.8, 38.1, and 41.7 billion U.S. dollars, respectively (see the previous table). From the standpoint of balance of payments, the non-official capital inflow could offset a part of the current account deficit. However, the current account itself was in surplus. This is manifest in the huge accumulation of foreign exchange reserve. To be exact, the foreign currency reserve of the central bank increased from 51.6 billion U.S. dollars in 1994 to 105 billion U.S. dollars in 1996. For China, where the shortage of foreign currency has long been a major concern, this reversal has come as a welcome relief.

Aside from foreign direct investments, we cannot ignore China's large outstanding foreign loans, which amounted to 116.3 billion U.S. dollars by the end of 1996. The repayment schedule of these foreign loans is expected to reach a peak soon.[4] Yi and Fang (1997) estimate that China has to pay out 63 billion U.S. dollars annually over the next 3–5 years, including repayment of principal, interest on loans, profit remittance expected for past foreign investments, and China's own foreign investments abroad.

The Asian financial crisis is a warning sign that we need to pay attention to the financial risk associated with international capital flows. So far, China has maintained a favorable balance in her current account, the capital inflow is mainly from foreign direct investment, and foreign debt is also predominantly long term. Therefore, China's foreign debt risk indicators have been kept consistently below the international safety warning line. It is necessary to note that although the debt risk indicator of South Korea was below the safety limit, the country eventually fell into insolvency and serious financial crisis. China faces many hidden dangers as well. In particular, the high ratio of bad debt in the banking system, including the loans associated with loss-making state-owned enterprises, is a hidden factor which may involve potential danger.[5]

3. *The Uncertain Role of Foreign Enterprises*

It is undeniable that direct foreign investments promoted the production and export of China's processed goods. What is interesting is the structural change associated with foreign direct investments, which can be readily observed. (1) There is an increasing market share of foreign capital enterprises in the rising industries and high-technology fields. (2) The market of high-profit industries has a tendency to be dominated by foreign enterprises. (3) The foreign enterprises intrude into traditional industries, with the effect of crowding out domestic investors. Statistics show that over half of the total sales of foreign enterprises are directed to the domestic market – strong evidence of the growing influence of those foreign enterprises. The most apparent example may be seen in electronic, telecommunication, and transportation equipment. Domestic sales of foreign enterprises in electronics alone represent 45.6% of the whole industry (see Niu, 1998). A few years hence, even larger foreign capital will come into China. As most of it will be targeted at the Chinese domestic market, the RMB revenue is bound to increase, while foreign currency revenue may decrease. On the whole, foreign enterprises will face a significant foreign currency imbalance. Whether the hundreds of billions of RMB in the hands of foreign firms will be used for reinvestment or transferred abroad will be an unpredictable and potentially destabilizing factor that may affect China's balance of payments and, in turn, significantly affect the RMB exchange rate.

VI. CONCLUSIONS

Two fundamental reasons explain why China did not need to depreciate her currency in the face of massive devaluations in the Southeast and East Asian countries. First, China has been accumulating foreign currency reserves so rapidly as to become the second largest holder of reserves in the world, after Japan. This accumulation of reserves has resulted from the current account surplus, due especially to the favorable balance of trade and large inflow of foreign capital for direct investment. Second, there is the perception that the RMB, which was devalued by 33% in 1994, does not seem to be over-valued in 1998. The 1994–1997 performance of export expansion, despite a stable or slightly rising RMB, bolstered the confidence that a change in the RMB was not warranted for maintaining the surplus in the balance of payments.

Although over-all considerations suggest that further devaluation is not necessary, at least for the time being, there are several other factors that China must take into account in making an eventual decision regarding the RMB. First, China is about to accelerate the process of bank reform, the success of which depends greatly on the stability of the RMB. China is, therefore, not likely to resort to devaluation, especially as the South-East Asian countries recover from their crisis. Another unknown factor has to do with when and whether Japan can successfully solve her own credit crisis and regain a growth trajectory, an eventuality that may profoundly influence China's domestic economy and the future of the RMB.

China also faces a potential currency risk, which may come about from two sources. (1) The insolvency of state-owned enterprises may adversely affect the banking system and (2) the capital outflow from payments of foreign debt with interest and profits remitted abroad by foreign companies, possibly inducing a substantial deficit in the capital account.

There is a need to keep a watchful eye on the development of trade surplus and capital inflow. So long as the official foreign exchange reserves can be maintained at the current level, the RMB does not need to be depreciated. However, what is crucial to avoid a financial crisis is not limited to external factors. Ultimately, China's success depends, to a great extent, on whether the process of reform makes the Chinese economy more efficient, significant growth is attained, corruption is controlled, and fairness and stability can be achieved in the society. If China is able to transform itself and realize reform, there is no reason why she may not avoid a vicious and competitive depreciation which might force many Asian countries into deeper financial crisis.

NOTES

1. In 1997, China overtook Japan as the country which accounts for the largest source of U.S. trade deficit.

2. China's official foreign reserves are deposited mainly abroad. The rate of return is close to the interest rate of short-term U.S. Treasury bills, hence far lower than the rate of return of domestic investments. See Wu (1998).

3. In terms of regional distribution, the direct foreign investments are concentrated in the eastern coastal areas. Four large coastal investment districts are already formed: the Zhujiang delta district (Guangdong), where the investments come mainly from Hong Kong, Macao and Taiwan; the Minnan golden triangle area (Fujian), where the investments come mainly from Taiwan; the Yangzi River delta district (Shanghai, Jiangsu, Zhejiang), where the investments come mainly from the USA, Japan, and EU countries; the Bohai coastal district, where the investments are mainly from Japan and South Korea. In general, the foreign capital investments of the two southern investment districts are mainly export-induced processing and assembling projects, in which the technical level is relatively low. The foreign capital investments in the two northern districts are mainly import-substitute projects that have a high density of capital and technology.

4. Most of China's foreign loans are invested in basic industrial projects. To assist the development of the midwestern areas, the distribution of favorable loans goes to these areas. According to the statistics, 47% of the loans from foreign governments and 40% of those from international financial institutions were used in construction projects of the middle and western areas in 1996. Of all the international capital borrowed, the share of the middle and western areas is 20%.

5. Even conservative estimates indicate that out of 70% of bank credits provided to enterprises, 10–15% ends up as bad debts. The ratio of delayed payments is even larger.

REFERENCES

Kwan, C. H. (1997). How China Responds to ASEAN's Currency Crisis. *Nomura Asia Focus*, (Winter).

Niu, N. (1998). An Analysis of the Effects of the Use of Foreign Capital in China. *Economics Research*, *5*, 22–29.

Yang, F. (1997). The Reform of the RMB Exchange Rate System and an Analysis of Its Fluctuation. *China in 1998: the Analysis of the Economic Situation and the Predictions*.

Liu, Guoguang, Beijing, the Social Science Documents Publisher (1998). The Exchange Rate and the Policy Option of Our Country in the New Economic Conditions. *Exchange Market References*, *3*, 2–10.

Yi, G., & Fan, M. (1997). An Analysis of the Determinants of the RMB Exchange Rate and Its Fluctuation. *Economics Research*, *10*.

Wu, J. (1998). An Analysis and Classification of the Scale of Foreign Currency Reserve. *Economics Research*, *6*, 20–29.

29. SOUTH ASIA: A NEW REGIONALISM

Saleem M. Khan

INTRODUCTION

To create a dynamic South Asian economy in the twenty-first century, the region needs the strategies of a "new regionalism." New regionalism's framework conforms to open regionalism and free-trade area (FTA) arrangements between the developing countries and industrially advanced nations. This paradigm is viewed as a solution to major international economic problems. It can prove to be an effective instrument for streamlining the development process in South Asia. The establishment of South Asian Free Trade Area (SAFTA) on the pattern of new regionalism and implementation of its economic agenda will help achieve trade expansion and strong macroeconomic fundamentals by the South Asian economy.[1] The SAFTA initiative and its potential achievements will promote "Asianization of South Asia," i.e. making it a member of Asian Pacific Economic Cooperation (APEC).[2]

The establishment of SAFTA and its eventual membership in APEC are key goals for the South Asian countries. The achievement of these goals would make it possible to address two of their most difficult issues, namely, "poor governance" and "regional conflicts." Problems of poor governance and long-standing conflicts in the region have broken down economic discipline and seriously undermined development prospects. FTAs between developing and industrialized countries are recognized as the most effective instruments in attaining acceptable levels of economic management and keeping policy initiatives on track (Melo & Panagarity, 1992). Thus, "good governance" along with better "economic discipline" secured through "Asianization of South

Restructuring Asian Economics for the New Millennium, Volume 9B, pages 545–561.
2001 by Elsevier Science B.V.
ISBN: 0-7623-0710-2

Asia" are critical to the long-term success of economic programs and a strong economy.

The scope of this paper includes the framework of new regionalism and its suitability to the economies of South Asia. The paper is organized in six sections. First, the challenges of good governance and conflict-resolution in the region. Second, experience under economic liberalization régimes. Third, the establishment of the South Asian Free Trade Area (SAFTA). Fourth, regional partnership for development. Fifth, the importance of memberships in Asian Pacific Economic Cooperation (APEC). Sixth, a summary and conclusions.

I. THE CHALLENGE OF GOVERNANCE AND CONFLICT RESOLUTION

The South Asian countries in the post-independence era have a record of poor governance and multifaceted regional conflicts. These factors have squandered economic resources, and continue to undermine economic discipline and constrain the process of economic development.[3]

The process of governance in most of the South Asian countries is flawed in many respects. Its roots are in sustaining corrupt and unaccountable political systems, vain and inefficient civil service bureaucracies, and entrenched interests and feudal culture. Economic and political implications of these problems are far reaching for the wellbeing and welfare of the people and the countries.

The public institutions, the legislators, civil service, judiciary and military are reluctant to share the right of governance with people. Interest group politics strengthens institutional control over the people. By virtue of their power, their taste for western life-style, and their political agenda, the methods and actions of interest groups are counter to the welfare of their countries and their people. Their rule symbolizes personal authority and lack of accountability. The political and economic system they run rests on centralized rule, weak institutions, populist policies and a culture of corruption. Their governing constrains national institutions, economic structures, the political system, and the legal system. The feudal culture and grip of entrenched interest continue to have depressing impacts on national life and have diminished the potential of economic systems.

Poor governance has seriously undermined all aspects of economic management in the region. The economic systems in most of the South Asian countries are inefficient and fractured. Economic life in Bangladesh, India, and

Pakistan in particular is part of a cycle which revolves around "demand-side" and "supply-side" of corruption. Demand-side corruption refers to solicitation of bribes by public officials when they deal with licenses, controls, investment project approval, imports, exports, employment, land purchases, hiring and dismissals, and virtually every other aspect of economic activity. Supply-side corruption refers to companies and individuals offering bribes to avoid red tape. Both demand-side and supply-side practices are common at all levels in government and have almost paralyzed every aspect of economic life. Some specific examples help to illustrate the extent of corruption and its impact on the economic system: in Pakistan, General Zia's Administration has left a political legacy of direct lending of non-performing loans from nationalized banks; Miss Bhutto's racket of special development funds for rural programs has grossly mismanaged public funds; and Sharif's cooperative and financial scandals have deprived the poor of their meager savings. Similar conditions prevail in other South Asian countries.

This culture of corruption in the region is reinforced by international contracts. The findings of a recent study indicate instances of bribery in more than 60 international contracts (May 1997 to April 1998) valued at $30 billion. Many OECD member countries still allow tax deductions for bribes paid to foreign officials (Financial Times, February 1999).

The failure to check corruption has led to fiscal imprudence. This is evident from expenditures of public funds on projects which have little social or economic value. Billions more are spent on creating symbols, like building prestigious projects, commissioning memorials and national celebrations. Building schools, hospitals, and housing for the poor receive less attention. Billions disappear in investment leakages to civilian and military contracts. This culture of corruption also inhibits the inflow of foreign direct investment (FDI).

There appears to be no internal propensity in South Asian countries to counter corruption, inefficiencies and abuse of power. The only ray of hope for improving governance in the region comes from global linkages which have lower tolerance for corruption and inefficiency. A beginning can be made through the channels of regional integration and linkage with the global economy. Global linkages in particular are expected to boost the economy and contribute toward good governance.

Another significant problem, which started or intensified after independence and has historically hindered the development prospects in South Asia, is unresolved regional conflicts. A list of the major disputes and dates in the region is shown in Table 1.

Table 1. Regional Conflicts.

Countries	Conflicts	Since
India – Pakistan	Kashmir dispute; Nuclear arm race	1947; 1972
Bangladesh – India	The river water and population migration	1972
Sri Lanka – India	Indian linkage with the Tamil – Sinhala conflict	Old
Nepal – India	Nepal's transit and trade through India	1947
Bhutan – Nepal	The people of Nepalese origin in Bhutan	Old
Pakistan – Bangladesh	Repatriations of Biharis	1972

Source: South Asian Regional Dialogue, 1994, Lahore, Pakistan.

Political will is needed to resolve these issues expeditiously, prior to expecting an agreement on a development agenda for the South Asia region. So far some countries have offered to discuss side issues, while ignoring the central ones. For example, the government of India would like to discuss trade and cultural ties with Pakistan before political issues. However, according to Bhabani Sen Gupta, "all confidence building dialogues that have met with success – the Pugwash Conference, the Dartmouth Conference between the United States and the former Soviet Union, the Helsinki Treaty in Europe, the bilateral talks between Japan and the former USSR, and between China and Russia" have taken decades to negotiate satisfactory outcomes (South Asian Regional Dialogue, 1994).

In the interest of peace, prosperity, and economic development, all governments in the region should initiate confidence-building measures through adopting flexibility in their policies and positions. For example, issues like Kashmir, nuclear proliferation, trade and transit between India and Nepal, sharing of river waters, the Chakma question (on which some progress has recently been made) between India and Bangladesh, and the Tamil issue in Sri Lanka should receive a high priority. Moreover, sincere efforts on the part of Asian leaders are needed to examine whether the current positions and policies of the governments of the region are serving the economic interests of the countries and of the region as a whole.

These difficult issues need to be taken up by the South Asian leaders on an urgent basis. Finalization and implementation of the SAFTA framework and APEC membership will surely help. Since the end of the Cold War there has been some change in thinking and economic strategies, and the leadership has taken initiatives in the areas of economic reforms and liberalization.

II. EXPERIENCE UNDER ECONOMIC LIBERALIZATION RÉGIMES

The ongoing programs of economic reforms and liberalization policies in South Asia fall within the framework of new regionalism. A review of these programs will contribute to the better understanding of economic problems. The program of reforms and liberalization, which began in the 1990s in South Asian countries, has been modest, and the process has been slow in promoting export-led growth and sustainable economic development. The programs of deregulation, privatization, and liberalization have influenced, to some extent, the growth of broadly based economic development in South Asia.

Deregulation of business and privatization of state enterprises so far have created some supply-side effects in the South Asian economies. The main causes of slow process and constraints are in poorly formulated strategies of reforms and resistance from the civil service bureaucracies. The pace of trade and investment liberalization is slow. A profile of recent tariff reform and investment liberalization policies in South Asian countries is interesting. Bangladesh began dispersion of tariff rates in 1989. Sri Lanka is continuing its earlier reform process, which was initiated in 1985, by reducing the dispersion in effective rates of protection. Pakistan began shifting in 1987 from a positive list of permissible imports to a negative list. Both India and Pakistan, in 1993, removed some restrictions on imports of capital and intermediate goods. Table 2 presents the tariff reduction régime in South Asia.

Prior to tariff reform, as seen in Table 2, the average nominal rate was about 80%, which dropped to 53%. In 1997, the region's average tariff rate declined to 34% (Financial Times, October 1998), and the number of tariff rates has also

Table 2. Tariff Reduction Régime.

	Average Nominal Tariff Rates		
Country	1 Pre-Reform	2 Post-Reform	3 Tariff Ratio
Bangladesh (1989, 1992)	94	50	0.53
India (1990, 1993)	128	71	0.55
Pakistan (1987, 1990)	68.9	64.8	0.94
Sri Lanka (1985, 1992)	31	25	0.81
AVERAGE	80.48	52.70	0.71

Source: The World Bank, 1994, Trade Policy Reform in Developing Countries Since 1985.

been reduced. Policy negotiations to reduce the future target to 18% rate are currently under way.

There has recently been some change in strategy and philosophy toward investment liberalization in South Asia. Initial steps were taken to create a hospitable environment to attract "efficiency-driven" foreign investment. In the earlier period of import-substitution in the region, foreign investment was seen as an instrument of external control in the economy. Thus, it was viewed as a régime of welfare-reduction for the people. Currently in the environment of export-led growth, foreign investment is increasingly being viewed an effective instrument of enhancing export capabilities. The evidence in favor of a positive correlation between FDI and export enhancement was seen (prior to financial crisis in 1998) in the East Asian economies, especially in Malaysia and Thailand. FDI was also considered vital for policy-making in China and Singapore (The World Bank, 1994).

Due to substantial benefits and in order to bring their investment régimes in conformity with the global economic reform agenda, South Asian leaders have liberalized foreign private investment rules. However, global investors have been reluctant to start capital projects. In Table 3, a comparative profile of investment is presented (except for India), indicating that foreign private investment inflows have been insignificant in South Asia. Moreover, the South Asian region, according to the World Bank figures, is substantially behind in terms of total and per capita investments, compared to the newly emerging nations of China and East Asia.

In summary, the impact of economic reforms and the trade and investment liberalization in the South Asian region so far has been mixed. Since the reforms were introduced in the late 1980s and early 1990s, initially the impact was positive, especially on the export-import pattern: from the export of high-value, innovative manufacturing goods to the import of capital and consumer goods. There was also a marginal expansion of exports. However, more recently export performance and investment activities have declined. Currently, India and Pakistan are experiencing account deficits of 7% of GDP, after witnessing some improvement in 1995 and 1996. Their share of world exports is less than 1% (India 0.6%) and manufactured exports average 75% (Table 4), but over 60% of this is accounted for by textiles, garments, and handicrafts (Financial Times, October 1998).

The reasons behind the poor performance are numerous; important among them are the slow pace of economic reforms, internal inefficiencies, external shocks, and lack of real progress on establishing free-trade area. South Asian economies remain the world's most highly regulated, state dominated and protected. Discouraging results of the on-going economic reforms indicate that

Table 3. Investment Inflows to South Asia: A Comparative Analysis.

	1 Net Priv. Cap Flows ($ Bil)	2 Priv. Cap. Flows per Capita	3 For. Dir. Inv ($ Bil)	3 For. Dir. Inv per Capita	4 Other Foreign Private Flows ($ Bil)	4 Other Foreign Private Flows per Capita	5 Gross Domestic Invest. Annual Growth Rate 1990–1997
Bangladesh	0.05	0.4	15 m	–0.1	—	13.4	
India	5.5	6	2.0	2	1.5	2	8.9
Pakistan	1.7	13	1.1	9	1.3	10	3.8
Sri Lanka	0.2	—	0.1	—	—	—	6.4
Thailand	4.1	71	2.3	40	5.9	102	10.3
Malaysia	6.7	333	5.8	305	6.3	332	15.1
Indonesia	7.4	40	4.5	24	6.9	37	10.0
China	46.6	39	38.0	32	6.7	6	14.1

Source: The World Bank, World Debt Tables:

1. World Bank (1998).
2. Column 1 divided by population in Table 1 for South Asian countries, World Bank, 1996.
3. Foreign Direct Investment, "World Debt Tables, 1995." For Pakistan State Bank "Annual Report." 1995–1996. Foreign Indirect Investment includes net changes in debt and in equity portfolio investment. For Pakistan, only portfolio investment is shown. It is therefore not strictly comparable.

Table 4. Export Performance.

	Average Annual Percentage of GDP		Export of Goods and Service	
	Export of Manufacturing		Percentage of Total	
	1980–1990	1990–1997	1980	1996
Bangladesh	7.7	15.7	68	—
India	5.9	13.7	59	74
Pakistan	8.1	4.4	48	84
Sri Lanka	6.8	8.4	19	73
Indonesia	2.9	9.2	2	51
Malays	10.9	14.0	19	84
Philippine	3.5	11.5	21	84
China	11.5	15.8	—	84

Source: The World Bank, 1998, World Development Report 1998/99.

the measures adopted so far have been inadequate to invigorate these economies and to boost their international positions. Are there more policy options left open for South Asia to catch up with the rest of the world? In this context, creation of a free-trade area and APEC membership should be examined.

III. SOUTH ASIAN FREE TRADE AREA

Trade among the South Asian countries, the seven SAARC members (Bangladesh, Bhutan, India, Maldives, Nepal, Pakistan, Sri Lanka), historically accounts for about 3% of their total trade. These countries are only hesitatingly implementing a South Asian Preferential Tariff Agreement, the intended precursor to a Free Trade Area.

In May 1995, hopes had risen when South Asian leaders in New Delhi discussed priority actions on a South Asian Free Trade Area (SAFTA). SAFTA was considered a dynamic instrument in promoting specialization and intra-regional trade. The program was expected to restore the pre-1947 economic activity, when the three major regional economies of Bangladesh, India, and Pakistan had enjoyed free trade status, and almost 80% of trade was intra-regional. Restoring the erstwhile economic ties in the region, while keeping global changes in perspective, made a good deal of economic sense. The plan included regional economic integration reducing tariff and other trade barriers. With a renewed interest in open regionalism, all parties understand that the establishment of SAFTA will promote a liberal trade environment and restore a balance between intra- and extra-regional trade. In the last five decades, the trade régime in South Asia has taken a stronger extra-regional orientation, primarily at the expense of trade within the region. However, new arrangements have negligible effect of trade diversion. Trade creation and trade expansion effects are expected to be large (Safadi & Yeats, 1994).[4]

At this point, it is appropriate to mention static and dynamic effects of the trade creation, cost-reduction, external economies and investment expansion arguments in support of SAFTA.[5] The hospitable economic climate which would be created by the establishment of SAFTA will provide an opportunity for the above effects to take hold and will break new ground for economic cooperation and expansion. Trade and investment in the region would expand. For instance, the establishment of SAFTA, which provides for internal tariff reduction in the region, has the following potential:

(i) Reduction in the pre-FTA tariffs, leading to greater specialization and cost-reduction in the region

(ii) Increase in intra-regional trade

(iii) Gradual opening of access to each other's markets
(iv) Initiation and development of joint projects
(v) Establishment of a common strategy to deal with global economic issues
(vi) Increase in official, corporate, and private contacts and investment activities
(vii) Macroeconomic stabilization
(viii) Strong economic growth

Achievement of these economic objectives over a period of five to ten years would certainly help to develop strong macroeconomic fundamentals and vigorous and stable economies. Additional positive side effects of economic integration will be the beginning of a lasting regional partnership for economic development. Clearly, a fully functioning SAFTA is sure to promote a broad based economic agenda.

IV. REGIONAL PARTNERSHIP FOR ECONOMIC DEVELOPMENT

Without much doubt, SAFTA would encourage economic partnership and cooperation. The rationale for building worthwhile economic relations among the countries of South Asia exists on the basis of complementarity of economic factors and employment of a given pool of capital resources. The economic profile of the potential economic relationship between India and Pakistan in this regard is interesting.

Factors Promoting Economic Relationship

The relatively large size of the South Asian economy, its diverse economic base, abundant resources, the large development potential of almost every economic sector, and the invaluable experience of its public and private enterprises in development and foreign investment make a strong case for closer regional relationships. The complementarity relationship based on factor endowment has a good chance of succeeding and can be a most effective instrument of development. A few ideas on the complementarity of factor endowments, inter-industry projects, intra-regional trade and investment are as follows.

First, complementarity of resources. The region is relatively rich in natural and capital resources and possesses great development potential. For instance, Pakistan possesses large deposits of natural gas and copper, which require a huge capital investment to develop for commercial use at home and abroad.

Pakistan is already building engineering goods and agro-based industries, and restructuring investment infrastructures. India can benefit through trade and direct investment in these sectors because it needs raw materials and agro-products, and possesses expertise and technology. Bangladesh, Nepal, Sri Lanka and other countries have rich and diverse resource bases and long lists of potential development projects. Overall, the region offers great economic opportunities in public and private sectors, which are mutually beneficial for all seven countries.

Second, the Indian experience of industrialization gives it a dynamic comparative advantage in certain intermediate capital goods and manufactures, to which Western technology has been adopted. The entire South Asian region can benefit from it. For instance, India has made advances in locally designed high-tech items like numerically-controlled machine tools, advanced industrial boilers, telecommunication equipment, computer memory chips, power generation, basic drugs, steel mills, and petro-chemical products. India has achieved maturity in other items like paints, pharmaceuticals, rubber, conveyors, textiles, transmission towers, and small-scale industries (Lall 1982). Moreover, the government is encouraging foreign companies – particularly U.S. and European firms – to invest in selected industries. The import of energy equipment, machine tools, scientific tools and instruments, electronic equipment and computers, chemical and petro-chemical equipment, railroad equipment, and petroleum exploration and development equipment is now being liberalized. Indian access to such a sophisticated technology and collaboration with the foreign companies would further enhance its industrial capabilities. I am sure all South Asian countries would welcome India's participation and investments in their economies on the basis of mutual gains.

Third, public and private enterprises' participation in joint ventures and cross-region investment projects will be mutually rewarding. Indian companies such as Bharat Heavy Electricals Limited (Government of India), Tata Exports, Kamani Engineering Corporation, and Hind Galvanizing and Engineering Company are multi-national enterprises which promote joint ventures. Pakistani companies like Kohi-e-Noor Enterprises have similar capabilities and experiences. Businesses with a global orientation in Bangladesh and Sri Lanka are also emerging. These companies would welcome joint ventures and investment opportunities throughout the region.

Fourth, a larger capital base and greater specialization will promote capital investments and efficiency. Public and private enterprises in Bangladesh, India, Pakistan, and Sri Lanka would have a larger pool of capital for joint projects, which would lead to the launching of capital-intensive projects and greater specialization. The Asian tiger countries of South Korea, Taiwan, Singapore, and Hong Kong can serve as a model. They have successfully achieved rapid industrialization and export-capabilities, primarily due to resource mobilization on the domestic front and through cross-country investments.

Closer economic links between South Asian countries and public and private enterprises in pooling capital resources would support capital projects in the region. Some ideas on economic collaboration among various enterprises in the regions are discussed next.

Potential for Collaboration: Model Projects

The above arguments provide the basis for a creative economic partnership. Under normal conditions, it appears difficult to initiate an economic relationship among the countries in the region, but an open climate and mutuality of economic gains make a strong case for collaboration. Clearly, project launching would involve a subsidy, either direct or indirect, to support a higher cause, namely economic collaboration among the countries, regardless of mundane concerns about costs, prices, technical quality, etc. For illustrative purposes, let us assume specific projects between two countries. Three model projects between India and Pakistan that seem feasible are the following.

First, joint venture in private sectors for setting up a heavy mechanical plant in Pakistan in collaboration with Indian and Pakistani companies. This project could be successful, especially if payment is not required in foreign exchange, at least not immediately. If the project succeeds and becomes profitable, part of the profit will have to be repatriated. In this case, equipment and technology would be supplied by the Indian company, classified as a capital transfer under private investment rules, and a local partner would supply the land, services and related indigenous costs. This project is likely to be based on the fact that the Indian company is an established enterprise and provides equipment of standard technical quality.

Second, a joint venture in the public sector may be established in Pakistan between two state enterprises, one each from India and Pakistan, to build power and distribution stations. In this case, some procurement is done in India either based on cost advantage or on subsidized prices. (The subsidy could come from either side; Pakistan buying expensive for collaboration sake or India selling cheaper for the same reasons.) This type of arrangement is not rare in bilateral or multilateral transactions.

Third, another project is an extension of the second, which may involve only a supply contract. It would amount to supplying a few pre-selected items for a given project, and closing that procurement to all bidding. In such a case, a decision by one country has to be made to buy supplies such as rails, loco

Table 5. Leading Factors in Regional Development.

Factors Promoting Regional Development	Complementarity of resources; public and private enterprises with international business experiences; larger capital pool; greater specialization.
Model Projects	
Private Sector	Joint ventures in heavy and small industry; energy and communication projects; supply projects; financial institutions.
Public Sector	Infrastructure development projects: water and power, transportation, communication.
Payment System	Cash or barter transactions; letters of credit in local currency denominated in foreign exchange; rupee credit agreements payable in specified terms.
Limitations	
Economic	Economics of collaboration; private sector shyness; Public sector limitations; financial resources constraints.
Political	Territorial disputes, geo-political conflicts, fear of economic domination, client state status, captive market concerns.

Source: Adopted from the text in the paper.

chassis, and iron billets which would provide substantial savings on transportation costs as well as a price advantage.

Payment System

An acceptable payment system must be established to ensure the success of an investment project. Two examples of such a payment system are as follows. First, the payment arrangements between two companies in two countries can be either on a cash or barter basis. The company at the buying end will open a three- or six-month letter of credit for the supplies at a correspondent bank equivalent to local currency, denominated in foreign exchange. In this case, the foreign exchange has to be officially pre-authorized in the country of the buying firm. Upon delivery, the payment is effected automatically by the correspondent bank.

A second payment arrangement could work in this way: a Bangladeshi company is given an Indian rupee credit equivalent for the value of the purchase of capital goods, payable on pre-agreed terms, at a given interest rate, and for a given number of years. The interest rate could be confessional, that is, below the market rate, subsidized by the Indian government. This is again a common practice in international transactions in addition to offering a price advantage. It may be noted that in this case, the sale of the goods has generated an international debt obligation for the Bangladeshi company, which is to be treated in the same way as any other debt obligation. The implication of this would be that for each payment, a Bangladeshi company would have to surrender a given amount of Bangladeshi takka (to buy the amount of payment in foreign exchange). The value of the Bangladeshi takka may fluctuate depending on foreign exchange rates, which would mean a larger Pakistani rupee amount each time, given the greater rate of devaluation of the Pakistani rupee relative to the Indian rupee.

Typically, economic deals require immediate payments and therefore would not be so easily handled. A public sector joint venture would be easier to set up and presumably would involve less official approval. In such a case, some elements of subsidy on both sides and easier payment terms would be the part of the agreement. Eventually, it would require payment in foreign exchange, and technical feasibility would be a pre-condition of such a deal.

V. BENEFITS OF APEC MEMBERSHIP

Within the scope of new regionalism, Khan argued in support of integration between South Asia and APEC: "Will the APEC bloc accommodate South Asia in its economic program? A positive response will not rest with APEC alone, but will largely depend on the economic imperatives which South Asia will create in the region, namely coordinating its economic policies to fit the East Asian and APEC paradigm" (Khan, 1996).

Why such a strong push for recruiting South Asia for APEC membership? As mentioned earlier, South Asia has unique challenges of national reconstruction, export-led expansion, poor governance and long-standing conflicts. Evidence so far is convincing about the region's inability to come to grips with these daunting tasks. In this regard, outside influence can be a catalyst. One can hope to import a friendly environment from APEC and other industrial countries.

APEC's regulatory framework sets standards of compliance for its members to policy guidelines and rules of the game. For example:

- Trade and investments liberalization policies of member countries should remain on track due to the economic linkage and agreement obligations.
- Free-trade area agreements generally influence trade policies of the member countries in the right direction, especially when trade policy is endogenous and subject to interest group politics.
- Harmonization of economic institutions within the FTA membership becomes a foregone conclusion.

- Developing countries benefit from the import of growth stimulating environment of their industrial partners.
- Developing countries benefit from guaranteed excess to larger markets.

It is expected that once the South Asian countries are subject to the rules of international treaty with large and rich partners, it will be hard for them to repudiate their obligations. Indirectly, such influences will also be beneficial for governance and conflict resolution.

Another critical development which cannot be overlooked by the South Asian leadership is economic globalism emerging on the international landscape. Economic globalism signifies four related patterns of change, which reinforce each other to produce growing economic linkages among all countries in the world. These patterns of change are trade and investment liberalization, the deregulation of international financial flows, internationalization of production systems, and a trend towards the harmonization of economic institutions among nations. These dimensions of change have created enormous opportunities and new challenges, especially for developing countries in the world economy. In the new global marketplace, only a strong and competitive economy stands to succeed. Clearly economic integration of the South Asian region with the global economy, along with APEC, have the potential for big economic gains. The South Asian countries need to seize "new opportunities and new challenges" offered by regional integration and emerging global economy. The stepping stone indeed is SAFTA.

Implementation of the above agenda will significantly advance the chances of South Asia joining APEC and would entail numerous tangible economic benefits to the region:

(i) Guaranteed access to the markets of the U.S.A, Canada, Japan, and other East Asian and South Pacific countries
(ii) Boost in foreign direct investment (FDI) from North America and Japan and other East Asian countries
(iii) Greater benefits of technology transfer, import of industrial raw materials and capital goods, and greater access to technical know-how
(iv) Positive impact on the stability and continuation of economic reforms in the South Asian economies
(v) Asianization of South Asia
(vi) Accelerated integration into the global economy

Indeed, South Asian conflicts and problems of governance could be eased by Asianization of South Asia, i.e. making them members of APEC. Moreover, South Asia will be gainfully integrated in the global economy.

VI. SUMMARY AND CONCLUSIONS

South Asian countries have difficulties in guiding their economies to enter the "take-off" phase of economic development. Past strategies of economic planning and public control did not produce desired outcomes. Trade and investment liberalization and market reforms approaches, which they adopted in the 1980s, have produced, at best, mixed results. The search for a workable development strategy is continuing for stimulating growth in the region and making it an active partner in the global economy.

For advancing the objectives of trade expansion and economic growth, the strategy of the new regionalism is widely recognized. Currently, negotiations are under way among South Asian leaders to launch a Free Trade Area (SAFTA) and to finalize regulatory arrangements by the year 2001. It is important to note that the South Asian Free Trade Area is being fashioned along the line of the North American Free Trade Agreement (NAFTA) (Dawn, December 1998).

The SAFTA approach appears to be an effective framework in addressing leading development issues as well as problems of poor governance and conflicts in the South Asia region. The SAFTA framework and implementation of its economic agenda are expected to promote trade, expand investment and develop strong macroeconomic fundamentals, making South Asian countries strong candidates for APEC membership. Once subject to the APEC regulatory framework, South Asian problems of poor governance and multifaceted conflicts are expected to be eased by Asianization of South Asia. In summary, the strategy of new regionalism – open regionalism and FTA with industrial countries – is most likely to advance the objectives of strong economy, good governance and economic discipline in South Asia.

NOTES

1. a. A Free Trade Area (FTA) is a preferential trading arrangement in which member countries agree to lower their import tariffs to other members of the FTA. Member countries retain the right to set their own tariff rates on imports from the rest of the world. Also, an FTA maintains rules of origin, designed to restrict intra-area trade of products originating in, or primarily produced in, the area.

b. Behind these recent trends are numerous factors that can be identified as the possible reasons. First, the growing dissatisfaction with multicultural trade negotiations as a means of achieving trade liberalization. Second, the General Agreement on Trade and Tariffs (GATT) negotiations which complicate the agenda of the multilateral trade negotiations (MTNs) due to diverse interests of a large number of participating countries. Third, GATT's *de facto* rule which member countries frequently use to block progress until their individual demands are met. Other evidence in trade and regional arrangements also confirm the trend toward regional agreements. About 46% of world trade and 50% of manufacturing is now conducted under some form of regional trade agreement. Besides, European Union (EU) regional arrangements cover approximately one third of world trade.

2. "Asianization of South Asia" refers to south Asian integration with East Asian countries. At present, APEC includes East Asia, South Pacific and North American economies.

3. Corruption, bribes and regional conflicts are universal problems. The nature of these problems is ominous to the development process in most countries in Africa, Asia and Latin America. Corrupt international influences, multi-national companies competition to get business contracts overseas, territorial disputes among newly independent countries and geo-politics among competing superpowers make these problems more complicated and difficult to handle. (Porta & Vannucci, 1999.)

4. Trade creation is the increase in exports to members of the FTA. Trade expansion is the increase in total exports for the region.

5. The static effects refer to "trade creation" which is increase in exports to AFT member countries. The dynamic effects refer to economies of scale, external economies, technical change, and investment. It is assumed that creation of the Free Trade Area in South Asia should lead to a larger internal market, permitting greater degree of specialization, and leading ultimately to a reduction in costs. This cost reduction can result from strong utilization of plant capacity, learning by doing, development of a pool of skilled labor and management, etc. Other dynamic effects, including external economies, technical change, and increase in investment, are important factors. Technological spillovers should take place when advancements in knowledge made by one economic unit are adopted by other economic units in FTA's member countries. Spillovers should also occur as FTA members adopt uniform standards which bring together experts from other member countries. These and other spillovers could decrease the cost of innovations and increase an industry's competitiveness. The technology gap and difference in average costs between members and non-members of the FTA could also increase. Related dynamic effects involve the possibility of increased technology transfer to South Asian region as an externality associated with export-led growth. This point is of particular importance because South Asian countries are pursuing export-led industrialization strategies. Significant potential exists for increase in intra-regional investment spending.

REFERENCES

Dawn (1998). Karachi, Pakistan. *Financial Times*, 1998 and 1999, New York.

Khan, S. M. (1996). South Asia and APEC: Potential for Growth Enhancement. In: Dutta-Hooley-Nasution-Pangestu (Eds), *Asia-Pacific Economic Cooperation: Theory and Practice Research in Asian Economic Studies* (Volume 7, Part B, pp. 441–459). JAI Press Inc.

Lall, S. (1982). Developing Countries as Exporters of Technology. Hong Kong: The Macmillan Press.

Melo, J., & Panagarity, A. (1992). *The New Regionalism*. Washington, D.C.: World Bank.

Riordau, E. M., & Srinivasin, T. A. (1996). *Pakistan's International Linkage: Evaluation and Prospects*. The World Bank.

Porta, D. C., & Vannucci A. (1999). *Corrupt Exchanges*. New York: Adline de Grugter.

Safadi, R., & Yeats, A. (1994). NAFTA. Its Effects in South Asia. *Journal of Asian Economics, 5*(2), 197–216.

South Asian Regional Dialogue (1994). *South Asia: Vision and Perspective*. Pakistan: Lahore.

The World Bank (1994). *East Asian Leadership in Liberalization*.

SECTION FIVE

30. THE ROLE OF FOREIGN DIRECT INVESTMENT FOR KOREA'S ECONOMIC RECOVERY AND FUTURE DIRECTIONS IN FOREIGN INVESTMENT PROMOTION POLICY

Yang-Taek Lim

I. INTRODUCTION

Due to a weak industrial foundations and vulnerable financial capabilities, Korea relied on foreign assistance for the nation's economic reconstruction immediately following the Korean War (June 1950–July 1953) which devastated the country.

In the late 1950s, Korea showed a set of chronic problems normally associated with import substitution: market saturation, low levels of manufactured exports, excessive dependence on imports, and serious deterioration of balance of payments.

The adoption of an outward-looking development strategy to counter these problems in the 1960s triggered the take-off of the Korean economy.[1] Since then, the Korean government policy has been a key ingredient in the entire process of economic development. A new emphasis on the export-oriented

Restructuring Asian Economics for the New Millennium, Volume 9B, pages 565–599.
2001 by Elsevier Science B.V.
ISBN: 0-7623-0710-2

growth strategy went hand in hand with the welcoming of foreign capital to finance economic development. Active mobilization of financial resources from home and abroad in combination with Korea's high-quality, low-cost manpower allowed the country to exhibit a dramatic economic performance.

In the 1970s, advanced countries began to raise trade barriers against exports of labor-intensive goods from developing countries. The oil crises also caused economic difficulties, accelerating inflation, weakening cost advantages of exports, undermining growth potential and aggravating the imbalance of trade.

During the time period of worldwide recession in the early 1980s, the economic stabilization had been emphasized as the primary goal of Korean government's economic policy. By the mid-1980s, relatively uniform incentives, rather than selective preference for a few strategic industries, were reinforced as the main economic policy instrument for the purpose of resource allocation for the whole industries. The success in Korean government's attempt to relieve inflationary pressures had an affirmative effect on Korean exports, and resulted in a sizable surplus in the current account of trade balance during the time period between 1986 and 1988. This led to the acceleration of important liberalization in Korea, which caused a return to a deficit in trade balance in 1989 due to a number of reasons including wage increases, the Korean currency appreciation, and increasing pressures for market opening from developed countries. The noticeable response to these changes is further liberalization rather than a recourse back to import-substitution.

In the late 1980s, faced with declining international competitiveness of manufacturing exports partly due to rising production costs, the Korean government and private business recognized the need for high technology. External and internal pressures intertwined together to trigger Korea's adoption of a new policy direction toward further liberalization.

Technological superiority became more important in enhancing international competitiveness in higher value-added industries, and foreign firms became more reluctant to share high technology with Korean firms as the technological gap narrowed.

Under these circumstances, the Korean government has chosen to encourage foreign direct investment (hereafter FDI) in Korea, recognizing that the business activity of high-tech foreign multinational firms in the local markets is an important source of technology transfer through learning by doing originally asserted by K. J. Arrow (1962) and R. E. Lucas (1993).

Despite a relatively minor role of FDI in Korea's economic development, many cases where foreign multinationals have contributed greatly to the technological improvement of Korean firms can be found. One of the most successful episodes, which reflects the role of FDI in the field of technology transfer, can be found in the Masan Export-Processing Zone (hereafter EPZ), where about 9,000 workers and technicians benefited from the opportunity of having an overseas training program until 1993. Subcontracting outside the Masan EPZ increased significantly, contributing to the value-added of products manufactured by foreign investors.[2]

On the other hand, capital inflow is an additional resource available to finance economic growth. However, it has been acknowledged that there exist inherent risks on relying excessively on external borrowings to accelerate economic growth. Without the efficient use of foreign capital, a country would never make a smooth transition from a debtor economy to a self-sustained one.

Due to inadequate domestic savings, the key question has been how to efficiently use foreign capital. In that sense, the Korean government intervened in the allocation of foreign resources in order to avoid duplication of investment by channeling borrowed funds into expanding social overhead capital (hereafter SOC), including power and electricity, communication, roads and harbors, as well as strengthening the major strategic industries, such as iron and steel, petro-chemicals, and electric-electronics.

Thus, foreign capital inflows have bolstered savings, investment, and growth in Korea. There exist various types of foreign capital inflows and their impact on domestic savings, capital formation, and long-term economic development can be quite different.

FDI is thought to have much different effects on long-term economic development than does borrowing from international capital markets. The way which industrialization has been financed in East Asian countries has taken different forms. Korea relied on foreign borrowings, whereas Singapore and Hong Kong on FDI.

Until the mid-1980s, most of long-term capital inflows needed for economic development was channeled through official loans, hence the role of FDI was not significant.

The lack of attention given by the Korean government to FDI can be explained as follows.

(1) FDI is essentially intrusive of territorial sovereignty of a state, and the Korean government has been fearful that the economy would become dominated by foreign interests.
(2) The Korean government would like to channel limited amount of capital resources to some strategic industries vital to long-term growth.

With this strategy in mind, the Korean government preferred foreign borrowings to FDI in which foreigners kept control of foreign resources. Over the period 1985–1995, Korea attracted only U.S.$8.8 billion in FDI, less than one-tenth the amount received by China.

Since the mid-1980s, however, Korea has been repaying its foreign debt, and FDI in long-term capital inflows has gradually increased its importance. Moreover, the Korean economy began to experience serious difficulties as a result of the side-effects of the economic plan to build up heavy and chemical industries in the 1970s. The new industrial strategy was designed to upgrade Korea's industrial structure as a whole by moving into more technology-and skill-intensive industries.

An important policy instrument of this technological upgrading was to liberalize the regulation on FDI. The Korean government implemented the automatic approval system which exempted certain categories of FDI projects from government screening before approval in 1984.

In 1992, business categories subject to notification were expanded to yield a notification-oriented system with approval as exceptions. In 1993 the Korean government has an active investment liberalization policy of FDI by expanding liberalization measures and has been introducing deregulation programs to promote FDI and provide an attractive environment.

In April 1995, the Korean government established a comprehensive service system for FDI by introducing an "One-Stop Service System" in Seoul and in the provinces. In March 1998, initiatives to reform the "Foreign Direct Investment and Foreign Exchange & Capital Transaction Systems" were announced.

Under the previously mentioned background, the recent changes in FDI policy result from several factors as follows.

First, Korea's restrictive economic policy has been facing increasing pressure from the international community, including international trade-related norms stipulated by WTO. There were intensified pressures for market liberalization from Washington, Brussels, and Geneva while the Uruguay Round (hereafter UR) of trade negotiations was in progress. These pressures increased even further with the completion of the UR negotiations.

Second, Korea's fear of an economy dominated by foreign interests may have been ameliorated by the strength of Korean firms as global players; preferential treatment or protection for Korean firms against foreign firms is no longer efficient and desirable even in dynamic sense.

Third, the Korean government has an incentive to introduce some foreign presence into the domestic economy for the efficient allocation of resources and enhancement of competitiveness of local companies.

In November 1997, Korea, which had long been the envy of many developing countries, was faced with a threat of a debt moratorium defies imagination.

From early in the year, the relation between receipts and payments of foreign exchange showed unstable movements. The large amount of deficit in current account and the slowdown of foreign capital inflows combined to bring about a sharp decrease in the country's foreign exchange reserves and in the exchange value of the Korean won. However, from April 1997, the Korean won strengthened temporarily against the U.S. dollar, thanks to the announcement of an early capital market opening schedule by the government and the narrowing deficit in the goods balance.

From the beginning of the third quarter, however, foreign investors' misgivings about the health of the Korean economy deepened, owing to the delay in handling Kia's financial difficulties, financial institutions' accumulation of bad loans, and the negative impact of the Southeast Asian currency crisis.

Accordingly, there was a large net outflow of foreign portfolio capital, new external borrowing became almost impossible, and Korean financial institutions faced substantial difficulty in rolling over their existing short-term debts in the international financial markets.

As a result, Korea found itself in financial crisis, lacking sufficient foreign currency liquidity to meet its maturing liabilities following a sharp decline in its foreign exchange reserves from early November 1997.

What brought about this large mismatch between demand and supply in the foreign exchange market was mainly the heavier foreign debt taken on to finance the deficit in current account, and the difficulty in coping with a flood of repayment demands because of the heavy reliance on short-term external borrowings.

Besides these factors, the building of expectations of a massive depreciation of the Korean won due to the persistent wide deficit in current account also played a large part in the further worsening of the foreign exchange situation.

The country's foreign exchange reserves, which had stood steady at around U.S.$30 billion until October 1997, declined sharply to U.S.$24.4 billion at the end of November and to U.S.$20.4 billion at the end of December 1997.

The reason they dwindled so rapidly was because the Bank of Korea was forced, as the lender of last resort, to provide support for the settlement of foreign claims on domestic financial institutions when demands for the redemption rather than the customary roll over of their maturing short-term foreign liabilities mounted from early November.

Most seriously, usable official foreign exchange reserves, which are official foreign exchange reserves less the BOK's deposits at overseas branches of domestic banks, decreased to just U.S.$7.3 billion as of the end of November as against U.S.$22.3 billion as of the end of October 1997.

Consequently, the government had to turn to the IMF to request a stand-by credit on November 21, 1997. An agreement was reached with the IMF on December 4 for the provision of an amount of some U.S.$21 billion.

In addition, major international financial institutions such as the IBRD and the ADB and also a number of developed countries including the United States and Japan indicated their readiness to provide an additional U.S.$36 billion, upon the conclusion of the agreement with the IMF. This meant that Korea was to receive in stages a total amount of U.S.$57 billion by way of the emergency rescue package.

With domestic demand imploding, the current account surplus reached U.S.$10.6 billion or some 14% of GDP in the first quarter of 1998. Much of this resulted from a precipitous drop in imports of machinery and equipment and consumer durables.

To date the rise in export prices has exceeded that of import prices and the usual "J" curve following devaluation has been absent. This development largely reflects comparatively "weak" increases in import prices, owing to depressed world oil and commodity prices.

Further, the collapse in imports of investment goods may have induced foreign suppliers to price to market. By contrast, export prices have risen sharply in local currency terms, as exporters boosted their profit margins to compensate for depressed domestic demand.

Customs data suggest that export volumes increased by some 10 to 12% in the first quarter of the year, though these figures included the one-time effects of the extraordinary nation-wide campaign to collect some U.S.$2.2 billion in gold to help pay off the nation's foreign debt. Nonetheless, it appears that the lion's share of the swing in the current account to date reflects the depressed state of the economy.

In effect, Korean capital markets have been fully open to foreign investors by July 1998. The desirability of large-scale foreign investment to help restructure Korean industry, as well as to upgrade managerial skills and technological standards to world class levels, is now indisputable.

However, foreign investors are also wary to see how legislative changes are implemented in practice. Indeed, a recent survey of foreign business leaders in Korea cited the potential for labor-management conflict as tile single most important obstacle. All in all, although a significant rise in FDI is possible following full capital market liberalization, the amounts will be minor compared with total corporate assets.

As in early 1998, much of these inflows in the beginning is likely to take the form of portfolio investment, mergers and acquisitions (M&As) and joint ventures. Hence, the catalytic role of FDI needs to be complemented by vigorous domestic corporate restructuring.

It is notable that a current account surplus of 1% of GDP is projected for 2003. This would imply cumulative current account surpluses of over U.S.$100 billion from 1998–2003 which would allow quick repayment of borrowings of some U.S.$35 billion from international agencies, and a build-up of official reserves to U.S.$80 to 90 billion (or 6 to 7 months of imports). However, the desirability of such a large build-up of foreign reserves is questionable, given their high opportunity costs.

Unlike loans, FDI has the effect of directly participating in business, not only influencing a country's domestic investment, economic growth, and trade balance, but also transferring production and business technology.

In consideration of the important role of FDI in the Korea's economic development, Yang Taek Lim (1988 and 1989) analyzed the determinants of FDI on Korea made by the three major investors (the United States, Japan, and Europe), and estimated their effects on domestic investment, economic growth, trade balance, and technical efficiency.[3]

The purpose of the current study is to investigate the current regime of Korea's FDI measures and propose some policy recommendations with an expectation its significant contribution to Korea's efforts for economic recovery.

For this purpose, in Section II the author shall discuss about the causes of Korea's financial crisis in the two aspects: the real side and monetary side, and the prospects of short and long term's Korean economy. Section III shall summarize the author's econometric study on the determinants of Korea's FDI and its macroeconomic effects on domestic investment economic growth, trade balance, and technical efficiency. In Section IV, the writer shall overview the Korea's FDI policy and its current regime. Finally, summary and conclusion shall be made in Section V.

II. KOREA'S FINANCIAL CRISIS AND ITS ECONOMIC PROSPECTS

Korea, which had long been the envy of many developing countries, was faced with a threat of a debt moratorium defies imagination. But it would be a mistake to blame this debacle solely on contagion from the financial crisis in Southeast Asia.

To be sure, by most criteria, Korea had sound macroeconomic fundamentals. However, owing to an excessively leveraged corporate sector and a weak financial system, they did not suffice to ride out the financial market firestorm sweeping through the rest of Asia.

Moreover, the operations of Korea's "floating" exchange rate system was in practice akin to an "adjustable peg" system, and monetary policy also proved to be inappropriate in a context of greater capital market openness.

Indeed, from August 1997 almost to the eve of the crisis, the authorities vainly attempted to prop up the won, while at the same time injecting substantial liquidity into the financial system to check tile wave of bankruptcies. In the event, policy inertia, inappropriate exchange rate goals and capital flight quickly exhausted Korea's limited foreign exchange reserves.

A. The Background of Korea's Financial Crisis

Prior to the late 1997 financial crisis, the Korean economy was marked by a puzzling dichotomy between a benign real economy and growing financial market tensions. Up to late October, the real economy appeared to be adjusting smoothly to the severe 1996 terms-of-trade shock and a cutback in business investment following a boom in the early 1990s.

These factors had slowed GDP growth from an unsustainably high rate of 9% in 1994–1995 to 7% in 1996. The first quarter of 1997, when GDP growth fell to 5.7%, appeared to mark a successful "soft-landing". Indeed, notwithstanding sluggish domestic demand, GDP growth during the first three quarters of 1997 still averaged over 6%, while industrial output growth was some 9% reflecting strong net exports.

Inflation, measured by the 4.3% rise in the private consumption deflator, was the lowest in a decade. Unemployment, albeit edging up to some 2.5% of the labor force, was very low by OECD standards.

At the same time, the current account deficit, which had soared to U.S.$23.7 billion in 1996 (almost 5% of GDP), had been halved by the third quarter of the year: and the capital account, although volatile, was recording small net inflows.

As in the past, the economy was firmly underpinned by cautious monetary and fiscal policies (with the budget oriented towards a balanced current position and a small surplus on the social security accounts).

The macroeconomy prior to the financial crisis gave few signs of imminent stress. In the pasts high nominal GDP growth had masked many of Korea's financial problems (and perhaps lulled regulators and foreign investors into complacency). However, the crucial pressure point between weak micro-economic structures and slower economic growth proved to be the corporate sector's weak balance sheet and cash flow positions. Insolvencies (especially among incorporated firms) were on the rise, as increasing gearing resulted in higher business break-even points, while slowing economic growth exacerbated cash-flow problems. Insolvencies soared during the course of 1997 and reached dangerous levels in early 1998.

(1) In the Real Side

The first critical fault line on the path to crisis was the rapid build-up of short-term domestic and foreign debt to finance the investment boom of the large conglomerates, known as *chaebols*, in the 1990s. By end-1997, Korea's 30 largest chaebols' average debt to equity ratio had soared to over 500%, 100 points higher than in 1996 and the five previous years. Such traditionally high leveraging reflected *inter alia* the chaebols' pursuit of rapid growth on a global scale by diversifying into capital-intensive industries, as part of an ambitious strategy to "leap frog" quickly up tile value-added chain into higher technology products.

This strategy had been successful in the 1970–1980s, when Korean companies were small, and achieving scale economies and establishing extensive distribution channels were critical to increasing productivity and shareholder value. But by the late 1980s, global competitive conditions had changed radically, and past strategies of debt financed growth became increasingly risky in the face of falling profitability.

Chaebols' governance structures were slow to internalize these basic changes in international competitive conditions, and shareholder value was systematically being destroyed from the late 1980s onwards. Indeed, rapid expansion in the late 1980s into a number of "prestige" capital-intensive, high-risk industries where Korean industry had weak technical or management comparative advantage, probably laid the seeds of the corporate sector's current dire situation. Worse, given the simultaneous entry of a number of chaebols into similar industries (for example, semiconductors, steel, consumer durables and especially automobiles), rates of return were quickly depressed by the rapid build-up of capacity and fierce competition. Given the limited size of domestic bond and equity markets and preferential access to credit from a docile banking sector, this industrial strategy left the chaebols with a legacy of excessively-leveraged balance sheets and ill-prepared for the rigorous of global competition.

Korea's non-financial corporate sector as a whole exhibits balance sheet characteristics similar to those of the chaebols, albeit with a debt-to-equity ratio of just under 400% (excluding the chaebols). Nonetheless, by end-1997 total corporate debt had risen 26.8% to 810.6 trillion won (around U.S.$600 billion) or 167% of GDP. A key feature in 1997 was the marked rise (from 9 to 28%) in financing coming from non-bank financial institutions (especially shaky "merchant banks"), reflecting weak bond and equity markets, as well as reluctance of banks to increase their lending activities.

Heavy debt service is a quintessential feature of fragile firms. Combined with rigid lay-of flaws, weak cash-flow and cross-debt guarantees, this is a recipe for serial bankruptcies and high systemic risk. Warning signs first appeared in mid-1996, when over-capacity emerged in key export sectors (following an investment boom concentrated in semiconductors, cars, steel and petrochemicals). Export prices softened, with semiconductor prices plummeting some 80%.

Notwithstanding a modest recovery in profit margins, a critical point was reached around mid-1997 when financial costs exceeded profits, and corporate cash-flow was caught in a savage squeeze.

Given the highly leveraged position of the corporate sector and resulting balance-sheet problems, the slowdown in growth in 1997 triggered a 50% jump in the number of insolvencies. Although large-scale bankruptcies in Korea have been quite rare, 8 of the 30 largest chaebols (representing around 4% of the assets of non-farm, non-financial business) foiled in 1997.

(2) In the Monetary Side

The crisis per se started in early July 1997 with Thailand's "surprise" decision to float its currency. This was followed a few weeks later by KIA Motor's request for a "debt work out" programs with its major creditors (involving some U.S.$8 billion) to avoid bankruptcy.[4] These events increased the sensitivity of investors to financial sector problems. Soon after, major international credit rating agencies that had foiled to foresee the Thai situation began to reassess countries with similar characteristics.

The second critical fault line was inconsistent monetary policy during the second half of 1997. As is well known, monetary policy has limited independence in globalized financial markets and the authorities must choose to target either domestic monetary conditions (interest rates or money growth) or the exchange rate. Policy can address different policy goals at any moment in time, but credibility and consistency require concentrating on a single overarching objective, such as low inflation or a fixed exchange rate. This basic principle was ignored in Korea.

Monetary policy in 1997, as in the past, was oriented towards achieving neutral conditions by supplying sufficient monetary growth (M_2 and MCT) to underpin output growth at around its potential, wale allowing "unavoidable" inflation and trend income velocity. This proved to be difficult. Although money growth was well sustained through 1997, this was misleading as it masked significant shifts (and distortions) in the allocation of credit. Bank loans to the 30 largest chaebols actually rose by 43% in the year to December, and indeed some 40% of the growth in bank credit over the second half of 1997 may have been emergency loans to distressed firms (at rates below market). Such non-market lending practices continued into 1998, resulting in an acute liquidity shortage for some healthy small and medium-sized firms.

Against this background, basing monetary policy on quantitative targets was difficult. as this approach risked ratcheting up the level of interest rates when demand and supply conditions shifted. Notwithstanding these complications, domestic monetary policy per se did not trigger the financial crisis.

On 25 August 1997, a high-risk decision was taken to "implicitly" guarantee the foreign liabilities of the merchant banks to facilitate their overseas borrowing needs (even though some of these institutions may have been close to insolvency). This guarantee foiled because in the wake of the KIA failure domestic and foreign financial institutions refused to increase their exposure to shaky merchant banks.

More importantly, the decision to underwrite the foreign liabilities of the banks meant that the Bank of Korea was trying to play the role of lender of last resort in U.S. dollars (similar in nature to Mexico's Tesobonos problem).

This high-risk strategy was compounded by the decision to prop up the won. From August to end-November 1997, the Bank of Korea lost at least U.S.$8 to 10 billion in foreign reserves through exchange market intervention, even though the won was theoretically floating within a predetermined band.

In short, through the latter part of 1997 monetary policy was being run in a fixed-exchange rate mode. This approach to policy may have reflected an illusion that the cautious dismantling of capital controls served to protect the economy from sharp swings in capital.

In fact, Korea's foreign liabilities had tripled since 1994, and its useable foreign reserves were less than a third of its short-term external liabilities Prior to the crisis (though the authorities may have been ignorant of the scale of external debt, owing to a chronic lack of transparency). With the benefit of hindsight, the quick adoption of a freely floating exchange rate (even as late as July 1997) might have avoided some of the worst excesses of the crisis. To be sure, a severe financial crisis and a loss of international confidence would still have been inevitable. And though it is impossible to say whether the attack on the won would have been tempered, the Bank of Korea would at least have been able to play the role of lender of last resort in domestic currency.

A final action, which added fuel to the flames, was an ill-judged decision to bail out KIA Motors in late October 1997 (after repealed public statements that the government would not do so). But by this time, foreign banks had already sharply reduced their credit lines, and foreign investors were quitting Korea in large numbers.

B. The Prospects of Korean Economy

On 17 November 1997, the government abandoned its attempts to support the won and two days later announced an emergency program to stem the financial crisis.

An U.S.$57 billion IMF stand-by agreement was announced on 3 December, 1997. The centerpiece of the stand-by was stringent macroeconomic-policy guidelines to choke off any second-round inflation effects from currency depreciation. An original aspect of this agreement was the detailed specification of microeconomic reforms aimed at opening up the Korean economy to greater domestic and world competition, reforming corporate governance structures and practices as well as improving transparency and reporting procedures.

The central focus of these initiatives was to speed the pace of restructuring and reform of the financial system and the chaebols. These initiatives were supported by measures to increase labor market flexibility, change Korea's outdated bankruptcy procedures and to open up the market for corporate control to foreign capital.

The financial crisis has had a surprisingly quick and severe impact on labor markets, the more so as large scale restructuring of the chaebols has yet to begin. Total employment plummeted by some 1.5 million from July 1997 to April 1998, while the unemployment rate rocketed from 2.2 to 6.7% despite a sharp drop in labor force participation.

The government has introduced pay cuts of 10 to 20% according to grade, and the vast majority of business has implemented plans to slash their payrolls and investment outlays. Wages and especially overtime and bonuses will thus be under intense pressure to save jobs.

However, this assumes that management and labor will share the burden of adjustment, and that sharply rising unemployment will be shouldered by society as a whole through social transfers to the jobless.

(1) The Short-Term Economic Prospects
Signs of more normal financial market conditions began to appear in late January 1998. By March 1998, corporate bond yields had dropped from their peak of almost 30% to 18%, and the won had stabilized at around 1,400 won to the dollar. Even so, with interest rates stuck at such punitive levels, the economy was on a razor's edge and pessimism in Korea (and South-East Asia) deepened.

The short-term economic prospects are thus unusually clouded and will depend crucially on how this "high interest rate conundrum" is resolved. Beyond that, how the economy performs will depend on how quickly economic agents adapt to the "new economic paradigm" in three areas:

(1) the corporate sector's adjustment to an era of high interest rates and intense competition;
(2) how households adapt to uncertainty concerning job security and pay; and
(3) How foreign investors react to investment opportunities following the unprecedented opening up of Korea's capital markets.

Survival of Korea's industrial base will thus require large-scale restructuring, wage cuts and labor shedding. Assuming that a 15% reduction in the wage bill is realized, a break-even point could be attained by late 1998, even though full year results will probably show a loss. But by 1999, quite large operating surpluses could be emerging. Even so, the scope for quickly reducing corporate debt-to-equity ratios under this central scenario is modest.

If 1997 figures for new share issues and foreign direct investment (mostly in the form of joint ventures and M&As) ale simply extrapolated, corporate gearing might drop from some 400 to 350% between 1997 and 1999. This figure might drop further to the 300 to 325% range when recent tax changes which encourage land and asset revaluation are included.

Nonetheless, these estimates underline the difficulty of bringing down debt-to-equity ratios to the government's suggested 200% target level quickly. Indeed, reaching this figure would require combined asset sales and foreign direct capital inflows of the order of U.S.$90 to 100 billion over the next two years.

Investment bank reports suggest a surge in foreign interest in buying parts of or entire Korean enterprises. Chaebols have already sold some of their overseas subsidiaries and real estate (for roughly U.S.$2 to 3 billion), and a few of their domestic operations (for some U.S.$4 to 5 billion). For some of the five largest chaebols, attaining the 200% debt-to-equity target by 1999 might be feasible though very difficult.

The Korean economy will be driven by the two powerful equilibrating forces over the next two years, as follows.

(1) nominal wage cuts will restore corporate profitability and damp job losses:
(2) while a drop in business investment will produce large on-going current account surpluses.

During the first few months of its mandate, the new government has introduced a wide range of policy measures, touching virtually every aspect of the economy, to create a "new economic paradigm". The goal of these reforms is to transform fundamentally an economy long based on economic dirigism into a modern, free market-oriented economy. Although many of the details are yet to be spelled outs the core feature of the new paradigm is to create the legal and institutional framework necessary for rational incentive structures to govern economic behavior in the two directions as follows:

(1) exposing the economy more fully to world competition, and
(2) Introducing effective governance structures into banks and business.

To be sure, other components of reform, such as measures to enhance labor market flexibility and more effective bankruptcy laws are also critical elements of reform. But without these core measures, their impact would be significantly less positive.

(2) The Long-Term Economic Prospects

Although the government has made an impressive start in putting a promising legislative framework in place, the challenge will be to implement these measures and change the attitudes of economic agents during a period of severe recession. The initial offsets of the financial crisis have been a collapse in business investment, industrial restructuring and large-scale labor shedding. These shocks might lower potential output growth from 6 to 7% prior to the crisis to between 3 and 4% per annum in 1998–1999 (consistent with scrapping 10 to 15% of business capital stock).

If microeconomic reform is not implemented promptly, the economy risks stagnation with growth in the 3 to 4% range, as Korea's structural weaknesses steadily sap potential output growth, and investors' confidence is undermined. However, the OECD's medium-term baseline (MTB)[5] assumes that reform is carried out quickly and that social cohesion is maintained. Nevertheless, the rate of potential output growth during the period 2000 to 2003 is projected at between 5 and 6%, somewhat below the pre-crisis rate, reflecting the three factors as follows.

(1) labor inputs will slow as the expansion of the working-age population decelerates from 2% in the first half of the 1990s to only 0.5% in the first year of the next decade.
(2) the national investment rate may fall as much as 6 percentage points from its average of 35% during the first half of the 1990s as the firms that survive the crisis become more sensitive to profitability in expanding their operations. Consequently, the contribution of capital inputs may be reduced by about half from the 2-percentage point average during the past decade.
(3) structural reforms are unlikely to have a significant impact on total factor productivity (hereafter TFP) growth immediately.[6] Judging by the experience of other OECD countries (such as New Zealand and the United Kingdom) this will take at least five years.

Thus, supply side factors suggest growth in the range of 5 to 6%, a rate that is assumed to be achieved by the end of the MTB scenario (1998 to 2003) as private consumption and fixed investment recover. Inflation is projected to be low and stable during the next five years.

By 2003, the unemployment rate might be back to 4%, even though discouraged workers re-enter the labor market. Nevertheless, unemployment would be higher than in the past, reflecting greater frictional unemployment in a more flexible labor market.

The Korean government will face significant spending pressures to finance higher unemployment and social welfare benefits and to rehabilitate the financial system, which alone may cost as much as 1% of GDP a year from 1998 to 2003. Nonetheless, the budget surplus could be back in the 3% range by 2003. However, a small surplus in the social security accounts is would not be sufficient to deal with the fiscal consequences of a rapidly aging population.[7]

At the same time, a current account surplus of 1% of GDP is projected for 2003. This would imply cumulative current account surpluses of over U.S.$100 billion from 1998–2003 which would allow quick repayment of borrowings of some U.S.$35 billion from international agencies, and a build-up of official reserves to U.S.$80 to 90 billion (or 6 to 7 months of imports). However, the desirability of such a large build-up of foreign reserves is questionable, given their high opportunity costs.

Beyond 2003, the productivity gains resulting from the new market-oriented paradigm and more efficient resource allocation might allow Korea to match its pre-crisis potential growth rate of 6 to 7% despite a one-third decline in inputs, as TFP in Korea continues to converge to the OECD leaders.

III. AN ECONOMETRIC ANALYSIS OF FOREIGN DIRECT INVESTMENT ON KOREA

There are three major theoretical approaches to FDI: (1) The microeconomic approach based on the perspectives of the companies concerned (2), the macroeconomic approach based on location advantages such as labor costs and market size, and (3) the eclectic theory considering both (1) and (2).

The typical example of the microeconomic approach theory is the industrial organization theory, which says that a business with monopoly power makes FDI to dominate a market in an imperfect competition situation. This theory has been developed by C. P. Kindleberger (1970), R. E. Caves (1971), and S. Hymer (1976). The monopolistic elements in the theory include the ability to differentiate products, marketing skills, management skills, patents, undisclosed technologies, and economies of scale.

The macroeconomic approach begins with a criticism of the microeconomic approach claiming that the latter does not move beyond the framework of the partial equilibrium analysis and therefore cannot identify the externalities and social cost of individual business' activities inflicted on the entire national economy. The macroeconomic theory tries to explain overseas direct investments from the perspective of a macroeconomic general equilibrium analysis, arguing that based on the theory of international specialization, direct investments flow to the countries with comparative disadvantages (K. Kojima, 1973, 1978, 1982).

The eclectic theory tries to explain overseas direct investments using both the company's competitive edges and the location advantages (J. Dunning, 1981), stating that an individual business makes overseas direct investments because it wants to combine its competitiveness in capital, technologies and management skills with the location advantages of other countries, including labor costs and local marketing costs.

Yang-Taek Lim (1988) proposed a new hypothesis in connection with the industrial-interdependent relationship between the home country (investor) and the host country (invested) to analyze the determinants of FDI in Korea (based on the outstanding amounts in balance, during the period of 1970–1985). Lim has named this the industrial-interdependent relationship hypothesis. This means that the direct investment by the home country will increase if the host country has a high import dependency on the exporting products made by the home country.

Therefore, policy makers should study not only how FDI can maintain a complementary relationship with domestic investment of the host country, but also how FDI can contribute to its economic growth.

A. The Macroeconomic Effects

The following is the summary of Yang Tack Lim's study (1988 and 1989) on the determinants of FDI in Korea and its macroeconomic effects, with respect to each of the foreign investors including the United States, Japan, and Europe.

(1) The Direct Investment by the United States

As hypothesized, the direct investment by the United States (FDI_U) showed a positive (+) effect for the average rate of profit and the growth rate of domestic shipment of the Korean manufacturing sector, while it showed a negative (−) effect for the average wage level (W) and the tax rate (t) of the host country.

This coincides with the findings by N. W. Bandera and J. T. White (1968) and A. E. Scaperlanda and I. J. Mauer (1969). The Scaperlanda and Mauer model (during the 1952–1966 period) showed that the GNP of EEC nations was the only significant variables in explaining the size-of-market hypothesis. They concluded that the major determinant in the American direct investments in EEC was the market size.[8] Furthermore, not only did the direct investment by the United States (FDI_U) showed significantly a complementary relationship with Korea's domestic investment (I), it also contributed to an improvement in Korea's trade balance.

According to the above analysis of the macroeconomic effects of FDI in Korea, it was the United States which most effectively pursued industrial and technological cooperations and settled a complementary relationship between the host country (the U.S). and the home nation (Korea).

Such an analysis is contrary to the study by K. Kojima (1984). He analyzed the effect of the previous year's FDI on the current year's exports. He claimed that the direct investment by Japan (FDI_J) played a big role in reducing Korea's deficit in the balance of trade with Japan, whereas the direct investment by the United States (FDI_U) hardly did anything to improve Korea's trade balance.

Related with the above, K. Kojima (1973, 1978, 1979, 1982) and K. Kojima and J. Ozawa (1984) named the industry (labor-intensive and light industry) with comparative advantage in direct investment the trade oriented FDI, while naming the host country's industry (capital-intensive and heavy chemical industry) with comparative disadvantage the anti-trade oriented FDI. Going further, they claimed that the trade oriented FDI develops the host country's comparative advantage industry (labor-intensive and light industry) while the home country specializes in its comparative advantage industry (capital-intensive and heavy chemical industry), thus both profit from international trade.

Furthermore, Kojima claimed that Japan was usually engaged in the trade oriented FDI targeting the export industry profiting both countries, whereas the United States made the anti-trade oriented FDI which usually targeted the host country's domestic industry.

However, it must be noted that Kojima has dismissed the current realities where a developing country's specialization in light industry brings about a subordinate relationship such as intensifying the dependency on capital goods including the machinery parts.

Concerning Kojima's study (1984), it should be noted that he compared the FDI in Korea with the absolute value of Korea's exports when analyzing its effects on Korea's trade balance, instead of Korea's *net* exports. The absolute value of Korea's exports is highly likely to be erroneous, especially when taking into consideration of it's industrial dependency on Japan.

(2) The Direct Investment by Japan

The average wage level (W) and the growth rate of domestic shipment (S/S) were statistically significant variables that showed negative (−) effects on the direct investment by Japan (FDI_J).

The observation that the increase of shipment by Korean businesses (S/S) induced a decrease in the direct investment by Japan (FDI_J) coincides with the findings by the Bank of Korea (1985) and J. Dunning (1981). According to the analysis by the Bank of Korea, an increase in sales by Korean businesses showed a negative (−) effect on FDI.

Taking into consideration of the monopolistic property of the Korean industry, the empirical result can be explained that the intention of Japanese businesses to extend their business into Korea had declined the higher the increase rate of shipment (S/S) by Korea's big businesses.

Moreover, the direct investment by Japan (FDI_J) showed significantly a complementary relationship with Korea's domestic investment (I). And it was estimated to have deteriorated Korea's trade balance. This empirical testing result may reflect the heavy dependence of Korea on the imports of intermediary products from Japan.

Such an analysis coincides with the case studies by S. Lall and P. Streeten (1978) and R. Cohen and J. Frieden (1981). According to these studies, among six developing countries during the 5–7 years at the end of the 1960s, the FDIs by 159 foreign businesses showed a negative (−) effect on the trade balance of the five countries (Columbia, India, Iran, Jamaica, and Malaysia), only missing Kenya. Only a handful of FDI in a host country contributed to its trade balance.

Meanwhile, according to the study by R. Cohen and J. Frieden (1981), the deficit in balance of payment produced by eight foreign motor companies in Brazil in 1974 accounted for 1/8 of the total deficit. FDI also proved to have an unfavorable effect on the balance of payment in Nigeria.

The reason why FDI results in a negative (−) effect on the trade balance of a host country can be explained as follows. First of all, the remittance from the home country surpasses the amount of original investment. Secondly, the outflow of foreign exchange is excessive due to the import of intermediary goods. Thirdly, the export of many investment companies including foreign investors is stagnant.

(3) The Direct Investment by Europe

The average rate of profit (π), the average wage level (W), and the tax rate (t) of the host country are all statistically significant explanatory variables that showed a positive (+) effect on the direct investment by Europe (FDI_E) .

Furthermore, the direct investment by Europe (FDI_E) had a significant, complementary relationship with Korea's domestic investment (I), but deteriorated Korea's trade balance.

B. Its Effect on Technical Efficiency

Following the approach of M. Blomstrm (1986), Yang Taek Lim (1989) measured the yearly technical efficiency index (E) for each of 79 industrial sectors in the Korean manufacturing industry during the periods of 1978, and 1982–1986.

As shown in Table 1, M. Blomstrm (1986) and Y. T. Lim (1989) had the same results except the effect on the growth rate of market size (MG). Thus, in explaining technical efficiency (E), the Herfindal index (H) representing industrial concentration showed a positive (+) effect, the rate of change in the highest level of labor productivity (ΔY^+) representing technical development showed a negative (−) effect, and the market share of foreign businesses in Korea (MS) showed a positive (+) effect.[9]

From the two studies above, we can know that industrial concentration (H) reflects economies of scale and specialization rather than the market share of big businesses in small open economies such as Mexico and Korea. This coincides with the two studies on the determinants of technical efficiency, B. Carlsson (1972) for the Sweden and M. Blomstrorm (1986) for Mexico.

Table 1. Determinants of Technical Efficiency (E) of Mexico and Korea.

	Country	Model	Constant	H	ΔY^+	MG	FS	R^2	Time Period	No. of Industrial Sectors
M. Blomstrorm (1986)	Mexico	Linear Non-logarithm	0.6396	0.2341 (0.0675)	–0.0714 (0.0143)	–0.0044 (0.0211)	0.1866 (0.0612)	0.2891	1970–1975	145
		Linear logrithm	–0.1853	0.1182 (0.0527)	–0.2293 (0.0429)	–0.0801 (–0.0569)	0.0566 (0.0190)	0.2530		
Y. T. Lim (1989)	Korea	Linear Non-logarithm	0.2734	0.5669 (11.112)	–0.0647 (4.930)	–0.0950 (2.634)	0.2544 (2.025)	0.7030	1978, 1982–1986	79
		Linear logarithm	0.6135	0.3568 (7.439)	–0.4342 (5.124)	–0.0084 (0.428)	0.0018 (0.260)	0.5515		

Notes:
(1) The number in parentheses each indicates the standard error for Blomstrorm, and the t-statistic for Lim.
(2) For the proxy variable of market growth(MG), Blomstrorm chose the time rate of change in the number of employees (ΔL) whereas Lim chose the percentage rate of change in fixed capital ($\Delta K/K$).
(3) For the proxy variable of market share(MS) of foreign businesses, Blomstrorm chose the relative ratio of the number of employees in foreign businesses to the total number of employees in the Mexican industry (L_f/L), whereas Lim chose the relative ratio of the fixed capital of foreign businesses to the total amount of fixed capital in the Korean industry (K_f/K).
(4) For the proxy variable of foreign share(FS), Blomstrorm chose all foreign businesses having more than 15% ownership by foreign investors whereas Lim chose those with more than 50% of foreign share.

It was the growth rate of market size of the host country (MG) that the two studies above showed a difference. The percentage rate of change in fixed capital of the host country ($\Delta K/K$) and its time rate (ΔK) showed negative ($-$) effects in the two studies of Blomstrorm and Lim, although statistically insignificant for $\Delta K/K$, and statistically significant at the 5% level for ΔK. Therefore, the growth rate of market size of the host country (MG) showed a negative ($-$) effect on technical efficiency (E) in the study of Yang Taek Lim (1989), whereas Blomstrorm claimed that this explanatory variable hardly affects technical efficiency.

Second, the other three explanation variables: the export ratio (x), the import ratio (m), and the tax ratio (τ) were introduced to reflect the degree of international competitiveness. Among these, the import ratio (m) and the tax ratio (τ) were found to be significant determinants. Industrial concentration (H or CR_4) decreased as the import ratio (m) increased, but the extent was minimal.

Furthermore, technical efficiency (E) of the host country decreased due to a deterioration in international competitiveness when the tax ratio (τ) was high, coinciding with the empirical result of B. Carlsson (1972) for the Sweden's case.

Therefore, we can know that an effective way to increase technical efficiency (E) in the host country is to lower the tax ratio (τ) rather than increase the import ratio (m).

Third, the market share of foreign businesses in Korea (MS) both raised and lowered technical efficiency (E) of the host country. Its technical efficiency was raised when the relative ratio of foreign fixed capital to domestic fixed capital (K_f/K) was selected, whereas it was lowered when the relative ratio of foreign shipment to domestic sales volume (S_f/S) was selected.

This result may reflect the fact that the learning effect of the host country was higher with high K_f/K, and the industrial-interdependent relationship between foreign and domestic businesses was intensified. On the other hand, the market share of the host country's big businesses would fall, the higher the relative ratio of foreign shipment to domestic sales volume (S_f/S); thus technical efficiency of the host country (E) due to economies of scale and specialization could fall.

Thus, technical efficiency of the host country (E) will rise in the industry where there are more FDI with a higher ratio of foreign fixed capital to domestic fixed capital (K_f/K) and a lower ratio of foreign shipment to domestic sales volume (S_f/S): likewise, its technical efficiency will fall in the industry where there are more FDIs with a lower K_f/K and the higher S_f/S.

Fourth, the growth rate of market size of the host country (MG) showed a negative (−) or a positive (+) effect on technical efficiency (E) of the host country according to the given model and the selected proxy variable.

IV. THE KOREAN GOVERNMENT'S POLICY OF FOREIGN DIRECT INVESTMENT AND ITS CURRENT RÉGIME

The basic law governing FDI in Korea is the Foreign Capital Inducement Act, which is accompanied by Presidential Decrees and working rules specifying matters under the Act and its enforcement measures. There are also Regulation on Foreign Investment which provide matters necessary for enforcement.

The conclusion of the UR negotiations in 1993 has led to great changes in the international economic climate. Since then, the need for the Korean economy to upgrade its industrial structure to enhance international competitiveness has been greater than ever.

In 1993 the Korean government has an active investment liberalization policy of FDI by expanding liberalization measures and has been introducing deregulation programs to promote FDI and provide a more hospitable environment.

In 1994, the processing period for notification was much shortened from 20–30 days to no more than 3 hours. The processing period for amplifications subject to approval was also reduced from 30 days to 5 days (15 days, if consultation with related ministries is required).

In February 1995, foreign investment procedures for trading firms, with the exception of Japanese trading firms, were also simplified from the previous approval system to the notification system.

In April 1995, the Korean government established a comprehensive service system for FDI by introducing an "One-Stop Service System" in Seoul and in the provinces. This system is now able to resolve grievances of foreign-controlled firms, arrange linkages to joint partners and provide comprehensive information and administrative services.

A. *"Foreign Investment Promotion Act"*

The Korean government continues to pursue further liberalization of FDI by conforming to international standards of investment protection, such as WTO/TRIMS, OECD Code and NTI (National Treatment Instrument).

In March 1998, initiatives to reform the "Foreign Direct Investment and Foreign Exchange & Capital Transaction Systems" were announced. In April 1998, a public hearing to discuss a proposed draft of the "Foreign Investment Promotion Act" was held. After the approval by the Cabinet, the draft of the "Foreign Investment Promotion Act" was submitted to the National Assembly on July 24, 1998 for approval. The major points of the Act are summarized as follows.

(1) Simplification of Notification and Registration Procedures
The Acceptance of FDI Notification System will be changed to a simple Notification System (Draft Article 5 and Article 6).

The Foreign Investment Company Registration System will be maintained in order to provide tax reduction or exemption incentives and other supports for foreign investors (Draft Article 21).

Notification and applications for registration can be submitted to the branches and headquarters of the Foreign Exchange Bank and the overseas offices, local offices, and the headquarters of KOTRA's Investment Promotion Center. Previously, applications could only be submitted to the headquarters of the Foreign Exchange Banks.

(2) Abolition of the Report on Customs Clearance of Foreign Capital and the Resident Agent Notification Requirement
The law requiring notification to the Minister of Finance and Economy within one month of the customs clearance of induced foreign capital will be abolished (Current Law Article 38).

The law requiring a non-resident to appoint a resident as an agent to submit notifications, applications, or reports regarding FDI transactions will be abolished (Current Law Article 10).

(3) Establishment of Foreign Investment Promotion Center
Within KOTRA, the Investment Promotion Center will be established to serve as the central institution in inducing FDI. (Draft Article 15, Paragraph 1). This Center shall deal with all matters of assistance for foreign investors and foreign investment enterprises. The Center shall provide substitute settlement[10] and direct settlement[11] of approval or authorization applications for foreign investors and foreign invested enterprises, guidance and support in all matters relating to FDI, and other assistance in the promotion of FDI and execution of investment surveys.

The Head of KOTRA shall hold the Right of Request to request the dispatch of public officials from related ministries and cooperation in matters related to FDI.

Related ministries and related institutions shall dispatch experienced officials to work under the Head of KOTRA (Draft Article 15, Paragraph 2 and Paragraph 6).

(4) Central Government Support for Local Government Activities to Induce FDI

Central government will support port local government activities to induce FDI through the following methods (Draft Article 14, Paragraph 1). Funds will be supplied for the creation of FIZs. Capital to purchase land, to be rented to foreign invested enterprises, will be lent. Purchase and rental fees of land will be reduced or exempted for foreign investors and foreign invested enterprises. Public subsidies for various purposes, such as job training, will be provided.

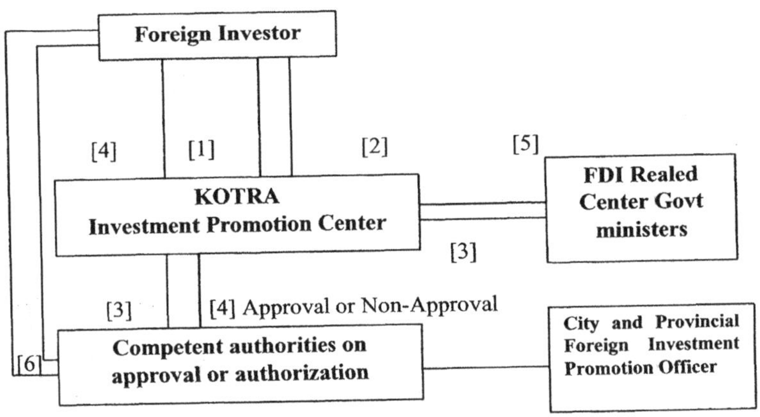

[1] Approval and authorization (e.g. the comprehensive process packages)

[2] Immediate settlement of directly settled civil affairs

[3] Substitute settlement of approval or authorization applications

[4] Settlement of approval or authorization (automatic approval upon lapse of time period determined by law)

[5] Report of the decision

[6] Monitoring of settlement procedures related to FDI

Fig. 1. The Comprehensive Process and the Automatic Approval System of the FDI Policy in Korea.

(5) Further Liberalization of Foreign Business Categories
The Korean government has also expanded the business categories of FDI by amending the enforcement decrees related to Foreign Capital Inducement Act. It abolished the approval system applied to reinvestment by foreign-controlled firms which infringed on labor-related decrees, and allowed foreign investors to acquire stocks owned by domestic partners of existing foreign-controlled firms. Procedures for stock sales of foreign investors and for disposition of capital were also simplified.

By January of 2000, the number of restricted businesses will be brought down to 21, while 1,078 categories will be fully open and another 47 partly open to foreign investment.

The Korean government has the authority to reject the foreign investment application only for reasons related to maintenance of public order, the protection of public health, morals and safety, the protection of its essential security interests, or the fulfillment of its obligations relating to international peace and security (Draft Article 14, Paragraph 1).

The Korean government firmly believes that further liberalization in currently restricted business categories is necessary. In the near future, the Korean government plans to speed up to the ongoing process of liberalization and establishing a timetable for business categories not yet scheduled to be liberalized by 2000.

B. Its Current Régime

The major points of the current régime of Korean government policy of FDI are summarized as follows.

(1) National Treatment for Foreign Investment Business
Unless otherwise specified In the laws, foreign investors and foreign-controlled firms are treated equally as Korean nationals and firms after an one-year waiting period. Tax exemption and deduction pertaining to Korean firms are equally applied to foreign-controlled firms.

The notification requirement for foreign invested enterprises, when wishing to engage in a additional businesses beyond those notified to the Ministry of Finance an Economy, will be abolished by the Foreign Investment Promotion Act.

(2) Guarantee of Overseas Transfer and Foreign Investors' Property
The overseas remittance of dividends from the stock or shares acquired by a foreign investor, and of the sales of proceeds of stocks or shares is guaranteed

in accordance with the contents of approval, the acceptance of the notification or the agreement at time of the remittance. The property rights of a foreign investor and a foreign-invested enterprise are guaranteed in accordance with the provisions of the laws.

(3) Protection of Intellectual Property Rights

The Korean government has a strong belief that effective protection of protect intellectual property rights (hereafter IPR) is critical to the fostering technological development in Korea and to attracting high-tech multinational corporations from abroad. The Korean government's efforts to IPR are being pursued in three ways:

(a) by penalizing IPR violators;
(b) by upgrading the legal framework and the institutions for IPR protection; and
(c) by raising public awareness of IPR.

As a result of such strong and continuous efforts since 1986, foreigners can now expert protection that is in line with international standards. In particular, Korea has enacted several amendments to its legislation in order to fully comply with WTO/TRIPS agreement before the end of the 1995.

(4) Taxation and Incentives for Foreign Direct Investment

The Korean government provides tax incentives and support for foreign-controlled firms which bring in advanced technology that is deemed necessary in achieving an advanced industrial structure. The basic framework for advanced technology eligible for financial and tax benefits was established in 1984. Since then, however, the industrial structure has changed and more advanced technology has emerged, necessitating the readjustment Korea's industrial development policy.

In 1995, the Korean government introduced a new incentive system in which the government's discretion is significantly reduced. Under the old system, foreign investors would not benefit from tax deduction and exemption unless investment were accompanied by advanced technology and tax exemption lasted for five years upon the occurrence of positive profits followed by 50% tax reduction in the subsequent three-year period.

Under the new incentive system, however, eligibility for tax benefits no longer depends on the types of technology initially provided by the investor. Korea has thus far signed bilateral tax treaties with 52 countries. Most of the recently signed treaties closely follow the guidelines set by the OECD Model Tax Convention.

In addition, the Law for the Coordination of International Tax Affairs (LCITA) was passed for enactment in the National Assembly in November 1995. Under this law, Korea's tax levying practices will be brought more in line with standards set by the OECD.

Under the Foreign Investment Promotion Act, the FDI incentive system shall be augmented as follows.

Tax Reduction or Exemption

Tax reduction or exemption on corporate and income tax on dividends for 10 years for FDI in Korea shall be augmented (See Table 2). Also, the tax reduction or exemption of local tax (Draft Article 9, Paragraph 4) will apply to acquisition tax, property tax, aggregate land tax, and registration tax. Previously, registration tax was not included.

Concerning the tax reduction or exemption period, local governments will have the autonomous power to grant tax reduction or exemption from anywhere

Table 2. Tax Reduction or Exemption on Corporate and Income Tax on Dividends for 10 Years for FDI in Korea.

Present	Planned
A business accompanying Advanced technology : reduction and exemption of taxes for 8 years 5 years at 100% the remaining 3 years at 50%	A business accompanying advanced technology, or service industries that support the manufacturing sector which strengthen the international competitiveness of a domestic business reduction and exemption of taxes for 10 years (7 years at 100%, 3 years at 50%)
A business located in a Free Export Zone (FEZ) 8 years for a business accompanying advanced technology 5 years for all other types of companies – 3 years at 100% – the remaining 2 years at 50%	A business located in a FIZ reduction or exemption of taxes for 10 years * The augmentation of FIZ incentives apply to the Masan and Iksan FEZs.

Source: Draft article 9, Paragraph 2 and Pargraph 3 of the Foreign Investment Promotion Act.

Table 3. The Present Local Government Property Rental System

Rent period	3 years for Administrative Properties 5 years for Miscellaneous Properties (Rents can be renewed)
Renting fees	Must be more than 5% of the value of the Properties

between 8 to 15 years. However, the tax reduction or exemption period and ratio will be higher than that of the previous law (5 years at 100%, the remaining 3 years at 50%).

A Foreign investor may check potential tax reduction or exemption incentives prior to deciding to invest. Presently, foreign investors may apply for tax reduction or exemption only after giving notification of their investment (Draft Article 9, Paragraph 7 and Paragraph 8).

In the case a foreign invested enterprise seeks to convert a farm or forestry land into a factory site, conversion fee shall be reduced or exempted. The criteria and ratio for reduction or exemption shall be stipulated by Presidential Decree.

Renting of National and Local Government Properties

Under the Foreign Investment Promotion Act, national and local government properties can be rented on the basis of private contracts. Previously, this was not allowed. Installment payments and delayed payments for the purchase of national and local government properties will be permitted.

Rent reduction or exemption is possible for national government properties in Foreign Investors Industrial Parks, National Industrial Parks, and FIZs (Draft Article 13, Paragraph 4).

As in the case of national government properties, the rental period of local government properties will be expanded to 50 years. Businesses eligible for rent reduction or exemption, as well as the rates to be applied, will be autonomously determined by local governments(Draft Article 13, Paragraph 5).

(5) Mergers and Acquisitions

FDI through mergers and acquisitions (hereafter M & A) was not permitted in Korea. Only portfolio investment was shares listed on the Korean Stock Market Exchange is allowed, but foreigner's purchases of listed shares were limited buy ceilings set by the Korean government. But under the current legislation,

M & A having the characteristics of FDI is almost completely liberalized, although stock market transactions will still be limited. However, with further progress in liberalization and with the gradual elimination of ceilings on stock market purchase, M & A in the form of stock market transactions is more widely open to foreign investors.

(6) Foreign Investors' Acquisition of Real Estate in Korea

High population density has been the reason behind strict government regulations of the real estate market in Korea. Moreover, the land price bubble that occurred in the late 1980s further strengthened the restrictions by creating such measures as tax disincentives or zoning regulations.

These regulations are equally applied to foreign and domestic investors, but foreign investors, including those enterprises whose ownership exceeds 50% of total share capital, are subject to additional restrictions in purchasing real estate properties in Korea.

Rules on land purchases by foreigners differ from those on purchases of other types of real estate. Non-residents are required to have authorization from the Ministry of Finance and Economy before purchasing real estate properties other than land pursuant to the Regulation on Foreign Exchange Management.

According to a new Act under the jurisdiction of the Ministry of Construction and Transportation, however, foreign-controlled firms are easily able to purchase land, as long as they do so for legitimate business purposes.

For foreign-controlled firms belonging to the manufacturing sector, only notification of purchases of factory sites are required for legitimate business operations. The title of ownership shall then be issued within fifteen days upon the notification. However, different rules apply to foreign-controlled firms in the service sector.

Notification is the only requirement for purchases that do not exceed the specified ceilings. These measures are all part of efforts made by the Korean government to reduce the soaring land prices and should not be viewed as discriminatory given Korea's real estate situation.

(7) Loans of Five Years or More

Under the current foreign investment law, loans of maturities more than three years are treated as commercial loans rather than FDI. Commercial loans are allowed only for imports of facilities and equipment by foreign- controlled firms in high-tech industries, small-and medium-sized firms in manufacturing industries, firms engaged in the construction of infrastructure, and firms that have already rapid existing loans.

Loans with maturities of more than three years are subject to approval by the Korean government, considering that various liberalization measures on capital movements may induce excessive capital inflows from abroad.

Under the new Foreign Direct Investment Law, loans with purpose of direct investment and maturities of five years or more will be classified as being tantamount to the FDI.

V. SUMMARY AND CONCLUSION

Unlike loans, FDI has the effect of directly participating in business, not only influencing a country's domestic investment, economic growth, and trade balance, but also transferring production technology and business management skill.

The basic direction of the Korean government policy of FDI is to foster further economic development by upgrading domestic industrial structure through FDI into high-tech manufacturing and service industries and by raising international competitiveness through the absorption of the state- of-the-art technologies.

The Korean government is currently undertaking a reform to amend the Foreign Capital Inducement Act. When completed, tax reform will bring the legislation more in conformity with the OECD standard. The new legislation will set Korea's FDI liberalization and deal with comprehensive incentives for and protection of FDI in Korea. To fulfill these goals, the government is seriously considering the inclusion of various reform packages in the legislation. The deregulation shall be executed in the directions as follows:

(1) The number of deregulated industries (an additional reduction in the number of prohibited or restricted industries) shall be increased. The industries already open to foreign capital and also widen their doors in practical terms.
(2) The investment permit procedures (an increase in the number of industries which can begin operations only with declarations to the authorities, and eventually, the elimination of permit requirements altogether) shall be simplified.
(3) The conditions imposed on foreigners' investment ratio shall be eliminated. Likewise, tax break or other benefits offered to foreign investors also shall be reduced and eliminated in the end so that foreign investors will be treated exactly like domestic ones.

However, the Korean government must recognize the importance of the improvement in the business environment for foreign investors. Korea's foreign investment climate was relatively less attractive than those of South East Asian countries which had greatly improved their investment climates after the second half of the 1980s.

FDIs in Korea have been done on a much smaller scale than Taiwan and ASEAN countries, not to mention China during the past few years. FDIs in Korea rose by 180% during the three years of 1989–1992 compared to the five years of 1984–1988: FDIs in Taiwan recorded an 250% increase and FDIs in Malaysia, Indonesia and Thailand recorded an 400%–500% increase during the same period. The FDIs in Korea accounted for 0.3% of GDP during 1984–1992, a very low figure compared to those for many other Asian countries.

High wages negatively affect FDIs. Stabilization of wages therefore can be considered as one of the surest way of attracting more FDIs to Korea. The traditional type of FDIs attempting to take advantage of low wages in assembly work will continue to decline. The critical factor for FDIs is the stability of industrial relations and wages.

Korea has already been losing her international competitiveness to China, Thailand, and other low-wage countries for simple labor-intensive assembly work. Thus it is being forced to shift to high-tech industries for joint ventures with foreign investment partners. It needs to have both trained scientists and technicians. The Korean government should support the expansion of institutes of higher learning. It should also offer a variety of intense support for re-training and re-education for technical staff in the private sector.

Improvements in the infrastructure are also essential for attracting more foreign capital. The returns on FDIs remain low because of high production costs partly attributable to saturated ports, airports, and the inland transportation network.

The OECD's medium-term reference scenario illustrates the large potential benefits of rapid economic reform and transforming Korea to a more market-oriented economy. From this perspective, Korea's financial crisis can be seen as a catalyst to structural reform which might have taken decades to implement under "business as usual" circumstances.

Based on the studies of Yang Taek Lim (1988 and 1989), the Korean government should pursue some incentive systems designed to activate FDIs to become complementary with domestic investment of the host country so that they can contribute to economic growth and improve trade balance of the host country.

In connection with this matter, H. W. Singer (1950) analyzed whether FDI in an underdeveloped country improved the welfare of the underdeveloped country or that of the developed nature. The multiplier effect caused by FDI was usually accrued to the home country (the developed nation) rather than the host country (the underdeveloped country).

Considering that FDI was usually made in the export industrial area, such an effect was enlarged when there was a big difference between the host country's productivity in the export industry and the productivity in the domestic industry. FDI could only contribute to the welfare of the home country(the developed nation), especially when that investment was made in the primary industry since terms of trade between the primary and the secondary industrial product gradually deteriorated.

Meanwhile, D. F. Burges (1978) analyzed the effect of FDI on income redistribution of the host country (the undeveloped country). Unlike the previous studies which concluded that the inflow of capital caused by FDI transferred income from capital to labor due to the decline in the rate of profit in capital, he claimed that income distribution of the host country (the underdeveloped country) differed according to the substitution elasticity between consumption and production.

Finally, Korean needs perseverance, courage and skill enough to enhance the economy's fundamental strengths (rather than simply international competitiveness), such as a strong sense of national identity and social cohesion, a high national savings rate, and a well-educated, diligent work force.

NOTES

1. According to J. Fei and G. Ranis(1975), Korea experienced the take-off in the early 1970s in the aspect of dualistic economy.

2. For a detail discussion, see H. Byun and Y. Wang (1995).

3. To analyze the determinants of FDI in Korea, Lim chronologically analyzed Korea's industry as a whole including the manufacturing industry during the period of 197–1985 and analyzed only the manufacturing industry during the same time span to investigate the economic effects of FDI in Korea. The reason for his choice of 1985 as the end of the period in the analysis was that there was a structural change in Korea's FDI policy from the positive system (1960–1983) to the negative system (1984–1992).

4. Financial market confidence was particularly shaken in January 1997 by the first such insolvency, that of Hanbo Steel (Korea's 14th-largest conglomerate). The scale of the ensuing bribes-for-loans scandal was stunning, even for a Korean Public long hardened to "cosy" arrangements: and foreign investors' confidence appealed to have been irrevocably shaken. This fragile situation calmed in Spring 1997, in part because Korean banks entered into a voluntary "Bankruptcy Avoidance Agreement" in April to avoid driving "solvent" firms into receivership (albeit at the costs of weakening their own balance sheets). But this respite proved short-lived.

5. The MTB assumes that the won will correct for overshooting and retrain the W 1200 level by 2000. Beyond 2000. the exchange rate has been assumed to remain constant in real terms.

6. TFP has contributed around 3 percentage points to growth since 1979 according to Yang-Taek Lim (1996) and Kim and Hong (1997). If the TFP contribution remains in that range, potential growth, taking account of labor and capital inputs, would be between 5 and 6%.

7. Although the government plans to increase the contribution rate by 3 percentage points every five years from its current level of 9%, the Social Security Fund will cease accumulating assets in 2008 and will move into deficit before 2030. To put the system on an actuarially-sound basis, fundamental reform, including some combination of a higher retirement age, less generous benefits and a more rapid increase in contributions, will be required.

8. The theoretical background of the determinants of FDI can be found in the context of industrial organization, trade complementarity, investment selection, and currency value advantage. Among the determinants of FDI based on industrial organization are two different theories, one being the market share hypothesis by A. E. Scaperlanda and I. J. Mauer (1969) and the other being the product life cycle hypothesis by R. Vernon (1966).

9. The same result above was shown in the closed economy model and the open economy model in which an additional explanatory variable, FDI was additionally introduced. It was the same whether the explanatory variables representing the degree of international competitiveness such as the export ratio (x), the import ratio (m), the tax ratio (τ) were additionally introduced.

10. Substitute settlement: upon submitting the appropriate application forms to KOTRA, it will settle applications with other related administrative institutions for foreign investors and foreign invested enterprises.

11. Direct settlement: upon submitting the appropriate application forms to KOTRA, it will directly settle applications, through dispatched public officials from related ministries at KOTRA for foreign investors and foreign invested enterprises.

REFERENCES

Aliber. R. Z. (1970). A Theory of Direct Foreign Investment. In: C. P. Kindleberger (Ed.), *The International Corporation*. Cambridge, Mass.: MIT Press.

Agarwal, J. (1980). Determinants of Foreign Direct Investment: A Survey. *Weltwirtschaftliches Archiv, 116*.

Arrow, K. J. The Economic Implications of Learning-by-Doing. *Review Economic Studies, 29*(1), 155–173.

Balasubramanyam, V. N. (1986). Incentives and Discentives for Foreign Direct Investment in Less Developed Countries. In: B. Balassa & H. Giersch (Eds), *Economic Incentives*. The McMillan Publishers, Ltd.

Bandera, V. N. J. T., & White U. S. (1968). Direct Investments and Domestic Markets in Europe. *Economica International, 21*.

Bank of Korea. Determinants of Foreign Direct Investment in Korea and its Economic Effects (1985). *Monthly Bulletin, 39* (Korean).

Blomstrorm, M. (1986). Foreign Investment and Productive Efficiency: The Case of Mexico. *Journal of Industrial Economics, 35*.

Brems, H. (1970). A Growth Model of International Direct Investment. *American Economic Review, LX*(3).

Buckley, P. J., & Casson, M. (1985). *The Economic Theory of the Mult-inational Enterprise*. New York: St. Martin Press.
Byun, H., & Wang, Y. (1995). Technology Transfer and Multinational Corporation: The Case of South Korea. *Journal of Asian Economics, 2*.
Caves, R. E. (1971). International Corporations: The Industrial Economics of Foreign Investment. *Economica, 38*.
Cohen, R., & Frieden (1981). The Impact of Multinational Corporation on Developing Nations. In: E. P. Reubens (Ed.), *The Challenge of the New International Economic Order*.
Cushman, D. O. (1988). Exchange Rate uncertain and Foreign Direct Investment in the U.S. *Weltwirtschaftliches Archiv, 124*(2).
Dunning, J. H. (1981). *International Production and the Mutinational Enterprise*. London: George Allen & Unwin.
Fei, J. C. H., & Ranis, G. (1975). A Model of Growth and Employment in the Open Dualistic Economy. *Journal of Development Studies, 57*.
Goldberg, M. A. (1972). Determinants of U.S. Direct Investment in the EEC: Comment. *American Economic Review, 62*.
Goldbrough, D. J. (1979). The Role of Foreign Direct Investment in the External Adjustment Process. *IMF Staff Papers, 26*.
Griffin, K. B. (1970). Foreign Capital, Domestic Savings and Economic Development. *Bulletin of the Oxford Institute of Economics and Statistics, 32*.
Haddad, M., & Harrison, A. (1987). Are There Positive Spillovers from Direct Foreign Investment? – Evidence from Panel Data for Morocco. *Journal of Development Economics, 69*.
Hymer, S. (1976). *International Operation of National Firm: A Study of Direct Foreign Investment*. Cambridge: The MIT Press.
IMF (1985). *Foreign Private Investment in Developing Countries*. Washington, D. C.: International Monetary Fund.
Kim, & Hong (1997). Accounting for Rapid Economic Growth in Korea, 1963–1995. Korean Development Institute.
Kindberger, C. P. (1969). *American Business Abroad: Six Lectures on Direct Investment*. New Haven: Yale University Press.
Krugman, P. (1994). The Myth of Asia's Miracle. *Foreign Affairs*.
Kojima, K. (1973). A Macroeconomic Approach to Foreign Direct Investment. *Hitotsubashi Journal of Economics, 14*(1).
Kojima, K. (1978). Direct Foreign Investment Between Advanced Industrialized Countries, *Hitotsubashi Journal of Economics, 18*(1).
Kojima, K. (1978). *Direct Foreign Investment*. New York.
Kojima, K. (1982). Macroeconomic versus International Business Approach to Foreign Direct Investment. *Hitotsubashi Journal of Economics, 23*(1).
Kojima, K., & Ozawa, T. (1984). Micro and Macro-Economic Models of Direct Foreign Investment: Toward a Synthesis. *Hitotsubashi Journal of Economics, 25*(1).
Lall, S., & Streeten, P. (1978). *Foreign Investment Transnationals and Developing Countries, 47*.
Lucas, R. Jr. (1993). Making a Miracle. *Econometrica, 61*(2).
Lim, Y.-T. (1988). Determinants of Foreign Direct Investment in Korea and Its Economic Effects. *The 22nd Annual conference of Korea International Economic Association*. (Korean).
Lim, Y.-T. (1989). Determinants of Technical Efficiency in Korean Manufacturing Industry. *The Annual Conference of Korea Economic Association*. (Korean).

Lim, Y.-T. (1989). *Technology Transfer Through Foreign Direct Investment.* Korea's Science Foundation. (Korean).

Lim, Y.-T. (1996). Export-led Development Strategy: the Korean Experience for India and South Asia. Paper presented at the International Conference on India's New Economic Policy held by American Committee of Asian Economics at Jawaharlal Nehru University, New Delhi.

Lim, Y.-T. (1996). An Econometric Study on Technological Progress, Innovation, Diffusion, Transfer, and their Impacts National Competitiveness of the Korean Manufacturing. The 8th Conference of Technology, Business Administration and Economics.

Lim, Y.-T. (1996). Korea's Liberalization Policy Directives amid Weakening Competitiveness. *Journal of Asian Economics, 7*(4).

Lim, Y.-T. (1998). The Role of Korea in the Asian Pacific Economic Cooperation. *Research in Asian Economic Studies, 8*, JAI Press Inc.

Loo, F. V. (1977). The Effect of Foreign Direct Investment on Investment in Canada. *Review of Economics and Statistics, 59.*

Lucas, R. E. Marketing a Miracle. *Econometrica, 61*, 251–272.

Lunn, H. (1993). Determinants of U.S. Direct Investment in the EEC. *European Economic Review, 21.*

Moore, M. O. (1993). Determinants of German Manufacturing Direct Investment: 1980–1988. *Weltwirtschaftliches Archiv, 129.*

OECD (1995). *Code of Liberalization of Capital Movements.* Paris: OECD.

Petirochilos, G. A. (1989). *Foreign Direct Investment and the Development Process: The Case of Greece.* Avebury: Gower Publishing Company, Ltd.

Riedel, J. (1975). The Nature and Determinants of Export-Oriented Direct Foreign Investment in a Developing Country of Taiwan. *Weltwirtschaftliches Archiv, 111*(3).

Root, F., & Ahmed, A. A. (1979). Empirical Determinants of Manufacturing Direct Foreign Investment in a Developing Countries. *Economic Development and Cultural Change, 27.*

Ruman, A. M. (1986). New Theories of Multinational Enterprise: An Assessment of Internalization Theory. *Bulletin of Economic Research, 38.*

Salter, W. E. G. (1960). *Productivity and Technical Change.* London: Cambridge University Press.

Scaperlanda, A. E., & Mauer, L. (1969). The Determinations on U.S. Direct Foreign Investment in the EEC. *American Economic Review, 59.*

Singer, H. W. (1950). U.S. Foreign Investment in Undeveloped Area: The Distribution of Gains Between Investing and Borrowing Countries. *American Economic Review, 40.*

Tsai, P. L. (1994). Determinants of Foreign Direct Investment and Its Impact on Economic Growth. *Journal of Economic Development, 19*(1).

UNCAD (1996). *World Investment Report.*

United Nations (1993). *World Investment Report.*

United Nations (1994). *World Investment Report.*

Voivodas, C. S. (1973). Exports, Foreign Capital and Economic Growth. *Journal of International Economics, 3*(4).

Wang, Z. Q., & Swain, N. J. (1995). The Determinants of Foreign Direct Investment in Transforming Economies: Empirical Evidence from Hungary and China. *Weltwertschaftliches Archiv.*

31. ARE FOREIGN FIRMS TECHNOLOGICALLY MORE ACTIVE AND PROGRESSIVE IN LESS DEVELOPED COUNTRIES?: EVIDENCE FROM THE INDIAN CHEMICAL INDUSTRY

Amit S. Ray

I. INTRODUCTION

The benefits and costs of transnational corporation (TNC) activities in developing countries have been extensively debated in the development economics literature.[1] The debate revolves around several key issues: resource transfer effects (typically capital, technology and skills), balance of payments effects, market structure effects and effects on national sovereignty. This paper focuses on one of them – the technological effects of TNC activities on host developing countries.

TNCs are a major channel of transferring technology internationally. Doubts can be raised about the appropriateness of such technology transferred through TNCs to less developed countries. It may also be argued that this may not be the most effective means of technology transfer from the host government's point of view.[2] Notwithstanding these controversial questions, a most serious cause for concern about TNC entry into less developed countries continues to

Restructuring Asian Economics for the New Millennium, Volume 9B, pages 601–614.

ISBN: 0-7623-0710-2

be *the effect that it may have on the technological development of the host less developed country.*

This can manifest itself at three levels. *First,* it depends on the nature and degree of technological interaction within the affiliates of a particular TNC. The *second* dimension is reflected in the technological linkages and spillovers created by the TNCs with other vertically linked and competing domestic enterprises. *Final* and perhaps the most crucial manifestation is to be found in the technological activities and behaviour of foreign firms in comparison with local ones. It is this third facet that we intend to examine in this paper. The questions that emerge are posed below.

Is it legitimate to suggest that foreign firms operating in less developed countries spend less on R&D compared to domestic firms? Does this mean that foreign firms do not promote local technological development? If they do, what kind of technological competence do they build? Do they indeed stress more on technological "know-how" and less on technological "know-why"? To what extent do they introduce technical changes in their operations? All these questions can be summarised under the broad question posed in the title: are foreign firms technologically more active and progressive in less developed countries?

To seek answers to the above questions, this paper presents an econometric analysis of the technological behaviour of foreign and domestic firms based on a firm-level data set from the Indian chemical industry. In the following section, we develop a conceptual framework for analysing technological behaviour of enterprises in less developed countries. In Section III, we describe our econometric methodology based on this conceptual framework. Section IV reports the results and analysis. Section V summarises and concludes.

II. A CONCEPTUAL FRAMEWORK

To understand the technological behaviour of firms, we should ideally view research and development (R&D) as a production process where research inputs are transformed into research outputs. Our intention here is to conceptualise such a research production function, which we have represented in a schematic diagram in Fig. 1.

Research input includes R&D spending, R&D employment and scientific and technological manpower in R&D. Indeed, one could argue that R&D spending is the key input which in turn determines the other input of R&D employment, particularly the extent of scientific manpower devoted to R&D.

Research output has traditionally been identified with major innovations or technological breakthroughs causing an outward shift of the technology

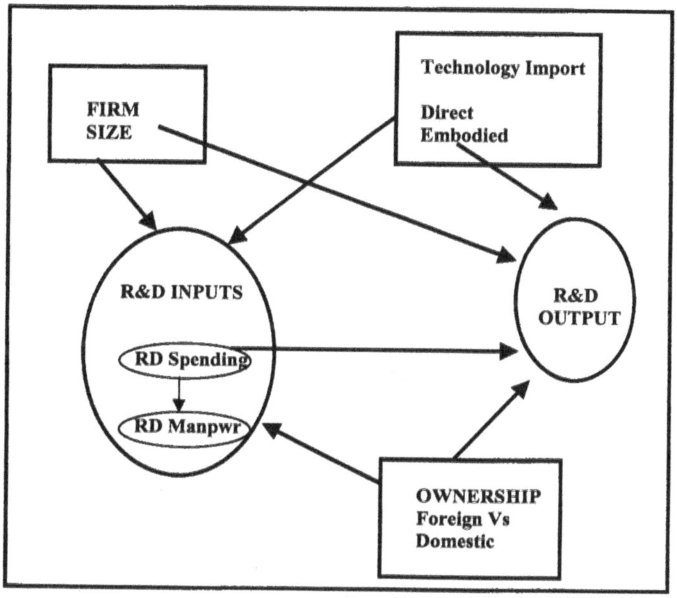

Fig. 1. The R&D Production Function: A Schematic Framework.

frontier. However, Rosenberg (1976) has strongly criticised this restrictive Schumpeterian usage of the term "innovation."[3] Subsequently, technological development has been broadly defined to encompass an enormous range of activities including diffusion, adaptation and implementation. The acquisition of technological capability, defined generally as the capacity to select, assimilate, adapt and improve given (imported) technologies, has now been acknowledged as a principal research output and an important source of technical progress, particularly in the context of less developed countries.[4] In fact, in these countries, most firms do not engage in R&D leading to major innovations and technological breakthroughs. We, therefore, restrict ourselves only to technological capability as the output of the research production function.

Following Lall (1985), we can categorise technological capability as know-how and know-why. This distinction proves to extremely useful in understanding technological activities of LDC enterprises. Know-how is acquired through "not only the assimilation of imported techniques (which itself can be a lengthy and active learning process) but also quality control (which also involves active technical effort), improved plant layout and production practices, slight modifications to equipment and tooling, trouble-shooting, the use of different raw materials and so on,"[5] all of which can be summarised as production engineering. Know-why is the next stage of technological development, which involves the understanding of the nature of the process and product technologies leading to the development of new, improved designs. Frontier R&D leading to major innovations follow this stage.[6] Both know-how and know-why have proved to be extremely important in determining the technological competitiveness enjoyed by less developed countries in international markets.

It appears from the above discussion that know-how and know-why can be achieved only through conscious technological effort and explicit investments in R&D. However, we cannot ignore the possibility of some technological learning, know-how in particular, which can be achieved through activities other than those in R&D, like shop floor practices and learning by doing. Unfortunately, it is difficult to model such factors in a research production function framework, given the limitation of data availability.

The R&D production function, however, is not a simple mapping of R&D inputs into technology outputs. Rather, it encompasses a complex set of factors, exogenous as well as endogenous to the firm. We consider some of the important ones, particularly in the context of a less developed country: *technology imports*, *scale* and above all *ownership (foreign versus domestic)*.

Technology Import

In a developing country, the extent of technology imports is likely to have a strong influence on the quantum of R&D activities of firms. The effect could be either negative or positive, depending on whether domestic technological effort acts as a substitute for or as a complement to imported technology. Imported technology may be divided into two categories. First, technology may be imported directly through technology purchase agreements or licensing on payment of royalty/technical fees. Second, through import of capital goods, embodied foreign technology could flow in. This distinction is crucial because the nature and extent of local R&D will depend on the form of technology import. It is commonly held that direct purchase of technology requires less R&D effort by the importing firm as opposed to import of embodied technology which demands complementary R&D effort by firms.

Apart from determining the research-input levels of R&D spending and/or R&D manpower, the extent of technology imports could also conceivably directly enter the research production function determining the level of research output for given quantities of inputs.

The Scale Effect

The scale effect in R&D production is well documented in the literature. The basic idea is rooted in the Schumpeterian hypothesis that "bigness and fewness encourage technological advancement."[7] This hypothesis identifies both firm-size as well as the degree of monopoly as determinants of R&D.[8] The scale effect determines not only the size of the firm's R&D set-up (the amount R&D inputs), but also the productivity of these R&D inputs (the amount research outputs produced per unit of research inputs). Here economies of scale, as well as the incentive to produce new knowledge, jointly determine the impact of firm size on research production.[9] There are numerous empirical studies attempting to estimate the relationship between firm size and R&D (inputs as well as outputs). The results are ambiguous, suggesting that the scale effect is more of an empirical question, not bound by any rigid theoretical hypothesis.

The Ownership Factor

This constitutes the central focus of this paper and brings us to the question of the role of TNCs in local technological development. All industrialising, less developed countries require large amounts of imported technology. TNCs provide a major channel of international technology transfer to host less developed countries. As Lall (1991) suggests, FDI, in appropriate conditions, can prove to be a very efficient means of transferring a package of capital, skills, technology, brand name and access to established international networks. There are, of course, other channels of arm's length technology transfer, notably licensing, which the non-affiliate enterprise in less developed countries utilises to import disembodied technology.

However, "passive" import of technology cannot result in indigenous technological development. Local R&D efforts are crucial to promote and acquire domestic technological capability. In this respect, how much do foreign firms differ from local firms? Technology transfer itself is a costly process entailing substantial transfer and assimilation costs, irrespective of whether the recipient is an affiliate or a domestic firm.[10] After a plant is in operation, technology creation begins in the form of technical know-how. According to Lall (1985), there is no reason to differentiate between the performance of foreign and local firms in the know-how phase. Both would undertake problem-solving activities leading to minor innovations and adaptations. It is possible to argue that foreign firms would actually perform better than local firms would in this stage because of their higher quality of technical and skilled manpower and their ready access to accumulated know-how of the parent firm.

However, when it comes to technical know-why, foreign firms (TNC affiliates) are likely to lag behind domestic firms. These firms bring in packaged technology from their parent firms and there is no need for them to acquire know-why leading to new designs and development. Such activities are performed in their centralised R&D, usually located in the industrial economies and transmitted to all affiliates. Whatever little R&D set-up they may have in their LDC affiliates would be geared toward know-how activities.

Domestic firms, on the other hand, depend on "unpackaged" imported technology acquired through arm's-length transactions, like licensing.[11] For these firms, R&D activities are centred on "know-why" simply in order to absorb and adapt foreign technologies properly. Unlike the foreign firms, they cannot rely on a continuous flow of basic design knowledge from a parent firm, and hence their conscious strategy to develop technological autonomy over time by concentrating their technological effort on know-why or "deeper" technological learning.

III. THE ECONOMETRIC METHODOLOGY

The Model

Based on the above conceptual framework, we formulate the following econometric model for our empirical analysis. While using the concept of research production function, we have acknowledged the influence of firm size, ownership and technology imports in the process. Implicit in our discussion was a presumption that these are treated as exogenous to the model. Accordingly, we maintain a fairly simple econometric structure and model the R&D behaviour of firms under the assumption that they have already reached their optimum decisions relating to size, technology imports and ownership. In other words, we treat the two major research inputs, namely, R&D spending and scientific and technical personnel in R&D, and the research output, namely, the number of minor innovations introduced, to be the only three endogenous variables in this model structure. The other relevant variables, like firm size, ownership and technology imports, are assumed to be exogenous to the model.[12]

Accordingly, we have an econometric model represented by the following three structural equations:

1. $RDS_i = \alpha_{11} + a_2 SZ_i + \alpha_3 MTD_i + \alpha_4 MTE_i + \alpha_5 FD_i + u_{1i}$
2. $RDM_i = \alpha_{21} + \alpha_{22} RDS_i + \beta_1 SZ_i + \beta_2 MTD_i + \beta_3 MTE_i + \beta_4 FD_i + u_{2i}$

3. $TC_i = \alpha_{31} + \alpha_{32}RDS_i + \alpha_{33}RDM_i + \gamma_1 SZ_i + \gamma_2 MTD_i + \gamma_3 MTP_i + \gamma_4 FD_i + \gamma_5(FD_i{*}RDS_i) + u_{3i}$

Here subscript-i denotes the i-th firm, u's denote white noise errors and the remaining variables are described below:

RDS	R&D Spending (research input)
RDM	R&D Manpower (research input)
TC	Technical Changes (research output)
SZ	Index of Firm Size
MTD	Direct import of disembodied technology
MTE	Import of embodied technology
FD	Foreign Ownership dummy

The Estimation Method

The model represents a recursive simultaneous equation system and can be estimated one at a time using OLS.

Data and Variables

To quantify the variables appearing in the above model, we have used two firm-level databases. The first one, obtained from the Department of Science and Technology, Government of India, contains information on R&D expenditure, R&D manpower and R&D output, while the second one, obtained from the Centre for the Monitoring of the Indian Economy, provides balance sheet data. We selected the set of common firms belonging to the chemical industry appearing in both databases and merged the two data to end up with a set of 75 observations (firms) in all. It is a cross-section pertaining to the year 1994–1995.

The chemical industry was selected for our analysis because in India chemicals (including drugs) as an industry group has the largest expenditure on in-house R&D,[13] and this industry also has significant participation of foreign firms.

The measurement of the variables included in our model is described below. *SZ* (firm size) is proxied by total sales of the firm. *RDS* (the research input of R&D spending) is calculated as the amount of expenditure on R&D normalised by firm size, i.e. total sales. *RDM* (the input of R&D manpower) is used to capture the extent of scientific and technical personnel in R&D. The variable is constructed as the number of such employees engaged in R&D as a fraction of total employment. *TC* (the research output) is captured by the number of minor technical changes introduced by the firm in terms of product development, process development and the development of import substitutes, again normalised by firm size. This variable is indeed an accurate reflection of technological capability as broadly defined earlier. Moreover, it reflects acquisition of technical know-how as opposed to know-why, in particular. Know-why could possibly have been captured by the number of scientific papers published, etc. Lall (1985) used the exports of disembodied technology by the firm as an instrument to capture technical know-why. Unfortunately, we do not have adequate data to construct a meaningful index of know-why for this study. *MTD* (import of disembodied technology) is captured by the extent of foreign currency payment of royalties and technical fees by the firm. *MTE* (import of embodied technology) is measured by the amount of capital goods' imports. *FD* is the foreign ownership dummy, which takes the value 1 if the firm in question is a foreign firm and 0 otherwise. In our model we have used this ownership factor in the production function equation (No. 3) not only as an intercept dummy, but also as a slope dummy for RDS. This would enable us to detect whether and how the slope of the R&D production function with respect to RDS varies with ownership.

IV. THE RESULTS

The results of our estimated model are reported in Table 1. Estimates of the research input equations are not so robust statistically. In fact, the RDS equation (No. 1) has a poor overall fit with very low value of adjusted R2 (0.03) and a statistically insignificant F-value. The RDM equation (No. 2) is somewhat better with adjusted $R^2 = 0.18$ and a significant F-value.

The coefficients of equation 1 indicate that foreign firms tend to spend less on R&D compared to domestic firms, while size or technology imports do not seem to matter in the determination of R&D spending.

Turning to equation 2, we discover that firms with larger technology imports employ less S&T manpower in R&D. This is perhaps in line with the commonly-held position that there is some degree of substitutability between technology purchase and R&D effort, although we do not get any confirmation of this proposition with respect to R&D spending. Another interpretation of this result rests on the nature of research effort required by firms with imported technologies. More emphasis is placed on assimilation and adaptation which makes it more critical to place S&T manpower in production operations rather than in R&D.

Equation 2 also reflects the positive scale effect on R&D manpower input. Larger firms employ a larger fraction of S&T personnel in R&D. This is in line

Table 1. Estimation of Research Production Function.

DepVariables	Eqn 1: RDS =		Eqn 2: RDM =		Eqn 3: TC =		Eqn 3A: TC =	
Intercept	256.9	(8.5)***	0.02	(2.1)**	–0.009	(0.3)	0.05	(1.8)*
SZ	–0.04	(0.3)	0.00009	(4.1)***	–0.0003	(2.9)***	–0.0002	(2.6)**
MTD	–2.22	(0.1)	–0.01	(2.9)***	0.37	(2.5)**	0.21	(1.9)**
MTE	–2.82	(1.1)	0.00002	(.04)	–0.0006	(0.3)	–0.0007	(0.3)
FD	–110.5	(1.9)*	–0.014	(1.1)	0.13	(2.6)***	–0.14	(2.9)***
RDS			0.0004	(1.6)	0.0003	(3.7)***	0.0002	(2.2)**
RDE					1.06	(2.3)**	0.49	(1.5)
FD*RDS							0.002	(8.1)***
Adjusted R^2	0.03		0.18		0.26		0.62	
F	1.6		4.14**		5.27***		16.73***	

Notes:
1. Figures given in parentheses are the absolute t-values.
2. The levels of significance of the t-values are indicated by the asterisks.
3. *** denotes statistically significant at 99% level.
4. ** denotes statistically significant at 95% level.

with the basic tenet of the Schumpeterian hypothesis. The ownership dummy with a negative coefficient and RDS with a positive one, confirming that foreign firms have less R&D manpower input and firms with larger R&D spending (i.e. larger R&D scale), have proportionately more S&T personnel in R&D. But these coefficients fail to reach acceptable significance levels.

The last two equations (3 and 3A) represent the research production function. In equation 3, we have considered the foreign ownership only as an intercept dummy, whereas in equation 3A, it is entered as a slope dummy with RDS as well. The results are robust with good overall fit as revealed by F-test and adjusted R2. In fact, the value of adjusted R2 for equation 3A is 0.62, which is remarkably high for cross sectional regressions. In these regressions, all coefficients with the exception of MTE are statistically significant.

The results are equally interesting. First, we observe that the basic input/output relationship is upheld: both the inputs of RDS and RDM are positive and significant in the estimated production function.

Firm size appears negative and significant. For given input levels, smaller firms produce more output from R&D. The efficiency of smaller firms in research production reflects the presence of diseconomies of scale. For the particular industry in question, namely chemicals, large scale is perhaps characterised by standardised mass production techniques with little scope of adaptation and introduction of technical changes. Small firms, on the other hand, use technologies, which are more amenable to modification and improvement. Although the result may appear to contradict the received Schumpeterian hypothesis that bigness encourages innovation, one must keep in mind that in the Indian chemical industry, we do not by any means consider "innovations" in the sense it is used in the Schumpeterian literature. Our technological output represents "minor" and "lower" forms of adaptation and improvement, where scale appears to act as a deterrent to achieving higher research output.

On the question of import of technology entering the research production function, the results show that direct technology import does matter while the import of technology embodied in imported capital goods does not have any effect on research inputs as well as outputs. Firms using more of imported technology are more productive in their research activity. MTD is positive and significant in the production function equations. This suggests that in less developed countries, although one could observe some degree of trade-off between technology imports and R&D effort, the technology importing firms cannot be described as technologically inactive. In fact, they appear to be more efficient in acquiring technological know-why and introducing minor innovations compared to firms depending more on indigenous technology. The reason could simply be the fact that imported technologies require greater know-how and are more amenable to minor innovations to make them suited to local conditions than domestic technologies.

We now take a close look at the coefficients of the ownership dummy. The results are revealing. We have reported above that foreign firms are found to devote less input to R&D activities than domestic firms. But in the production function equation 3, when FD is applied only as an intercept dummy, it comes up with a positive and highly significant coefficient. This suggests that foreign firms are more productive in their research activities, notwithstanding their lower expenditure on R&D. In equation 3A, when FD is applied as an intercept dummy as well as interactive with RDS as a slope dummy, we discover even more fascinating results. The coefficient of (RDS*FD) is positive and significant, while that of FD is negative and significant. The research production function (*f*: rds → tc) of foreign firms has a lower intercept but a steeper slope than that of the domestic firms.

Foreign ownership, per se, has a lowering effect on R&D activities. We have already seen that their propensity to spend on R&D is relatively lower than that of the domestic firms. However, the efficiency with which the input of RDS is converted into the research output of TC is remarkably higher in foreign firms. This is not surprising if we delve deeper into the nature of R&D in less developed countries.

We have already mentioned that foreign firms in less developed countries concentrate more on know-how than know-why. The results then reveal a perfectly consistent picture. Foreign firms do not spend large amounts on R&D in India. Perhaps they do not need to. The kind of technological activities (emphasising on know-how) they are engaged in may require lower investments in R&D compared to firms which concentrate more on know-why. Our results, however, clearly show that foreign firms are much more efficient in generating know-how, per unit of R&D spending, than their domestic counterparts.

V. CONCLUSION

This paper has dispensed with one of the major concerns regarding TNC entry into less developed countries. The hypothesis – that TNC affiliates in less developed countries are technologically inactive and do not promote local technological development – is discarded. The results of our econometric analysis, based on a data set of Indian chemical firms, demonstrate that foreign firms are actively engaged in technological pursuits. Although their propensity to spend on R&D may be less than that of the domestic firms, they are more efficient and productive in converting research inputs into research outputs. In this paper, we have confined our attention to technological know-how as the only research output. Indeed, the technological activities of TNC affiliates have a clear thrust on know-how, and we find that they acquire know-how more efficiently than their domestic counterparts. The domestic firms, on the other hand, are believed to concentrate their technological effort on know-why, although in this paper we have not been able to test this proposition econometrically.

Skeptics could argue that know-why, rather than know-how, constitutes the key to industrial success of less developed countries. In that respect, transnational corporations, with their thrust only on know-how, cannot really contribute much to the development of domestic technological capability of host less developed countries.

Others, however, suggest that know-how creates a distinct competitive edge for less developed countries in the international markets. This know-how driven technological competitiveness is at the root of the industrial success of the East Asian newly industrialised countries. Even Japan's technological progress began with its successful know-how activities, which was later followed by know-why and subsequently by major innovations.

Ultimately, the attitude towards TNCs, insofar as their technological impact is concerned, boils down, to a large extent, to the preference between know-why and know-how. However, I feel that this debate between know-how and know-why does not lead us very far. Clearly, one is not a substitute for the other, and there is hardly any trade-off between the two. Indeed, successful know-why presupposes a substantial degree of know-how.

As Lall (1984) suggested, in countries like India, know-why has been overemphasised at the cost of know-how, even at the early stages of technological development. This has certainly led to indigenous learning of basic design (mostly through reverse engineering) and has generated some degree of technological self-reliance. But the country remained at a technological disadvantage, not only with respect to the quality of the technology in use but also with respect to the efficiency with which it is operated. Perhaps this would not have happened if our policy regime emphasised equally on know-how as well as know-why.

In fact, if we are to emphasise know-how as well as know-why, TNC affiliates need not be kept out. On the contrary, if they are efficient in generating know-how, they should be equally efficient in generating know-why, and basic research, if they so desire. Given the comparative advantage that India can offer in this regard with its large pool of scientific and technological manpower, TNCs might actually find it profitable to locate their centralised

R&D activities, at least in part, in India. There is growing evidence of such tendencies among TNCs. But this requires a long-term commitment of hospitality towards TNCs on the part of the government. Since R&D requires huge investments by TNCs, and their global operations are essentially driven by their R&D activities, they cannot afford to be under any uncertainties regarding their long term existence and operations in India. This must, therefore, be put into the policy agenda for progressive industrialisation and development.

In reality, all these considerations notwithstanding, the actual choice between know-how and know-why boils down to ideological preferences and so does the attitude towards TNCs.

ACKNOWLEDGMENT

I am grateful to Saon Roy and Saradindu Bhaduri for helping me in preparing the data set used for the econometric analysis presented in this paper.

NOTES

1. See Helleiner (1989) for a comprehensive review of this literature.
2. See, for instance, Mansfield et al. (1982).
3. He has four grounds: "(1) We confine our thinking about innovations to characteristics which are likely to be true only of major innovations. (2) We focus disproportionately upon discontinuities and neglect continuities in the innovative process. (3) We attach excessive importance to the role of scientific knowledge and insufficient importance to engineering and "lower" forms of knowledge. (4) We attach excessive significance to early stages in the process of invention and neglect the crucial later stages."
4. See Lall (1978, 1985), Bell et al. (1984), Katz (1984, 1987), Fransman and King (1984), Gonsen (1998).
5. Lall (1985), p. 116.
6. The distinction made between know-how and know-why is not meant to be watertight. There can be a significant overlap of the two categories of technological capability and one need not necessarily be independent of the other.
7. See Fischer and Temin (1973).
8. Dasgupta (1986) clarifies that whereas Schumpeter seems to be suggesting that large size has distinct advantages, he recognises that monopoly power and large firm-size are not identical.
9. Nelson (1986).
10. See Teece (1976), Lall (1985).
11. Of course, some of the domestic firms may not import technologies but develop their own (by imitation).
12. However, we must acknowledge that these variables should ideally be endogenised to the firm's decision making process where optimum size, technology imports (and perhaps ownership pattern) as well as R&D levels are jointly and

simultaneously determined outcomes of the firm's optimisation programme (see, for instance, Kamien & Schwartz (1975). Accordingly, modelling of R&D behaviour should ideally be integrated with the rest of the decision making of the firm within a complex simultaneous equation structure. However, we do not attempt such an integrated econometric modeling exercise in this paper.

13. See Department of Science & Technology (1997), Table 5.3.

REFERENCES

Bell, M. et al. (1984). Assessing the Performance of Infant Industries. *Journal of Development Economics, 16*, 101–128.

Dasgupta, P. (1986). The Theory of Technological Competition. In: J. E. Stiglitz & G. F. Mathewson (Eds), *New Developments in the Analysis of Market Structure*. Macmillan, London.

Department of Science & Technology (1997). *Research and Development Statistics, 1994–95*, Govt of India.

Fischer, F. M., & Temin, P. (1973). Returns of Scale in Research and Development: What does the Schumpeterian Hypothesis Imply? *Journal of Political Economy, 81*, 56–70.

Fransman, M., & King, K. (Ed.) (1984). *Technological Capability in the Third World*. Macmillan, London.

Gonsen, R. (1998). *Technological Capabilities in Developing Countries*. Macmillan, London.

Helleiner, G. (1989). Transnational Corporations and Direct Foreign Investment. In: H. Chenery & T. N. Srinivasan (Eds), *Handbook of Development Economics Volume II*. North Holland, Amsterdam.

Kamien, M. I., & Schwartz, M. L. (1975). Market Structure and Innovation: A Survey. *Journal of Economic Literature, 13*, 1–37.

Katz, J. M. (1984). Domestic Technological Innovations and Dynamic Comparative Advantage. *Journal of Development Economics, 16*, 13–37.

Katz, J. M. (Ed.) (1987). *Technology Generation in Latin American Manufacturing Industries*. Macmillan, London.

Lall, S. (1978). Transnationals, Domestic Enterprises and Industrial Structures in Host LDCs: A Survey. *Oxford Economic Papers, 30*(2), 217–248.

Lall, S. (1984). India's Technological Capacity: Effects of Trade, Industrial, Science & Technology Policies. In: M. Fransman & K. King (Eds), *Technological Capability in the Third World*. Macmillan, London.

Lall, S. (1985). *Multinationals, Technology and Exports*. Macmillan, London.

Lall, S. (1991). Explaining Industrial Success in the Developing World. In: V. N. Balasubramanyam & S. Lall (Eds), *Current Issues in Development Economics*. Macmillan, London.

Mansfield, E. et al. (1982). *Technology Transfer, Productivity and Economic Policy*. W. W. Norton & Co., New York.

Nelson, R. (1986). Evolutionary Modelling of Economic Change. In: J. E. Stiglitz & G. F. Mathewson (Eds), *New Developments in the Analysis of Market Structure*. Macmillan, London.

Rosenberg, N. (1976). *Perspective on Technology*. Cambridge University Press, New York.

Teece, D. J. (1976). *The Multinational Corporation and the Resource Cost of Technology Transfer*. Ballinger, Cambridge MA.

32. LOCATIONAL DETERMINANTS OF JAPANESE FOREIGN DIRECT INVESTMENT*

Shujiro Urata and Hiroki Kawai

I. INTRODUCTION

The economic crisis in East Asia, which was triggered by the currency crisis in Thailand in July 1997, derailed many East Asian countries from their rapid economic growth path. Being faced with a shortage of foreign exchange, Thailand, Indonesia and Korea had to ask the International Monetary Fund (IMF) for a rescue operation. In an attempt to recover from the serious economic situation, these countries adopted tight fiscal and monetary policies under the guidance of the IMF. Together with the restructuring of the weak financial sector, which was believed to be a major cause of currency and economic crises, these measures have resulted in substantial slowdown in economic activities in these countries.[1] Economic slowdown in Thailand, Indonesia, and Korea, in turn, has had serious repercussions in other East Asian countries through close inter country economic linkages, which were built upon rapid expansion of foreign trade and foreign direct investment (FDI) inside the East Asian region. It was somewhat ironic that close intra-regional linkage was one of the factors that led to rapid economic growth in the pre-crisis period. The economic crisis reversed this growth mechanism.

Recognizing the substantial contribution that FDI makes to economic growth of the host countries of FDI through various channels such as capital formation and technology transfer, it has become important for East Asian economies to

* Parts of this article also have been published in *Small Business Economics.*

Restructuring Asian Economics for the New Millennium, Volume 9B, pages 615–641.

ISBN: 0-7623-0710-2

attract FDI, in order to recover from the crisis and to get back on the growth path. To attract FDI, East Asian countries have liberalized restrictions on FDI, which had been imposed to protect and promote domestic industries. Moreover, a number of East Asian countries have introduced various kinds of incentives including preferential tax treatment to make them attractive for FDI. Although these policy measures would be important for promoting FDI inflow, one needs to know other factors that determine FDI inflow, in order to successfully attract FDI.

In light of the current economic crisis in East Asia and the possible role that FDI can play in economic recovery in the region, this paper attempts to identify the characteristics of host countries that have successfully attracted FDI. This analysis would be useful for policy makers in East Asia and in other parts of the world, who are interested in promoting FDI. Because of data availability, we examine the case of Japanese FDI. We adopted two different approaches to examine the issue. One approach utilizes the results of a questionnaire survey conducted by the Ministry of International Trade and Industry (MITI) of the Japanese government. Specifically, we examine the response of Japanese firms to questions on the motives of their FDI and the problems they are faced with in their foreign operation, in order to discern the characteristics of the countries that are attractive to Japanese firms. Despite their usefulness, survey results in tabulated form cannot provide the precise measure of the importance of various factors in attracting FDI. To deal with this problem and to complement the analysis based on the questionnaire survey, we carry out a statistical analysis to examine the importance of various characteristics of FDI recipient countries in affecting decisions of Japanese firms on the location of their FDI.

The structure of the paper is as follows. Section II presents a brief overview of the recent changes in Japanese FDI with a focus on its FDI in Asia, in order to set the stage for the following analysis. Sections III and IV examine the motives of Japanese FDI and the problems faced by Japanese firms in their overseas operation, respectively. Section V carries out a statistical analysis to identify the locational determinants of Japanese FDI. Finally, Section VI presents some concluding observations.

II. RECENT TRENDS OF JAPANESE FOREIGN DIRECT INVESTMENT[2]

II.1. Rapid Expansion of Japanese FDI in the 1980s and Subsequent Slowdown in the 1990s

Japanese FDI increased on a large scale and underwent major changes in its regional and sectoral composition in the latter half of the 1980s (Fig. 1, and

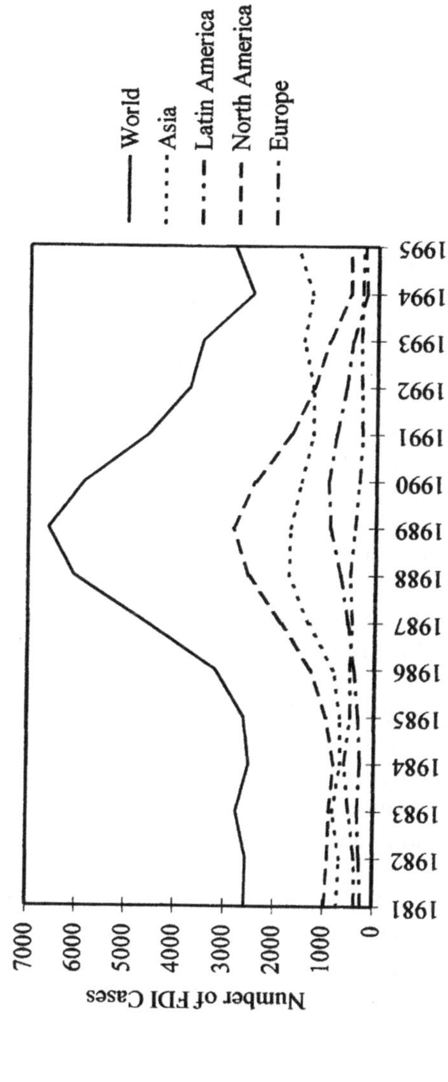

Fig. 1. Japanese Foreign Direct Investment.

Tables 1–3). The number of annual FDI cases increased sharply from around 2,500 in the early 1980s to more than 6,000 in the latter half of the 1980s. Equally as dramatic as the size of the boom was the pace at which Japanese FDI declined after reaching a peak in 1989. The decline in annual FDI cases continued through 1994, when the number of annual FDI cases amounted to less than 40% of the value recorded in 1988. From 1994 through 1997, the year of the economic crisis, the number of annual FDI cases remained more or less stable at low levels (not shown in the figure).

One identifies both "push" and "pull" factors behind the recent developments of Japanese FDI. The push factors are those in the investing country, that is Japan in this case, while the pull factors are those in the recipient countries. We will take up the push factors in this section and the pull factors in the next section in explaining the recent developments of Japanese FDI.

Several push factors can be identified for the rapid growth of Japanese FDI in the latter half of the 1980s. The rapid and steep appreciation of the yen against other currencies was the most important macroeconomic factor leading to the expansion of Japanese FDI in the second half of the 1980s. The yen appreciated by 37% between 1985 and 1988 on a real, effective basis. The drastic yen appreciation stimulated Japanese FDI in two ways. One way was the dramatic "relative price" effect, and the other was the "liquidity" or "wealth" effect. The relative price effect substantially reduced the international price competitiveness of Japanese products, resulting in a decline in Japan's export volume. To cope with the new international price structure, a number of Japanese manufacturing firms moved their production base to foreign countries, especially to East Asia, where production costs were lower.

Yen appreciation had a positive impact on Japanese FDI through the "liquidity" or "wealth" effect as well. To the extent that yen appreciation made Japanese firms relatively more "wealthy" in the sense of increased collateral and liquidity, it enabled them to finance FDI relatively more cheaply than their foreign competitors. A number of FDI projects in real estate were undertaken by Japanese firms by taking advantage of the liquidity effect.

Another important push factor was the emergence of the "bubble" economy in Japan. Indeed, the liquidity effect discussed above was strengthened by the bubble economy, in which the prices of assets such as shares and land increased enormously. Indeed, the average share prices more than doubled in four years from 1985 to 1989, as the index of share prices increased from 45.7 in 1985 to 117.8 in 1989. The Bank of Japan injected liquidity into the economy to deal with the recessionary impact caused by the drastic yen appreciation. Active fiscal spending for the same purpose of reflating the economy was an additional factor leading to the bubble economy.

A general rise in Japanese firms' managerial and technological capabilities in international business, which had been accumulated through past experiences such as exporting and FDI, was a natural underlying factor behind the surge of Japanese FDI. It is also important to note that a number of Japanese firms followed their business customers that invested overseas. A case in point is FDI by subcontracting firms that followed their parent companies, which had undertaken FDI, to maintain business. Furthermore, the labor shortage in Japan necessitated some Japanese firms, especially small and medium sized firms, to move their operation abroad.

The decline in Japanese FDI in the early 1990s resulted mainly from the burst of the bubble economy in 1989. The burst of the bubble economy reduced the capability of Japanese firms for undertaking FDI by making it difficult for Japanese firms to raise funds for FDI. Indeed, the mechanism that led to rapid FDI expansion in the latter half of the 1980s reversed itself in the 1990s, to result in the decline in Japanese FDI. The depreciation of the yen also contributed to the decline.

II.2. Japanese Foreign Direct Investment in Asia

Japanese FDI in the second half of the 1980s was directed largely to North America and Europe, mainly in non-manufacturing sectors such as services and real estate. These two regions together absorbed more than 50% of Japan's FDI cases during the period.[3] A main pull factor behind active FDI in real estate was availability of attractive assets, which satisfied speculative demand of Japanese investors. As for FDI in manufacturing, trade friction was an important motive. To cope with the restrictive measures such as anti-dumping duties imposed on Japanese exports, Japanese manufacturing producers set up production bases in Europe and in North America to serve these markets.

Although a smaller share of Japan's FDI went to Asia in the 1980s, investments in manufacturing were relatively active. The 1990s have seen some changes in the patterns of Japan's FDI. First, the share of Asia, particularly East Asia including the NIEs (Newly Industrializing Economies), ASEAN (Association of South East Asian Nations) countries and China, in Japanese FDI started to increase sharply (Table 1). Indeed, the share of Asia in Japan's total FDI cases increased rapidly from 25.6% in 1990 to 6.9% in 1995. Major pull factors behind Japanese FDI in East Asia include the region's robust economic growth, low unit labor costs, and trade and FDI liberalization and pro-FDI policies.

Since the mid-1980s, geographical distribution of Japan's FDI to Asia has changed significantly, from the Asian NIEs to ASEAN4, and then to China and other Asian countries (Table 2).[4] The NIEs attracted FDI until the late 1980s by

Table 1. Destinations of Japanese FDI in the World.

	Number of Cases			Regional Composition (%)		
	1981–1985	1986–1990	1991–1995	1981–1985	1986–1990	1991–1995
Number of Cases						
World	12,978	26,308	17,134	100	100	100
Asia	3,566	7,103	6,958	27.5	27.0	40.6
Latin America	2,285	2,207	1,527	17.6	8.4	8.9
Middle East	80	23	57	0.6	0.1	0.3
Africa	389	348	223	3.0	1.3	1.3
North America	4,517	10,986	5,010	34.8	41.8	29.2
Europe	1,399	3505	2,395	10.8	13.3	14.0
Oceania	742	2136	964	5.7	8.1	5.6

Note: Reported basis.
Source: Ministry of Finance.

Table 2. Destinations of Japanese FDI in Asia.

	Number of Cases			Country Composition (%)		
	1981–1985	1986–1990	1991–1995	1981–1985	1986–1990	1991–1995
Number of Cases						
Asia	3,566	7,103	6,958	100	100	100
NIEs	2,089	3,634	1,639	58.6	51.2	23.6
Hong Kong	742	1338	747	20.8	18.8	10.7
Korea	236	565	162	6.6	8.0	2.3
Singapore	720	784	463	20.2	11.0	6.7
Taiwan	391	947	267	11.0	13.3	3.8
ASEAN4	1,147	2,700	2,222	32.2	38.0	31.9
Indonesia	405	492	669	11.4	6.9	9.6
Malaysia	336	570	447	9.4	8.0	6.4
Philippines	88	226	318	2.5	3.2	4.6
Thailand	318	1,412	788	8.9	19.9	11.3
China	202	648	2,842	5.7	9.1	40.8

Note: Reported basis.
Source: Ministry of Finance.

FDI promotion policies. Policy makers in Korea, Taiwan, and Singapore, in particular, promoted inward FDI in their pursuit of high-tech industrialization. These countries enjoyed positive growth brought about by the simultaneous expansion of trade and inward FDI.

Japanese FDI in the Asian NIEs reached a peak in 1988. The Asian NIEs started to lose some of their cost advantages due to rapid wage increases and currency appreciation. Firms in Japan and other advanced economies therefore started to look to other East Asian countries such as ASEAN4 as hosts for investment. One important factor in attracting FDI in manufacturing to ASEAN4 has been the shift of development strategies from inward-oriented to outward-oriented ones by ASEAN4 countries, which was carried out through their unilateral liberalization of trade and FDI policies. Such regime changes have been prompted by the earlier success of outward-oriented policies by the NIEs.

FDI inflows into China have also grown quickly since 1990 due to China's gradual but persistent economic reforms, liberalization in trade and FDI policies, and its political and social stability despite the Tiananmen Square incident in 1989. As of 1995, China was the largest recipient of Japanese FDI in Asia. The attractiveness of China as a host to FDI has increased recently because some ASEAN countries have lost their attractiveness mainly due to the rapid increase in the production costs including wages, material and service costs, which in turn resulted from the currency appreciation, shortage of manpower, emergence of serious bottlenecks in infrastructure and other factors.[5] It should be noted that these are some of the important factors leading to the economic crisis in some countries.

Since the 1980s, a distinct characteristic of Japanese FDI in Asia is the large share of manufacturing in comparison to other regions (Table 3). The share of manufacturing was around 50% through the 1980s, and then it started to increase in the 1990s and exceeded 70% in 1995. Among the manufacturing sub-sectors, textiles and electric machinery increased their respective shares in the 1990s, to register 20.8 and 14.0% in 1995.[6] Similar to the pattern observed for Japanese FDI as a whole, geographical distribution of Japanese FDI for most manufacturing sub-sectors shifted from the NIEs to ASEAN4 countries and to China over the 1980–95 period.[7] This shift was most pronounced in the textile sector.

III. MOTIVES BEHIND JAPANESE FDI IN ASIA

Several factors that promoted Japanese FDI in the latter half of the 1980s were explained in the previous section. This section examines closely the motives

Table 3. Sectoral Composition of Japanese FDI.

	Number of Cases						Sectoral Composition (%)					
	World			Asia			World			Asia		
	1981–85	1986–90	1991–95	1981–85	1986–90	1991–95	1981–85	1986–90	1991–95	1981–85	1986–90	1991–95
Total	12,978	26,308	17,134	3,566	7,103	6,958	100	100	100	100	100	100
Food	399	683	476	156	304	283	3.1	2.6	2.8	4.4	4.3	4.1
Textiles	274	659	1633	150	417	1,414	2.1	2.5	9.5	4.2	5.9	20.3
Wood and pulp	156	322	233	64	193	119	1.2	1.2	1.4	1.8	2.7	1.7
Chemicals	477	774	524	279	366	299	3.7	2.9	3.1	7.8	5.2	4.3
Ferrous and non-ferous metals	348	750	622	141	427	419	2.7	2.9	3.6	4.0	6.0	6.0
General machinery	502	951	649	186	401	334	3.9	3.6	3.8	5.2	5.6	4.8
Electric machinery	613	1,422	1079	255	734	716	4.7	5.4	6.3	7.2	10.3	10.3
Transport machinery	228	619	459	112	198	269	1.8	2.4	2.7	3.1	2.8	3.9
Other manufacturing	655	1484	1193	312	800	780	5.0	5.6	7.0	8.7	11.3	11.2
Manufacturing total	3,652	7,664	6,868	1,655	3,840	4,633	28.1	29.1	40.1	46.4	54.1	66.6
Agriculture	251	317	201	64	91	68	1.9	1.2	1.2	1.8	1.3	1.0
Fishery	154	211	147	67	117	85	1.2	0.8	0.9	1.9	1.6	1.2
Mining	285	361	335	31	92	91	2.2	1.4	2.0	0.9	1.3	1.3
Construction	312	334	200	184	153	99	2.4	1.3	1.2	5.2	2.2	1.4
Commerce	3,728	4,252	2,276	739	1,009	677	28.7	16.2	13.3	20.7	14.2	9.7
Banking and insurance	431	1,446	827	83	239	228	3.3	5.5	4.8	2.3	3.4	3.3
Services	1,037	3,330	2,394	447	579	498	8.0	12.7	14.0	12.5	8.2	7.2
Transportation	2,186	2,083	1,364	127	193	158	16.8	7.9	8.0	3.6	2.7	2.3
Real estate	516	5,923	2,362	48	662	309	4.0	22.5	13.8	1.3	9.3	4.4
Other non-manufacturing	231	52	4	23	14	0	1.8	0.2	0.0	0.6	0.2	0.0
Non-manufacturing total	9,131	18,309	10,110	1,813	3,149	2,213	70.4	69.6	59.0	50.8	44.3	31.8

Note: Reported basis.
Source: Ministry of Finance.

behind Japanese FDI in Asia by using the results of a questionnaire survey, because these motives influence the pattern of geographical distribution of Japanese FDI, which is our main concern in this paper.

Several questionnaire surveys on the motives of Japanese firms for undertaking FDI are conducted on a regular basis. The most comprehensive is a questionnaire survey conducted by the Ministry of International Trade and Industry (MITI) of the Japanese government.[8] Table 4 summarizes the results of the 1992 MITI survey conducted on the motives for Japanese FDI in Asia, Latin America, and the world as a whole.

One common motive behind Japanese FDI in the three regions is the importance of local sales. Indeed, as many as 50–70% of the respondents indicated local sales as one of their motives for undertaking FDI in these regions. For the Asian affiliates, local sales was an important motive, particularly for the sectors producing the materials used for further processing such as chemical products, iron and steel, and non-ferrous metals. This observation indicates that the level and/or the growth of local sales influences the investment decision of Japanese firms.

A large proportion of respondents identified the use of local labor as their motive for FDI in Asia.[9] This observation suggests that Japanese firms have shifted their production base to Asia in order to produce labor-intensive products for exports. Japan has long lost its comparative advantage in labor-intensive products, so Japanese firms are taking advantage of abundant labor in the Asian host countries.[10] Japanese FDI in textiles may be a typical example reflecting such an FDI strategy on the part of Japanese firms. Indeed, as many as 80% of respondents in textiles, noted the use of local labor as their motive for FDI in Asia.

Despite the fact that machinery products are capital and technology intensive, a large proportion of the respondents in the machinery sectors undertook FDI in Asia to take advantage of local labor. This seemingly inconsistent behavior of Japanese firms may be explained by their strategy of breaking up the entire production process into several sub-processes and locating labor-intensive sub-processes in labor abundant Asian countries.

The fact that the use of local labor as a motive for Japanese FDI in Asia appears to reflect a rational behavior of Japanese firms from the point of view of comparative advantage in Asia. Richly endowed with labor, Asian countries have a comparative advantage in the production that requires labor-intensive techniques. This observation points to the differences between the expectation of the host countries on the one hand and the actual behavior of foreign firms on the other hand regarding the types of technologies utilized in the host countries. The host countries interested in upgrading their technological

Table 4. Motives Behind Japanese Foreign Direct Investment in Asia and Latin America.

(Percent)

	World			Asia			Latin America		
	Use of Local sales	FDI Promotion Local Labor	Use of Policies by Hosts	FDI Promotion Local sales	Use of Local Labor	FDI Promotion Policies by Hosts	Local sales	Local Labor	Policies by Hosts
Total industry	66.1	23.7	10.8	65.6	45.4	18.3	52.5	27.3	18.8
Manufacturing	69.6	43.6	21.5	62.4	65.0	28.0	68.1	52.8	40.3
Food	50.0	29.6	5.6	53.2	48.4	9.7	36.4	54.5	9.1
Textiles	55.6	69.6	18.7	50.8	80.6	17.7	63.6	63.6	22.7
Wood and pulp	33.3	33.3	11.1	20.0	46.7	6.7	0.0	50.0	0.0
Chemical products	75.8	29.0	15.5	77.7	44.6	21.2	55.6	11.1	22.2
Iron and steel	84.6	41.8	6.6	82.7	59.6	5.8	75.0	25.0	25.0
Non-ferrous metals	77.2	46.7	28.3	82.6	76.1	43.5	60.0	80.0	40.0
General machinery	73.6	39.3	20.9	64.4	64.4	24.1	85.7	42.9	71.4
Electric machinery	71.0	43.6	23.5	59.6	70.6	32.0	77.5	47.5	55.0
Transport machinery	74.1	41.7	29.9	68.8	65.6	40.0	66.7	66.7	33.3
Precision instruments	66.7	32.0	10.7	45.5	60.6	24.2	50.0	0.0	0.0
Petro and coal products	50.0	25.0	0.0	50.0	50.0	0.0	100.0	0.0	0.0
Other manufacturing	67.5	55.6	27.3	55.2	69.2	34.0	75.0	75.0	56.3

Note: The figures indicate the percentage share of the firms indicating the motive in total number of surveyed firms. Other motives reported include exports to third countries, exports to Japan, acquisition of raw materials, information collection, etc.
Source: MITI, *Kaigai Toshi Tokei Soran [Comprehensive Statistics on Japanese Foreign Direct Investment]*, No. 5, 1994.

capability would like foreign firms to bring in high technologies with a hope that these countries would gain a comparative advantage in high value added production. However, foreign firms are generally interested in exploiting comparative advantage currently possessed by the host countries.

FDI promotion policies by the host government appear to have played an important role in attracting Japanese FDI in Asia and Latin America, since one out of four Japanese firms in manufacturing undertook FDI in response to the incentives given to FDI. However, there are wide sectoral variations, as to the importance of FDI promotion policies in FDI decision making on the part of Japanese firms. In general, FDI promotion policies have an important impact on Japanese investors' decision in metal and machinery sectors. Indeed, the high response rate observed for the metal and machinery sectors in Asia and Latin America reflects the fact that the metal and machinery sectors have been the targets of industrial promotion policies in a number of countries in these regions.

IV. THE PROBLEMS ENCOUNTERED BY JAPANESE FIRMS IN ASIA

An investigation of the problems that are faced by overseas affiliates of Japanese firms would provide useful information on the locational determinants of Japanese FDI. This is because the firms would select the location of their investment where the probability of encountering problems is minimal. Below, two kinds of problems are investigated. One is regulations imposed on foreign direct investment, and the other concerns the economic environment under which Japanese firms conduct their business.

Table 5 shows the frequency of the response given by Japanese firms to some of the problems in their overseas operation. To begin with the problems associated with the regulations on FDI, one finds that approximately 10% of the respondents experienced such problems, regardless of the locations of their operation.[11] Among the manufacturing sub-sectors, a relatively high response rate was reported for the Asian affiliates in transport machinery. This apparently reflects the restrictive FDI policies adopted for transport machinery in some Asian countries, in order to promote local automobile production.

Turning to the problems concerning economic environment of the host countries, one observes that the shortage of skilled labor was experienced by a large number of respondents, in particular those operating in Asia.[12] Indeed, one out of two Asian affiliates indicated that they suffer from the shortage of skilled labor. High inflation, underdevelopment of infrastructure, and that of supporting industries were each regarded as a problem by approximately one

Table 5. The Problems Faced by Japanese Firms in Various Regions.

(Percent)

	World						Asia						Latin America					
	FDI regu-lation	Political instability	High inflation	Under-devel-oped infra-structure	Under-devel-oped support industries	Shortage of skilled labor	FDI regu-lation	Political instability	High inflation	Under-devel-oped infra-structure	Under-devel-oped support industries	Shortage of skilled labor	FDI regu-lation	Political instability	High inflation	Under-devel-oped infra-structure	Under-devel-oped support industries	Shortage of skilled labor
Total industry	8.9	13.3	22.5	16.9	17.7	36.3	10.2	15.9	31.5	31.1	28.3	50.4	13.1	59.1	74.0	34.0	18.6	25.6
Manufacturing	10.2	14.6	25.9	23.3	28.4	45.0	11.2	15.9	32.7	35.7	35.8	54.6	15.5	66.3	76.2	36.6	26.7	31.7
Food	6.3	5.3	17.3	14.7	8.0	49.3	6.8	2.7	16.2	24.3	13.5	51.4	2.0	60.0	80.0	20.0	0.0	20.0
Textiles	10.0	22.1	51.3	44.2	27.4	50.4	9.8	13.9	48.1	51.9	30.4	55.7	15.3	70.6	82.4	41.2	11.8	41.2
Wood and pulp	14.6	8.1	41.7	20.8	33.3	58.3	16.7	0.0	33.3	25.0	50.0	58.3	10.0	100.0	100.0	0.0	0.0	0.0
Chemical products	8.6	12.8	22.3	20.4	12.8	37.9	9.2	14.8	27.8	31.3	13.9	47.0	25.0	75.0	100.0	25.0	0.0	25.0
Iron and steel	6.2	20.5	28.2	23.1	10.3	43.6	6.3	21.1	26.3	47.4	10.5	36.8	2.5	50.0	100.0	0.0	0.0	0.0
Non-ferrous metals	13.0	9.4	20.3	23.4	26.6	46.9	16.5	3.2	29.0	45.2	35.5	64.5	30.0	100.0	75.0	25.0	25.0	25.0
General machinery	8.0	11.3	19.1	12.1	31.9	52.5	8.5	11.5	25.0	19.2	46.2	48.1	12.3	53.8	69.2	30.8	38.5	53.8
Electric machinery	10.8	13.5	27.3	21.2	32.4	48.4	12.2	16.5	36.9	29.6	41.5	63.1	16.2	57.1	61.9	61.9	42.9	42.9
Transport machinery	15.1	20.5	27.5	25.0	43.0	36.5	17.1	30.4	35.7	45.2	50.4	45.2	21.3	66.7	73.3	20.0	46.7	13.3
Precision instruments	6.5	20.8	12.5	20.8	27.1	33.3	6.7	23.8	23.8	33.3	57.1	47.6	—	100.0	100.0	100.0	0.0	100.0
Petro and coal products	10.0	33.3	66.7	33.3	16.7	16.7	6.7	33.3	66.7	66.7	33.3	33.3	—	100.0	100.0	0.0	0.0	0.0
Other manufacturing	8.4	12.8	21.0	28.0	28.0	46.9	9.1	12.0	27.3	39.3	35.3	56.7	10.9	72.7	72.7	45.5	27.3	18.2

Note: The figures indicate the percentage share of the firms indicating the problem in total number of surveyed firms. Other problems listed include regulations, labor relations, and etc.
Source: MITI, *Kaigai Toshi Tokei Soran [Comprehensive Statistics on Japanese Foreign Direct Investment]*, No. 5, 1994.

third of the respondents. In comparison with the affiliates in other regions, a relatively high proportion of the affiliates in Asia face the problem of the underdevelopment of supporting industries. Thirty percent of Asian affiliates are concerned with the problem of underdeveloped supporting industries, while the corresponding share is lower, at 20%, for the affiliates in Latin America. Among the manufacturing sub-sectors, the machinery sub-sectors, which use a number of parts and components, suffer from a lack of supporting industries.

High inflation is a particularly serious problem for the affiliates in Latin America, because as many as 74% of the respondents indicated this problem. High inflation was indicated as a problem by approximately 30% of the Asian affiliates, a significantly smaller proportion compared with the case for the Latin American affiliates, but a larger proportion compared with the affiliates in developed regions.[13] These differences in the seriousness of the inflation problem obviously reflect the differences in the rates of inflation in these regions.

Political instability, which largely reflects the governance capability, is a serious problem in Latin America, as 60% of the respondents in Latin America felt such a problem. In contrast, only 16% of the Asian affiliates responded that political instability was a problem.

V. THE DETERMINANTS OF FDI LOCATIONS BY JAPANESE FIRMS[14]

The examination of the motives of FDI by Japanese firms and the problems they face in their overseas operation in the previous sections revealed some important factors that attract FDI by Japanese firms. Some of the important factors that would attract FDI by Japanese firms include the availability of labor, presence of a large local market, macroeconomic stability, availability of infrastructure and supporting industries, and investor-friendly FDI policies. In this section, the importance of these factors is examined in detail by the use of a statistical analysis. Before conducting the analysis, a brief review of previous studies is in order.

V.1. Previous Studies

Several recent studies examined the determinants of the location of Japanese FDI by considering the characteristics of the host countries under the framework of the conditional logit model. Fukao and Chung (1996) and Wakasugi (1997) examined the determinants of Japanese manufacturing FDI, and Tokunaga and Ishii (1995), and Fukao and Yue (1997) examined the determinants of FDI by Japanese electronics firms. As an indicator of a firm's decision on FDI, Fukao and Chung, and Wakasugi used the number of FDI cases by industry, reported to the Ministry of Finance, while Tokunaga and Ishii, and Fukao and Yue used the number of FDI cases by Japanese electronics firms, compiled from firm-level data sets. Fukao and Chung and Fukao and Yue analyzed the determinants of Japanese FDI at global level, while Tokunaga and Ishii, and Wakasugi examined the determinants at regional (East Asia) level, in addition to their analysis at global level.

There are some variations in their findings, but major common findings include the following. In the global location analysis, high wages are found to discourage Japanese FDI, while the presence of large local market attracts Japanese FDI. However, these relationships are not strong for the regional location analysis. The availability of infrastructure was found to attract Japanese FDI in the global FDI decision, but it was not important in the local FDI decision. Industry agglomeration was shown to be an important element for attracting Japanese FDI, probably indicating the importance of supporting industries in the decision making of Japanese FDI. Fukao and Chung found that low country risk attracts Japanese manufacturing FDI.[15]

V.2. The Model and the Hypotheses on the Determinants of FDI Location

(1) The Model[16]

To model the location of Japanese FDI, we assume that Japanese firms undertake FDI in a country where they can maximize their profits after evaluating relevant characteristics of alternative locations. Let us describe the profit (π) of firm i obtained from undertaking FDI in country j as (1).

$$\pi_{ij} = a_0 X_{1j}^{a1} \cdots X_{mj}^{am} \cdot e^{uij} \qquad (1)$$

where a's are unknown parameters, Xsj (s = 1, . . . , m) are variables describing the characteristics of country j (j = 1, . . . , n), and u_{ij} is a random disturbance term.

Given profit equation (1) and assuming that u_{ij} are independently and identically distributed with Weibull density functions, then we obtain that the probability of undertaking FDI in country j is given by equation (2) (McFadden, 1993)

$$P_{ij} = \frac{\exp\left(\sum_{k=1}^{m} a_k \ln X_{kj}\right)}{\sum_{s=1}^{n} \exp\left(\sum_{k=1}^{m} a_k \ln X_{kj}\right)}. \qquad (2)$$

Expressing the number of FDI selections made by Japanese firms in country j as Wj (j = 1, . . . , n), we obtain the probability of observing such FDI pattern as equation (3).

$$L = \prod_{i} \prod_{j=1}^{n} P_{ij}^{Wj}. \tag{3}$$

This type of model is called the conditional logit model, and the parameters (a's), which indicate the characteristics of potential host countries to Japanese FDI, are estimated by the maximum likelihood estimation method, which maximizes the likelihood function (3).

(2) The Hypotheses

Taking account of the results of the survey examined above and the results of the previous studies, we undertake a statistical analysis of the determinants of the location of Japanese FDI by analyzing the characteristics of the host countries that have successfully attracted Japanese FDI. As to the characteristics of the host countries, we examine the effects of the following variables on Japanese FDI, exchange rate, exchange rate volatility, wage rate, market size, macroeconomic stability, labor quality, infrastructure, agglomeration (cumulative FDI cases by Japanese firms), and governance of the host country government. In the remainder of this section, we first discuss the hypotheses on the determinants of Japanese FDI location and the expected signs of the estimated coefficients on explanatory variables before discussing the estimated results in the next section.[17]

The exchange rate is an important determinant of FDI location for several reasons. First, a country whose currency depreciates is likely to attract FDI, as the depreciation makes it easier for foreign firms with foreign currency denominated assets to invest in the depreciating country by increasing the value of their assets in terms of depreciating currency. Second, for the firms interested in export production, depreciation of the currency of a host country increases the attractiveness of that country as a host to FDI, because depreciation tends to improve export competitiveness of the products produced in that country. Following these observations, we expect that the exchange rate of the host country (denoted by EXR), which is constructed as the value of currency per Japanese yen, to be positive.

Large fluctuations in the exchange rate tend to discourage FDI inflow, as they increase uncertainty associated with economic environment of the host country. Several studies have found the inhibiting effect of exchange rate volatility on foreign trade.[18] But, to the knowledge of the authors, there have not been any studies that examined the effect of exchange volatility on FDI. Following the discussions above, we expect the estimated coefficient on exchange rate volatility (EXRV) to be negative.

One of the important motives of Japanese manufacturing FDI has been found to utilize low-wage local labor in the MITI survey discussed above, and therefore the expected sign of the wage variable (WAGE) is negative. Judging from the result of the MITI survey that shows the importance of local sales motive behind Japanese FDI, the coefficient on the market size, here proxied by purchasing power parity adjusted GDP (GDP), is expected to be positive. A number of Japanese firms in the MITI survey noted that inflation is one of the problems they face in overseas operation. Accordingly, we include the consumer price index as an indicator of inflation (CPI) in our analysis to test the statistical validity of this observation. The expected impact of inflation on Japanese FDI is negative.

Shortage of skilled labor was found to be a serious problem for Japanese firms operating overseas in the MITI survey. One would therefore expect that Japanese FDI would be attracted to an economy where high quality labor is available. Given the difficulty in measuring the quality of labor, we use the secondary education enrollment ratio (EDU) as a proxy for skilled labor. Based on the discussion above, the expected sign of the estimated coefficient on EDU is positive. Infrastructure plays an important role for attracting FDI. Various indicators such as the availability of transportation and communication services may be used for the measurement of infrastructure. Among these indicators, we use the level of electricity generation per person (ELEC) as a proxy for infrastructure, because most Japanese manufacturing firms regard the availability of electricity as a key factor for producing high quality products. We expect the coefficient on electricity to be positive. It should be added that electricity generation and other indicators of infrastructure are highly correlated.

Agglomeration of Japanese FDI would attract new Japanese FDI for several reasons. A potential Japanese investor would think that a country where a substantial number of Japanese FDI have already undertaken to be a safe and suitable place for investment. In such a country, potential Japanese investors may also expect abundant business opportunities with Japanese firms, with whom they feel most comfortable to do business. We measure the extent of agglomeration by the number of cumulative FDI cases by Japanese firms (FDI), and we expect the estimated coefficient to be positive.

Governance capability of the host government has an important impact on the decision of FDI for several reasons. First, in spite of recent liberalization in the FDI regime in many economies, FDI is still subject to various government regulations. Second, investing firms are concerned with the security of their

FDI, as FDI involves substantial commitment in the forms of financial and human resources. We measure the quality of governance capability by incorporating the following five indicators: government repudiation of contracts, risk of expropriation, corruption, law and order tradition, and bureaucratic quality. Government repudiation of contracts and risk of expropriation are indicators of government credibility.[18] Law and order tradition, and government repudiation of contracts measure the presence or absence of peaceful mechanisms for adjudicating disputes, and therefore they may be interpreted as proxies for the security of property and contract rights. Corruption and bureaucratic quality are considered as proxies for the efficiency of the government in providing public services. In addition, they appear to have implications on the degree of uncertainty regarding the credibility of government commitments.

In order to derive an explanatory variable, which captures the essential properties of these five indicators, we carry out a factor analysis. From the analysis, we obtain the first principal component, which is constructed as a weighted average of the five indicators with more or less similar weight. As the governance variable (GOV) is constructed in such a way that high value indicates high quality of governance, we expect the estimated coefficient to be positive.

V.3. Empirical Results: An Application of the Conditional Logit Model

To examine the importance of the characteristics of host countries for the decision making of FDI location by Japanese firms, we estimated the determinants of Japanese FDI by using the conditional logit model. In the estimation, we consider 117 countries as possible sites for Japanese FDI.[19] The choice of 117 countries depended on their importance as a host to Japanese FDI and the availability of necessary data for the estimation. In addition, we performed analyses on subset of these countries, developed and developing countries, and Asian countries. The analysis was conducted for four manufacturing sub-sectors, textiles, general machinery, electric machinery, and transport machinery, which account for a dominant share of Japanese FDI.

The results of the estimation are shown in Table 6. The estimated coefficients of the exchange rate (EXR) are shown to have mixed signs. EXR is positive for textiles and transport machinery, as expected, and it is statistically significant only for textiles. According to these findings, the exchange rate does not play an important role in the determination of the location of Japanese FDI. Exchange rate volatility (EXRV) has a negative impact on attracting Japanese

Table 6. Locational Determinants of Japanese FDI (1980–1994).

1. Textile

	All Sample		Developed Economies		Developing Economies		Asia	
	coefficients	t-statistics	coefficients	t-statistics	coefficients	t-statistics	coefficients	t-statistics
EXR	3.5E-08	3.133***	–0.709	–0.536	4.02E-08	3.575***	–0.020	–1.577
EXRV	–0.588	–1.548	–5.385	–0.401	–0.335	–0.963	–3.111	–1.459
LnWAGE	–2.615	–12.788***	–0.382	–0.426	–3.055	–12.972***	–3.746	–11.549***
LnGDP	0.175	2.966***	1.006	4.987***	0.277	1.816*	0.268	1.765*
CPI	–0.042	–1.001	–0.411	–0.102	–0.040	–0.952	–0.154	–0.880
EDU	–2.426	–3.875***	–0.109	–0.055	–2.522	–3.749***	–1.226	–1.641*
LnELEC	1.016	5.964***	1.072	1.820*	1.637	10.010***	1.435	7.730***
LnCFDI	0.698	9.226***	0.139	0.860	0.983	10.373***	0.992	11.040***
GOV	13.073	8.307***	3.300	0.572	13.531	9.144***	10.915	6.741***
Pseudo R2	0.465		0.410		0.555		0.581	
n.o.b.	15468		1838		13630		13234	

2. General Machinery

	All Sample		Developed Economies		Developing Economies		Asia	
	coefficients	t-statistics	coefficients	t-statistics	coefficients	t-statistics	coefficients	t-statistics
EXR	–0.008	–1.064	–1.083	–1.308	–0.005	–0.691	–0.002	–0.285
EXRV	–0.585	–1.477	–0.322	–0.167	–0.277	–1.728*	–6.096	–1.916*
LnWAGE	–1.169	–6.599***	–0.329	–0.859	–1.543	–7.050***	–1.715	–7.038***
LnGDP	0.488	10.496***	0.980	12.477***	–0.207	–1.041	–0.243	–1.406
CPI	–0.131	–1.486	–2.034	–1.945*	–0.074	–1.308	–0.794	–1.803*
EDU	–1.030	–2.401**	2.535	3.228***	–2.469	–4.257***	–2.259	–3.723***
LnELEC	0.089	0.805	–0.471	–1.142	0.880	6.150***	1.006	6.182***
LnCFDI	0.394	9.974***	0.184	2.773***	0.612	9.394***	0.667	9.613***
GOV	7.870	6.914***	0.790	0.311	10.902	8.809***	10.373	7.852***
Pseudo R2	0.222		0.438		0.231		0.261	
n.o.b.	23264		13296		9968		9472	

Table 6. Continued.

3. Electric Machinery

	All Sample		Developed Economies		Developing Economies		Asia	
	coefficients	t-statistics	coefficients	t-statistics	coefficients	t-statistics	coefficients	t-statistics
EXR	–1.08E-06	–0.888	–1.062	–1.881*	–1.05E-06	–0.893	–0.003	–0.564
EXRV	–1.002	–3.927***	–14.157	–2.839***	–0.614	–2.683***	–7.674	–3.458***
LnWAGE	–1.152	–10.864***	–0.593	–1.802*	–1.532	–12.295***	–1.642	–11.199***
LnGDP	0.245	7.611***	1.071	14.747***	–0.326	–2.967***	–0.353	–2.231**
CPI	–0.017	–0.653	–0.581	–0.592	–0.027	–1.125	–0.827	–1.424
EDU	–1.780	–6.374***	2.571	3.470***	–2.935	–8.580***	–2.790	–7.637***
LnELEC	0.386	5.335***	–0.062	–0.316	0.963	11.746***	1.093	11.096***
LnCFDI	0.519	18.273***	0.235	3.839***	0.709	17.565***	0.715	17.194***
GOV	8.732	12.840***	–0.065	–0.028	11.810	17.260***	10.887	14.283***
Pseudo R2	0.195		0.475		0.238		0.266	
n.o.b.	46761		18412		28299		27061	

4. Transport Machinery

	All Sample		Developed Economies		Developing Economies		Asia	
	coefficients	t-statistics	coefficients	t-statistics	coefficients	t-statistics	coefficients	t-statistics
EXR	5.52E-09	0.391	–0.160	–0.650	1.42E-08	0.919	–0.012	–1.657*
EXRV	–1.108	–3.083***	–1.056	–0.737	–0.854	–2.370**	–14.077	–3.900***
LnWAGE	–0.929	–7.107***	–0.394	–0.977	–1.395	–9.526***	–2.428	–10.697***
LnGDP	0.445	10.657***	0.990	10.831***	–0.046	–0.821	–0.104	–1.720*
CPI	–0.068	–1.214	0.106	1.258	–0.048	–1.887*	–0.667	–1.656*
EDU	–1.224	–3.387***	4.121	4.505***	–2.990	–6.912***	–1.583	–3.235***
LnELEC	0.375	3.815***	0.372	1.672*	0.637	5.907***	0.620	4.575***
LnCFDI	0.443	12.836***	0.254	3.320***	0.485	10.427***	0.587	11.281***
GOV	2.529	3.111***	4.406	1.731*	6.505	7.501***	5.165	5.648***
Pseudo R2	0.200		0.500		0.178		0.247	
n.o.b.	25463		12504		12909		11524	

Note: '*', '**', and '***' indicate statistical significance at 10, 5, and 1%, respectively.
Source: Authors' estimation.

FDI in electric machinery, and transport machinery, as expected. FDI discouraging effect is particularly strong for FDI in developing countries.

The estimated coefficients of the wage rate (WAGE) are negative for all the industries, as expected, and all of them are statistically significant. It is important to note that WAGE has an expectedly negative impact on Japanese FDI in developing countries and in Asian countries. These results, which indicate that Japanese firms select a country with low-wage labor as a site for their investment are consistent with an earlier observation from the MITI survey that the use of local labor is one of the important motives of undertaking FDI by Japanese firms in Asia.

Market size (GDP) has an expected positive sign in all the industries and it is statistically significant. Market size is a particularly important characteristic to attract Japanese FDI in developed countries. Indeed, for the three machinery sectors the coefficients on GDP turn out to be negative for Japanese FDI in developing countries. These findings appear to show that Japanese firms undertake FDI in developing countries to produce products not for local market but for exporting. The estimated coefficients on inflation (CPI) are mostly negative, as expected, but only a few coefficients are statistically significant.

The availability of skilled labor (EDU), expressed by the secondary school enrollment ratio, has an unexpected negative impact on Japanese FDI in most cases. A comparison of the results covering developed countries and developing countries brings out an interesting contrast that EDU has an importantly positive impact on Japanese FDI in developed countries but not in developing countries. This finding indicates that Japanese firms investing in developed countries give importance to the availability of highly educated population, while those investing in developing countries are interested in using low-skilled, low-wage labor. The combination of different motives regarding the use of local labor by Japanese firms in developed countries and those in developing countries are reflected in these contrasting results.

Electricity generation (ELEC) is shown to be an important factor in attracting FDI as the estimated coefficients on electricity are positive and statistically significant in many cases. This finding indicates that the availability of a well-developed infrastructure is important for attracting Japanese FDI. As expected, ELEC has a significant impact on the FDI decision making of the locations among developing countries.

The estimated coefficients on agglomeration (CFDI) are positive and significant in all the industries except in the case of textiles in developed countries. This observation indicates the importance of inter-firm relations for Japanese firms in the form of inter-firm transactions and information exchange. These findings may indicate the importance of supporting industries in machinery sectors, as they require a large number of reliable parts and components in their production, a large part of which are supplied by other Japanese firms in the region. This observation is consistent with the result of the MITI survey indicating the lack of supporting industries as one of the problems in operating in Asia.

Governance (GOV) has an expected positive coefficient with statistical significance in all the industries, supporting the validity of the observation that good governance of the host government promotes Japanese FDI. Governance is especially important for Japanese firms interested in investing in developing countries.

VI. CONCLUSIONS

Our analysis of the determinants of FDI location by Japanese firms shows that host country factors play a very important role in attracting Japanese FDI and probably FDI from other sources as well. Specifically, we found that abundance of low-wage labor, availability of good infrastructure, industrial agglomeration, and good governance to be key factors for successfully attracting Japanese firms.

These findings provide the crisis-stricken East Asian countries with valuable suggestions, in order for them to recover from the crisis and to get back on the growth path by attracting FDI. Construction of good infrastructure such as electricity generation, transportation and communication services, and establishment and management of reliable institutions such as bureaucracy and legal system are important for attracting FDI. Indeed, these factors play important roles for achieving sustainable economic growth in developing countries.

A lack of financial and human resources makes it difficult for developing countries to carry out these tasks. To construct good infrastructure and to establish good governance, developing countries should utilize economic and technical assistance from developed countries. Furthermore, to improve governance, or to reduce political risk, it may prove effective for developing countries to commit themselves to bilateral and multilateral investment agreements. Finally, developing countries are well advised to manage their economies properly, so that they can avoid economic uncertainties reflected in high inflation and large fluctuations in exchange rate, which are detrimental to FDI inflows.

NOTES

1. A number of studies have examined the East Asian economic crisis. Among them, the World Bank (1998) provides a comprehensive analysis.

2. This section extends Urata (1993a) and Kawai and Urata (1998). Although the discussions in these papers refer to the value of FDI rather than the number of FDI cases, the essence of the discussions in these papers can apply to those in this paper. This is because the Japanese FDI patterns in terms of value and in terms of the number of cases are similar.

3. In terms of value, these two regions absorbed more than 60% of Japan's FDI, indicating the average size of Japanese FDI in terms of value in developed regions is greater than that in developing regions.

4. This observation applies to new FDI. A lack of data precludes one from obtaining accurate statistics, but there are signs showing that Japan's FDI undertaken with reinvested earnings has continued to grow in the ASEAN countries. See, for example, Okamoto and Urata (1997) for the case of Malaysia.

5. See Urata (1993b) for a detailed discussion.

6. The figures for 1995 are not shown in the table. In terms of cumulative value from 1986 to 1995, electric machinery has the largest share among the manufacturing subsectors, followed by textiles and chemicals.

7. See Urata and Kawai (1997) on this observation.

8. The MITI conducts a comprehensive survey of overseas activities of Japanese firms every three years starting 1980. The results of the survey are published under the title of Kaigai Toshi Kokei Soran [Comprehensive Survey of Overseas Activities of Japanese Firms]. In the 1992 survey, a questionnaire was sent to 3,378 Japanese multinationals, 1,594 of whom responded. The respondents covered the activities of 7,108 overseas affiliates. The MITI also conducts an annual survey with the more limited number of questions except for the years of Comprehensive Survey. The results of the survey are published under the title of Wagakuni Kigyo no Kaigai Jigyo Katsudo [Overseas Activities of Japanese Firms]. Motives of FDI are asked in the comprehensive surveys but not in the annual surveys.

9. There are some variations regarding the importance of securing inexpensive labor as an FDI motive among the Asian countries. Based on the results of its survey of Japanese multinationals, the Export-Import Bank of Japan (1996) reports that for as many as 60% of the affiliates in China, Indonesia, Vietnam, India, and the Philippines noted that securing inexpensive labor was one of their motives behind their establishment, while the corresponding figures are much smaller for the affiliates in Thailand, Malaysia, Singapore and others.

10. Although not shown in the table, the share of exports in total sales of Asian affiliates is significantly higher than the corresponding shares for the affiliates in other regions. For example, for 1992 the share of exports in total manufacturing sales of the Asian affiliates was 33.9%, while the corresponding figure for all the affiliates in the world was 23.3% (MITI).

11. A survey by the Export-Import Bank of Japan (1996) reveals that local legal system and procedures for investment approval were serious problems in China and Vietnam.

12. The shortage of skilled workers, a lack of adequate infrastructure, and underdevelopment of supporting industries were shown to be major problems faced by Japanese firms in many Asian countries (The Export-Import Bank of Japan, 1996).

13. The corresponding proportions for the affiliates in North America and in Europe are 3.8 and 14.7%, respectively.

14. This section draws on Urata and Kawai (2001).

15. In their study of the determinants of FDI locations by U.S. manufacturing and electronics firms, Wheeler and Mody (1992) find that risk has a discouraging effect but the effect is very small.

16. Several studies have applied this type of model to explain the locational determinants of FDI. See, for example, Woodward (1992) and Head, Ries, and Swenson (1995).

17. The definitions of the explanatory variables and their data sources are presented in Appendix Table 1.

18. For example, see Thursby and Thursby (1987) and Cushman (1988).

19. See Knack and Keefer (1995) on these observations. They examined the effect of quality of institutions, measured by these indicators, on economic growth and private investment, and found that quality of institutions has a positive impact on these two economic variables.

20. Appendix Table A2 lists the sample countries.

REFERENCES

Cushman, D. O. (1988). U.S. Bilateral Trade Flows and Exchange Risk during the Floating Period. *Journal of International Economics*, *24*(3/4), 317–330.

Export-Import Bank of Japan (1996). *EXIM Review*, *16*(1).

Fukao, K., & Yue, X. (1997). Denki Meka no Ricchi Sentaku" [The Locational Selection of Japanese Electronics Firms]. *Mita Gakkai Zasshi* [Mita Journal of Economics], *90*(2), 11–39 [in Japanese].

Fukao, K., & Chung, H. (1996). Chokusetsu Toshi Aitekoku no Kettei Yoin: Wagakuni Seizogyo ni Kansuru Jissho Bunseki [The Determinants of FDI Recipients: An Analysis of Japanese Manufacturing Industry], *38*, *Financial Review* [in Japanese].

Head, K., Reis, J., & Swenson, D. (1995). Agglomeration benefit and location choice: Evidence from Japanese manufacturing investments in the United States. *Journal of International Economics*, *38*, 199–222.

Kawai, M., & Urata, S. (1998). Are Trade and Direct Investment Substitutes of Complements? An Empirical Analysis of Japanese Manufacturing Industries. In: H. Lee & D. Roland-Holst (Eds), *Economic Development and Cooperation in the Pacific Basin: Trade, Investment and Environmental Issues*. Cambridge: Cambridge University Press.

Knack, S., & Keefer, P. (1995). Institutions and Economic Performance: Cross-Country Tests Using Alternative Institutional Measures. *Economics and Politics*, *7*(3), 207–227.

McFadden, D. (1974). Conditional Logit Analysis of Qualitative Choice Behavior. In: P. Zaremka (Ed.), *Frontiers in Econometrics*. New York: Academic Press.

Okamoto, Y., & Urata, S. (1997). Japan's Foreign Direct Investment in Malaysia in the 1990s. In: K. Sugiyama & S. Leong (Eds), *Revitalization of Japan's Economy: Implications for Malaysia*. Malaysia: Institute of Strategic and International Studies (ISIS).

Thursby, J. G., & Thursby, M. C. (1987). Bilateral Trade Flows, the Linder Hypothesis, and Exchange Risk. *Review of Economics and Statistics*, *60*(3), 488–505.

Tokunaga, S., & Ishi, R. (1995). Nihon Kigyo no Gurobaru oyobi Higashi Ajia niokeru Chokusetsu Toshi Kettei ni Kansuru Keiryo Bunseki: Kondisshonaru Logit Moderu niyoru Takokuseki Kigyo no Ricchi Sentaku Bunseki [An Econometric Analysis of the Determinants of Japanese FDI in the World and in East Asia: An Application of the Conditional Logit Model to the Locational Choice of Multinational Enterprises]. In: K.

Ohno & Y. Okamoto (Eds), *EC, NAFTA, Higashi Ajia to Gaikoku Chokusetsu Toshi: Tojo Kokueno Eikyo*. The Institute of Developing Economies, Tokyo [in Japanese].

Urata, S. (1993a). Japanese Foreign Direct Investment and Its Impact on Foreign Trade in Asia. In: T. Ito & A. O. Krueger (Eds), *Trade and Protectionism*. Chicago: University of Chicago Press.

Urata, S. (1993b). Obstacles to Further Economic Growth in East Asia and Japan's Economic Assistance. *Japan Review of International Affairs*, 7(40), 297–315.

Urata, S., & Kawai, H. (1997). Governance and the Flow of Japanese Foreign Direct Investment. Presented at a World Bank Workshop on Governance and Private Investment in East Asia, Hakone, Japan.

Urata, S., & Kawai, H. (2001). The Determinants of the Location of Foreign Direct Investment by Japanese Small and Medium-sized Enterprises. *Small Business Economics*, forthcoming.

Wakasugi, R. (1997). Nihon Kigyo no Chokusetsu Toshi: Shijo Yoin to Kigyo Tokushuteki Yoin no Jissho Bunseki [FDI by Japanese Firms: An Empirical Investigation of Market Characteristics and Firm-Specific Characteristics]. *Mita Gakkai Zasshi* [Mita Journal of Economics], *90*(2), July, Keio University, 40–58. [in Japanese].

Wheeler, D., & Mody, A. (1992). International Investment Location Decisions: The Case of U.S. Firms. *Journal of International Economics*, *33*, 57–76.

Woodward, D. P. (1992). Locational Determinants of Japanese Manufacturing Startups in the United States. *Southern Economic Journal*, 690–708.

World Bank (1998). *East Asia: The Road to Recovery*.

APPENDIX

Appendix Tables A1 and A2 appear on the following pages.

Table A1. Summary Statistics of Explanatory Variables.

	EXR (local/yen)		EXRV		CPI (%)	wage		GDP (billion 1987$)		Electricity (KWh)		Education (%)		CFDI		Governance	
	1981	1994	1981	1994	1981/1994	1981	1994	1981	1994	1981	1994	1981	1994	1981	1994	1981	1994
Latin America	0.076	25,345,434	1.306	0.307	13.7	0.160	0.189	28	36	1,055	1,614	42	51	496,987	3,288,635	0.0	1.8
Middle East	0.593	14.204	0.070	0.104	7.8	na	na	34	41	1,276	2,348	47	58	301,305	647,856	–5.4	1.5
Africa	0.500	17.179	0.068	0.091	9.1	na	na	7	9	225	288	23	30	308,264	1,589,036	–4.4	0.1
North America	0.651	1.419	0.060	0.043	3.4	0.743	1.291	2,082	2,905	11,092	13,893	92	96	4,899,046	92,152,647	6.5	6.2
Europe	0.647	2.225	0.068	0.053	5.2	0.728	1.430	191	265	4,654	5,438	82	91	257,646	4,833,219	5.0	5.6
Oceania	0.407	1.367	0.044	0.049	5.4	0.614	0.990	42	60	6,006	7,975	65	75	618,068	5,601,649	5.8	6.5
Asia	0.454	2.180	0.076	0.048	6.1	0.150	0.287	39	100	270	661	38	45	653,247	4,732,353	0.1	3.1
NIES	0.635	1.278	0.057	0.039	3.8	0.089	0.440	45	134	1,573	4,435	71	87	884,473	7,454,323	3.0	5.0
Hong Kong	0.470	1.402	0.051	0.042	6.7	0.109	0.348	33	71	2,596	4,412	65	71	1,095,110	12,748,128	6.7	5.0
Korea	0.543	1.382	0.072	0.044	4.6	0.070	0.453	79	233	1,038	3,712	81	93	1,136,698	4,868,914	–0.2	5.3
Singapore	0.658	1.026	0.051	0.028	1.8	0.141	0.456	15	37	3,224	6,842	61	84	936,156	8,481,126	6.1	5.2
Taiwan	0.869	1.301	0.054	0.043	2.1	0.072	0.402	54	196	2,214	5,629	64	88	369,926	3,719,122	4.9	4.7
ASEAN	0.415	1.634	0.056	0.043	5.6	0.039	0.069	38	81	208	570	39	50	1,521,358	8,285,181	–1.9	2.2
Indonesia	0.252	1.860	0.056	0.049	6.8	na	0.031	56	129	67	281	31	43	4,423,776	18,911,273	–4.8	2.2
Malaysia	0.600	1.474	0.053	0.034	2.7	0.041	na	25	57	763	1,988	49	59	650,356	5,615,145	4.0	2.6
Philippines	0.252	1.818	0.058	0.053	9.5	0.029	0.101	34	41	372	404	64	79	614,928	2,149,568	–5.4	0.3
Thailand	0.556	1.384	0.056	0.037	3.5	0.046	0.074	36	99	322	1,234	29	37	396,371	6,464,736	0.6	2.9
China	0.300	3.277	0.051	0.043	7.1	0.008	0.018	141	521	311	779	45	52	12,021	6,149,888	0.5	3.7
Other Asia	0.405	2.531	0.060	0.054	7.9	0.253	0.456	58	113	163	368	31	35	16,996	180,117	–1.8	1.3

Table A1. Continued.

	EXR (local/yen)		EXRV		CPI (%)	wage		GDP (billion 1987$)		Electricity (KWh)		Education (%)		CFDI		Governance	
	1981	1994	1981	1994	1981/1994	1981	1994	1981	1994	1981	1994	1981	1994	1981	1994	1981	1994
India	0.438	3.425	0.050	0.060	7.3	0.420	0.445	192	372	187	423	31	37	39,390	331,998	−1.0	2.1
Pakistan	0.373	2.486	0.060	0.063	6.4	na	0.512	23	47	222	463	15	21	7,030	142,064	−5.5	−0.4
Bangladesh	0.381	1.839	0.057	0.045	6.8	0.118	0.445	14	23	30	84	18	19	5,927	125,494	−6.5	−1.6
Sri Lanka	0.429	2.375	0.073	0.049	8.6	0.220	0.420	5	9	125	246	57	74	15,638	120,913	−1.9	−0.6

Source: World Development Indicators, 1997 (World Bank), Financial Statistics (IMF), Yearbook of Labor Statistics (ILO), International Country Risk Guide (Political Risk Services).

Notes:

(1) EXR: local/yen index, 1987 = 1.0, EXRCV: Coefficient of Variation on Exchage Rate, 5 years average, CPI: annual growth rate, %, wage: wage rate, 1987U.S. = 1.0; Electricity: Percapita Electricity Production, kWh, Education: Secondary School Enrollment Ratio, CFDI: cumulative FDI, million yen.

(2) Governance (1st principal component of GOV1–GOV5), GOV1 (Government repudiation of contract), GOV2 (Risk of expropriation), GOV3 (Corruption), GOV4 (Law and Other Tradition), GOV5 (Bureaucratic quality). High score indicates better governance.

Table A2. The List of Countries Used in the Analysis.

1	United States	41	Hong Kong	80	Hungary
2	Canada	42	Taiwan	81	Romania
3	Mexico	43	Vietnam	82	Finland
4	Panama	44	Korea, Rep.	83	Cyprus
5	El Salvador	45	Nepal	84	Russian Federation
6	Brazil	46	Brunei	85	Australia
7	Argentina	47	China	86	Fiji
8	Paraguay	48	Iran, Islamic Rep.	87	New Zealand
9	Chile	49	Israel	88	New Caledonia
10	Peru	50	Kuwait	89	Papua New Guinea
11	Dominican Republic	51	Lebanon	90	Western Samoa
12	Venezuela	52	Saudi Arabia	91	Egypt, Arab Rep.
13	Bolivia	53	United Arab Emirates	92	Morocco
14	Bahamas, The	54	Afghanistan	93	Zimbabwe
15	Colombia	55	Bahrain	94	Liberia
16	Guatemala	56	Qatar	95	Tanzania
17	Ecuador	57	Syrian Arab Republic	96	Sudan
18	Nicaragua	58	Iraq	97	Nigeria
19	Costa Rica	59	United Kingdom	98	Cote d'Ivoire
20	Trinidad and Tobago	60	France	99	Madagascar
21	Bermuda	61	Germany	100	Kenya
22	Puerto Rico	62	Belgium	101	Ethiopia
23	Honduras	63	Ireland	102	Zambia
24	Suriname	64	Switzerland	103	Uganda
25	Jamaica	65	Portugal	104	Ghana
26	Guyana	66	Netherlands	105	Cameroon
27	Uruguay	67	Italy	106	Zaire
28	India	68	Luxembourg	107	Rwanda
29	Pakistan	69	Spain	108	Gabon
30	Bangladesh	70	Greece	109	Sierra Leone
31	Sri Lanka	71	Malta	110	Gambia, The
32	Myanmar	72	Austria	111	Mauritania
33	Malaysia	73	Norway	112	Senegal
34	Singapore	74	Yugoslavia, FR	113	Swaziland
35	Thailand		(Serbia/Montenegro)	114	Libya
36	Indonesia	75	Denmark	115	Guinea
37	Macao	76	Iceland	116	Niger
38	Philippines	77	Sweden	117	Tunisia
39	Cambodia	78	Turkey		
40	Lao PDR	79	Poland		

33. FOREIGN DIRECT INVESTMENT AND TECHNOLOGY FLOWS IN ASIA AND THE PACIFIC REGION IN THE 1990s: AN ANALYSIS OF TRENDS, PATTERNS AND POLICIES

Momtaz Uddin Ahmed

1. INTRODUCTION

The renewed optimism in the role of FDI as sources of capital flows, technology transfer, management know-how, access to export markets and faster economic growth has led to great surge of FDI flows globally and between regions during the mid 1980s and 1990s. Many Asian countries have become recipients of these large private capital flows, especially FDI, which has contributed to their catching up process through capital accumulation and technology transfer. Indeed, the optimism associated with the prospects for capital flows, technology transfer, management know-how, access to export markets and faster economic growth which grater globalization should bring has given birth to renewed interest in the role of the transitional corporations as engines of economic growth. According to UNCTAD, some 40,000 parent firms and approximately 270,000 foreign affiliates controlled an FDI stock of U.S.$2.7 trillion, equivalent to 10% of the world GDP in 1995. The size, nature, and influence of these cross-border transactions on the world economy has prompted a recent World Bank study (Brewer, 1991) to describe the

Restructuring Asian Economics for the New Millennium, Volume 9B, pages 643–668.

ISBN: 0-7623-0710-2

phenomenon as a new FDI era – an era marked by a greater recognition of the benefits of FDI.

Foreign direct investment brings to the host country not only capital and foreign exchange, but it also facilitates the import of new technology in the form of new products and new production processes. The greatest benefit to the host country is the access to the knowledge that helps overcome the managerial gap and technological gap. New production techniques accompany the inflow of private capital and facilitate diffusion of technological knowledge in the economy. In addition, foreign private investment may promote new skills through training imparted to the local workforce, and knowledge gained by these workers can be transmitted to other members of the labour force employed by local firms. Through externalities and spillovers, technology transfer thus improves the international competitiveness of an economy and contributes to the process of economic development.

All these arguments carry considerable weight. Therefore, it is necessary to deliberate on ways and means of promoting technological flows in association with the flows of investible resources. Given the adoption of private sector-led strategy by the governments in Asia and the Pacific region in the recent years, it is also substantive to analyse how the private sector could ensure needed technology flows in association with the private capital flows.

The present paper analyses the trends and patterns of FDI flows and technology transfers in the Asian region and highlights the policy support and incentive structures provided by these countries to attract FDI and encourage technology transfer. The paper begins with an overview of the trends and patterns of FDI flows into the ESCAP region in terms of countries and economic sectors.[1] The nature, mode, and appropriateness of technology transfer are analysed in section 2. The policies and institutional arrangements made by the host countries in the ESCAP region to attract FDI flows and encourage technology transfer are discussed in section 3. The concluding section draws together important findings and proposes some policy measures for boosting FDI flows and ensure transfer of appropriate technologies to the developing countries.

2. TRENDS AND PATTERNS OF FDI FLOWS IN THE COUNTRIES OF ESCAP REGION IN THE 1990s

2.1. Recent FDI Flows in the ESCAP Region: An Overview

An unprecedented surge of financial and investment flows has taken place in the 1990s, both globally and in the ESCAP region. The accelerated and sustained growth in the long- term financial flows, especially to the developing countries, is attributed almost entirely to the growth in the private capital flows which nearly quadrupled between 1990–1995 (UN, 1997).

The developing economies in the ESCAP region experienced over a threefold increase in the total net resource flows in the 1990s, from U.S.$38.2 billion in 1990 to U.S.$120.78 billion in 1995. During the same period, aggregate net resource flows to all developing countries more than doubled (Table 1) from 101.9 billion U.S. dollars in 1990 to 231.3 billion U.S. dollars in 1995, registering a percentage increase of 128% in value terms. Concomitantly, FDI flow grew nearly four fold *globally* from U.S.$25 billion to $90.3 billion with *ESCAP region* recording nearly five fold increase from $11.5 billion to $55.5 billion. In percentage terms, the share of the ESCAP region in the total net resource flows increased from 38 to 52% and that in the FDI increased from 46 to 62% between 1990 and 1995.

Another notable feature observed from the data in Table 1 is that in addition to increase in the net resource flows, there has been a significant change in the composition of such flows to the developing countries. FDI now constitutes the dominant source of external finance in place of long- term debt which was the major source in the early 1990s. As seen from the table, FDI now contributes to nearly half of the aggregate inflows.

Table 1. Aggregate Net Flows to Developing Countries and the Share of Developing Economics in the ESCAP Region.

(in Billion U.S.$)

Flow	1990	1991	1992	1993	1994	1995
Aggregate	101.9 (37.6)	127.1 (35.8)	155.3 (40.4)	207.2 (40.2)	207.4 (47.8)	231.3 (52.2)
Net long debt	43.7 (45.0)	47.0 (52.1)	62.7 (47.8)	64.1 (31.0)	60.0 (50.8)	86.2 (52.9)
FDI	25.0 (46.0)	35.0 (41.1)	46.6 (47.9)	68.3 (56.8)	80.1 (55.2)	90.3 (61.7)
Portfolio	3.7 (64.9)	7.6 (13.2)	14.1 (39.1)	45.6 (44.1)	34.9 (53.9)	22.9 (61.8)
Grants	29.4 (16.0)	37.5 (14.7)	32.0 (15.3)	29.4 (15.3)	32.5 (16.9)	32.9 (17.6)

Note: Figure in parentheses are percentage shares of the ESCAP region.
Source: UN ESCAP, Economic and Social Survey of Asia and the Pacific, 1997.

The overall inflow of both private capital and FDI has been uneven among the countries of the ESCAP region with such flows being highly concentrated in the countries of East Asia, primarily China (Table 2). While the share of total flows of public and private debt has gradually declined over the years for most of the countries in the region including the six least developed countries, the net flow of total private investment has remained above 40% in 19 out of 32 countries and above 30% in the other four countries. Of the total portfolio investment, the major recipients have been India, Malaysia, the Philippines, the Republic of Korea, and Vietnam, and to a lesser extent, Indonesia, Pakistan and Thailand. In the rest of the ESCAP region, the inflow is rather negligible.

The FDI inflow as share of GDP has also increased over the years in the economies of the ESCAP region. As will be noted from Table 3, the FDI inflows as proportions of GDP registered an upward trend for all individual countries during the period 1984–1989 and 1990–1994. The rate of growth between the two periods, however, has been uneven among the individual countries, reflecting very sharp increases in the countries of East and Northeast Asia compared to other Asian countries.

The developing economies in Asia witnessed almost a four fold rise in FDI flows, from an annual average of U.S.$13.5 billion during 1985–1990 to U.S.$51.7 billion during 1991–1996, with the total inflow reaching a peak of U.S.$84.3 billion in 1996 (Table 4). In contrast, the FDI flows to East, South-East and South Asian countries rose to a record high annual average of U.S.$50 billion during 1985–1990, registering a percentage increase of over 316%. In absolute terms, the rise was from U.S.$21.22 billion in 1991 to $81.24 billion in 1996, accounting for nearly two-thirds of the total inflows (128.74) to the developing countries in 1996. What is notable, of the record U.S.$81.2 billion netted by the countries of East, South-East and South Asia, China alone accounted for over half of the total flows (42.3 billion) in 1996. Since 1992, China overtook Singapore in attracting FDI and continued to remain the largest FDI recipient country in the region since then. However, Singapore maintained its second portion till date since then.

During 1991–1996, the other Asian countries experiencing steady growth in FDI inflows were Cambodia, Hong Kong, India, Indonesia, South Korea and Vietnam. However, the ASEAN economies as a separate group experienced a significant decline in their relative share of FDI inflows among the region from 61% during 1990–1991 to roughly 30% during 1994–1996.

The Pacific island economies succeeded in attracting an average FDI inflow of U.S.$300 million during 1991–1996, reaching a peak of U.S.$590 million in 1995. While Papua New Guinea continues to be the largest FDI recipient

Table 2. Aggregate Net Resource Flow in ESCAP Region, 1985–1994 (Annual averages). (in Million of U.S.$)

Region/economies	Total	Debt	FDI	Portfolio equity	Grants	Total	Debt	FDI	Portfolio equity	Grants
	1985–1989					1990–1994				
Least Developed Country										
Bangladesh	1,414.2	781.0	1.4	0.0	631.4	1470.8	626.6	6.6	9.4	828.6
Bhutan	28.3	13.5	0.0	0.0	14.8	34.9	2.1	0.0	0.0	32.7
Cambodia	—	—	—	—	—	142.4	11.0	31.2	0.0	100.2
Lao	175.8	145.4	1.2	0.0	29.4	172.2	78.6	28.6	0.0	65.0
Maldives	15.6	0.2	3.0	0.0	12.4	33.1	13.1	7.0	0.0	13.0
Mynmar	273.8	197.2	1.2	0.0	75.6	108.8	41.2	3.2	5.8	58.2
Nepal	289.4	159.4	1.0	0.0	15.1	40.9	14.0	4.6	0.0	22.3
Samoa	16.1	0.8	0.2	0.0	18.1	29.1	–0.2	14.2	0.0	14.9
Solomon Island	33.5	10.6	4.7	0.0	18.1	29.1	–0.2	14.2	0.0	16.6
Vanuatu	27.3	2.7	7.9	0.0	16.8	44.3	5.2	24.2	0.0	14.9
East and North-East Asia										
China	8,253.8	5,560.6	2,487.0	0.0	206.0	27,285.4	9,395.2	16,062.2	1,608.0	219.8
Mongolia	—	—	—	—	—	84.8	45.3	7.0	0.0	32.0
Korea, south	–2,043	–2,667	579.8	42.0	2.2	6,018.6	2,704.6	818.4	2,492.4	3.2
South-East Asia										
Indonesia	3,001.4	2,343.0	442.2	39.8	176.4	6,653.6	3,516.8	1,693.0	1,187.8	255.8
Malaysia	–74.4	–963.0	798.8	56.4	33.4	5544.4	185.2	4173.6	1139.6	46.4
Philippines	1,129.0	486.0	389.0	50.6	294.0	2,506.2	1,044.0	613.0	564.4	285.2
Thailand	1,885.6	598.2	731.8	420.6	135.0	4,752.0	2,206.2	1,788.0	614.6	143.4
Viet Nam	—	—	—	—	—	323.2	26.0	39.4	89.5	186.2

Table 2. Continued

Region/economies	Total	Debt	FDI	Portfolio equity	Grants	Total	Debt	FDI	Portfolio equity	Grants
	1985–89					1990–1994				
South and South-West Asia										
India	5314.0	4480.0	155.8	83.2	595.0	5449.2	3243.2	269.4	1381.2	554.0
Iran	–285.0	–210.2	–83.2	0.0	8.4	199.0	249.0	–113.8	0.0	63.6
Pakistan	1102.6	615.2	152.2	0.0	335.6	2139.0	1177.8	322.4	336.4	302.4
Sri Lanka	482.0	264.4	36.4	0.0	181.6	603.0	287.0	115.0	22.4	178.6
North and Central Asia										
Armenia	—	—	—	—	—	122.9	50.22	0.0	0.0	72.7
Azarbaizan	—	—	—	—	—	72.2	33.7	0.0	0.0	27.4
Kazakstan	—	—	—	—	—	461.3	305.0	145.0	0.0	11.3
Kyrgyzstan	—	—	—	—	—	106.2	63.8	3.3	0.0	18.5
Tajikistan	—	—	—	—	—	111.9	90.1	3.3	0.0	18.5
Turkmenistan	—	—	—	—	—	96.1	110.0	0.0	0.0	3.2
Uzbekistan	—	—	—	—	—	231.0	181.0	45.0	0.0	7.0
Pacific Island economies										
Fiji	24.6	–8.8	16.8	0.0	17.2	28.5	–28.2	39.8	0.0	16.8
Papua New guinea	567.4	181.2	124.8	0.0	261.2	442.8	46.0	138.8	0	266.2
Tonga	11.1	1.7	0.1	0.0	0.4	16.0	2.4	1.0	0.0	12.6

Source: UNESCAP, Economic and Social Survey of Asia and the Pacific, 1997, based on World Debt Tables 1994–1995 and 1996: External Finance for Developing Countries, Vol. 2: Country.

Table 3. Rate of FDI Inflows to GDP in ESCAP Region, 1984–1994. (Percentage)

Region/Economy	1984–1989	1990–94
Least Developed Countries		
Bangladesh	0.01	0.03
Cambodia	—	1.7
Lao	0.1	2.6
Maldives	3.2	2.6
Mynmar	0.01	0.01
Nepal	0.04	0.1
Samoa	—	4.0
Solomon Islands	3.1	8.7
Vanuatu	7.4	14.4
East and North East Asia		
China	0.7	3.6
Hong Kong	3.0	1.7
Mongolia	—	0.3
South Korea	0.4	0.3
Taiwan Province of China	0.7	0.6
South-East Asia		
Brunei Darussalam	—	0.1
Indonesia	0.5	1.3
Malaysia	2.4	7.8
Philippines	1.0	1.5
Singapore	10.3	9.7
Thailand	1.3	1.7
Viet Nam	0.02	0.5
South and South-West Asia		
India	0.1	0.1
Iran	–0.02	–0.02
Pakistan	0.4	0.7
Sri Lanka	0.6	1.2
North and Central Asia		
Armenia	—	0.03
Kazakhshtan	—	0.3
Kyrgystan	—	0.04
Tajikstan	—	0.1
Uzbekistan	—	0.1
Pacific Island Economies		
Fiji	1.4	3.0
Papua New Guinea	4.4	3.9
Tonga	—	0.7

Table 3. Continued

Region/Economy	1984–1989	1990–94
Other ESCAP Members		
Australia	2.1	1.7
Japan	0.004	0.05
New Zealand	0.5	4.3
Russian Federation	—	0.1
Turkey	0.3	0.5

Source: UNESCAP, Economic and Social Survey of Asia and the Pacific, 1997, based on World Investment Report 1996, UNCTAD.

among the Pacific island countries in the 1990s, her share reached nearly 77% of the regions total in 1995.

2.2. *Trend of FDI Flows by Broad Economic Sectors*

Lack of adequately disaggregated statistics at individual industry levels precludes detailed analysis of the distribution of FDI flows or stocks by industry in the region. The only level of disaggregatation available is at the sectoral level. Unfortunately, data on sectoral distribution of FDI is also scant and affected by distortions.[2]

In both East Asia and ASEAN member countries, traditionally the manufacturing industries sector has traditionally been the major recipient of FDI inflows. Within manufacturing, electrical goods, electronics and chemical goods industries tended to remain predominate. After manufacturing, services, agriculture, fisheries and forestry and coustruction and public utilities came next. For example, in the Republic of Korea and Taiwan, over 80% of Japanese FDI during 1955–1989 have been in manufacturing, mainly comprising chemicals, electronics, textiles and electrical products. Similarly, 60% of Japanese FDI in four large members of ASEAN – Indonesia, Malaysia, Philippines and Thailand – and in China has been in manufacturing (Chen, 1993). In Hong Kong and Singapore, on the contrary, the attention of Japanese FDI has been more on the service sectors. In fact, since the 1980s, there has been a marked increase of FDI in the non-manufacturing sectors, especially in trade, banking and insurance and services. On the one hand, it seems to have been due to structural transformation of the host countries and, on the other hand, due to relaxation of restriction on FDI in services. Between 1982 and 1986, there was almost even distribution of FDI between manufacturing and

Table 4. FDI Inflows, by Host Region and Economy, 1985–1996. (in Million U.S.$)

Host region/ economy	1985–1990 (Annual average)	1991	1992	1993	1994	1995	1996
World	141,930	158,936	173,761	218,094	28,738	316,528	349,227
Developed countries	116,744	114,792	119,692	138,762	142,395	2,058,676	208,226
Developing ountries	24,736	41,696	49,625	73,045	90,462	96,330	12,8741
Latin America and the Caribbean	8,145	15,356	16,204	18,072	26,974	25,424	38,563
Developing Europe	49	195	231	269	369	369	571
Asia	13,492	23,129	29,632	50,924	57,507	65,249	84,283
CentralAsia	—	—	140	195	393	837	1,149
Armenia	—	—	—	—	8	12	34
Azerbaizan	—	—	—	—	22	275	601
Georgia	—	—	—	—	8	6	40
Kazakstan	—	—	100	150	185	280	310
Tajikstan	—	—	—	—	10	13	13
Turkmenistan	—	—	—	—	100	100	80
Uzbekistan	—	—	40	45	50	120	55
South, East and South-East Asia	12,357	21,228	27,668	47,278	55,718	65,175	81,241
Afghanistan	—	—	—	—	—	—	—
Bangladesh	2	1	4	14	11	2	9
Brunei	—	1	4	14	6	7	9
Cambodia	—	—	33	54	69	151	350
China	2,654	4,366	11,156	27,515	33,787	35,849	42,300
Hong Kong	1,597	538	2,051	1,667	2,000	2,100	2,500
India	169	155	233	574	1,314	1,929	2,587
Korea, South	705	1,180	727	588	809	1,776	2,308
Lao	2	7	8	30	59	88	104
Macao	—	3	2	3	—	2	2
Malaysia	1,054	3,998	5,183	5,006	4,342	4,132	5,300
Maldives	4	7	7	7	6	5	7
Mongolia	—	—	2	8	7	10	5
Manmar	28	238	171	149	91	115	100
Nepal	2	2	1	4	6	5	5
Pakistan	167	257	335	347	419	639	690
Philippines	413	544	228	1,238	1,591	1,478	1,408
Singapore	2,952	4,887	2,204	4,686	5,480	6,912	9,440
Sri Lanka	37	48	123	195	166	63	170

Table 4. Continued

Host region/ economy	1985–1990 (Annual average)	1991	1992	1993	1994	1995	1996
Taiwan	879	1,271	879	917	1,375	1,559	1,402
Viet Nam	30	229	385	523	742	2000	2,156
West Asia	1,135	1,900	1,823	3,452	1,396	–763	1,898
Iran	–130	23	–170	–50	2	17	10
The Pacific	181	264	407	89	116	590	375
Fuji	28	15	51	29	65	67	49
Kiribati	—	—	—	–1	—	—	1
New Caledonia	7	3	17	20	10	17	13
Papua New Guinea	130	203	294	–2	–5	453	230
Solomon Islands	6	15	14	13	11	18	21
Tonga	—	—	1	2	2	1	23
Vanatu	9	25	26	26	30	31	36
Western Samoa	1	3	4	2	3	2	4
Least Developed Countries (Total)	555	1,830	1,459	1,743	994	1,024	1,603
LDCs (Asia)	21	837	937	1,155	252	148	674
LDCs (The Pacific)	17	44	45	40	44	51	62

Source: UNCTAD, World Investment Report, 1997.

services in the Republic of Korea. However, manufacturing became more prominent than services between 1987 and 1991 because of sharp increase of FDI in electrical, electronics and chemical products (Chen, 1993).

In Indonesia, Philippines, Thailand and Malaysia, a broadly identical trend of sectoral distribution of FDI is noted (Yue, 1993) during the mid 1980s and early 1990s, with manufacturing claiming the largest share of FDI inflows followed by services, agriculture, fisheries and forestry, construction and public utilities. Within manufacturing, the investment concentrated mainly in chemicals, basic metal products, textiles and transport equipment.

However, a markedly different pattern can be noted in the sectoral distribution of FDI in the South Asian countries, reflecting relatively early stages of their industrial development and the impact of the past economic policies. For the sub-region as a whole, the FDI inflows have been generally modest and are heavily concentrated (90%) in manufacturing, with services receiving only 5%. While the skewed composition is largely influenced by the sectoral distribution in India, a more balanced distribution between manufacturing and services can be noted in Pakistan, Sri Lanka and Bangladesh

(Lall, 1993). The composition of FDI within manufacturing also reflected relative stages of industrial development in these countries. Endowed with a relatively advanced industrial base, India attracted the most FDI into heavy industries. In contrast, Bangladesh and Sri Lanka, lacking a strong industrial base, attracted FDI flows mainly into simple export-processing activities like ready-made garments and other assembly activities.

2.3. Technology Transfer and FDI Flows

2.3.1. Some Common Concerns

Technology is usually defined as knowledge about methods of production of a given commodity in different endowment situations, and means of improving and introducing new methods. The developed countries are the prime source of technology because of huge R&D expenditures associated with it and incurred by these countries. In the modern world, the fastest and the most efficient way of accessing improved technology is through transfer from the industrialized world to the developing ones. In this process TNCs, through private investments, play an important role.

There are differences of opinion about the type, volume and conditions of technology transfer. These controversies generally relate to issues as to whether such transfers are on favourable terms to the host countries and whether such technologies are appropriate to the host country circumstances and requirements. Since factor endowments, in relation to which the developed countries have been upgrading their technologies, are different from those prevailing in the developing host countries, there is a concern that host countries may suffer production biases leading to unemployment, income inequality, and distortions in technology choice (Lall & Streeten, 1977). It is also alleged by the critics that the prices for technology and know-how which are generally dictated by TNCs on the basis of their superior strength and negotiating skills may not always be favourable for the host country.

2.3.2. Evolution in the Technology Transfer Paradigm

The conceptual framework for analysing technology transfer has been somewhat fluid, given that the policy environment and circumstances leading to technology transfer to developing countries have been changing over time and are different between countries. The framework for technology transfer in the past, as presented by Qinn (1969), has been simple and has revolved around the production presence of the Trans National Corporation (TNCs). In contrast, it has become significantly more complex in recent years and includes difficult issues as noted by Lan and Young (1996). These include:

- Technology is no longer confined to the technological knowledge associated with production, but includes organisational know-how in such fields as finance, marketing and management skills.
- Production and innovation are separated. Greater emphasis is therefore placed on quality rather than the quantity of FDI in evaluating technology transfer to host countries (Dunning, 1994).
- The dynamics of international transfer has widened from a one-way flow from home to host countries to a global and interactive process of technology generation and application. Technology transfer not only occurs after maturity but appears at innovation within innovation-network model (Ostry & Gestrin, 1993). Technology generation and diffusion may take place simultaneously. FDI can perform two roles, either as a "downstream distributor of technology" or an "upstream hunter of technology."
- Accessing technology is both difficult and expensive. Costs include not only direct costs such as royalty payments and tax concessions, but also a range of indirect costs such as communication and training costs derived from resistance of foreign technology, lower level of entreprenureship, education or absorptive capacities, etc.
- The world-wide liberalisation of FDI policies has changed the international business environment. The policy emphasis has shifted from focusing on *firms' obligations and government's rights* to one *emphasising firms' rights and government's obligations.*

2.3.3. Recent Dominant Modes of Technology Transfer

The economic growth of every nation is inextricably linked to successful international transfer of technology. There are different modes of international transfer of technology. These include: (i) import/purchase of capital goods and embodied technology, (ii) foreign direct investment, (iii) technology licensing agreements, (iv) turnkey projects, and (v) technical assistance and cooperation. No single method of technology acquisition is best for all countries. Depending upon each country's technological needs, capabilities and market conditions, the effective method of technology transfer tends to be different.[3] For example, in the early years of industrialisation, Japan built her technological capabilities primarily through licensing, turnkey projects, reverse engineering of imported inputs and goods supported by overseas on-the-job training (OJT), and study and analysis of foreign technological literatures (Kakazu, 1990). In the Republic of Korea, on the other hand, turnkey plants and machinery imports played the dominant role, followed by licensing agreements and foreign direct investment as avenues of technology transfer. While FDI is noted to have played a more important role than other modes of technology transfer in

Singapore and Thailand, heavy reliance on licensing, and technical agreements with the multinationals (MNCs) is marked in India and Indonesia (Dahlman et. al., 1987). Historical experience thus suggests that the most successful and effective mode of technology transfer involves a combination of all of the various available avenues of transfer.

An overriding consideration determining the mode of technology transfer is the cost involved in such transfers. For example, embodying technology transfer through capital goods imports is considered the most important and the cheapest source of technology acquisition for the developing Asian economies (Kakazu, 1990). However, this mode of technology acquisition requires established local engineering capabilities to perform reverse engineering, i.e. disassembling and reassembling of imported machinery.

Licensing arrangements, though suiting local needs, are relatively more costly and involve more complex and time consuming processes. Turnkey projects are the easiest way of technology acquisition, but this mode is not very helpful for building local technological capabilities.

Technology Transfer Through FDI and MNCs Foreign direct investment, particularly in the form of joint ventures, has become an increasingly important source of technology acquisition in most Asian economies in the recent years. By attracting FDI, a country acquires not only needed capital and hardware technology but also software managerial skills and marketing know-how. It is important to distinguish two aspects of technology transfer by the multinationals through FDI. First, there is the direct effect on the affiliate in the host country and on the host economy through technology transfer by the parent company. Second, there is the additional positive spillover effects through demonstration to other producers in the host economy of new technologies and management methods. This is the indirect effect of stimulating local firms in technology acquisition and improvement through competition.

The indirect benefits of externalities, generally referred to as "spillovers" may occur in many ways. The MNCs may increase the degree of competition among firms in the host country market and thereby force the inefficient domestic firms to become more productive and efficient through investing in physical or human capital. The MNCs may also undertake the training of labour and management which cannot be replicated in domestic firms or purchased from abroad. Another important avenue for positive spillover effects is the upgrading of local production facilities and suppliers of services to meet the higher standards of quality control, reliability and speed of delivery required by the technology and operating procedures of the foreign-owned companies.[4]

It is relevant to note that despite playing an important role as a vehicle of technology transfer, FDI faces some serious criticisms as well. For example, the MNCs are held responsible for creation of an enclave industrial structure, particularly through making highly capital-intensive investments in the free trade zones, control of local industries and markets by foreign capital, exploitation of natural resources, and reluctance on the part of the foreign investors to transfer core technology and management know-how. These are highly controversial issues attracting the attention of a large number of researchers arguing both for and against MNCs as modes of technology transfer to the developing nation.[5]

2.3.4. Dominant Modes of Technology Transfer by the Countries of the Asia-Pacific Region

Different Asian economies followed very different technology strategies commensurating the differences in their national innovation system.[6] A very significant difference in this respect relates to the extent to which the countries of East and South-East Asia in particular have relied on FDI as a mode of technology acquisition. Singapore, for example, has relied the most on FDI, which is indicated by the fact that currently the stock of foreign capital in the country's economy is 91.7% of GDP. At the other extreme, the share of foreign capital stock to GDP is only 4.9% in Taiwan and a meager 2.1% in the Republic of Korea (Dahlman, 1994). In Hong Kong, this share is reported to be 22.2% in the recent years.

All of these four countries, however, displayed remarkable similarity in their technology acquisition efforts by relying very heavily on technology licensing to acquire new knowledge and skills. In Singapore and Hong Kong, the licensing is done largely between the subsidiaries of the MNCs and their parent companies. In Korea and Taiwan, on the contrary, such licensing is done by the domestic firms. Very high dependence on the imports of capital goods has been another common technology acquisition strategy pursued by all of these four East Asian countries. Again, all four economies made extensive use of sending students abroad for higher studies in the science-oriented disciplines.

The major difference in the national innovation system of the four countries lies in their domestic technological efforts indicated particularly by their Research and Development, or R&D, efforts. For example, while Singapore and Taiwan spent 0.9% and 1.2% of their GNP on R&D, respectively, in 1990, Hong Kong spends so little on R&D that there is no published figure on it. At the other end of the spectrum, the Republic of Korea spent 1.9% of her GNP on R&D activities, which is noted to be 20–30% below the proportions spent by the OECD countries (Dahlman, 1994). Another notable feature of the recent domestic technology efforts made by these countries is that nearly 80% of R&D activities is undertaken by the private sector since 1990, except in Taiwan where 50% of her R&D expenses originate from the public sector. Finally, all of these four countries made very high levels of investments in development of technical human capital which helped them to effectively acquire, assimilate and diffuse modern technology in their economies.

Next to the East Asian "Gang of Four," the Asian NIEs, especially Thailand, Indonesia and Malaysia greatly benefited from large export-oriented inflows of FDI since the mid-1980s. While the developing East Asian countries are noted to have attracted four waves of foreign investment in the post World War II Period, the third wave beginning in the mid-1980s (and preceded by the first and second waves of 1960 and 1970 respectively) involved the transfer of labour intensive operations to East and South-East Asia in the wake of appreciations of the yen and some currencies of the NIEs. Initially dominated by Japan, the wave eventually included substantial flows from the NIEs (Wells 1993) and the regional ratio of inward foreign direct investment to GDP more than tripled (Petri, 1997). The fourth and the most significant FDI wave flowing to the Asian countries involves the current investment boom in China, with the net FDI inflows jumping from a figure of U.S.$3.5 billions in 1990 to U.S.$37.5 billions in 1995. According to the latest UNCTAD figures quoted in The Daily Star (Bangladesh, 31st December 1997), China attracted FDI inflow of a record U.S.$42.3 billion in 1996. During the last few years, however, much of this FDI flow is going to Vietnam rather than to Thailand, Malaysia and Indonesia.

The Flying Geese Paradigm. Analysing the trade-investment nexus in the context of East Asian economies, Petri (1997) notes the existence and operation of various mutually reinforcing linkages between outward-oriented trade and investment policies, which help to stimulate additional trade which in turn promotes further trade-oriented investments. The international linkages so created played a historically important role in the Asian region's economic progress along the lines predicted by Kaname Akamatsu's "flying geese" model in the 1930s. According to the "flying geese" model, countries gradually move up in technological development by following the pattern of countries just ahead of them in the development process. Under this scenario, Korea and Taiwan took over leadership in textiles and apparels from Japan as Japan moved into the high-tech sectors of electronics, automobiles and other capital goods. A decade or so later, Korea and Taiwan were able to upgrade to electronics and auto components manufacturing countries, with Thailand, Indonesia and Vietnam taking over textiles and apparels.

This illustrates the growing acceptance of a product cycle model of economic development based on the principle of comparative advantage. The "flying geese" hypothesis refers to a changing pattern of comparative advantage in Asia, linked to FDI as an important modality of relocation of the production of certain goods mentioned above, that no longer enjoy comparative advantage in the home country compared to the host Japanese firms relocated first to the Asian NIES and then to the ASEAN countries.

The technology strategies adopted by the countries of South-East Asia, especially Thailand, Indonesia and Malaysia, exhibit strong similarities with those followed by the East Asian countries. All three countries acquired much of new the technologies through licensing agreements and royalty payments. While they also relied heavily on imports of capital goods, Malaysia invested heavily in tertiary education for development of technically qualified human capital. However, in terms of the overall domestic technical efforts, all three countries have yet to go a long way in developing R&D infrastructures and training higher level technical personnel, both of which are reflections of their relatively low level of industrial development compared to the "Gang of Four".

As noted earlier, China is moving full speed ahead, taking large strides in acquiring Western technology, particularly by attracting FDI ever since broader opening of her economy to the West in the 1980s. In addition to licensing foreign technology at a very rapid pace (the stock of FDI to GNP rising to 5.5% in 1990 from almost a non-existent base prior to 1980s), China is also investing very heavily in building domestic technological capabilities. For example, China is reported to have 4500 R&D institutions, one million scientists and engineers involved in R&D activities, with over 45% of them being engaged in industrial research (Dahlman 1994).[7]

Although FDI flows across national borders have registered a sharp rise in the 1990s, increasing by about four times the growth of world commodity trade, the countries of South Asia lagged far behind their other Asian neighbours. For example, in 1994, the inflows into South Asia were less than one quarter of the total FDI flows into 4 NIEs or the ASEAN-4 individually (Lloyd, 1996). The performance of the Pacific island economics is even worse, attracting only one-twentieth of the modest FDI flows going to the South-Asian countries in 1994 (Table 5).

The dismal performance of the South Asian and Pacific countries in attracting FDI inflows in the 1980s and 1990s is attributed primarily to their historical preference for import substitution and inward-looking industrialisation policies over the outward-oriented export-led industrialisation strategies. All South Asian countries were far behind their East and South-East Asian

Table 5. Foreign Direct Investment in Selected Countries of Asia and Pacific Regions (1989–1994). (in Million U.S.$)

	1989	1990	1991	1992	1993	1994	1989–1994
Newly Industrializing	5,609	7,693	7,330	3,957	6,521	7,772	38,882
Economics	1,118	788	1,180	727	588	809	5,210
Korean	2,887	5,575	4,879	2,351	5,016	5,588	26,290
Singapore	1,804	1,330	1,271	879	917	1,375	7,376
Taipei, China							
China, People's of	3,393	3,487	4,366	11,156	27,515	33,787	83,704
Central Asia Republics							
Kazakshtan	—	—	—	473	445	918	
Kyrgyz Republic[a]	—	—	—	1	42	43	
Southeast Asia	4,668	8,399	8,038	9,304	9,499	8,223	46,151
Indonesia	682	1,093	1,482	1,777	2,004	2,109	9,147
Malaysia	1,668	2,332	3,998	5,183	5,006	4,348	22,535
Philippines[b]	563	530	544	228	763	1,126	3,754
Thailand	1,775	2,444	2,014	2,116	1,726	640	10,715
South Asia	580	455	454	805	1,155	2,140	5,589
Bangladesh	2	3	1	14	4	11	35
India[c]	350	165	148	344	600	1,314	2,921
Pakistan	210	244	257	335	346	649	2,041
Sri Lanka	20	43	48	122	195	116	595
Pacific Islands	232	258	258	382	101	112	1,343
Fuji	8	80	15	50	49	69	272
Papua New Guinea	203	155	203	291	1	4	857
Solomon Islands	12	10	15	14	24	9	83
Vanatu	9	13	25	27	27	30	131
Total	14,502	18,293	20,446	25,604	45,264	52,521	176,630

Note:
a. Data include portfolio investment.
b. Data for 1994 refer to net foreign direct investment.
c. Data refer to net foreign direct investment z.
Source: Asian Development Bank (1996).

neighbours in adopting policies to open up their markets for both commodities and capital. These countries also suffer from low levels of development of physical and social infrastructures, small size (except India) and slow growth of the domestic economy. As a result, their domestic technological capability in terms of both availability of scientific manpower and R&D facilities is limited. To these are added labour unrest and political instability in some countries (i.e. Bangladesh) which lead to frequent interruption of working days and consequent production loss. Only India has large domestic market and successfully developed indigenous technological capability to the extent that she exports small-scale technologies abroad. However, India's industrial products being much less competitive in the international market indicates the existence of a puzzling gap between indigenous technological capability and product competitiveness. (Lall, 1993).

2.3.5. FDI and Technology Transfer: the Real Issues

As noted in the beginning, FDI impacts the Macroeconomic performance of the host country in many complex ways. It acts as a source of savings to augment capital accumulation. It is a mechanism for transfer of technology and an agent for the transformation of the host country's industrial structure and commodity composition of exports. FDI may also lead to an increase in the productive capacity of the economy of the host country though augmenting human capital formation or development of activities based on natural resources. These are all very convincing theoretical arguments but very difficult to be supported by empirical evidence. As very aptly noted by Lloyd (1996), regrettably, empirical research has lagged far behind the theories of FDI and MNC behaviour. Methodological problems and data limitation involved in quantifying the impacts of technological change and in estimating the Macroeconomic transformation process preclude proliferation of empirical studies attempting detailed impact assessment.

Analysing the role of FDI in the process of Asian industrialisation in the 1980s, Lloyd (1996) observed that increased intra-Asian movements of capital and labour have been instrumental in transforming the economics of the East and South-East Asian countries through development of new industries and products. The cases of development of the electronics industries in the Republic of Korea and Taiwan and in Penang in Malaysia and Guadalajara in Mexico are cited as examples of development of new industries and products as a result of transfer of technologies by the MNCs to their affiliates in these countries (Lloyd, 1996).

Similarly, the MNCs have been identified as major sources of export growth in many of the Asian economies. For example, the shares of foreign affiliates in the national exports were as high as 57% in Malaysia, 91% in Singapore, 24% in Hong Kong and 17% in Taiwan in the late 1980s and 1990s. This TNC-assisted export growth is said to have been instrumental in maintaining high rates of growth of exports and real output in the Asian countries during the period under study.[8]

3. POLICIES AND INSTITUTIONS DETERMINING FDI FLOWS AND TECHNOLOGY TRANSFER IN THE ESCAP REGION

There is an ongoing debate concerning what policy measures and institutional arrangements should be adopted by the developing countries to attract FDI flows and encourage the MNCs to directly transfer technologies and also to increase the potentials for spillover effects.

In order to encourage private financial and investment flows, the countries of Asia and the Pacific have put in place a diverse range of policy initiatives over time. It is difficult to determine the relative importance of such policy mixes as all have played a part in attracting private investment flows, especially FDI. However, the recent upsurge of inter-Asian, investment flows is commonly ascribed to the policy reforms introduced in the following areas: (i) liberalisation of trade and investment régimes attracting FDI, (ii) improvement of macroeconomic performance, (iii) provision of elaborate support services and incentive package targeted to attract foreign investment, and (iv) improvement of domestic technology effort to strengthen technology absorption capacity. We discuss these policies in turn.

3.1. Liberalisation of Investment Régimes through Market-oriented Reforms

With the pendulum of public opinion starting to surface in favour of FDI since the 1980s as an instrument of economic growth,[9] the developing countries began courting it, especially in the face of rising real interest rates, the debt crisis, and the virtual disappearance of voluntary bank lending.

While various forms of restrictions relating to admission, establishment, ownership and control applying to FDI in the past began to be significantly liberalised by the Asian developing countries since the mid-1980s, the relaxation of controls on inward FDI has been particularly rapid in the East Asian nations, followed by their South-East Asian neighbours, particularly Indonesia, Malaysia, and Thailand. The relaxation measures included several elements, i.e. greater rights of establishments for foreign investors, removal of performance requirements on foreign corporations, privatisation, deregulation and reductions in administrative controls on capital and factor income movements. Further, exchange rate adjustments and liberalisation of commodity trade régimes at a faster rate in these countries greatly facilitated inter-Asian

FDI flows. The macroeconomic stability, high rates of output growth, outward orientation, and market-oriented government policies combined together to enhance investors confidence. Both location specific advantages and a favourable policy environment encouraged inter- and intra-regional mobility of capita and technology, positive interaction between trade and investment, and created dynamic clusters of innovation and growth (Petri, 1997).

The speed of liberalisation of capital flows and trade in goods and services gained momentum in the South Asian countries in the 1990s. The Pacific island economies followed their other Asian neighbours and proceeded gradually with the foreign investment liberalisation measures (ADB, 1996/97).

The effective implementation of FDI policies is critically dependent upon having a favourable regulatory framework. There is evidence that bureaucratic controls and regulations often create long delays in approval of investment projects and in gaining access to utilities in the South Asian countries (Wadhva, 1996). A much better regulatory framework prevailing in the Asian NIEs and the ASEAN member countries made them attractive to foreign investors.

3.2. Promotion of FDI through Incentives

In addition to liberalisation of investment régimes, the Asian countries offer various incentives to attract FDI. These incentives are broadly grouped into three categories: fiscal, financial and others. Generally, these special incentives are widespread and used to attract FDI in specific industries or in some designated areas of the country, particularly export processing zones (EPZs).

In the East Asian countries, the EPZs are termed as "export platforms" which are used to create an enclave economy hospitable to foreign investors and integrated into the global economy without the problems of infrastructure, security, rule of law, and trade policies that plague the rest of the economy. The Asian countries introduced several variants of the export platforms including EPZs, bonded warehouses, special economic zones, and duty drawback systems. The governments supported these institutions with appropriate macroeconomic policies that strengthened the incentives for labour-intensive exports particularly through liberalised trade and payment régimes. However, the efficacy of these incentive schemes in attracting FDI has been debatable on both theoretical and empirical grounds (Naya, 1990). Consequently, there is a preference for selective use of such facilities as instruments of FDI promotion also on the ground that the incentives are a small concern in the decision of the MNCs to invest. It is argued that the MNCs are more concerned with a stable economic environment, developed infrastructure, skilled labour at competitive prices, and an appropriate legal and regulatory framework.

3.3. Macroeconomics Policy Environment

A stable macroeconomic environment characterised by the absence of large budget deficits, excessive monetary expansion and repressed financial systems is a critical prerequisite for strengthening and maintaining the confidence of the foreign investors. Any economy suffering from the symptoms of chronic instability and indicating future problems of inflation, exchange rate fluctuations and overall poor performance scare away the foreign private investors of all categories. As noted earlier, a stable macroeconomic environment and high rates of growth of outputs and exports have been the important driving forces behind the great upsurge of FDI flows into the East Asian and some of the South-East Asian countries in the 1990s. This is referred to as the domestic "virtuous circle" which asserts that the domestic policy reforms creating a market-friendly open economy attracts inflow of foreign investments including technology and management skills which increase the competitiveness of domestic production. A domestic "virtuous circle" can indeed explain how a stable and open economic environment facilitate sustainable high rates of economic growth.

3.4. Domestic Technology Absorption Capacity

The development of technology absorption capabilities in the host countries is a critically important determinant of successful transfer of technologies. Analysing the decisions of the TNCs regarding location of their R&D activities in a number of Asian-Pacific countries (Japan, Hong Kong, India, Indonesia, Malaysia, the Philippines, Singapore, Taiwan and Thailand), Kumar (1996) concludes that the TNCs prefer to locate their R&D activities in the countries offering large markets, adequate technical resources and elaborate infrastructural facilities. It is also essential that the domestic firms have the requisite learning capabilities. The implication is that increased investments need to be made in human development through education and training, in industrial research, and development of the state-of-the-art technology so that a "virtuous circle" of competition, productivity and technology growth can take place and generate spillovers from "learning by doing." Empirical evidence available from other country case studies (i.e. Korea and Thailand) also suggest that in order to effectively acquire, assimilate and diffuse foreign technology, local technological conditions and capabilities must be developed to undertake the reverse engineering tasks and master embodied technology obtained through various modes of transfer (Lee, 1987).

Unfortunately, the development of indigenous innovative capability which is critically dependent upon R&D efforts is still at very low levels in most of the South Asian and Pacific island economies, especially compared to their East Asian neighbours. The Republic of Korea's experience is often cited as a classical example of a close relationship between R&D efforts and technological capability. And yet another useful lesson learned from Korea's experience is that the contribution of the private sector to R&D expenditures has been substantial, increasing from 32% in 1980 to 82% in 1986 (ADB, 1995).

In addition to low R&D efforts, lack of a conscious and aggressive technology strategy, dearth of skilled and technical personnel at various levels, lack of technical information systems, inadequate inter-industry linkages, unfavourable attitudes of the entrepreneurs, and bureaucratic regulations, etc. are other major problems inhibiting growth of the "national innovation system" in many Asian developing countries. This suggests the need for transfer of technological capabilities from the developed Asian countries to those countries in need. The establishment of a regional technology network system may perhaps play a vital role in this process. This is an area where private sector efforts should be supported and co-ordinated jointly by the public sector and various regional development organisations.

4. CONCLUSIONS AND POLICY RECOMMENDATIONS

In tandem with the marked increase in the foreign capital flows globally between the 1980s and 1990s, many Asian countries have become recipients of large private capital flows, especially FDI. Among various benefits brought to the recipient countries by such capital flows, transfer of technology to the host countries has figured prominently. Various forms of technology transfer have contributed to the recipients technological modernisation and productivity growth, with FDI playing the dominant role in most of them. With the exception of Indonesia and Philippines, where primary sectors absorbed 82% and 29% of inward FDI stock, it has concentrated primarily in the manufacturing and service sectors in the other Asian countries.

While a mix of policies and incentives have been adopted by the Asian countries to attract FDI, a stable macroeconomic environment, liberalised trade and investment régimes, a well-developed domestic technological base and a host of fiscal, financial and other incentives have been the major attractions for the FDI flows. However, given the inter-country as well as inter-regional differences in the stage of development, market size, and domestic technological capabilities, some of the Asian countries (i.e. East and South-East Asia) have been more successful then the others (South Asia and Pacific islands) in capturing FDI inflows. Both groups of countries now face formidable challenges to continue to maintain their shares of FDI flows and the direct technological benefits and indirect spillover effects accompanying them. For the less successful countries, the task is relatively more daunting in view of the fact that they have to increasingly depend on the private capital flows in the future since ODA is not expected to be enough and easily available as it was in the past. For the more successful countries, the challenge is to continue to attract FDI flows to sustain the current flow.

The implication is that both groups of countries in the Asian-Pacific region have to evolve appropriate investment and trade strategies both individually and jointly to enhance their prospects for integration with the global economic system and their share of foreign private investment and inter-related technology flows. These challenges have become especially formidable for the East and South-East Asian countries in the wake of currency crises recently engulfing their economies. While highly topical as well as pertinent to any discussion on the economics of the region, this falls outside the scope of the present paper. Nevertheless, none would perhaps deny the inevitable consequences such as loss of investor's confidence, tightening of the fiscal stance, sharp increase in the interest rate and in inflation etc. affecting the economies of the region and thereby having a dampening effect on investments and ultimately on economic growth. Under the circumstances, the prospects for FDI inflows in these countries during the period beyond the 1990s may remain bleak, at least during the medium term or until such time when a turn around in the economic growth prospects takes place under a stable exchange rate régime, an improved export competitiveness, favourable current account position, and ultimately high economic growth.

NOTES

1. The paper analyses only inflows of FDI in the ESCAP region. The outward investment flow in Asia which registered a substantial upward trend from U.S.$8 billion during 1985–1990 to U.S.$30 billion during 1991–1996 (Appendix Table 1) falls outside the purview of the present paper.

2. There is statistical distortion arising from incomplete coverage of some sectors and different realisation rates achieved by different sectors. Again, the actual sectoral distribution does not necessarily reflect comparative advantage of the host country as the distinction is affected by selective FDI policies of the countries concerned.

3. Further, as technology and economic conditions change, new modes of technology transfer are developed and used. A comprehensive discussion of the various modes and models of technology transfer is available in Dahlman (1994) and Lan et al. (1996).

4. An elaborate discussion on the role of MNCs in technology transfer and on the potential for spillovers to the local firms, is available in Yoon et al. (1995).

5. See, for a recent survey of literature providing an update on the nature of controversies concerning the role of MNCs, Enos et al. (1997), Kakazu (1990) and Lan Ping et al. (1996).

6. A country's "national innovation system" is defined broadly to include FDI policies and the network of public and private institutions and agents supporting or undertaking scientific and technological activities including R&D activities, technology diffusion and creation of technical human capital.

7. For an update on the nature and magnitude of FDI flows and the attendant technology flows to North-East China, the reader is referred to Ping et al. (1996).

8. For further details on the impacts of FDI and technology transfer on the overall Macroeconomic transformation process of the host economies, see ADB (1995), UNCTAD (1994) and (1995) and the citations therein.

9. In the late 1960s through the mid-1990s, the MNCs came under severe criticism in the developing countries and were viewed as "suction pumps" designed to perpetuate an exploitative economic system. This period, therefore, witnessed a proliferation of restrictions on FDI inflows in the developing countries, with many of their critics (i.e. Caves (1982), Oman (1993) providing necessary support to the move through highlighting various socio-economic costs associated with FDI.

REFERENCES

Asian Development Bank (ADB) (1997). *Asian Development Outlook, 1996/97*. Manila.

ADB (1995). *Technology Transfer and Development Implications for Developing Asia*. Manila, May.

Asian and Pacific Economic Co-operation (APEC) (1995). Economic Committee, Foreign Direct Investment and APEC Economic Integration, APEC Secretariat.

Ariff, M., & Hill, H. (1989). *Export-oriented Industrialisation: The ASEAN Experience*. Sydney: Allen and Unwin.

Brewer, T. L. (1991). *Foreign Direct Investment in Developing Countries; Patterns, Policies and Prospects*. World Bank: Washington, D.C.

Caves, R. E. (1982). *Multinational Enterprise and Economic Analysis*. Cambridge University Press.

Chen, Y. K. (1993). Foreign Direct Investment in East Asia. *Asian Development Review, 11*(1).

Dahlman, C. J. (1994). Technology Strategy in East Asian Developing Economies. *Journal of Asian Economies, 5*(4), 541–572.

Dunning, J. H. (1994). Multinational Enterprises and Globalization of Innovative Capacity. *Research Policy, 23*(1), 67–88.

Enos, J. L. (1989). Transfer of Technology. *Asian-Pacific Economic Literature, 3*(1), 3–37.

Enos, J., & Lall, S. et al. (1997). Transfer of Technology: An Update. *Asia-Pacific Development Journal*.

ESACP (1997). *Economic and Social Survey of Asia and the Pacific*. New York: United Nations.

Hill, H. (1995). Indonesia's Great Leap Forward? Technology and Policy Issues. *Bulletin of Indonesian Economic Studies, 31*(2), 83–123.

Kumar, N. (1996). Intellectual Property Protection, Market Orientation and Location of Overseas R&D Activities by Multinational Enterprise. *World Development, 24*(4), 673–688.

Kakazu, H. (1990). Industrial Technology Capabilities and Policies in Asian Developing Countries. *Asian Development Review, 8*(2).

Lall, S., & Streeten, P. (1977). *Foreign Investment, Transnationals and Developing Countries*. Oxford University Press: Oxford.

Lall, S. (1993). Foreign Direct Investment in South Asia. *Asian Development Review. 11*(1).

Lall, S. (1995). Industrial Strategy and Policies on Foreign Direct Investment in East Asia. *Transnational Corporations, 4*(3), 1–26.

Lloyd, P. J. (1996). The Role of Foreign Investment in the success of Asian Industrialization. *Journal of Asian Economics, 7*(3), Fall.

Lan P., & Young S. (1996). Foreign direct investment and technology transfer: a case study of foreign direct investment in North-east China. *Transnational Corporations, 5*(1), April.

Naya S. (1990). *Private Sector Development and Enterprise reforms in Growing Asian Economies*. ICEG.

Oman, C. (1984). *New Forms of International Investment in Developing Countries*. OECD: Paris.

Petri, P. A. (1995). The Interdependence of Trade and Investment in the Pacific. In: Chen, K. Y. et al. (Eds), *Corporate Financial Links and Foreign Direct Investment in Asia and the Pacific*. Harper: Australia.

Petri, P. A. (1997). Asian Development Strategies for a Global Economy. In: *IDE, Asia's Challenge in the Coming Century*. Tokyo.

Quinn, J. B. (1969). Technology Transfer by Multinational Companies. *Harvard Business Review, 47*(6), 147–161.

UNCTAD (1990). Periodic Report 1990: Policies, Laws, and Regulations on transfer, application and development of technology. *UNCTAD/ITC/TEC, 16*, New York and Geneva, United Nations.

UNCTAD (1996). *World Investment Report, 1996*. New York and Geneva.

UNCTAD (1997). *World Investment Report, 1997*. New York and Geneva.

UNCTAD (1997). *Trade and Development Report, 1997*. New York and Geneva.

Wadhva, C. D. (1996). *Foreign Direct Investment Policies and Related Institution-Building: the Experience of India*. September.

Yoon, H. et al. (1995). Technology Transfer and Multinational Corporations: The Case of South Korea. *Journal of Asian Economics, 6*(2), Summer.

Young, S., Hood, N., & Peters, E. (1993). Multinational Enterprises and Regional Economic Development. *Regional Studies, 28*(7), 657–677.

Yue, C. S. (1993). Foreign Direct Investment in Asian Economies. *Asian Development Review, 11*(1).

Zhao, H. (1995). Technological Imports and Their Impacts on the Enhancement of China's Indigenous Technological Capability. *Journal of Development Studies, 31*(4), 508–602.

APPENDIX

Table A1. FDI Outflows, by Home Region and Economy, 1985–1996. (in Million U.S.$)

Home region/ economy	1985–1990 (Annual Average)	1991	1992	1993	1994	1995	1996
World	155,578	198,143	201,465	239,090	251,117	338,729	34,684
Developed Countries	145,005	189,782	179,671	204,818	209,726	291,271	294,732
Developing Countries	10,554	8,324	21,695	34,067	40,711	47,034	51,469
Africa	1081	962	441	750	627	647	786
Latin America and the Caribbean	1,354	–453	2,561	2,264	4,171	3,919	3,850
Asia	8109	7,819	18,695	31,042	35,913	42,537	46,816
South, East and South-East Asia	7,378	8,151	17,380	30,280	34,804	41,627	45,675
China	697	913	4,000	4,400	2,000	2,000	2,200
Hong Kong	2,062	2,825	8,254	17,773	21,437	25,000	27,000
India	6	–11	24	41	49	38	43
Indonesia	11	13	52	356	609	603	512
Korea, South	771	1,500	1,208	1,361	2,524	3,529	4,188
Malaysia	281	389	514	1,325	1,817	2,575	1,906
Pakistan	11	–4	–12	–2	1	6	2
Philippines	3	–26	5	374	302	399	182
Singapore	610	526	1,317	2,021	3,104	3,906	4,800
Sri Lanka	1	5	2	7	8	7	8
Taiwan	2861	1854	1869	2451	2460	2678	3069
Thailand	64	167	147	233	493	886	1760
The Pacific10	–4	2	6	4	9	6	
Fiji	13	–4	2	6	4	9	6
Papua New Guinea	–2	—	—	—	—	—	—
Ass LDCs	59	351	30	21	51	23	30
LDC (Asia and the Pacific)	—	—	—	—	—	—	—

Source: UNCTAD, World Investment Report, 1997, FDI/TNC database.

34. AN ANALYSIS OF THAILAND'S CAPITAL FLOWS

Wiboonchutikula Paitoon, Tubtimtong Bangorn, Lakshmi Raut and Chaivichayachat Bundit

1. INTRODUCTION

Thailand is currently facing a severe recession resulting from the currency and financial crisis starting in 1997. Most would attribute the crisis to over-borrowing from abroad for financing growth of unproductive and speculative sectors. In Thailand, it is not the first time that the country experienced economic problems from excessive foreign borrowing. Actually, it had suffered from a financial and debt problem before in the early 1980s. At that time, the problem came from large foreign borrowing in the public sector as the Thai government borrowed heavily for financing the fiscal deficits that grew yearly to a peak of 3.5% of GDP in 1982.

Thailand avoided a large-scale debt crisis as occurred in Latin America by changing the exchange rate system in 1984 from pegging to the U.S. dollar to a system that fixed the Thai baht to a basket of currencies. The Thai government also considerably cut its spending and in 1986 a limit was actually set on the magnitude of foreign borrowing in the public sector. This fiscal discipline resulted in a rapid decline in both the government expenditure and the interest payments on foreign loans. In fact, in the second half of the 1980s when exports grew highly at the rate of 20% a year, real GDP also grew at double digit rates for many consecutive years. In addition, the government revenue rose as the government tax collection increased in large volume. The government budget went into surplus and the problems of public debt soon

Restructuring Asian Economics for the New Millennium, Volume 9B, pages 669–715.
2001 by Elsevier Science B.V.
ISBN: 0-7623-0710-2

disappeared. Actually, throughout 1987 to 1995 the government had its budget in surplus every year without interruption.

The high growth and stable macroeconomic environment since the late 1980s provided enough confidence for Thailand to open up it international financial market. From 1989 to 1993 the Bank of Thailand followed a series of financial market liberalization efforts. First, the interest ceiling on deposits and lending of commercial banks and financial institutions were abolished. Second, foreign exchange controls were freed by allowing foreign exchange earners to open their accounts in foreign currencies. Meanwhile, nonresidents were allowed to open their baht account in Thailand. Third, commercial banks and finance companies were allowed to increase their variety and scope of activities. Lastly, in 1993 the capital flows were liberalized under the Bangkok International Banking Facilities (BIBF) scheme. Qualified local and branches of foreign banks were granted licenses to borrow in the international financial market. The incentive was for investors in Thailand to borrow across borders at a reduced cost and for increased investment to stimulate real income growth (Vichyanond, 1994).

The impact after the opening up of the international financial markets was that Thailand's net capital inflows increased by three times from 1990 to 1995. The structure of capital flows was also changed from direct foreign investment as a major component of the inflows to be dominated by private loans of both the banking and non-banking sectors. Nonresident bath accounts also increased tremendously to gain from interest rate differentials under Thailand's essentially fixed exchange rate system. Some foreign investors also opened the nonresident baht accounts to deposit the savings temporarily before making their investment in the stock market.

All would have been well if Thailand could have continued its miraculous growth with stability that began in the late 1980. Unfortunately, from late 1995 to the middle of 1997, Thailand's economic conditions worsened rapidly. Inflation rose in 1995 but subsisided in 1996. Current account deficits increased to over 8% of GDP in 1995 and persisted for the next two years. Export growth turned from a rate of almost 20% per year to a negative rate in 1996 and declined further in early 1997. On top of all that, there was a scandal in a commercial bank that gave large loans to a group of borrowers without sufficient collateral. With the real estate sector also in a slump, threat of increased nonperforming loans at both the banking and the financial institutions almost led to a run in the deposits. Furthermore, the creditworthiness of the financial sector, as rated by international rating agencies, worsened by the month, and the private sector found it increasingly difficult, if not impossible, to borrow from abroad to cover their increased debt. As the economic malaise continued, the government also had difficulty deciding or implementing a policy. Therefore, political credibility declined and became another factor contributing to the drying-up of capital inflows.

Eventually, deepened and widespread economic and political problems led to a ripe timing for attacking Thailand's currency. The first Thai baht attack was in early 1997 and soon a few more followed. The Bank of Thailand tried hard to defend the baht so as not to increase the foreign debt burden of both the banking and nonbanking sectors which were, in fact, already in enough trouble. As a result of the action, Thailand's foreign reserves were depleted quickly. At the end, the Bank of Thailand had to lead the baht float in July 1997 in order to avoid using up all the foreign reserves. After floating the baht, Thailand went into a currency and financial crisis, and it had to seek loans from the IMF to cover the official reserve position. Also, it had to accept the requirement of the IMF to impose an economic policy package that was designed to be implemented with the access of the loans.

The interesting question is, therefore, whether foreign capital transaction liberalization had played a part in leading Thailand into the financial crisis. Just as investors voiced concerns about some economic problems in the mid-1990s, their confidence was shattered, and the capital flows suddenly dried up. In other words, while foreign capital flows might help Thailand promote economic growth, these flows could be volatile and thus harmful to the stability of the economy. This paper intends to analyze Thailand's capital flows in three sections. In the first section we use time series data of Thailand's foreign capital flows to examine the nature of volatility of the various types of capital flows. In the second and the third sections, we analyze econometric factors determining capital inflows and discover their impact on both growth and stability. Our quantitative analysis will provide implications for policies that are beneficial for managing Thailand's capital flows in the future.

2. NATURE OF THAILAND'S CAPITAL FLOWS

Tables 1 and 3 provide data on Thailand's net capital flows and capital inflows to Thailand from 1985 to 1996. The capital flows are divided by type of instruments namely, direct foreign investment, portfolio investment, private loans, nonresident baht accounts, other private loans, and borrowing in the banking system. These flows are also classified by source country, namely, the U.S., Japan, EU, Hong Kong, Singapore, and others. These tables show clearly that Thailand's net capital flows changed their composition from direct and portfolio investments to private borrowing in the banking sector and in the nonresident baht accounts. In particular, after 1993 loans in the banking sector,

Table 1. Net Private Capital Flows by Type, 1980–1997. (Billion Baht)

Year	Total	Bank	Total Non Bank	Direct Investment	Portfolio Investment	Private Loans	Non-Resident Baht A/C	Others
1980	22.59	–9.62	32.21	3.82	1.03	11.28	2.59	13.50
1981	7.21	–7.73	14.94	6.36	0.02	17.69	3.00	–12.13
1982	10.05	–7.14	17.19	4.34	0.61	8.43	3.68	0.13
1983	34.14	15.45	18.68	8.19	0.34	4.20	5.33	0.62
1984	42.86	1.84	41.03	9.62	–0.09	24.57	8.26	–1.34
1985	–4.33	–14.24	9.91	4.38	–3.86	2.11	10.81	–3.53
1986	–13.03	–21.97	8.94	6.88	2.52	–3.33	9.67	–6.80
1987	26.15	5.94	20.21	4.71	12.86	–16.01	10.59	8.06
1988	104.21	21.49	82.72	27.35	11.19	4.64	21.72	17.83
1989	155.31	–7.72	163.02	44.41	36.66	46.93	28.10	6.92
1990	301.78	48.05	253.73	61.12	11.51	114.89	34.31	31.90
1991	293.36	6.61	286.74	47.11	3.85	142.71	52.43	40.65
1992	255.82	49.05	206.78	50.30	14.10	69.16	55.28	17.94
1993	292.38	45.19	247.20	34.46	122.63	–45.56	107.26	28.41
1994	363.03	346.76	16.27	4.37	27.50	–134.85	96.41	22.84
1995	524.01	279.68	244.33	29.06	81.72	38.09	84.16	11.29
1996	176.77	126.77	50.00	36.82	88.24	138.02	73.76	–286.86
1997	78.46	61.50	16.96	26.55	40.63	29.03	91.74	–170.98

Source: Bank of Thailand.

Table 2. Change in Composition of Net Private Capital Flows, 1986–1996. (Percentage)

Net Capital Flows	1986–1989	1990–1992	1993–1996
Bank	11.1	17.5	60.8
Non Bank			
Direct Investment	25.0	17.6	7.1
Portfolio Investment	13.1	18.5	15.2
Loans	27.4	19.9	0.9
Non-Resident Baht Account	17.2	21.8	16.1
Others	6.2	4.7	0.1

Source: Bank of Thailand.

together with nonresident baht accounts, constituted over three quarters of the total net flows.

Table 4 shows that most capital flows into Thailand came from Japan, Hong Kong, Singapore and the U.S. Furthermore, while direct foreign investment came mostly from Japan, most of the rest of the inflows came from Singapore and Hong Kong. However, the financial flows from Hong Kong and Singapore did not originate entirely from these two countries. In fact, they are offshore financial centers acting as intermediaries for investors and borrowers from many other countries. Besides Japan, which was very active in the banking activities in Singapore and Hong Kong, it is very difficult to precisely determine the ultimate source of the inflows channeled through these two financial centers into Thailand.

Table 5 shows net capital flows of direct foreign investment and portfolio foreign investment by invested sector from 1987 to 1997. There was a major change in the sectors that foreign investors invested in Thailand over the past decade. In the late 1980s, about half of total direct foreign investment was in the industrial sector, most production of which was for export. However, for four to five years before Thailand's economic crisis, about 40% of total direct foreign investment was invested in the real estate sector. The same is true for the portfolio investment in Thailand. From 1990 to 1992, about 40% of portfolio foreign investment was in the industrial sector. From 1993 to 1996, most portfolio investment was shifted to the real estate sector. If we consider that the real estate sector is actually a nontraded good sector which could easily be manipulated by speculators, the concentration of investment in this sector could expose foreign investors to both foreign exchange and speculative risks.

Table 3. Private Nonbank Capital Inflows by Type, 1980–1996.
(Billion Baht)

Year	Total	Direct Investment	Portfolio Investment	Private Loans	Non-Resident Baht A/C	Others Capital Flows
1980	99.401	9.259	1.096	30.269	2.799	55.978
(%)	(100.0)	(9.3)	(1.1)	(30.5)	(2.8)	(56.3)
1981	116.515	9.342	0.277	33.028	3.998	69.870
(%)	(100.0)	(8.0)	(0.2)	(28.3)	(3.4)	(60.1)
1982	124.328	9.597	0.615	42.624	6.372	65.120
(%)	(100.0)	(7.7)	(0.5)	(34.3)	(5.1)	(52.4)
1983	122.844	13.994	0.042	34.827	8.628	65.353
(%)	(100.0)	(11.3)	(0.3)	(28.3)	(7.0)	(53.1)
1984	160.386	16.977	2.416	70.438	10.308	60.247
(%)	(100.0)	(10.6)	(1.5)	(43.9)	(6.4)	(37.6)
1985	139.193	10.167	4.079	51.122	13.133	60.692
(%)	(100.0)	(7.3)	(2.9)	(36.7)	(9.4)	(43.7)
1986	112.684	10.526	3.054	48.084	10.855	40.165
(%)	(100.0)	(9.3)	(2.7)	(42.7)	(9.6)	(35.7)
1987	130.065	12.541	17.148	27.659	11.359	61.358
(%)	(100.0)	(9.6)	(13.2)	(21.3)	(8.7)	(47.2)
1988	204.592	32.738	27.754	45.287	25.337	73.476
(%)	(100.0)	(16.0)	(13.6)	(22.1)	(12.4)	(35.9)
1989	348.522	53.079	64.796	103.128	30.270	97.249
(%)	(100.0)	(15.3)	(18.6)	(29.7)	(8.7)	(27.7)
1990	540.109	77.267	87.642	185.646	40.178	149.376
(%)	(100.0)	(14.3)	(16.2)	(34.4)	(7.4)	(27.7)
1991	967.451	94.128	58.586	347.210	306.084	161.443
(%)	(100.0)	(9.7)	(6.1)	(35.9)	(31.6)	(16.7)
1992	1,340.172	135.068	86.375	368.376	576.483	173.870
(%)	(100.0)	(10.1)	(6.4)	(27.5)	(43.0)	(13.0)
1993	2,944.924	67.340	277.253	460.950	1,946.960	192.421
(%)	(100.0)	(2.3)	(9.4)	(15.7)	(66.1)	(6.5)
1994	6,370.151	62.039	225.916	44.096	5,804.325	233.775
(%)	(100.0)	(0.9)	(3.3)	(6.5)	(85.8)	(3.5)
1995	11,501.126	76.746	248.393	533.703	10,370.215	272.069
(%)	(100.0)	(0.7)	(2.2)	(4.6)	(90.2)	(2.3)
1996	16,376.059	103.369	250.755	635.430	15,092.368	294.137
(%)	(100.0)	(0.6)	(1.5)	(3.9)	(92.2)	(1.8)
Change in composition, 1980–1986						
1980–1990	100.0	10.4	5.5	31.8	7.4	45.0
1990–1993	100.0	9.1	9.5	28.4	37.0	16.0
1994–1996	100.0	0.7	2.3	5.0	89.4	2.5

Source: Bank of Thailand.

Table 4.1. Net Direct Foreign Investment by Source Country, 1987–1997. (Billion Baht)

	1987	1988	1989	1990	1991	1992	1993	1994	1995	1996	1997
TOTAL	9.040	27.964	45.698	64.695	51.389	53.691	43.812	33.241	49.887	57.472	117.552
Japan	3.269	14.608	18.762	27.931	15.593	8.572	7.733	3.091	13.856	13.250	44.071
U.S.A.	1.816	3.185	5.220	6.154	5.919	11.788	7.236	3.909	6.471	10.870	23.031
Hong Kong	0.796	2.795	5.716	7.027	11.566	14.549	4.898	8.004	6.948	5.444	15.704
Taiwan	0.687	3.136	5.062	7.160	2.754	2.221	1.237	2.074	2.405	3.492	6.135
ASEAN	0.531	1.647	2.812	6.666	6.576	7.170	1.522	4.919	3.989	7.804	9.132
– Singapore	0.537	1.572	2.748	6.136	6.469	6.722	1.545	4.630	3.394	6.969	8.300
E.U.	0.940	2.248	3.819	4.212	3.964	6.887	6.092	2.636	4.651	4.162	10.487
Others	1.005	0.345	4.307	5.545	5.018	2.504	15.094	8.608	11.567	12.450	8.992

Source: Bank of Thailand.

Table 4.2. Net Portfolio Foreign Investment by Source Country, 1987–1997. (Billion Baht)

	1987	1988	1989	1990	1991	1992	1993	1994	1995	1996	1997
TOTAL	12.862	11.185	36.659	11.508	0.928	11.512	67.850	–10.283	52.759	28.437	122.034
Japan	0.105	1.187	0.192	1.268	–0.763	–1.145	0.531	–0.115	1.000	0.562	1.005
U.S.A.	0.981	2.688	1.654	6.094	0.536	–0.705	3.745	4.593	1.172	1.204	–13.716
Hong Kong	7.712	–0.403	11.764	9.012	7.301	20.634	10.165	5.705	6.497	–4.465	42.149
Taiwan	0.001	0.099	0.703	3.176	–0.003	–0.092	–0.230	–0.568	–0.507	0.084	–0.438
ASEAN	1.193	3.982	12.090	1.037	–2.353	–1.881	51.179	–1.935	36.115	26.269	57.118
– Singapore	1.191	3.975	12.037	0.941	–2.307	–1.850	51.130	–2.169	36.619	26.278	57.039
E.U.	2.801	3.500	9.258	24.994	–1.763	–7.067	0.321	–20.734	3.169	3.803	33.071
Others	0.069	0.132	0.998	–34.074	–2.026	1.768	2.140	2.771	5.313	0.980	2.845

Source: Bank of Thailand.

Table 4.3. Net Private Loans by Source Country, 1991–1997. (Billion Baht)

	1991	1992	1993	1994	1995	1996	1997
TOTAL	15.858	10.979	8.897	1.873	2.695	–2.877	4.720
Japan	3.127	0.791	0.423	–3.950	1.400	–2.815	–1.368
U.S.A.	1.512	0.170	2.147	0.387	0.139	–1.454	0.600
Hong Kong	4.433	3.295	0.578	1.640	0.605	0.908	3.275
Taiwan	0.079	0.019	–0.003	–0.147	–0.017	0.108	2.198
ASEAN	4.442	4.915	0.505	3.321	–0.105	1.687	–1.145
– Singapore	4.438	4.783	0.667	3.321	–0.050	1.629	–1.101
E.U.	1.122	1.351	2.524	0.218	0.883	–1.179	0.468
Others	1.143	0.439	2.722	0.403	–0.210	–0.132	0.692

Source: Bank of Thailand.

Table 4.4. Net Non Resident Baht Accounts by Source Country, 1992–1996. (Billion Baht)

	1992	1993	1994	1995	1996
TOTAL	44.52	67.83	51.14	84.16	76.76
Japan	2.44	–6.80	11.29	2.75	–11.39
U.S.A.	–1.17	–24.22	–98.17	–6.00	–49.76
Hong Kong	10.13	–30.14	9.55	11.14	10.55
Taiwan	1.56	4.73	9.55	11.14	10.55
ASEAN	27.70	71.82	69.78	25.19	89.01
– Singapore	27.72	71.27	68.43	22.66	82.00
E.U.	6.24	52.03	10.17	1.69	–18.42
Others	–2.39	0.42	38.97	38.26	46.24

Source: Bank of Thailand.

Therefore, it is interesting to find out whether these types of foreign investments might be as volatile as other short-term inflows.

According to the conventional belief, both bank loans and nonresident baht accounts are short-term flows, while direct and portfolio investment are long-term flows. The short-term inflows tend to be speculative and easily reversible, while the long term inflows are based on economic fundamentals, and the flows are reversed only when the fundamentals change. Therefore, the change in Thailand's capital flow composition might be considered as a factor explaining

Table 5.1. Net Direct Foreign Investment by Sector, 1987–1997. (Billion Baht)

	1987	1988	1989	1990	1991	1992	1993	1994	1995	1996	1997
Financial Institution	442.8	2,576.3	2,843.2	4,530.8	6,822.5	6,555.1	1,641.8	171.2	642.8	1,822.7	24,559.0
Trade	853.3	3,881.5	6,821.9	12,928.5	7,726.4	7,096.0	5,546.0	8,561.0	11,111.6	13,797.6	28,440.0
Construction	1,349.1	1,841.0	6,925.5	3,300.9	3,306.4	14,534.3	3,853.2	1,751.6	906.1	1,782.5	6,648.0
Mining and Quarrying	192.0	472.6	575.1	1,139.2	2,072.8	3,125.5	3,175.7	1,310.3	1,418.6	489.6	934.0
Agriculture	285.9	315.2	603.4	762.7	597.8	–150.6	330.1	–157.7	232.3	51.2	71.0
Industry	4,749.2	16,162.4	21,866.1	31,003.4	23,839.6	9,259.4	11,430.2	12,873.1	14,114.3	17,941.8	44,652.0
Service	748.5	1,109.0	1,593.5	2,054.0	1,654.7	2,150.5	468.1	1,403.5	2,186.1	3,162.2	6,675.0
Investment	—	—	—	-	-	195.3	–405.1	3,670.2	–1,954.3	2,456.8	—
Real Estate	42.9	1,419.1	7,108.4	8,421.2	3,618.9	9,698.5	17,592.4	11,862.6	21,245.8	19,054.0	2,107.0
Others	—	186.4	360.5	554.3	1,750.9	1,227.0	178.9	–8,204.8	–16.4	629.6	3,466.0
TOTAL	9,043.7	27,963.5	45,697.6	64,695.0	51,390.0	53,691.0	43,811.3	33,241.0	49,886.9	61,188.0	117,552.0

Source: Bank of Thailand.

Table 5.2. Net Portfolio Foreign Investment by Sector, 1990–1996. (Billion Baht)

	1990	1991	1992	1993	1994	1995	1996
Financial Institution	1,163.4	256.2	290.5	1,641.8	171.2	642.8	1,822.7
Trade	10,099.9	6,248.1	5,431.5	5,136.4	7,039.4	10,715.6	14,551.0
Construction	3,209.1	2,144.2	14,329.5	3,500.5	1,498.8	832.4	1,425.3
Mining and Quarrying	1,124.8	2,076.4	2,788.6	2,906.4	1,108.9	1,214.0	527.0
Agriculture	416.3	185.6	111.9	351.7	–95.3	278.3	84.1
Industry	20,648.6	17,316.7	6,254.9	7,543.7	11,541.8	15,085.8	19,850.0
Service	1,079.4	1,351.9	1,956.7	812.8	1,533.7	2,037.9	8,806.4
Investment	0.0	0.0	172.9	–305.4	919.9	–2,163.3	756.8
Real Estate	4,784.8	4,669.8	10,173.6	13,134.8	15,872.1	18,544.4	18,909.4
Others	473.5	1,283.4	1,201.9	192.3	–8,222.5	4.1	3,731.0
Total	42,999.8	35,532.3	42,712.0	34,915.0	31,368.0	47,192.0	70,463.7

Source: Bank of Thailand.

parts of the current financial and currency crisis. In this section, we aim to examine the nature of Thailand's capital flows following the methodologies used by Claessens et al. (1995), Chuhan et al. (1996) and Walsh et al. (1998).

Table 5.3. Net Private Loans Sector, 1990–1995. (Billion Baht)

	1990	1991	1992	1993	1994	1995
Financial Institution	9,783.1	12,395.8	11,556.0	22,113.1	13,518.6	49,047.4
Trade	21,192.9	16,198.9	4,860.7	–561.3	–13,464.6	10,100.0
Construction	3,442.2	2,418.5	186.7	442.3	–743.4	–403.2
Mining and Quarrying	–243.6	647.8	–318.1	–858.7	–771.5	31.5
Agriculture	1,834.4	51.5	690.5	–692.2	–284.6	371.8
Industry	47,118.4	77,133.6	45,105.1	26,378.9	–1,665.6	55,060.7
Service	2,534.4	1,799.2	1,669.4	–106.6	825.3	8,121.8
Investment	0.0	5,336.5	–3,233.5	2,190.2	–1,369.7	17,113.2
Real Estate	19,212.5	27,768.6	6,514.5	–4,554.4	10,221.5	11,171.5
Others	10,014.2	1,658.3	2,126.9	29.7	2,490.0	–472.7
Total	114,888.5	145,408.7	69,158.2	44,381.0	8,756.0	150,142.0

Source: Bank of Thailand.

We use monthly data of net capital flows classified by type from January 1991 to December 1997 for our study. We choose this period of time because in 1990, Thailand liberalized the foreign exchange market and interest rate structure. In 1993, the Bank of Thailand liberalized the banking sector and established BIBF in order to facilitate foreign borrowing and to help reduce funding costs. Finally, starting in 1997, Thailand experienced the worst economic crisis and recession in decades after the second World War.

2.1. Persistency

We examine the hypothesis that changes in the composition of the net capital flows in the decade before Thailand's economic crisis matter, and it could explain part of the ongoing currency and financial problems. As shown earlier, Thailand increasingly relied on private foreign borrowing in the 1990s, and, therefore, the net capital flows were dominated by debt instead of equity investment. We suspect that portfolio investment, bank loans, nonresident baht accounts, and other private loans, which are generally used for financing short-term investments, are more volatile than direct foreign investment and private loans, which are generally used for financing long-term investments. In the literature, short-term flows are sometimes referred to as "hot money," in the sense that they are speculative and likely to flow in and out quickly; whereas the long-term flows are known as "cool money," in the sense that they are more likely to be persistent or to keep flowing in for a continuing period of time. We would like to examine empirical validity of such belief.

To do so, we apply autocorrelation functions of the time series analysis to our monthly data of capital flows, separated by type and by time period. If the capital flows were persistent and not volatile we expect the autocorrelation to be positive. On the contrary, if the flows were not persistent or they were volatile, we expect the auto-correlation to be zero or negative. The parameter estimates are shown in Table 6. From 1990 to 1993, capital flows in the form of direct foreign investment, bank loans, and nonresident baht accounts exhibit low autocorrelations with signs changing from month to month. Meanwhile, net flows in the form of portfolio investment and private loans show positive autocorrelations for a certain time span but the coefficients turned negative afterwards. From 1994 to 1997, except for private nonbank loans, the autocorrelation coefficients of the rest of the capital flows were not significantly different from zero. For some types of the flows, the autocorrelation coefficients seemed to alternate their signs from one lagged period to another. Therefore, our data suggest that almost all flows, both short-term and long-term, seem to become more volatile or less persistent after the early 1990s.

Table 6.1. Autocorrelation of Private Capital Flows by Type, 1990–1997.

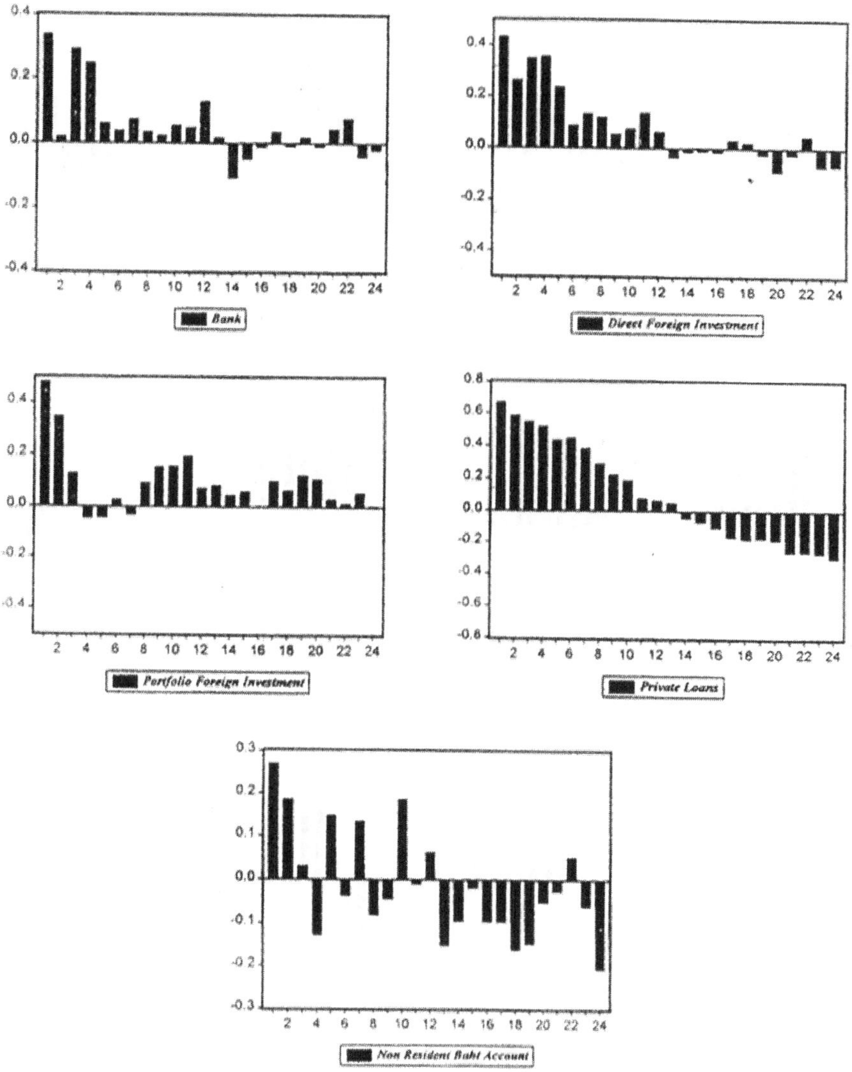

Table 6.2. Autocorrelation of Private Capital Flows by Type, 1990–1993.

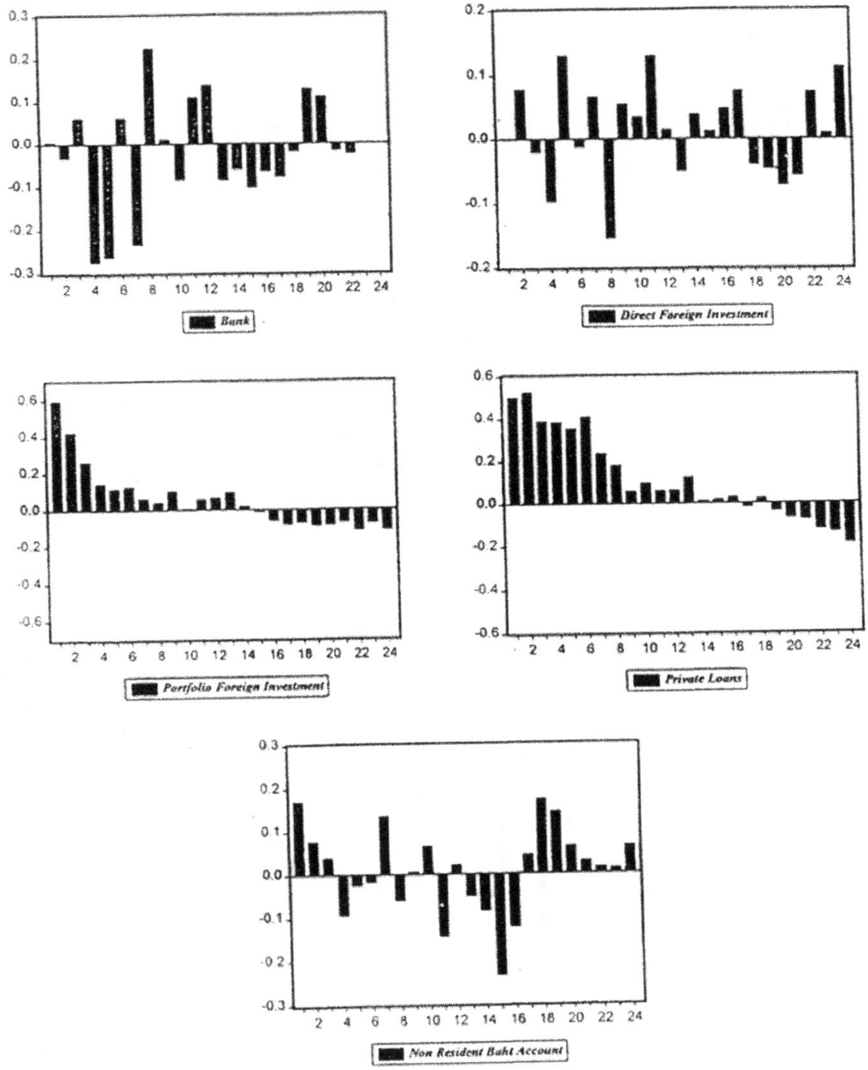

Table 6.3. Autocorrelation of Private Capital Flows by Type, 1990–1997.

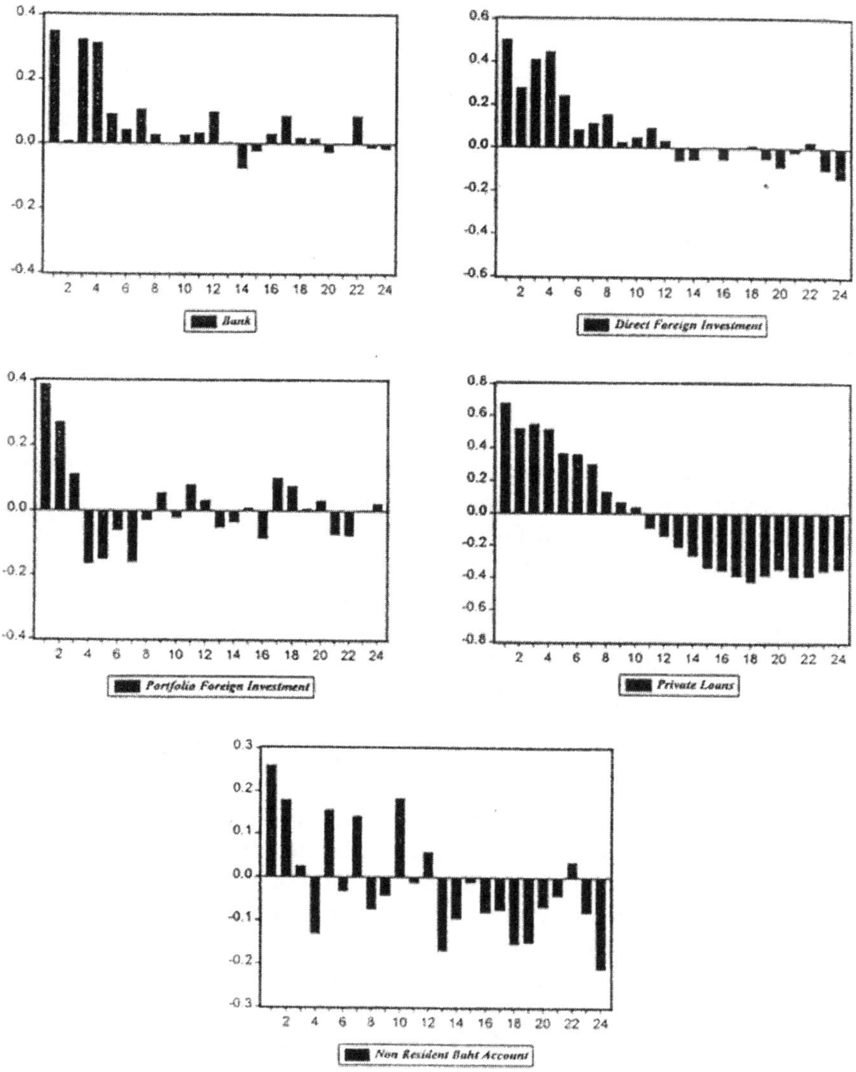

Table 7. Q Statistics and Significance Levels.

	Jan 1994–Dec 1997	Jan 1990–Dec 1993	Jan 1990–Dec 1997
Bank	19.831	12.463	24.204
Prob.	0.228	0.712	0.085
Direct Investment	44.320	5.303	64.252
Prob.	0.000	0.994	0.000
Portfolio Investment	18.331	36.443	49.546
Prob.	0.305	0.003	0.000
Private Loans	116.140	67.126	214.390
Prob.	0.000	0.000	0.000
Non Resident Baht Account	14.634	11.241	26.695
Prob.	0.552	0.794	0.045

To test whether the autocorrelations, which were individually estimated to have low values, were different from zero jointly, we estimated autocorrelations up to lag 15 and computed Q-statistics on the joint significance of the 15 autocorrelations for each type of capital flows. Table 7 shows that from 1990 to 1993 the Q-statistics of private nonbank loans and portfolio investment were higher than those of direct foreign investment, bank loans, and nonresident baht accounts. From 1994 to 1997, private, nonbank loans had the highest value of Q-statistics while the value of the rest of the capital flows remained low. This confirms the earlier finding that when we decompose our analysis into two subperiods, namely, one before and the other after 1993, we find that all types of capital flows became more volatile after 1993.

Another method we use for detecting whether different types of capital flows were similar in terms of their persistency is the augmented Dickey-Fuller unit root test with optimal lags being judged by the Akaike Information Criterion. The test examines each type of capital flows in terms of its stationarity. If the capital flow series differed in their stationarity, then they might support the notion that capital flows were dissimilar. That is, some flows might be more persistent than others.

Table 8 shows the augmented Dickey-Fuller test statistics for the entire period of 1990 to 1997 and the breakdown periods of 1990–1993, 1994–1996, and 1995–1997. For the entire period, all but one type of capital flows (namely private loans) was able to reject the nonstationarity hypothesis. For the subperiod of 1990–1993, none was able to reject the nonstationarity hypothesis. However, for the later subperiods of either 1994–1997 or

Table 8. Test of Nonstationarity.

	Jan 1990–Dec 1997	Jan 1990–Dec 1993	Jan 1994–Dec 1997
Bank	–1.801	–4.222	–1.262
Number of lags	2	0	1
Direct Investment	–3.815	–4.824	3.097
Number of lags	0	1	6
Portfolio Investment	–5.715	0.909	4.901
Number of lags	0	2	3
Private Loans	–0.534	–1.255	–0.322
Number of lags	3	1	2
Non Resident Baht Account	–3.114	–4.355	–2.218
Number of lags	4	0	4

1995–1997, there were more types of flows that the nonstationarity hypothesis could not be rejected. Again, we may conclude that the flows became more volatile in the latter subperiod, and they were increasing similarly in terms of their instability.

The stationarity tests and autoregressions both address the issue of persistence in a univariate analysis. However, if we set our analysis in a multivariate framework, we will be able to detect some relationships among the capital flows. The detected relationships will suggest whether the flows had any differences in terms of their persistency. For example, one flow might have an effect on both its own future and that of other flows' future. In contrast, for another flow, it might have an effect on its own future, but it was not influenced by any other flows. In this case, we may interpret that the latter flow was more persistent than the former flow.

We use Granger causality test to test the above relationships and to detect whether there were differences among capital flows. Table 9 shows that during 1990–1993, except for direct foreign investment, each of the rest of the flows was caused by at least one other flow. In contrast, there is no evidence that direct foreign investment was Granger-caused by any other flows. However, from 1994–1997, we see that all flows were Granger-caused by each other, implying that there were no differences among flows. This implies that the flows were getting similar in terms of their volatility after the early 1990s. In other words, before 1993, except for direct foreign investment, each of the rest of the flows followed other flows, while direct foreign investment did not. But after 1993, all flows followed one another, and they became less persistent.

Table 9. Granger Causality Among Flows.

			Prob. F
Jan 1990–Dec 1993			
Portfolio Investment	Cause	Non Resident Baht Account	0.010
Non Resident Baht Account	Cause	Portfolio Investment	0.013
	Cause	Private Loans	0.014
Jan 1994–Dec 1997			Prob. F
Bank Loans	Cause	Direct Investment	0.013
	Cause	Non Resident Baht Account	0.089
Direct Investment	Cause	Private Loans	0.023
	Cause	Non Resident Baht Account	0.042
Portfolio Investment	Cause	Bank	0.012
	Cause	Direct Investment	0.097
Private Nonbank Loans	Cause	Direct Investment	0.033

We next use a vector autoregression (VAR) to examine the relationships among all flows. Each VAR has five equations, one for each type of flows. The equations express each flow its own past values and those of the other flows. Table 10 shows the results for 1990–1993 and 1994–1997. It is clearly shown that direct foreign investment was different from other flows: that the variation of direct foreign investment could not be explained by contemporaneous changes in other flows, while the rest seem to influence each other. Here it shows that direct foreign investment had characteristics slightly different from other flows in term of its persistency. Thus, while it is true that the nature of direct foreign investment in terms of its volatility become more similar to other short-term capital flows after early 1990s, the multivariate results seem to suggest that, after all, direct foreign investment was different from other flows in the sense that it responded less to the disturbances in other flows than other types of capital flows did.

2.2. *Volatility*

We also test the predictability of each type of capital flows by computing root mean square errors and the Theil Inequality coefficient. Our hypothesis is that long-term flows are more predictable than short-term flows. It is easier to capture systematically the patterns of long-term flows than the short-term flows, and it is easier to predict the long-term flows by simply using their past value. In our investigation, we test all forms of capital flows with different

Table 10. VAR Estimation of Capital Flows.

	Jan 1990–Dec 1993		Jan 1994–Dec 1996		Jan 1994–Dec 1997	
	Coefficient	S.E.	Coefficient	S.E.	Coefficient	S.E.
Dependent variable is Bank Loans						
Bank Loans	0.4501	0.3383	–0.3489*	0.2741	0.2999	0.2468
Direct Investment	–1.7506	0.1727	–1.2793	2.0324	–5.1652*	2.1275
Portfolio Investment	0.3271	0.9184	0.1196	0.5570	1.0118*	0.5725
Private Loans	0.9013*	0.4409	–0.7448*	0.3040	–0.1654	0.4073
Non Resident Baht Account	0.5672	0.1345	–0.2794	0.2528	0.1903	0.2342
R^2	0.2483		0.2147		0.3375	
Dependent variable is Direct Investment						
Bank Loans	–0.0612	0.0519	0.0014	0.0242	–0.0158	0.0290
Direct Investment	–0.1007	0.2647	–0.1725	0.1795	0.5827	0.2498
Portfolio Investment	–0.0160	0.1408	0.0133	0.0492	–0.0041	0.0672
Private Loans	–0.0327	0.0676	0.0222	0.0269	–0.0247	0.0478
Non Resident Baht Account	–0.1128	0.2062	0.0003	0.0223	–0.0294	0.0275
R^2	0.1179		0.0047		0.3312	
Dependent variable is Portfolio Investment						
Bank Loans	0.2124	0.1879	0.1269*	0.0755	0.0240	0.0673
Direct Investment	–1.1245	0.2647	0.0554	0.5599	0.3655	0.5796
Portfolio Investment	1.0574*	0.5102	–0.1483	0.1534	–0.1276	0.1560
Private Loans	–0.3959*	0.2449	0.1744*	0.0838	0.0653	0.1110
Non Resident Baht Account	–0.1736	–0.2323	0.1488*	0.0697	–0.0521	0.0638
R^2	0.4585		0.2992		0.0560	
Dependent variable is Private Loans						
Bank Loans	–0.0866	0.2222	0.0066	0.1304	0.0189	0.0705
Direct Investment	1.2385	1.1346	–0.1650	0.9666	–1.4594*	0.6072
Portfolio Investment	–0.3012	0.6033	–0.0734	0.2649	0.0676	0.1634
Private Loans	–0.0196	0.2896	0.7064*	0.1446	0.6912*	
Non Resident Baht Account	–1.4431*	0.8834	0.0465	0.1203	0.0861	0.0669
R^2	0.3465		0.4983		0.5964	
Dependent variable is Non Resident Baht Account						
Bank Loans	0.1280*	0.0973	0.3949*	0.2398	–0.0043	0.2110
Direct Investment	0.1154	0.4966	1.6469	0.1778	1.1006	1.8182
Portfolio Investment	–0.4203	0.2641	–0.2107	0.4873	–2.9897	0.4893
Private Loans	–0.0246	0.1268	0.2401	0.2660	0.1497	0.3481
Non Resident Baht Account	0.3374	0.38681	0.2926	0.2212	0.0270	0.2002
R^2	0.2190		0.1794		0.0240	

* Denotes reject of the null hypothesis at 5% significance level.

types of ARIMA (p,d,q) to search for suitable representative models. We finally find that AR(3) is the most appropriate model in our analysis. Next, we computed the Theil Inequality coefficients. If the coefficient is close to zero, it implies a perfect fit of the model. If, in the opposite, the coefficient is close to one, it implies that the estimated time series models do not work well. Our test results are shown in Table 10. For all subperiods, direct foreign investment is the only type of capital flows that was most predictable, while bank loans and nonresident baht accounts had the highest coefficients, implying the least predictable.

The above result is confirmed by computing the volatility index based on the ARCH and GARCH models. The ARCH model of Engle (1982) assumes that movements of capital flows are subject to volatility clustering. It, therefore, creates heteroscedasticity and volatility when large changes in capital flows are followed by large changes in either direction. The GARCH model (Bollerslov, 1986) generalizes the above ARCH model by allowing the current conditional volatility to depend on both error terms of the ARCH model and the past conditioned volatility. Hence, the model takes into account the volatility that comes from one extreme flow followed by another, and thus, measures the volatility more efficiently.

We firstly construct the volatility index from the mean of the variance of GARCH (1,1) for each type of capital flows. Then we compute the index in percentage term in order to compare degrees of volatility among the flows. The result is shown in Table 11. For all subperiods, the volatility index of bank loans was the highest, followed by nonresident baht accounts, private loans, portfolio investment and direct investment. In the end, both bank loans and nonresident baht accounts were the most volatile capital flows, and the volatility was intensified in the few years before the currency and financial crisis in 1997.

3. DETERMINANTS OF THAILAND'S FOREIGN CAPITAL FLOWS

In order to find determinants of each type of foreign capital flows, we use the cointegration method to find a long-run relationship between each type of the flows and factors that significantly influence it. The estimation method follows three steps. Firstly, we use the Dickey and Fuller unit root test to test for stationarity of the capital flows data. If there are autocorrelation problems, we apply the Augmented Dickey-Fuller test method to correct them before we proceed to the next step. Secondly, we find the long-run relationships among the variables by constructing the Johansen's likelihood ratio test to search for an optimal lag and numbers of cointegration vectors used in the model. Thirdly, we construct the error-correction mechanism to explain the short run adjustment process towards the long run equilibrium.

3.1. Direct Foreign Investment

In the 1980s, direct foreign investment was the major component of Thailand's capital flows. Direct foreign investment, mainly from Japan and the Asia NICs, whose price competitiveness and access to world markets had deteriorated, flowed into Thailand in large amounts in the late 1980s. The contribution of direct foreign investment increased from 5% during 1970 to 1986 to about 10% during 1987 to 1990. Of all the foreign investment inflow, about 50% was invested in the manufacturing sector, concentrated in the electronic and the labor intensive goods industries producing for export. At that time, Thailand's relatively low wages, foreign investment promotion, and GSP privileges, added to the already favourable investment climate, made it a major foreign investment recipient.

From 1991 to 1996, Thailand's capital flows had changed their composition from direct foreign investment to portfolio, and in the most recent year, to

Table 11. Volatality Index of Capital Flows.

	Mean of Conditional Variance	(%)
1990.1–1997.12		
Bank Loans	1180000000	100.00
Direct Investment	8427308	0.71
Portfolio Investment	66822876	5.66
Private Loans	163000000	13.81
Non Resident Baht Account	521000000	44.15
1990.1–1993.12		
Bank Loans	435000000	100.00
Direct Investment	16997096	3.91
Portfolio Investment	61722262	14.19
Private Loans	125000000	28.74
Non Resident Baht Account	105000000	24.14
1994.1–1997.12		
Bank Loans	1710000000	100.00
Direct Investment	22603468	1.32
Portfolio Investment	90154692	5.27
Private Loans	190000000	11.11
Non Resident Baht Account	780000000	45.61

private borrowing in both the banking and nonbanking sectors. Direct foreign investment declined at the rate of about 2% a year during 1991 to 1996. Major investors from Japan and Asian NICs reduced their direct foreign investment in Thailand in response to prolonged recession in Japan and the strategy of shifting their export base from Thailand to lower-wage countries such as China, Vietnam, India, and Mexico. It is interesting to note that the sectors the foreign investors invested in Thailand were also subject to changes in the first half of the 1990s. As mentioned earlier, in the late 1980s, about half of the total direct foreign investment was in the industrial sector. However, for four to five years before Thailand's crisis, about 40% of total direct foreign investment was invested in the real estate sector. The source countries were also changed from Japan to an unspecificed group of countries aggregated as "others" in the table.

Survey articles on determinants of direct foreign investment in LDCs can be found in Agarwal (1980) and De Mello, Jr. (1997). Here, we postulate that Thailand's direct foreign investment is dependent upon factors grouped into two categories. The first group includes characteristics of the host country, namely, Thailand's real GDP growth, production costs, and domestic policies. The second group includes factors that push foreign investors to invest in Thailand, such as home country's real income growth, and capital cost in the host country in comparison with that in Thailand.

In the first group we use the following variables for measuring the host country's pull factors: (1) real GDP growth reflecting the size of the domestic market as well as the rapid expansion of the economy (the higher Thailand's real GDP growth the greater direct foreign investment flowing into the country can be expected); (2) real wages representing Thailand's comparative advantage as a low labor cost country, suitable for direct investment in labor-intensive goods for export to a third country; (3) real depreciation of the Thai baht favoring price competitiveness of Thailand's exports and attracting foreign investors using Thailand as the export base; and (4) Thailand's openness policies represented by export promotion and import liberalization, eventually leading to increased export and import as a percentage of GDP. The more open the host country's economy, the more direct foreign investment it can attract.

The second group of variables representing the push factors in the home country includes : (1) real GDP growth of the investing countries (it is presumed that high growth in the home country leads to a greater possibility for investment expansion from home to abroad); and (2) differential investment cost between the host and the home countries. Here we use differences between the U.S. government long-term bond yield and Thailand's discount rate as the proxy. The U.S. government bond yield represents a summary measure of the

Table 12. Determinants of Direct Foreign Investment.

Table 12.1. Ordinary Least Squares (OLS) Results.
(Dependent Variable is FDI)

Variable	Coefficient	Std. Error	t-Statistic	Prob.
GGDP	0.792371	0.311313	2.545258	0.0244
IMP/GDP	1.794374	0.793094	2.262499	0.0414
RWAGE	−0.520157	0.694736	−0.748712	0.4674
REXC	−0.326389	0.903879	−0.361097	0.7238
USG	−0.501226	1.944873	−0.257716	0.8007
C	4.243241	66.7172	0.0636	0.9503
AR(1)	0.729363	0.247691	2.944644	0.0114

R-squared	0.823989	Mean dep. var	17.6164
Adjusted R-squared	0.742754	S.D. dep. var	19.71086
S.E. of regression	9.99724	AIC	4.873835
Sum squared resid	1299.282	Schwarz criterion	5.222341
Log likelihood	−70.11712	F-statistic	10.1432
Durbin-Watson stat	1.701164	Prob(F-statistic)	0.000286
Inverted AR Roots	0.73		

long-term investment returns to foreign investors in their home country, and Thailand's discount rate measures the opportunity cost of borrowing in the host country (see Wang & Swain, 1995).

From the above hypothesis, we specify our direct foreign investment function in the following form:

$$FDI = f(GGDP, RWAGE, REXC, IM/GDP, ORGDP, IND)$$

where FDI = direct foreign investment, GGDP = real GDP growth of Thailand, RWAGE = real wage rate, REXC = real exchange rate, IM/GDP = import per GDP, OGGDP = real GDP growth of the investing countries, and IND = differences between the U.S. government long-term bond yield and Thailand's discount rate.

We use time series data for the period of 1977 to 1995 for estimating the above function, and the final results with the best fit are shown in Table 12. We find that there was a long run positive relationship between direct foreign investment and Thailand's real GDP growth, real depreciation of local currency, and the openness policy. However, Thailand's direct foreign investment was inversely related to the country's increased real wages and the

Table 12.2. Dickey and Fuller Unit Root Test.

Variable	At level	First difference	Variable	At level	First difference
FDI	−1.4858 [0] (−3.0199)	−3.7293 [0] (−3.0294)	RWAGE	0.9656 [4] (−3.0659)	−3.5030 [3] (−3.0659)
GGDP	−6.5624 [0] (−3.0199)	−10.668 [0] (−3.0294)	REXC	−2.1796 [0] (−3.0199)	−4.0547 [0] (−3.0294)
IMP/GDP	−1.2388 [0] (−3.0199)	−5.1998 [0] (−3.0294)	USG	−1.1798 [0] (−3.0199)	−3.5740 [0] (−3.0294)

opportunity cost of foreign investors investing in their home market rather than in Thailand. In other words, Thailand's direct foreign investment was determined by the host country's growth, cost competitiveness, openness

Table 12.3. Cointegration Test.

12.3A: Cointegrating LR test based on Maximum Eigenvalue of the stochastic matrix.

Eigenvalue	Likelihood Ratio	5 Percent Critical Value	1 Percent Critical Value	Hypothesized No. of CE(s)
0.957916	143.3195	94.15	103.18	None **
0.78243	79.95757	68.52	76.07	At most 1 **
0.672588	49.4529	47.21	54.46	At most 2 *
0.566383	27.12218	29.68	35.65	At most 3
0.34362	10.41032	15.41	20.04	At most 4
0.094711	1.990016	3.76	6.65	At most 5

*(**) denotes rejection of the hypothesis at 5%(1%) significance level.
L.R. test indicates 3 cointegrating equation(s) at 5% significance level.

12.3B: Estimated cointegrating vector.

FDI	GGDP	IMP/GDP	RWAGE	REXC	U.S.G	C
1	−2.003803	−3.610039	0.452757	10.69629	1.226677	36.82994
	−0.7218	−0.39219	−0.17011	−2.80264	−0.85275	
Log likelihood	−306.4597					

Table 12.4. Empirical Estimates of ECM.

		D(FDI) = –0.2959*Error + 1.3659
SE. =	(–0.0599)	(–1.9093)
T-stat. =	(–4.9418)	(–0.7154)
		R-squared = 0.57569 SE. = 8.538824

policies, and the opportunity cost of the foreign investors' investment at home in comparison with investing abroad.

By estimating adjustment parameters in the error correction model, we find that they are negative and highly significant. If there is any discrepancy between direct foreign investment and its determinants in the short-run, it will be eliminated in the long-run and the speed of adjustment is about 29% per year.

3.2. Portfolio Foreign Investment

Foreign portfolio investment in Thailand increased significantly during the economic boom in the late 1980s, accounting for 13% of total net capital flows. After Thailand opened up the capital account in the early 1990s, it grew even more rapidly and it constituted over 17% of the overall net flows (see Tables 1 to 3). From the late 1980s to the early 1990s, most of portfolio foreign investment came from Hong Kong, Singapore, the U.K., and the U.S. After 1993, investment from Singapore accounted for over 60% of the total portfolio foreign investment, followed by Hong Kong and the U.K. Before 1992, most investment was in the industrial and the trade sectors. After 1992, investment in the real estate sector jumped, and it became the sector that absorbed the most of the portfolio investment.

The determinants of portfolio foreign investment are found by revising Chaivichayachat's (1996) model, which is based on the portfolio adjustment theory extended to the international economy version. He finds that the determinants of portfolio equity foreign investment are inflation rates, price per earning ratio, private investment index, interest rate differentials, and the relative risk between the stock exchange of Thailand and the New York stock exchange. We revise the above model and use yearly data to find the long-run relationship between the portfolio investment and its determinants by using the cointegration method and the error correction model.

We postulate that possible determinants of portfolio foreign investment include both macroeconomic factors attracting the investment and factors that directly affect investment returns, and in turn motivate foreign investors to mobilize the funds to Thailand. The first set of factors includes Thailand's real GDP growth, inflation rate, current account balance, foreign exchange reserves, and foreign exchange risk. The second set of factors include growth of real income of the investing countries, expected returns of investment in Thailand's stock market, and differences of asset yields in the host and the home countries. Finally, the portfolio investment function can be written in the following form:

$$FPI = f(GGDP, CB, ECPI, FR, EREXC, OGGDP, ERSET, DAY)$$

where GGDP = real GDP growth of Thailand, ECPI = expected GDP inflation rate, CB = current account balances, FR = foreign exchange reserves, EREXC = foreign exchange risk, OGGDP = growth of real income of the investing countries, ERSET = expected returns of investment in Thailand's stock market, and DAY = differences of asset yields in the host and the home countries.

The model with best parameter estimation results is presented in Table 13. We find that factors that significantly determine Thailand's portfolio foreign

Table 13. Determinants of Portfolio Foreign Investment.

Table 13.1. Ordinary Least Squares (OLS) Results.
(Dependent Variable is FPI)

Variable	Coefficient	Std. Error	t-Statistic	Prob.
ECPI	1.649552	0.846805	1.947971	0.0774
GGDP	2.041273	0.39941	5.110725	0.0003
EREXC	−1.486286	0.698717	2.127588	0.0579
ERSET	1.526696	0.687986	2.21908	0.0487
DAY	−9.073485	3.744459	2.423177	0.0338
C	−142.2217	156.738	−0.907385	0.3837
AR(1)	0.706278	0.196544	3.593488	0.0042

R-squared	0.751295	Mean dep. var	18.047
Adjusted R-squared	0.615638	S. D.dep. var	33.09318
S. E. of regression	20.51675	AIC	6.327785
Sum squared resid	4630.308	Schwarz criterion	6.67404
Log likelihood	−75.49096	F-statistic	5.538193
Durbin-Watson stat	1.950081	Prob(F-statistic)	0.007223
Inverted AR Roots	0.71		

Table 13.2. Dickey and Fuller Unit Root Test.

Variable	At level	First difference	Variable	At level	First difference
FPI	2.2252 [3] (–3.0818)	–5.1417 [2] (–3.0818)	EREXC	–1.5271 [0] (–3.0400)	–4.1957 [0] (–3.0521)
ECPI	1.7463 [4] (–3.1003)	–3.4760 [3] (–3.1003)	ERSET	–3.4251 [0] (–3.0400)	–7.0138 [0] (–3.0521)
GGDP	–6.1611 [0] (–3.0400)	–10.169 [0] (–3.0521)	DAY —	–2.0050 [2] (–3.0659)	–3.4802 [2] (–3.0818)

investment during 1977 to 1995 is reduced to five variables, namely, the real GDP growth rate, expected inflation, expected change in the Thai currency, expected returns on investing in Thailand's stock market, and the interest rate

Table 13.3. Cointegration Test.
13.3A: Cointegrating LR test based on Maximum Eigenvalue of the stochastic matrix.

Eigenvalue	Likelihood Ratio	5% Critical Value	1% Critical Value	Hypothesized No. of CE(s)
0.920763	115.7798	94.15	103.18	None **
0.833615	70.14424	68.52	76.07	At most 1 *
0.652672	37.86212	47.21	54.46	At most 2
0.522062	18.82736	29.68	35.65	At most 3
0.259987	5.538439	15.41	20.04	At most 4
0.006582	0.118861	3.76	6.65	At most 5

*(**) denotes rejection of the hypothesis at 5%(1%) significance level.
L.R. test indicates 3 cointegrating equation(s) at 5% significance level.

13.3B: Estimated cointegrating vector.

FPI	ECPI	GRGDP	EREXC	ERSET	DAY	C
					3.06773	—
1	–1.202291	5.708735	2.416238	3.426286	3.067738	–53.07268
	–0.44848	–2.18865	–4.96827	–1.07638	–2.93277	
Log likelihood	–291.1842					

Table 13.4. Empirical Estimates of ECM.

		D(FPI) = –0.3795*Error + 4.54
SE. =	(–0.1048)	(–6.9097)
T-stat. =	(–3.6199)	(–0.6570)
		R-squared = 0.450241 SE. = 29.31553

differentials. Additionally, the estimated error correction terms also imply that the speed of adjustment of discrepencies between short-run and long-run equilibrium is approximately 38% a year.

3.3. Private Loans

Private loans, mostly in the form of public borrowing, was the largest component of Thailand's net capital flows in the first half of the 1980s. The borrowing was so much that the country almost fell into a major debt crisis, as in many Latin American countries during the time. After learning from past mistakes, Thailand's fiscal policy became more self-disciplined, and foreign borrowing in the public sector was restrained to a manageable level. However, since the late 1980s, foreign borrowing in the private sector increased. After the country adopted the BIBF scheme in 1993, borrowing in the banking sector together with the nonbanking sectors, increased to account for over 70% of the total foreign flows. Most loans came from the financial centers in Singapore and Hong Kong. Although it is difficult to trace the ultimate source of these loans, it is likely that the majority of them came originally from Japan since Japanese banks play a dominant role in the international bank lending in these two financial centers. It is also difficult to be precise on the sectors that the loans went to because much of the funds were distributed to different sectors passing through the commercial banks and the financial institutions. However, Table 5 suggests that a large portion of the funds went to the real estate sector after 1993.

The studies of determinants of private foreign loans are few, and Kengchon (1995) stands out as a valuable study in the case of Thailand's foreign borrowing during 1970 to 1989. His regression specification is based on the neoclassical investment model with a financing constraint. Foreign loans are dependent upon factors that determine both the demand and the supply sides of loans. On the side of the borrowing country, the factor that leads to an increase in the demand for loans is expected real GDP growth rate. Those that lead to a decrease in the demand are available domestic savings, and foreign exchange

Table 14. Determinants of Privte Loans.

Table 14.1. Ordinary Least Squares (OLS) Results.
(Dependent Variable is FPL)

Variable	Coefficient	Std. Error	t-Statistic	Prob.
GGDP	3.868137	1.01123	3.825181	0.0015
DEBT	–5.620368	3.472688	–1.618449	0.1251
ISGAP	9.152577	3.655304	2.503916	0.0235
OTHERS	–0.634864	0.28628	–2.21763	0.0414
C	75.42167	69.13184	1.090983	0.2914
AR(1)	0.695983	0.190327	3.656772	0.0021
R-squared	0.622774	Mean dep. var	13.555	
Adjusted R-squared	0.504891	S. D.dep. var	53.31544	
S. E. of regression	37.51488	AIC	7.476476	
Sum squared resid	22517.86	Schwarz criterion	7.774033	
Log likelihood	–107.4579	F-statistic	5.282975	
Durbin-Watson stat	1.624505	Prob(F-statistic)	0.004704	
Inverted AR Roots	0.7			

risk. On the supply side, the determinants are liquidity situation in the world financial markets and creditworthiness of the borrowing country. We revise the above model and postulate that Thailand's foreign loans depend on the country's real GDP growth rate, the investment-saving gap, the domestic and world interest rate differentials, creditworthiness, and the availability of other types of foreign capital substitutable for the foreign loans.

Our model of foreign private loans is therefore specified in the following form:

Table 14.2. Dickey and Fuller Unit Root Test.

Variable	At level	First difference	Variable	At level	First difference
FPL	2.4929 [4] (–3.0400)	–8.8277 [2] (–3.0294)	ISGAP	–2.7014 [0] (–3.0038)	–5.2663 [0] (–3.0114)
GGDP	–6.8274 [0] (–3.0038)	–10.609 [0] (–3.0114)	OTHERS	0.0048 [1] (–3.0114)	–8.4271 [0] (–3.0114)
DEBT	–2.1649 [3] (–3.0294)	–4.3074 [0] (–3.0114)			

Table 14.3. Cointegration Test.

14.3A: Cointegrating LR test based on Maximum Eigenvalue of the stochastic matrix.

Eigenvalue	Likelihood Ratio	5% Critical Value	1% Critical Value	Hypothesized No. of CE(s)
0.897956	87.77524	68.52	76.07	None **
0.637672	37.56351	47.21	54.46	At most 1
0.305336	15.22896	29.68	35.65	At most 2
0.223929	7.213781	15.41	20.04	At most 3
0.071688	1.636532	3.76	6.65	At most 4

*(**) denotes rejection of the hypothesis at 5%(1%) significance level.
L.R. test indicates 3 cointegrating equation(s) at 5% significance level.

14.3B: Estimated cointegrating vector.

FPL	GGDP	DEBT	ISGAP	OTHERS	C
1	–44.38015	–3.772925	–43.86603	0.833577	525.0179
–20.4415	–6.41749	–18.8393	–0.47029		
Log likelihood	–384.1238				

$$FPL = f(GGDP, ISGAP, IND, CR, OTHER)$$

where GGDP = real GDP growth rate of Thailand, ISGAP = the investment-saving gap, IND = domestic and world interest rate differentials, CR = creditworthiness, and OTHERS = the availability of other types of foreign capital substitutable for the foreign loans.

We use yearly data from 1977 to 1995 for estimating the above model, and the cointregration and error correction results are shown in Table 14. The best fitted equation has only three statistically significant variables, namely, real

Table 14.4. Empirical Estimates of ECM.

		D(FPL) = 0.1155*Error + 1.7548
SE. =	(–0.0339)	(–9.6935)
T-stat. =	(–3.4045)	(–0.1810)
		R-squared = 0.3668 SE. = 45.4667

GDP growth rate, investment-saving gap, and the availibility of other types of capital flows. However, short-run adjustments to the long-run equilibrium appear to be divergent.

3.4. Nonresident Baht Account

Private capital flows in the form of nonresident baht accounts increased rapidly after Thailand's foreign exchange control was greatly relaxed in 1991. Foreign investors are allowed to bring in these funds and deposit them in a nonresident baht account opened at Thailand's commercial banks. These funds can be withdrawn for investment, lending, paying for exports, or transferring to other baht accounts. The ultimate purpose of all the above permission is for facilitating trade and investment in the productive sector. In the 1980s, the average net capital flow in the form of nonresident baht accounts was about 10.4 billion baht a year, accounting for only 7% of the total private nonbank flows. In the 1990s, it was increased to 80.2 billion baht a year and accounted for about 60% of the total flows. In the 1980s, most of funds in nonresident baht account came from the U.S., Singapore, Hong Kong, the U.K., and Japan. In the 1990s, almost half of the funds came from Singapore, with the rest mainly coming from Hong Kong and the U.K.

Table 15.1. Ordinary Least Squares (OLS) Results.
(Dependent Variable is NRB)

Variable	Coefficient	Std. Error	t-Statistic	Prob.
TVOL	2.578334	0.372288	6.925637	0.0000
RSET	0.086445	0.110373	0.78321	0.4500
EREXC	−3.792817	1.98535	−1.910402	0.0825
RDEP	42.80398	6.69559	6.392862	0.0001
OTHERS	−0.204949	0.045543	−4.500168	0.0009
C	−68.87969	30.78714	−2.237287	0.0469
AR(1)	−0.838185	0.217428	−3.854995	0.0027

R-squared	0.911675	Mean dep. var	29.8055
Adjusted R-squared	0.863497	S. D.dep. var	34.80145
S. E. of regression	12.85784	AIC	5.393209
Sum squared resid	1818.566	Schwarz criterion	5.739465
Log likelihood	−67.07978	F-statistic	18.92326
Durbin-Watson stat	2.563966	Prob(F-statistic)	0.000033
Inverted AR Roots	−0.84		

Table 15.2. Dickey and Fuller Unit Root Test.

Variable	At level	First difference	Variable	At level	First difference
NRB	–0.1709 [0] (–3.0400)	–4.3326 [0] (–3.0521)	EREXC	–1.5271 [0] (–3.0400)	–4.1957 [0] (–3.0521)
TVOL	–1.3095 [0] (–3.0400)	–5.7309 [0] (–3.0521)	RDEP	–1.3376 [0] (3.0400)	–4.0220 [3] (–3.1003)
RSET	–3.5969 [0] (–3.0400)	–6.9813 [0] (–3.0521)	OTHERS	–3.3333 [2] (–3.0659)	–3.6731 [3] (–3.1003)

The determinants of capital flows in the form of nonresident baht accounts are different from other types of flows in that they are short-term almost by definition. They are deposited in local commercial banks to gain from domestic

Table 15.3. Cointegration Test.

15.3A: Cointegrating LR test based on Maximum Eigenvalue of the stochastic matrix

Eigenvalue	Likelihood Ratio	5% Critical Value	1% Critical Value	Hypothesized No. of CE(s)
0.96944	145.6461	94.15	103.18	None **
0.879793	82.86117	68.52	76.07	At most 1 **
0.775876	44.72752	47.21	54.46	At most 2
0.544078	17.80754	29.68	35.65	At most 3
0.161642	3.66974	15.41	20.04	At most 4
0.027188	0.496153	3.76	6.65	At most 5

*(**) denotes rejection of the hypothesis at 5%(1%) significance level.
L.R. test indicates 3 cointegrating equation(s) at 5% significance level.

15.3B: Estimated cointegrating vector.

NRB	TVOL	RSET	EREXC	RDEP	OTHERS	C
1	–3.452888	–0.289536	7.659068	–52.75636	0.334983	32.82504
	–0.1847	–0.03791	–0.85095	–2.84314	–0.0247	
Log likelihood	–324.4305					

Table 15.4. Empirical Estimates of ECM.

		D(NRB) = 0.0189*Error + 4.628
SE. =	(–0.0143)	(–3.1381)
T-stat. =	(–1.3230)	(–1.4748)
		R-squared = 0.0986 SE. = 13.3141

and foreign exchange rate differentials, for speculation in the changes of foreign exchange rates, and for awaiting other trade and investment opportunities. Therefore, by the interest parity condition and the portfolio adjustment theory, we can postulate that factors determining net flows of nonresident baht accounts are domestic, and foreign interest rates spreads, real exchange rate changes, trade volume, returns on investment in Thailand's stock market (if the investors should shift from the nonresident baht account deposit to portfolio investment) and the supply of other types of capital flows. Specifically, the model can be written as follows:

$$NRB = f(IND, REXC, TVOL, RSET, OTHERS)$$

where IND = domestic and foreign interest rates spread, REXC = real exchange rate changes, TVOL = trade volume, RSER = return on investment in Thailand's stock market, and OTHERS = the supply of other types of capital flows.

Our estimation results are shown in Table 16. The estimated parameters of all postulated variables are statistically significant, and we can conclude that the major determinants of the net capital flows in the form of nonresident baht accounts were differentials of the Thai and foreign interest rates, changes of real exchange rates, returns on investment in Thailand's stock market, and the availability of other types of capital flows. The estimated error correction adjustment parameters are positive. If short-run disturbances exist, they seem to be divergent from the long-run equilibrium, suggesting that this type of capital flows is rather unstable.

4. IMPACT OF THAILAND'S FOREIGN CAPITAL FLOWS

4.1. Use of a Growth Accounting Framework

In our earlier paper (Wiboonchutikula et al. (1995)), we used the growth accounting methodology to find the impact of capital flows. Within the

Table 16. Regression Estimates for Aggregate Gross Foreign Capital Inflows to Thailand.

Variables	Industries			
	Light	Heavy	Petro-chemical	Overall
Constant	0.2190	0.0170	0.1070	0.0650
Absolute T Stat.	2.8900	0.0860	2.5700	0.8100
Y90–95	–0.1170	0.0030	0.0280	0.0110
Absolute T Stat.	2.6000	0.0140	0.6800	0.1100
Labor	–0.0040	0.0180	0.0004	0.0800
Absolute T Stat.	1.8000	1.7000	0.3200	1.7000
Capital	–0.2750	–0.2900	0.0360	–0.5760
Absolute T Stat.	0.3600	0.1200	0.2300	1.0100
FI	–1.3080	–0.1620	–0.0880	0.1930
Absolute T Stat.	0.9300	0.1700	0.7530	0.6200
DFI	1.3970	–0.2240	0.0360	–0.2540
Absolute T Stat.	1.7900	0.2000	0.2800	0.6200
R-square	0.6380	0.1470	0.0100	0.0640

Source: Wiboonchutikula Paitoon, Lakshmi Raut, and Bangorn Tubtimtong (1996).

aggregate production function framework, the main determinants of output Y_{it} of industry i in time period t are domestic capital stock K_{it}, foreign capital stock F_{it}, labor L_{it} as follows:

$$Y_{it} = A_{it} L_{it}^{\alpha 2} K_{it}^{a21} F_{it}^{\alpha 22}$$

$$A_{it} = B_{it}\left[1 + \eta\left(\frac{FI}{Y}\right)_{it}\right] \tag{1}$$

where A_{it} is the total factor productivity level of industry i in period t. Presumably, the sectors in which foreign capital is invested has higher productivity compared to the rest of the economy. In the above specification, we have assumed that the total factor productivity parameter, A_{it}, is endogenously determined by the share of foreign direct investment in GDP, the output due to productivity differential of the sector where foreign capital is invested as compared to the rest of the economy, B_{it}, denotes the residual total factor productivity level.

Let us reinterpret our model in Feder's (1982) framework (which he developed to study the effect of export). More specifically, we assume that the marginal products of labor and capital in the foreign investment sector are

$(1+\alpha)$ times higher than those of the rest of the economy; and that marginal and average productivity of labor within the rest of the economy are approximately equal. Then, it can be shown that $\delta = \eta/(1-\eta)$. By taking the natural logarithm and then the first difference of this production function, using the approximation that $\log(1+z) = z$ when z is small, and denoting the natural logarithm of an upper case variable by its lower case, and the difference a variable by a dot over it we obtain the following equation:

$$Y_{it} = \alpha_{0t} + \alpha_1 \dot{i}_{it} + \alpha_{21}\left(\frac{I}{Y}\right)_{it} + \alpha_{22}\left(\frac{FI}{Y}\right)_{it} + \eta\Delta\left(\frac{FI}{Y}\right) + \varepsilon_{it}$$

$$= \alpha_{0t} + \alpha_1 \dot{i}_{it} + \alpha_2\left(\frac{I}{Y}\right)_{it} + \alpha_4\Delta\left(\frac{FI}{Y}\right) + \varepsilon_{\iota T} \qquad (2)$$

where (FI/Y) is the average annual change in the foreign direct investment/output ratio during period t, and I is the domestic investment rate. In this specification, if $\alpha_3 + \alpha_4 = 0$, then the sector with foreign capital does not have higher factor productivity relative to the rest of the economy.

Our study categorizes Thailand's industries into three broader groups: light, heavy, and petro-chemical. The estimate results are shown in Table 16. With the exception of the light industry, there is no statistical evidence for the hypothesis that sectors with a higher rate of total (direct as well as portfolio) foreign investment has higher productivity growth. In the light industry, however, it appears that sectors with higher total foreign capital flows are associated with higher productivity growth. The causality of whether foreign capital flows were higher to the sectors which had higher productivity growth, and thus more attractive for investment, or whether foreign capital flows into a sector led it to have higher productivity growth is not clear from these results. Further research along these lines will be very useful.

4.2. Use of the VAR Model

We also use the nonstructural vector autoregressive (VAR) model together with the impulse response function to study the impact of changes in each type of capital flows on growth and stability. The stability variables are represented by inflation, current account balance, and interest rates. The VAR model is expressed in the following form:

$$NFI_{i,t} = \alpha + \sum_{j=1}^{n} \beta j NFI_{i,t-j} + \sum_{j=1}^{n} \delta j GGDP_{i,t-j} + \sum_{j=1}^{n} \gamma j CPI_{i,t-j}$$

$$+ \sum_{j=1}^{n} \eta j ISGAP_{i,t-j} + \sum_{j=1}^{n} \pi j DISCOUNT_{i,t-j} + \varepsilon t$$

where NFI_i = net foreign capital flows, GGDP = growth rate of real GDP, CPI = consumer price index, ISGAP = investment saving gap, DISCOUNT = discount rate, i = each type of foreign capital flows; i = 1 : bank (BANK); i = 2 : direct foreign investment (DFI); i = 3 : portfolio foreign investment (PFI); i = 4 : private loans (LOAN); i = 5 : nonresident baht account (NR); and i = 6 : total of net foreign capital flows.

The above model is estimated by using the yearly data from 1977 to 1995. The results of estimating the model using the OLS method are shown in Table 17. The growth of real GDP determined all types of capital flows except for bank loans. Inflation determined portfolio foreign investment and nonresident baht accounts. The balance of current account represented by investment-saving gaps determined direct foreign investment.

After constructing and estimating all of the above equations in the VAR model, we are now ready to use the impulse response function to simulate the dynamic impact of changes in each type of capital flows on variables representing growth and stability. The method is to allow for one standard deviation shock in the innovation of each flow, where the shock comes from an unanticipated change in each type of capital flows. The results are shown in Tables 18 to 25. For easy interpretation, we also show the percentage distribution of components of forecasting errors in order to determine the impact of changes in each type of capital flows on all the growth and stability variables.

A change in most types of capital flows had an impact on real GDP growth and current account balances. However, the effects on inflation and interest rates were quite little. An unanticipated shock in portfolio foreign investment and the nonresident baht accounts had more dynamic impact on real GDP growth than other types of capital flows. Meanwhile, direct foreign investment and private loans had a relatively large impact on the current account balances represented by the investment-saving gaps.

5. CONCLUSION

Foreign capital of all types flowed into Thailand at a rapid rate from the late 1980s to the first half of the 1990s following the country's policy of opening

Table 17. Impact of Capital Flows by VAR.

Dependent Variable	Total	Bank	Direct Investment	Portfolio Investment	Private Loans	Non Resident Baht A/C
AR(1)	1.2492*	1.2161*	0.538*	0.3356	0.3509	1.2797*
T-stat	8.672	2.0721	2.7579	–0.5377	1.124	8.7277
GGDP(–1)	–2.2059*	7.3469	0.5972*	–2.4513*	2.8134*	–1.0339*
T-stat	–1.9689	1.5758	2.366	–4.3116	2.3558	–7.5369
ISGAP(–1)	–19.4303	12.6665	2.3711*	2.001	–0.7972	–1.5706
T-stat	–2.76	0.5965	1.5388	0.3937	–0.0786	–1.3217
CPI(–1)	0.2219	–0.6449	0.2591	0.8802*	0.9844	0.3154*
T-stat	0.1338	–0.2005	1.7026	1.7685	0.879	2.0883
DISCOUNT(–1)	4.6174	–14.8544	–1.376	–4.4662	13.0954	1.2443
T-stat	0.5159	–0.4445	–0.7005	–0.5776	0.8307	0.6805
R^2	0.9648	0.6981	0.8873	0.7772	0.6152	0.9859
	–	–				
Log likelihood	–86.4728	–82.2383	–59.6576	–64.293	–76.5011	–41.7634

Table 18. Impulse Response to One SD Innovation and Variance Decomposition of Bank Loans.

Response of Bank Loans

Period	BANK	GGDP	ISGAP	CPI	DISCOUNT
1	58.184	0.000	0.000	0.000	0.000
	–10.623	0.000	0.000	0.000	0.000
2	30.814	15.337	8.480	–3.724	–6.639
	–15.766	–10.731	–11.886	–8.303	–11.632
3	51.728	6.140	–10.223	11.203	7.442
	–28.334	–7.698	–14.277	–7.319	–9.393
4	32.237	10.872	4.343	0.886	–10.146
	–32.703	–13.922	–17.695	–9.762	–11.677
5	45.262	8.037	–6.065	13.625	2.770
	–45.577	–11.449	–19.317	–10.040	–11.684
6	38.031	9.524	2.681	9.196	–7.119
	–48.634	–16.271	–19.483	–10.381	–11.840
7	45.955	9.116	–0.886	16.805	–0.767
	–61.670	–15.620	–21.462	–12.945	–12.654
8	46.357	9.991	3.614	16.754	–4.940
	–67.535	–19.685	–21.251	–13.068	–12.208
9	53.050	10.625	3.244	21.700	–2.518
	–82.037	–21.140	–23.658	–17.744	–13.550
10	57.839	11.702	5.746	23.963	–4.129
	–93.329	–25.222	–24.743	–19.824	–13.566

Variance Decomposition of Bank Loans

Period	S.E.	BANK	GGDP	ISGAP	CPI	DISCOUNT
1	1.000	58.184	0.000	0.000	0.000	0.0000
2	2.000	68.556	5.005	1.530	0.295	0.9377
3	3.000	87.743	3.545	2.291	1.810	1.2919
4	4.000	94.757	4.356	2.175	1.561	2.2542
5	5.000	106.406	4.025	2.050	2.877	1.8554
6	6.000	114.025	4.203	1.840	3.156	2.0055
7	7.000	124.421	4.067	1.550	4.475	1.6882
8	8.000	134.341	4.041	1.402	5.394	1.5833
9	9.000	146.500	3.927	1.228	6.730	1.3609
10	10.000	159.903	3.830	1.160	7.895	1.2090

Table 19. Impulse Response to One SD Innovation and Variance Decomposition of Direct Foreign Investment.

Response of Direct Foreign Investment

Period	DIRECT	GGDP	ISGAP	CPI	DISCOUNT
1	6.655	0.000	0.000	0.000	0.000
	–1.109	0.000	0.000	0.000	0.000
2	5.887	3.076	3.117	0.365	–0.648
	–1.750	–1.578	–1.417	–0.330	–0.763
3	3.944	–1.121	0.992	0.822	0.000
	–1.863	–1.386	–1.704	–0.460	–0.807
4	3.665	0.918	2.030	0.991	–0.085
	–1.922	–1.462	–1.504	–0.473	–0.553
5	2.701	–1.197	0.806	1.122	0.102
	–1.920	–1.354	–1.500	–0.502	–0.553
6	2.642	0.105	1.367	1.166	0.018
	–1.798	–1.266	–1.333	–0.515	–0.439
7	2.156	–1.042	0.667	1.209	0.099
	–1.733	–1.138	–1.245	–0.539	–0.411
8	2.168	–0.256	0.999	1.216	0.040
	–1.640	–1.055	–1.145	–0.566	–0.359
9	1.918	–0.895	0.607	1.228	0.083
	–1.598	–0.950	–1.071	–0.595	–0.340
10	1.944	–0.431	0.807	1.225	0.047
	–1.556	–0.893	–1.016	–0.626	–0.316

Variance Decomposition of Direct Foreign Investment

Period	S.E.	DIRECT	GGDP	ISGAP	CPI	DISCOUNT
1	6.655	100.000	0.000	0.000	0.000	0.0000
2	9.934	80.007	9.587	9.844	0.135	0.4260
3	10.824	80.670	9.148	9.132	0.691	0.3588
4	11.685	79.054	8.466	10.855	1.313	0.3131
5	12.132	78.292	8.827	10.511	2.073	0.2975
6	12.546	77.643	8.261	11.016	2.802	0.2784
7	12.847	76.861	8.536	10.774	3.558	0.2715
8	13.126	76.357	8.215	10.901	4.266	0.2610
9	13.367	75.697	8.371	10.719	4.959	0.2556
10	13.593	75.235	8.194	10.716	5.606	0.2483

Table 20. Impulse Response to One SD Innovation and Variance Decomposition of Portfolio Foreign Investment.

Response of Portfolio Foreign Investment

Period	PORT	GGDP	ISGAP	CPI	DISCOUNT
1	14.031	0.000	0.000	0.000	0.000
	–2.480	0.000	0.000	0.000	0.000
2	1.073	–12.861	0.370	1.532	–1.986
	–7.199	–3.388	–2.981	–0.988	–2.740
3	–9.104	12.893	9.359	–0.399	–4.381
	–8.652	–7.783	–3.764	–1.491	–3.229
4	13.582	–1.674	–7.894	2.259	8.207
	–13.588	–10.756	–7.258	–2.451	–5.533
5	4.221	–14.658	–0.497	1.111	–3.554
	–16.339	–15.973	–8.825	–1.808	–7.210
6	–13.953	12.476	11.073	–0.488	–6.403
	–22.458	–23.799	–13.055	–2.716	–9.124
7	12.180	4.265	–7.213	2.059	8.906
	–32.382	–23.504	–18.940	–3.138	–15.007
8	9.816	–19.495	–4.758	1.718	–1.060
	–30.104	–35.938	–17.926	–2.338	–15.569
9	–18.046	10.788	13.902	–0.914	–9.892
	–46.783	–45.625	–28.540	–4.840	–19.794
10	8.888	11.427	–5.291	1.778	9.194
	–55.773	–42.988	–33.948	–4.608	–29.031

Variance Decomposition of Portfolio Foreign Investment

Period	S.E.	PORT	GGDP	ISGAP	CPI	DISCOUNT
1	14.031	100.000	0.000	0.000	0.000	0.0000
2	19.231	53.541	44.721	0.037	0.635	1.0660
3	26.942	38.697	45.684	12.086	0.345	3.1877
4	32.372	44.407	31.912	14.319	0.726	8.6358
5	35.982	37.319	42.424	11.609	0.683	7.9653
6	42.531	37.473	38.970	15.087	0.502	7.9679
7	45.946	39.138	34.254	15.392	0.631	10.5850
8	51.129	35.291	42.200	13.296	0.623	8.5908
9	57.863	37.281	36.424	16.154	0.511	9.6301
10	60.608	36.131	36.754	15.485	0.552	11.0785

Table 21. Impulse Response to One SD Innovation and Variance Decomposition of Private Loans.

Response of Private Loans

Period	LOANS	GGDP	ISGAP	CPI	DISCOUNT
1	28.858	0.000	0.000	0.000	0.000
	-5.101	0.000	0.000	0.000	0.000
2	16.669	4.486	14.309	3.626	6.538
	-9.029	-5.810	-6.940	-3.628	-6.329
3	-11.384	-11.078	7.818	8.538	12.052
	-12.305	-7.056	-7.950	-4.856	-6.201
4	-0.261	-5.335	6.639	1.247	-1.805
	-9.056	-5.215	-6.648	-3.766	-7.268
5	3.757	0.119	5.948	1.968	0.692
	-8.489	-5.675	-4.534	-2.495	-4.387
6	-2.793	-3.382	3.338	3.597	3.109
	-5.216	-3.714	-3.960	-3.013	-4.598
7	0.026	-2.060	2.817	1.671	-0.482
	-3.697	-3.148	-3.525	-2.241	-3.311
8	1.453	-0.428	2.696	1.714	0.019
	-4.046	-2.767	-2.992	-1.901	-2.429
9	-0.360	-1.357	2.010	2.188	0.833
	-2.370	-1.971	-2.556	-2.023	-2.337
10	0.263	-1.093	1.839	1.655	-0.103
	-1.816	-1.806	-2.295	-1.826	-1.518

Variance Decomposition of Private Loans

Period	S.E.	LOANS	GGDP	ISGAP	CPI	DISCOUNT
1	28.858	100.000	0.000	0.000	0.000	0.0000
2	37.302	79.821	1.447	14.715	0.945	3.0724
3	43.852	64.495	7.429	13.826	4.475	9.7758
4	44.726	62.002	8.564	15.494	4.379	9.5603
5	45.324	61.064	8.340	16.810	4.453	9.3330
6	45.905	59.898	8.673	16.916	4.955	9.5569
7	46.070	59.469	8.811	17.169	5.051	9.4994
8	46.206	59.220	8.768	17.409	5.159	9.4438
9	46.330	58.909	8.807	17.504	5.355	9.4256
10	46.410	58.710	8.832	17.601	5.464	9.3937

Table 22. Impulse Response to One SD Innovation and Variance Decomposition of Non Resident Baht Account.

Response of Non Resident Baht Account

Period	NON	GGDP	ISGAP	CPI	DISCOUNT
1	3.291	0.000	0.000	0.000	0.000
	−0.582	0.000	0.000	0.000	0.000
2	2.442	−4.330	−1.247	0.653	0.597
	−1.308	−0.980	−0.664	−0.416	−0.701
3	6.657	−2.453	−0.490	−0.715	−1.010
	−1.590	−1.069	−1.149	−0.680	−1.157
4	6.968	−7.764	−2.185	0.467	0.542
	−2.877	−2.178	−1.788	−0.892	−1.559
5	13.293	−7.861	−1.924	−0.971	−1.173
	−4.204	−3.196	−2.792	−1.376	−2.394
6	17.108	−15.492	−4.206	0.008	0.174
	−7.189	−5.442	−4.209	−1.965	−3.466
7	28.212	−19.694	−5.044	−1.506	−1.568
	−11.360	−8.722	−6.445	−2.977	−5.226
8	39.622	−32.851	−8.754	−0.896	−0.574
	−18.881	−14.483	−9.764	−4.371	−7.704
9	61.634	−45.900	−11.936	−2.721	−2.538
	−30.509	−23.663	−14.912	−6.580	−11.515
10	89.765	−71.716	−18.949	−2.811	−2.169
	−49.889	−38.789	−22.709	−9.795	−17.091

Variance Decomposition of Non Resident Baht Account

Period	S.E.	NON	GGDP	ISGAP	CPI	DISCOUNT
1	3.291	100.000	0.000	0.000	0.000	0.0000
2	6.155	44.334	49.493	4.106	1.127	0.9397
3	9.486	67.909	27.525	1.995	1.043	1.5283
4	14.286	53.729	41.668	3.219	0.567	0.8179
5	21.181	63.832	32.731	2.290	0.468	0.6787
6	31.608	57.961	38.722	2.799	0.210	0.3078
7	47.042	62.132	35.007	2.413	0.197	0.2501
8	70.284	59.614	37.530	2.632	0.105	0.1187
9	104.888	61.296	36.001	2.477	0.114	0.1119
10	156.761	60.231	37.046	2.570	0.083	0.0692

Table 23. Impulse Response to One SD Innovation and Variance Decomposition of Net Foreign Capital Flows.

Response of Total

Period	TOTAL	GGDP	ISGAP	CPI	DISCOUNT
1	29.521	0.000	0.000	0.000	0.000
	–4.920	0.000	0.000	0.000	0.000
2	31.306	–9.712	–27.038	0.572	2.176
	–9.308	–8.648	–6.844	–1.052	–3.463
3	21.956	–1.945	–32.140	1.085	–4.996
	–11.487	–9.931	–10.613	–2.073	–5.076
4	15.457	–3.600	–34.727	3.375	–7.278
	–13.801	–9.852	–12.425	–2.863	–5.071
5	9.983	–3.379	–32.237	5.990	–7.755
	–14.955	–10.025	–13.876	–3.349	–5.195
6	7.865	–6.104	–29.386	8.346	–6.646
	–15.386	–8.878	–15.151	–3.508	–4.980
7	7.671	–7.714	–26.490	10.101	–5.164
	–15.130	–8.649	–15.972	–3.565	–4.749
8	9.285	–9.836	–25.243	11.248	–3.747
	–14.708	–8.119	–16.777	–3.638	–4.552
9	11.497	–11.043	–25.347	11.925	–2.842
	–14.449	–8.435	–17.380	–3.848	–4.454
10	13.911	–12.124	–26.874	12.347	–2.459
	–14.736	–8.829	–18.209	–4.223	–4.431

Variance Decomposition of Total

Period	S.E.	TOTAL	GGDP	ISGAP	CPI	DISCOUNT
1	29.521	100.000	0.000	0.000	0.000	0.0000
2	51.788	69.037	3.517	27.257	0.012	0.1766
3	65.015	55.208	2.321	41.733	0.036	0.7025
4	75.823	44.746	1.932	51.660	0.224	1.4377
5	83.639	38.199	1.751	57.311	0.697	2.0412
6	89.844	33.871	1.979	60.366	1.467	2.3162
7	94.978	30.961	2.431	61.796	2.444	2.3682
8	99.908	28.845	3.166	62.232	3.476	2.2809
9	105.016	27.305	3.971	62.150	4.436	2.1376
10	110.678	26.163	4.775	61.850	5.238	1.9739

Table 24. Impulse Response to One SD Innovation of Each Capital Flow.

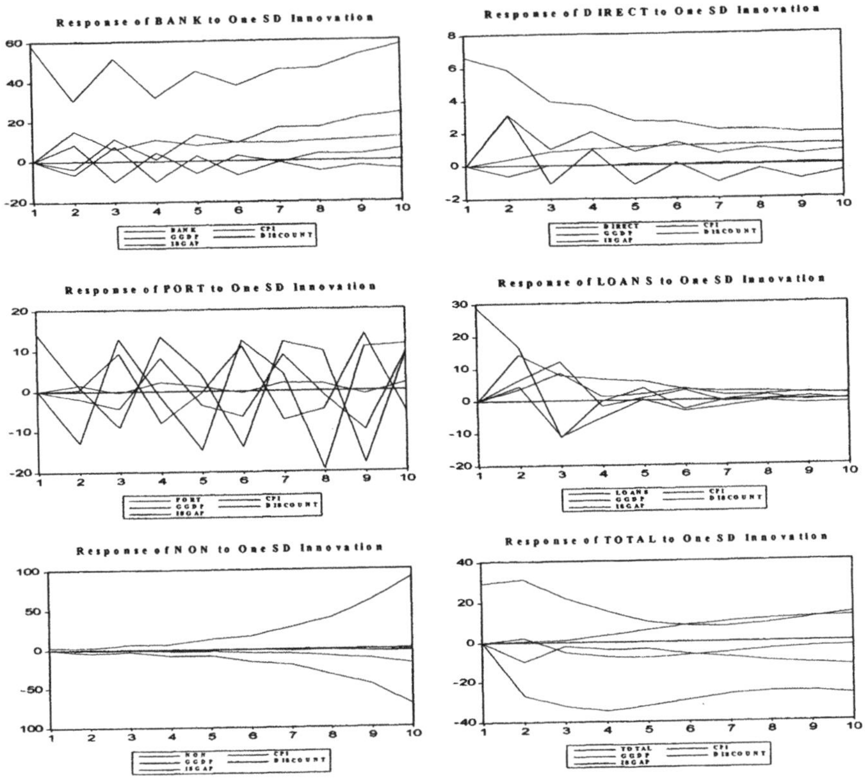

up the external financial sector. Investors were also attracted by Thailand's sound economic fundamentals, namely, high growth, low inflation, and stable exchange rates. However, from the early 1990s, the major components of the private capital flows were drastically changed from direct and portfolio foreign investment to borrowing in the banking sector and deposits in the nonresident baht accounts. As foreign investors grew suspicious of Thailand's macroeconomic stability and export growth in the mid-1990s, capital inflows quickly dried up, culminating in a severe currency and financial crisis in 1997. This study analyzes all aspects of Thailand's capital flows using the various econometric methods in order to learn how the change in Thailand's capital flow structure might play a part in the country's current economic crisis.

Table 25. Variance Decomposition of Each Capital Flow.

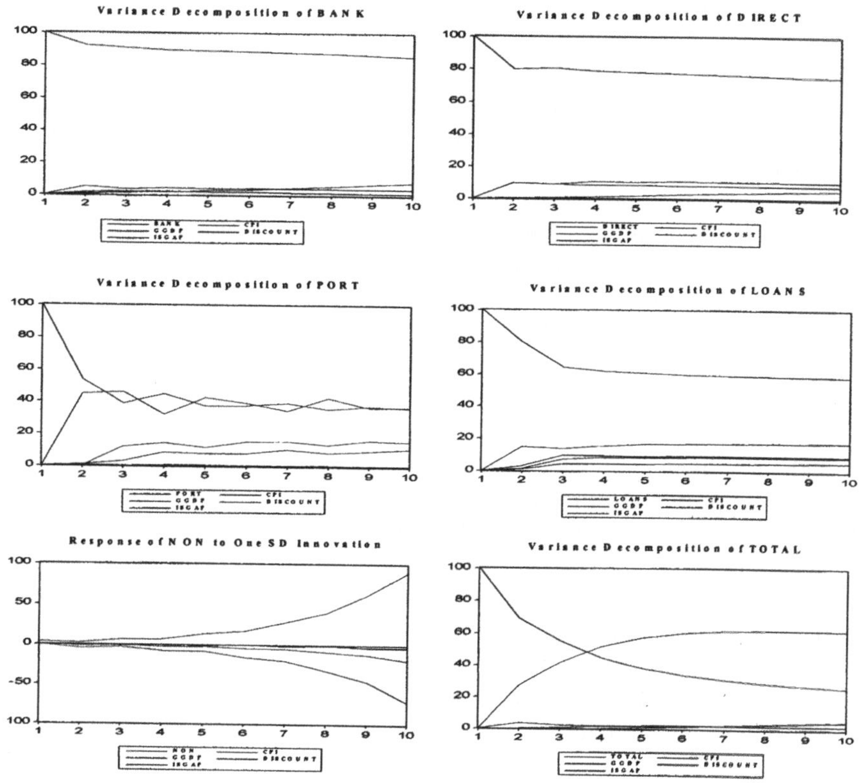

Our study on the nature of Thailand's capital flows in the 1990s shows that in a univariate framework, all types of capital flows, both long-term and short-term flows, were quite similar in their persistency or volatility. However, based on the multivariate results, direct foreign investment responded less to disturbances in other flows than other types of capital flows did. This implies that direct foreign investment was more persistent than other flows. Furthermore, by computing the volatility index based on the ARCH and GARCH models, the results show that bank loans and capital flows in the form of nonresident baht accounts were more volatile than other flows. In all models, the findings are consistent: capital flow volatility increased in the years immediately preceding Thailand's crisis in 1997.

All types of capital inflows were attracted by Thailand's high real GDP growth rates and stable exchange rates. Additional variables that determined direct foreign investment were production costs and the openness policy. Portfolio foreign investment responded significantly to economic stability and factors directly affecting investment returns. Bank loans reacted to current account balances, and nonresident baht accounts were sensitive to interest rate differentials.

We also find that most types of foreign capital flows contributed to affected overall production growth, but they did not have much effect on productivity changes of industries except for light industries. An unanticipated shock in portfolio foreign investment and the nonresident baht accounts had more dynamic impact on real GDP growth than other types of capital flows. Meanwhile, direct foreign investment and private loans had a relatively large impact on the current account balance, as represented by the investment-saving gap.

Although opening up the capital account can potentially benefit growth, the desirable impact is sensitive to macroeconomic policies, a strong banking and financial system, and the general economic and political conditions. In Thailand, as the financial sector and its supporting institutions were not yet developed, the capital inflows could easily be used for financing speculative sectors and industries supported by government protection or assistance. As Thailand is integrating into the world economy, a wrong policy is quickly and severely punished. It is also very difficult and increasingly costly to protect any sectors which are not internationally competitive and institutions which are not efficient.

NOTE

Paper prepared for presenting in the International Conference on "A MacroEconomic Core of an Open Economy for Progressive Industrialization and Development in Asia in the New MillenNium", held in Bangkok, Thailand, 16–18 December, 1998.

ACKNOWLEDGMENTS

The authors are grateful to Chulalongkorn University's Rajadapiseksompoj Research Fund for financial support of this project and for participants of this conference for comments on earlier draft of this paper.

REFERENCES

Agarwal, P. J. (1980). Determinants of Foreign Direct Investment. *Welwirtschaftliches Archiv*, Band 116, Heft 4.

Agarwal, R. N. (1998). Inflow of foreign Portfolio Liberalization in Japan and the Perception of Japanese Investors. Institute of Developing Economies, Working Paper, No. 311.

Bollerslev, T. (1986). Generalized Autoregressive Conditional Heteroscedasticity. *Journal of Econometrics, 31*.

Cardoso E., & Goldfajn, I. (1998). Capital Flows to Brazil: The Endogeneity of Capital Controls. *IMF Staff Papers, 45*(1).

Chaivichayachat, B. (1996). *The Characteristics and Determinants of Foreign Portfolio Investment in Thailand*, M.A. Thesis, Faculty of Economics, Chulalongkorn University.

Chuhan P., Perez-Quiros, G., & Popper, H. (1996). Do Short-Term Investment and Direct Investment Differ? *Policy Research Working Paper*, No. 1669, October.

Claessen, S., Dooley, M., & Warner, A. (1995). Portfolio Capital Flows: Hot or Cool. *The World Bank Economic Review, 9*(1).

Cochrane H. J. (1998). What do the VARs mean? Measuring the Output Effects of Monetary Policy. *Journal of Monetary Economics, 41*.

De Mello, Jr., & Luiz, R. (1997). Foreign Direct Investment in Developing Countries and Growth: A Selective Survey. *Journal of Development Studies, 34*(1), October.

Engle, R. (1982). Autoregressive Conditional Heteroscedasticity with Estimates of Variance of United Kingdom Inflation. *Econometrica, 50*.

Feder, G. (1982). On Exports and Economic Growth. *Journal of Development Economics, 35*.

Fernandez-Arias E. (1996). The New Wave of Private Capital Inflows: Push or Pull? *Journal of Development Economics, 48*.

Fernandez-Arias E., & Montiel, P. J. (1996). The surge of Capital Inflows to Developing Countries: An Analytical Overview. *The World Bank Economic Review, 10*(1).

Kengchon C. (1995). *Thailand Perspective on Foreign Loans*. Thailand Development Research Institute, Monograph.

Krueger, A. O. (1997). Nominal Anchor Exchange Rate Policies as a Domestic *Distortion. NBER Working Paper No. 5968.*

Levin, A., & Raut, L. (1997). Complementarities between Exports and Human Capital in Economic Growth: Evidence from Semi-Industrialized Countries. Economic Development and Cultural Change, 46(1), October.

Taylor P. M., & Sarno, L. (1997). Capital Flows to Developing Countries: Long and Short Term Determinants. *The World Bank Economic Review, 11*(3).

Vichyanod P. (1994). *Thailand's Financial System: Structure and Liberalization*. Thailand Development Research Institute, Monograph.

Walsh M. D., & Yu-Gen Tsou, G. (1998). Forecast Index Volatility: Sampling Interval and Non-Trading Effect. *Applied Financial Economics, 8*.

Wang Q. Z., & Swian, N. J. (1995). The Determinants of Foreign Direct Investment in Transforming Economies: Empirical Evidence from Hungary and China. *Weltwirtschaftliches Archiv*, Band 131, Heft 2.

Wiboonchutikula, P., Raut, L., & Tubtimtong, B. (1996). *The Nature and Impact of Foreign Capital Flows into Thailand*. Paper presented at the Fifth Convention of the East Asian Economic Association, Bangkok, Thailand.

SECTION SIX

35. GENERAL EQUILIBRIUM ASSESSMENTS OF TRADE LIBERALIZATION IN APEC COUNTRIES

Hiro Lee, David Roland-Holst and Dominique van der Mensbrugghe

1. INTRODUCTION

Asia-Pacific Economic Cooperation (APEC) countries have embarked on the important liberalization process in recent years. At the 1994 summit, APEC leaders delivered the Bogor Declaration, agreeing to remove trade and investment barriers by 2010 for developed members and 2020 for developing members. In Osaka in 1995, they agreed on the Action Agenda for implementing the objectives. In 1996, APEC leaders adopted the Manila Action Plan for APEC (MAPA), which included the individual and collective action plans to liberalize trade and investment in the region starting in 1997.

The primary impetus behind the APEC process is a vision of open multilateral trade that can more fully realize the immense potential of economies that are home to over 40% of the world's population. Attaining this vision will entail a reorganization of economic activity around the Pacific that more fully exploits the diverse resources, technologies, and tastes of this vast region. At the national level, such a transition may imply dramatic adjustments in specific economic activities and policies, and resistance to such change will pose a challenge to reformers. There is, however, a clear consensus that all

Restructuring Asian Economics for the New Millennium, Volume 9B, pages 719–742.

ISBN: 0-7623-0710-2

APEC members will ultimately benefit from this process, and empirical economists can facilitate reform by elucidating the detailed benefits and costs of APEC trade reform.

This chapter contributes to the policy dialogue by evaluating the effects of APEC trade liberalization on member country real GDP, sectoral output, exports and imports using an 18-region, 16-sector dynamic calibrated general equilibrium (CGE) model of the global economy. The current work extends our earlier study (Lee et al., 1999) in two respects. First, we have updated all the data used in our model from 1992 to 1995 using the GTAP database, version 4 (McDougall et al., 1998). Second, we have modified our model to allow for imperfect substitutability between domestically produced goods and exported goods within a given sector. The next section provides an overview of APEC countries' trade patterns and summarizes the extent of trade distortions. Section 3 contains a brief description of the APEC model used for quantitative assessments. In Section 4, we present the aggregate and sectoral results of the APEC trade liberalization experiment, and the final section offers conclusions.

2. APEC COUNTRIES' TRADE PATTERNS AND PROTECTION RATES

2.1. Trade Patterns

In this section, we provide an overview of trade patterns within APEC and with respect to the rest of the world. Table 1 presents a world trade matrix, where the world is disaggregated into 15 APEC countries/regions – Australasia (ANZ: Australia and New Zealand), Japan (JPN), China including Hong Kong (CHN), Korea (KOR), Taiwan (TWN), Singapore (SGP), Malaysia (MYS), Thailand (THA), Indonesia (IDN), the Philippines (PHL), Vietnam (VNM), Canada (CAN), the United States (USA), Mexico (MEX), and Chile (CHL) – and 3 non-APEC regions – the rest of Latin America (LAT), Europe (EUR), and the rest of the world (ROW).[1]

For the great majority of the APEC members, intra-APEC trade accounted for more than two-thirds of total trade in 1995. On the export side, in addition to Canada and Mexico (which each sold approximately three-quarters of their total exports to the United States), the ratio of intra-APEC to total exports exceeded two-thirds in Australasia and all the Asian members with the exception of Vietnam. On the import side, the ratio of intra-APEC to total imports was particularly large in China (73%), Taiwan (79%), Singapore (74%), Malaysia (74%), and Vietnam (81%). By contrast, Chile has a relatively small presence in Asia-Pacific markets, with intra-APEC trade shares of 50%.

Table 1. World Trade Matrix, 1995 (Millions of U.S. dollars).

	Importing Country										
Exporting Country	ANZ	JPN	CHN	KOR	TWN	SGP	MYS	THA	IDN	PHL	VNM
Australasia (ANZ)[a]	6,957	21,293	4,833	5,944	3,483	2,360	2,205	1,354	1,982	979	138
Japan (JPN)	13,723	...	50,253	36,780	31,573	25,648	16,869	20,731	9,739	7,307	1,080
China (CHN)[b]	5,765	47,455	30,737	9,182	6,923	8,057	2,779	3,448	2,828	2,236	1,054
Korea (KOR)	2,291	25,488	19,120	...	4,336	5,840	2,888	2,618	3,099	1,509	1,303
Taiwan (TWN)	2,531	16,065	31,643	2,896	...	5,548	3,934	3,497	1,879	1,317	1
Singapore (SGP)	3,746	13,549	12,660	3,212	5,951	...	13,587	4,799	2,422	1,921	1,577
Malaysia (MYS)	1,506	10,276	4,930	2,220	2,104	14,480	...	2,683	768	656	258
Thailand (THA)	1,036	14,016	5,425	1,231	1,431	5,916	1,716	...	1,198	560	481
Indonesia (IDN)	1,164	13,979	3,542	3,321	1,809	3,688	1,025	763	...	667	318
Philippines (PHL)	296	4,617	1,529	643	360	1,131	467	638	239	...	121
Vietnam (VNM)	230	2,025	540	217	6	418	115	66	175	49	...
Canada (CAN)	1,337	13,051	3,868	2,514	1,350	515	523	577	579	312	28
United States (USA)	15,310	82,794	26,919	32,821	21,861	17,803	9,889	9,260	3,734	5,928	326
Mexico (MEX)	130	2,689	399	338	63	185	52	355	124	189	1
Chile (CHL)	95	3,664	415	1,073	745	108	98	190	201	52	2
Other Latin Amer (LAT)	826	9,712	4,282	2,577	1,593	934	1,143	1,017	872	587	40
Europe (EUR)	22,314	65,967	46,832	22,338	17,006	19,433	15,179	20,035	12,834	7,129	1,076
Rest of World (ROW)	4,863	66,204	20,601	18,026	3,616	11,733	3,376	7,466	5,290	4,012	425
APEC[c]	56,117	270,961	196,814	102,393	81,994	91,697	56,146	50,979	28,967	23,682	6,689
Non-APEC	28,003	141,882	71,714	42,942	22,215	32,100	19,698	28,519	18,995	11,728	1,541
World	84,120	412,843	268,528	145,335	104,209	123,798	75,844	79,498	47,963	35,410	8,230

These trade flows are evaluated at world export (FOB) prices in millions of 1995 U.S. dollars.

[a] Australia and New Zealand.

[b] Includes Hong Kong. The figure in the third row and the third column is the sum of China's exports to Hong Kong and Hong Kong's exports to China.

[c] Excludes Brunei, Papua New Guinea, Peru, and Russia.

Source: GTAP database, Version 4.

Table 1. Continued.

Exporting Country	Importing Country									
	CAN	USA	MEX	CHL	LAT	EUR	ROW	APEC	Non-APEC	World
Australasia (ANZ)	1,430	6,272	231	165	1,030	11,095	6,587	59,628	18,713	78,341
Japan (JPN)	8,838	131,377	3,932	1,188	9,119	85,504	30,777	359,040	125,400	484,440
China (CHN)	5,613	62,464	767	1,073	7,151	63,327	23,657	190,382	94,135	284,517
Korea (KOR)	2,258	27,108	1,003	652	5,872	19,509	14,527	99,513	39,908	139,421
Taiwan (TWN)	2,181	31,417	717	214	1,949	19,535	4,483	103,838	25,967	129,806
Singapore (SGP)	850	22,816	267	98	1,772	17,792	13,475	87,457	33,039	120,496
Malaysia (MYS)	943	15,644	385	81	856	11,425	5,387	56,936	17,667	74,604
Thailand (THA)	740	12,467	98	84	1,235	12,595	8,718	46,399	22,549	68,948
Indonesia (IDN)	448	7,801	117	110	900	9,264	3,968	38,751	14,132	52,884
Philippines (PHL)	392	7,475	70	47	521	5,482	1,086	18,025	7,089	25,114
Vietnam (VNM)	61	309	16	13	187	1,902	407	4,239	2,496	6,735
Canada (CAN)	...	148,178	1,075	345	3,596	16,166	4,921	174,253	24,683	198,936
United States (USA)	119,100	...	48,597	3,997	47,789	201,219	53,882	398,337	302,890	701,226
Mexico (MEX)	2,867	63,394	...	534	4,838	5,077	2,301	71,319	12,216	83,535
Chile (CHL)	155	1,970	193	...	3,255	4,699	810	8,961	8,764	17,725
Other Latin Amer. (LAT)	2,294	43,371	1,815	3,800	35,266	41,560	12,988	74,865	89,814	164,679
Europe (EUR)	20,482	199,394	7,802	4,135	49,410	1,610,485	313,484	481,955	1,973,379	2,455,334
Rest of World (ROW)	4,063	60,099	1,038	808	12,954	238,539	89,036	211,619	340,528	552,148
APEC	145,876	538,692	57,469	8,602	90,069	484,593	174,986	1,717,079	749,648	2,466,727
Non-APEC	26,839	302,863	10,656	8,743	97,629	1,890,584	415,508	768,440	2,403,721	3,172,160
World	172,716	841,555	68,125	17,346	187,699	2,375,177	590,493	2,485,519	3,153,369	5,638,888

The United States, a country geographically linked to the world's three largest trading regions (East Asia, Europe, and the Americas) had the second lowest intra-APEC export and import ratios (57 and 64%, respectively) in 1995. On average, 70% of APEC countries' exports and imports were intraregional in 1995.

While exports to and imports from the United States and Japan accounted for large percentages of trade for developing-country APEC members, trade among them has also become significant. Singapore accounted for 19.4% of Malaysia's exports, and China (including Hong Kong) accounted for 13.7 and 24.4% of Korea and Taiwan's exports in 1995. In the past several years, China's trade with these neighboring countries has increased dramatically.

2.2. *Import Protection and Export Tax/Subsidy Rates*

Sectoral rates of nominal import protection and export tax/subsidy rates for the 15 APEC countries/regions are summarized in Tables 2 and 3, respectively. The import protection rates are the sum of sectoral tariff rates and *ad valorem* equivalents of quantitative restrictions (QRs) on imports, which are computed from the GTAP database. The average protection rates in 1995 (the last row of Table 2) range from 1.4% in Singapore to 19.3% in the Philippines, and sectoral protection rates differ significantly across APEC. The most notable sector is rice and wheat, where the rates range from zero or negative in a number of countries to 535% in Japan.[2] In other agriculture, they are very high in Japan, Korea, Taiwan, and Malaysia, whereas in processed food they are quite high in Vietnam, Thailand, and the Philippines.[3]

Developing-country members have substantially lowered trade barriers on a variety of manufactured products, yet some of them still maintain relatively high tariff rates. A number of manufacturing sectors, for example, are still highly protected in the Philippines, Thailand, and China. In simple manufactures (e.g. textiles, clothing, and footwear), developed countries tend to impose trade barriers to protect unskilled workers. Nevertheless, the import protection rates on textiles and clothing are higher in developing members than in developed members.

On the export side, Malaysia imposes export taxes on all goods and services with the exception of rice and wheat and processed food (Table 3). Its average export tax rate is 13.2%. Several APEC countries' export subsidy rates on rice and wheat are very high, but these reflect large domestic-world price differentials on the highly protected sector.[4] It is also worth noting that, although many members rely on heavy export tax and subsidy instruments in the grain sectors, this does not represent a significant macro trade distortion for

Table 2. Import Protection Rates in Major APEC Countries, 1995 (Percent).

	Products	ANZ	JPN	CHN	KOR	TWN	SGP	MYS	THA	IDN	PHL	VNM	CAN	USA	MEX	CHL
1	Rice and wheat[a]	0.3	535.0	−14.5	66.0	68.0	34.9	85.2	59.2	0.0	70.8	5.2	0.0	1.2	−17.5	−23.3
2	Other agriculture	2.4	65.9	7.6	45.0	49.2	17.6	45.4	25.7	6.4	18.0	8.5	0.6	4.4	0.9	5.9
3	Coal, oil, and gas	0.1	0.7	3.0	4.2	5.7	2.7	2.8	2.8	3.4	1.1	21.6	6.0	0.6	0.7	8.8
4	Other mining	0.5	0.0	1.4	1.8	0.9	0.0	1.7	1.6	3.7	4.8	1.7	0.0	0.1	3.2	8.4
5	Processed food	4.0	30.9	11.4	26.0	28.9	20.3	34.2	53.1	9.2	45.2	68.3	6.4	9.9	−2.0	10.1
6	Textiles and clothingb	14.6	6.8	30.9	6.9	8.6	1.4	17.4	24.1	14.0	23.0	28.1	11.2	9.9	3.4	10.4
7	Wood and paper	6.5	0.7	13.6	5.2	4.0	0.4	9.4	10.9	6.0	21.7	13.1	0.5	0.5	1.1	9.8
8	Chemicalsc	6.4	2.2	14.6	7.5	5.6	1.3	8.0	16.4	8.0	26.0	4.8	1.5	2.9	2.6	9.9
9	Metals and prod.	7.7	0.9	12.4	5.9	5.8	0.0	9.4	11.5	7.1	20.4	5.8	1.6	2.0	3.0	10.0
10	Machinery and equip.	7.4	0.4	12.7	8.0	6.4	0.0	6.4	9.9	4.5	25.0	4.5	1.0	1.9	3.1	10.5
11	Transport equip.	11.2	1.6	38.4	4.8	18.2	2.8	14.5	37.8	27.2	19.4	25.5	0.8	1.4	3.4	10.5
12	Other manufac.	10.2	1.3	24.8	7.5	7.8	0.1	11.5	25.2	10.4	27.8	18.4	1.3	3.0	7.0	10.2
13	Construction	...	...	...	...	...	...	...	...	...	...	...	...	...	...	...
14	Electricity	...	...	...	...	...	...	...	...	...	...	...	...	...	...	...
15	Trade and transp.	0.3	3.3	0.0	0.0	0.0	0.0	0.0	0.0	0.0	0.0	0.0	0.0	0.0	0.0	0.0
16	Other services	0.1	2.9	1.8	0.2	0.0	0.0	0.0	0.0	0.0	0.0	0.0	0.0	0.0	0.0	0.0
	Weighted average	6.1	9.1	14.5	8.1	8.3	1.4	9.0	13.1	6.7	19.3	17.2	1.6	2.4	2.3	8.1

These rates include ad valorem equivalents of quantitative restrictions on imports.

[a] Include processed rice.

[b] Includes leather and footwear.

[c] Include plastics and rubber products.

Source: GTAP database, Version 4.

Table 3. Export Tax and Subsidy Rates in Major APEC Countries, 1995 (Percent).

	Products	ANZ	JPN	CHN	KOR	TWN	SGP	MYS	THA	IDN	PHL	VNM	CAN	USA	MEX	CHL
1	Rice and wheat[a]	–0.1	–83.5	32.7	–51.6	–56.8	0.0	–52.2	–55.7	–0.6	–44.1	4.4	–0.3	–1.5	29.5	13.7
2	Other agriculture	–2.7	–12.5	2.4	–0.3	–0.7	0.0	13.3	–1.0	0.0	–0.3	13.5	–0.6	0.6	3.8	0.0
3	Coal, oil, and gas	1.7	0.0	19.6	0.0	0.0	0.0	13.7	0.0	0.0	0.0	0.7	0.0	6.1	0.0	1.3
4	Other mining	0.0	0.0	–0.9	0.0	0.0	0.0	13.6	0.0	0.0	0.0	3.1	0.2	3.9	0.0	0.0
5	Processed food	–3.0	–4.4	2.2	–1.6	–0.7	0.0	0.0	–5.7	0.0	–0.9	4.7	–3.0	0.0	1.9	0.0
6	Textiles and clothing[b]	0.0	0.0	–1.2	0.3	0.5	0.2	15.5	1.3	0.6	21.5	2.6	0.0	0.3	0.0	0.0
7	Wood and paper	0.3	0.0	–5.5	0.0	0.0	0.0	13.7	0.0	0.0	0.0	5.7	0.1	1.0	0.0	0.0
8	Chemicals[c]	0.2	0.0	–10.8	0.0	0.0	0.0	13.7	0.0	0.0	1.3	1.9	0.0	1.5	0.0	0.0
9	Metals and prod.	0.0	0.0	–7.3	0.0	0.0	0.0	13.7	0.0	0.0	0.0	0.4	0.0	0.7	0.0	0.0
10	Machinery and equip.	1.0	–0.1	–5.0	0.0	0.0	0.0	13.7	0.0	0.0	2.0	1.9	0.1	0.8	0.0	0.2
11	Transport equip.	–0.2	0.1	–0.9	0.4	0.0	0.1	13.0	0.0	0.0	0.0	1.9	0.0	0.5	0.1	0.8
12	Other manufac.	1.5	0.0	30.3	0.0	0.0	0.0	13.7	0.0	0.0	1.1	4.0	0.4	0.5	0.0	0.0
13	Construction	...	...	...	...	...	...	...	...	...	...	...	...	...	...	...
14	Electricity	...	...	...	...	...	...	...	...	...	...	...	...	...	...	...
15	Trade and transp.	0.1	0.0	0.0	0.0	0.0	0.0	21.4	0.0	0.0	0.0	3.2	0.2	10.0	0.0	0.0
16	Other services	0.1	0.0	0.0	0.0	0.0	0.0	13.7	0.0	0.0	0.0	26.3	0.1	4.9	0.0	8.9
	Weighted average	–0.5	–0.1	–0.8	0.0	0.0	0.0	13.2	–3.2	0.1	2.4	4.4	–0.1	2.2	0.2	0.5

Positive number indicates export taxes and negative numbers indicate export subsidies.
[a, b, c] See Table 2.
Source: GTAP database, Version 4.

any country. Trade distortions on other agriculture, manufactures, and services are the main determinants of economywide export bias.

3. BRIEF DESCRIPTION OF THE APEC MODEL

A CGE model is an empirical tool that is well suited to evaluating new trading arrangements for several reasons. First, it captures extensive indirect effects, such as interindustry linkages between sectors and trade linkages between countries and regions. Second, it can evaluate the effect of removing trade barriers on resource allocation and structural adjustment in each country. Third, it can detail the impacts on both member and nonmember countries and thereby better elucidate implications for the negotiating environment.

The APEC model used in this study is a dynamic CGE model of the global economy. It is, to a large extent, based upon OECD's LINKAGE model (OECD, 1997). One of the key features of the model is that goods are differentiated by region of origin and are modeled as imperfect substitutes. On the import side, this is reflected by the implementation of the so-called Armington assumption where a constant elasticity of substitution (CES) specification is used to incorporate imperfect substitution of imported goods with respect to domestically produced goods. A symmetric specification is used to model export supply, the latter being implemented with constant elasticity of transformation (CET) functions.[5]

As defined in Section 2, the APEC model contains 15 APEC and 3 non-APEC regions. The model is calibrated to social accounting matrices (SAMs) of the 18 regions, which are constructed from the GTAP database, version 4. The original database provides 1995 data on input-output, value added, final demand, bilateral trade, transport and protection data for 45 regions and 50 sectors. This has been aggregated into an 18-region, 16-sector data set for the implementation of the APEC model.

The model spans the period 1995–2020. It solves every year from 1995–2010 and every five years from 2010–2020. While the model relies on sequential static computation of equilibria, intertemporal trends are specified for factor growth (labor) and accumulation (capital), as well as changes in productivity. Land is assumed to be price-responsive, however, with no time trend on the supply curve.

All sectors are assumed to be perfectly competitive and operate under constant returns to scale. Production technology is modeled mainly by a nesting of CES functions. The model has three kinds of factors of production: labor, capital, and sector-specific fixed factors (e.g. land in agricultural sectors). Labor supply is assumed to be fixed in all regions and for all time periods, and the wage rate adjusts to insure equilibrium in the domestic labor market. While we assume no international migration, labor is free to move across all sectors of the economy. Thus, there is a single equilibrium wage rate.

Within each period, capital is classified as being either *old* or *new*. New capital is generated by the previous period's investment. This vintage structure of capital allows for differentiating the substitution possibilities across inputs by the age of capital. Similar to labor, *new* capital is assumed to be perfectly mobile across sectors, and there is a single economywide rate of return on capital.

All income generated by economic activity is assumed to be distributed to consumers. A single representative consumer allocates optimally his/her disposable income among the consumer goods and saving. The consumption/saving decision is static: saving is treated as a good, and its amount is determined simultaneously with the demands for the other goods. The price of saving is set arbitrarily equal to the average price of consumer goods.

The model is calibrated on exogenous growth rates of real GDP, population, labor productivity, and an autonomous energy efficiency improvement in energy use.[6] In the baseline scenario, the dynamics are calibrated in each country/region by imposing the assumption of a balanced growth path. This implies that the ratio between labor and the capital/fixed-factor bundle (in efficiency units) is held constant over time.[7] When the APEC trade liberalization scenario is simulated, the growth of capital is endogenously determined by the saving-investment relation.

4. EMPIRICAL ASSESSMENTS

In this section, we examine both aggregate and sectoral effects of APEC trade liberalization. To assess the implications of regional trade liberalization, we first establish a baseline scenario that assumes no trade liberalization during the 2000–2020 period. We then run a simulation on nondiscriminatory APEC trade liberalization; i.e. developed members remove import and export distortions by 2010, and developing members remove them by 2020 on a Most-Favored Nation (MFN) basis.[8]

In contrast to a free trade area where each member country removes bilateral trade barriers on imports from other members, trade liberalization by APEC members is nondiscriminatory toward the rest of the world. Each member submits individual action plans (IAPs) every year, which provide a blueprint for implementing liberalization and facilitation in APEC (Yamazawa, 1997). The general perception among the APEC leaders is that regional integration should be nondiscriminatory toward the rest of the world, which is consistent with the process of multilateral trade liberalization as envisioned under the World Trade Organization (WTO).[9]

Three caveats should be mentioned with regard to the APEC scenario. First, it is assumed that APEC countries' liberalization coincides with the Uruguay Round (UR) commitments during 1995–2000. However, a number of countries (e.g. Chile, China, Indonesia, and the Philippines) have committed to tariff reductions that are significantly larger than the UR commitments (Yamazawa, 1997). Second, the baseline scenario does not incorporate conceivable reductions in trade distortions beyond the year 2000 under the new WTO Round. The first caveat would underestimate the impact of APEC trade liberalization while the second would overestimate it. Third, the assumption that all members remove trade barriers on agricultural products by 2010/2020 might be too optimistic. For example, Japan, Korea, and the Philippines have excluded liberalization of rice and some other agricultural products from their IAPs. In particular, it is highly unlikely that Japan would liberalize its rice market by 2010. Thus, these caveats must be borne in mind when interpreting the simulation results.

4.1. Impact of APEC Trade Liberalization on Real GDP Growth

Table 4 summarizes the impact of APEC trade liberalization, on an MFN basis, on real GDP. It indicates percentage changes in real GDP relative to the baseline in 2005, 2010, 2015, and 2020, as well as absolute changes (billions of 1995 U.S.$) in 2020. By the year 2020, real GDP of developed and developing APEC members would increase by $42 billion and $83 billion, respectively (the last column of the table). In addition, since there would be no trade diversion under nondiscriminatory liberalization, the non-APEC regions would also be able to capture nontrivial gains in real GDP ($16 billion). The gains in real GDP are distributed very unevenly, however. In 2020, the Philippines would realize a 3.8% increase in real GDP over the baseline projection, followed by Thailand (1.6%), Vietnam (1.4%), Singapore (1.3%), and Taiwan (1.1%). In percentage terms, an increase in real GDP is very small in Japan, Canada, the United States, and Mexico.[10]

The real GDP gains reported in this chapter are significantly smaller than those obtained in our earlier study (Lee et al., 1999) for two major reasons. First, the model used here is calibrated to the 1995 database, whereas we used the 1992 database in the previous study. During the three-year period, some APEC countries reduced trade barriers significantly, resulting in much lower trade distortions in the base year. For example, Thailand lowered its average tariff rate from 31.6 to 13.1%, and Indonesia from 12.3 to 6.7% during

Table 4. Changes in Real GDP relative to the Baseline Values.

Country/Region	Percentage changes 2005	2010	2015	2020	Absolute changes in 2020[a]
Australasia	0.1	0.2	0.5	0.7	5.8
Japan	0.1	0.2	0.2	0.2	13.0
China (incl. Hong Kong)	0.2	0.4	0.7	0.9	38.8
Korea	0.1	0.3	0.4	0.5	6.6
Taiwan	0.2	0.5	0.8	1.1	11.8
Singapore	0.2	0.6	1.0	1.3	3.4
Malaysia	0.3	0.6	0.8	0.9	3.2
Thailand	0.3	0.7	1.2	1.6	6.9
Indonesia	0.0	0.1	0.3	0.4	2.1
Philippines	0.4	1.2	2.4	3.8	8.2
Vietnam	0.3	0.7	1.1	1.4	0.7
Canada	0.0	0.0	0.0	0.1	0.6
United States	0.0	0.1	0.1	0.2	22.8
Mexico	0.0	0.0	0.0	0.0	0.2
Chile	0.0	0.2	0.3	0.5	1.2
Other Latin America	0.0	0.0	0.0	0.1	2.4
Europe	0.0	0.0	0.0	0.1	9.2
Rest of World	0.0	0.0	0.0	0.1	4.2
Developed APEC	0.0	0.1	0.2	0.2	42.2
Developing APEC	0.1	0.3	0.5	0.7	83.0
Non-APEC Countries	0.0	0.0	0.0	0.1	15.9

[a] Billions of 1995 U.S. dollars.

1992–1995. Second, some modifications in the structure of the APEC model would affect simulation results. Most importantly, the newly incorporated assumption of imperfect substitutability between domestically produced goods and exported goods, which are represented by CET functions, would reduce the impact of the removal of trade distortions.

While countries with higher initial protection rates generally achieve greater efficiency gains from trade reform, the extent of welfare gains depends upon several other factors. Singapore has the lowest average rate of protection (with the exception of Hong Kong which is aggregated into China), but its real GDP gains are relatively large. This is because its export to GDP ratio and intra-APEC trade share are both extremely high, and an APEC-wide trade liberalization would enable it to capture a relatively large gain through export expansion.

Canada and Mexico gain very little from APEC trade liberalization. This is because about three-quarters of Canadian and Mexican exports were destined to the United States in 1995, and the U.S. tariff rates on Canadian and Mexican products were already quite low.[11] Thus, the benefits for Canada and Mexico are expected to be very small because of their low trade shares with non-U.S. APEC members.

A major reason why the U.S. gains (in percentage terms) are small might be because liberalization of service trade is excluded from our experiment. The frequency of NTBs in various categories of services in APEC countries suggests that the magnitude of barriers to trade in services may be extremely large (APEC & PECC, 1995). However, there is no proper method to convert frequency ratios into *ad valorem* equivalents, and no attempt has been made in the present study. Service exports accounted for approximately one-quarter of U.S. exports in 1995, and its share in total exports would have been much greater in the absence of regulations in its trading partners. Since the U.S. has comparative advantage in services, service trade liberalization is expected to bring substantial benefits.

Another limitation of this study is that we have only considered trade liberalization. Liberalization on foreign direct investment (FDI) is expected to bring additional gains. Lee and Roland-Holst (1998) show that, in the context of U.S-Japan trade, capital mobility increases the welfare gains to both countries that accrue from bilateral trade liberalization. Petri (1997) conducts APEC trade and FDI liberalization experiments and finds that an exclusion of FDI liberalization would diminish global welfare gains resulting from APEC liberalization by \$60 billion, or 23% of full liberalization.[12] These results confirm our *a priori* expectation that the removal of investment barriers would lead to additional real output and income gains, which could be substantial for developing members.

4.2. *Sectoral Results*

Although the real GDP results of the liberalization scenarios indicate the overall gains in the standard of living resulting from the removal of trade distortions, economywide efficiency gains are rarely distributed uniformly across sectors. Trade liberalization might lead to a sharp contraction of output and employment in highly protected activities, and the adversely affected sectors are likely to strongly oppose trade reform.

In many of the previous studies assessing the impact of APEC trade liberalization (e.g. APEC, 1997; McKibbin, 1998; Yang et al., 1998), sectoral effects are not evaluated. However, aggregate results reveal only part of the story and can give misleading signals about the political feasibility of trade accords. Since trade policy is often formulated from the bottom up, a modern view of national interest, such as that based on trade reciprocity and open multilateralism, might encounter conflicts with established domestic interests.

Table 5 provides absolute and percentage changes in sectoral output, exports, and imports resulting from APEC liberalization compared with the projected baseline values in 2020. Since rice and wheat are the most protected products in many East Asian members, the removal of trade distortions in these products can lead to extreme adjustments. In particular, Japan's output of rice and wheat is estimated to contract by 56% while its imports would rise by almost 700% compared with the baseline values in 2020. By contrast, countries that export relatively large shares of rice and wheat would experience sharp increases in output. Driven by a surge in exports, the output of rice and wheat in Australasia, Canada, and the United States is expected to rise by 108, 69, and 49%, respectively.

The agricultural exporters would generally experience reductions in manufacturing output because labor and capital are drawn into the agricultural sectors.[13] For example, the United States would experience reductions in growth rates of manufactures with the exception of processed food, wood and paper, and chemicals. However, increases in output of agricultural sectors and service-oriented sectors (sectors 13–16) would more than offset the reductions in manufacturing output.

In China, Asian NIEs (Korea, Taiwan, and Singapore), and the ASEAN-4 countries (Malaysia, Thailand, Indonesia, and the Philippines), exports and imports increase in all manufacturing sectors. Not only would they expand production of labor-intensive manufactures (e.g. textiles and clothing), but most of the Asian developing countries also increase output of the great majority of capital-intensive manufactures.

Korea and Taiwan's results are somewhat similar to Japan's as agricultural sectors contract (relative to the baseline case) and all manufacturing sectors expand except transport equipment in Taiwan. One notable difference is that the reductions in agricultural output in these two countries are significantly smaller than in Japan mainly because of their much lower initial protection rates on agricultural products.

In China, removing the trade distortions would result in a fall in agricultural output, posing a potential problem on food supply in the long run. Real output of a number of manufacturing and service-oriented sectors would increase over the baseline level, where Hong Kong's comparative advantage in manufactures and services might be contributing significantly to these results.

Table 5. Changes in Sectoral Output, Exports, and Imports relative to the Baseline, 2020 (Billions of 1995 U.S. Dollars, Percent).

		Australasia						Japan						China (incl. Hong Kong)					
		Output		Exports		Imports		Output		Exports		Imports		Output		Exports		Imports	
		($b)	(%)	($b)	(%)	($b)	(%)	($b)	(%)	($b)	(%)	($b)	(%)	($b)	(%)	($b)	(%)	($b)	(%)
1	Rice and wheat	6.2	108.4	5.2	182.4	0.0	−6.5	−61.8	−55.7	−0.1	−89.0	74.4	691.9	−1.6	−0.7	0.0	17.4	−0.8	−17.1
2	Other agriculture	2.3	3.8	−0.1	−0.7	0.3	11.6	−28.2	−11.1	−0.1	−9.3	36.1	57.2	−9.0	−1.2	0.5	2.5	0.2	0.7
3	Coal, oil, and gas	0.5	1.0	−0.1	−0.4	0.3	3.1	1.4	1.9	0.2	8.6	−1.2	−0.7	13.0	2.7	2.7	11.9	−0.7	−3.7
4	Other mining	−0.5	−2.5	−0.4	−3.2	0.0	1.1	0.6	1.8	0.0	4.0	0.1	0.4	4.3	2.5	1.0	8.7	−1.0	−5.8
5	Processed food	7.0	8.8	5.4	22.5	0.4	7.1	−8.7	−1.3	0.4	14.1	19.9	23.2	−1.2	−0.3	4.2	15.5	1.7	5.4
6	Textiles, clothing	−1.4	−7.0	−0.2	−4.1	2.9	17.7	0.9	0.3	3.1	21.0	11.3	11.0	34.4	4.0	50.0	15.2	38.0	21.7
7	Wood and paper	−0.5	−0.9	−0.1	−2.1	0.9	8.4	3.6	0.6	0.5	7.2	−0.4	−0.7	1.5	0.4	2.7	6.4	2.2	5.6
8	Chemicals	−0.4	−0.7	0.1	0.4	1.8	7.2	7.5	0.8	5.1	7.2	−0.4	−0.6	−10.4	−1.1	2.2	2.0	9.7	6.9
9	Metals and prod.	−1.1	−1.6	−0.2	−0.9	0.8	8.1	16.9	2.1	4.2	7.8	−0.1	−0.1	−0.1	0.0	4.0	3.6	3.6	4.6
10	Machinery	−1.6	−3.6	−0.3	−2.1	3.5	6.3	40.4	2.2	27.0	5.8	0.5	0.3	13.8	0.8	29.7	7.1	13.1	3.8
11	Transport equip.	−1.5	−4.4	−0.1	−2.0	2.7	10.7	22.0	4.7	17.8	11.8	−0.8	−2.1	−23.7	−7.0	1.2	5.1	13.2	21.1
12	Other manufac	−0.7	−3.7	0.0	−1.5	1.4	13.9	3.6	1.0	2.4	6.5	1.5	3.2	12.8	1.9	18.3	14.0	7.0	17.5
13	Construction	3.8	3.2	. . .	. . .	. . .	. . .	8.7	0.4	. . .	. . .	. . .	. . .	5.3	0.6	. . .	. . .	. . .	. . .
14	Electricity	0.3	1.6	. . .	. . .	. . .	. . .	1.6	0.7	. . .	. . .	. . .	. . .	3.7	1.0	. . .	. . .	. . .	. . .
15	Trade and transp.	1.3	0.3	0.0	−0.1	1.2	3.2	8.5	0.3	3.4	4.1	4.7	1.7	28.5	1.2	23.9	7.8	−2.6	−3.1
16	Other services	1.7	0.3	−0.2	−1.1	0.2	1.7	−0.7	0.0	0.5	1.7	0.6	0.9	8.4	0.6	4.3	6.6	−1.5	−4.0

Table 5. Continued.

		Korea						Taiwan						Singapore					
		Output		Exports		Imports		Output		Exports		Imports		Output		Exports		Imports	
		($b)	(%)	($b)	(%)	($b)	(%)	($b)	(%)	($b)	(%)	($b)	(%)	($b)	(%)	($b)	(%)	($b)	(%)
1	Rice and wheat	–3.4	–4.5	0.0	–63.1	2.0	101.5	–1.4	–7.1	–0.2	–71.4	0.6	116.6	0.0	88.1	0.0	67.6	0.0	–0.4
2	Other agriculture	–5.2	–5.5	0.0	0.1	8.5	36.4	–3.0	–6.9	–0.1	–4.5	5.1	44.5	–0.4	–4.8	0.0	–0.7	0.5	8.3
3	Coal, oil, and gas	1.6	1.5	0.3	3.1	1.3	2.5	1.0	3.0	0.0	0.4	1.4	11.4	0.7	1.4	0.4	1.4	1.5	6.2
4	Other mining	0.3	1.6	0.0	2.3	0.1	1.6	0.2	2.6	0.0	3.9	0.1	4.5	0.0	1.4	0.0	0.3	0.1	3.5
5	Processed food	0.5	0.3	0.4	10.4	2.3	18.6	3.8	7.5	2.4	34.7	2.1	23.4	1.8	10.6	1.9	19.5	1.0	11.1
6	Textiles, clothing	22.8	15.1	14.3	23.0	2.0	9.2	30.8	25.5	21.3	31.7	2.7	20.1	0.8	7.3	0.7	9.1	0.9	7.6
7	Wood and paper	0.4	0.4	0.5	6.7	0.5	3.4	0.5	0.7	0.8	4.5	0.9	6.9	0.4	1.7	0.2	2.4	0.3	5.0
8	Chemicals	8.8	3.6	4.2	9.7	2.1	5.1	16.1	7.9	7.5	12.6	3.9	9.4	2.2	3.6	2.0	4.2	1.4	3.8
9	Metals and prod.	4.8	1.7	2.3	6.9	2.2	4.8	0.7	0.3	2.1	5.2	2.4	7.1	1.4	5.0	0.8	5.1	0.9	3.7
10	Machinery	6.7	1.6	9.1	5.4	5.5	4.1	1.4	0.4	4.6	2.2	8.2	5.7	8.3	3.3	7.9	3.4	7.2	3.4
11	Transport equip.	5.1	4.2	4.6	10.6	0.0	0.3	–1.5	–2.0	0.6	3.4	3.5	14.7	0.4	2.8	0.4	3.8	0.5	2.8
12	Other manufac	1.5	1.5	1.6	7.8	0.8	7.7	3.5	5.3	3.3	12.6	1.0	10.2	0.7	3.1	0.6	3.3	1.0	4.3
13	Construction	1.5	0.4	...	...	...	...	3.9	3.0	...	...	...	...	1.6	5.2	...	...	...	...
14	Electricity	0.2	0.6	...	...	...	...	1.3	3.4	...	...	...	...	0.2	4.3	...	...	...	...
15	Trade and transp.	–3.4	–0.9	1.4	2.3	–0.3	–0.8	–4.3	–1.3	–0.6	–2.4	0.9	4.9	1.3	0.6	0.2	0.2	0.6	7.9
16	Other services	–5.9	–0.8	0.3	1.4	–0.6	–2.0	–3.4	–0.5	–0.3	–2.2	0.5	1.7	1.7	1.2	–0.1	–0.6	0.7	2.3

Table 5. Continued.

		Malaysia						Thailand						Indonesia					
		Output		Exports		Imports		Output		Exports		Imports		Output		Exports		Imports	
		($b)	(%)	($b)	(%)	($b)	(%)	($b)	(%)	($b)	(%)	($b)	(%)	($b)	(%)	($b)	(%)	($b)	(%)
1	Rice and wheat	−1.8	−10.2	0.0	−35.6	1.9	95.5	−9.4	−44.0	−5.1	−63.6	0.3	62.8	−0.1	−0.2	0.0	3.0	−0.4	−12.3
2	Other agriculture	−1.8	−4.7	0.0	0.3	2.7	36.8	1.0	2.4	1.1	12.8	0.6	11.4	0.0	0.0	0.2	2.2	0.0	−0.4
3	Coal, oil, and gas	−2.3	−4.3	−1.1	−4.5	0.1	2.6	−0.3	−1.6	0.1	6.8	−0.7	−4.0	1.7	2.6	1.3	3.8	0.2	2.0
4	Other mining	−0.3	−3.9	−0.1	−3.8	0.0	2.1	0.3	4.9	0.3	7.5	−0.2	−5.4	0.2	0.9	0.1	1.1	0.0	2.4
5	Processed food	0.9	2.5	1.8	11.4	1.0	16.9	1.3	2.7	2.3	13.2	2.1	32.7	−0.6	−1.1	0.1	2.0	0.3	9.3
6	Textiles, clothing	2.2	11.5	2.0	18.8	1.0	12.7	5.3	8.4	4.5	17.3	1.3	20.1	3.9	9.6	3.3	13.3	1.4	18.2
7	Wood and paper	1.7	5.0	1.7	9.1	0.1	2.5	0.0	0.0	0.4	7.2	0.2	3.9	1.3	2.8	1.1	5.0	0.2	4.1
8	Chemicals	3.2	10.1	2.5	17.7	0.4	1.9	0.5	1.7	1.2	10.1	1.2	4.8	0.3	0.7	0.5	5.6	1.2	5.8
9	Metals and prod.	−0.1	−0.4	0.5	4.7	1.0	4.8	0.1	0.8	0.4	9.0	0.8	2.9	−0.1	−0.3	0.3	4.6	0.5	3.7
10	Machinery	13.6	9.0	13.3	9.5	3.7	2.5	7.0	6.7	6.5	9.8	2.8	3.6	0.6	1.1	0.6	5.2	0.4	0.9
11	Transport equip.	−1.0	−3.3	0.6	6.2	0.5	3.6	−4.5	−10.6	0.2	6.1	4.6	21.6	−1.6	−11.8	0.0	0.9	1.7	15.5
12	Other manufac	1.1	3.5	1.4	7.7	0.6	6.0	0.4	1.3	1.1	8.7	1.1	16.5	0.0	−0.1	0.2	3.5	0.4	10.2
13	Construction	−1.5	−2.4	...	...	...	...	1.5	2.7	...	...	...	...	1.7	1.2	...	...	...	...
14	Electricity	0.1	1.1	...	...	...	...	0.2	1.5	...	...	...	...	0.0	0.1	...	...	...	...
15	Trade and transp.	−1.7	−1.5	0.4	1.4	0.1	5.1	2.5	1.7	3.6	8.6	−1.6	−7.9	−0.7	−0.4	0.3	2.6	−0.1	−0.9
16	Other services	−1.8	−2.1	0.0	−0.6	−0.4	−1.8	0.2	0.2	0.3	5.3	−0.6	−5.0	−0.7	−0.5	0.1	1.2	0.0	−1.7

Table 5. Continued.

		Philippines						Vietnam						Canada					
		Output		Exports		Imports		Output		Exports		Imports		Output		Exports		Imports	
		($b)	(%)	($b)	(%)	($b)	(%)	($b)	(%)	($b)	(%)	($b)	(%)	($b)	(%)	($b)	(%)	($b)	(%)
1	Rice and wheat	−2.1	−11.8	0.0	−45.7	1.0	55.8	1.1	22.1	0.8	59.2	0.0	14.1	4.5	68.9	4.3	79.0	0.0	−18.1
2	Other agriculture	−0.1	−0.2	0.4	23.1	0.0	1.2	−0.8	−5.2	0.0	0.4	0.0	4.5	0.0	0.0	0.2	2.2	0.2	2.6
3	Coal, oil, and gas	1.7	14.0	0.4	27.5	−0.4	−5.6	1.5	19.7	1.3	21.9	0.6	20.1	0.1	0.1	0.1	0.4	0.8	6.7
4	Other mining	1.4	22.4	0.6	25.2	0.0	0.9	0.0	−1.9	0.0	4.3	0.0	−4.6	0.0	−0.2	0.0	−0.1	0.0	−0.3
5	Processed food	−1.7	−3.4	1.1	21.1	1.0	15.3	−1.3	−16.5	−0.1	−2.3	1.9	51.4	−0.6	−0.9	0.1	0.8	0.6	5.9
6	Textiles, clothing	6.4	42.1	4.4	54.5	1.3	19.0	2.1	24.2	1.7	30.4	0.9	23.9	−1.5	−6.1	−0.2	−3.3	2.9	14.1
7	Wood and paper	0.9	9.1	0.5	25.7	0.1	5.1	−0.1	−1.5	0.0	5.5	0.1	7.5	−0.7	−0.5	−0.3	−0.5	0.2	0.8
8	Chemicals	0.8	4.1	0.5	20.7	0.8	6.7	0.2	6.6	0.1	16.1	0.1	1.5	0.7	0.8	0.2	0.7	0.8	2.0
9	Metals and prod.	2.5	26.5	0.9	28.9	1.5	18.7	0.0	−1.9	0.0	5.1	0.0	−1.6	−0.4	−0.5	0.0	−0.2	0.3	1.1
10	Machinery	9.7	32.6	9.2	33.1	6.7	18.9	0.0	0.5	0.0	4.9	0.0	0.6	−0.8	−0.8	−0.4	−0.7	0.7	0.6
11	Transport equip.	0.6	27.9	0.4	41.7	0.4	5.8	−0.2	−15.0	0.0	4.1	0.3	8.3	0.4	0.3	0.5	0.5	0.4	0.6
12	Other manufac.	1.1	22.6	1.0	32.6	0.3	10.1	0.0	−0.7	0.0	8.1	0.1	10.9	−0.3	−1.6	0.0	−0.7	0.5	3.0
13	Construction	1.4	9.7	...	...	...	...	0.2	1.2	...	...	...	...	0.4	0.2	...	...	...	...
14	Electricity	0.1	1.6	...	...	...	...	0.0	−0.2	...	...	...	...	−0.1	−0.2	...	...	...	...
15	Trade and transp.	1.6	1.6	3.3	19.8	−1.9	−17.0	0.2	0.8	0.5	5.0	0.0	−0.7	−0.4	−0.1	0.3	1.0	0.3	0.8
16	Other services	2.2	2.2	2.8	14.0	−0.4	−13.2	−0.4	−2.6	0.0	0.7	0.0	−2.6	−0.9	−0.2	0.0	−0.1	0.0	0.0

Table 5. Continued.

		United States						Mexico						Chile					
		Output		Exports		Imports		Output		Exports		Imports		Output		Exports		Imports	
		($b)	(%)	($b)	(%)	($b)	(%)	($b)	(%)	($b)	(%)	($b)	(%)	($b)	(%)	($b)	(%)	($b)	(%)
1	Rice and wheat	12.8	48.8	10.3	80.7	–0.1	–11.2	0.0	–2.4	0.0	2.9	0.0	9.2	0.0	–0.5	0.0	7.1	0.0	2.1
2	Other agriculture	34.2	7.6	23.1	40.9	1.9	5.7	0.1	0.2	0.2	3.3	0.0	0.7	0.2	0.7	0.2	4.4	0.0	1.5
3	Coal, oil, and gas	2.8	0.6	0.2	1.2	1.5	1.0	1.3	1.2	0.7	3.0	0.0	–0.1	0.1	1.4	0.0	9.1	0.1	3.4
4	Other mining	–0.1	–0.1	0.0	–0.3	0.0	0.0	0.1	0.7	0.0	1.8	0.0	1.5	1.1	5.7	0.7	6.7	0.0	4.8
5	Processed food	4.0	0.5	3.1	6.8	4.8	10.9	0.1	0.1	0.2	4.9	–0.2	–5.3	–0.1	–0.2	0.2	3.3	0.1	4.0
6	Textiles, clothing	–15.1	–4.1	–0.4	–1.2	31.9	15.9	–0.8	–1.3	–0.2	–2.1	0.3	3.8	–0.4	–2.2	0.0	6.2	0.4	9.3
7	Wood and paper	1.6	0.2	0.1	0.1	1.2	1.3	0.2	0.4	0.1	2.0	0.0	–0.2	0.7	2.8	0.6	5.7	0.1	3.6
8	Chemicals	1.1	0.1	1.7	1.1	5.0	3.4	0.3	0.3	0.4	2.5	0.2	0.9	0.0	–0.1	0.2	5.8	0.2	3.4
9	Metals and prod.	–3.5	–0.4	0.1	0.2	2.7	2.3	0.7	1.1	0.4	2.7	0.2	1.4	2.2	6.4	1.8	9.1	0.1	3.8
10	Machinery	–19.8	–1.2	–3.1	–0.6	26.7	4.2	1.3	1.3	1.4	1.9	0.7	1.0	–0.1	–2.1	0.0	4.3	0.4	3.3
11	Transport equip.	–0.2	0.0	0.3	0.2	8.4	3.5	1.1	1.7	1.0	2.8	0.3	1.6	0.0	–1.0	0.0	7.4	0.3	2.8
12	Other manufac	–3.7	–1.4	0.1	0.4	8.3	7.0	–0.3	–1.0	0.0	0.5	0.5	8.3	–0.1	–2.0	0.0	4.5	0.2	8.1
13	Construction	13.5	0.6	...	...	...	...	0.1	0.2	...	...	...	...	0.5	1.3	...	...	...	...
14	Electricity	0.8	0.3	...	...	...	...	0.0	–0.1	...	...	...	...	0.0	0.4	...	...	...	...
15	Trade and transp.	6.4	0.2	1.7	0.9	5.1	3.0	–0.7	–0.2	0.7	2.0	–0.1	–1.2	0.0	0.0	0.5	5.6	–0.1	–2.9
16	Other services	16.1	0.2	0.4	0.2	0.3	0.2	–1.0	–0.4	0.0	1.0	–0.1	–1.3	–0.8	–0.7	0.1	3.0	–0.1	–3.1

Large structural adjustments occur in ASEAN countries, particularly in the Philippines. Textile and clothing output would increase in all six ASEAN countries reported in Table 5, ranging from 7.3% in Singapore to 42.1% in the Philippines. Machinery is another sector that expands in all the ASEAN countries. In the Philippines APEC trade liberalization would lead to output increases in all manufacturing sectors in excess of 20% over the baseline values in 2020.

Relatively small structural adjustments are predicted to occur in Mexico and Chile. In Mexico, output growth is higher in fossil fuels, metals and products, machinery, and transport equipment over baseline projections, whereas it is lower in rice and wheat, textiles and clothing, and other manufactures. The sectoral results for Chile are consistent with our *a priori* expectations on output adjustments for a resource-abundant country. Real output growth is faster under the liberalization scenario in other agriculture, fossil fuels, other mining, wood and paper, and nonferrous metals (aggregated into metals and products), largely driven by new export demand. Real output growth becomes slower in textiles and clothing, machinery, and other manufactures.

Although not reported in this chapter, we also conducted a discriminatory liberalization experiment. Standard deviations of changes in real output relative to the baseline are not significantly different between the discriminatory and nondiscriminatory scenarios in most of the APEC countries/regions. For products with comparative disadvantage, such as agriculture and processed food in Japan and clothing in developed members, the shares of intra-APEC imports are extremely high. Thus, even though these products suffer greater output losses under nondiscriminatory liberalization, additional contractions are relatively small.

5. CONCLUSION

At the turn of this millennium, most of the nations bordering the Pacific have embarked upon an ambitious plan for open multilateralism. Although the aggregate benefits from more efficient regional specialization are readily apparent, more detailed adjustment costs *en route* to Pan-Pacific free trade are more difficult to ascertain but unlikely to be negligible in domestic policy agendas. For this reason, implementation of this trade reform agenda can be facilitated by a deeper understanding of these adjustment patterns, including the magnitude and incidence of their economic costs.

In that spirit, this chapter has provided general equilibrium estimates of the impact of APEC trade liberalization on real GDP, sectoral output, exports and imports. Compared with the baseline scenario where no trade liberalization is assumed during 2000–2020, real GDP of developed and developing APEC members is predicted to increase by $42 billion and $83 billion, respectively, by the year 2020 while that of non-APEC members would increase by $16 billion. The estimates based on our dynamic CGE model are not forecasts, however. They depend upon the model structure, parameter values, and policy scenarios. The present model does not incorporate such features as scale economies or human capital in the production function. The inclusion of these factors with dynamic specification is likely to result in a substantially larger impact of liberalization.[14] In addition, we have only considered liberalization of merchandise trade and did not include liberalization of service trade or investment in this study. Thus, our results may be considered a lower end of the full impact of APEC liberalization.

APEC members submit individual action plans (IAPs) each year, providing their own liberalization and facilitation plans for the short-, medium- and long-term horizons and unilaterally reduces its trade barriers accordingly. However, the implementation of IAPs is non-binding and several member governments are thus reluctant to remove trade barriers on politically sensitive sectors, particularly when the domestic economy is experiencing a recession or crisis. Nonetheless, if each government implements an adjustment program, including the training of workers in depressed sectors, the social costs of economic transition could be mitigated. Overall, APEC trade liberalization would produce trade expansion in most product categories, especially inexpensive imports at the expense of high-priced domestic products.

Although the assessments of APEC liberalization would be enhanced by extension of our model, as well as by more careful evaluation of IAPs, our results provide some important policy implications. First, despite large disparities in per capita income, nondiscriminatory liberalization promises substantial benefits to the APEC member countries and people in the Pacific Basin. These benefits appear to outweigh the adjustment costs of attaining a higher and more sustainable growth trajectory. Second, while the adjustments may be difficult for some groups, they are necessary if each of the member economies and the region as a whole is to realize its full economic potential. A dynamic economy cannot avoid experiencing structural adjustments, inasmuch as technological innovation and growth-induced changes in consumption and production patterns would require such adjustments. Finally, while APEC liberalization is a good long-term prescription for regional growth, speeding up the process would also be good first aid for the East Asian economies that are currently experiencing economic crisis. Economies dealing with both recession and the prospect of globalization should focus their resources on the recovery of export-oriented activities to secure a more sustainable basis for economic recovery and future growth.

NOTES

1. These data are based on the Global Trade Analysis Project (GTAP) database. See Gehlhar et al. (1997) and McDougall et al. (1998) for detailed descriptions of the GTAP database. Due to the data limitations, Brunei, Papua New Guinea, and Peru are aggregated into ROW. Russia, which is newly admitted to APEC in 1998, is also aggregated into ROW.

2. In version 4 of the GTAP database, the observed domestic-world price gap is applied at the commodity level to estimate import protection and export tax/subsidy rates. Thus a negative protection rate might result (e.g. rice and wheat in China, Mexico, and Chile) when the domestic price is lower than the world price.

3. These are largely caused by the imposition of import quotas on a number of agricultural products in these countries.

4. Japan's export subsidy rate of 83.5% on rice and wheat is significantly smaller than its import protection rate of 535%. This is because heavily protected paddy rice and wheat have negligible amount of exports compared to processed rice. In GTAP database, Japan's export subsidy rate on processed rice is set to zero whereas its import protection rates on processed rice is the same as that on paddy rice.

5. Note that the CET export specification was not implemented in the *Linkage* Model. Hence, differences in model results can partially be attributed to this change in model specification. Further, the trade elasticities used in this analysis were somewhat reduced from those used in the previous study.

6. Real GDP and population growth rates are based on the World Bank's latest projections (as of May, 1999).

7. This involves computing in each period a measure of Harrod-neutral technical progress in the capital/fixed-factor bundle as a residual, given that the growth of the labor force (in efficiency units) is pre-determined. This is a standard calibration procedure in dynamic CGE modeling.

8. Only positive tariffs and negative export distortions (i.e. subsidies) are phased out.

9. See, e.g. Lloyd (1996), Oxley (1996), Tan (1998), and Yamazawa (1996).

10. Studies evaluating the effects of alternative trade liberalization scenarios among Asia-Pacific countries include Brown et al. (1996), Lee and Woodall (1998), Lee et al. (1999), Lewis et al. (1995), Yang et al. (1998), and Young and Chye (1997). These studies generally find that, in percentage terms, both discriminatory and non-discriminatory liberalization by East Asian or APEC countries would lead to welfare gains to developing countries (e.g. China and ASEAN) that are significantly greater than those to developed countries. Recent studies assessing the impact of the Uruguay Round (e.g. Francois et al., 1996, 1997; Goldin et al., 1993; Harrison et al., 1996; Hertel et al., 1996; Yang et al., 1997) also show substantial variations in the distribution of world welfare gains across regions.

11. While we only summarize APEC countries' average protection rates by commodity in Table 2, the GTAP database provide protection rates by trading partner and by commodity.

12. Other relevant work in this area includes Walmsley (1999), who modifies the standard GTAP model and incorporates the existence of foreign ownership of capital and land. She finds that the foreign ownership of assets has a significant effect on the results of trade liberalization in the Asia-Pacific region.

13. This result crucially depends upon the assumption that labor is homogeneous and perfectly mobile across sectors. Had we disaggregated labor by type and skill, labor mobility would have been limited and many of the manufacturing sectors might not have contracted.

14. Francois et al. (1997) show that the welfare gains resulting from the Uruguay Round agreement under increasing returns to scale and monopolistic competition could be almost three times as large as those when constant returns and perfect competition are assumed.

ACKNOWLEDGMENTS

We thank Narongchai Akrasanee, Shujiro Urata, and other participants of the International Conference on "A Macroeconomic Core of an Open Economy for Progressive Industrialization and Development in Asia in the New Millennium," held in Bangkok, 16–18 December 1998, for their helpful comments.

REFERENCES

Asia-Pacific Economic Cooperation (APEC) (1997). *The Impact of Trade Liberalization in APEC.* Singapore: APEC Secretariat.

Asia-Pacific Economic Cooperation (APEC) and Pacific Economic Cooperation Council (PECC) (1995). *Surveys of Impediments to Trade and Investment in the APEC Region.* Singapore: PECC for APEC Secretariat.

Brown, D. K., Deardorff, A. V., & Stern, R. M. (1996). Computational Analysis of the Economic Effects of an East Asian Preferential Trading Bloc. *Journal of the Japanese and International Economies, 10,* 37–70.

Francois, J. F., McDonald, B., & Nordström, H. (1996). The Uruguay Round: A Numerically Based Qualitative Assessment. In: W. Martin & L. A. Winters (Eds), *The Uruguay Round and the Developing Countries.* Cambridge: Cambridge University Press.

Francois, J. F., McDonald, B., & Nordström, H. (1997). The Uruguay Round: A Global General Equilibrium Assessment. In: D. Robertson (Ed.), *East Asian Trade After the Uruguay Round.* Cambridge: Cambridge University Press.

Gehlhar, M., Gray, D., Hertel, T. W., Huff, K. M., Ianchovichina, E., McDonald, B. J., McDougall, R., Tsigas, R. E., & Wigle, R. (1997). Overview of the GTAP Data Base. In: T. W. Hertel (Ed.), *Global Trade Analysis: Modeling and Applications.* New York: Cambridge University Press.

Goldin, I., Knudsen, O., & van der Mensbrugghe, D. (1993). Trade Liberalization: Global Economic Implications. Paris and Washington, D.C.: OECD and World Bank.

Harrison, G. W., Rutherford, T. F., & Tarr, D. G. (1996). Quantifying the Uruguay Round. In: W. Martin & L. A. Winters (Eds), *The Uruguay Round and the Developing Countries.* Cambridge: Cambridge University Press.

Hertel, T. W. (Ed.) (1997). *Global Trade Analysis: Modeling and Applications*. New York: Cambridge University Press.

Hertel, T. W., Martin, W., Yanagishima, K., & Dimaranan, B. (1996). Liberalizing Manufactures Trade in a Changing World Economy. In: W. Martin & L. A. Winters (Eds), *The Uruguay Round and the Developing Countries*. Cambridge: Cambridge University Press.

Lee, H., & Roland-Holst, D. (1998). Cooperative Approaches to Shifting Comparative Advantage: The Case of Bilateral Trade between the United States and Japan. In: H. Lee & D. W. Roland-Holst (Eds), *Economic Development and Cooperation in the Pacific Basin: Trade, Investment, and Environmental Issues*. New York: Cambridge University Press.

Lee, H., Roland-Holst, D., & van der Mensbrugghe, D. (1999). Quantitative Analysis of APEC Liberalization Using Calibrated General Equilibrium Modelling. In: M. E. Kreinin, M. G. Plummer & S. Abe (Eds), *Asia-Pacific Economic Linkages*. Amsterdam: Elsevier.

Lee, H., & Woodall, B. (1998). Political Feasibility and Empirical Assessments of a Pacific Free Trade Area. In: H. Lee & D. Roland-Holst (Eds), *Economic Development and Cooperation in the Pacific Basin: Trade, Investment, and Environmental Issues*. New York: Cambridge University Press.

Lewis, J. D., Robinson, S., & Wang, Z. (1995). Beyond the Uruguay Round: The Implications of an Asian Free Trade Area. *China Economic Review, 6*, 35–90.

Lloyd, P. J. (1996). Regional Trading Arrangements and Regional Integration. *Asian Economic Journal, 10*, 1–28.

McDougall, R., Elbehri, A., & Truong, T. P. (Eds) (1998). Global Trade, Assistance, and Protection: The GTAP 4 Data Base, West Lafayette: Center for Global Trade Analysis. Purdue University.

McKibbin, W. J. (1998). Regional and Multilateral Trade Liberalisation: The Effects on Trade, Investment and Welfare. In: P. Drysdale & D. Vines (Eds), *Europe, East Asia and APEC: A Shared Global Agenda?* Cambridge: Cambridge University Press.

OECD (1997). The LINKAGE Model, mimeo. OECD Development Center, Paris.

Oxley, A. (1996). Political Hurdles to the Realisation of the Bogor Declaration: The Need to Revisit 'Open Regionalism'. Paper presented at the Conference on International Consortium of APEC Study Centers, Manila, May 9–10.

Panagariya, A. (1998). Should East Asia Go Regional? In: H. Lee & D. W. Roland-Holst (Eds), *Economic Development and Cooperation in the Pacific Basin: Trade, Investment, and Environmental Issues*. New York: Cambridge University Press.

Petri, P. A. (1997). Foreign Direct Investment in a Computable General Equilibrium Framework. Paper presented at the Brandeis-Keio Conference on "Making APEC Work: Economic Challenges and Policy Alternatives". Keio University, Tokyo, March 13–14.

Tan, K. Y. (1998). Regionalism in the Pacific Basin: Strategic Interest of ASEAN in APEC. In: H. Lee & D. W. Roland-Holst (Eds), *Economic Development and Cooperation in the Pacific Basin: Trade, Investment, and Environmental Issues*. New York: Cambridge University Press.

Walmsley, T. L. (1999). Incorporating International Capital Ownership into the GTAP Model: Results for Asia-Pacific Trade Liberalisation. Preliminary Working Paper No. IP-72, Centre of Policy Studies and the Impact Project, Monash University.

Yamazawa, I. (1996). APEC's New Development and Its Implications for Nonmember Developing Countries. *Developing Economies, 34*, 113–137.

Yamazawa, I. (1997). APEC's Progress toward the Bogor Target: A Quantitative Assessment of Individual Action Plans Report, Japan National Committee for Pacific Economic Cooperation and APEC Study Center, Hitotsubashi University, September.

Yang, Y., Duncan, R., & Lawson, T. (1998). Trade Liberalisation in the European Union and APEC: What If the Approaches Were Exchanged? In: P. Drysdale & D. Vines (Eds), *Europe, East Asia and APEC: A Shared Global Agenda?* Cambridge: Cambridge University Press.

Yang, Y., Martin, W., & Yanagishima, K. (1997). Evaluating the Benefits of Abolishing the MFA in the Uruguay Round Package. In: T. W. Hertel (Ed.), *Global Trade Analysis: Modeling and Applications*. New York: Cambridge University Press.

Young, L. M., & Chye, K. M. (1997). Free Trade in the Pacific Rim: On What Basis? In: T. W. Hertel (Ed.), *Global Trade Analysis: Modeling and Applications*. New York: Cambridge University Press.

36. TRADE AND INDUSTRIALIZATION OF THAILAND IN 2020[1]

Juanjai Ajanant

I. INTRODUCTION

Thailand was able to grow on average of about 6–7% per annum in the 1960s and 1970s. From the mid-1980s to the early 1990s, the economy was growing over the 10% mark. Despite the robust growth throughout the decades, the economy is susceptible to many inherent weaknesses. The 1997 financial meltdown that took place in Thailand sends a strong signal that accumulated weaknesses within the system have finally handcuffed the true potential for industrialization of the country. Thailand by choice did not develop manufacturing industries on a broad base. Unlike many countries in 18th century Europe, that began their industrial revolution on strategic industries such as the iron and steel industry and capital machinery industry, Thailand, originally an agrarian society, leaped forward into industrialization on a different path. Instead, the industrialists began to invest in light industries focusing on food-processing and textiles. All of these industries relied on imported capital machinery and foreign know-how. The textile industry also required raw-materials – polyester fiber and cotton yarn – from abroad, as the local supply did not meet technical requirements. As the industrialization was underway, the private sector began to invest in rubber-based, wood-based, jewelry, automotive parts, computer peripherals, electronics, electrical appliances, steel products, and petrochemical industries.

Industries were established in Thailand with active state involvement. In fact, the initial push for industrialization was delivered with concerted efforts from the government. Prior to 1960, most production capacities were in the domain

Restructuring Asian Economics for the New Millennium, Volume 9B, pages 743–772.

ISBN: 0-7623-0710-2

of public enterprises. Outside of the retail and wholesale commerce, there was no private sector participation in industrial production. There was enough interest among businessmen to invest, but the government under Field Marshall Pibulsongkram was reluctant to permit ethnic Chinese to be involved in the production.[2] The ending of the Pibulsongkram period was followed by another dictatorial government under Field Marshall Sarit Thanarat. This strong man must be credited as the man behind the big push toward production by the private sector. It was during his brief tenure as head of the government from 1959 to 1963 that many economic laws were promulgated to set up the investment and economic planning boards. Many agencies that were established then became the hot bed of ideas on development and industrialization during the following decades.

In terms of promotional effort from the state, at the risk of over-simplification, we can subdivide the four decades into two periods. From the 1960s, the industrialization process was encouraged with an intention of substituting imports. Before 1960, it was difficult to name a business/industry managed by Thai private businessmen. Almost all productive units were operated by public enterprises. It was believed necessary to follow the inward-looking policy in the initial years. The country was short of capital, technology, entrepreneur, raw-materials, and unskilled labour. The capital shortage is well-known and typical of any developing country at the time. The intellectual foundations for this approach were provided by Holis Chenery who was writing his famous articles on the two-gap theory with his colleagues. While many people worked in the private sector, most Thai graduates of that period joined the civil service or public enterprises as they were the main employers of trained people. Labourers toiling on farms had to be trained to perform on the shop floor. The training task normally was to last several years before the high labour absentee rate dropped. After the first oil shock in 1973/1974, there was solid demand for Thai products in international markets. Most manufacturers began shifting their output to the export markets. By the late 1970s, it became clear that inward-looking industrialization had reached its useful limits. By the early 1980s, the government decided belatedly to shift from the inward-looking process to the outward-looking process to accommodate export prospects. This period saw a close cooperation between the public and private sectors. Businessmen were actually demanding the state to change its policy measures to fit with the reality. The outward-looking process transformed the Thai economy and put into place a system that promotes industry that has remained largely intact.

The shift from the inward oriented policy to an outward oriented policy was very slow, and sometimes the old measures have not been legally discarded. In most cases, policymakers have attempted to bypass the old legal labyrinth by creating a new route. As we shall see later, some of the new measures and old measures actually complicate the system. Some pundits attribute this complex system to an aversion to meddling with the legality of policy measures in the overall economy. In addition, in terms of the contribution to economic surplus, the manufacturing sector could not produce at the most lowest cost and relied upon tariff protection while the surplus sector (the agriculture) was being taxed. In short, the spectacular growth of the manufacturing industry was achieved in part at the expense of the agricultural sector. This paper is intended to discuss two crucial issues. The first half of this paper will examine the pitfalls of trade and industrialization that has taken root since the mid-1960s. Subsequently, we shall offer an alternative concept to trade and industrialization for the coming decades.

II. MAJOR PITFALLS OF INDUSTRIALIZATION

This section will appraise the past performance of the trade régime and the industrialization process since the 1960s. As the industry was still embryonic in the initial phase, the economic surplus came from the agriculture. The rapid growth of the economy in the early 1960s was based on the performance of the agrarian sector as light industries took root. Primary commodities such as rice, tin, and rubber buttressed the economy while industrialization was actively promoted. Thailand followed the standard international practice of the time by enacting disincentive measures for the agriculture in favour of budding industries. Industries were producing output to replace imports in their initial phase. Exports did not show any concrete trend in this period. The real contribution of the manufactured sector in export revenues began to show by the mid-1970s as export growth was initiated. Manufactured export growth was rapid in the 1980s, and in certain periods, the contribution of manufactured export led overall exports to achieve double-digit growth. By the early 1990s, export growth was already over 14% per annum and eventually began to attenuate by the late 1990s. Therefore, the growth dimension of industrialization was very impressive.

There were many studies in the 1980s linking growth and exports of the country, pointing to the close relationship between the two parameters. Some studies indicated that if export grew by one percentage point, then GDP growth studies would be about one-half a percentage point. Such was the case during the period when the degree of openness of the economy was high as measured by the percentage of foreign trade in the gross domestic product. While internal commerce had its own life, the foreign sector of the economy was the prime mover of economic prosperity. As Bhagwati (1996) notes, if the economy had been closed, the expansion of demand would have been surely constrained by the growth in agriculture which has not exceeded 4% anywhere over a sustained period of time.[3] Colin Bradford (1988) hypothesized that export growth was promoted by economic growth.[4] His hypothesis was plausible, but the bulk of evidence pointed to the opposite direction.

There were some drawbacks to the rapid growth of industries achieved in the economy. Table 1 shows the trade account from 1961 to 1995. Throughout the entire period, there was chronic deficit. Since the floatation of the baht in 1997, trade account has shown positive numbers resulting from a sharp decline on the import side. Yet these results underscore that Thai manufacturers have to import in order to export. Even when we combine services account into the trade account, the current account also shows deficits in the same period. The current account in 1998 has also shown some positive numbers due to inflows of direct foreign investment. In Table 2, we separate imports of intermediate inputs and raw materials from total imports. Here one can see that about one quarter of Thai merchandise imports constitutes raw materials and intermediate products. The inability of Thai manufacturers to integrate backward is perhaps due to the unwillingness of joint-venture partners to shift the upstream production. Manufacturing export growth shows Thai manufacturers and labour are capable of processing many imported intermediate inputs into finished products. But that perhaps suggests the limits of industrialization in the trade régime.

When industrialization took place, one of the many objectives was to create job opportunities for the Thai people. In the 1960s, the population was at the 30 million mark, with over one-half of the population under the working age. In 1996, according to the ADB, the population was recorded at 60 million.[5] Starting from the late 1970s, birth control was vastly advocated, and today population growth of Thailand is about 1.5% per annum. On average, the labour supply would be expanding at 200,000 persons per annum in the early period to 600,000 persons per annum in the latter years. Table 3 illustrates employment in the manufacturing sector from 1973–1996. In the first eight years through 1980 employment in the sector remained below 2 million persons in all but two years. It took nine years more to increase employment to the 3 million point and only three additional years to reach the 4 million point. By 1996, employment had reached the 4.5 million point. Therefore, the demand for labour was growing at approximately 6% per annum. Since there are no capital figures in the archives, we do not know the capital-labour ratio of the sector. But the rate of supply of labour to the economy was growing more rapidly than the rate of demand. The excess supply of labour is being pushed back to the agricultural sector and tertiary sectors (see Table 4). This is not

Table 1. Current Account and Trade Account.

(Unit: Million Baht)

Year	Export	Import	Service	Current Account
1961	9,622.70	–10,062.10	320.10	180.70
1962	9,434.50	–11,241.50	508.40	–1,298.60
1963	9,577.70	–12,547.00	686.20	–2,283.10
1964	12,165.00	–14,015.00	732.20	–1,117.80
1965	12,663.50	–15,091.00	1,443.80	–983.70
1966	13,817.20	–18,172.00	4,107.10	–247.70
1967	13,808.10	–22,188.00	5,913.10	–2,466.80
1968	13,227.60	–24,103.00	6,188.30	–4,687.10
1969	14,254.20	–25,966.00	5,853.50	–5,858.30
1970	14,269.70	–27,009.00	6,036.20	–6,703.10
1971	16,697.10	–26,749.00	5,404.10	–4,647.80
1972	21,750.20	30,875.00	6,583.00	–2,541.80
1973	31,252.50	–42,184.00	6,836.40	–4,095.10
1974	44,364.50	–64,525.70	6,160.80	–11,483.40
1975	60,361.20	–71,446.10	1,642.50	–6,924.40
1976	70,462.80	–96,004.80	2,405.20	–20,617.80
1977	82,250.80	–109,956.10	4,279.10	–20,906.20
1978	106,881.20	–153,463.50	3,237.90	–40,823.40
1979	132,040.50	–190,025.30	11,144.90	–44,317.90
1980	150,218.20	–216,000.10	6,042.40	–57,216.50
1981	157,230.40	–193,319.60	8,795.00	–24,770.20
1982	145,076.10	–234,278.50	16,758.40	–69,919.00
1983	173,520.00	–242,283.60	15,199.40	–51,038.20
1984	191,703.00	–253,337.60	15,252.60	–43,855.00
1985	231,481.40	–245,690.30	14,969.60	3,288.70
1986	298,099.10	–341,376.30	28,713.40	–12,034.80
1987	399,230.20	–501,400.80	54,376.60	–45,264.00
1988	509,924.90	–647,802.30	68,897.80	–66,448.60
1989	583,206.30	–832,606.90	63,528.30	–183,337.30
1990	720,545.00	–967,808.00	67,919.00	–176,811.00
1991	815,202.00	–1,020,582.00	72,279.00	–130,567.00
1992	921,433.00	–1,143,108.00	77,142.00	–141,998.00
1993	1,118,049.00	–1,344,831.00	38,712.00	–185,534.00
1994	1,381,660.00	–1,755,456.00	76,643.00	–294,616.00
1995	1,378,902.00	–1,796,549.00	111,998.00	–303,111.00

Source: Bank of Thailand.

surprising as we believe most industries have adopted production techniques in favour of capital relative to the use of labour.

Table 2. Intermediate Product and Raw Material (I & R) and Growth. (Unit: Million Baht)

Year	(I&R)	Growth
1974	16,105.00	20.34719818
1975	20,219.00	24.89506333
1976	26,921.00	9.044530036
1977	29,598.00	31.95862069
1978	43,500.00	3.998940678
1979	45,312.00	15.42323845
1980	53,575.00	–10.24569923
1981	48,596.00	26.89472576
1982	66,474.00	4.509215233
1983	69,613.00	8.128332366
1984	75,772.00	10.15142352
1985	84,333.00	29.60047146
1986	119,792.00	34.42378857
1987	182,676.00	23.1067765
1988	237,571.00	16.65462174
1989	285,044.00	13.51610476
1990	329,592.00	0.523651861
1991	331,327.00	5.172038764
1992	349,398.00	11.45155404
1993	394,584.00	22.5687951
1994	509,593.00	–7.595556766
1995	473,619.00	4.57540175
1996	496,328.00	

Source: Bank of Thaialnd.

We believe conomists may regard this capital-labour ratio to be contrary to the factor proportions theory that encourages the use of abundant resources to be used intensively. In the real world, availability of technology is not divisible as depicted by a smooth isoquant. There are some technologies that will fit with the market size and financial capacity of an enterprise. Some labour-using technologies may not be suitable to achieve the optimum cost on a long-term basis. Incidentally, as Thai industrialists have embarked upon the international setting, the scale of output tends to favour the capital-intensive and technology-intensive techniques that discourage the use of an abundant factor. For example, an ethylene cracking plant producing 600,000 tons of output annually requires only 200 workers to perform the operation. By contrast, a tuna cannery producing 400 tons of canned items on a daily basis requires 7,000 persons to

Table 3. Employment in Manufacturing Sector.

Year	Manufacturing
1973	1,506.40
1974	2,125.40
1975	1,958.90
1976	1,514.00
1977	1,879.10
1978	1,740.20
1979	2,177.30
1980	1,788.90
1981	2,088.10
1982	2,404.70
1983	2,536.70
1984	2,283.90
1985	2,152.00
1986	2,300.00
1987	2,738.70
1988	2,611.10
1989	3,104.30
1990	3,132.60
1991	3,802.00
1992	4,054.70
1993	4,179.00
1994	4,348.30
1995	4,608.20
1996	4,513.00

Source: Ministry of Labor and Social Welfare.

man the operation. Thai entrepreneurs cannot always find the labour-intensive techniques to fit the factor-proportionality. They can only match market demand with the available technologies, regardless of whether those are capital-intensive or otherwise. Therefore, one cannot give a full mark for employment creation as there are often mixed results of the industrialization.

Employment creation in this fashion may have mixed results, but when it comes to the use of scientists and engineers in the manufacturing sector, the performance is below par. In the 1960s when President Park Chung Hee of South Korea embarked on the modernization program, one of the key parameters to the success of the Korean industrialization was the number of scientists and engineers coming out of universities. The emphasis on science and technology in Korea and other newly industrialization countries (NICs) was to achieve independence in industrial knowledge, without which it would

Table 4. Employment by Sector, All Industries, 1994–1995.

Industry	1994
Municipal Areas	Total Employment 5,539,700
1. Agriculture, Forestry, Hunting and Fishing	211,400
2. Mining and Quarrying	5,500
3. Manufacturing	1,262,900
4. Construction, Repair and Demolition	301,800
5. Electricity, Gas, Water and Sanitary Services	89,600
6. Commerce	1,558,000
7. Transport,Storage and Communication	391,300
8. Services	1,714,000
9. Activities not Adequately Described	4,800
Non-municipal Areas	22,693,700
1. Agriculture, Forestry, Hunting and Fishing	12,189,100
2. Mining and Quarrying	59,700
3. Manufacturing	3,267,600
4. Construction, Repair and Demolition	1,993,600
5. Electricity, Gas, Water and Sanitary Services	93,300
6. Commerce	2,355,900
7. Transport, Storage and Communication	540,400
8. Services	2,190,100
9. Activities not Adequately Described	3,600
Total employed persons	28,233,400
Municipal Areas	total employment 6,078,300
1. Agriculture, Forestry, Hunting and Fishing	94,200
2. Mining and Quarrying	4,700
3. Manufacturing	1,484,900
4. Construction, Repair and Demolition	509,900
5. Electricity, Gas, Water and Sanitary Services	79,900
6. Commerce	1,679,700
7. Tranaport, Storage and Communication	444,600
8. Services	1,765,700
9. Activities not Adequately Described	14,200
Non-municipal Areas	22,976,700
1. Agriculture, Forestry, Hunting and Fishing	11,754,600
2. Mining and Quarrying	59,300
3. Manufacturing	3,354,500
4. Construction, Repair and Demolition	2,139,100
5. Electricity, Gas, Water and Sanitary Services	114,100
6. Commerce	2,594,800
7. Tranaport, Storage and Communication	581,100
8. Services	2,377,000
9. Activities not Adequately Described	1,900
Total, Employed Persons	29,055,000

Source: Ministry of Labor and Social Welfare.

be impossible for developing countries to catch up with the developed countries. By contrast, the emphasis on science and technology in Thailand has lagged behind the NICs. While universities in Thailand have been able to train many graduates in the science and technology fields, they have not been employed in the real sector. The implication of Table 8 is that there are few people who are working in these fields. Human resources in this field appear to be well behind many countries in the region.

While the capital-intensive techniques are pursued with vigour, the accumulation of core knowledge to furthering the scientific knowledge of industry is lagging behind. Before World War II, most western countries were spending around 4% of GDP in R&D. Whether this had anything to do with the armaments or not, we do not know. The level of R&D expenditure (Table 5) indicates that the country spent less than U.S.$100 thousand per annum.

Table 5. R&D Expenditure in Thailand.

(Unit: Million Baht)

Year	Value
1976	1,166.00
1977	1,277.00
1978	1,468.00
1979	1,331.00
1980	1,507.00
1981	2,549.00
1982	3,271.00
1983	1,656.00
1984	2,104.00
1985	2,416.00
1986	2,020.00
1987	2,664.00
1988	2,504.00
1989	2,908.00
1990	3,076.00
1991	3,228.00
1992	3,484.00
1993	3,716.00
1994	3,756.00
1995	3,974.00
1996	4,085.00
1997	4,178.00

Source: Office of National Research.

Expenditures by firms on in-house researches are not calculated into these figures. Few firms have in-house laboratories and the budget toward this item is not a top priority. The reasons that discourage the spending on R&D are well known. If the technologies are patented, then the technology owners would transfer, at a cost, all technical details to the licensers. If there is no patent, the process is very old, and there is no impetus to seek patentable techniques. Most people in the Thai society believe that knowledge is powerful. In the same

Table 6. Corporate Income Tax.

(Unit: Million Baht)

Year	Corp tax
1967	845.00
1968	979.00
1969	1,182.00
1970	1,298.00
1971	1,455.00
1972	1,557.00
1973	1,760.00
1974	2,090.00
1975	3,628.00
1976	3,734.00
1977	4,695.00
1978	6,458.00
1979	7,837.00
1980	9,612.00
1981	13,448.00
1982	12,779.00
1983	13,198.00
1984	14,616.00
1985	15,390.00
1986	15,522.00
1987	17,623.00
1988	27,351.00
1989	38,755.00
1990	58,658.00
1991	74,934.00
1992	85,586.00
1993	103,038.00
1994	134,783.00
1995	157,430.00

Source: Bank of Thailand.

breath, people believe that knowledge is a free good, and we should not pay for the use of knowledge. In the commercial world, Thai businessmen who use a patented process normally pay for the use of that patent throughout the period through a special technology agreement. The government in the 1980s was not aware of the extensiveness of the piracy issue and refused to pass the intellectual property rights laws as demanded by many trading partners. Debates on insignificant points were pedantic and did not change how business was conducted in any way.

But to provide a balanced view to the above, one is inclined to mention the role of direct foreign investment (DFI) in the economy. Thailand lacks indigenous capital knowledge such that technology had to be imported. Panagariya (1998a) notes that imports of superior technology can provide both a higher level of income and a higher rate of growth.[6] The level effect can be

Table 7. Gross National Investment and Gross National Saving.
(Unit: Million Baht)

Year	GNI	GNS
1975	75,747.00	49,840.00
1976	78,444.00	60,155.00
1977	102,540.00	83,797.00
1978	126,950.00	77,378.00
1979	160,287.00	86,420.00
1980	193,060.00	100,144.00
1981	225,638.00	98,836.00
1982	223,155.00	125,675.00
1983	276,069.00	130,354.00
1984	291,215.00	139,977.00
1985	298,404.00	151,539.00
1986	293,236.00	172,879.00
1987	262,347.00	240,973.00
1988	508,354.00	366,101.00
1989	651,175.00	475,883.00
1990	902,978.00	530,118.00
1991	1,073,877.00	634,535.00
1992	1,131,345.00	677,261.00
1993	1,266,221.00	753,336.00
1994	1,462,112.00	867,679.00
1995	1,742,814.00	895,583.00
1996	1,919,014.00	1,071,300.00

Source: NESDB, BOT.

Table 8. Number of Scientists and Engineers in Thailand.
(Unit: Persons)

Year	Scientist	Engineer
1988	343	2,574
1989	529	2,911
1990	489	3,459
1991	307	3,692
1992	257	5,281
1993	218	6,025
1994	283	5,779
1995	236	6,307
1996	n.a	8,688
1997	n.a	10,133

Source: Office of National Statistics.

seen directly in the shifting down of supply curve. As long as the extra cost of technology imports is below the extra surplus generated by the downward shift in the domestic supply curve, there will be a net gain in the society.

But it is important to note that the benefits of the DFI are less in the presence of trade barriers. This is because at least a part of the investment will be of the tariff-jumping variety. Such investment may locate in the import-competing sector. This is harmful to the extent that the import-competing sector has already become overextended due to the trade barriers. In addition, any benefits arising from imports of superior technology are likely to be limited by the size of the domestic market. The petrochemical industry in Thailand relies on protection and domestic market to survive international competition. By contrast, in the absence of trade barriers, investment is more likely to locate in the export sector which is unconstrained by the domestic market.

Before the Uruguay Round MTN was concluded in April 1994, the Commerce Ministry had established the Department of Intellectual Property that registers all patents. During the short period of operations from 1992, the number of patents has grown significantly. At the last count there are 4,779 total patents registered in Thailand. Foreign patents number 4,057, and Thai patents are 722. Of these numbers, the majority shown in Table 9 is listed under the design heading. There is no special category for sub-patents, and, therefore, we have no knowledge whether these Thai patents are major patents or sub-patents. While we have made strides in the right direction, it is too late to debate the merits of intellectual property rights in the 1990s when most of the

Table 9. Number of Patents Granted to Thai and Other Nationalities.

				Inventions												
	Design			Chemistry			Engineering			Total			Grand Total			
Year	Thai	Foreign	Total	Thai	Foreign	Total	Thai	Foreign	Total	Thai	Foreign	Total	Thai	Foreign	Total
1992	72	115	187	4	133	137	7	55	62	11	188	199	83	303	386
1993	83	79	162	3	170	173	6	110	116	9	280	289	92	359	451
1994	51	192	243	4	261	265	7	159	166	11	420	431	62	612	674
1995	100	212	312	0	231	231	1	238	239	1	469	470	101	681	782
1996	168	303	471	7	394	401	11	472	483	18	866	884	186	1169	1355
1997	176	249	425	4	267	271	18	417	435	22	684	706	198	933	1131
Total	650	1,150	1,800	22	1,456	1,478	50	1,451	1,501	72	2,907	2,979	722	4,057	4,779

Source: Intellectual Property Department.

technologies are foreign technologies. Thailand will not be able to develop her local technologies as long as the society cannot prioritize the basic ingredients of industrialization.

Due to the relatively slower growth of its domestic market, Thai industries have, since the mid-1980s, tilted markedly toward the export market. Within the export system, there are many incentive measures that promote exports. These include tax rebates, tax withdrawals, tax exemption, and access to a lenient export financing system. In addition, both the Department of Customs and the Office of the Board of Investment are empowered to return import duties to exporters, so long as import duties were paid prior to importation. Table 11 illustrates the number of tax refund cases under Article 19(2) of the

Table 10. Saving by Household, Private Sector and Public Sector.

(Unit: Million Baht)

Year	New Saving	Private Sector		Public Sector	
		Household	Corporate	Government	Public Enterprise
1974	63,494.00	37,815.00	17,633.00	6,877.00	1,169.00
1975	49,840.00	42,071.00	3,078.00	3,512.00	1,179.00
1976	60,155.00	44,062.00	4,277.00	9,883.00	1,933.00
1977	83,797.00	62,529.00	9,156.00	9,062.00	3,050.00
1978	77,378.00	58,598.00	6,970.00	9,062.00	2,748.00
1979	86,420.00	68,864.00	8,902.00	6,170.00	2,484.00
1980	100,144.00	75,256.00	13,456.00	10,531.00	901.00
1981	98,836.00	72,935.00	14,724.00	9,174.00	2,003.00
1982	125,675.00	113,011.00	13,317.00	3,384.00	2,731.00
1983	130,354.00	96,102.00	16,793.00	10,066.00	7,393.00
1984	139,977.00	105,974.00	16,717.00	5,703.00	11,583.00
1985	151,539.00	124,809.00	15,595.00	3,320.00	14,455.00
1986	172,879.00	134,729.00	17,980.00	4,750.00	15,420.00
1987	240,973.00	161,224.00	31,815.00	29,404.00	18,530.00
1988	366,101.00	211,138.00	44,262.00	85,373.00	25,328.00
1989	475,883.00	267,435.00	61,870.00	112,848.00	33,730.00
1990	530,118.00	213,168.00	92,357.00	182,678.00	41,915.00
1991	634,535.00	255,434.00	102,025.00	234,145.00	42,931.00
1992	677,261.00	270,924.00	138,503.00	222,290.00	45,544.00
1993	753,336.00	271,554.00	169,336.00	260,403.00	52,043.00
1994	867,679.00	246,543.00	228,273.00	333,281.00	59,582.00
1995	895,583.00	296,110.00	238,385.00	290,978.00	70,110.00
1996	1,071,300.00	357,500.00	226,200.00	377,800.00	69,800.00

Source: NESDB.

Table 11. Number of tax-rebate and value under Article 19(2) of Customs Act.

(Unit: Million Baht)

Year	Number of Applications	Value of Rebates	Value of Export under Article 19(2)
1987	66,579	3,916.19	n.a
1988	71,993	5,493.74	n.a
1989	108,068	8,550.95	n.a
1990	164,845	11,878.00	127,394.00
1991	188,226	12,777.00	127,930.00
1992	208,760	18,732.00	202,676.00
1993	262,332	18,616.00	268,158.00
1994	357,160	18,942.00	451,609.00
1995	383,412	17,369.00	649,267.00
1996	369,997	15,725.47	754,660.60
1997	424,698	13,132.67	945,860.21

Source: Customs Department.

Customs Act. In general, all corporations in Thailand pay a minimum of 30% of their profits as corporate taxes, and they can also use annual operating losses to offset the future taxable income. The tax contribution of companies in Thailand, including the manufacturing sector, was initially quite small. In 1967, shown in Table 6, it was Baht 845 million. By 1975, this figure amounted to Baht 3.6 billion and reached Baht 13.44 billion in 1981. Between 1981 and 1995, the corporate income tax climbed to reach Baht 157 billion in 1995. Currently the corporate income tax is not a substantial amount compared to the value-added tax that contributes over 46% of the tax revenue. One would have hoped that as the industries grow up they will be the ones that provide fiscal strength to the economy.

It is harsh to judge the performance of the industries in accordance with the criterion that we have considered. But that is the only yardstick that we have to measure the performance in positive economic terms. In normative terms, the economic policies that the country pursued during the course of the last 39 years is unbalanced in favour of manufactured producers. The early planners were convinced that to amortize any investment, producers must earn over 30% gross margin. Thus, high tariffs would be sufficient to do the trick. Through the high tariff protection in the early period of industrialization, consumers were suffering from the consumer loss due to high domestic prices of consumer goods. Producers enjoyed the luxury of a barrier to trade to charge an amount equal to CIF plus the tariff in commodities that had no rivals in the local market. This problem was acute when most tariff rates were in excess of 40% *ad valorem*. This burden remained when the trade régime moved from the inward-looking towards the outward-looking path. Instead of dismantling tariff barriers to liberalize the manufacturing sector, the authorities chose to maintain the tariff system. It was after Thailand joined the GATT and after 1994 that the excessive rates of tariff began to abate. The current simple average rate of tariff in all 96 chapters of tariff lines is now at 18.49%, and these reduced tariffs should offer some relief to consumers.

The type of régime that Thailand has pursued also hinged on the ability of the Finance Ministry to collect revenue from various sources. The Customs Department has traditionally collected over 15% of government revenue. This is a remnant of the early 1950s, when the government could not design an internal tax system to collect sufficient revenue. Instead, it relied on border tax revenues to boost the income of the ministry. In the 1970s and 1980s, the ramifications of the import duties were enormous, such that local producers were allying themselves with the Finance Ministry.[7] Since local producers were reluctant to face liberalization, they found a convenient ally in the Finance Ministry. The introduction of the value-added system changes this picture drastically. The ministry is no longer counting on the tariff revenue to boost government income. In tune with the global trend of trade liberalization, the trade régime has become more liberal than ever. Currently domestic producers are finding themselves pleading with the Finance Ministry for protection. It is a rather unique relationship that has turned 180 degrees in a span of one decade.

The regional dispersion of the manufacturing sector in Thailand has been discussed at length by many authors. Only modest commentary is necessary. By the early 1980s, it was found that the industrialization of the country took place together with the urbanization of the Bangkok Metropolitan Administration (BMA). Entrepreneurs tend to concentrate their production activities in Bangkok and neighbouring provinces. Some cite the geographical convenience to the port for inbound and outbound merchandise as the decisive factor. Many mentioned the availability of utilities and labour within the zone as the attraction. The Ministry of Industry developed industrial estates with promotional privileges for producers and achieved a certain level of success. There are now industrial estates in several provinces outside of BMA, such as in the eastern seaboard and in Nakhorn Ratchasima. The effort by the BOI to promote the relocation of industries into Zone III (comprising 60 provinces) was met with reluctance from the business community.

During the 1980s by NESDB attempted to map out growth centers in all regions of the kingdom. However, the urbanization of the BMA has grown by leaps and bounds while the urbanization of other major cities has been somewhat limited. If BMA has a population over 5 million, the next major cities such as Nakhorn Ratchasima and Chiangmai can only boast about 1 million people in their respective domains. The influx of migratory workers from rural areas into the BMA has been an established pattern for many decades. There are at least three attractive points to working in the BMA. First, the minimum wage in the BMA is higher than any province in the country. Second, it is easier for migratory workers to find a paying job in the BMA. Third, the availability of utilities and life conveniences in the BMA is more widespread than in the rural areas. Of course, maintaining a comfortable life in the BMA is more difficult as its cost of living is higher than those in other provinces. Still, the net inflow of rural people into major cities continues to be the standard today. One would have wished that living in Bangkok should not be markedly different from living in Chiangmai and other provinces. The BMA is full of industrial belts lying to the north, the east, and the south of the city center. This pattern is similar to Birmingham, Manchester, and Liverpool in England in the Victorian era. The only missing link is that Thailand has as yet no other major cities apart from Bangkok.

III. A NEW PARADIGM

Intellectual and scientific advances, Thomas Kuhn showed in his *The Structure of Scientific Revolution*, consists of the displacement of one paradigm, which has become increasingly incapable of explaining new or newly discovered facts, by a new paradigm, which does account for those facts in a more satisfactory fashion. "To be accepted as a paradigm", Kuhn wrote, "a theory must seem better than its competitors, but it need not, and in fact never does, explain the facts with which it can be confronted".[8]

Before we begin to discuss the new paradigm for trade and industrialization, it is essential to discuss the changing external environment that necessitates fresh thinking on Thailand's industries and trade. The trading environment which has existed since the 1930s up to the end of the Uruguay Round evolved around tariffs and non-tariff barriers. For sure, there were other issues as well, but the main focus has been on tariffs. From the end of World War II until 1994, the tariff rates of major countries have declined markedly. Lavergne calculated that the tariff declined from the first round of MTN by more than one-third at the end of the Tokyo Round.[9] The Uruguay Round also concluded with further reduction of tariff rates by another 37%. The decline of tariffs stimulates the total volume of trade by many folds. About two-thirds of total global trade is conducted between the OECD countries. The remaining trade is between the North and the South.

The decline of tariff rates in the economies around the globe also gives rise to non-tariff barriers and other technical barriers. Non-tariff barriers used to be simple and not as complicated as at present. Today many countries have resorted to administered practices, such as surveillance and monitoring. Many countries have also conducted dumping investigations, even though there is no clear evidence of dumped products in their markets. Michael Fingers (1993) notes that the major industrial countries led by the U.S. have the longest and most extensive experience with anti-dumping procedures and remedies. However, as developing countries have liberalized their traditional trade régimes, they have begun to turn to modern forms of administered protection, particularly anti-dumping mechanisms and procedures to appease domestic vested interests. Though the number of anti-dumping cases initiated by developing countries remains considerably smaller than in advanced countries, they are turning to potential anti-dumping remedies at rates fast approaching the advanced countries.[10] Fingers also regarded the administered remedies to be effective prompting importers faced with uncertainties to switch to imports from other suppliers.

In recent years, the quality aspect of standardized products has become the central issue of many major importing nations. The introduction of the ISO system, HACCP and GMP means that small firms may not be able to internalize the incremental costs of improvement. Firms are being pushed to be either regional or global players in their respective fields. It also signals the end of small and medium firms at the global level. Firms in developing countries are faced with a dilemma: to compete in a world market, they have to become a global scale through merger and/or rapid internal expansion. This route is very difficult, as it requires heavy funding in a short span of time. Most firms will not become world players since heavy investment is beyond their capacities.

The proliferation of free trade agreement (FTA) and other economic groupings since 1990 also changes the trading scenario in a surprising way. In a world with high tariffs and without free trade areas, it was convenient to classify a country's products into exportable or importable. The tariff level of the country can neatly separate the two. The FTA – with free flows of goods across borders with preferential tariffs – implies that some merchandise is no longer importable or exportable. Goods produced in Mexico must compete with goods from Canada and the U.S. The pulp and paper industry in Thailand will soon be forced to compete head-on with low-cost pulp from Indonesia under the AFTA scheme. Fortunately, the AFTA covers only relatively smaller portions of the overall trade of ASEAN nations; otherwise, there would be more trade conflicts. Furthermore, in the near future, there is a great likelihood that many multinational companies (MNC) will exploit AFTA for their benefits. The case in point is the ethylene cracking plants by Exxon and Mobil established in Singapore. These petrochemical plants will be eligible to ship their products to all markets of the ASEAN.

The liberalization process that the Uruguay Round established is being followed up by the WTO. The WTO, in its operation since 1995, has conducted many negotiations over a wide range of issues. Some issues link trade to the environment, labour standards, human rights, investment, and competition policy. It is the industrialized nations that set the tone on these issues. This is a déjà vu of the previous rounds of the GATT. Apparently, many developing countries are reluctant to join in the negotiations. Countries like India and Brazil regard some of the negotiation issues as the neo-colonization of the South. The WTO might be an effective world body in moving several issues to the negotiating table in a short span of operation. But in the area of conflict resolution, the WTO is being bombarded with many complaints. At the last count, the WTO has been handling more dispute cases (150) in three years than the 47 years under the GATT. While one-half of the 150 cases are under investigation, the number of complaints to the Dispute Settlement Body means that trade conflicts are rising.

International agreements also signal the end of subsidies. Countries are not allowed to subsidize their exports and some domestic outputs that have implications for trade. In addition, many countries begin to monitor the exchange rate of the exporting countries vis-à-vis the U.S. dollar and other major currencies. Trade imbalances are being addressed through exchange rate manipulation. The Plaza Accord exemplifies this type of intervention in the market when major trading nations could not force the yen to appreciate through market mechanisms. Major trading nations are also watching the development of the exchange rates of counterparts closely. This is to halt the manipulative practices in pegging the exchange rate below the real effective exchange rate. Export promotion through undervaluation of the currency is not encouraged by major trading partners.

One can argue that all trading nations face the same external environment. Yet one cannot overlook that Thailand faces an increasing number of rivals in the international markets in the 1990s. In the 1970s, Thai products could replace the products of Taiwan, South Korea, and ASEAN countries in major markets. In the 1990s, Thailand is competing with mainland China, Pakistan, Vietnam and other ASEAN countries. It shows that the type of industries that

Thailand set up can be established elsewhere at an alarming rate. To worsen the situation, Thailand can no longer claim to have the lowest cost producers in many categories of merchandise. The rapid rise of labour costs, land prices, utilities, and raw-materials reduces the cost competitiveness of Thai industries. To complicate future trading prospects, Thailand stands to lose many more GSP privileges extended by the EU to a wide range of exports. This factor alone will surely dampen export prospects in coming years.

The changing external and domestic environment implies that Thailand must change to fit with the new milieu. Hence, we must think of a new paradigm. The old paradigm that the Thai people used to introduce modernity to Thai society is perhaps obsolete now. Today we are hearing more from environmentally concerned people who promote sustainable development, especially when the trend is almost irreversible from the natural resource standpoint. We may have lost our forested areas to the point that they cannot be revived. Some people are promoting organic fertilizer and organic living. These represent active, albeit small, intellectual movements in society. Of course, when the early planners embarked upon the industrialization of the country, they had a choice of modernity. But the final selection was based on the most effective cost method and based on a commercial scale. The organic method would have produced a lower growth rate which would not have been sufficient to amortize the loans which the government owed to the multilateral agencies in the 1960s. The organic method was not selected when the Malthusian prediction was real in a country that had over 3% growth of population per year.

The main assault on the industrialization and trade paradigm must be further exposed to show its pitfalls. The previous section has already shown the mixed results from the industrialization. Some parameters are in line with expectations such as growth. Other parameters such as employment, trade and current accounts, use of abundant factor, development of science and technology base and human resource are failing the test. The conclusion is that industrialization has achieved a hollow success.

The new paradigm must follow from the basic premise that Thailand has a large pool of unskilled labour, a small pool of skilled labour, a vast industrial area, large arable land suitable for agricultural production, plenty of water resources, many days of sunshine, low indigenous technology base, and high cost of capital. The theory of factor proportions dictates that we should be producing with the abundant factors intensively to attain the low cost objective. Thus, we must start from the agricultural sector and extend this to the other sectors. Many will see this as the de-industrialization of the country. However, both Theodore Schultz[11] and later, John Mellor, argued that in order for the economy to be able to embark upon the industrialization process, the agriculture sector must be promoted first.

Therefore, we must revolutionize the farming sector with new technologies from planting, harvesting, post-harvest damage control, and marketing. It appears that the traditional way of rice farming, that went back over 4,000 years from the archaeological evidence in the Northeast and the Sakai Cave in the South, has hardly changed over centuries.[12] Some people want to maintain the traditional way of farming as a part of rural life. Leaving aside this portion of the populace, the new technologies would only be possible when the domestic terms of trade are in favour of farm production. Ethnic Chinese did not enter the farming sector in Thailand but remained commercial traders of the farm product due to these unfavourable terms of trade coupled with uninsured risk. Like all Asian farms, the average farm size in Thailand is about one tenth of those in the well-developed countries. The small size is compatible with low-technology presently applied by farmers. But to achieve a better yield per acre, some new thinking must be introduced.

The agricultural production must consist of large acreage, a large pool of workers with the application of machinery, and effective marketing channels. Our farms must be managed by competent professionals. More importantly, the ability of these farms to produce low-cost, high-margin exports of farm produce should not be limited arbitrarily by government. Presently, rice exports of the country are still subject to premiums (export tax). Except in rare cases of direct home consumption, the Ministry of Commerce should allow market mechanisms to prevail. Thai politicians are known to boast about Thailand being one of four countries in the world that has net export of staples. But they do not know the true potential of the agriculture, especially in the human food business.

Non-human food, such as ingredients to the feeds industry, must obey international prices. In the past, price distortions in the form of price guarantees to farmers for low-yield crops resulted in the imposition of tariff or seasonal quota restrictions. Crops such as soy beans and oil palm have been buttressed by the state when they were not able to compete with the imports. Price distortions must be removed at all points to allow the markets to allocate resources more efficiently. One must remember that distortions are costly to the society.

The agricultural sector has manifold roles. We believe the sector, which has already employed a substantial number of people, can create more jobs than the industrial sector. When we think of industry, we tend to think of the ability to absorb many people. Evidently, Thai industries cannot accomplish this. Neither has there been an alternative to subsistence farming in the society. Capital owners loathe the farming sector for a number of reasons. First, they regard owning a farm as a low profit enterprise unless, of course, there is a rapid land price increase within a short interval, such as in the early 1990s. Second, most businessmen coming from the trading class view farming as a loss leader. Farmers require a long lead time from the time of planting to the time of harvesting. Price movements in between are largely unpredictable, and there is no mechanism to remove this risk. Third, business views state intervention to be the stumbling block to reliance on market mechanisms. Particularly for major commodities relied upon by consumers, there are strong arguments that the state cannot allow prices to become volatile. Intervention tends to moderate the ups and downs in a cycle. There is a low possibility of earning extra profits from this type of policy when you are operating a farm. Hence, farmers and traders prefer to become middlemen in the process.

There is an opportunity for commercial farming on a large scale. We are thinking of 5,000 acres as an optimal size. We would like to consider for discussion's sake an arbitrary size for Thai farms. It is envisaged that commercial farming will provide numerous benefits to the country. First, we believe controversially that large-sized farms will be able to employ more people than standard-sized firms. Commercial farming could be used for creating employment alternatives for a large section of the population. Second, the creation of commercial farming can be used to provide internal commerce for the nation. Hitherto, the farming sector has been linked to the export market via the local merchants in rural areas. There is limited horizontal integration in the process. Currently, surplus commodities are being distributed from Bangkok to other provinces, even though Bangkok does not produce any commodities. Horizontal commerce would more efficiently stem from the farms. Third, it is expected that surplus commodities will be processed into exportables. It means that some proportion of arable land will focus on domestic staple food; Some will concentrate on horticulture, and others will focus on export markets. Commercial farming should help raise GDP per capita both by providing employment to the people and by increasing rural incomes through reliance on higher valued commodities.

If we target the agricultural sector to be a leading sector in the new paradigm, we must also discuss the role of the manufacturing sector. We believe the Thai manufacturing sector has been serving a small group of people. It either serves families of wealthy people or new business groups with close connections to commercial banks. Most projects follow the initiatives of foreign partners as they have access to better technologies and intermediate inputs and raw materials. This reduces the role of Thai businessmen to organizers of labour inputs to complement the capital. Due to low efficiency, it became necessary to consider providing industries with incentives in various forms. Many promoted firms, after the domestic resource cost (DRC) scrutiny, would have failed the test without state protection.

We examine whether there is a need to continue to provide infant-industry protection. The infant industry argument has provoked many debates in the past and will continue to do so in the future. Unfortunately, most studies of the Thai case are not sufficiently robust to provide a clear picture of infant industry promotion.

A bulk of empirical studies on the infant industry argument have relied on the case of Korea. There are lessons to be learned from these debates. In the views of Larry Westphal (1990)[13] and Howard Pack (1986),[14] in addition to export orientation, targeted infant industry promotion also played a crucial role in Korea's development. A principal means of infant industry promotion has been protection of the domestic market. At their inception, targeted industries were granted absolute protection via import controls. This approach gives the domestic industry a guaranteed market. At the same time, the government insisted that protected firms export a swiftly growing proportion of their output at world prices. Unlike the sales in protected domestic markets, these latter sales were not subsidized and encouraged the firms to achieve productivity growth necessary to compete at world prices.

Pangariya (1998b) described a slightly modified version of this infant industry protection that was also provided by Singapore when it went through a very brief period of "import-substitution".[15] Rather than require firms to export an increasing proportion of their output, Singapore kept their infants on their toes by committing to a strategy whereby infant industries which fail to grow within a short, pre-specified period will lose protection automatically. Amsden (1989),[16] Wade (1990),[17] and Rodrik (1995)[18] all subscribe to the importance of the infant-industry promotion in the case of Korea. Rodrik downplayed the significance of exports in the development of Korea. He argued that since exports were only 5% of the GDP in Korea in 1960, it could hardly serve as the engine of growth.

The Bhagwati-Krueger-Little school of thought on the infant-industry provides the other side of the argument. Bhagwati (1996)[19] and Little (1996) provide a detailed defense of this position. They both agree that industrial policy played a role in South Korea but question the claim that its contribution was positive. Little, based on a study by Dollar and Sokoloff,[20] notes that "TFP growth in most capital-intensive sectors (many the object of industrial policy promotion) was less than half of that in the most labour-intensive sectors.

Electrical goods; rubber, leather and plastic products; furniture; and clothing and footwear all show above average TFP growth."

Panagariya (1998a) views the controversy surrounding the case of Korea to be unresolved at the moment as both schools of thought have not proved their case beyond doubt.[21] Yet he regards the infant industry promotion to be less beneficial in the long run and to be avoided. Moral hazard and the inability of the government to manage in a complex situation tend to reduce the merits of the infant industry promotion. While this lesson is clear in the case of Korea, it is difficult to foresee the elimination of infant-industry promotion in Thailand. The governments of Thailand throughout the last four decades have advocated this line of policy, and efforts to change this strategy abruptly would be faced with resistance from the investment promotion agency and protected infants. Yet, it is unlikely that the promotion of infant industries will survive the onslaught of Multinational Agreement on Investment (MAI). We judge that the threat of MAI on the infant-industry promotion is greater than the arguments by prominent economists.

However, if the country chooses to promote infant industries, there are three lessons: (1) At any time, it must target a small number of industries. Targeting too many industries is bound to spread government and entrepreneurial talent too thinly. Moreover, the willingness to grant such protection with relative ease, especially during the difficult times, gives invitation to ever increasing numbers of industries to seek infant-industry protection; (2) The criterion for picking industries should be their ability to rapidly increase the share of export in total sales to some benchmark level. Such a strategy ensures that the industries already on the verge of achieving comparative advantage are the ones targeted. By contrast, an import-substitution approach to infant-industry protection is likely to pick industries at the bottom end of the comparative advantage ladder; (3) Targeted industries must be credibly informed that protection is strictly temporary. Credibility should be established by a withdrawal of protection from any industry failing to achieve benchmark levels of export at various stages.

IV. NEW POLICY DIRECTION

The following section will concentrate on summarizing the policy implications of the above-mentioned arguments. The new policy directions will be subdivided into two parts: macroeconomic stabilization and new directions at the ministerial level.

Macroeconomic Stabilization

It has long been a tradition for government officials to focus on growth of the economy. The pro-growth school of thought advocates a higher growth rate via more direct foreign investment and quick increases in exports. Trade theorists used to believe that trade and investment are substitutes.[22] Incidentally, these two parameters tend to complement one another in an obscure way. Rapid growth tends to attract more foreign investment into an economy which, in turn, will further rapid growth in a subsequent period. The real difficulty with the high-growth syndrome is Thailand's stabilization policies are not effective. To facilitate the operation of macroeconomic policies, trade liberalization and other domestic liberalization must also be undertaken. There are strong arguments for free flows of merchandise, but many studies including by Edwards (1993)[23] argue for a cautious approach to permitting free movement of capital before the completion of motion all other reforms.

The government should therefore aim at a warranted growth rate. What is the warranted growth rate? Here we are departing from the Harrod-Domar type of warranted growth rate. Our warranted growth rate must be the growth rate that reduces the trade deficit to a minimum and continues to service loans owed by the government to internal and external sources. This warranted growth rate must be based on moderate export growth rates to major importing countries. Hence, we must aim at the growth rate that exceeds the growth rate of population but remains lower than the export rate in any given year. This translates into a growth rate of 5–7% per annum.

The fiscal expenditure of the government must be on the low side. Instead of aiming at a deficit budget of 6% of GDP (Tables 7 and 10), the target is to set the deficit at a lower rate, say 4% of GDP. Collection efficiency must be improved at the Revenue Department and other revenue collecting agencies. On the other hand, on the spending side there is a real need to improve on the fiscal responsibilities of the agencies. While there has not been studies of the accountability of many projects in the past, it is recommended that this feature be improved. We believe the government should also aim to become smaller. In the age where downsizing is politically correct, the Thai government has not thought about downsizing. It should aim to cut down on the budget toward the civil service activities. The first to be chopped will be the activities that can be outsourced without major upheaval in the system. Should they want to promote early retirement for some civil servants, the government should endorse it.

Monetary policy must aim to neutralize the expansion of non-productive activities in the system. Strict regulation and supervision of non-productive activities must be monitored. In the past, commercial banks have advocated their own lending activities which appear to be contrary to the national aims. We suggest that the activities should be synchronized through an improved system of communications between the private sector and the public sector. The central bank and the finance ministry should review debt/equity ratios across the business sectors to set the maximum standards for loans. To complement moderate growth, the authorities can set benchmark levels of debt/equity ratios for industries. This aims to stave off the explosion of over-investment in some sectors that lack real apparent demand. At the limit, the central bank must review the maximum monetary expansion within the economy so that both growth and inflation balance is achieved.

The macroeconomic stabilization should be supported with an exchange rate system that can be verified at any time to be aligning to the real effective exchange rate. The quasi-pegging or the so-called "pegging via a basket of major currencies" is not operational in the next millennium. While the world is searching for a new system of exchange, the central bank must be promoting the diversification of risks associated with trading under the U.S. dollar area, the Euro areas, and other currency areas. This promotion can take the form of reduction of nominal cost of hedging in the international transactions. It is advised that the monetary authorities monitor the issuance of debt instruments by Thai business enterprises to foreign creditors. In the past, the Finance Ministry has monitored the country's sovereign debt closely, and are recommended that the same treatment apply to the private system. This does not imply that we are opposed to the movement of capital but want to prevent the over-exposure of Thai private debt to foreign creditors.

Science and Technology

There are two major components in the science and technology field. First, we believe the training of engineers and scientists must take a top priority in terms of budget allocation. Public universities must be allocated funds to promote graduates in science and technology. With limited financial resources, training of liberal arts, social science, humanities and other areas must be reduced to accommodate this. Private universities with less financial endowment can fill in the gap left by privatizing the activities of public universities. Second, public universities, along with the Ministry of Science and Technology, must spearhead research and development in various fields so that these works will lead to more major and minor patents and other significant increases in intellectual capital.

Labor and Skills

One of many lessons that we learn from the financial crisis is that labor suffers the most among all people in this society. The Labour Ministry lacks a data base on employment and unemployment. Statistics on employment have been a black hole in our economic management. We believe many international aid agencies are willing to fund this data compilation. The objective is to solve two related activities. The first is the conceptualization of a comprehensive social safety net for the unemployed. The labour ministry is willing to admit that there were 2 million unemployed at the end of 1998. This figure is only the tip of the iceberg. There are many unemployed and underemployed persons including disguised employment in the rural sector. We believe the government should design a social safety net to support the unemployed persons. It is no longer acceptable to argue that extended families of Thailand can support displaced people during economic downturns. Family institutions are not supposed to replace the responsibility of the government.

The skill increment to low-skilled labour must be improved rapidly. While there is argument that Thai labour cost is becoming more expensive, the productivities among all classes of labour have not been upgraded on the same scale. Industrialists expect a higher skill level to be commensurate with higher pay. Training is not sufficiently widespread. It should be noted that, as intensive capital techniques are used, the skill level will have to be higher too. Training labour to possess more skills will complement reliance on a higher level of technologies.

Distortion Removals

There are many distortions in the Thai economy that provide ample room for inefficient Thai firms to survive. At the same time, the same distortion may burden the other groups of people. The first best policy for a small country regarding distortions is to remove all distortions. As the economy is heading toward lower tariffs in coming years, this is the chance to remove remaining distortions. The practice of changing quota restrictions (QR) into tariff quota restrictions (TRQ) must end soon, and the government can adopt tariffication of all classes of merchandise.

In designing the export promotion system in 1985, the government confused business by using tax withdrawals and tax rebates to offset built-in business taxes. With the introduction of the value-added tax system, tax rebates for manufactured goods are no longer necessary. The government can end the tax rebate system at any time. Tax withdrawals under Article 19(2) are the standard practice among manufactured exporters. Perhaps this system should be extended to agriculture exports whose documents show appropriate documentation to the customs officers. This would provide a level playing field for all products of the country.

The government must address the bias against the primary products from agriculture. The elimination of all export taxes and the rice premium is in the offing. Price guarantees of inefficient produce must also end, even when the constitution permits such a price guarantee. The Ministry of Agriculture should be looked to map out a new strategy to promote the role of agriculture in economic development. If it means local production of fertilizer from methane at world prices, the Ministry of Industry should be looked to make provision for the production of methane. New species of seeds and other innovative technologies for farmers should be provided at nominal charge. The Commerce Ministry should provide market information and risk coverage to farmers at reasonable prices.

Review of Targeted Industries

There are many industries that no longer deserve to receive protection by the Ministry of Industry or the Investment Agency. The automobile assembly industry is one of the targeted industries. Its original aim was to provide local assemblers to process CKD parts into automobiles at lower cost. Today, almost all assembly plants are foreign-owned. This has nothing to do with nationalism. There is no need to provide protection to assemblers and parts makers under AFTA. The standard practice of assigning value to parts must be scrapped as technology owners are very unlikely to transfer their knowledge to Thai partners. It is futile to force technology owners to part with their knowledge when there is no commercial reason to justify it. The best procedure would be for the review board to agree with the board of investment officials on the time frame to end the protection of targeted industries.

Improved Trade Diplomacy

In the age where trade negotiations under the auspices of the WTO are neverending, the government must be prepared to secure the national interest through better information. Information will provide the government an effective response to any threat to market access. At present, the early warning system is not functioning. The case in point is the removal of GSP by the EU for many classes of Thai products. It is not the fault of our ambassador to the WTO who is negotiating in Geneva without touching base with research groups. It is proper that researchers in various fields dealing with trade and environment, trade and competition, multinational agreement on investment and other important issues be passed on to trade negotiators to reflect national policy on these issues. We will not discuss who should take the lead in trade diplomacy for the country. This sensitive issue can be decided at the highest level.

NOTES

1. Presented at The 22nd ACAES International Conference on Asian Economics. Theme "A Macroeconomic Core of an Open Economy for Progressive Industrialization and Development in Asia in the New Millenium".

2. James C. Ingram (1971). *Economic Change in Thailand, 1850–1970*. London: Oxford University Press.

3. Jagdish Bhagwati (1996). "The Miracle That Did Happen: Understanding East Asia in Comparative Perspective", delivered on May 3, 1996 in honour of Professors T. C. Liu and S. C. Tsiang, Ithaca, Cornell University.

4. Colin I. Bradford, Jr., "NICs and the Next-Tier NICs as Transitional Economies", in Colin Bradford, Jr. and William H. Branson, (1987), *Trade and Structural Change in Pacific Asia*. Chicago: National Bureau of Economic Research. Bradford argued that growth induce changes in factor intensities that bias towards trade.

5. Asian Development Bank (1998). *Key Indicators of Developing Asian and Pacific Countries 1998* (Volume XXIX). Manila: ADB.

6. Arvind Panagariya (1998a). "Openness: Growth and Recovery in Asia", Workshop on Asian Economic Outlook, Manila: ADB.

7. Narongchai Akrasanee and Juanjai Ajanant (1986). "Manufacturing Industry Protection in Thailand: Issues and Empirical Studies", in Christopher Findlay and Ross Garnaut, The Political Economy of Manufacturing Protection: Experience of ASEAN and Australia, Sydney: Allen and Unwin.

8. Thomas Kuhn (1962). *The Structure of Scientific Revolution*. Chicago: University of Chicago Press.

9. Lavergne, R. P. (1983). *The Political Economy of U.S. Tariffs: An Empirical Analysis*. New York: Academic Press.

10. J. M. Fingers (1993). *Antidumping: How it works and who gets hurt*. Ann Arbor, Michigan: University of Michigan Press.

11. Theodore W. Schultz (1964). *Transforming Traditional Agriculture*. New Haven and London: Yale University Press.

12. Stephen Oppenheimer (1998). *Eden of the East*. London: Weidenfeld and Nicholson.

13. Larry E. Westphal (1990). "Industrial Policy in an Export-Propelled Economy: Lessons from South Korea's Experience", *Journal of Economic Perspectives* 4, Summer.

14. Howard Pack and Larry E. Westphal (1986). "Industrial Strategy and Technological Change: Theory versus Reality", *Journal of Development Economics*, 22.

15. Arvind Panagariya (1998b). "Trade Liberalization in Asia", University of Maryland, mimeograph.

16. Alice Amsden (1986). *Asia's Next Giant: South Korea and Late Industrialization*. New York: Oxford University Press.

17. Robert Wade (1990). *Governing the market: Economic Theory and the Role of Government in East Asian Industrialization*. Princeton: Princeton University Press.

18. Dani Rodrik (1995). "Getting Interventions Right: How South Korea and Taiwan Grew Rich", *Economic Policy* 20.

19. Jagdish Bhagwati, (1996). op. cit.

20. Dollar, D. and Sokoloff, K (1990). "Patterns of Productivity Growth in South Korean Manufacturing Industries, 1963–1979", *Journal of Development Economics*, 33.

21. Panagariya (1998a). op. cit., pages 33–35.

22. See Robert A. Mundell (1957). "International Trade and Factor Mobility", *American Economic Review*, 67.

23. Sebastian Edwards (1993). "Openness, Trade Liberalization and Growth in Developing Countries", *Journal of Economic Literature*, 31.

37. ALTERNATIVE INDUSTRIAL DEVELOPMENT PATHS FOR INDONESIA: SAM AND CGE ANALYSES[1]

Romeo M. Bautista, Sherman Robinson and Moataz El-Said[2]

I. INTRODUCTION

Indonesia is currently in a deep political and economic crisis. One wonders, however, whether the situation was not any worse in the mid-1960s (just before the New Order government assumed power), given the country's economic stagnation, rapid inflation, and neglect of infrastructure since the early 1950s. Subsequently, the Indonesian economy grew impressively for most of the past three decades. Real GDP increased at an estimated average annual rate of well over 7% between 1970 and 1996 (based on World Bank data). Nevertheless, among Southeast Asian market economies, Indonesia still ranked lowest in 1996 – before the recent (and ongoing) crisis – in income per capita and level of industrialization. There is a continuing need to address longer term issues of economic development and industrialization in Indonesia even as the country faces difficult problems of crisis management and structural adjustment.

In this paper, we examine the economy-wide effects of three alternative growth paths for Indonesia's industrial sector using SAM (social accounting matrix) multiplier analysis and CGE (computable general equilibrium) modeling. The context is the immediate post-crisis period – most likely to be

Restructuring Asian Economics for the New Millennium, Volume 9B, pages 773–790.
2001 by Elsevier Science B.V.
ISBN: 0-7623-0710-2

in the next millennium – represented in our study by a modified benchmark data set for 1995 (see below). Special attention is given to the overall income and equity effects, considering that egalitarian growth has become a particularly important development objective in Indonesia. The model simulations involve the promotion of productivity growth and capital formation focused on two industrial sub-sectors – labor-intensive (or light) manufactures and processed food – and the agricultural sector (i.e. crops and livestock). Since the early 1980s when oil exports, Indonesia's principal foreign exchange earner, began to suffer from sharply declining real prices, the government has encouraged export diversification into light manufactured goods – with significant results on export earnings, industrial production, and labor employment. Food processing, which has traditionally been the largest component of Indonesia's manufacturing sector, serves to enhance national food security and is characterized by relatively strong production linkages that can provide the basis for large output increases in the entire economy. On the other hand, what Adelman (1984) has termed "agricultural demand-led (ADL) industrialization" is promoted by income growth among farm households, which if broadly based, has substantial consumption linkages that can create a mass market for domestically produced goods, including in particular labor-intensive manufactures, and provide the impetus to a rapid and equitable growth of the national economy (Mellor, 1995).

Economy-wide modeling to analyze the growth and distributional effects of alternative development paths is preferable to a partial-equilibrium approach. The latter abstracts from many important factors that operate simultaneously and interactively, many of which are difficult to anticipate. Quantitative studies on the macro and distributional effects of development policies, such as the early work on South Korea by Adelman and Robinson (1978), typically find that there are strong interactions among various sectors of the economy that influence the direction and magnitude of policy effects.

The SAM (social accounting matrix) framework is a useful starting point for economy-wide analysis, which we employ to focus on the demand side. In the next section, we briefly describe the benchmark Indonesian SAM and calculate the multiplier (direct and indirect) effects of an exogenous income injection to each of the sectors being promoted by the alternative industrial development strategies. These income multipliers give indication of the relative strength of economy-wide linkage effects for different production sectors, assuming no supply constraint. We also calculate the income multipliers associated with different household groups, which have implications for the relationship between growth and equity.

Next, we present the structure of our CGE model of the Indonesian economy, which incorporates nonlinearities and endogenous prices that are ignored in SAM analysis. The CGE model is used subsequently to generate the comparative results of simulation experiments involving three stylized industrial development strategies. A benchmark social accounting matrix (SAM) for 1995 is modified to represent initial conditions for the model simulations after an assumed recovery of the Indonesian economy from the crisis. The paper ends with some concluding remarks.

II. THE BENCHMARK SAM AND INCOME MULTIPLIERS

A simplified framework for economy-wide analysis is shown in Fig. 1. It traces the circular flow of incomes from product markets through factor payments to households and back to product markets through expenditures on final goods. Additionally, income flows involving producers, government, rest-of-the-world, and the capital account are included in the diagram.

A social accounting matrix describes quantitatively, in a square table, the income flows taking place in an economy – such as those represented in Fig. 1 – during a specified period of time.[3] Each account in the SAM is represented by a row and a column of the table; expenditures are shown in the columns and receipts in the rows. The SAM can be expressed either algebraically as accounting identities (stating that receipts must equal expenditures for each account), or as numbers that represent the data base for a given benchmark period (typically a year). The numerical SAM integrates national income, input-output, flow-of-funds, and foreign trade statistics into a comprehensive and consistent data set, as exemplified in Table 1 by an aggregate version of the official Indonesian SAM for 1995.

In the present study, we make use of a benchmark Indonesian SAM which has been adjusted from the official 1995 SAM to conform to our desired aggregation level and to reflect equilibrium conditions after Indonesia has achieved economic recovery. It distinguishes 17 production sectors (activities/commodities), 6 factors, and 7 household groups (see Table 2), with three accounts for government, one account each for enterprises, capital, and rest-of-the-world (ROW).[4] For present purposes, we identify the three crop and livestock sectors as the direct beneficiary of an agricultural demand-led industrial development strategy; similarly, the food processing and light manufacturing sectors are assumed to benefit directly from the policy regimes promoting the two other industrialization paths. The equity effect arising from each strategy will be evaluated in terms of the comparative income changes for

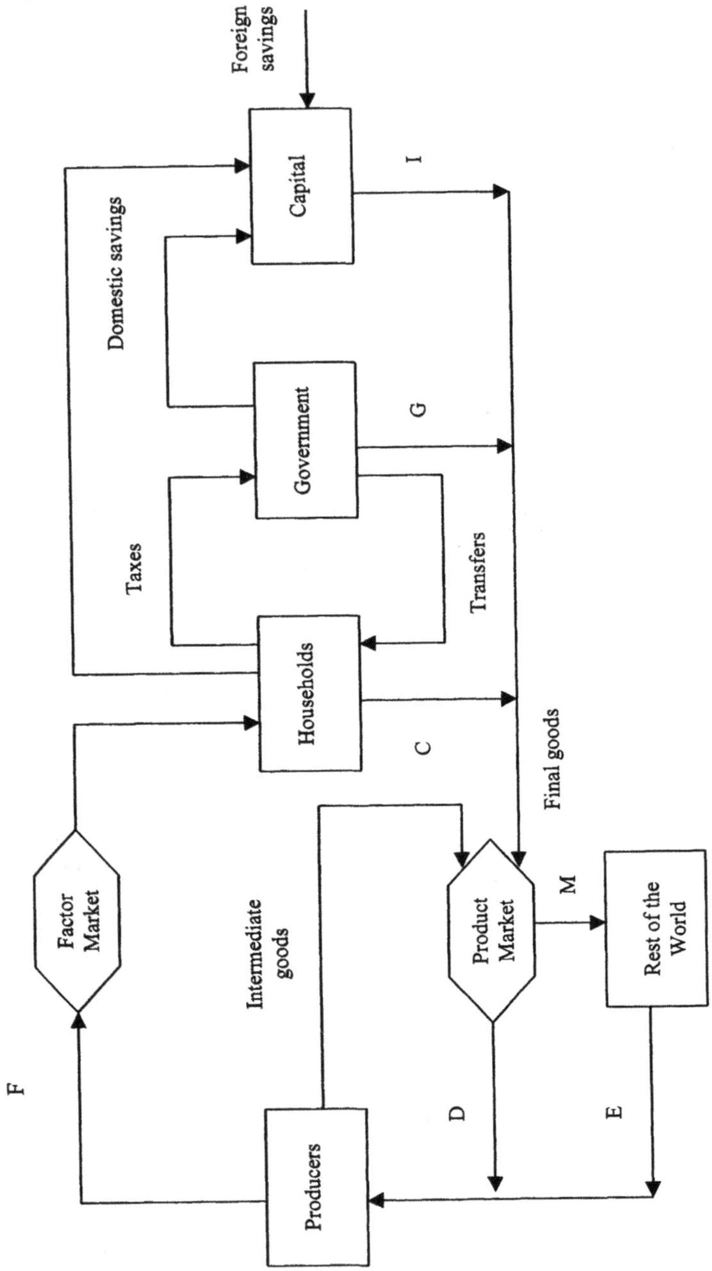

Fig. 1. Economywide Circular Income Flow.

Table 1. Aggregate SAM for Indonesia, 1995. (Trillions of Indonesian Rupiah).

	Expenditures										
	Value Added			Suppliers		Institutions					
	(1)	(2)	(3)	(4)	(5)	(6)	(7)	(8)	(9)	(10)	Total
Receipts											
Value Added											
(1) Labor				262							262
(2) Land				32							32
(3) Capital				217							217
Suppliers											
(4) Activities					976					122	1,099
(5) Commodities				563		360		36	152		1,110
Institutions											
(6) Households	262	32	92			2		8		6	402
(7) Enterprises			125							11	136
(8) Government				25	7	4	40			(6)	69
(9) Capital						37	43	25		47	152
(10) World					127		53				180
Total	262	32	217	1,099	1,110	403	136	69	152	180	

Table 2. Disaggregation of the Benchmark Indonesian SAM for 1995.

Activities/commodities (17)		
Food crops	Other mining	Utilities
Other crops	Food processing	Trade and transport
Livestock	Light manufacturing	Banking
Forestry	Fertilizer	Public administration
Fishery	Other manufacturing	Other services
Oil	Construction	
Factors (6)		
Agricultural labor		
Nonagricultural labor: production, clerical, professional		
Capital		
Land		
Households (7)		
Rural: farm-worker, small-farm, large-farm, nonfarm low-income, nonfarm high-income		
Urban: low-income, high-income		

the various household groups, with special attention to farm-worker, small-farm, nonfarm low-income, and urban low-income households.

Assuming exogeneity in some accounts (usually the government, capital, and ROW accounts), the algebraic SAM can be transformed into a multi-sectoral, demand-driven model of the economy in which the linkages among sectoral production, household incomes and expenditures, foreign trade, and macroeconomic balances are systematically taken into account. The SAM is partitioned so that the total income (row sum) in each endogenous account is equal to the sum of products of the expenditure coefficient and corresponding income plus the total exogenous income from the government, capital, and ROW accounts; that is,

$$Y = A_n Y + X \tag{1}$$

where Y is a column vector of total incomes in the endogenous accounts, X is a column vector of total exogenous incomes (the exogenous accounts in the partition), and A_n is the expenditure coefficient matrix pertaining to the endogenous accounts which is assumed fixed in conventional SAM modeling.

Equation (1) can be solved for Y in terms of X as follows:

$$Y = (I - A_n)^{-1} X = M_a Y \tag{2}$$

where M_a is the SAM multiplier matrix. Equation (2) can be used to calculate the endogenous incomes associated with any constellation of total exogenous incomes, given M_a. Also, the effects on Y arising from any given changes in X (e.g. an exogenous income injection in any production sector or in any household group) can be derived from equation (2). Each cell in the multiplier matrix indicates the total (direct and indirect) income change in the endogenous row account induced by an exogenous unit-income injection in the column account. It captures both the Leontief (input-output) production linkages and the consumption expenditure linkages induced by changes in production activities through their effect on household incomes.

Based on our benchmark Indonesian SAM for 1995, the calculated income multipliers, representing the induced effects on GDP at factor cost, are as follows: 2.45 for food crops, 2.30 for nonfood crops, and 2.28 for livestock; 1.93 for processed food; and 1.71 for light manufactures. They correspond to the sum of the six factor-payment entries along each production-sector column in the multiplier matrix. Thus, SAM-based analysis allows us to infer that an increase in income of crop and livestock producers by one million Rupiahs will lead to a rise in GDP (at 1995 prices) by about 2.3 million Rupiahs, while the same income increase in the food processing and light manufacturing sectors will lead to GDP increases that are smaller by 16 and 26%, respectively. Evidently, the demand stimulus generated by agricultural growth significantly exceeds that by growth in either of the two industrial sectors. This finding lends support to the hypothesis that there are strong macro-linkages from rising agricultural incomes; a hypothesis favored by advocates of agriculture-based development.

The SAM model can also be applied to the analysis – again, focusing on the demand side – of the direct and indirect effects of exogenous income injections to different household groups. It is often noted that household expenditures of less affluent households are heavily oriented to locally produced, labor-intensive goods and services. By contrast, the consumption patterns of higher income households favor capital-intensive products of urban industry and imported goods. The latter implies relatively weaker and less labor-intensive linkages in the domestic economy. On this basis, it has been argued, with ample empirical evidence in developing countries,[5] that pro-equity growth measures do not necessarily hinder a favorable impact on overall income growth.

The calculated GDP multipliers for the seven household groups distinguished in the Indonesian SAM are shown in the first column of Table 3. It is notable that the three most affluent household groups – large-farm, nonfarm high-income rural, and high-income urban – are associated with GDP multipliers that are smaller than those for the lower income households. This result indicates that greater income benefits accruing to the latter households from any source (agricultural or nonagricultural) of economic growth would

Table 3. Income multipliers by household group.

	Gross domestic product	Manufacturing output
Rural households		
Farm-worker	1.673	1.560
Small-farm	1.614	1.505
Large-farm	1.569	1.378
Nonfarm low-income	1.601	1.514
Nonfarm high-income	1.538	1.457
Urban households		
Low-income	1.676	1.474
High-income	1.428	1.313

have a larger impact on overall income growth. Similarly, the comparative values of manufacturing output multipliers, shown in the second column of Table 3, suggest that income increases for less affluent household groups represent a more potent demand stimulus to industrial growth.

III. THE CGE MODEL

The CGE model of the Indonesian economy that we use in this study is adapted from a more disaggregated, agriculture-focused model developed earlier in Robinson et al. (1998) to analyze the economy-wide effects of trade liberalization and exchange rate changes under alternative rice policy regimes in Indonesia. Our model consists of five blocks of equations which are given in the Appendix below. It follows roughly the standard neoclassical specification of general equilibrium models (Dervis et al., 1982, Robinson, 1989).

Markets for goods (or products), factors, and foreign exchange respond to changing demand and supply conditions which are influenced by government policies and the external environment. The model is Walrasian in that it determines only relative prices and other variables in the real sphere of the economy. Sectoral product prices, factor prices, and the foreign exchange rate are defined relative to an aggregate consumer price index, which serves to define the *numeraire*.

The production technology is represented by nested CES (constant-elasticity-of-substitution) and Leontief (fixed-coefficient) functions. Domestic output in each sector is a CES function of value added and aggregate intermediate input use. Value added is a CES function of the primary factors, while intermediate input use is defined by fixed input-output coefficients. It is assumed that land is mobile between the two crop sectors and that agricultural labor and nonagricultural production labor are substitutable.

Profit-maximizing behavior of producers determines factor demand. Factor market distortions are included, with the average return for a factor differing from the marginal revenue product of that factor in specific sectors. Each sector is assumed to produce differentiated goods for the domestic and export markets, sectoral output being a CET (constant-elasticity-of-transformation) function of the amounts sold in the two markets. Subject to this transformation function, producers maximize revenue from sales. Similarly, imported and domestic products are differentiated at the sectoral level. The composite (consumption) good is a CES aggregate, and consumers minimize the cost of obtaining a given amount of composite good. Such product differentiation permits two-way trade and gives some realistic autonomy to the domestic price system (de Melo and Robinson 1981). The associated price links are portrayed in the price transmission mechanism shown in Fig. 2.

Based on the small-country assumption, the domestic price of sectoral imports is represented in terms of the foreign price, exchange rate, and tariff rate. The country is also assumed to be small on the export side; the domestic price of sectoral exports is determined by the world price, exchange rate, and any applicable export tax (or subsidy).

The four components of sectoral demand are intermediate, consumption, investment, and government. Fixed input-output coefficients determine intermediate demand. Household consumption demand is based on the linear expenditure system. Inventory investment in volume terms is exogenous, while fixed investment is the difference between total investment and inventory demand in nominal terms. Government consumption of sectoral products is in fixed shares of total government consumption in volume terms.

Aside from the supply-demand balances in the product and factor markets, three macroeconomic balances are specified in the model: (i) the fiscal balance, showing that government savings is the difference between government revenue and spending; (ii) the external balance, equating the supply and demand for foreign exchange; and (iii) the equality between total investment and total savings. For purposes of simulating alternative industrial development paths, we specify a simple, neutral, macro closure whereby the ratios of investment and government consumption expenditures *in nominal terms* to total absorption are assumed to remain the same as in the base model. The external balance is exogenous.

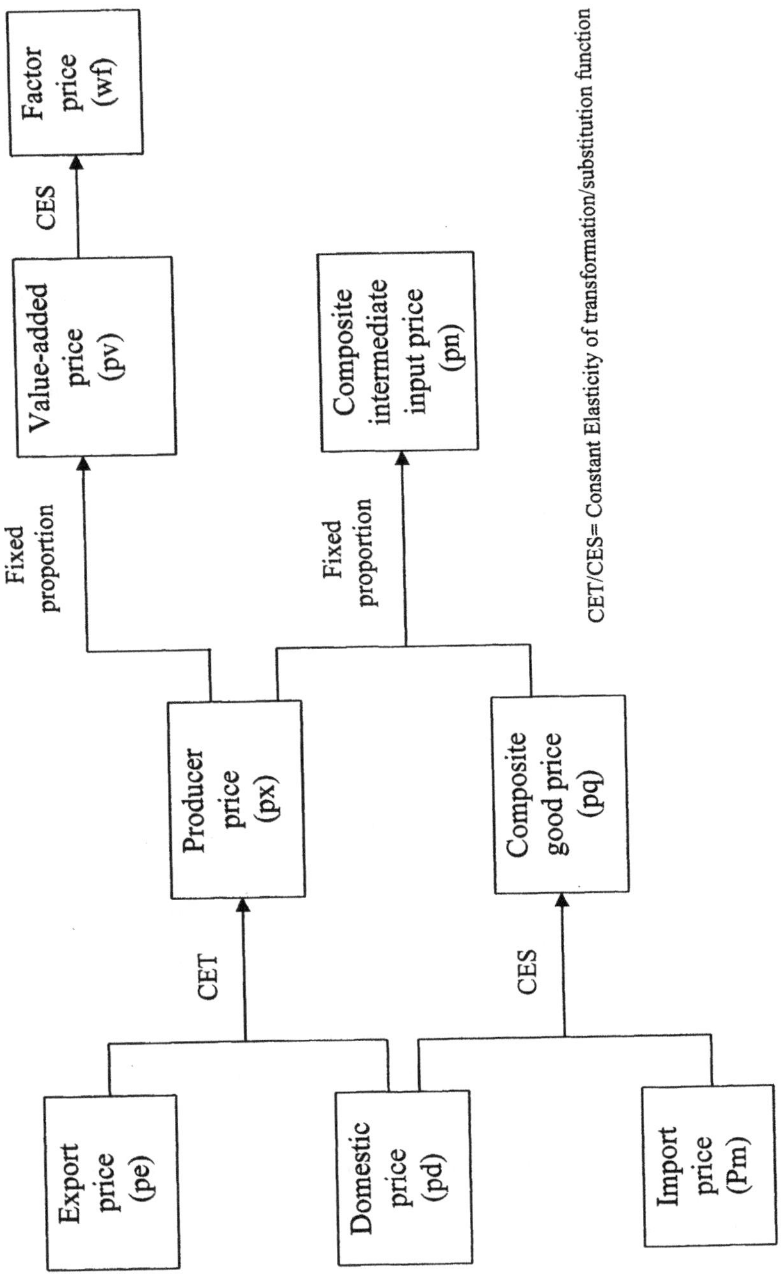

Fig. 2. Domestic Price Transmission Mechanism.

IV. MODEL SIMULATIONS AND RESULTS

Our stylized representation of the Indonesian economy in the immediate post-crisis period is one in which net capital inflow and remittances to enterprises are reduced to zero which, based on the CGE model, is associated with a depreciation of the real exchange rate by about 30% from the 1995 benchmark. We modify the base model to reflect the changed economic structure after the crisis, which then represents the initial conditions that are perturbed by exogenous shocks corresponding to the alternative industrial development paths assumed in the model simulations. The simulation results should be interpreted therefore in reference to this post-shock base.

Implementation of the three industrialization strategies can be expected to have differential effects on two basic determinants of sectoral production: (1) the capital stock (land for agricultural sectors), as a result of domestic investments being made more attractive for the favored sectors; and (2) total factor productivity (TFP), related to the likely improvement in sectoral infrastructure and support services. Specifically, capital and land investments of Rp 30 trillion (in 1995 prices) are postulated for the relevant sectors in the three simulations; also, an exogenous direct increase in real value added of Rp 30 trillion from sectoral TFP growth is assumed in each simulation experiment. Under the ADL industrialization scenario, output gains from land improvement and TFP growth will accrue to three production sectors (food crops, nonfood crops, and livestock), which are allocated in accordance with their land and value added shares, respectively. In a dynamic model, changes in sectoral capital stock and (perhaps) total factor productivity would be endogenously determined. Introducing "by hand" these assumed (direct) sectoral effects in our static CGE model allows us to examine, in an exploratory manner, the economy-wide income and equity effects of the three alternative industrialization paths for Indonesia.

The results of the three simulation experiments are shown in Table 4. They indicate deviations from the modified base values, given the simulated changes in the relevant sectors. The comparative effects on real GDP bear out the strong macro-linkages of agricultural growth. ADL industrialization is seen to generate a larger GDP increase than either the food processing-based (FPB) or light manufacturing-based (LMB) industrial growth path. The ADL advantage is even greater if it is assumed, as in the classical "vent-for-surplus" growth model, that output in the food and nonfood crop sectors (dominated by rice and rubber, respectively) are fully tradable.[6] As can be discerned from the last row of the table, however, the share of manufacturing in GDP declines with ADL development and rises under FPB and (even more so) LMB industrialization.

The equity impact is not clear-cut. It is somewhat surprising that, except for the large increase in farm-worker household income, the ADL scenario is associated with lower real incomes of farm households.[7] The explanation is that the increases in agricultural output from the postulated total productivity growth and land improvement lead to a substantial terms of trade decline (by 21% from the modified base value). Preventing the latter from happening by the assumption of full tradability of crop output is seen to generate the expected favorable income effects for the three farm household groups relative to the rural nonfarm and urban households. Without the latter assumption, food processing-based industrial growth improves farm household incomes better than both the ADL and LMB scenarios; however, the equity impacts on rural nonfarm and urban households are unfavorable. A final observation is that LMB industrial growth leads not only to the lowest increase in real GDP among the three scenarios but also the most inequitable distribution of income gains – large-farm, rural nonfarm, high-income, and urban high-income households being the chief beneficiaries. This result is attributable to the

Table 4. CGE Model Simulation Results of Alternative Industrialization Paths.
(in Percent Changes from Modified Base Values)

	Agricultural demand-led (ADL)	Food processing-based (FPB)	Light manufacturing-based (LMB)
Real GDP	4.9 (6.4)	3.7	3.3
Household incomes			
Rural:			
Farm-worker	20.6 (92.6)	48.7	–7.1
Large-farm	–3.2 (16.5)	10.2	2.9
Small-farm	–3.2 (10.2)	6.2	9.0
Nonfarm, low-income	4.4 (9.2)	3.4	0.1
Nonfarm, high-income	0.6 (3.8)	7.8	15.2
Urban			
Low-income	13.3 (5.0)	0.0	–1.5
High-income	10.3 (4.7)	4.8	5.1
Manufacturing value added (at base prices)	3.0 (6.3)	4.6	5.5

Note: Numbers in parantheses are the corresponding results assuming that food and non-food crop sector products are fully tradable.

relatively high proportion of factor payments in the light manufacturing sector in Indonesia accruing to higher-income households in the benchmark period.

V. CONCLUSION

This paper has explored the economy-wide income and equity effects of three alternative industrial development paths for Indonesia, in a post-shock environment. The results of SAM multiplier analysis indicate relatively strong macro-linkages of agricultural demand-led industrialization, yielding a significantly larger increase in real GDP compared to that arising from industrial development oriented to either food processing or light manufacturing. Another important finding is that the three higher-income rural and urban household groups have smaller GDP and manufacturing output multipliers, suggesting that the distribution of income benefits is a potentially significant influence on growth of the national economy and the manufacturing sector.

The simulation results based on CGE modeling, which takes account of nonlinearities and supply constraints that are ignored in SAM analysis, bear out the dominant influence of demand linkages in showing that ADL industrialization is associated with a larger GDP increase than the two other industrial development paths. However, to preserve the income gains for farm households and improve equity, it would be necessary to prevent the agricultural terms of trade from deteriorating – for example, through improvement of the country's ability to export farm products. Otherwise, food processing-based industrial growth raises farm household income by more than the two other development scenarios. Finally, while industrialization based on light manufacturing shows the most significant increase in the ratio of manufacturing value added to GDP, it is also associated with the smallest GDP increase and the worst equity effect.

NOTES

1. Paper presented at the International Conference on a Macroeconomic Core of an Open Economy for Progressive Industrialization and Development in Asia in the New Millennium, sponsored by the American Committee on Asian Economic Studies and Chulalongkorn University on 16–18 December 1998 in Bangkok.

2. *Romeo M. Bautista, formerly Research Fellow, Trade and Macroeconomics Division, International Food Research, 2033 K Street, N.W. Washington D.C. 20006 U.S.A. Sherman Robinson, Director, Trade and Macroeconomics Division, International Food Research, 2033 K Street, N.W. Washington D.C. 20006 U.S.A. Fax: (202) 467–4439; E-Mail: S.Robinson@CGIAR.ORG. Moataz El-Said, Research Analyst, Trade and Macroeconomics Division, International Food Research, 2033 K Street, N.W.

Washington D.C. 20006 U.S.A. Fax: (202) 467–4439; E-Mail: M.El-Said@CGIAR-.ORG.

3. See Pyatt and Round (1985) for an early discussion of the SAM structure, and Robinson and Roland-Holst (1988) for perspectives on SAM-based modeling.

4. The disaggregate SAM is too large to be reproduced here, but is available from the authors on request.

5. Among others, see Mellor (1976) on India, Adelman on South Korea (1984), Bautista (1997) on the Philippines, and Delgado et al. (1994) on a number of sub-Saharan African countries.

6. Meaning that the substitution elasticities between sectoral domestic product and imports, and also between domestic use and exports, are infinite.

7. The large percentage changes in farm-worker household income shown in Table 4 arise in part from its very low initial value (only 3.2% of total household income in the modified base solution).

REFERENCES

Adelman, I. (1984). Beyond export-led growth. *World Development, 12*, 973–986.

Adelman, I., & Robinson, S. (1978). *Income distribution policy in developing countries: A case study of Korea*. Oxford: Oxford Univ. Press.

Bautista, R. M. (1997). Income and equity effects of the Green Revolution in the Philippines. *Journal of International Development, 9*, 151–168.

Delgado, C., Hazell, P., Hopkins, J., & Kelly, V. (1994). Promoting intersectoral growth linkages in rural Africa through agricultural technology and policy reform. *American Journal of Agricultural Economics, 76*, 1166–1171.

de Melo, J., & Robinson, S. (1981). Trade policy and resource allocation in the presence of product differentiation. *Review of Economics and Statistics, 63*, 169–177.

Dervis, K., de Melo, J., & Robinson, S. (1982). *General equilibrium models for development policy*. Cambridge: Cambridge University Press.

Mellor, J. M. (1976). *The new economics of growth*. Ithaca: Cornell University Press.

Mellor, J. M. (1995). *Agriculture on the road to industrialization*. Baltimore: Johns Hopkins Univ. Press.

Pyatt, G., & Round, J. (Eds) (1985). *Social accounting matrices: A basis for planning*. Washington, D.C.: The World Bank.

Robinson, S. (1989). Multisectoral models. In: H. Chenery & T. N. Srinivasan (Eds), *Handbook of Development Economics*, Vol.II. Amsterdam: Elsevier Science Publishers.

Robinson, S., El-Said, M., & San, N. N. (1998). Rice policy, trade, and exchange rate changes in Indonesia: A general equilibrium analysis. *Journal of Asian Economics, 9*, 393–423.

Robinson, S., & Roland-Holst, D. W. (1988). Macroeconomic structure and computable general equilibrium models. *Journal of Policy Modeling, 10*, 353–375.

APPENDIX

Appendix Tables 1–6 appear on the following pages.

Table A1. Definition of Parameters and Variables in the GCE Model for Indonesia.

Parameters

	Symbol	Definition
A	a_i^c	Armington function shift parameter
	a_i^d	CES shift parameter
	$\alpha_{i,f}$	CES factor share parameter
	a_i^T	CET function shift parameter
	$a_{i,j}$	Input-output coefficients
B	$b_{i,j}$	Capital composition matrix
	$\beta_{i,h}$	Marginal budget shares (LES)
C	$cwts_i$	Consumer price weights
D	δ_i	Armington function share parameter
	$depr_i$	Depreciation rates
	$dwts_i$	Domestic sales price weights
E	$exrb_i$	Base exchange rate (Rupiah per US dollar)
F	$fmap_{hh,f}$	Factors to household map
G	γ_i	CET function share parameter
	$\gamma_{i,h}$	Subsistence minima (LES)
	$gles_i$	Government consumption shares
K	$kshr_i$	Shares of investment by sector of destination
M	$make_{i,j}$	Make matrix coefficients
P	pvb_i	Base value added price
	$pwmb_i$	Base import price
	pwm_i	World market price of imports (in dollars)
	pwe_i	World price of exports (in dollars)
	$pwts_i$	Price index weights
	pxb_i	Base output price
R	ρ_i^c	Armington function exponent
	ρ_i^p	CES production function exponent
	ρ_i^T	CET function exponent
S	$sremit_{hh}$	Remittance shares
	$strans_{hh}$	Government transfer shares
	$syenth_{hh}$	Share of enterprise income to households
	$syent_f$	Enterprise shares of factor income
	$sytr_{hh}$	Share of household income transferred to other households
T	tc_i	Consumption tax (+) or subsidy (-) rates
	te_i	Tax (+) or subsidy (-) rates on exports
	th_{hh}	Household tax rate
	tmb_i	Base tariff rate
	tm_i	Tariff rates on imports
	txb_i	Base indirect tax
	tx_i	Indirect tax rates
Y	$ymap_{h,hh}$	household to households map

Variables

	Symbol	Definition
C	CD_i	Final demand for private consumption
	CH_h	Household disposable income
	$CONTAX$	Consumption tax revenue
D	DA_i	Domestic activity sales
	$DEPREC$	Total depreciation expenditure
	DK_i	Volume of investment by sector of destination
	DST_i	Inventory investment by sector
E	E_i	Exports
	$ENTSAV$	Enterprise savings
	$ENTTAX$	Enterprise tax revenue
	$ENTTF$	Enterprise transfers abroad
	ESR	Enterprise savings rate
	ETR	Enterprise tax rate
	$EXPTAX$	Export tax payments
	EXR	Exchange rate
F	$FBOR$	Government foreign borrowing
	$FDSC_{i,f}$	Factor demand by sector
	$FLABTF$	Labor transfers abroad
	$FSAV$	Net foreign savings
	FS_f	Factor supply
	$FXDINV$	Fixed capital investment
G	$GDPVA$	Value added in market prices
	$GDTOT$	Total volume of government consumption
	GD_i	Final demand for government consumption
	$GOVTAB$	Government consumption to total absorption ratio
	$GOVSAV$	Government savings
	$GOVTH$	Government transfers to households
	GR	Government revenue
H	$HHSAV$	Household savings
	$HHTAX$	Household tax revenue
I	ID_i	Final demand for productive investment
	$INDTAX$	Indirect tax revenue
	INT_i	Intermediates uses
	$INVEST$	Total investment
	$INVTAB$	Investment to total absorption ratio
M	MPS_{hh}	Marginal propensity to save by household
	M_i	Imports
P	PC_i	Consumer price of composite goods
	PDA_i	Domestic activity goods price
	PDC_i	Domestic commodity goods price
	PE_i	Domestic price of exports
	$PINDCON$	Consumer price index
	PK_i	Price of capital goods by sector of destination
	PM_i	Domestic price of imports
	PQ_i	Price of composite good
	PV_i	Value added price
	PX_i	Average output price
Q	Q_i	Composite goods supply
R	$REMIT$	Remittances
	$REMITENT$	Enterprise remittances
	$RGDP$	Real GDP
S	$SAVING$	Total savings
	SPC_i	Variable subsidy
T	$TABSORB$	Total absorption
	$TARIFF$	Tariff revenue
W	$WFDIST_{i,f}$	Factor price sectoral proportionality ratios
	WF_f	Average factor price
X	X_i	Domestic output
Y	$YENT$	Enterprise income
	$YFCTR_f$	Factor income
	YH_h	Household income

Table A2. Price Equations.

#	Equation	Description
1	$PM_i = pwm_i \cdot (1 + tm_i) \cdot EXR$	Import prices
2	$PE_i = pwe_i \cdot (1 - te_i) \cdot EXR$	Export prices
3	$PDA_i = PE_i$	Export Price, perfect substitutes
4	$PDC_j = \sum_i make_{if} \cdot PDA_i$	Definition of commodity prices
5	$PQ_i = \dfrac{PDC_i \cdot CD_i + PM_i \cdot M_i}{Q_i}$	Composite good prices
6	$PX_i = \dfrac{PDA_i \cdot DA_i + PE_i \cdot E_i}{X_i}$	Producer prices
7	$PV_i = PX_i \cdot (1 - tx_i) - \sum_j a_{ji} \cdot PC_j$	Value added prices net of indirect taxes
8	$PK_i = \sum_j b_{ji} \cdot PC_j$	Composite capital good prices
9	$PINDCON = \sum_i cwts_i \cdot PC_i$	Consumer price index

Table A3. Quantity Equations.

#	Equation	Description
10	$X_i = a_i^D \cdot \left[\sum_f \alpha_{i,f} FDSC_{i,f}^{-\rho_i^P} \right]^{-\frac{1}{\rho_i^P}}$	CES production function
11	$FDSC_{if} = X_i \cdot \left[\dfrac{\alpha_{if} \cdot PV_i}{(a_i^D)^{\rho_i^P} \cdot WF_f \cdot WFDIST_{if}} \right]^{\sigma_i^P}$	Demand function for primary factors (First order condition for profit maximization where $\sigma_i^P = \dfrac{1}{\rho_i^P + 1}$)
12	$INT_i = \sum_j a_{ji} \cdot X_j$	Total intermediate use
13	$DA_i = \sum_j make_{ij} \cdot DC_i$	Commodity/activity relationship
14	$X_i = a_i^T \left[\gamma_i E_i^{\rho_i^T} + (1 - \gamma_i) D_i^{\rho_i^T} \right]^{\frac{1}{\rho_i^T}}$	Gross domestic output as a composite good
15	$X_i = E_i + D_i$	Gross domestic output, perfect substitutes
16	$E_i = D_i \left[\dfrac{PE_i (1 - \gamma_i)}{PDA_i \cdot \gamma_i} \right]^{\frac{1}{\rho_i^T + 1}}$	Export supply
17	$Q_i = a_i^C \left[\delta_i M_i^{-\rho_i^C} + (1 - \delta_i) D_i^{-\rho_i^C} \right]^{-\frac{1}{\rho_i^C}}$	Total supply for a composite good
18	$M_i = D_i \left[\dfrac{P_i^d \cdot \delta_i}{P_i^m (1 - \delta_i)} \right]^{\frac{1}{1 + \rho_i^C}}$	First order condition for cost minimization of composite goods

Table A4. Income Equations.

#	Equation	Description
19	$YFCTR_f = \sum_i WF_f \cdot FDSC_{if} \cdot WFDIST_{if}$	Factor income
20	$YENT = \sum_f syent_f \cdot YFCTR_f + REMITENT \cdot EXR + PREMY$	Capital income
21	$YH_{hh} = \sum_f fmap_{hh,f} \cdot (1 - syent_f) \cdot YFCTR_f + sremit_{hh} \cdot (REMIT - FLABTF) \cdot EXR + strans_{hh} \cdot GOVTH + \sum_h ymap_{hh,h} \cdot sytr_h \cdot YH_h + syenth_{hh} \cdot (YENT - ENTTAX - ENTSAV - ENTTF \cdot EXR)$	Household income
22	$CH_{hh} = (1 - th_{hh}) \cdot (1 - MPS_{hh}) \cdot YH_{hh} - \sum_h ymap_{hh,h} \cdot sytr_h \cdot YH_{hh}$	Household disposable income
23	$TARIFF = \sum_i tm_i \cdot pwm_i \cdot M_i \cdot EXR$	Tariff revenue
24	$CONTAX = \sum_i (tc_i - SPC_i) \cdot PQ_i \cdot Q_i$	Consumption taxes
25	$INDTAX = \sum_i tx_i \cdot PX_i \cdot X_i$	Indirect taxes
26	$EXPTAX = \sum_i te_i \cdot pwe_i \cdot E_i \cdot EXR$	Export tax
27	$HHTAX = \sum_h th_h \cdot YH_h$	Household taxes
28	$DEPREC = \sum_i depr_i \cdot PK_i \cdot FDSC_{i,capital}$	Depreciation expenditure
29	$ENTTAX = ETR \cdot YENT$	Enterprise taxes
30	$ENTSAV = ESR \cdot YENT$	Enterprise savings
31	$HHSAV = \sum_h MPS_h \cdot YH_h \cdot (1 - th_h)$	Household savings
32	$GR = TARIFF + CONTAX + INDTAX + HHTAX + FBOR \cdot EXR + ENTTAX + EXPTAX$	Government revenue
33	$SAVING = HHSAV + ENTSAV + DEPREC + GOVSAV + EXR \cdot FSAV$	Total savings

Note: f = set of factors
hh = h = set of households

Table A5. Expenditure Equations.

#	Equation	Description
34	$PC_i \cdot CD_i = \sum_h PC_i \cdot \gamma_{i,h} + \beta_{i,h} \cdot (CH_h - \sum_j PC_j \cdot \gamma_{j,h})$	Private consumption
35	$GD_i = gles_i \cdot GDTOT$	Government consumption
36	$FXDINV = INVEST - \sum_i PC_i \cdot DST_i$	Fixed investment
37	$PK_i \cdot DK_i = kshr_i \cdot FXDINV$	Real fixed investment by sector of destination
38	$ID_i = \sum_j b_{ij} \cdot DK_j$	Investment final demand by sector of origin

Table A6. Market Clearing and Macro Economic Closures.

#	Equation	Description
39	$Q_i = INT_i + CD_i + GD_i + ID_i + DST_i$	Goods market equilibrium
40	$FS_f = \sum_i FDSC_{i,f}$	Factor market equilibrium
41	$GR = \sum_i PC_i \cdot GD_i + GOVSAV + GOVTH$	Fiscal balance
42	$\sum_i pwm_i \cdot M_i = \sum_i PWE_i \cdot E_i + FSAV + FBOR + REMIT + ENTTF - FLABTF + REMITENT$	External balance
43	$SAVING = INVEST$	Saving- investment balance
44	$GDPVA = \sum_i PV_i \cdot X_i + INDTAX + TARIFF + CONTAX$	Value added including indirect taxes
45	$TABSORB = GDPVA + EXR\left(\sum_i pwm_i \cdot M_i - \sum_i pwe_i \cdot E_i\right)$	Total absorption
46	$RGDP = \sum_i (pvb_i + txb_i)pxb_i \cdot X_i + tmb_i \cdot exrb \cdot pwmb_i \cdot M_i$	Real GDP
47	$GOVTAB = \frac{\sum_i PC_i \cdot GD_i}{TABSORB}$	Government consumption to total absorption share
48	$INVTAB = \frac{\sum_i PC_i \cdot ID_i}{TABSORB}$	Investment to total absorption share

38. IMPERFECT COMPETITION AND TECHNOLOGY ADVANCE: IMPLICATIONS FOR INDONESIAN PRACTICE

Robert H. Aten[1]

INTRODUCTION

Technology advance is often thought about in highly sophisticated terms – building airplanes and computers. In highly developed countries, this characterization may be partly true. In developing countries such as Indonesia, building less sophisticated information into processes of industrial production provides technology advance and helps achieve more rapid economic recovery and growth. As technology advance is modeled in recent economic literature, it encompasses both these perspectives. Moreover, the information content consists of two components – company specific information (often discussed in the business-school literature as the "core competence" of a company), and technical information that has become more generally available and cannot be confined within a particular company (usually modeled as a public or social good in the economics literature).[2] Modeling such information treats social good information as extremely important to economic growth. Moreover, imperfect competition is usually required to sustain profits and long-term economic growth in such models, and so the behavior of social-good information provides a central justification for the realism of such models. Important theoretical insights underlie such models, although substantial

Restructuring Asian Economics for the New Millennium, Volume 9B, pages 791–825.
2001 by Elsevier Science B.V.
ISBN: 0-7623-0710-2

empirical work has been slow to emerge. This paper is designed to explore some of the implications of these approaches for technology policy and imperfect competition in Indonesia. The core hypothesis that underlies this paper is that much technology-based information can be and is transferred to developing countries such as Indonesia through commercial transactions, usually relying on multinational corporations and the discipline engendered by meeting international standards through an export orientation. These processes help generate more rapid economic growth. But the core benefit to such growth is generated through the adaptation and utilization of technological information.

Indonesia has been criticized for its various economic inefficiencies. This paper particularly addresses those that arise from the competitive structure of some of Indonesia's industries and their relationship to its government policies intended to sustain Indonesian technology advance. The problem is that Indonesia's traditional strategy is partially misplaced. The problem arises in part because of the stage of Indonesian development and in part because specific inward-looking Indonesian nationalistic policies have been inappropriately defended as economically useful by some Indonesian policymakers.

International trade aspects implied by policies like these domestic Indonesian policies are among those being addressed internationally by a working group of the World Trade Organization (WTO).[3] The link between competition policy and trade policy needs additional clarification, although for a number of years more open trade policy has been conceived of as likely the most successful technique for bringing technology to developing countries. Other factors often thought to generate economic growth (exports, etc.), while necessary processes in efficient economic growth, nonetheless rely on improved technology transfer by means of improved access to information as the core source of developing country economic growth.

So, growth theory suggests that imperfect competition is not all bad, if it is is related to the bringing of technology to a developing country that sustains growth. In Indonesia, however, imperfect competition normally has not occurred as is justified by economic theory to provide a forum to transfer technological information efficiently, as is sustained by the logic of recent economic theory. Instead, imperfect competition is the direct result of government interventions of one kind or another in the private economy, sometimes directly to encourage technological advance in ways that economic theory suggests are unworkable. The author believes these interventions, even when intended to improve technological advance in Indonesia, in fact inhibit such advance, and hence inhibit Indonesian economic recovery and growth. The author believes Indonesian economic growth has occurred in the past by improving the quality of its labor force, by exploiting natural resources, and by putting underemployed peasants to work more efficiently on the land and in the formal sector. And as a result of technological transfer.

For several decades, Indonesia has generally pursued what are perceived as good and useful macroeconomic policies, although industrial, technology, and competition policies have often been less desirable. Over the past year, substantial and desirable changes in Indonesian national economic policy have occurred in the direction of more open markets and more transparent decision-making. These changes have often occurred as a direct result of adoption of IMF and World Bank recommendations by the GOI. The focus of this paper is that additional changes should be made in Indonesian economic policies that will encourage additional economic advance in Indonesia through reliance on an enhanced rate of transfer of technology.

The general economics literature of recent years stresses the importance of building institutions that support the structure of a free market economy, such as reliable fast-acting, non-corrupt legal institutions. However, the bent of the current economics literature in the field of industrial organization is perhaps best characterized as much less certain about the virtues of a pure free market approach to aspects of competition policy under consideration in this paper compared with, for example, 1997–98 IMF recommendations to Indonesia about its policies regarding industrial organization.

THE ROLE OF TECHNOLOGICAL CHANGE IN ECONOMIC GROWTH

Export-led economic growth is well established as a core proposition sustaining developing country economic growth. However, the empirical facts of international trade are better explained by taking market structure firmly into account. This literature is summarized in Helpman and Krugman (hereafter, H&K, (6)) who suggest that "conventional trade theory seems to be inadequate in accounting for empirical observation: its apparent failure to explain the volume of trade, the composition of trade, the volume and role of inter-firm trade and direct foreign investment, and the welfare effects of trade liberalization." (6) H&P believe that increasing returns and imperfect competition aspects of the international economy are central to explaining these phenomena. Thus, given the relative success of Indonesia in opening its economy to trade and the additional upside potential suggested in the economics literature from the beneficial impacts of technology transfer, it makes sense to consider the technology aspect of these matters first theoretically and then with respect to Indonesia.

There are divergent views on how technological change takes place in developing countries better to help shape economic growth. A World Bank report on the then-extraordinary economic successes of the Asian tiger economies of a few years ago lays out the case.[4] (18) As we shall see, the Bank believes there are a number of clearly defined market failures that prevent markets in technology from operating successfully in developing countries. And the standard prescription for reacting to such market failure has traditionally been appropriate and responsive government intervention. Perhaps the principal economic advocate of a stronger and more dynamic view than that of the Bank is Sanjaya Lall, which will be discussed in more detail. (11) The market failure framework from which both Lall and the World Bank *Miracle* study approach technological innovation and economic growth is standard in economics.

Of the four market failures in resource allocation regarding industrial policy set forth in the *Miracle* study, two have direct application to the dynamic issues of technology policy. These are the imperfect appropriability of company-level investments in knowledge and skills, and the inability of individual investors to act rationally when there are technologically interdependent investments. These problems can be seen respectively as leading to underinvestment in company-specific skills (because these are social goods whose benefits are not appropriable to the company), and underinvestment in technology companies by investors (because investor time horizons do not encompass sufficient time for technological innovations to be sustained and brought to markets).[5] Together, these deficiencies reduce reliance on technology and thus reduce the pace of economic growth.

> Lall argues that the World Bank has oversimplified these issues, because:
> the mastery and use (of technology) require the recipient to invest in new skills, technical information, organization methods and external linkages. The process continues over time, and varies by technology. (11)

These technology development processes take place over long periods, and it is not easy to separate companies successfully utilizing technology from those that are not while the process of company development is still ongoing. Thus, governments have difficulty in determining how to respond to perceptions of the need for specific government intervention in response to these market failures. Moreover, Lall also argues that the necessary process of learning to utilize technology may be slowed and distorted in developing countries, because the circumstances in which companies operate in such countries are often hostile to such processes. This discussion suggests to Lall that companies operating in developing countries will tend to underinvest in technologies that have "costly, prolonged, and risky learning periods. This will also (adversely) affect the process of technological deepening: entering more complex technologies, increasing local content, or undertaking more demanding technological tasks (say, from simple final-assembly technology to design and development activity." (11)

Lall argues that "simply improving factor markets without offsetting market failures to learning within firms (sic) can lead to narrow and shallow technological development."[6] (11)

Lall believes that the case for investment in such circumstances goes: "beyond simply coordinating individual investment decisions when there are externalities. The nature of the externalities is also important – when certain industry 'clusters' generate strong benefits for the economy in term of technological learning, spillovers, and dynamism, there may be a case for promoting them over others that have more limited or static effects." (11)

In contrast with the modestly interventionist approach found in the World Bank *Miracle* study, Lall recommends a five-stage more heavily interventionist rationale for the promotion of improved "industrial policy" in developing countries, which he believes encompasses why policies of import substitution have failed and policies of export orientation have succeeded as forms of government intervention. He believes his program is a major step beyond "getting prices right" and toward the promotion of what he regards as a healthy and dynamic learning process.

Lall's view is that "(1) Interventions in factor and product markets have to be closely coordinated and integrated; one without the other may be ineffective, even counterproductive. Factor-market policies as recommended by new growth theories cannot provide a complete explanation of rapid industrial development by indigenous enterprises since they ignore the costs of learning and the variety of market failures faced. (2) Distortions introduced by interventions must be offset. In particular, protection must be accompanied by competitive pressures to enter world markets. This is what traditional import substitution strategies failed to provide (presumably this refers to the Korean experience). (3) Since intervention resources are limited, only a few activities should be supported at any one time. Intervening in a large number of unrelated activities risks waste and failure. (4) Since learning is a cumulative and incremental process, interventions must aim to support activities that have a base in existing skills and knowledge in a country. New technological "leaps" must be modest, based on realistic assessments of what is feasible within reasonable periods of time. (5) The line between market friendly and selective interventions is almost impossible to draw. Each market may be subjected to a combination of functional and selective policies." (11)

There is some truth in Lall's viewpoint, but your author believes that the national policies that should result from analyses such as those of Lall are considerably less interventionist than those recommended by interventionists such as Lall. The reasons have to do with the inadequacies of government decision making. Instead of directly addressing Lall's analysis, the author generally plans to provide a more affirmative substitute approach.

ONE OBVIOUS BUT DIFFICULT STRATEGY TO ENCOURAGING TECHNOLOGY UTILIZATION: GROWING COMPANIES

The most obvious factor left out of Lall's analysis is the exchange rate and financial crisis in East and Southeast Asia (E/SE) since the spring/summer of 1997. This crisis has probably been most intense in Indonesia, where the crisis has settled into the inadequate and inadequately supervised banking and financial market systems.[7] As of early 1999, the free fall in the Indonesian economy has slowed to what is perhaps an economic bottom and is at worst a slow decline. This ongoing economic crisis makes it relatively easy to dismiss the prior interventionist strategies encapsulated in the arguments of Lall – which are largely justified by the past "successful" behavior with respect to industrial policy of certain Asian countries that have relied upon interventionist government industrial strategies. These arguments (and the corresponding sections of the World Bank's *Miracle* report) should now be seen as encompassing much wishful thinking.

There is a very strong economic and technical case against developing countries attempting to carry out sophisticated technology-based industrial investment strategies designed directly to grow companies that will rely on technical information and will generate technology-based economic growth. First, many unforeseen things can go wrong, as has most obviously occurred in the E/SE Asian nations that relied on such strategies. Interventionist Japan has been without a significant economic recovery for more than eight years, almost entirely missing the world economic expansion of the 1990s. The remainder of Asia, including substantially interventionist Korea, has relied on Japan as a major market for economic strategies/exports (about one third of Indonesia's major country exports traditionally go to Japan).

The continuation of Japan's economic and financial crisis for so many years is not normally seen as related to its interventionist industrial policy. However, in the view of the author, the Asian economic crisis might have been headed off or been resolved much more rapidly if several Asian governments had not been distracted from their obligations to their banking systems by trying to over-manage sophisticated industrialization. The Asian crisis occurred directly because these nations had both weak financial institutions and experienced significant failures of government to manage and respond. Asian governments that long resisted banking reform could have had the capacity and insight to understand and contain the weaknesses of their banking and financial markets. However, this could only have occurred through better government supervision of banking. In turn, such improved supervision might have occurred had governments not been heavily engaged in industrial policymaking which often had the effect of directing bank subsidies to government-sponsored companies. The result was often internal government struggles between defenders of the industries receiving such subsidies and those advocating improved banking regulation and supervision and actions to resolve financial problems. Such struggles certainly delayed sensible government actions to end banking crises. Obtaining the necessary resolution to act sensibly and take the ugly steps necessary to resolve banking crises is always difficult, as the U.S. government delays in addressing the U.S. savings and loan crisis in the early 1980s attest.

Secondly, in any event, if such governments cannot manage their banking systems, what gives them the hubris to think they can micromanage their industrialization processes? Governments must manage banking systems because banks have the capacity in effect to print money and an incentive to overlend because their deposits which they put at risk are other people's money and the banks retain the profits they make from lending. Thus, without appropriate regulation, banks can simply speculate with other peoples' money, keep the gains, and transfer the losses to government. Nonetheless, it is difficult for governments to do what they must do in banking regulation, and their capacities to do are minimized when governments are also trying to grow companies and carry out industrialization policies relying on high technology. Third, many Asian governments such as Indonesia possess weak human and technical skills, and have difficulty carrying out those functions that governments must carry out. And sophisticated highly educated human talent – the relative lack of which for its size is probably one of Indonesia's greatest weaknesses – must be directed into making technology-based interventionist strategies workable if such strategies are pursued.[8] These profound limitations make it very difficult to believe that governments such as Indonesia can successfully help their private sectors organize and carry out the sophisticated kinds of functions that Lall so carefully documents are required in order to assure appropriate utilization of technological advance.[9]

Fourth, Lall himself lists five lessons for policy that all governments (and for the author, particularly the Government of Indonesia (GOI)) should consider before adopting polices of protection and other government interventions to encourage technology-based economic development. These are that: (a) developing countries lack sufficient information to run the kinds of intervention policies necessary to sustain technology transfer that is required to use technology advance to generate/sustain economic growth, (b) developing countries lack the skills within government to design and carry out such interventions,[10] (c) that such countries lack the flexibility to admit mistakes, (d) there is a strong possibility that government decisionmaking will be sectionalized because of the existence of technology policies, and (e) there is a strong adverse impact of corrupt behavior by government officials.

In the author's view, this last point settles the implications of Lall's views on interventionist policies in Indonesia. Lall says,

> venality can distort the most liberal regime, not just interventionist ones. The solutions, if any, lie in larger political and social processes . . . but certainly a corrupt government should not be intrusted to undertake detailed industrial policy.[11]

By all accounts, Indonesia has recurring severe problems of governmental/private-sector corruption that remain unsolved. Even Lall, the strong economic interventionist, states clearly he would argue that national technology policy should not involve detailed government intervention in the face of such problems – presumably in Indonesia.

The major problem with the analysis so far as it would apply to Indonesia is that without such government intervention (not desirable), some would argue there is little basis for quickly achieving necessary technology inputs that would help economic growth resume and continue. After under/unemployed peasants are put to work, and natural resources are exploited, there is little that remains as a strategy to resume and increase Indonesian economic growth without reliance on technology. For the next several years, the key strategy for Indonesia is putting people back to work – largely in export-oriented businesses.

Lall's list of five problems suggests strongly that little can be done to embody technology in an economy – including Indonesia – without solving a range of difficult technical problems, in his view particularly difficult if left to the private sector in developing countries. Dismissal of interventionist views such as those of Lall for Indonesia is undoubtedly warranted at present because of the over-optimism they imply with respect to the ability of government to plan and carry out technology-based industrialization strategies. Moreover, in any event, Indonesia probably lacks sufficient high-level trained human capacity to solve these problems.

Lall's discussion of technology advance is reasonably sophisticated, except that he appears to fail to understand certain management developments of the last couple of decades that have led first Japanese and then U.S. manufacturing companies to adopt very sophisticated processes of managing human resources and technology. For example, no one any longer advocates organization of companies into functions or activities that are not also profit centers. However, the limitations of Lall's analyses only strengthen the author's case that government interventions in the economy to promote technology advance are extraordinarily difficult to carry out.[12]

Economists accept the critical role of technology/information in economic growth. It is not easy to dismiss the implications for Indonesian policy of the systematic market failures that occur with respect to the necessary conditions for successful technology-based economic growth as conceptualized/documented in sources such as the *Miracle* report and Lall's work. The result is a dilemma: to achieve sustained economic growth (beyond that provided by relatively easy exploitation of cheap labor and natural resources) apparently requires government action to assure technology transfer and the embodiment of technology, and yet the GOI lacks the capacity carry out a strategy that could yield that result.

MULTINATIONAL CORPORATIONS

All is not lost, for not all possible strategies for achieving sustained economic growth through technology utilization have been considered. We next turn to the role of multinational corporations (MNCs).[13] The case will be advanced that World Bank and Lall both have been too concerned with encouraging an increased role for domestic corporations in developing countries that might compete with MNCs.

It is very difficult for developing nations directly to establish and sustain policies that will "grow" domestic companies that rely on technology. This limitation should mean that more attention is paid by developing country policymakers to other strategies for obtaining additional embodied technology. One key technique available to Indonesia is that it might encourage MNCs to transfer more technology. The problem has been the reluctance to rely on MNCs for technology because of the desire to sustain domestically owned activities and to retain the fruits of development for domestic owners. This analysis ignores the major and largely successful efforts Indonesia has carried out – not consistently – over a number of years since the late 1960s to attract multinational corporation investment.

The existence and behavior of MNCs in developing countries have often been subject to a number of national policy concerns, concerns that are being raised again in Indonesia. In a sense, the author's views about technology and economic growth in Indonesia lead him to believe that such corporations are a principal vehicle for helping Indonesia to return to a pace of reasonably rapid economic growth.

There is room for optimism – increased reliance by the GOI on encouraging appropriate behavior from MNCs may help provide the key technological information that will eventually generate additional sustained economic growth. There is evidence (discussed in the next section) that American-based MNCs tend to respond to appropriate regimes that protect their intellectual property by transferring more and sophisticated technologies to businesses in developing countries that are their partners. Lall seems to prefer that governments act to require such a result. Lall favors such a more activist policy, as he is not confident MNCs will respond to the incentives discussed here. He does not cite statistical evidence for his doubts.

Next, we discuss the theory of MNCs. Simply, a MNC is a company that operates in more than one nation. How are such companies; to be distinguished from national companies? To begin with, MNCs normally have to have a serious justification before entering a national market. After all, they are competing in such national markets with domestic companies that are likely to have substantial advantages. National companies are likely to know local factor and product markets well, and therefore have the capacity in principle to make more efficient decisions about resource allocation and production than multinational corporations are likely to be able to make. Moreover, such national corporations are likely to have substantial insights and capacities in dealing with national politics. With these advantages, how can MNCs compete with national corporations in national markets?

For one thing, MNCs, have access to efficiencies in production themselves across national boundaries, and have economies of scale in certain aspects of their operations. In many circumstances, production at the plant level does not involve substantial significant economies of large-scale production, so national and multinational corporations will face about the same circumstances at the plant level. However, MNCs can achieve efficiencies in such activities as finance, headquarters operations, and research and development (technology advance). MNCs are able to spread the costs of these activities over a broad multinational production base. These activities provide additional efficiencies for MNCs that give them an ability to offset the normal advantages of national companies and therefore compete with them in national markets.

These differing comparative advantages to both national and multinational corporations mean that the detailed capability of national corporations to compete successfully with MNCs and vice versa will generally depend on the facts of the situation. But economic theory suggests that one of the advantages of certain MNCs – their key role in technology advance – is critical to shaping the factors that lead to national economic growth. In the case of developed economies, such advance arises either from new technology or technology transferred from elsewhere. In developing countries normally only technology transfer is available as a source for economic growth that does not rely on such factors as exploitation of natural resources or putting under/unemployed peasants to work. The Indonesian experiments with forcing technology development by building high technology companies with public monies have been expensive, and judged by outsiders to be relatively unsuccessful (9, pp. 187–255).

The reliance of economic growth on technology-related factors in developing countries is at the heart of the explanation for economic growth in modern dynamic economic growth theory. Thus, it is worth stating again that the theoretical advantage of MNCs includes a theoretical advantage in technology generation and utilization. So, developing country governments such as Indonesia interested in technology-based economic growth should normally seek ways to encourage multinational corporations to share the technologies they possess.

In contrast, Lall argues that such companies are generally unwilling to share technologies and therefore must be forced to do so, or that national companies that have such technologies must be created through domestic public policy actions. His policy conclusion is difficult to accept, because economists normally believe market transactions in competitive markets and not government policy interventions are needed to help countries attain economic efficiency and growth. Luckily, there is a literature that addresses how to encourage MNCs to share significant technologies.

THE IMPORTANCE OF REASONABLE NATIONAL RULES AND NATIONAL TREATMENT: THE CASE OF INTELLECTUAL PROPERTY RIGHTS

Numerous factors under the control of developing countries enable them to encourage technology-based growth relying on the technology advances of MNCs. These factors include tax policy, relevant expenditure policy by government, government regulatory regimes, control over corruption, democratic decisionmaking rules and procedures, etc. In addition, country location, natural resources, and size of domestic markets are other factors not much under the control of developing countries that matter to MNCs considering investments. Indonesia is well endowed with these favorable factors. While all these national policies and endowments matter to the framework for economic growth, to keep this paper within some modest bounds, only one of these potential issues will be addressed – Indonesian national rules with respect to intellectual property.[14] The reason for the selection is that this approach is key to providing an appropriate response to the key claim made by Lall – who believes that such corporations will not provide substantial sophisticated technology to developing countries.

The contrasting view of the author is that without improved and acceptable intellectual property rules, MNCs will not be willing to share their intellectual property with subsidiaries, through licensing, etc. in developing countries, particularly including Indonesia. In general, intellectual property to a MNC is at the heart of the core competence that its owners, officers and managers believe makes them unique and their products marketable at high prices in a competitive world. The key issue is the extent to which such technology will be shared.

Econometric work carried out by Edwin Mansfield clarifies for a number of nations, mostly in Asia and including Indonesia, the impact of appropriate intellectual property protection and the relationship of those rules to the magnitudes of foreign direct investment (12). The logic of the relationship is that foreign direct investment is a sensible means of transferring technology to developing countries. However, MNCs, particularly U.S. MNCs, are unlikely to want to transfer much sophisticated technology that constitutes their core competence or other significant technology unless there are strong protections in the recipient nation for the intellectual property involved.

Mansfield's statistical evidence shows that U.S. companies in several broad industry groupings consistently invest much more heavily in nations in which intellectual property rights protection is available.[15] These industry groupings are chemical industries, transportation equipment, electrical equipment, food, metals, and machinery. Data are available on the views of executives of major corporations with respect to the strength of the intellectual property rights protection for 17 developing nations. With these data, Mansfield examines industry views on the strength of intellectual property protection to ascertain the percentage of U.S. companies believing that such protection is too weak to allow them to invest. Categories of investment considered are the transfer of their newest and most effective technology in a joint venture with local partners, to a wholly owned subsidiary, or to unrelated companies. Except for the category of transfer of technology to a wholly owned subsidiary (where Indonesia is about in the middle of the list), Mansfield reports that Indonesia is near the bottom of the list of seventeen developing nations in all other cases. Thus, it is clear that the perception of American executives who make foreign direct investment (FDI) decisions is that protection of intellectual property rights in Indonesia is judged much worse than many other countries (although

India is at the bottom of the list). That is, in considering whether to transfer sophisticated intellectual property to Indonesia, executives of MNCs must in general take decisions that they believe will put their core competences at risk of being stolen by their competitors.

Mansfield also reports on econometric work that attempts crudely to measure the loss in FDI when intellectual property rights protection is considered as weak. (13) This FDI loss may be viewed as a proxy for the extent to which companies avoid transferring technology to nations with weak intellectual property rights protection. His estimate suggests that about $200 million in FDI is lost in a year by a country like Indonesia because of weak intellectual property rights protection. That is, the econometric work carried out by Mansfield suggests that, with respect to Indonesia in the mid-1990s, foreign direct investment was about $200 million lower because of the weaknesses in the intellectual property regime in Indonesia as perceived by executives of multinational corporations that would be making these investments.

The obvious conclusion is that Indonesia is likely to be able to attract significantly more FDI when its economic recovery occurs if it continues to follow policies that sustain a more open and transparent economic policy regime to MNC investment by providing better intellectual property rights protection.

AN APPROPRIATE SOLUTION: SELF-LIMITING MONOPOLY POWER

Indonesia is rightly concerned to sustain or accelerate its pace of technological advance. Indonesia's current President Habibie has a long history as a cabinet minister of favoring large government investments to generate rapid technology advance in Indonesia, but at substantial budgetary cost. This approach may not be the strategy Indonesia will continue to adopt should it want directly to continue to encourage technological advance. In the wake of the decline in the real exchange rate of the rupiah against the dollar in the last year, Indonesian companies almost certainly are much better protected from foreign competition than they were a year or so ago, so such policies hardly seem useful in the current economic situation, and have – by themselves – been totally discredited among economists. Even Lall opposes protection in isolation.

Traditionally, Indonesia has invested heavily with public funds to support the advance of certain technology-based industries, such as aircraft manufacture and shipbuilding. Indonesia's current budget stringency arises from the adverse impacts of the economic crisis, because domestic political concerns have meant that available GOI resources are being used to finance subsidies to such activities as food and fuel. This stringency has reduced the ability of the GOI to provide direct subsidies to technology-based industries, as has been traditional. However, the experience of certain European nations which are not technological innovators but nonetheless maintain a high pace of economic and technical advance suggests that there are other more efficient ways to achieve a rapid pace of technological advance in Indonesia[16] (14).

One main problem with standard Indonesian strategies is the experience in the Western world with the behavior of companies. The kinds of private companies that generate sustained technology advance that Indonesia desires to have are normally motivated by the desire to seek repeated instances in which they have a temporary monopoly in the goods or services they sell, and act aggressively to carry out research and development and product innovation to attain a market advantage that will yield such a temporary monopoly position. To provide Indonesian companies with a legal monopoly or some form of government-sponsored protection does not provide them with an economic structure within which companies that generate technology advance are likely to emerge. The resulting incentives provided for company behavior are all wrong.

There has been a role in the West for government financial support in the form of subsidies for private activities that have led to sustained technology advance. However, despite the economic disincentives that were provided by subsidies, the result generally has been to preserve the main focus of these companies in promoting and sustaining technology advance. The easiest example is the American aerospace companies that housed major projects designed to seek objectives to serve the missions of the U.S. Defense Department and the U.S. National Aeronautics and Space Administration. Moreover, in many of these cases, the most advanced technologies were not in the major aerospace companies. What these companies have is a management style and capacities that are adapted to (1) permit them to deal successfully with government procurement rules and regulations, and (2) organize and carry out very large projects that utilize technology and skills they acquire largely from smaller technology-based companies that often came and went as technology advance ebbed and flowed.[17] All this suggests that a model in Indonesia of a large company supported by government spending will not necessarily generate a rapid pace of technology advance. (9), pp. 187–225.

The temptation to Indonesia and other developing nations is to take more direct action to assure that their nationals control technology and economic growth. These issues should be considered in the context of the efficiency losses that occur when the monopolist/oligopolist has sufficient market power to ensure that sales occur when prices exceed marginal costs. State owned enterprises, monopolies sanctioned by government rules, or natural monopolies all have this capacity. However, there is also a more dynamic circumstance that has a more mixed pedigree. Rapid technological change gives a company the opportunity to create, build and market products that are technologically more advanced than those of its competitors[18] (3). The result is that such a company obtains market power – the ability to sell its products at prices well above the efficiency point where marginal costs equals price. This market power tends to be self limiting over time because such companies are usually pursued by competitors who provide similar technology-based products, thus eventually eroding the market power of the initial innovator. In some industries with advanced technologies, the pace of technological innovation is so rapid that the advantage conferred to the innovator is often no more than a matter of months. While such technological advantages are eventually limited in the marketplace, they provide the foundation for dynamic efficiencies in production, and are the core of continual technological advance.

In contrast, and consistently with the standard literature, Indonesian imperfect competition has usually arisen directly or indirectly because of government fiat creating monopolies, an approach standard economic theory clearly suggests usually leads over time to a strategy that implies significant retardation in the pace of economic advance. In response to the Indonesian economic crisis, International Financial Institutions (IFIs, including the World Bank, the Asian Development Bank, and the International Monetary Fund) initially pressed views that aimed to help resolve these problems. As the financial, banking, and exchange-rate regimes were gradually seen to be in more and more difficulty, these latter issues became more dominant. Thus, competition policy matters have appeared to fade into the policy background. Indonesian President Habibie when he was Minister of Research and Development sought to encourage Indonesian economic growth through reliance on government subsidies to technology-based companies. This view has traditionally been attacked as inefficient in Indonesia (and more generally elsewhere), and has now been at least temporarily abandoned as the GOI can no longer stand the necessary budgetary subsidies and would face difficulties justifying them under the guidance of the IMF. However, the questions are likely to revive under the justification that prebumi (native Indonesian) businesses require government economic support, and that economic protection is the way to proceed to avoid the necessity for government budget subsidies. While the IFIs would resist this approach, their resistence is likely to be less fierce than with regard to alternatives such as manipulation of the exchange rate, which was also seriously been considered by the GOI in the fall of 1998.

Thus, what current Indonesian competition policy exists tends to inhibit Indonesian technological advance, a substantial contrast with the United States where there is less tolerance for substantial government-induced imperfect competition.[19] The policy question for Indonesia is whether this difference in national approaches is welfare enhancing or represents a stage in Indonesian economic growth, or is merely mistaken. There is reason to believe that rigorous pressure to provide a competitive environment would help to generate exactly the kinds of companies able and interested in sustaining technology advance that Indonesia has tried and so-far failed to obtain through GOI subsidy.

SPECULATION ABOUT WHAT IS TO BE DONE

Indonesia is at choice. The International Financial Institutions led by the IMF are pressing Indonesia to continue to seek macroeconomic growth by opening itself still further to international trade and investment. This approach is consistent – indeed required – with a strategy of seeking to obtain advanced technology through technology transfer. (14) Permitting or encouraging economic protection is a sure way to fail to build the kinds of companies that are economically efficient and generate innovation.

Traditionally, advocates of tight government control over those activities of companies that tend to create monopolies and oligopolies have contended savagely with defenders of business. Often such political debate has spilled over to influence academic economic investigations, with resulting controversial policy implications.[20]

A serious contradiction lies at the root of the standard debate within the economics profession about merger/competition policy. Arnold Harberger showed long ago that standard measured efficiency losses due to such factors as monopoly/oligopoly are normally relatively small. After some debate, most recent literature has continued to suggest that such efficiency losses are small. For a number of years, this standard conclusion has appeared to make debates about competition policy less a matter of economic efficiency and more a matter of the allocation of power (a political science question) and the resulting effects on the distribution of income/wealth (an equity issue). Little in the normal confused public debate about antitrust/competition policy shows that the available empirical evidence has yet much changed the political economy of this traditional debate. Company size alone appears not to be a significant inhibition to efficient behavior. But size with no incentives for efficient behavior is probably another matter.

Recent developments within macroeconomic theory have explored the key importance of understanding better how economic growth is generated. In the newer literature, there is reliance on concepts such as the endogenous influence of information and the role of workers in research and technology (in addition to the standard reliance on increased stocks of labor and capital) to help explain economic growth. These newer macroeconomic models often utilize imperfect competition in their explanations of economic growth, as it is necessary to provide the incentives for profits that are required to sustain and justify a continued pace of investment in activities that lead to further technological advance.

These evolving differences in viewpoint can perhaps be partially reconciled through investigation of the long-term implications of international differences in competition policy for the success of nations in achieving economic growth. Rigorous competition policies such as those traditionally pursued in the United States help remove straightforward efforts to seek monopoly/oligopoly from the panoply of U.S. corporate strategic practice. For some decades, a major remaining technique that has been legally defensible and hence available for U.S. companies to attain a monopoly position is to become a technology-based company and seek to obtain temporary monopolies through bringing new and more sophisticated products to market more rapidly than its competitors. The new products are often based in part on research based on internal corporate understanding of technology advance or on exploiting research funded in universities.

The relevant economic theory suggests that the principal long-term benefit to U.S. style of competition policy has been to help generate a U.S. corporate sector focused (as for example the U.S. high-end manufacturing/communications sectors largely are) on the achievement of growth through technological progress – a strategy central to what may be a successful long-term approach to managing long-term economic growth. In the absence of rigorous competition policy, companies in other nations (until recent years) often achieve traditional monopoly/oligopoly power with little difficulty. However, these latter approaches are not forms of imperfect competition that sustain economic growth in the way that the newer macroeconomic theory suggests that temporary technology-based monopoly/oligopoly does. Thus, rigorous enforcement of competition policy may turn out to be critical to achieving long-term economic growth, and thus critically important to achieving economic growth. This is a role for competition policy that is substantially different from the standard "trust busting" role.

The United States made a major comeback in advanced manufacturing over the past decade or more after thorough defeats were imposed on many U.S.

companies by Asian companies in the early-to-mid 1980s. The U.S. manufacturing comeback largely relied on a combination of improved management helping to generate increased worker productivity and temporary monopolies/oligopolies using advanced technologies. In contrast to much of E/SE Asia (except Japan), in the United States rigorous competition policy prevents companies from seeking/obtaining a dominant market position via monopoly/oligopoly practices. The major relaxation of competition policy in the 1980s and early 1990s in the United States does not contradict this perspective. American companies are used to the regular ebb and flow of rigorous antitrust enforcement and as a result are not likely to change core behavior because antitrust policy changes for a few years. Thus, the long-term strategies described in this paper here would likely continue regardless of the pace of antitrust enforcement. Rigorous competition policies may in the long run benefit those nations' companies that successfully adapt to following long-term strategies of economic growth based on reaping rewards from temporary imperfect competition through continuing innovations rather than relying on monopolies/oligopolies (a conclusion that is attractive but not yet proven).

It can be suggested that this partial implicit strategy for carrying out competition policy is a useful organizing device for Indonesian decision making. The strategy about to be discussed is only partial as it does not fully take into account the range of in between behavior. This strategy is also the key to an alternative framework for Indonesian policy to Lall's approach. Indonesian policymakers should consider the establishment and enforcement of a strong and vigorous competition policy. The goal of such a policy would be to provide the right kind of incentives – to build over time the right kind of competitors among Indonesian companies.[21]

The public policy goal for this sort of competition policy would be to encourage the creation and growth of businesses that rely on technology advance to sustain economic growth. And such businesses cannot be created through direct government action. And certainly the business sector will not be very happy with this sort of rigorous competition policy enforcement.

What does such a policy regime encompass? First, any government decision to pursue this kind of approach would also require as a precondition the elimination as rapidly as is possible of the publicly generated reasons that have favored certain companies in Indonesia or have generated monopolies or special positions for certain companies. There is a possible lesson for current issues in macroeconomic and competition policy in East/Southeast (E/SE) Asia. Substantial economic growth has been achieved in the past by relying on rapid technological transfer that permits putting labor and capital to work, although in the early days much of the labor involving providing full-time work to previously unemployed peasants. Manufacturing industries captured in the 1980s from the United States are apparently not now underpinning a current long-term basis for continuing super-rapid Asian economic growth (partially because demand for Asian products has weakened cyclically and perhaps because there may be limits to the continuing pace of long-term growth in many industries on which E/SE Asia now relies). It is possible that such industries perhaps are or are becoming "sunset" industries or industries in which there remains little monopoly power that, as the products are near-commodities. The result has been a tendency to over produce in such an industry, as a range of competitors over optimistically believe they will be able to share the monopoly profits previously earned, just as these profits are going away.

Second, such a policy regime would not seek a favored position of Indonesian companies through special tariffs/government rules. The practices of this nature that do exist should be eliminated. Third, such a policy would provide strong intellectual property rights protection to go along with other approaches already in place to opening the Indonesian economy. Such protection would be designed to encourage companies investing in Indonesia through FDI to bring their "core competences" with them. Fourth, the current openness/transparency (such as it is) and related benefits of Indonesian macroeconomic policymaking should be retained and expanded in support of good standard macroeconomic policy. (9)

Business in Indonesia faces a number of complex problems. These include short-term macroeconomic problems including negative economic growth (and its implication of a lack of domestic demand by Indonesians for Indonesian products), continuing inflation (although moderated from the levels of 1998), and massive unpaid foreign debt denominated in dollars. Domestic Indonesian businesses are still over regulated, although less so than in the past. The remaining regulation is partially a hangover from the import substitution period in the late 1970s and early 1980s. It should be noted that these points apply to the industrial system in Indonesia and not to its banking system. The latter has been and continues to be dangerously under regulated substantively.

The source of the rationale for Indonesian industrial regulations goes back in its history. There are two major components: the discredited import substitution rationale and the impulses toward economic nationalism that previously helped cause the erroneous import-substitution rationale to be so thoroughly adopted in Indonesia. These rationales for misguided policies are still supported by quite active proponents in Indonesia.

Fears of predatory behavior by large domestic and international companies on small undercapitalized Indonesian companies, often including state enterprises, are the core of the rationale for the reliance on import substitution policies. There is normally a fear that such local enterprises will not be able to reform sufficiently to face international competition. Hence, there is an impulse toward relying on protectionist measures in GOI policymaking circles.

There remains a real separation between the Indonesian still-constrained domestic market and the capacity of firms located in Indonesia to sell relatively freely in international markets. Yet, the developing international market is generating links to Indonesian domestic producers as well. In the early and mid-1980s, there was no significant link in the Indonesian input output table between the industries that manufacture for the domestic market and industries that export. By the early 1990s, such a link had been shown to be statistically significant. Thus, domestic Indonesian manufacturing companies were beginning to support the export of products from Indonesia – thus providing components for such exports.[22]

Moreover, the U.S. experience of the 1950s through 1980s (after which the United States began to rely much more heavily on international trade as its source of growth) has shown that long-term economic growth is certainly feasible for a large self-contained society trading mostly with itself. Although the United States relies significantly on international trade and investment as a major source for its economic growth, that is a relatively recent development. Throughout the period of rapid U.S. economic growth in the 1950s and 1960s, U.S. dependence on international trade remained in the low single digits. Thus, it is reasonable that Indonesian economic growth could eventually occur on the internally-based pattern of the United States when the U.S. economy was opening up in the 1950s and 1960s. Your author's view is that one necessary factor key to such growth in Indonesia is the transfer of technology. Moreover, the U.S. economy was becoming more open throughout its comparable period. Eventual domestic-led growth in Indonesia is therefore not a suggestion that the Indonesian economy should become closed – quite to the contrary.

If Indonesia were to decide to utilize its government regulatory power to help the private sector generate businesses that have the sort of characteristics that support economic growth, how would it go about doing this? One policy strategy, that has been pursued in the United States, is to take economic power away from businesses in all ways except when they use innovation to produce new products that give them economic power temporarily.[23]

The competition policy problem remains. If government is to tolerate some temporary market power by technology oriented businesses, it is still necessary to think about managing the monopoly-generating aspects of all this. One possibly useful strategy for thinking about policy matters in this environment is to utilize the concept of contestability. Suppose policy changes are made to ensure that markets become contestable (full pure contestability in a monopolistic market means that all barriers to entry into that market on the part of firms other than the monopolist are eliminated). Then even if the monopolist decides to raise prices to attempt to exploit its monopoly power, because there are no barriers to entry, other firms can enter and undercut the higher monopoly prices. As a result, the monopoly firm will fear to take advantage of its monopoly power because if it does it will lose market share to entering competitors. As a result, the theoretical expectation is that the monopoly firm will often charge prices close enough to the competitive price to deter other firms from entering the market. That is, the monopolist will behave as if it were a competitive firm in a competitive market. The consequence of a successful effort to make a monopoly market contestable is that the continued existence of a monopoly in a market does not lead to high prices.

Contestability approach is controversial. The principal argument against this approach is the existence of capital costs (including sunk costs), in the presence of which contestability is harder to defend theoretically. Yet, the policy framework suggested by contestability is interesting, nonetheless. It suggests that all efforts should be made to reduce or eliminate barriers to entry. Yet, sometimes these can be directly addressed, as when they are government sponsored. Reduction of such barriers moves policy concerns in the direction of gradually promoting competition, if not to contestability.

This contestable markets rationale for policy should be seen as a limiting case – like that for perfect competition. Despite this, simulations/experimental methods in economics testing for the existence of contestable markets have suggested that this limiting case has substantial explanatory power. (15) This approach could provide a theoretical basis for tolerating (or even encouraging) companies that seek temporary monopolies through technological advance.

In Indonesia, contestability suggests a strategy for dealing with an important political/economic problem that has serious ethical components. Large Indonesian conglomerates have monopoly power, and are owned by ethnic Chinese, many of whom have lived in Indonesia for generations. In the policy regime being put into place in 1999 to deal with competition policy issues, there appears to be a strong "trust busting" component in the public discussions that will inevitably be seen as aimed at these companies with significant market power. Instead, if the GOI could manage to look through the prisms suggested by this paper, such policies might appear as partially anti-growth.

The policy framework discussed so far suggests considering an alternative regime to be put into place for dealing with companies. The alternative approach would be to eliminate the statutory and regulatory advantages given to such companies in the past. Instead, Indonesia should seek ways to eliminate barriers to entry to encourage an improved competitive policy regime. Adoption of this approach would prevent scarce Indonesian intellectual and legal capacities being wasted by being aimed at antimonopoly activities that probably have little economic payoff. Government policymakers would then not be wasting time and energy making more judgments than are necessary about the competition policy regime. The main problem with antimonopoly activities is that such a strategy in Indonesia may also have anti-competitive results.

APPLICATION TO INDONESIA: A TRANSITION TO EMPIRICAL WORK

What can be said about companies at present operating in Indonesia with respect to reasonable technology policies in Indonesia? There is much detail but also little clarity. In part this is because it is difficult to generalize too much about the complex models that underlie much recent theoretical work. In part it is because of the sheer geographic size and human scale of the nation and its businesses.

Hal Hill produced a recent pre-crisis study of Indonesia's industrial transformation (9). Hill reports that, by the mid-1990s compared with the mid-1960s, while the economy as a whole had increased six fold, manufacturing had increased a staggering 18- fold, from about 8% of GDP to overtaking agriculture to become the largest sector in the Indonesian economy about 24% of GDP in 1996. This rapid growth in the manufacturing sector can be considered nothing short of phenomenal. However, the policy regime under which it occurred involved a range from "blatant instances of rent-seeking and corruption" often without careful consideration of the difficult issues that arise involving state ownership versus market orientation.

As Hill says, and the author agrees, while macroeconomic policies have generally been good, at the microeconomic level, these policies have been offset by

> a range of ineffectual, and in some instances, downright malign policies and programs . . . Large projects owned by the most powerful citizens in the country . . . . have been able to operate more or less independently of the usual policy rules . . . . From the late 1970s, import projection was granted in a selective, discretionary manner. And all firms had to deal with a bureaucracy which involved complex, opaque and corrupt procedures. (9), pp. 7–8.

This is not an environment designed to create companies that are interested in the use of technology to generate economic growth. And of course if the above analysis of how economic growth occurs generally is correct, this paper is another beginning to the discussion. There needs to be more specific application to Indonesia. Certainly, putting underemployed peasants to work full time and exploiting natural resource endowments has helped to generate much economic growth. And opening the economy to international trade and foreign direct investment has brought reliance on advanced technology as international standards have spread throughout the Indonesian economy.

A principal Indonesian anxiety is for Indonesian ownership of the fruits of Indonesia, particularly its natural resources. There is a vaguely worded constitutional provision suggesting that Indonesian resources belong to the Indonesian people – perhaps to the Indonesian government. While Indonesian economic policy has nonetheless generally supported the view that there are sufficient economic benefits to permitting a gradual opening of the open economy, as usual the losers in this policy process – the Indonesian businesses that would carry out the same tasks to the extent they were carried out – are certainly better connected in Indonesian policy circles than the winners. The winners would largely be the Indonesian people benefitting from lower prices, more jobs, a wider availability of goods and services, as part of a sustainable economic recovery.

Policies favoring large businesses through protection often have adverse effects on small businesses. And in the current environment, small business is an increasing proportion of the employment of Indonesians employed in the economic recovery. The main effects of efficient development on the small company have been carefully identified by Snodgrass and Biggs (17, hereafter S&B). If, after economic stabilization occurs in Indonesia, and economic recovery begins, the main pattern of general economic development set forth by S&B for small businesses is followed in Indonesian development over the next decade or more, economies of scale in production are likely to account for much of the economic growth that occurs in the manufacturing sector as Indonesia's GDP per capita recovers from the current recession lows and later starts an economic recovery and rises from $800 to $2,000 per capita.[24]

For most nations, there is a pattern in the nature of industrialization.[25] There are many anomalies by sector, as can be seen in the discussion of Indonesian manufacturing. As per capita income grows, S&B argue that industrialization shifts from the early industries of food, beverages, tobacco, textiles, and clothing to middle industries of wood and wood products, chemicals and rubber products, and non-metallic industries. The early industries are usually highly inefficient, serve local markets, involve little in the way of returns to scale, and can operate successfully in the highly unstructured economic environments nearly always found in low income countries such as Indonesia.

S&B believe the middle industries involve strong returns to scale and contribute as much as 40% of growth as GDP rises from $300 per capita to

$1,000 per capita. Indonesia passed through the latter point, and then substantially regressed as the result of the economic crisis. These strong returns to scale of necessity involve the existence of some imperfect competition. As Indonesia returns to and follows the normal pattern of industrialization, during and immediately after the economic recovery, the middle industries will contribute substantially to economic growth. They will begin to phase out as contributors to growth as the resulting expansion continues. And early industries such as shoe manufacturing and textiles can be expected to seek government protection as their position declines and they become uncompetitive. There are already examples from the middle industry of chemicals that serves textiles. There are no significant reasons for providing subsidies or economic protection to the middle industries in the quite probably vain hope that they will continue to impact Indonesian economic growth successfully. But the policy temptation to do so will be strong. However, it will give up the potential for additional economic growth for preservation of mature industries with little upside growth possibility.

The author's view is that the late industries kicked in on schedule in Indonesia at about $750 per capita (these are normally industries such as paper and printing, basic metals, metal products, and machinery, many of which are already substantial contributors to Indonesia's GDP growth). These industries have regressed as a result of the economic crisis. These industries (unless controlled or monopolized) grow faster than GDP from $750 per capita until industrialization becomes less important as full development has occurred. This approach occurs as other service-oriented sectors grow more rapidly. S&B believe these late industries account for about 80% of the increase in industry's share after incomes reach $750 per capita.

These late industries are successful in large measure because they rely on economies of scale in production. Such economies create market power – oligopoly or monopoly. Indonesia should think through the competition policy regime under which they will operate. These industries imply a rising average firm size as economic growth (measured by per capita incomes) increases. Indeed that outcome is what the cross country evidence shows. Why does this result occur? Adam Smith said specialization of labor, and no one has entirely gainsayed him. Another way of saying that is that economies of scale and/or of scope are occurring. S&B believe that other potentially relevant explanatory variables include random shocks and historical accidents, differences in efficient firm size within industries, infrastructure costs, foreign trade effects, demand fluctuations, the impacts of human capital and other scarce factors of production, technology, and the costs of organizing and managing transactions.

Because of Indonesia's huge physical scale, these differences are likely to be exacerbated in the Indonesian context. Moreover, the competition policy regime Indonesia puts into place can shape how rapidly the late industries come into play. Continued acceptance of FDI and the technology advance it brings will encourage a rapid pace of growth to this process. An anti-foreign "trust-busting" regime could delay the potential for economic growth in the late industries that could otherwise encourage a more rapid pace of Indonesian modernization.

It is important to make that competition policy regime sufficiently sophisticated. It is important for the industrial policy regime in Indonesia to be clear – that technology transfers as the late industries come into play will best sustain the Indonesian economic recovery and generate additional economic growth.

Competition policy regimes will have to differ by industry. The degree of concentration, the pre-existing industry structure, the nature of the technology involved will all shape how Indonesia should decide its competition policies. Transparency and openness for policy are particularly important in an area as naturally murky as competition policy. It will be very difficult to fit a "one size fits all" policy approach to this area. Careful economic study of the behavior and potential for the various sectors of the Indonesian economy before government acts on competition policy affecting those sectors will pay strong dividends not only in the form of better policy but also in the form of better understanding of that policy and support for its implementation.

Imperfections in factor markets allow inefficient small firms to exist in the presence of superior technology. Inefficient small firms are often squeezed out as income rises and production generally becomes more efficient. After the economic recovery advances substantially, many small firms in Indonesia will gradually disappear because they are too inefficient to compete in the more integrated Indonesian markets that are partially already available and are certainly coming. However, these inefficient firms probably haven't yet realized they are non-competitive in broader markets, as they are just starting to face them.

SOME LIMITED EMPIRICAL EVIDENCE

Empirical evidence is available regarding the characteristics of industrial establishments in Indonesia[26] (10). Evidence is available for numbers of establishments, total number of employees, and output increases for all classes of industrial establishments in Indonesia during the period, 1992–94, for small establishments (less than 20 employees) and very large establishments (more

3,000 employees, of which there were 100). These are critical years, since they are the years in which Indonesia was recovering from the economic slowdown engendered by the large government-induced rise in Indonesian interest rates to control inflation, which slowed growth in the early 1990s. It might be argued that the behavior of business in these years are (and should be) a precedent for the years of economic recovery to come.

In 1992–1994, the percentage rates of increase for the key data (noted above) for both large and small establishments were significantly smaller than they were for the companies in the middle (in the various classifications of non-small and non-large establishments). The exception is that, in value added terms, the large establishments did approximately match the behavior of other data categories. However, there does appear to be a rapid tailing off in the rate of increase in value added that small establishments are providing to Indonesian economic growth (Only a 13.7% increase in growth in value added in 1993–94 compared with totals in no other category of slightly less than 19% growth in value added in 1993–94). The tentative conclusion from the Indonesian data on its last economic recovery appears to be that the very smallest of industrial establishments and the very largest did not do as well as the rest of Indonesian industrial establishments. For the smaller establishments, economic theory provides a rationale for inefficiency. For the largest of establishments, there is the substantial possibility that has been implied in this paper – that the varying results obtained for establishment size, employment changes, and output changes may suggest the possibility of inefficiency.

It is also possible that the large establishments could be in mature industries – and hence unable inherently to realize normal rates of economic growth. In general, it seems doubtful that is the case in as young an economy as Indonesia. Perhaps the most serious possibilities are in textiles, shoes, etc., the very footloose industries. However, the recession-engendered decline in Indonesia's wages (measured internationally) has made such industries competitive in Indonesia for a long time to come. However, if such large industries are so mature there is little room for additional economic growth from them, that is a particularly strong reason for eliminating government subsidies and protection benefits, and refusing to provide additional such benefits.

Inefficiencies in the Indonesian economy are quite possibly brought on by past government intervention that principally has benefited the largest establishments by guaranteeing market position. Economic theory suggests that the result is likely to be to make such establishments less efficient in their operations, thus leading to the relatively inefficient results just reported. Moreover, such intervention is most likely for the largest of companies because they are likely to be able to afford the efforts involved to influence government to favor them. In addition, government cannot intervene on a retail basis with smaller companies, so that special government treatment (no matter how justified or rationalized) is most likely to occur favoring the largest of companies. However, once such companies receive protection or other favors, the likelihood that they will remain efficient and highly competitive (if they ever were) is minimal. Thus, it is likely that in a society in which there is some economic protection, it will have its most debilitating effects on the largest and most politically well connected establishments. The data show that conclusion for the largest establishments.

These data therefore suggest an important potential role for the GOI in eliminating anticompetitive behavior that will be particularly important in this economic recovery – as it could have been in the last economic recovery. The idea is that competition policy should try to get government out of the way in areas of the Indonesian economy where standard government intervention of the kind Indonesia has regularly indulged in will probably have the effect that the growth in value added in assisted industries in Indonesia will be relatively low. The beneficiaries of good Indonesian competition policy are in the smallest establishments where theory from other nations and knowledge of Indonesian behavior suggests there is normally likely to be much inefficiency. The harm that will be generated by bad Indonesian competition policy will be in the largest of establishments where government intervention is often attempted to favor winners and normally to leads to inefficiency as a byproduct of the intervention.

LESSONS FROM THE UNITED STATES

This paper has made a case for increasing the pace of Indonesian economic recovery and eventual growth by providing continued openness and reliance on technology transfer and by trying to grow technology-based companies without favoring them in the GOI decision making process. Suppose the strategy that has been advocated in this paper is correct and adopted in Indonesia. A concern could arise that the unwinding of the monopoly positions in Indonesia to encourage more technology-based corporations over time would create massive losses in jobs, slow innovation, and slow economic growth in the short-term when it is needed most. The author believes these problems will not arise.

There is no large-scale sustained Indonesian experience regarding such deregulation. However, in general the arguments that can be expected to be made in Indonesia about these matters parallel those made in the United States when it underwent a wave of economic deregulation in the late 1970s and early 1980s. Charles Winston has provided data that show that U.S. industry has adjusted very successfully to economic deregulation. He shows that "deregulation is a long-term process from which society will continue to reap benefits as firms continue to adjust to free market competition and as more and more industries are more fully deregulated." (19) Winston argues coherently that the adjustment process will occur over an extended period, and that consumer benefits will rise over that period. Cost reduction and product improving innovations will occur in industries that have not adopted them previously, and markets will become substantially more competitive.

In the United States, as a result of deregulation, Winston reports there have been real economic benefits: load factors in airlines increased by about 10%, trucking carriers have substantially reduced their empty miles, real operating costs per mile of railroads have declined by 60%, deregulation on the number and location of branches in banking has reduced operating costs more than 8%, and real operating and maintenance expenses in transmission and distribution of natural gas have fallen roughly 35%. (19) These successful experiences in past deregulation are now generating pressures for additional deregulation in the United States to achieve similar benefits in still regulated fields such as telecommunications, the production and delivery of electric power, and cable television. There are other examples and other potential economic benefits from further economic deregulation that lie ahead in the United States where there is also local government regulation, such as for taxis and occupational licensing – problems that will arise more forcefully in Indonesia as decentralization of its government occurs.[27]

Arguments could be raised in Indonesia that the transition costs of moving to a regime of increased competition are too high or that the economic benefits of such a change will be fleeting. Such views are contradicted by the on-going experience of the United States in the 20 years since it started to move to a much more competitive economic policy regime. The implications for Indonesia seem clear. The empirical arguments for deregulation in Indonesia (or for opposing additional regulation by such means as by insisting that the Indonesian distribution network be run largely through or by cooperatives, or by imposing some other non-market regime) can be generalized from the U.S. experience. There is no reason for Indonesia – facing a long, slow climb from its economic devastation – to choose deliberately not to achieve all the economic efficiency it can handle.

The U.S. experience of economic deregulation reports an economic gain after 10 to 15 years of an additional 10–15% increase in the size of the regulated industries resulting from successful decisions by these industries to carry out innovations and institute productivity increases – decisions that did not occur while they were regulated. In the Indonesian circumstances, this result suggests that replication of the U.S. approach in Indonesia – large-scale deregulation and a refusal to reregulate – could have large benefits. The U.S. experience suggests that paralleling the U.S. approach could lead to a potential increase of key sectors of the Indonesian economy compared with what it would otherwise be of between ten to 15% over the next ten to 15 years, all else equal. That might be nearly as much as a $40 billion increment in the size of the Indonesian economy, just from making the right choices with respect to policies promoting economic efficiency now. Such a translation of the experience of the United States to Indonesia is possibly a low-side estimate of the potential benefits of suitable competition policy, as the Indonesian industries affected are probably not mature industries as their counterparts are in the United States. Indonesia should not lightly throw such benefits away.

CONCLUSION

This paper supports the main line economic policy consensus about the importance of technology transfer from MNCs as a spur to economic growth in developing countries. Generally, it makes the case that interventionist industrial policies seem far less justifiable in the light of the Asian economic crisis, particularly given the enormous importance of salvaging the banking systems in crisis countries and the difficulty of making such decisions when advocates of industrial policy within government have a stake in the outcome. Appropriate protection of intellectual property rights will provide a principal vehicle for Indonesia to obtain the necessary information to help it grow.

This paper suggests more controversially that strong competition policy enforcement is a central key to economic growth. To be effective, such a policy regime must take a strong line favoring inclusion of all businesses, including state-owned enterprises, cooperatives, and small businesses, within the purview of the competition policy agency. The strategy is that by taking away anticompetitive options from business executives, they will eventually be brought to learn that there is one remaining way to achieve a monopoly position – and that is to become highly expert in the management and encouragement of technology as a key to their growth. And that process will provide increased technology to support Indonesian economic growth.

Indonesian economic growth coming out of the 1991–92 slowdown was particularly supported by middle-sized companies, rather than small companies or very large companies. This history suggests that a repetition may be the appropriate strategy for Indonesia coming out of its current recession. There is no direct empirical evidence in Indonesia about the importance of assuring a competitive policy regime. However, in the United States in the 1970s and

1980s, a regime of large-scale economic regulation of certain industries was eliminated or greatly reduced. The results have been a demonstrated major increase in U.S. economic growth as these industries shook of regulatory shackles. The strong suggestion is that Indonesia would presumably benefit from the removal of its shackles as well.

NOTES

1. Ph.D., Senior Public Finance Advisor, USAID/Jakarta, Indonesia.

2. A public or social good has certain relevant characteristics. Unlike a private good such as an apple, consumption of a social good by one person does not diminish its availability for consumption by another party. In this case, then, general technological information useful in one company is also useful to another company, and the first company is not harmed by its use in a second unrelated company. Moreover, the difference in the efficiency condition for the production of a social good as compared with a private good has standard policy implications. For a private good, the efficiency condition is that marginal benefit equals marginal cost. For a social good, the efficiency condition is that the sum of the marginal benefits equals the marginal cost. This difference leads directly to the standard conclusion that a social good is likely to be under supplied in competitive markets because no one company can capture all the benefits. This factor provides the standard justification, for example, for government subsidies to university research and development activities, which produce information with social good characteristics.

3. The WTO Working Group on Trade and Competition Policy is chaired by Frederic Jenny, France. The charter of the group is to study "issues raised by Members relating to the interaction between trade and competition policy, including anti-competitive practices, in order to identify any areas that may merit further consideration in the WTO framework."

4. The current perspective in Indonesia is from a massive economic dislocation and collapse from major declines in exchange rates, high inflation, and pervasive failures in banking systems and industry, particularly manufacturing for the Indonesian domestic market. The lesson appears to be that optimism about the ability of developing county governments, (even advised by the International Financial Institutions (IFIs)) to manage the process of technology development and continue to attain rapid economic growth, is less promising than a few years ago. Many of the candidates for success and emulation cited in the Bank's study appear to have done badly over the past several years, e.g. Japan, Korea. The East Asian economic "miracle" looks more like a bubble at present. It will be recollected that Indonesia was considered for a number of years to be a second-generation economic tiger, or tiger cub.

This paper only addresses selected technology-policy recommendations found in the *East Asian Miracle*, rather than the wide range of other ideas discussed there.

5. It is difficult to see the latter deficiency in the empirical behavior of investors in late 1998, given the enormous favoritism that has been shown to technology-based companies during the recent incredible run-up in American stock prices (probably also a bubble).

6. *Ibid.*, p. 11. Italics in original. These views of Lall encompass his response to the main thrust of the *Miracle* technology-based recommendations. The 'sic' is provided because among executives of industrial companies, firms are law firms. Lall is discussing, in their parlance, companies.

7. Lall of course wrote before the crisis, so it is hard to fault him for not foreseeing it, as many others (including the author) did not. However, it is hard to defend Lall's interventionist recommendations in current circumstances.

8. In fairness to Lall, he argues strongly for good macroeconomics and investment in human resources. He is simply more optimistic than the author with respect to the capacities of Asian governments to carry out his ambitious technology programs.

9. Lall, *op.cit.*, pp 27–58. Lall discusses these matters with some care. He is enamored of the Korean experience with respect to the management of technological and economic advance through close government collaboration with large industrial corporations. It is probably unfair to Lall (but hard to resist remarking on) how difficult the Asian economic crisis has been on Korea, as compared with, say, Taiwan, where the government interventions have been – with certain exceptions – relatively less intensive.

Your author has strong views about the limitations of government, based on the limited capacity he has seen from very competent public officials who tried and often failed to achieve sensible policy outcomes for the United States government during his past 25 years of work. He has also watched the behavior of developing country governments for a number of years, and seen little in such countries that is different and that suggests strong capacities to manage sophisticated technology processes.

10. Such interventions are very unlikely to yield additional GDP growth. If not, they seem like an enormous waste of critical resources available to developing countries such as Indonesia – investment dollars and trained manpower. For a couple of specific analyses that lead to the view that such interventions usually accomplish little, see (2) and (4). Both studies argue that Japanese market intervention gained little and probably cost economic welfare.

11. Lall, *op. cit.*, pp. 21–23. This point certainly applies to technology-based policies.

12. These views of Lall's analyses are based on the personal experiences of the author working with senior executives of more than 80 companies among the *Fortune* 500 U.S. manufacturing companies on these and related matters for several years during the early 1990s.

13. Export orientation is another source for technology provision to developing countries, as their exports must meet world standards. To do so, such exports must embody technology – in the broad sense that word is used in this paper. This strategy is not considered separately in this paper, as it is in the view of the author an additional way of examining the role of technology transfer.

14. The selection is also made because it is relatively unrecognized by the GOI as a serious problem, is an area where Indonesia's problems remain serious, and yet straightforward solutions are under the control of the GOI.

15. This is based on a sample of 94 companies. Mansfield has traditionally had very good access to the views of senior U.S. company executives.

16. The author provides evidence (not entirely compelling) that technology transfer in OECD nations makes it possible for those nations that do not invest in technology but

are hospitable to receiving the transfer of technology are able to keep up rates of economic growth at about the same pace as those who invest heavily in technology.

17. Sometimes a smaller technology based company would win enough Defense Department contracts to become a major company responsible for the organization and execution of larger contracts. Sometimes a larger company would fail to win enough contracts and be merged out or drop back to become a smaller company. But the pattern generally remains that the most advanced technologies used were in the smaller companies rather than Boeing, etc. Source: Interviews during 1990–93 by Dr. Aten with senior executives of more than 80 such companies.

18. A relative of the standard Shumpeter argument. The case that size alone provides for technological advance that Shumpeter advanced does not seem to have significant economic relevance.

The United States has recently brought an antitrust case against the Microsoft Corporation which is ongoing as this paper is written. Note that the legal defense Microsoft is mounting in the current anti-trust case the United States government is bringing against it relies in part on a variant of this argument – that Microsoft is enhancing GDP growth in the United States by bringing technology to bear rapidly and fruitfully in the computer field.. However, the Federal government's position is that Microsoft has also violated other rules, including predatory pricing, and illegal (under U.S. laws) utilization of its monopoly position to gain market advantage. Antitrust actions should probably not be an option for Indonesian competition policy in the near term until after it clearly alters its views on industrial intervention. Until then, such policies will not be credible.

19. There is an ongoing task force in Indonesia addressing competition policy issues under the auspices of the GOI. It is not yet publically clear to what extent this activity is motivated as an effort to increase competition (which could encourage the sorts of technology-based economic growth that are the focus of attention in this paper) or as an effort simply to punish past monopolies (which might be serious distraction from efforts to get the Indonesian economy moving again), possibly for ethnic reasons. The legislation will almost certainly be limited in that state-owned enterprises, small businesses, and cooperatives will be excluded from its purview. Moreover, there appears to be too little discretion given to the Commission that will manage this process not to act if market shares are too high. In addition, the penalties are calculated as a share of profits and are labeled as criminal penalties. This approach means that damages may not be calculated, but rather penalties will be assessed simply because market shares are judged too large. These judgments rely on the analyses of Steve Marks, USAID PEG project, 1999.

In the United States, there are still ongoing struggles at the state and local level about economic regulation, although it is largely eliminated (except for ongoing efforts to preserve competition) at the national level. However, social regulation has been on the rise in the United States.

20. Examples of this can be drawn from issues on merger policy. An article by Dennis C. Mueller (an advocate of strong/tight government control over company merger behavior) sets an uncompromising tone for competition policy. See (16). In another article, Robert Smiley discusses carefully the results of analytical work regarding American merger policy that address the extent to which, if any, efficiency gains are obtained from mergers and acquisitions. *Ibid.* To a non-specialist, the wide variety of differing experiences with regard to merger/antitrust policies that has been

reported over the last few years for European countries suggests that merger policy in Europe has changed substantially over the past 20 years or so generally toward the more interventionist stance toward such policies toward business which was standard in United States practice (except for the United Kingdom, which became much more permissive towards mergers in the 1980s) and has been renewed in the United States in recent years. For example the case the U.S. government recently brought against Microsoft suggests a strategy of stronger antitrust enforcement in the United States.

Three theoretical hypotheses about motivations for mergers occur in the relevant economic literature: (1) mergers lead to market-power increases and to higher prices; (2) mergers reduce production/transactions costs, or as a means to rationalize production, thus increasing economic efficiency; and (3) mergers are conducted under a rationale for industrial organization different from profit maximization. One example of the third hypothesis would be that mergers are conducted to increase firm size subject to a profit constraint, so that managements are able to benefit financially from the standard linkages between additional firm size and increased renumeration opportunities for management. The standard judgment from the literature appears to be that articles by Mueller and Smiley that report and interpret empirical evidence on the behavior of firm shares that does not successfully support or refute any of these hypotheses. This limitation of the empirical work (relatively normal in economics) leaves room for differing interpretations on the appropriateness of the differing stances for competition policy.

21. Any competition policy actually adopted must consider major issues beyond the scope of this paper which is limited to certain of the implications of technology transfer. There are other legitimate sources of monopoly power, including natural monopolies, which do not arise from technology advance. Thus, the policies discussed in the text should only be considered as a partial solution to monopoly powers, rather than a complete response.

22. For the USAID-funded TIPP project in the Indonesian Ministry of Industry and Trade, William (Ted) James and Natsuka Fugita carried out input-output work that provides support for these conclusions.

23. This strategy was perhaps pursued purely accidentally by academics and policy analysts who really were opposed to large businesses simply because they are large.

24. The discussion over the next couple of pages relies heavily on S&B. S&B report there was a clear interventionist bias in policy favoring small firms in the economics literature involving small firms in the late 1960s. S&B believe that policy bias led India (and after India under the influence of Indian economists in international organizations, much of the developing world) astray. By not following the Indian policy lead in this area, Indonesia missed the debilitating adverse effects on economic growth of imposing a strong regulatory environment leading to an overreliance on such firms. More recently, donor organizations have also contributed to policy confusion by supporting (on what S&B believe to be erroneous) efficiency grounds an equity view involving the desirability of poverty alleviation through microenterprise promotion. No one can argue with the moral strength of the poverty alleviation view through continued support of microenterprises. However, the technical economic support for the likelihood of that perspective is much weaker.

25. S&B treat as probably not replicable such exceptional cases as the nations of Japan, Italy, and Taiwan where small business has retained an important role, despite successful development processes. The principal point S&B make is that such small

businesses must also become as efficient as their larger competitors to remain competitive as development proceeds.

26. Data from the *Indonesian Industrial Survey* for 1991–94 yield varying results by establishment size, measured by the number of employees in an establishment. Establishments are location specific components of firms. Thus, a single firm may consist of a number of establishments. Good empirical evidence of the behavior of Indonesian industry is also to be found in (9). The period 1992–94 is worth separate study in the current environment since it encompasses the most recent Indonesian economic recovery.

27. Indonesia also faces significant regulatory opportunities for increased growth and efficiency in its telecommunications and electric-power production industries, where efficiencies and interconnection prices had been too high compared with international norms, and might be changed, provided suitable competition policy is adopted. The decline in the rupiah has made Indonesia's telecommunication costs more competitive with those of its neighbors, and probably too low for sustainability.

ACKNOWLEDGMENTS

The author is grateful to Mr. Gary Goodpaster, COP, United States Agency for International Development (USAID)-funded PEG project in Indonesia, and Mr. Paul Brietsky, PEG project in Indonesia, Dr. Steve Marks, PEG project in Indonesia and Dr. Kelly Bird, PEG project in Indonesia for their helpful comments. This paper represents the views of the author only which should not necessarily be construed as those of the USAID, where the author works.

REFERENCES

Aten, R. H. (1996). Macroeconomic Theory Divergences Between Developed and Less Developed Countries. In: R. Hooley (Ed.), *Research in Asian Economic Studies* (pp. 133–144). Greenwich, CN: JAI Press.

Baldwin, R. E., & Krugman, P. R. (1992). Market Access and International Competition: A Simulation Study of 16 K Random Access Memories. In: G. Grossman (Ed.), *Imperfect Competition and International Trade*. Cambridge, MA: MIT Press.

Cohen, W. M., & Levin, R. C. (1989). Empirical Studies of Innovation and Market Structure. In: R. Schmalensee & R. Willig (Ed.), *Handbook of Industrial Organization* (pp. 1059–1105). Amsterdam: North-Holland.

Dixit, A. K. (1992). Optimal Trade and Industrial Policies for the U.S. Automobile Industry. In: G. Grossman (Ed.), *Imperfect Competition and International Trade*. Cambridge, MA: MIT Press.

Graham, E. M., & Richardson, J. D. (Eds) (1997). *Global Competition Policy*. Washington, D.C.: Institute for International Economics.

Grossman, G., & Helpman, E. (1991). *Innovation and Growth in the Global Economy*. Cambridge Mass: MIT Press.

Helpman, E. (1993). Multinational Corporations and Trade Structure. In: G. Grossman (Ed.), *Imperfect Competition and International Trade* (pp. 285–302). Cambridge, MA: MIT Press.

Helpman, E., & Krugman, P. R. (1985). *Market Structure and Foreign Trade*. Cambridge, MA: MIT Press.

Hill, H. (1997). *Indonesia's Industrial Transformation*. Singapore: Institute of South East Asian Studies.

Indonesian Industrial Survey (1992–1994). Jakarta, Indonesia: Indonesian Central Bureau of Statistics.

Lall, S. (1996). *Learning from the Asian Tigers: Studies in Technology and Industrial Policy*. New York: St. Martin's Press.

Mansfield, E. (1994). *Intellectual Property Protection, Foreign Directo Investment, and Technology Transfer*. Washington, D.C.: The World Bank (International Finance Corporation). Discussion Paper 19.

Mansfield, E. (1995). *Intellectual Property Protection, Direct Investment, and Technology Transfer: Germany, Japan, and the United States*. Washington, D.C.: The World Bank (International Finance Corporation). Discussion Paper 27.

Ochoa, O. A. (1996). *Growth, Trade and Endogenous Technology: A Study of OECD Manufacturing*. New York: St Martin's Press. Index.

Plott, C. (1989). An Updated Review of Industrial Organization: Applications of Experimental Methods. In: R. Schmalensee & R. Willig (Eds), *Handbook of Industrial Organization* (Chap. 19, Vol. II). Amsterdam: North Holland Press.

Mussati, G. (Ed.) (1995). *Mergers, Markets and Public Policy: Studies in Industrial Organization*. Kluwer Academic Publishers: Boston. No index.

Snodgrass, D. R., & Biggs, T. (1996). *Industrialization and the Small Firm: Patterns and Policies*. San Francisco, CA: International Center for Economic Growth.

Winston, C. (1998). U.S. Industry Adjustment to Economic Deregulation. *The Journal of Economic Perspectives*. *12*(3), 89–110.

The World Bank (1993). *The East Asian Miracle: Economic Growth and Public Policy*. New York: Oxford University Press.

39. HEALTH SERVICES SYSTEMS AND THE CONSEQUENCES FROM THE GENERAL AGREEMENT ON TRADE IN SERVICES (GATS)

Wattana S. Janjaroen and Siripen Supakankunti

I. INTRODUCTION

Free trade is built around international specialization and based upon comparative advantage. It is usually described by terms such as "*liberalization*" and "*globalization*." Free trade has long been presumed good by the existence of the General Agreement on Tariffs and Trade (GATT). GATT is used as an international instrument, whose objectives are to promote and regulate the liberalization of international trade through "rounds" of trade negotiations. The Multilateral Trade Negotiation held under GATT led to the establishment of an international organization known as World Trade Organization (WTO). WTO has international legal status and regulates all matters related to international trade among members. This organization provides the principal governmental contractual obligations prescribing how governments should frame and implement their trade policy.

The principal instrument consists of multilateral agreements that are binding upon countries when they join WTO. The WTO Agreement has 29 legal agreements. These cover everything from agriculture to textiles and clothing and from services to government procurement, rules of origin and intellectual properties.

Restructuring Asian Economics for the New Millennium, Volume 9B, pages 827–846.

ISBN: 0-7623-0710-2

Presently free trade or trade liberalization is one of the favorite topics of discussion among political leaders around the world. Many people almost automatically think that free trade is a good thing for all countries to practice. The logic of comparative advantage is, for the most part, not contested, and opens up borders for easy import flows which can create problems for countries, unless they can also raise exports to other countries at the same rate as or faster than imports (Khor & Daly, 1993). The rich and strong (developed) countries with big companies usually take advantage of trade liberalization, while the poor and weaker (developing) countries most often end up losing. Sub-Saharan Africa, the world's poorest region, suffered a total $55.9 billion income losses during 1987–1989 (Khor, 1993).

The result of trade liberalization is increased competition and reduced cost. Some countries may end up importing cheaper products including capital and produce nothing (Daly, 1993; Khor, 1993; Bhagwati, 1993). It is not true that "free trade" has been a great benefit to every country.[1]

However, Agreements from the Uruguay round are not all for "free trade." The strong countries succeeded in making a restrictive, conditioned agreement on intellectual property rights, known as TRIPS (Trade-Related Intellectual Property Rights). These results will hinder the growth of developing countries' technological capacity and enable the strong countries to get a monopoly on power and benefit derived from intellectual property rights.[2]

International trade in services is a rapidly growing area within the global economy, accounting for an increasing share of products in both developed and developing countries. Therefore, trade in services was the main focus of the multilateral trade negotiations during the Uruguay Round. The General Agreement on Trade in Services (GATS) was one of the major results of these negotiations.[3]

International trade in services covers transportation, telecommunications, insurance, travel and tourism, and legal and education and health care services. Initially, many countries, especially the developing countries, were reluctant to include trade in services (13 of them) in the Uruguay Round negotiations because international trade in services is significantly different from that in goods (see Table 1).

As a member of WTO, Thailand also participated in the multilateral trade negotiations. It has made some specific commitments on service liberalization with the exception of the health care sector (Table 1). However, it plans to make commitments consistent with GATS in the year to come.[4]

Although improvements in health status, health coverage and access to health care are apparent throughout the world, these improvements may not benefit all. Consequences of trade liberalization potentially create more

Table 1. Summary of Industry-Specific Commitments Scheduled by Asia/pacific Trading Partners, By Industry, Under GATS.

	Australia	Hong Kong	India	Indonesia	Korea	Malaysia	New Zealand	Philippines	Singapore	Thailand
Distribution	x	x			x		x			x
Education	x						x			x
Enchanced Telecomunication	x	x	x	x	x	x	x	x	x	x
Audiovisual		x	x		x	x	x		x	x
Courier		x						x	x	
Health care	x		x			x	x		x	
Accounting/ Finance	x	x			x	x	x		x	x
Advertising	x	x			x	x	x		x	x
Legal	x					x	x			x
Architectural and Engineering	x		x	x	x	x	x		x	x
Construction	x	x	x	x	x	x	x		x	x
Transportation	x				x		x	x		x
Travel/ Tourism	x	x	x	x	x	x	x	x	x	x

Source: U.S. International Trade Commission: "General Agreement on Trade in Services: Examination of the Schedules of Commitments Submitted by Asia/Pacific Trading Partners", Publication 3053, August 1997.

disparities between the developing and the developed countries. In the case of Thailand, study has shown that the structural changes of output resulting from trade in services liberalization is negative, even though some service sectors have positive annual output growth (Chirathivat, 1998). Therefore this paper will attempt to explore what will happen if Thailand commits to free trade in health care services.[5] Part 2 will explore the substance of GATS. The impact on and impediments to health care service transactions will be investigated in Part 3. The potential of health care service sectors, to which Thailand should make a commitment, will be assessed in Part 4. Finally, policy revisions should be made before committing to GATS.

II. WHAT ARE HEALTH SERVICES UNDER GATS?

International trade in services is a rapidly growing activity in the world economy that opens up new possibilities in the health sector. Health service policy has established relationships between social and commercial elements in addition to creating scientific, professional, efficiency and ethical considerations. Trade in services should be guided strongly by the objective of improving the health status and living condition of the population, especially in the developing countries.

The term "services" is generally described differently from physical commodities. Services are intangible and non-transferable economic goods. The Agreements cover all internationally- traded services, including health care services. GATS define four different ways of providing international services:

- **Cross-Border Trade**
  Services can be supplied from one country to another. The growth of information technology and telecommunications has made possible the provision of health services across borders, namely *telemedicine*. The patient can consult senior physicians, or local clinics can send radiological images by satellite for rapid interpretation by specialists abroad, and medical students can follow the most up-to-date courses without cost of travel. Local health services management can access specialized data and information through computer-based information and communication systems (Adams & Kinnon, Marconini, 1998; WHO Regional Committee Document, 1998).
- **Consumption Abroad**
  Consumption abroad means that consumers or firms can make use of health services in another country. Patients might seek health care abroad for specialized treatments that are not available in their home country, to have better quality at lower prices, or obtain alternative medicine. Others might go to certain developing countries to benefit from lower-price treatment of equal

quality such as medical treatment and dental outpatient care or paramedical services, or to benefit from "exotic" or exclusive therapies or for more affordable services not covered by health insurance, such as cosmetic surgery. (Adams & Kinnon, 1998; Walvaardt, 1998).

- **Commercial Presence**
  Commercial presence is a foreign company setting up subsidiaries or branches to provide services in another country. Foreign investment in health so far is usually in hospital operations or management or in health insurance. A common pattern of investment for foreign providers is to enter into a joint venture with local partners, which helps secure good understanding of local characteristics and access qualified local health personnel. Some foreign firms might integrate medical care delivery and financing through contracts with physicians and hospitals and linkage with insurance companies (Adams & Kinnon, 1998). For example, Thailand, India, Indonesia, Sri Lanka and Nepal opened their markets for foreign collaboration in various forms, i.e. through bilateral agreements for cost containment and achieving better health services (WHO Regional Committee Document, 1998).
- **Temporary Presence of Natural Persons, as Suppliers of Services**
  This represents an individual professional's travel from his own country to supply services or work in another country. This area of international trade in services seems to be essential to developing countries, i.e. Southeast Asian countries. Qualified health care professionals such as physicians, pharmacists, dentists, and nurses from developing countries can migrate to seek higher income and better living and working conditions.

Since "services" are generally described as being distinct from physical goods, GATS has two distinctive components: *General Obligations* and *Specific Commitments*.

General Obligations. The GATS Agreement requires member countries to treat trading partners equally under the principle of *Most Favored Nation Treatment (MFN)*. When GATS came into force, some countries already had preferential services agreements they had signed with trading partners. The agreements permitted member countries to make exemptions to MFN obligations in "*MFN Exemption Lists*," covering specific measures which WTO members were unable to offer initially with their first set of commitments. In order to protect the general MFN principle, exemptions can be made once, and nothing can be added to the lists. These exemptions will be reviewed after five years (in 2000) and should not last for more than ten years.

The Specific Commitments. The GATS Agreement allows member countries to choose the service sectors and activities for which they wish to apply market access, called the "*market access commitments*." Members can indicate these services sectors and activities in the schedule of specific commitment and place conditions and limitations, called the "*market access limitation*." An example of the special commitment is that governments can choose the services which they make market accessible and national treatment commitments. In other words, member countries are not obliged to open all service sectors or lift all barriers to international trade in services, but must specify those sectors and limitations within which member countries wish to open free trade under the Agreement in the schedule. One of the main principles of GATS is to achieve progressive liberalization of trade in services through successive negotiation (WHO Regional Committee Document, 1998).

III. HOW DOES THE GATS AGREEMENT AFFECT THE HEALTH SECTOR?

Trade in health services is a slowly growing activity; only one-fourth of WTO Members (32 out of 134) have made health sector market access commitments under GATS. In the WHO Southeast Asia Region, many countries, including Thailand, did not make health sector access commitments.

Many governments are faced with the complexity of providing health services to their populations. In industrial countries, rising health care costs, combined with an increasing aging population, have reduced public spending on social programs. Health services trade offers countries the opportunity to enhance their health systems through trading health technology in areas where countries have comparative advantages. Developing countries might improve their infrastructure, upgrade medical knowledge and technological capacity to satisfy foreign demand, and increase foreign demand and earn more foreign currency.

A number of questions remain, and there are no clear answers. Government health authorities have to do many things to improve national health services and benefit the local population. Various health service sectors depend on many factors, such as cost structure, the quality of health personnel, facilities and infrastructure, natural endowments and cultural and geographical considerations. The question is how one can balance and compromise to meet the objectives of profitability and resource use to generate improvement in the population's health . . . which is the goal of every health system.

The goals of public health, identified by WHO, are *equity in access to care, efficient use of resources* and *quality of care*. This section will attempt to assess the possibility of a free trade consistent with the objectives of public health and the consequences.

Opportunities and consequences of international trade in health services can be discussed in four modes of supply as defined in the GATS Agreement.

1. Cross-Border Trade

In recent years, the rapid growth of telecommunications and information technology has tremendously expanded the potential for providing health services across borders. Such trade can be practiced in the form of telemedicine, using interactive audio visual and data communication, which includes care delivery, diagnosis and treatment and medical education (Adams & Kinnon, 1998). This method can be substituted for direct contact between health care providers and patients or direct consultation among providers. Commercial telemedicine services exist both in developed and developing countries. Examples of telemedicine services exist between Arab Gulf Countries and the United States and telemedicine links between University Hospitals in Norway and hospitals in Russia (Peterson, 1997). France, United Kingdom, and Australia also provide services by using telemedicine and tele-education.[6] China has experience providing tele-diagnosis services to patients in Taiwan, Macao and other countries of Southeast Asia (Xing, 1998).

Telemedicine and information technology develop quickly in rich countries, but the developing or poor countries may need this technology most to bridge the gaps that conventional means of giving services cannot meet.

However, it is not easy to judge whether increased use of telemedicine in developing countries would lead to more *equity* in accessing to health services. If the cost of telemedicine is covered by the public sector through taxation (normally indirect taxation), it might not be considered *vertical equity.*[7] Further consideration about realizing equitable access[8] to services concerns mobility of health professionals. Availability of human resources in the health system might move towards telemedicine if the opportunities of earning higher wages, upgrading skills or improving career prospects are better than in conventional medical services. This will reduce equity overall if it is not utilized in the appropriate area. In fact, clear government policy on the place of telemedicine in the health care system is needed; remote areas and underserved populations with inaccessible services, are a significant consideration for an equity system.

Use of telemedicine obviously improves the *quality* of the health system, by providing timeless and effective health interventions and improving the training of health providers.[9] A general practitioner could seek advice or expert opinion anywhere in the world while attending a patient. Telemedicine can provide rapid and reliable diagnosis that local facilities might not have the skill or equipment to supply.

When assessing the cost of telemedicine carefully, the *efficiency* is debatable. Cost of telemedicine services not only includes communications infrastructure, equipment and operation, but also training of skilled personnel to run a communications system. The sources of funding in this area come from both public and private sectors. But capital investment, solely from private funding, is very rare. Telemedicine services often receive government subsidies through tax exemptions on technological equipment. Therefore using public funds for telemedicine raises the question of cost effectiveness. Investment in less sophisticated types of care (conventional ones) may be more efficient in term of reduced morbidity and mortality and as a result, more cost effective (Wolvaardt, 1998; Warner, 1998; Adams & Kinnon, 1998).

2. *Consumption Abroad*

At present, patients might go to other countries to seek health care abroad for various reasons. Patients with a high ability to pay might wish to take advantage of advanced, specialized treatment unavailable at home or avoid long waiting lists in their home countries.

Some developing countries might try to attract foreign patients in order to increase foreign exchange earnings, provide employment for health care personnel and related career and financial benefits from economies of scale that would help to upgrade their health service sector as a whole. For example, India can offer "super specialties" such as cardiovascular surgery and certain exclusive alternative medicine therapies with highly qualified medical personnel and a well-developed pharmaceutical sector. India's advantage is competitive prices, which are estimated to be around 1/5 to 1/10 of those in industrial countries for the same intervention or treatment (Prassad, 1997).

In view of rising health care costs in developed countries along with an increasing aging population, some developing countries can offer special health packages to retired persons from developed countries during temporary stay in their countries. Both sides benefit: the developed country from better containment of health services costs and the host country from increased revenues (Diaz & Butkevicinene, 1998).

3. *Commercial Presence*

The domestic health sector may open its health services to the foreign market to provide health-related services to clients in other countries. This can result in investment in hospital operation or management or in health insurance. Most health services providers will not invest in developing countries where only few people can afford private treatment. In common practice, most providers of health services invest in foreign countries through joint ventures with local partners to ensure access to qualified trained local medical health personnel and a better understanding of local culture and characteristics.

"Managed care services" is another technique for penetrating foreign markets. It integrates financing and delivery of medical care through contracts with physicians and hospitals and links with insurance companies (UNCTAD, 1998).

Foreign commercial presence in the health sector, in the form of investment in hospital or health insurance schemes, might improve health services delivery. In most developing countries, only the small portion of population with high ability to pay benefits. If the government is able to watch closely and regulate the health sector, including private providers, there may be general public health benefit. That is the poor might benefit from better access to health care if resources were reallocated within the public sector as the result of the greater use of the private sector by those who could afford to pay.

The presence of foreign commercial firms (with large amounts of capital) needs highly qualified health personnel, which might cause an internal brain drain from the public to the private sectors. Countries facing real shortages of skilled health personnel would end up with fewer skilled physicians and nurses working in public sector to serve the majority of the population. The health system will become more two-tier, with different standards for different population groups (UNCTAD, 1998; Adams & Kinnon, 1998).

Therefore increased foreign presence in health service management may decrease *equity* in access to health services.

An increase in foreign commercial presence in hospital and health management might improve *quality* through introduction of better management techniques and information systems. With the perception of better quality, the government may allocate more resources to high technology services rather than fulfilling broader social demands, which in turn would make it difficult to maintain good quality public services.

The impact of foreign commercial presence on the country's efficient use of health sector resources may vary. Foreign investment in health care i.e. hospital, is likely to increase the overall level of funding in the sector, and the government is able to reallocate public funds in a more *efficient* and equitable manner.

Foreign commercial presence should increase competition in the delivery and financing of health services. Market failures in the health sector means greater competition among providers does not guarantee improved efficiency. That is, the volume of health services may increase because supplier-induced demand, which might contribute to cost escalation.

From the public health point of view, (equity, quality and efficiency), if governments allow foreign commercial presence and strong competition, they need to provide a strong effective regulatory framework and appropriate incentives for the private sectors, including foreign firms. It is very essential that governments first need to be *clear on national policies on health and health care financing*, and only then determine the scope for an expansion of foreign presence within their countries (UNCTAD, 1998).

4. *Temporary Presence of Natural Persons as Service Suppliers*

This area of international service trade is increasing in its importance to the countries in Southeast Asia and developing countries. The health services sector is labor-intensive and largely based on universal scientific knowledge. There are shortages of health personnel in many countries. Many qualified health professionals migrate to seek better living standards, career opportunities and higher remuneration which they cannot get in their home countries. Hence, the movement of health personnel may remove the shortage in the more developed countries.

Many countries have experienced both an inflow and outflow of health personnel. Doctors and nurses from Philippines and Thailand migrate to U.S. to work as physicians and live better, which creates a short supply of physicians and nurses in their home countries. In another words it causes a "brain drain" problem in the original country. (Mejia, Pizurki & Rayston, 1979). This will create shortage of health personnel. Although we have free trade in health services, migration of health personnel to other countries can be impeded by professional licensing requirements. In many countries, including Thailand, doctors and nurses cannot practice without a license and visa for entering the country.

It is obvious that the migration of health personnel will have an impact on *equity* (if it creates shortages in the home country) and reduce access to services that used to be provided by the migrants. If there is an excess supply of health personnel, their migration may increase *efficiency more* than equity.

Temporary movements of health personnel could improve the *quality* of care if the returnees resume their practice in their home countries. The quality of care may suffer if the home country loses the best health personnel. The migration of health personnel will create more cost to home countries, since in most countries education of health personnel is mainly subsidized by public funds and requires a big amount of investment. The original countries subsidize the other countries without compensation. Hence this entails additional cost to society and is less *efficient*. However, costs may be partially offset by remittances that migrants send home. (Adams & Kinnon, 1998).

One can see that trade liberalization in health services causes both positive and negative impacts on health systems of countries. There is increasing interest in the possibility that trade in health services might increase foreign exchange earnings. The government has to make choices carefully to reconcile commercial considerations with social priorities to ensure the population's *equity in accessing good quality and efficient services.*

IV. THAILAND AND POTENTIAL GATS COMMITMENTS IN HEALTH SERVICES SECTOR

In Thailand, like many rapidly developing countries, the service sector is the biggest, around 57 to 59% of GDP average per year from 1980 to 1994, and most rapidly growing sector of the economy, important in supporting manufacturing growth, output and employment (Chirathivat, 1998). To the present, Thailand has made commitments on international trade in only eleven services sectors, such as, telecommunications, construction, financial services, transportation, education, etc. (see Table 1), but not in health services.

Health services activities are delivered through public and private providers. The major purpose and expected outcome of an efficient health system are to improve the health of the population by ensuring equity in accessing adequate health care. At present, with the economic crisis, the Thai Government is faced with a complex set of factors and has to assess how changes in economic conventions can be managed in order to improve health services and benefit the population.

Trade liberalization in health services offers countries opportunities to enhance their health systems through the generation of additional financing resources, to improve infrastructure by using resources resulting from satisfying foreign demand and movement of qualified health personnel, and to upgrade medical knowledge and technology capacities. The competitive position of health services among local public and private providers and other countries will mainly depend on various factors: cost structure, the quality of health facilities and infrastructure, the availability of skilled human resources, the natural endowment and cultural and geographical specifics. Developing countries like Thailand have potential in terms of trade in this health sector.

The Thai health care systems are characterized by two main types: modern medicine and traditional medicine, but the role of traditional medicine is now declining. Thailand has a market-oriented health care system. Although public providers play the major role in providing health care services, use of private hospitals and clinics continues to increase, from 11,495 in 1989 to 11,988 in 1994 (NSO). The government provides equal opportunities for both private and public facilities based on market competition. However, when focusing on health care resource distribution, it is found that private health care facilities are more concentrated in Bangkok and the big provinces. Health personnel are scarce and poorly distributed countrywide. The growth of the private health sector is making the government sector worse because of an outflow of public health personnel to the private sector in the past 5 years. Health care financing schemes in Thailand cover about 70% of the total population. Diversity of health services, modern and traditional medicine, public to private or self care, with free consumer choice of provider, are strengths of Thai health system.

This section will try to explore the present situation in Thailand along with 4 modes of supply under GATS, the health services area in which Thai has comparative advantages and the potential impact on the Thai health system of making agreements on trade in health services.

Cross-border trade

At present, Thailand has one telemedicine project. It is national, aimed at providing health care in remote areas as well as continuing education for physicians. This project has a network of 3 teaching public hospitals, 14 regional hospitals, 7 provincial hospitals and 20 community hospitals (Singkaew & S. Chaichana, 1998). In early 1998, a hospital in United States demonstrated heart surgery via satellite to a private hospital in Bangkok; physicians in both countries observed the process at the same time.

Studies show that telecommunication offers a significant opportunity to face and alleviate the health problems within and between countries. They have also spread awareness and understanding of global interdependence in health and environmental issues. Telecommunication tools and services could be used to improve the *equity of access to quality health care,* the extent and quality of education and training of human resources, *the cost-effective surveillance of diseases and services* and technological developments for affordable diagnosis and treatment by poor countries (Mandil, 1998).

To date, Thailand has no specific plan for cross border trade in telemedicine. If Thailand needs or wants to progress in this area, there are three issues to be considered and discussed carefully before a plan is formally adopted.

First, conventional health practice is a face-to-face encounter between healer and patient which has laws and regulations intended to safeguard the interests and concerns of the health care consumers, and at the same time to protect the profession and individual practitioners. For telemedicine, some aspects of ethical and legal questions remain. For example, in real practice, what would concern the responsibilities of the managers, users and intended beneficiaries, and in particular of the provider and recipient of telemedicine services.

Second are the problems of licensure for cross-border medical practice. In Thailand, in compliance with the Act on Medical Care Institution B.E.2504, information on the professional qualifications of health personnel must be provided before setting up a new hospital or clinic in Thailand. This might impede the growth in telemedicine between Thailand and other countries.

Third, telemedicine services that are between one-to-many or many-to-many sites often require a "gatekeeper" to direct and monitor or control the link involved and to ensure that each request for the service is properly responded to within a pre-set response time (Mandil, 1998). The gatekeeper will be considered commercial transaction. This directly affects cross-border telemedicine trade in Thailand, because of the laws and regulations governing work permits, foreign investment and other such commercial transactions.

Consumption abroad

Even though Thailand has not made any commitment on trade in health services, people from neighboring countries arrange inpatient visits. Wealthy people and foreigners who work in international organizations visit private and public teaching hospitals, while the poor from neighboring countries migrate into the country for health services in provincial hospitals along the border.

After the economic crisis occurred in 1997, the civil government health benefit scheme was reformed. Government officials could no longer get health care services from private hospitals. If a government official wishes, he needs to self pay for the private services. This puts the private hospitals in a worse situation. Most of the private hospitals, especially in Bangkok, are the capital intensive investments with high quality health personnel and high technology medical equipments.[10] Most of them are underutilized now.[11] Most of the large size private hospitals are capable and willing to provide health services for consumers abroad. The common areas of health care services for foreigners are acute care, physical check up, dentistry, long term care and health promotion. These are very promising areas for foreign exchange earnings to the country if it makes a commitment on international trade in health services.[12]

Apart from this, about 5 million people who came to Thailand as tourists and businessmen in 1997 got sick during their journeys and have to receive health care services. Some private hospitals also provide dental care and cosmetic surgery to foreign customers. Most of them said that services they got cost less with equal or better quality than those provided in their own countries.

There is good potential to combine health services with tourism. A health service package, i.e. health check up, can be sold with a tour package. Long term stay (1–3 months) with health benefit programs in Thailand is popular among the elderly population from Europe and Japan. The disposable income of these people is estimated to range from U.S.$12,000 to U.S.$20,000 per annum with an additional U.S.$5,000 per annum available in health care benefits. If health insurance benefits were to be portable, this advantage would be further enhanced.[13]

There are potential advantages that international trade holds for Thailand. It generates more foreign exchange earnings as well as more job opportunities in linkage industries (i.e. tourist industry, food industry, insurance, hotel business, etc.).[14]

Despite the potential advantages that exist from free trade, some impact on the health system should be considered.

- The equity of local people in accessing health care service might be disturbed since the number of health professionals is limited and not evenly distributed throughout the country. Therefore the ratio of health personnel to population may worsen.
- The creation of a two-tier system with high quality service to foreign clients with higher ability to pay.
- The potential of importing dangerous infectious diseases such as HIV/AIDS.

Commercial Presence

In Thailand, foreign-owned private hospitals or clinics are not permitted unless they form a joint venture with Thai partners. It is a requirement of the Ministry of Trade that the foreign maximum share is 49% of the total investment. With economic crisis, money from foreign investment is important. If this joint venture requirement is removed, there might be a monopoly in the private health care market. Therefore, the point that creates a win-win situation for both foreign investors and home countries needs to be researched in detail.

Temporary Presence of Natural Person as a Services Supplier

The inflow of medical personnel from abroad will increase equity in accessing health care services as well as improve the quality of services for local people. However, language, culture and medical license requirements will impede this situation.

On the other hand, there might be a brain-drain of health personnel from the public to the private sector and to hospitals abroad.[15] Nevertheless, some types of medical facilities, such as fitness centers, clinics and health promotion

Table 2. Potential Areas of Trade Initiatives in Thailand.

Cross-border Trade Telemedicine Teleeducation	**Movement of consumers** Medical and dental service Health promotion + tourism Traditional healers Non emergency care – elective and chronic care – cosmetic
Commercial presence Hospital and Clinics Health management services Pharmaceutical research and development	**Movement of personnel** Skilled health personnel Consultants

centers can be run without professional supervision. Their licenses are granted directly and local administration, the Ministry of Public Health or the Ministry of Trade controls them. Some health and health-related services i.e. Chinese healers, chiropractic, are outside the control of professional council or national committee. They might provide poor quality treatment for clients, which is not cost-effective.

V. CONCLUSION

The essence of the service sector in the Thai economy is based on its role as a source of foreign earnings, boosting macro economic prosperity and enhancing the country's international competitiveness. The challenge for developing countries, including Thailand, in future negotiations is to obtain gains in those areas where they have a comparative export advantage.

Discussion in this paper indicated that there are many complexities in free trade in the health services sector, the Specific Commitment and Market Access Commitments under the GATS agreement allowing member countries to restrict some health services from free trade in order to maintain the basic objectives of public health.

Table 3 provides conclusions about the potential impact of international health services trade on Thai health systems.

Policy-makers need to compare the different options available in the context of national priorities. The above matrix sets out schematically some of the key issues, presenting the mode of supply along the vertical axis and the health policy objectives along the horizontal.

Table 3. International Trade in Health Services: Trade-Off for Thai Health Systems.

Modes of Trade	Health Policy Objectives		
	Equity	Quality	Efficiency
Cross border	Serving remote areas	Improved quality	Might need Substantial Investment
Movement of Consumers Inflow of foreign Patients	"crowding out" nationals	Improved quality	
Foreign Commercial Presence	Possible "two-tier" System		Might (possible) free up resources
Movement of Persons supplying Services	Reduced access to Service	Loss of quality	Loss of public investment through foreign exchange remittances

Source: Modified from O. Adams and C. Kinnon, 1998.

For future negotiations, the Thai government has to increase its awareness of the following key aspects of health services trade at multilateral and other negotiating rounds and observe tradeoffs between the policy objectives for each particular mode of supply.

1. Promote of the awareness of the potential benefits and disadvantages of globalization, especially on GATS.
2. Establishing of specific institution body including government, private sector, NGO, and society will serve the purpose of collecting data, information and studying, analyzing the positive and negative consequences of trade liberalization in health services. This body would act as a prime mover in creating national mechanism, principles and guideline based on current knowledge to be discussed and balanced with the values of different stakeholders. These results of discussion can be used for public empowerment and informed decision-making by all involved. Specific issues, which need prompt considerations, are as follows:
   - Procedural solutions to consequential development of telemedicine and insurance services.

- Ease of some regulations and laws on medical and health services industries to enhance health services value in a way that minimizes the impact on the health system. Establish links between commercial presence and movement of personnel (service providers), since these two modes of supply are closely interdependent in the health sector.
- Aspects of domestic regulation through licences go beyond the specific commitments on trade in services. If the established national requirements cannot be met by the foreign service suppliers, the Thai market will be closed to them. On the other hand, if the government wishes to import the specialized medical services, it needs to recognize the qualifications of their providers. Therefore, the government needs to carefully develop comparable national regulations to facilitate the process of international recognition of national medical and health personnel qualifications to create the basis for future free trade.
- The progressive taxation rate imposed on foreign market systems should be utilized to create equity in accessing health care services for local people.
- Encourage participation of society in the decision making process related to trade liberalization and the use of the health resources. This would help to assess the acceptability of new policy.

3. Capacity strengthening of national institute through training and research in international health as related to trade liberalization.
4. Develop comprehensive plans with feasible benchmark to prepare the country to effectively participate in trade liberalization based on a win-win situation. This benchmark can serve as criterion for monitoring and evaluation of the plans aiming at fulfillment of the GATS required by the year 2010 A.D.
5. Governments should operationalize its commitment to trade liberalization by earmarking essential resources to support and maintain the optimal functioning of the prime mover and national mechanism.

NOTES

1. The economic crisis in many countries, including Thailand, is partly the product of the free trade.
2. The local drug industry is an example. Table A shows that Thailand has RCA less than Germany, Switzerland and Singapore.
3. The Multilateral Agreements on Trade in Goods include the Agreement on the Application of Sanitary and Phytosanitary Measures, Agreements on Technical Barriers to Trade, General Agreement on Trade in Services (GATS) and Agreement on Trade-Related Aspects of Intellectual Property Rights.

Table A. RCA of medical and pharmaceutical product by countries.

Yrs	RCA(Ger)	RCA(Switz)	RCA(U.S.)	RCA(Thai)	RCA(Sing)	RCA(Mal)
1984	1.648067	7.606859	1.657842	0.183912	0.662499	0.154684
1985	1.562768	7.08988	1.621384	0.173839	0.720859	0.138107
1986	1.40277	6.540413	1.558156	0.130688	0.62309	0.154433
1987	1.412753	6.789687	1.366131	0.127535	0.519315	0.143237
1988	1.356544	6.078945	1.226335	0.135049	0.415306	0.127221
1989	1.361008	6.36515	1.002356	0.101996	0.405206	0.12464
1990	1.338889	6.219965	0.967708	0.106750	0.361487	0.115394
1991	1.349896	6.258226	0.917512	0.103893	0.309335	0.105478
1992	1.273918	6.361359	0.894669	0.131270	0.286501	0.084794
1993	1.412419	6.329672	0.887864	0.241065	0.354233	0.076074
1994	1.43611	6.309272	0.847222	0.134984	0.358635	0.081203
1995	1.380216	6.426892	0.773525	0.153399	0.349767	0.074803

Note: RCA = Revealed Comparative Advantage

4. At present, only 32 out of 134 WTO Members negotiated and gave specific commitments to health sector services.

5. From 180 sectors of Thai industries are grouped into 38 industrial sectors and be categorized into four types of productive products. Medical and health care services are considered as the final primary production which require inputs from other industrial sectors.

Table B. Type of Productive Sectors.

FINAL MANUFACTURE	INTERMEDIATE MANUFACTURE
• Drug and Medicine • Medical Equipment • Milk and Diary Products	• Paper, Paper Product and Printing • Chemical Industry
FINAL PRIMARY PRODUCTION	**INTERMEDIATE PRIMARY PRODUCTION**
• Medical Services	• Banking, Insurance Services • Sanitary and Similar Services

6. G-7 Information Society, G-7 Pilot Project Report, 1997.

7. Indirect taxation is regressive, therefore the poor might end up paying more than their economic capacity.

8. Equitable access can be generalized as "equal utilization of health services for the same need".

9. Detail in: Health Information and Telemedicine, unpublished document EB99/INF.DOC./9, WHO, Geneva.

10. The private health sector in Bangkok has more GAMMA KNIFE, CT Scans, Mammograms etc. than England.

11. Private hospitals which own GAMMA KNIFE equipment, stated that the utilization rate of this equipment is only 50%.

12. Information from the research project: "Preliminary Study on Trade Liberalization in Health Services Sector: Its Consequences on Social and Health Care System in Thailand" by authors of this paper and team. Final report is forthcoming.

13. Ibid. (12)

14. The study in (12) showed that the backward linkage multipliers on value added and employment of medical services sector were found above the average (Table C).

Table C. Inter-Industrial Backward & Forward Linkage Multipliers.

Industrial Sector	Backward	Forward	Backward Linkage Multipliers on Value Added	Backward Linkage Multipliers on Employment
Pharmaceutical Sector	1.000964	0.724107	0.810235	0.717215
Medical Equipment	0.924528	0.677482	0.774642	0.603248
Medical services	0.914213	0.644901	1.117509	1.342994

15. The movement of health personnel from developing countries to developed countries may occur for better living standards, higher income and better technology and equipment in health care practice. For example, doctors and nurses from India, Philippines, Thailand, migrate to United States, England and countries in Europe. The result makes the doctor-population and nurse-population ratio worsen. Therefore, the ability of local people to access health care services e will be less.

ACKNOWLEDGMENTS

Authors would like to thank Professor Chitr Sitti-Amorn (M.D., Ph.D.), Dean, College of Public Health, Chulalongkorn University for his incisive comments on this paper.

REFERENCES

Adams, O., & Kinnon, C. (1998). A public health perspective. In: *International Trade in Health Services: A development perspectives*. United Nations Conference on Trade and Development, Geneva.

Bhagwati, J. (1993). The Case for Tree Trade. *Scientific American*, November.
Chirathivat, S. (1998). Thailand's Trade in Service Liberalization : GATS-AFTA-APEC. *Asian Economics Studies, 8.*
Daly, H. E. (1993). The Perils of Free Trade. *Scientific American*, November.
Diaz, D., & Butkevicinene, J. (1998). GATS commitments in the health service sector and the scope for future negotiation. In: *International Trade in Health Services: A development perspectives*. United Nations Conference on Trade and Development, Geneva.
Diaz, D., & Hurtado, M. (1994). International trade in health services: main issues and opportunities for the countries of Latin America and the Caribean. Washington, Technical Reports Series No. 33, Pan American health Organization.
Khor, M. Free trade – or whom? *The Third World Economics magazines*. Malaysia.
Majia, A., Pizurki, H., & Royston, E. (1979). Physician and nurse migration: analysis and policy implications. Geneva, World Health Organization.
Mandil, S. H. (1998). Telehealth: What is it? Will it propel cross border trade in health services? In: *International Trade in Health Services: A development perspectives*. United Nations Conference on Trade and Development, Geneva.
Marconini, M. (1998). Domestic capacity and international trade in health services: the main issues. In: *International Trade in Health Services: A development perspectives*. United Nations Conference on Trade and Development, Geneva.
Peterson, S. (1997). *Telemedicine in Norway, today and in the future*. 3rd International Conference on the Medical Aspects of Telemedicine, Kobe, Japan.
Prassad, H. A. C. (1997). Healthcare exports under consumption abroad mode: opportunities, obstacles and challenges for developing countries in general and India in particular. Unpublished document, Indian Institute of Foreign Trade, New Delhi.
Regional Committee Document (1998). *International Trade Agreements and Their Implication on Health*, WORLD Health Organization, September.
Singkaew, S., & Chaichana, S. (1998). The Case of Thailand. In: *International Trade in Health Services: A development perspectives*. United Nations Conference on Trade and Development, Geneva.
The National Statistical Office, Bangkok, Thailand.
U.S. International Trade Commission (1997). Genaral Agreement on Trade in Services: Examination of the Schedules of Commitments Submitted by Asia/pacific Trading Partners, Investigation No. 332–374. Washinton D.C. 20436, August.
Warner, D. (1998). The globalization of medical care. In: *International Trade in Health Services: A development perspectives*. United Nations Conference on Trade and Development, Geneva.
Wolvaardt, G. (1998). Opportunities and challenges for developing countries in health services sector. In *International Trade in Health Services: A development perspectives*. United Nations Conference on Trade and Development, Geneva.
Xing, H. (1998). The case of China. In: *International Trade in Health Services : A development perspectives*. United Nations Conference on Trade and Development, Geneva.

40. THE ASIAN ECONOMIC CRISIS: IMPLICATIONS FOR EMPLOYMENT, LABOUR MARKETS AND POVERTY*

Piyasiri Wickramasekara**

I. INTRODUCTION

The past two decades have witnessed unprecedented growth in a number of Asian economies, which has been referred to as the "East Asian miracle." The successful growth experience of the Republic of Korea, Taiwan (China), Hong Kong, China and Singapore – known as the "four tigers" – has been widely documented. A second group of economies comprising Malaysia, Thailand and Indonesia were well on their way to attain 'newly industrialized economy' (NIE) status by the turn of the century. "Asia's future will not be a replay of its past. The economic and social landscape of Asia is about to be transformed again," stated the ADB publication *Emerging Asia* (ADB, 1997), which set out to examine Asia's 'great economic and social transformation' and 'the prospects for its continuation'. Sadly enough it has become true too soon but not in the positive manner predicted by the Asian Development Bank, or by anybody else for that matter. The dramatic about-turn of the Asian miracle economies has spawned considerable research and debate on the causes, mechanisms and solutions. There is an extensive literature on the subject, especially on the causes and financial aspects but the social dimension of the crisis is also receiving increasing attention.[1] The present paper does not intend

Restructuring Asian Economics for the New Millennium, Volume 9B, pages 847–884.

ISBN: 0-7623-0710-2

to go into these broad issues. The limited objective of this paper is to discuss the employment and labour market implications of the crisis in the context of the most affected countries: Indonesia, the Republic of Korea and Thailand. The paper is divided into five sections. The first briefly touches on the background of the crisis. The second and third parts deal with the impact of the crisis on employment and poverty. The next part discusses the impact on two important groups: women and migrant workers. The final section raises some policy issues.

The crisis, which has led to a serious economic downturn in these economies in the past one year or so, started in Thailand and rapidly spread to Malaysia, Indonesia and the Philippines. The Republic of Korea was the last major casualty in the process in Asia. The downturn was triggered by a crisis in the finance sector. While there are obvious country-specific differences in the unfolding crisis, the common elements have been the accumulation of substantial foreign debt by the private sector and unsound investments at home resulting in the collapse of financial firms, massive capital outflows and a debt repayment crisis. This in turn led to substantial falls in the value of national currencies.

As an immediate response, the three most affected countries (Indonesia, the Republic of Korea and Thailand) received assistance from the International Monetary Fund in the form of a bailout package ranging from U.S.$17 billion (Thailand) to U.S.$57 billion (the Republic of Korea) to restore macro-economic, financial and exchange stability. As usual, the IMF package comes with a number of conditions – adoption of austerity measures on a large scale to ensure monetary and fiscal discipline, and structural adjustment programmes. In this process, the worst hit are the workers who have to face massive layoffs, unemployment, falls in real wages and loss of numerous fringe benefits. The irony of the situation is that workers have to pay the price for a crisis, which they did not create in the first place. According to the International Confederation of Free Trade Unions (ICFTU): "With millions of jobs lost and inadequate social protection, the Asian crisis is a stark illustration of the negative effects of globalization."[2]

While the crisis was initially perceived as a currency and debt crisis, later developments showed that it was the culmination of several developments building up over a number of years: gradual erosion of competitiveness, fragility of the banking system, defects in corporate governance and absence of proper regulatory controls, among others.

There has been considerable interest in the growth recovery process. Initially there was optimism that the crisis was a short term one similar to the Mexican crisis – a "V" shaped crisis with a sharp downturn followed by an equally sharp upturn. Now it is recognized that the recovery path will be long. The IMF had projected in May 1998 an average contraction of 2.7% for the most seriously affected countries (Indonesia, Malaysia, the Republic of Korea and Thailand) which was revised in September to 10.4%. It is, therefore, believed that the crisis may be "U-shaped," with protracted recovery time.

Table A1 (Tables with prefix A refer to Appendix tables.) provides some orders of magnitude on growth trends based on IMF and other forecasts. It shows that recovery is going to be slow and that while the Republic of Korea and Thailand will fare better than Indonesia, it will take considerable time to return to pre-crisis levels. In line with expectations, the most serious impact is on sectors which showed 'bubble' growth – finance and banking, construction, and manufacturing in addition to some service sectors. For instance, in the case of Indonesia, the contraction in the construction sector in 1998 was 36% over the 1997 level.

II. IMPLICATIONS OF THE CRISIS FOR EMPLOYMENT

In order to understand the impact of the crisis, it is important to review the pre-crisis situation relating to employment and labour markets in the countries concerned. Tables A2, A3 and A4 provide some relevant indicators.Out of the countries under concern, the Republic of Korea had eliminated labour surpluses with rapid transformation of the economy. The share of formal sector and wage employment was also high. In Malaysia, too, rapid growth of manufacturing had reduced the importance of the agricultural sector as a source of employment. In contrast, both Indonesia and Thailand still had more than 50% of their labour forces in agriculture. While agriculture contributes only 11% to GDP in Thailand, more than half the labour force is engaged in agriculture.

This gap between the GDP share and the employment share of agriculture is a broad indicator of the low productivity of agriculture or the large income disparity between urban and rural sectors. The share of wage employment was around 40% in Thailand (1997) and even lower in Indonesia (about 30%). With the exception of Indonesia and the Philippines, countries in the region had enjoyed nearly full employment conditions for seven to eight years, as evidenced, in both Malaysia and Thailand, by the presence of a large foreign work force.

It was inevitable that the type of economic downturn suffered by the countries would be translated into a deep social crisis with rising layoffs, unemployment and poverty. In short, economic downturn meant that the demand for labour was reduced to a substantial extent. The impact on employment can be gauged by examining one or more of the following: labour force participation; open unemployment and retrenchments; reduced hours of work and underemployment; decline in real wages and earnings; and changes in the quality of employment. The impact would also depend on which categories are considered: the employed; the unemployed and retrenched; new entrants to the labour force; and male and female workers.

2.1. Indonesia

The most seriously affected economy is Indonesia, which even in the pre-crisis period had sizeable employment problems. The employment challenge consists of several factors: direct job loss; new additions to the labour force at 2.5% per annum; returning migrant workers, especially from Malaysia; and increases in underemployment through swelling of rural and informal sectors.

The economic downturn in Indonesia has been very sharp with the IMF growth forecast for 1998 at a negative 15%. There are several differing estimates of unemployment available. Table 2.1 provides a summary of these estimates. Official estimates of unemployment are based on an assumed relationship between GDP and employment. It is estimated that a 1% decline in GDP leads to a loss in employment of about 400,000. On this basis, the government stated that 1.4 million jobs were lost in 1997. The National Development Planning Agency (BAPPENAS) in June 1998 projected a 13.6% open unemployment rate by the end of 1998. The Ministry of Manpower (MoM) estimate is higher at 14.8%. The ILO/UNDP Task Force estimate is the lowest. The main difference lies in the assumed rate of GDP decline and the treatment of the informal sector. The Task Force estimate is the lowest because it assumes that half of the displaced workers would be absorbed into the informal sector.

There was no indication of a significant increase in unemployment according to the national surveys conducted in February and August 1998 which confirms the lower estimate. The National Labour Force Survey (SAKERNAS) conducted in October 1998 reported only 5.5% unemployment overall and 9% in urban areas, both slightly higher than the 1997 figures of 4.9 and just over 8% respectively.[3] This confirms the ILO/UNDP Task Force assumption of a shift from formal to informal employment.

Information on layoffs and retrenchments is also incomplete. The Ministry of Manpower had approved only 180,079 retrenchments during October 1997 and June 1998 (see Table 2.2). This is believed to be a gross underestimate of actual retrenchments that had taken place because of the rigid procedures for termination of employment, which encouraged vast under-reporting by

Table 2.1. Indonesia: Alternative Estimates of Crisis-induced Unemployment in 1998.

	Persons (million)			Percentage		
	MoM[1]	BAPPENAS[2]	Task Force[3]	MoM[1]	BAPPENAS[2]	Task Force[3]
Backlog 1997	5.80	5.80	2.48	42	47	27
New entrants 1998	*2.70*	*2.80*	*1.40*	20	23	15
Sub-total Job Seekers	8.50	8.60	3.88	62	69	42
Displaced Workers	5.20	3.84	5.41	38	31	58
Total Unemployment (U)	13.70	12.44	9.29[4]	100	100	100
Labour Force (LF)	92.60	91.53	92.60			
Unemployment Rate (U/LF)	14.8%	13.6%	10.0%			

Source: ILO/UNDP 1998.

Notes (reproduced from above source):

(1) Ministry of Manpower (MoM): Assumes 0% economic growth in 1998 and uses reported dismissals.

(2) BAPPENAS: Assumes 10% contraction in 1998 and uses sectoral elasticities.

(3) Task Force: Assumes 30% contraction in 1998 in incorporated sectors and uses employment elasticities for wage employment only.

(4) Important remark: Task Force estimate of 5.4 million displaced workers includes 2.6 million workers re-absorbed in formal/informal employment. Therefore open unemployment is limited to 6.7 million persons or 7.2% of labour force.

Table 2.2. Indonesia: Approved Retrenchments: October 1997 – June 27, 1998.

Period	Retrenchments		In process		Sluggish	
	Firms	Workers	Firms	Workers	Firms	Workers
4th quarter 1997	93	41 716	10	2 068	11	6 523
1st quarter 1998	305	35 420	61	6 772	137	44 901
2nd quarter 1998	318	31 767	25	4 513	47	6 399
Total	716	108 103	96	13 353	195	57 823

Source: Ministry of Manpower (cited in: Oey Gardiner & Dharmaputra 1998).
Notes: Overall there were 1,007 firms seriously affected by the monetary crisis, involving 180,079 workers. Seven banks were liquidated, involving 2,804 workers. Seven banks have been taken over, involving 36,947 workers.

employers to the Ministry even in normal times. (Oey-Gardiner & Dharmaputra, 1998).

Apart from direct job loss, the level of underemployment in Indonesia has been generally high. Absorption of laid-off workers into the rural and informal sectors would obviously raise the level of underemployment in these sectors. A number of surveys carried out by the World Bank, UNICEF and other agencies have shown that the regional dimension of the labour market impact is very important. The impact was much more severe in Java, especially in the urban areas.[4]

Another unknown in the employment challenge is the number of returning migrant workers. Given that the bulk of those going to Malaysia are undocumented migrants, monitoring return migration is difficult. The estimate of about 750,000 Indonesian workers in Malaysia would imply that the return flow would be high, thereby placing a further burden on job creation.

2.2. Thailand

When the crisis occurred, Thailand had recorded impressive growth since the mid-eighties, which was reflected in substantial growth in employment and reduction of poverty. The open unemployment rate (which includes only those unemployed and actively seeking work) had been below 1% since 1988, while the total unemployment rate (including those not seeking work) had been below 2% since 1992. Thailand had thus virtually reached a full employment situation by mid-nineties. The labour market had tightened with labour shortages occurring in both the low- and high-skill segments. The employment structure was becoming diversified with more jobs created in the modern sector of the economy which helped absorb increasing numbers of women workers, migrant workers from the rural sector, as well as those in low productivity informal sector jobs. Thailand became a net importer of (largely unskilled) labour in the early 1990s. By 1997, it was estimated that there were some 1.3 million foreign workers, most of them from Myanmar.

Yet there were several structural weaknesses marring this impressive growth record. While open unemployment was low until 1997, the rural sector had been characterized by a high degree of underemployment, especially in the form of seasonal inactivity. Regional inequalities had been rising. The quality of jobs generated also left much to be desired in that the bulk of the employed – almost two-thirds of the total – were in the unorganized and informal sectors, where low wages, poor working conditions, and lack of social protection affect most workers. A major thrust is needed to raise productivity and quality of employment in these sectors. In terms of educational attainment, almost 80% of the Thai labour force possess only a primary level of education or none at all.

The recent economic downturn has accentuated these tendencies. IMF forecasts put the GDP decline at around 6% in 1998. Rising unemployment coupled with large-scale layoffs in the formal sector has been the major labour market impact of the crisis in Thailand. There is still considerable debate on the actual extent of job loss. The Committee on Labour Force, Employment and Unemployment Estimation, set up by the Ministry of Labour and Social Welfare, estimated that the unemployment rate would rise to 4.4% in 1998 from 1.9% in 1997. The February 1998 Round of the Labour Force Survey (which represents the dry season) has reported total unemployment reaching 4.6%, compared to only 2.3% in February 1997 (Table A5). This shows almost a doubling of unemployment levels within a year. The number of seasonally inactive persons has also shown a marked upward trend over the last few seasons. The total unemployment rate including the seasonally inactive rose to 8.5% and 11.2% respectively in the February and May rounds of the Labour Force Survey, 1998. The rate has rarely gone above 5% in previous years. The 1998 August open unemployment rate at 3.4% is more than three times the rate observed for the same month in the preceding year. Chart A1 shows trends in unemployment rates over the 1996–98 period.

Another important point is the observed decline in the labour force participation rate between February 1997 and February 1998, from 53.1% to 52.7%. This may represent discouraged workers who have opted to withdraw from the labour force. The August 1997 labour force participation rate

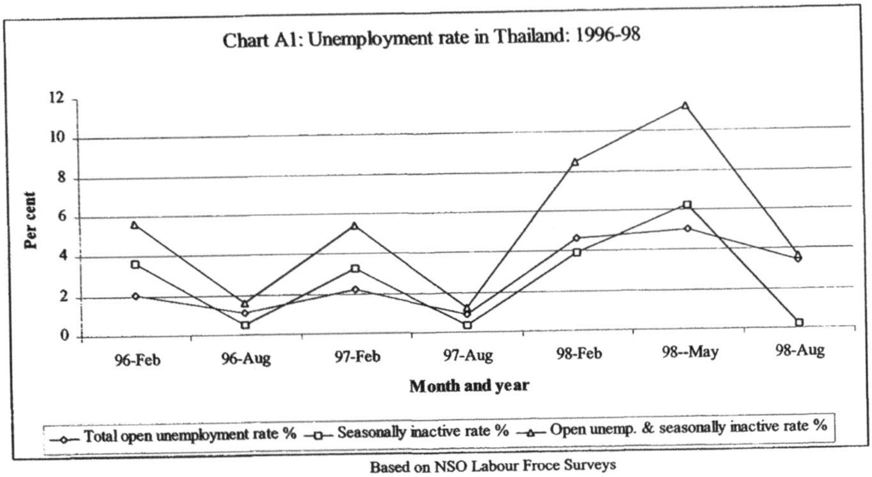

Chart A1. Unemployment rate in Thailand: 1996–1998.

(representing the wet or busy season) also shows a decrease from 55.3% to 54.5% in August 1998 confirming this trend.

The 1998 February Labour Force Survey included additional questions on unemployment to ascertain the employment impact of the crisis since January 1997 (NSO, 1998). The data collected showed a decline in employment in the manufacturing and construction sectors and an increase in employment in the service and commercial sectors. This may indicate a movement of labour from the formal to the informal sector. In February 1998, almost 90% of the unemployed were formerly employed workers and the bulk of them were farmers and craftsmen/labourers.

A survey of enterprises by NESDB and private sector organizations (cited in Teeranat & Voravidh, 1998) has reported lay-offs in almost every manufacturing subsector in the last two quarters of 1997. The total number out of work was 422,000 (manufacturing – 151,457; modern service – 17,572; construction – 252,500)[5]. The average layoff ratio was 24.4% at the end of the fourth quarter of 1997. The food and automobile parts sectors seem to be severely hit by the crisis. Their lay-off ratios were 37.1 and 35.1% respectively. In the modern service sector, the security and finance subsector had reported a lay-off rate of 45.9%, while the construction sector had a ratio of 50.5%.

Kakwani (1998) has made an estimate of the impact of the crisis on employment and real incomes using NSO data from the first and third rounds of the National Labour Force surveys from 1992 to February 1998. On the basis of a trend fitted to seasonally adjusted data, he estimates the crisis impact as the deviation from the trend in February 1998. The interesting finding is that the crisis impact has been widespread and not confined to the urban sector. Unemployment and underemployment have seriously affected the rural sector. While his approach represents a rigorous one, there are several problems with his interpretation. Obviously, all deviations from the trend cannot be attributed to the crisis. Moreover, the 1997 August situation itself captures part of the crisis impact. The interpretation of results is also very mechanistic, implying an unwarranted precision in findings which is unfortunate, especially in regard to income data (quoted up to two decimal points!). While the author himself has admitted that the crisis impact cannot be measured only from this single season, this is overlooked in the various generalizations. The crucial test would be results from the 1998 August season. At the same time, some definitions used are non-standard. For instance, the 'long term unemployed' are defined as those who did not find work within one month. This is obviously too short a period for job search. In OECD countries, the long-term unemployed are defined on the basis of one-year reference period while China uses a six-month criterion which is much more realistic.

2.3. Republic of Korea

The Republic of Korea, an OECD economy, is among the first tier of newly industrialized economies in Asia. It had enjoyed high and sustained growth for nearly three decades and full employment conditions had been well-established by the late 1980s. The crisis was, therefore, unexpected and sudden, as has been its impact. Korea's GDP growth decelerated by 3.9% in the first quarter of 1998 and by 6.6% in the second quarter. IMF forecasts show an overall GDP growth contraction of 7% for the year as a whole. The dramatic rise in unemployment and layoffs is a major feature. Over a one-year period, the unemployment rate rose from 2.2% (June 1997) to 7% (June 1998) as seen in Table A6. This was the highest rate in 31 years. By the third quarter of 1998, the total number unemployed amounted to 1.6 million.

The most adversely affected by current labour market trends are workers in the age group 40 to 60 years old. In November 1998, the number of unemployed in this age group amounted to 495,000 – a fourfold increase on the same month in 1997. According to the Korea Employers' Federation estimates, more than 100,000 jobs will be lost from the Chaebol workforce and from affiliated subcontractors under a restructuring programme.[6] Public employment also may be reduced by about 100,000 or so given government plans to cut

30% of local government workers and 11% of central government workers during 1999.

Another disturbing fact is the change in the composition of employment, which strongly suggests some deterioration in the quality of employment. Table 2.3 shows labour market adjustments at work which show growth of irregular and temporary work at the expense of regular work. Women seem to have borne the brunt of this change with the highest percentage decline in regular workers. For men, the biggest decline is in the daily workers category.

Table 2.3. Republic of Korea: Changes in Employment by Status of Workers.
(in thousands)

	1997 July	1998 July	% change*
Male	8,112	7,473	–7.9
Regular workers	5,143	4,815	–6.4
Temporary workers	1,884	1,763	–6.4
daily workers	1,085	895	–17.5
Female	5,237	4,629	–11.6
Regular workers	1,955	1,507	–19.7
Temporary workers	2,373	2,228	–6.1
daily workers	909	831	–8.6

* July 1998 compared to July 1997; Source Chang Pilwha, 1998.

By industry, the major decline in employment has been observed in manufacturing (15.1%) and in construction (22.9%). By occupation, production workers were affected severely. For women workers, clerical workers' category also fell sharply (see Table 2.4).

2.4. Malaysia

At the time of onset of the crisis, Malaysia was far ahead of both Indonesia and Thailand in its race towards 'newly industrialised economy' (NIE) status. With a much higher per capita income and a sizeable modern sector, it had enjoyed near full employment conditions for a number of years. Among the crisis-affected countries, it is unique in that it did not opt for a bailout package from the IMF. Yet the economy has experienced a severe downturn in 1998. The GDP growth was –2.8% in the first quarter but increased to –6.8% in the second quarter. The IMF estimate for the whole year is –4.0%.

Table 2.4. Republic of Korea: Number of Workers (in thousands) By Occupation, July 1997–July 1998.

Sex and Occupational category	July 1997 (1)	July 98 (2)	Change* 97–98
	In thousands		Per cent
Male	12,581	11,915	–5.3
Professional, administrative	2,703	2,707	0.1
Clerical	1,193	1 275	5.3
Service, sales	1,903	1,948	2.4
Agriculture and fishery	1,244	1,312	5.5
Mechanical, machine operator, unskilled	5,538	4,693	–15.3
Female	8,808	8,084	–8.2
Professional, administrative	1,052	1,065	1.2
Clerical	1,383	1,129	–18.4
Service, sales	2,972	2,780	–6.5
Agriculture, fishery	1,183	1,221	3.2
Mechanical, machine operator and unskilled	2,218	1,889	–14.8

* July 1998 compared to July 1997. Source: Pilwha, 1998.

The assessment of the employment and income impact is, however, difficult due to lack of adequate information, partly due to problems of data transparency. Official figures on retrenchments reported (see Table 2.5) may not indicate a serious impact but these may be underestimates of the actual extent of displacement, as in other countries.

There are indications of rising retrenchments, although the trend seems to have slowed down in the second quarter of 1998. According to government estimates, only 80,000 workers had been retrenched between July 1997 to end

Table 2.5. Malaysia: Retrenchments, January 1997 to June 1998.

Period	Year	Number
January–June	1997	6,363
July–December	1997	8,930
January–March	1998	15,821
April–June	1998	10,676

Source: Ministry of Human Resources.

of 1998. The situation according to industry type is more revealing. In common with other crisis-affected countries, manufacturing, construction and financial services are the hardest hit sectors. Most retrenchments are also in the urban areas around Kuala Lumpur and Penang. The government estimate is based on compulsory reporting of retrenchments by employers and do not include contract workers, casual workers and temporary workers who are laid off. (Chandran, 1998). Thus, it may underestimate retrenchments substantially. The figures also do not take into account the substantial numbers of documented and undocumented migrant workers who lost their jobs, most of whom may have returned to their home countries. The presence of a sizeable foreign work force was obviously a cushion against large-scale job losses for local workers. According to government estimates, unemployment is likely to rise to 6.7% by the end of 1998 from a pre-crisis level of only 2.7%. This represents additional unemployment to the tune of 300,000 workers (Chandran, 1998).

III. IMPACT ON WAGES AND POVERTY

All the affected countries had recorded impressive gains in poverty reduction over the past decade or so. The magnitude of the present crisis has not only seriously eroded these gains but also contributed to some reversal. This is to be expected given that most wage workers affected by the crisis are dependent on their jobs as the primary source of income. In addition, real wages and incomes have been affected by rising inflation, partly as a result of structural adjustment measures. This section attempts a review of wage and poverty trends, which are closely related to employment trends outlined above.

3.1. Wage Trends

Reliable statistics or data series on wages are difficult to obtain in most countries. In Thailand, the NSO Labour Force Survey collects limited wage data in each round. The Ministry of Labour and Social Welfare has a wage data series but their reliability and coverage and their comparability with NSO data are not known. Nevertheless there is little doubt that real wages would have declined in all countries for two reasons.

In the crisis situation, wage increases have been rare. In fact, employers have resorted to wage cuts to avoid retrenchment, in some cases with the consent of employees. A survey of wage bargaining in 5,156 establishments by the Korea Labour Institute revealed that 66% had managed to achieve a wage freeze while 19% had agreed on wage reductions. A wage increase was limited to only 16% of establishments. (KLI, 1998). In the third quarter of 1998, establishments with ten or more employees recorded an 8.1% fall in nominal wages compared to the same period in the previous year. In real terms, the fall in wages is 14%. Special payments (including bonuses) recorded a drop of 34% compared to the third quarter of 1997. The Tripartite Social Accord reached in March 1998 in the Republic of Korea among workers, employers and the government also had induced some degree of labour market flexibility. In Thailand, 23% of those changing jobs between January 97 and January 1998 quoted reduction of wage/benefit and dissatisfaction with payments as the major reason for the change (NSO, 1998). It is reported that over 60% of workers are facing cuts in real and nominal wages, including withdrawal of bonuses, wage freezes and cuts in overtime work (Chandran, 1998).

In all countries, sharp price increases have led to erosion of real wages. The largest increase occurred in Indonesia, at 60%. In Indonesia, the purchasing power of the minimum wage dropped dramatically from 6.3 kilos of rice to 2.6 kilos between January 1997 and mid-June 1998 (see Table 3.1).

For Thailand, Kakwani (1998) found that the average real wage and the total wage (including overtime and bonuses) had declined since February 1997 (see Table 3.2). He attributes declines of Baht 506 and 629 per month in these wages to the crisis – which represent deviations from the long-term trend.

Table 3.3 indicates the real wage trends for the economies concerned according to the Economist Intelligence Unit forecasts.

The general implication is that all these countries had enjoyed positive real wage growth until 1997 which is now being reversed during 1998–99. The decline is highest for Thailand.

Table 3.1. Purchasing Power of Daily Minimum Wage in terms of Rice Equivalent, Indonesia.

Period	Rice Price (Rupiah/kg)	Purchasing power Kg of rice
January 1997	925	6.27
December 1997	1220	4.75
May 1998 (pre Riots)	1350	4.3
18 May 1998 (during Riots)	1450	4
30 May 1998 (post Riots)	1750	3.31
15-June 1998	2200	2.64

Source: ILO/UNDP 1998.

Table 3.2. Wage Trends, Thailand (Baht per month).

Average real wage	1995	1996	1997	1998
Dry season (February)	5,447	5,547	5,734	5,397
Wet season (August)	5,873	5,796	6,015	
Crisis index				–506
Total wage				
Dry season	5,974	6,039	6,273	5,825
Wet season	6,445	6,336	6,604	
Crisis index				–629

Source: Kakwani 1998.

3.2. *Impact on Poverty*

What are the implications for poverty? According to the President of the World Bank: "*The true impact of the crisis comes less on the people in the financial sector, but rather on the millions of people just near the poverty line.*"[7] The economic collapse and sharp inflation, which resulted in widespread riots and the emerging food security issues in Indonesia, are a stark illustration of the reality of unfolding poverty.

It is also only in the case of Indonesia that new poverty assessments of poverty have been made following the crisis. Indonesian poverty estimates also vary widely, partly due to the poverty line adopted. The official poverty line – which had shown a drastic reduction in the population living in poverty from 29% in 1990 to 11% in 1996 – has been criticized as too low to be credible. This is apparent because the poverty incidence in countries such as Malaysia

Table 3.3. Real Wage Trends (per cent).

Year	Malaysia	Republic of Korea	Thailand
1996	5.8	6.8	2.3
1997	4.2	4.3	1.4
1998	–1.1	–5.7	–8.2
1999	–0.9	–2.1	–4.2
2000	0.7	1.9	2.4

Source: compiled from EIU country forecasts for the 1998 fourth quarter.

and Thailand (using higher poverty level definitions) is higher than in Indonesia. According to more realistic estimates, more than half the population lived in the neighborhood of the poverty line even before the crisis (ILO/UNDP, 1998).

The ILO/UNDP Task Force used more internationally comparable poverty lines and made estimates of urban and rural poverty for 1998 and 1999. The results are reported in Table A6. It shows a staggering number of almost 100 million below the poverty line at the end of 1998 – a poverty incidence of 48% – which is more than a four-fold increase from the official figure of 11% in 1996.

It has subsequently been shown that these initial projections were too pessimistic. A SMERU study reviewing field survey data from a number of surveys in various parts of Indonesia has suggested a much lower rate of increase in poverty incidence – from 11% to 14% or so. (Poppele et al., 1999). The ILO/UNDP 1998 estimate has been criticized on the ground that it looked only at the impact of inflation on the poverty line and not on nominal incomes. The SMERU researchers (Poppele et al., 1999) draw the conclusion that the social impact of the crisis has been less dramatic than earlier suggested. Still people in urban areas have been hard hit more than those in rural areas. They go on to add:

> People on Java appear to have been more e(a)ffected and are bearing the brunt of the crisis, both in comparison to more isolated islands with less linkage to the formal, modern economy (Maluku) or islands with export commodities (large parts of Sulawesi, Sumatra). The new data also shows that pre-crisis economic status or poverty rates are not good indicators of how much any given region or household has been affected by the crisis. While some of the poor are doing worse, others appear to be better off and many of the newly emergent urban middle classes are hit the worst of all.

The NESDB Development Evaluation Division has found that the long-term trend in poverty reduction has been slightly reversed according to 1998 data (Kakwani & Jaroenjit, 1998). The poverty rate has increased by 1.4% between 1996 and 1998.

In view of the controversial nature of poverty incidence trends, it is useful to look at some estimates prepared by the IMF and the World Bank. The IMF estimates are shown in Table 3.4.

According to this, roughly 11–12% of the population in the three countries will join the ranks of the poor due to lower real incomes and job losses. For all countries, unemployment is the main cause of additional poverty, though inflation accounts for 43% in Indonesia. In the Republic of Korea and Thailand, job loss is the main cause accounting for 80 to 87% of poverty.

Table 3.4. IMF Estimate of Crisis-Induced Poverty in Indonesia, the Republic of Korea and Thailand (per cent of population).

	Indonesia	Republic of Korea	Thailand
Poor before the crisis	11.3	15.7	15.1
Additional poor due to real income decline	4.8	1.6	2.3
Additional poor due to unemployment	0 to 6.4	0 to 10.5	0 to 9.3
Total additional poor	4.8 to 11.2	1.6 to 12.1	2.3 to 11.6
Share of unemployment contribution to additional poverty	57	87	80

Source: IMF World Economic Outlook October 1998.

A World Bank study (World Bank, 1998a) also comes up with another set of poverty increase estimates on the basis of a simulation exercise. The estimate is based on two factors: extent of GDP contraction and trend in inequality. The use of the second factor is based on the premise that a rise in inequality will have an adverse impact on poverty. Table 3.5 summarizes the main findings. The report concludes: "*A 10% contraction in aggregate GDP between 1998 and 2000 would add millions to the ranks of the poor . . . even with no change in inequality, the most likely growth scenarios (1998–2000) imply a halt or a sharp reversal in a 20-year long trend in poverty alleviation.*" (p. 21). If there are increases in inequality, the projections show a much worse situation.

IV. IMPACT OF THE CRISIS ON SELECTED GROUPS

4.1. Crisis and Women Workers

Gender disparities in labour force participation, sectoral employment, wages and working conditions were common in all the countries in the region even before the crisis. While fast growth had opened up modern sector job opportunities to women, these were mostly in occupations demanding low skills and with limited prospects for upward mobility (garments, electronics, food processing, etc). Table 3.4 provides some limited data on women in the labour market.

The influence of long-run factors make it difficult to isolate the impact of the crisis on women. An ILO/AIT project has carried out important research on the situation based on some country studies (ILO/ROAP, 1998b)[8]. The study comes to the general conclusion that women were affected more severely than men.

Table 3.5. World Bank Poverty Projections: Crisis-affected Countries. (Poverty incidence in per cent)

		10% contraction in GDP between 1998–2000				Alternative growth rate and no inequality	
		Year 2000					
Country	Poverty line	1997 level	No change in inequality	10% increase in inequality	10% decrease in inequality	Alt. Growth rate	Poverty Incidence
Indonesia	$1 a day	6.6	13.2	19.6	6	–15	16.3
Malaysia	$2 a day	19.9	25.7	31.4	18.3	0.3	21.8
Philippines	$1 a day	21.5	29.1	34.1	22.6	8.7	20.3
Thailand	$2 a day	14.7	20.2	27.5	10.5	–5.5	17.6

Source: World Bank 1998a.

Table 4.1. Women and the Labour Market: Crisis-affected Countries.

Country	Year	Unemployment rate % of labour force		Underemployment % (mostly for 1997)		Wage ratio FW/MW per cent	Labour force per cent
		Men	Women	Men	Women		
Indonesia	1997	4.1	5.6	27.5	51.6		37
Republic of Korea	August 1998	8.5	5.8	3.3	7.8	54.4	40
Malaysia	N/A.					69.0	37
Philippines	1998	12.2	15.2	25.4	17.5		46
Thailand	Aug-97	0.91	0.9	0.13	0.12	80.0	38

Source: ILO estimates based on national sources: last col. WDR 1998.

Women occupied an important position in some sectors seriously affected by the crisis such as manufacturing (textiles and garments, electronics and machinery), real estate, retail and wholesale trade, and financial services and insurance. In Korea, the unemployment rate for women rose from 1.8% to 5.8% during September 1997 to September 1998. But the Korea Labour Institute has pointed that this figure is an underestimate because an increasing number of women who have been laid-off are being counted as economically inactive.[9] The ILO/AIT report explained that women were often targeted first for retrenchment because they were not perceived as primary bread winners.

Labour market flexibility has affected women workers more than men in the form of shift into more precarious forms of employment and accepting wage cuts. This is illustrated by figures from the Republic of Korea, where the number of regular women workers decreased by 19% over the past year or so, while the decrease was only 6.4% for men (Table 2.4).

Social expenditure cuts, especially education and health, are likely to affect women and girls more. Girls are likely to be pulled out of the school system before boys. Women have to supply services for the family that were previously supplied by the public system. The crisis' impact on the rural sector, as more workers return there, holds adverse implications for women and families. While more attention has been focused on the state of the urban economy and its problems, the ILO/AIT research found that the rural poor and women have borne a significant part of the burden of the economic crisis: "The family rice bowl, largely produced and managed by women, is supporting the unemployed workers" – at a time when remittances to rural areas have drastically fallen. Women workers who had migrated to jobs abroad as well as in the cities lose their jobs and return to the rural sector. There is evidence that economic difficulties are leading to an increase in trafficking of women and children.

In all affected countries, women form a sizeable proportion of the informal sector work force and unpaid family workers. Homeworkers, weavers and traditional crafts people have been losers in the crisis according to country studies. The risks of the market are passed on to home-based workers who have to accept lower orders and piece rates. The position in Thailand and Indonesia has been particularly bad in this respect.[10]

The ILO/AIT country studies showed clear-cut evidence of adverse consequences for women only in the case of the Republic of Korea. It is quite possible that women were absorbed into lower quality employment instead of losing jobs outright in other countries. However, given the preliminary nature of the results, the situation in other countries has to be explored further before arriving at firm conclusions.

4.2. Crisis and Migrant Workers

The first half of the 1990s saw a substantial growth in labour migration within the Asian region reflecting demand from fast growing countries. ILO estimates show that there were over 6.5 million foreign workers in these countries (ILO/ROAP, 1999). Since many countries have highly restrictive policies concerning the import of unskilled and semi-skilled workers, the undesirable consequence was that a large proportion of workers were undocumented or irregular migrants who entered receiving countries without valid work permits.

Among the countries affected by the crisis, the Republic of Korea, Malaysia and Thailand represent largely labour-receiving countries whereas Philippines and Indonesia represent labour-sending countries. Given the serious employment problems encountered by migrant-receiving countries, there has been a significant impact on migration flows in the region, which has taken several forms (ILO/ROAP, 1998a; SCM, 1998). Workers in the construction sector were particularly affected. The Republic of Korea offered an amnesty for illegal workers to leave voluntarily, and many took advantage of this. The legal trainee scheme under which workers were admitted as trainees to enterprises for a fixed period of time has also been downsized.

The major migration issue relates to the presence of large numbers of Indonesians in Malaysia and Myanmar workers in Thailand, amounting to about one million in each case and largely undocumented. The natural tendency on the part of both Malaysia and Thailand was to repatriate foreign workers, especially undocumented workers, "to save jobs for the locals" given strong political pressures in the wake of rising domestic unemployment. Some groups have voiced concerns on the treatment meted out to migrant workers, particularly in detention centres, and possible human rights violations (Human Rights Watch, 1998). The vulnerability of these workers increased if they opted to remain behind illegally. Some employers took advantage of this to hold back accrued wages. It is also difficult to draw the line between migrant workers and political refugees in the case of some undocumented workers in both countries. The case of Myanmar workers was especially desperate given that many faced persecution at home. However, massive deportations have not occurred to the extent expected and ILO estimates show a return of about one million workers overall (see Table 4.2).

The driving force behind much of this migration, which has not been greatly reduced by the crisis, has been the persistent mismatch between available jobs and those demanded by local workers. This partly explains the lower-than-expected repatriations. Local workers have not been keen to go into these jobs involving arduous and risky work with low pay. Migrant workers have

Table 4.2. Impact of the Financial Crisis on Numbers of Migrant Workers (in Thousands).

Receiving economy	No. of migrant workers Pre-crisis 1997	Mid-1998
Hong Kong (China)	300 (9.4)*	300 (9.2)
Japan	700 (1.0)	680 (0.9)
Rep. of Korea	267 (1.2)	150 (0.7)
Malaysia	1,700 (19.8)	1,300 (14.7)
Singapore	450 (23.9)	400 (20.6)
Thailand	1,260 (3.7)	800 (2.3)
Total	4,677	3,630

Figures in brackets indicate percentage of the labour force.
Source: ILO Estimates (cited in ILO/ROAP 1999).

generally occupied jobs paying one third to one half of wages paid to Thai workers. Both Thailand (rice milling and fishing industry) and Malaysia (plantation sector) have, therefore, eased some of the restrictions initially imposed. While documented workers did not face the same type of problems as their undocumented counterparts, work permits of many workers are unlikely to be renewed, according to official pronouncements. A study on the Philippines showed that its migrant workers would be largely unaffected by the present crisis given that the Philippines has been able to diversify the countries of overseas employment (Bohning, 1998).

At the same time, there can be increased pressures for more clandestine migration given the bleak prospects at home. There is some evidence of its occurrence in the case of Indonesia and Myanmar.

Thus, the basic issues are orderly management of migration flows and protection of migrant workers. Collaborative and joint action on the part of governments of the countries of origin and destination are essential in this respect.

V. POLICY RESPONSES AND OPTIONS

It is obvious that there are no short-cut solutions (*aside from another Asian miracle!*) to the employment and poverty problems stemming from the economic crisis. Speedy economic recovery through structural adjustment and sound economic management is the medium- and longer-term solution. As part of the IMF bailout programme, Indonesia, Thailand and the Republic of Korea are implementing major macroeconomic restructuring and adjustment programmes. Malaysia established a National Economic Action Council (NEAC) in 1997 consisting of all economic ministers, representatives of private sector business, the Malaysian Trade Union Congress and consumer organizations to advise on economic recovery programmes. The NEAC introduced the National Economic Recovery Plan in July 1998, which addressed restoring exchange rate and macroeconomic stability, boosting economic growth and revitalising affected sectors.

Yet given the potential explosive nature of the social impact, many governments had to attempt a variety of short-term and medium-term responses to mitigate the social costs. It is heartening to note that the international development agencies and banks clearly recognise this as a priority issue. The ILO has proposed a broad range of actions to counter the social impact (ILO/ROAP, 1998a; ILO/ROAP, 1999). The World Bank and the Asian Development Bank are assisting affected countries in the region via loans for social sector programmes covering education, health and human resource development. The strategy should consist of both short-term measures to cushion the adverse impact and medium- and longer-term measures to restructure the economies towards sustainable growth. The ILO has discussed in detail the components of such an approach to contain the social costs of the crisis (ILO/ROAP, 1998a; Eddy Lee, 1998). Social protection and social dialogue are essential components of the process.

The crisis has exposed the serious inadequacy of existing labour market institutions and social protection systems in most of the countries affected. The existing social protection systems cover only a small portion of the labour force and only cater to a limited range of contingencies. Informal sector and rural sector workers are normally outside the formal social security schemes. While unemployment has emerged as a major problem in all countries, only the Republic of Korea has an unemployment insurance scheme, albeit a limited one. While the period of fast growth was the obvious time to build up such schemes, the ILO (ILO/ROAP, 1998a; Eddy Lee, 1998) has shown that they can be established at reasonable cost even in a time of crisis.

Given the painful process of adjustment, adequate consultation and dialogue among workers, employers and governments are essential to work out more acceptable and equitable distribution of burdens of adjustment. The Tripartite Social Accord of the Republic of Korea is a good example of this process. In all affected countries, employers, workers and the general public are calling for transparency in agreements and conditionalities reached with the IMF under structural adjustment loans.

Addressing social and labour market problems of the magnitude of those experienced in the crisis-affected countries is, however, no simple matter. I shall only highlight some elements of active labour market policies which are being discussed or adopted by these countries. It is important to note that active labour policies can be effective only within sound macroeconomic recovery programmes.

Job creation and management of unemployment and layoffs: Job creation is undoubtedly a key priority for all the affected countries. Both the public sector and the larger private sector establishments are no longer in a position to absorb labour in large numbers in the immediate future. Therefore, a number of employment promotion measures may be necessary, ranging from emergency job creation programmes to small and medium enterprise development. There is considerable experience in Asia in sustainable micro credit schemes for poverty alleviation[11]. Given the crucial role of the informal and rural sectors as a cushion during the crisis period, active support policies for these sectors are essential. With regard to the informal sector, the removal of regulatory and administrative controls on its operation would go a long way. Community-level job-creation initiatives are already under way in the affected countries.

Short-term employment and income generation through guaranteed employment schemes is another measure, which has been adopted immediately. These can be conceptualized as self targeting social safety nets for the unemployed poor. The World Bank has provided assistance to both Indonesia and Thailand to launch such programmes. Thailand is again reverting to the use of labour-based infrastructure creation programmes, which in the early 1990s were considered unsuitable in the context of labour shortages. It is interesting that even the Republic of Korea has also launched a massive public works programmes to absorb unemployed workers in diverse areas such as repair of social welfare facilities, building computer databases and dredging rivers and reservoirs. Malaysia claims to have found reemployment for about 80% of the retrenched workers. As shown earlier, statistics of retrenched workers omit several categories of workers. The tight labour market which existed prior to the crisis and the repatriation of large numbers of migrant workers could explain the high rate of reemployment there rather than public action.

Employment services: Employment services are a means of improving labour market processes. In the context of mounting job losses, the public employment services in the various countries have received a new lease of life. Employment services in the developed countries carry out four core functions: the production and dissemination of labour market information; the provision of vocational guidance and counselling; the administering unemployment insurance; and planning and managing active labour market programmes. (ILO, 1998). Of the affected countries, it is only in the Republic of Korea that the scope of the employment service is broad enough to cover all these functions. Even there, an ILO mission found that the administrative capacity of the employment service is inadequate to deal with the wide range of functions under the crisis. In Thailand, the employment service has traditionally been concerned with routine job seeker registrations and placements, mostly for low-skilled new entrants to the labour market. The service was, therefore, ill-equipped to cope with the recent challenge of mass unemployment. Apart from the routine job-seeker registration, it has to play a more pro-active role in counselling and vocational guidance, job search and mobility assistance, and training and retraining. The Ministry of Labour and Social Welfare, Thailand, established a Mass Layoff Centre at the very outset of the crisis to provide assistance to enterprises and laid-off workers. It was based on the concept of "one-stop services" which are becoming popular in meeting the needs of job seekers. The provincial level employment service centres were strengthened at the same time. The shortage of qualified staff to manage these expanded services is emerging as a serious constraint. In actual practice, it is mostly unskilled and semi-skilled workers who utilise public employment services. Given the magnitude of the challenge, private employment agencies are also being promoted, especially to cater to white collar workers. Another area is the strengthening of overseas employment services, in the Republic of Korea and particularly Thailand, as a temporary measure to relieve domestic unemployment.

Improved labour market information: The demand from policy makers, employers, workers and the general public for timely and improved labour market information following the crisis has been striking. The actual extent of job loss and the rate of unemployment, timeliness and transparency of existing labour market information sources and the lack of early warning indicators have been areas of major concern initially. Given the predominance of the unorganized sector in both Indonesia and Thailand, the emphasis on a single indicator such as the open unemployment rate is obviously misplaced. For the Republic of Korea, however, the open unemployment rate seems to have mirrored the changing economic fortunes closely. Nevertheless, the crisis has had a salutary effect in exposing the inadequacies in coverage and frequency of existing sources. Monthly labour force surveys – found in Japan, the Republic of Korea, and Hong Kong (China) – are, perhaps, luxuries for countries such as Thailand and Indonesia. Thailand has now expanded the Labour Force Surveys to cover one more round (November) and the data processing time has been reduced to three months or so from about one year. Still, statistics on layoffs (planned and actual) are not readily available and primary data would initially have to be generated through new surveys with the cooperation of workers' and employers' organizations. They may later be built into regular reporting systems or labour force surveys. Philippines has already started collecting layoff statistics on a regular basis.[12] At the same time, information has to be collected from enterprises. Establishment surveys and thematic surveys would be necessary. There is also scanty information on the labour market situation in the rural and informal sectors which are acting as cushions for retrenched and unemployed workers. In all cases, there is a strong case for gender-disaggregated information, which still seems to be the exception rather than the rule. New statistical initiatives may be hard to sell during troubled times but Thailand has responded well to the new demands.

It is generally agreed that the existing monitoring mechanisms failed to provide quick and reliable information on the social impact of the economic crisis – particularly, poverty and welfare trends and community responses. For analysing these impacts, one has to move beyond conventional sources such as labour force surveys. There are several initiatives towards rapid appraisal methods and increasing emphasis on field-based data gathering and qualitative sources of information. While these cannot compete with scientific national level surveys for generating macro-level information, they provide important and quick feedback to policy makers and planners on the impact of programmes at the local level. It highlights the need for some trade-off between quantitative and qualitative information gathering – which hard-core statisticians may find difficult to accept. Indonesia is experimenting with SMERU – Social Monitoring and Early Response Unit – an agency supported by the World Bank and a number of donor agencies. Its main purpose is providing qualitative information about the social impacts of the current crisis as they emerge drawing upon a variety of sources. Apart from its own information network which undertakes rapid appraisals in specific localities and regions, the Unit draws upon information generated by collaborating NGO networks and rapid assessment teams. Under the auspices of the Ministry of the Interior, Thailand also has implemented a community unemployment register in selected provinces.

At the same time, the fact remains that even available information is not properly disseminated or utilised due to lack of capacity, lack of transparency and poor coordination. There is a need to enhance the capacity of government agencies for monitoring the labour market and formulating active labour market policies based on available information. The crisis has also highlighted the need to share information.

Training and retraining policies: Training and retraining programmes for the unemployed and retrenched workers have been a popular response in the affected countries. It is a visible and tangible measure, which can be launched quickly. Yet the experience in developed countries has shown that training is no panacea to labour market problems. Evaluation research in European countries has shown that labour market prospects of trainees have not improved much under labour market training programmes. The Republic of Korea has now embarked on an ambitious programme of training and retraining for displaced workers. Thailand also has placed emphasis on this option. For best results, however, training should be based on a careful analysis of demand for new skills. As an example, Korea is training people in promising areas as millenium bug specialists (Y2K) and patent management specialists.(MOL Korea, 1999). For guarantee of improved job prospects, training imparted has to be of reasonable duration and quality. It is also important to have a strong linkage to the production system (ILO, 1998). The Republic of Korea is trying to improve the links between training and employment by evaluating job placement results of training institutions and providing them with incentives. Links can be established between training, credit and entrepreneurship development programmes using a package approach. Thailand has to assess the role of such short term training programmes in the context of its long-term problem of upgrading the low skill profile of the work force. The sense of urgency of implementation of new training and retraining programmes naturally makes it difficult to adequately address these issues.

NOTES

* Paper presented at the International Conference on "A Macroeconomic Core of an Open Economy for Progressive Industrialization and Development in Asia in the New Millenium" jointly organized by the Faculty of Economics, Chulalongkorn University, the American Committee on Asian Economic Studies (ACAES) and the Chulalongkorn Economics Association, 16–18 December 1998, Bangkok, Thailand.

** The responsibility for the views expressed in this paper lies solely with the author and not with his employer, the International Labour Office. He is grateful to Ms Penny Ferguson of ILO/EASMAT for editorial assistance. e-mail: wickramasekara@ilo.org

1. See ILO/ROAP 1998a, *The Social Impact of the Asian Financial Crisis*; Eddy Lee, *The Asian financial crisis: the challenge for social policy*, ILO, Geneva, 1998; World Bank, *Social Consequences of the East Asian Financial Crisis* by Tamar Manuelyan and Michael Walton, September 1998. World Bank website; IMF paper on policy analysis and adjustment. *Mitigating the social costs of the economic crisis and the reform programs in Asia* by Gupta, S. et al., IMF, June 1998. See Prof. Roubini's webpage on other aspects of thte Asian crisis at the following web address: http://www.stern.nyu.edu/~nroubini/asia/AsiaHomepage.html

2. International Confederation of Free Trade Unions, The social crisis behind the financial crisis, ICFTU Online, Internet.

3. Information supplied by Dr Chris Manning, Australian National University.

4. See the SMERU reports on the Internet: www.smeru.or.id

5. Teeranat and Voravidh 1998 use the term 'unemployment' in this context but my view is that it represents layoffs.

6. EIU Economic Review, Korea First Quarter 1999.

7. James D. Wolfensohn, quoted in the Bangkok Post, February 1, 1998.

8. This section draws upon ILO/ROAP 1998b.

9. Cited in: Gender Dimensions of the East Asia Crisis, East Asia and Pacific Region, The World Bank, January 1999.

10. Women homworkers and the Asian crisis, Newsletter, Southeast Asia HOMENET, 1998.

11. Wickramasekara, Piyasiri 1998, Evaluation of Special Employment Programmes in Asia, Resource paper presented at the Asian Productivity Organization Seminar on Measures for Rural Employment Generation, 19–24 October 1998, Hanoi, Vietnam.

12. Personal communication from the Director of the Bureau of Labour and Statistics, Department of Labour and Employment, Manila.

REFERENCES

ADB. (1997). *Emerging Asia: Changes and Challenges*. Asian Development Bank, Manila.

Bohning, W. R. *The Impact of the Asian Crisis on Filipino Employment prospects abroad*. SEAPAT, ILO, Manila.

Chandran, P. (1998). *Malaysia in Crisis*. Asian Labour Update, Issue No. 29, Sept.-Dec. Asia Resource Monitor Centre, Hong Kong.

Human Rights Watch (HRW) (1998). *Bearing the brunt of the Asian economic crisis: the impact on labor rights and migrant workers in Asia*, Vol. 10, No. 02. New York, March.

ILO (1998). *Korea; labour markets and social protection in a period of economic crisis: reform and development*, Preliminary report of a mission from the International Labour Office, August 1998 (restricted).

ILO/ROAP (1998a). *The social impact of the Asian financial crisis*, technical report for discussion at the High Level Tripartite Meeting on Social Responses to the Financial Crisis in East and South-East Asian Countries. Bangkok, 22–24 April.

ILO/ROAP (1998b). *AIT/ILO summary of research on the gender impact of the economic crisis in East and Southeast Asia*, prepared under the ILO/AIT Research project on the gender impact of the economic crisis in East and South-east Asia. ILO Regional Office for Asia and the Pacific, Bangkok, November.

ILO/ROAP (1999). *Towards full employment: Prospects and problems in Asia and the Pacific*, technical report for discussion at the Asian Regional Consultation on Follow-up to the World Summit for Social Development. Bangkok 13–15 January, ILO Regional Office, Bangkok.

ILO/UNDP (1998). *Employment challenges of the Indonesian economic crisis*. ILO Jakarta Office, Jakarta, June 1998.

IMF (1998). Gupta S. et al. *Mitigating the social costs of the economic crisis and the reform programs in Asia*, IMF paper on policy analysis and adjustment. IMF, June.

IMF (1998). *World Economic Outlook*, October.

Jeanne F. I. I. (1998). *The impact of the economic crisis on women workers in the Philippines: social and gender dimensions*, working paper prepared under the ILO/AIT Research project on the gender impact of the economic crisis in East and South-east Asia. ILO Regional Office for Asia and the Pacific, Bangkok, November.

Kakwani, N. (1998). *Impact of economic crisis on employment, unemployment and real income*. Development Evaluation Division, NESDB and ADB, Bangkok, September.

Kakwani, N., & Pothong, J. (1998). *Impact of the Economic Crisis on the Standard of Living in Thailand*. Development Evaluation Division, NESDB and ADB, Bangkok, 1998.

Lee, E. (1998). *The Asian Financial Crisis: The Challenge for Social Policy*. International Labour Office, Geneva.

KLI (1998). *KLI Quarterly Labor Review, 11*(4), 4/4. Korea Labor Institute, Seoul.

Mayling, O.-G., & Dharmaputra, N. (1998). *The impact of the economic crisis on women workers in Indonesia: Social and gender dimensions*, working paper prepared under the ILO/AIT Research project on the gender impact of the economic crisis in East and South-east Asia. ILO Regional Office for Asia and the Pacific, Bangkok, November.

MOL Korea (1999). *Employment Policy in Korea, National paper 8* presented by the Ministry of Labour, Republic of Korea, Asian Regional Consultation on Follow-up to the World Summit for Social Development. Bangkok 13–15 January, ILO Regional Office, Bangkok.

NESDB/World Bank (1998). *Competitiveness and Sustainable Economic Recovery in Thailand, Volume 1*: proceedings of the Conference "Thailand's Dynamic Economic Recovery and competitiveness", National Economic and Social Development Board (NESDB), Bangkok, May.

NESDB/World Bank (1998). *Competitiveness and Sustainable Economic Recovery in Thailand*, Volume 2, Background papers for the Conference "Thailand's Dynamic Economic Recovery and competitiveness", National Economic and Social Development Board (NESDB). Bangkok, May.

Pilwha, C. (1998). *The impact of the economic crisis on women workers in the Republic of Korea: Social and gender dimensions*, working paper prepared under the ILO/AIT Research project on the gender impact of the economic crisis in East and South-east Asia. ILO Regional Office for Asia and the Pacific, Bangkok, November.

Poppele, J., Sudarno, S., & Lant, P. (1999). *Social Impacts of the Indonesian crisis: New Data and Policy Implications: A SMERU Report*. Social Monitoring and Early Response Unit, Jakarta, Indonesia. (Internet URL of document: http://www.smeru.or.id/report/frreport2)

SCM (1998). The impact of the crisis on migration in Asia: conference report, by G. Battistella and Maruja Asis. In: Scalabrini Migration Centre (SCM), *Asian Migrant*, April-June, Manila.

Siamwalla, A., & Orapin, S. (1998). *Responding to the Thai Economic Crisis*. A paper prepared for the United Nations Development Programme, Thailand, UNDP Working Paper, Bangkok.

Talib, R. (1998). *The impact of the economic crisis on women workers in Malaysia: Social and gender dimensions*, working paper prepared under the ILO/AIT Research project on the gender impact of the economic crisis in East and South-east Asia. ILO Regional Office for Asia and the Pacific, Bangkok, November.

Teeranat, K., & Charoenloet, V. (1998). *The impact of the economic crisis on women workers in Thailand: Social and gender dimensions*, working paper prepared under the ILO/AIT Research project on the gender impact of the economic crisis in East and South-east Asia. ILO Regional Office for Asia and the Pacific, Bangkok, November.

UNDP (1998). *Human Development Report 1998*. Oxford University Press, New York.

World Bank (1998a). *Social Consequences of the East Asian Financial Crisis*, by Tamar Manuelyan and Michael Walton, September.

World Bank (1998b). *World Development Indicators 1998*. Washington.

World Bank (1999). *Thailand Social Monitor: Challenges for Social Reform*. World Bank Thailand Office, Bangkok, January.

World Bank EAP (1999). *Gender Dimensions of the East Asia Crisis, East Asia and Pacific Region*, The World Bank, Washington, January.

APPENDIX

Table A1. GDP Growth Trends in Asia (%).

Country	1990	1995	1996	1997					1998 (actual)		1998 forecasts		
				Q1	Q2	Q3	Q4	Full year	Q1	Q2	IMF	Govt.	EIU
Thailand	11.6	8.7	6.4					−0.4	−8		−6.5	−7.0	−6.0
Indonesia	9	8.2	8	8.5	6.8	2.5	1.4	4.6	−6.2		−13.5	−10 to −15	
Korea, Rep. of	9.5	8.9	7.1	5.6	6.6	6.1	4.0	5.5	−3.9	−6.6	−5.0	−4.0	−7.9
Malaysia	9.6	9.5	8.6	8.5	8.4	7.4	6.9	7.8	−2.8	−6.8	−4.0	−1 to −2	−3.5
Philippines	3	4.8	5.7	5.5	5.6	5.0	4.8	5.1	1.7		1.0	3.0	1.4
Viet Nam	4.9	9.5	9.3								4.0		
Singapore	9	8.8	7	4.0	8.5	10.6	7.7	7.8	5.6	1.9	−0.5		−0.5
Hong Kong, China	3.4	3.9	4.9	5.9	6.8	6.0	2.7	5.3	−1.9		−3.0		−2.0
China	3.8	10.5	9.7					8.8			5.5	−1.7	
Japan	5.1	1.5	3.9					0.8			−1.7		

Sources: International Monetary Fund (IMF): *World Economic Outlook*, Mar. and Oct. 1998; *World Economic Outlook*, Interim Assessment, Dec. 1997;
The Economist Intelligence Unit (EIU): Country Risk Service, 1st, 2nd, 3rd quarters 1998 and 4th quarter 1997.
Adapted from Eddy Lee 1998.

Table A2. Distribution of Total Labour Force by Sector (percentages).

Country	Agriculture		Industry				Services	
	Total		Total		Manufacturing		Total	
	1980	1997	1980	1997	1980	1997	1980	1997
Bangladesh	72.6	60.1	8.7	21.8	7.4	19.9	18.7	18.1
Bhutan	94.4	94.0	1.3	0.5	1.2	0.6	4.3	5.5
Brunei Darussalam	5.1	—	31.1	21.6	4.1	61.0	63.8	79.7
Cambodia	75.7	72.7	6.6	8.1	5.4	6.8	17.7	19.3
China	74.2	70.9	14.0	15.8	10.3	11.8	11.8	13.3
Hong Kong, China	1.3	0.6	49.8	27.2	41.3	17.8	48.9	72.2
India	69.5	60.1	13.1	18.1	10.7	14.9	17.4	21.8
Indonesia	57.8	53.6	12.1	14.5	8.9	11.3	30.1	31.9
Japan	11.0	4.3	34.6	33.9	24.1	24.0	54.4	61.8
Korea, DPR	44.8	34.0	29.2	32.9	21.2	24.1	26.0	33.0
Korea, Republic of	37.1	5.7	26.5	41.1	20.9	31.0	36.4	53.2
Lao, PDR	79.6	77.2	5.5	6.8	4.2	4.6	15.0	16.0
Malaysia	40.8	19.2	18.8	25.8	13.1	18.4	40.5	55.0
Maldives	50.1	20.2	29.0	32.7	24.9	27.9	20.9	48.1
Mongolia	39.8	27.3	21.0	23.4	15.9	17.7	39.2	49.3
Myanmar	75.8	71.6	8.2	10.9	6.9	7.7	16.0	17.5
Nepal	93.8	93.6	0.5	—	0.4	—	5.7	6.4
New Zealand	11.2	9.8	32.6	19.6	24.0	13.0	56.2	70.8
Pakistan	63.2	45.5	13.2	21.5	8.2	14.1	23.7	33.0
Papua New Guinea	82.5	77.0	5.8	7.1	2.8	4.3	11.8	16.1
Philippines	52.3	41.7	15.1	15.5	10.7	9.9	32.6	42.8
Singapore	1.6	(0.3)	41.7	32.2	26.0	30.0	56.8	68.1
Sri Lanka	51.9	46.3	17.8	22.9	10.5	16.5	30.3	30.8
Thailand	70.9	59.8	10.3	16.3	7.8	11.6	18.8	23.9
Vietnam	73.2	70.1	13.2	14.5	11.1	12.3	13.6	15.3

Source: ILO, *World Employment Report* 1998/99, Geneva, 1998, extracted from Table 3, statistical annex.

Table A3. Long-term Structural Change.

	Agriculture Value added		Labour force in agriculture		Urban population		Trade	
	% of GDP		% of total labour force		% of total population		% of GDP	
	1970	1996	1970	1996	1970	1996	1970	1996
Asia								
Bangladesh	55	30	81	65	8	19	21	39
Cambodia	—	51	79	74	12	21	14	69
China	34	21	78	72	17	31	5	40
Hong Kong, China	—	—	4	1	88	95	181	285
India	45	28	71	64	20	27	8	27
Indonesia	45	17	77	55	18	37	29	51
Japan	6	2	20	7	71	78	20	17
Korea, DPR	—	—	55	39	54	72	—	—
Korea, Republic of	25	6	49	18	41	82	37	69
Lao, PDR	—	52	81	78	10	21	—	65
Malaysia	29	13	54	27	34	54	80	183
Maldives	—	—	—	—	—	—	—	—
Mongolia	—	31	48	32	45	61	—	89
Myanmar	38	60	78	73	23	26	14	3
Nepal	67	42	94	94	4	11	13	60
New Zealand	12	—	12	10	81	86	48	59
Pakistan	37	26	59	52	25	35	22	37
Papua New Guinea	37	26	86	79	10	16	72	101
Philippines	30	21	58	46	33	55	43	94
Singapore	2	—	3	—	100	100	232	356
Sri Lanka	28	22	55	48	22	22	54	79
Thailand	26	11	80	64	13	20	34	83
Vietnam	—	27	77	71	18	19	—	97

Source: World bank, World Development Indicators 1998, Washington DC, 1998.

Table A4. Labour Market Indicators for Selected Asian and Pacific Economies. (Annual Growth Rates in Percentage)

Country	Unemployment rate			Employment growth rate		Labour force growth rate		GDP growth rate		Growth rate of real wages in manufacturing
	1987	1993	1996	1987–96	1993–96	1987–96	1993–96	1993–97	1997	1990–96
Bangladesh	1.2	—	2.5	1.2		2.4	2.2	4.9	5.7	
China	2	2.6	3	2.2	1.7	1.5	1.1	10.4	8.8	5.5
Fiji	9.3	5.9	5.4	2.8	1.6	2.8	3.1	2.0	−1.0	4.3
Hong Kong, China	1.7	2	2.8	1.3	2.4	1.4	2.7	4.9	5.2	0.0
India	3.4	2.3		2.4		2.2		6.9	5.0	–5.5
Indonesia	2.6	2.7	4.1	2.2	2.3	2.4	2.7	7.1	4.6	
Korea, Rep. of	3.1	2.8	2.6	2.6	2.3	2.5	2.2	7.5	5.5	7.1
Malaysia	7.3	3	2.5	3.8	4.4	3.3	4.2	8.7	7.5	4.6
Pakistan	3.1	4.7	5.4	1.9	1.9	2.2	2.2	4.3	3.1	–5.7
Philippines	9.1	8.9	7.4	3.1	3.9	2.9	3.4	5.0	5.1	–2.0
Singapore	4.7	2.7	3	3.6	3.2	3.4	3.3	8.5	7.8	6.3
Sri Lanka	14.1	14.7	11.3	1.7	3.3	1.0	1.9	5.3	6.3	–0.4
Thailand	5.9	1.5	1.1	1.7	0.1	1.2	–0.1	5.6	–0.4	3.3

Source: ILO, *World Employment Report* 1998/99, Geneva 1998.

Table A5. Thailand: Number and Percentage of Population by Labour Force Status, Whole Kingdom, 1996–98.

(Labour Force Surveys)

	1996		1997		1998		
Labour Force Status	Round 1 (Feb)	Round 3 (Aug)	Round 1 (Feb)	Round 3 (Aug)	Round 1 (Feb)	Round 2 (May)	Round 3 (August)
	Number ('000)						
Total	59,750	60,045	60,351	60,649	60,949	61,098	61,248
Total labour force	31,898	32,750	32,000	33,561	32,143	32,170	33,353
1. Current labour force	30,741	32,586	30,964	33,455	30,892	30,168	33,276
1.1 Employed	30,099	32,232	30,266	33,162	29,413	28,555	32,138
(1) At work	28,088	31,760	28,309	32,715	26,959	25,765	31,461
(2) With job but not at work	2,011	472	1,957	448	2,454	2,790	677
1.2 Unemployed	641	354	698	293	1,479	1,613	1,138
(1) Looking for work	120	110	180	96	403	492	477
(2) Available/not looking for work	522	244	518	196	1,077	1,121	662

Table A5. Continued.

(Labour Force Surveys)

Labour Force Status	1996 Round 1 (Feb)	1996 Round 3 (Aug)	1997 Round 1 (Feb)	1997 Round 3 (Aug)	1998 Round 1 (Feb)	1998 Round 2 (May)	1998 Round 3 (August)
	Number ('000)						
2. Seasonally inactive labour force	1,158	164	1,036	106	1,251	2,002	77
Not in labour force > 13 years of age	13,745	13,119	14,335	13,238	14,889	14,978	13,913
1. Household work	4,007	3,539	4,195	3,450	4,341	4,270	3,590
2. Study	5,473	5,519	5,811	5,580	6,090	6,048	5,913
3. Too young/old or incapable of work	3,379	3,377	3,463	3,517	3,661	3,838	3,624
4. Others	885	684	866	690	797	822	767
Not in labour force < 13 years of age	14,107	14,176	14,015	13,850	13,917	13,050	13,983
Labour force participation rate %	53.4	54.5	53.0	55.3	52.7	52.7	54.5
Total open unemployment rate %	2.01	1.08	2.18	0.87	4.60	5.01	3.41
Seasonally inactive rate %	3.63	0.50	3.24	0.31	3.89	6.22	0.23
Open unemp + seasonally inactive %	5.64	1.58	5.42	1.19	8.49	11.24	3.64

Source: NSO, Labour Force Surveys, various years.

Table A6. Republic of Korea: Trends in Employment and Unemployment by Sex.

	Year and month	Population aged 15 and over	Total economically active	Economically active Population: Employed	Economically active Population: Unemployed	Economically inactive population	EAP[1] Rate (%)	E[2] Rate (%)	UE[3] Rate (%)
		Number in thousands							
Total work force	1993	32 400	19 803	19 253	550	12 597	61.1	97.2	2.8
	1994	32 939	20 326	19 837	489	12 614	61.7	97.6	2.4
	1995	33 558	20 797	20 377	419	12 761	62.0	98.0	2.0
	1996	34 182	21 188	20 764	425	12 994	62.0	98.0	2.0
	1997	34 736	21 604	21 048	556	13 132	62.2	97.4	2.6
	Jan. '98	35 031	20 645	19 711	934	14 368	58.9	95.5	4.5 (4.1)
	Feb. '98	35 073	20 760	19 526	1 235	14 312	59.2	94.1	5.9 (4.7)
	Mar. '98	35 108	21 270	19 892	1 378	13 838	60.6	93.5	6.5 (5.3)
	April'98	35 146	21 561	20 127	1 434	13 585	61.3	93.3	6.7 (6.1)
	May '98	35 188	21 717	20 226	1 492	13 470	61.7	93.1	6.9 (7.0)
	June '98	35 229	21 712	20 183	1 529	13 517	61.6	93.0	7.0 (7.7)
	July '98	35 267	21 650	19 999	1 651	13 617	61.4	92.4	7.6 (8.6)
	Aug. '98	35 302	21 442	19 864	1 578	13 860	60.7	92.6	7.4 (8.1)

Table A6. Continued.

	Year and month	Number in thousands					EAP[1] Rate (%)	E[2] Rate (%)	UE[3] Rate (%)
		Population aged 15 and over	Total economically active	Economically active Population		Economically inactive population			
				Employed	Unemployed				
Women workers	1993	16 753	7 913	7 738	175	8 840	47.2	97.8	2.2
	1994	17 023	8 159	8 005	155	8 864	47.9	98.1	1.9
	1995	17 307	8 363	8 224	139	8 944	48.3	98.3	1.7
	1996	17 593	8 568	8 434	134	9 025	48.7	98.4	1.6
	1997	17 866	8 843	8 639	204	9 023	49.5	97.7	2.3
	Jan. '98	18 003	8 068	7 752	317	9 935	44.8	96.1	3.9
	Feb. '98	18 024	8 140	7 725	415	9 884	45.2	94.9	5.1
	Mar. '98	18 044	8 436	7 997	439	9 608	46.8	94.8	5.2
	April'98	18 065	8 615	8 151	464	9 450	47.7	94.6	5.4
	May '98	18 086	8 708	8 231	476	9 378	48.1	94.6	5.5
	June '98	18 107	8 702	8 207	495	9 405	48.1	94.3	5.7
	July '98	18 125	8 623	8 084	539	9 502	47.6	93.7	6.3
	Aug. '98	18 142	8 517	8 020	497	9 625	46.9	94.2	5.8

Table A6. Continued.

		Number in thousands							
				Economically active Population					
	Year and month	Population aged 15 and over	Total economically active	Employed	Unemployed	Economically inactive population	EAP[1] Rate (%)	E[2] Rate (%)	UE[3] Rate (%)
Men workers	1993	15 647	11 890	11 515	375	3 757	76.0	96.8	3.2
	1994	15 916	12 167	11 832	334	3 750	76.4	97.2	2.7
	1995	16 251	12 433	12 153	280	3 818	76.5	97.7	2.3
	1996	16 590	12 620	12 330	290	3 969	76.1	97.7	2.3
	1997	16 870	12 761	12 409	352	4 109	75.6	97.2	2.8
	Jan. '98	17 028	12 577	11 959	617	4 451	73.9	95.1	4.9
	Feb. '98	17 049	12 621	11 801	820	4 428	74.0	93.5	6.5
	Mar. '98	17 064	12 834	11 895	938	4 230	75.2	92.7	7.3
	April'98	17 081	12 946	11 976	970	4 135	75.8	92.5	7.5
	May '98	17 102	13 010	11 995	1 015	4 092	76.1	92.2	7.8
	June '98	17 122	13 010	11 976	1 034	4 112	76.0	92.1	7.9
	July '98	17 142	13 027	11 915	1 112	4 115	76.0	91.5	8.5
	Aug. '98	17 161	12 925	11 844	1 081	4 235	75.3	91.6	8.4

Note: 1. EAP: Economically active population; 2. E: Employment; 3. UE: Unemployment.
Source: NSO Korea, cited in Pilwha 1998.

Printed and bound by CPI Group (UK) Ltd, Croydon, CR0 4YY

16/09/2026

14963401-0007